NO LONGER THE PROPERTY
OF THE
UNIVERSITY OF R. I. LIBRARY

Encyclopedia of Western Colonialism since 1450

FIRST EDITION

Encyclopedia of Western Colonialism since 1450

FIRST EDITION

VOLUME 2
F-O

Thomas Benjamin
EDITOR IN CHIEF

MACMILLAN REFERENCE USA
An imprint of Thomson Gale, a part of The Thomson Corporation

THOMSON

GALE

Detroit • New York • San Francisco • San Diego • New Haven, Conn. • Waterville, Maine • London • Munich

Encyclopedia of Western Colonialism since 1450

Thomas Benjamin, Editor in Chief

© 2007 Thomson Gale, a part of The Thomson Corporation.

Thomson, Star Logo and Macmillan Reference USA are trademarks and Gale is a registered trademark used herein under license.

For more information, contact
Macmillan Reference USA
An imprint of Thomson Gale
27500 Drake Rd.
Farmington, Hills, MI 48331-3535
Or you can visit our Internet site at
http://www.gale.com

ALL RIGHTS RESERVED
No part of this work covered by the copyright hereon may be reproduced or used in any form or by any means—graphic, electronic, or mechanical, including photocopying, recording, taping, Web distribution, or information storage retrieval systems—without the written permission of the publisher.

For permission to use material from this product, submit your request via Web at http://www.gale-edit.com/permissions, or you may download our Permissions Request form and submit your request by fax or mail to:

Permissions
Thomson Gale
27500 Drake Rd.
Farmington Hills, MI 48331-3535
Permissions Hotline:
248-699-8006 or 800-877-4253 ext. 8006
Fax: 248-699-8074 or 800-762-4058

Since this page cannot legibly accommodate all copyright notices, the acknowledgments constitute an extension of the copyright notice.

While every effort has been made to ensure the reliability of the information presented in this publication, Thomson Gale does not guarantee the accuracy of the data contained herein. Thomson Gale accepts no payment for listing; and inclusion in the publication of any organization, agency, institution, publication, service, or individual does not imply endorsement of the editors or publisher. Errors brought to the attention of the publisher and verified to the satisfaction of the publisher will be corrected in future editions.

LIBRARY OF CONGRESS CATALOGING-IN-PUBLICATION DATA

Encyclopedia of Western colonialism since 1450 / Thomas Benjamin, editor in chief.
    p. cm.
    Includes bibliographical references and index.
    ISBN 0-02-865843-4 (set hardcover : alk. paper) – ISBN 0-02-865844-2 (vol 1 : alk. paper) – ISBN 0-02-865845-0 (vol 2 : alk. paper) – ISBN 0-02-865846-9 (vol 3 : alk. paper)
    1. Colonies–History–Encyclopedias. 2. Imperialism–History–Encyclopedias. 3. Postcolonialism–Encyclopedias. 4. Europe–Territorial expansion–Encyclopedias. I. Benjamin, Thomas, 1952-
    JV22.E535 2007
    325'.303–dc22   2006010042

This title is also available as an e-book.
ISBN 0-02-866085-4
Contact your Thomson Gale representative for ordering information.

Printed in the United States of America
10 9 8 7 6 5 4 3 2 1

Editorial Board

EDITOR IN CHIEF

Thomas Benjamin

Professor of Latin American history at Central Michigan University

ASSOCIATE EDITORS

Benjamin C. Fortna

Lecturer in the modern history of the Near and Middle East at the University of London, School of Oriental and African Studies

Chima J. Korieh

Assistant professor of history at Rowan University in Glassboro, New Jersey

Anthony McFarlane

Professor of Latin American History in the History Department and in the School of Comparative American Studies at the University of Warwick, UK

Hendrik E. Niemeijer

Research supervisor in History at Leiden University in the Netherlands

Editor-in-chief of Itinerario, European Journal of Overseas History

Eileen Scully

Professor of history at Bennington College in Vermont

Editorial and Production Staff

PROJECT EDITOR

Jenai Mynatt

CONTRIBUTING EDITORS

Mark Drouillard
Rachel J. Kain
Christine Slovey

EDITORIAL TECHNICAL SUPPORT

Mark Springer

MANUSCRIPT EDITORS

Anthony C. Coulter
Judith Culligan
Gina Renee Misiroglu

ADDITIONAL EDITORIAL SUPPORT

Judith Clinebell

PROOFREADERS

Laura Patchkofsky

Diane Sawinski
Julie Van Pelt

TRANSLATOR

Loes Nas

INDEXER

Laurie Andriot

PRODUCT DESIGN

Kate Scheible
Tracey Rowens

IMAGING

Dean Dauphinais
Lezlie Light
Michael Logusz
Christine O'Bryan

GRAPHIC ART

XNR Productions

RIGHTS ACQUISITION AND MANAGEMENT

Ronald Montgomery
Shalice Shah-Caldwell
Andrew Specht

COMPOSITION

Evi Seoud
Mary Beth Trimper

MANUFACTURING

Wendy Blurton

DIRECTOR, NEW PRODUCT DEVELOPMENT

Hélène Potter

PUBLISHER

Jay Flynn

Contents

F

FACTORIES, SOUTH AND SOUTHEAST ASIA

Between the sixteenth and eighteenth centuries, European trading companies from Portugal, the Dutch Republic, England, Denmark, France, Sweden, and the Austrian Netherlands founded numerous trading factories in Asian port cities. These settlements varied in their form from simple business offices to strong fortifications, but had in common their central function: to provide access, whenever possible privileged, to indigenous commodity markets. Furthermore, the factories operated as supply centers and provided military protection. Accordingly, they were manned with administrative, mercantile, and military personnel. Spread over the whole of South and Southeast Asia and organized hierarchically, they made up the backbone of the European trading networks in Asia.

Europe's expansion into Asia in the early modern period never strove for the type of colonialism known from the late nineteenth and early twentieth centuries: Commercial profit rather than territorial expansion was the central aim of the chartered companies. Because Asia was characterized by established state systems, most European factories could only operate with the permission and protection of local rulers. Only in a few exceptional cases were the companies able to achieve control over port cities. As a rule, negotiations over trade agreements between European representatives and the local authorities were an essential first step. Agreements permitted European settlements and factories, and regulated the local commercial organization. The results of negotiations varied depending on the local situation. Strong local rulers were able to dictate conditions, refuse privileges, and determine the location of a new factory. Some local rulers allowed several competing factories under their control (e.g., in Bantam and Makassar), but mostly they were interested in reliable long-term trading contacts achieved through a privileged agreement with one single European partner. In places where indigenous rulers were weak or European military presence was strong, Europeans were able to force local rulers to accept unequal contracts. In these cases, the factory remained nominally under the ruler's protection, but became the actual authority (as, for example, on the Moluccas).

During the sixteenth century the Portuguese built up the first European factory network, with its center in Goa and important secondary factories in Diu, Malacca, and Macau. During the seventeenth century, with only a few exceptions (Goa, Macau, Timor), the Portuguese were displaced by Dutch and English trading companies—namely, the Dutch Verenigde Oost-Indische Compagnie (VOC) and the English East India Company (EIC). The heart of the Dutch factory system was Batavia, which in 1621 became the residence of the governor-general. On the next level of the VOC hierarchy, the fortified residences of governors (in Ambon, Banda, Ternate, Makassar, Malacca, Semarang, Cochin, and Colombo) ensured a strong Dutch position. Less important factories were led by directors (exclusively an economic position in the Dutch system) or simple residents who ran small settlements without military relevance.

The first English attempts to establish the EIC in Indonesia failed due to competition from the Dutch. The EIC's first center, in Bantam, was lost as early as 1682, and the factories in the Moluccas quite a bit earlier.

Only some peripheral factories remained (Bencoolen on Sumatra, Balambangan off North Borneo). The EIC's main focus shifted to the Indian subcontinent, where residencies in Madras, Calcutta, Bombay, and Pondicherry were established.

Due to the VOC's dominance in Indonesia and the power of China and Japan's emperors, the greatest number of factories in Asia existed in India. Here, smaller European trading empires established limited networks—as with France (headquartered in Pondicherry) or Denmark (headquartered in Tranquebar)—or had to content themselves with isolated factories, as with Sweden or the Austrian Netherlands (the Oostende-Company).

Hypothetically, factories passed through five stages of development (see Rothermund, 1981). Initially, a factory would obtain goods for a company by purchasing whatever it found on the local market. In its second stage of development, a factory would zero in on specific items it wanted from the local population; it would produce samples to demonstrate its wants and use subscription payments to encourage focused production. In its third stage, it would begin to finance orders in advance, which allowed the company to implement standardization and quality control. Next, it began to intervene in the production process, in order to speed it up and thus increase the quantity of exports. Finally, it took over the organization of production by instituting a putting-out system, in which workers produced goods at home under company supervision and using company-supplied tools. This model most closely fits the textile trade in India, where these stages of development led ultimately to the economic system in which India became a British Crown Colony. Thus, the factories represented the core of the later territorial colonialism. Unlike India, settlements based on the spice trade normally finished their development at the third stage, as was the case with most of the Dutch factories in the Malay Archipelago.

The above remarks help explain the importance of factories for later colonial development, but they do not cover the whole spectrum. Depending on the function of a particular factory in a company's system and on the level of influence European representatives were able to achieve in particular local communities, divergent developments were also possible. Additionally, differences in the strategies and aims pursued by companies facing differing local conditions produced varying outcomes. Thus, the establishment of factories could lead to aggressive policies, as in Makassar where the VOC, after first attempting to control the spice market by offering the highest prices, later conquered the port in order to eliminate local competition. The subsequent establishment of a fortified factory under a governor solidified the factory's new function. Thus, the economic and political influence of European factories varied depending on local conditions and European strategies. Their cultural influence remained minimal, however, as factories were always primarily a key instrument of early modern mercantile expansionism.

SEE ALSO *Bullion Trade, South and Southeast Asia; English East India Company (EIC); Sugar Cultivation and Trade; VOC (Verenigde Oost-Indische Compagnie).*

BIBLIOGRAPHY

Arasaratnam, Sinnappah. "European Port-Settlements in the Coromandel Commercial System, 1650–1740." In *Brides of the Sea: Port Cities of Asia from the Sixteenth to Twentieth Centuries*, edited by Frank Broeze. Honolulu: University of Hawaii Press, 1989.

Bassett, David K. "Early English Trade and Settlement in Asia, 1602–1690." In *Britain and Netherlands in Europe and Asia, Vol. 3*, edited by John S. Bromley and Ernst H. Kossmann. London: Chatto and Windus, 1968.

Farrington, Anthony. *Trading Places: The East India Company and Asia, 1600–1834.* London: British Library, 2002.

Foster, William. *English Factories in India, 1618–1669.* 13 vols. Oxford, U.K.: Clarendon, 1906–1927.

Furber, Holden. *Rival Empires of Trade in the Orient, 1600–1800.* Minneapolis: University of Minnesota Press, 1976.

Rothermund, Dietmar. *Asian Trade and European Expansion in the Age of Mercantilism.* New Delhi: Manohar, 1981.

Société Jean Bodin, ed. *Les grandes escales*, Vol. 2: *Les temps modernes.* Brussels: Éditions de la Libraire Encyclopédique, 1972.

Jürgen G. Nagel

FEDERATED STATES OF MICRONESIA

Following a popular referendum in 1978, the Federated States of Micronesia (FSM) began to be organized as an independent nation in 1979. After a seven-year transitional period, complete independence was achieved in 1986. This relatively new nation consists of more than six hundred islands with a total land area of just over 700 square kilometers (about 270 square miles). Yet, it extends across more than 2,735 kilometers (about 1,700 miles) of the western Pacific Ocean and includes over a million square miles of ocean. It is therefore understandable that the federal government would concede a great deal of autonomy to the governments of the four states (listed from west to east): Yap, Chuuk, Pohnpei, and Kosrae.

The federal government concerns itself with foreign relations, international trade, and disputes between the states. The governments of the individual states manage almost every other aspect of governance. Both the federal and state governments have been loosely modeled on the three-branch structure of the U.S. government. The legislature is, however, unicameral rather than bicameral, and includes one senator from each state who is elected to a four-year term and ten senators apportioned according to population who serve two-year terms.

Known previously as the Caroline group, these islands were first visited by Portuguese traders early in the sixteenth century. The islands were then colonized by the Spanish, who had established settlements in the Philippine Islands as a counter to Portuguese and, somewhat later, Dutch influence in the East Indies (present-day Indonesia). The Spanish controlled the islands for more than three centuries. Following their defeat in the Spanish-American War (1898) and the loss of such Pacific possessions as the Philippines and Guam, the Spanish sold the islands in 1899 to Germany, which was anxious to establish a colonial presence that would suggest its growing parity with France and the United Kingdom. But after only a decade and a half, after the outbreak of World War I in 1914, Japan opportunistically declared war on Germany and seized control of the Caroline Islands as well as other German possessions in the Pacific. In 1920 the United Nations extended a formal mandate to the Japanese administration of the islands.

Unlike the Spanish, the Germans had begun to develop the islands economically, establishing copra production (dried coconut meat that is rendered to oil) as a major export industry. Under the Japanese, this economic development accelerated, with the introduction of sugarcane processing plants and mining enterprises. The downside of this prosperity was the extensive Japanese immigration into the islands, which ultimately reduced the indigenous peoples to about two-sevenths of the total population. In any case, any progress achieved under the Japanese civilian government was undercut when the Japanese military seized power and ruthlessly exploited all available resources to support Japan's war effort. Japanese preparations to defend the islands, and the eventual American conquest of them left the islands devastated on almost every level, from the topographical to the economic.

Through the United Nations, the United States was granted a trusteeship over many of the island groups in the western Pacific, including the Carolines. Although the United States did much to reconstruct and to improve the islands' infrastructures, the sustained infusion of considerable foreign aid did not promote the development of self-sustaining economic enterprises. Thus, although the islanders seem to have been well prepared for political independence, they have not achieved economic independence. The continued close relationship between the United States and the Federated States of Micronesia is reflected in the Compact of Free Association, which declares that the citizens of the two nations do not require visas to travel across each other's borders.

SEE ALSO *Pacific, American Presence in; Pacific, European Presence in.*

BIBLIOGRAPHY

Brower, Kenneth. *Micronesia: The Land, the People, and the Sea.* Baton Rouge: Louisiana State University Press, 1981.

Darrach, Brad, and David Doubilet. "Treasured Islands." *Life* (August 1995): 46–53.

Falgout, Suzanne. "Americans in Paradise: Anthropologists, Custom, and Democracy in Postwar Micronesia." *Ethnology* 34 (Spring 1995): 99–111.

Friedman, Hal M. "The Beast in Paradise: The United States Navy in Micronesia, 1943–1947." *Pacific Historical Review* 62 (May 1993): 173–195.

Friedman, Hal M. "Arguing over Empire." *Journal of Pacific History* 29 (1994): 36–48.

Hanlon, David. *Remaking Micronesia: Discourses over Development in a Pacific Territory, 1944–1982.* Honolulu: University of Hawaii Press, 1998.

Hezel, Francis X. "The Church in Micronesia." *America* 18 (February 1995): 23–24.

Kluge, P. F. *The Edge of Paradise: America in Micronesia.* New York: Random House, 1991.

Malcomson, S. L. "Stranger than Paradise." *Mother Jones* 14 (January 1989): 19–25.

"Micronesia: A New Nation." *U.S. News & World Report* (October 15, 1984): 80–81.

Montoya, R. T. "The Foreign Aid Cancer." *Vital Speeches of the Day* 1 (August 1987): 616–618.

Parfit, Michael . "Islands of the Pacific." *National Geographic* 203 (March 2003): 106–125.

Patterson, Carolyn Bennett. "In the Far Pacific: At the Birth of Nations." *National Geographic* 170 (October 1986): 460–500.

Peoples, James G. "Political Evolution in Micronesia." *Ethnology* 32 (Winter 1993): 1–17.

Rainbird, Paul. "Taking the Tapu: Defining Micronesia by Absence." *Journal of Pacific History* 38 (September 2003): 237–250.

Schwalbenberg, Henry M., and Thomas Hatcher. "Micronesian Trade and Foreign Assistance." *Journal of Pacific History* 29 (1) (1994): 95–104.

Woodard, Colin. "After Uncle Sam Goes Home: Trouble in Paradise." *Christian Science Monitor* (August 11, 1998): 6.

Woodard, Colin. "America's Half-Forgotten Islands." *Christian Science Monitor* (December 27, 1999): 6.

Martin Kich

FIJI

Fiji is a group of islands in the South Pacific Ocean. The Dutch navigator Abel Janszoon Tasman (ca. 1603–1959) reached some of the Fijian islands in 1643, and eighteenth-century visitors included James Cook (1728–1779) and William Bligh (1754–1817). Sandalwood, valued in China, drew European traders to Fiji in the early nineteenth century; missionaries also arrived at this time.

By the 1860s, Europeans, Americans, and colonial Australians began to negotiate substantial land sales with Fijian chiefs. A leading chief, Cakobau (1815–1883), attempted to form a centralized indigenous government in 1871, but the demands of investors, planters, traders, and Fijians proved irreconcilable. Fearing anarchy, Cakobau ceded Fiji to the British Crown in 1874.

British rule in Fiji was characterized by a romanticized view of indigenous Fijians, and a desire to promote Fiji's economy using imported labor from India. Fijians thus retained control of land and local government, and British governors prided themselves on their knowledge of Fiji's language and customs. This practice of Aindirect rule would be adopted in other parts of the British Empire.

By the 1960s decolonization was accelerating in other parts of the British Empire, but Fiji's small size and plural society were perceived to be barriers to rapid independence. Fiji had been described as a three-legged stool: Fijian land, Indian labor, and European government. The British perceived their role as crucial to the protection of indigenous Fijian interests, especially after the 1940s when Indians began to outnumber Fijians. Independence came in 1970, but unfinished business from the colonial period, especially the country's race-based approach to identity and political representation, continues to haunt Fijian politics.

SEE ALSO *Pacific, American Presence in; Pacific, European Presence in.*

BIBLIOGRAPHY

Derrick, Ronald. Albert. *A History of Fiji*. Suva, Fiji: Government Printer, 1957.

Scarr, Deryck. *Fiji: A Short History*. Sydney, Australia: Allen & Unwin, 1984.

Jane Samson

FINANCING, DEBT, AND FINANCIAL CRISES

From the 1700s to the 1900s, the Middle Eastern economy underwent a transformation brought about through an alteration in its economic relationship with Europe and the global economy. This process of alteration began with European commercial penetration, which expanded to include financial and then political penetration. This process facilitated a pattern of dependence that stifled Middle Eastern economic growth and income.

Europe's Industrial Revolution prompted its commercial penetration of the Middle East, where Europeans desired trade expansion and exerted political pressure to limit commercial restrictions. Europe's financial penetration of the Middle East, particularly in Egypt and Turkey, began during the mid-nineteenth century when both had demonstrated their inability to finance reforms through existing revenues.

European credit institutions capable of mobilizing extensive funds as loans for foreign governments were developing simultaneously. Egypt and Turkey became dependent on foreign loans, enabling European states, banks, and companies to maneuver for larger concessions while expanding trade. During the peak of European imperialism, Egyptian and Ottoman bankruptcy became means to developing international financial regimes in both areas, restricting their financial sovereignty. Middle Eastern economic dependence on Europe was reinforced through political might and, in Egypt, direct political control.

EARLY COMMERCIAL RELATIONSHIP

From 1500 to 1800, the Middle East experienced growth in key economic sectors, but this growth paled in comparison to Europe's, leaving the Middle East with a relative sense of decline. Capitalist industrialization remained absent in the region while expanding rapidly in Europe. Consequently, the economic gap between the Middle East and Europe widened from the seventeenth century onward, shifting the economic balance of power in Europe's favor. During the early eighteenth century, the Middle Eastern economy was stagnant in terms of investment and income, techniques and methods of organization, and production levels. The region's resources were underutilized, and it suffered from poor transport and irrigation systems.

The trade reduction following the discovery of the Cape of Good Hope route to India, effectively eliminating the Middle East's role as a crossroads of trade between Europe and the Far East, corresponded to the decline of Venice's control of the Mediterranean and its control by Britain and France. This established a new pattern of global trade where European manufactured goods were exchanged for Middle Eastern raw materials.

Under the protection of the Capitulation Treaties, which were a series of agreements between the Ottomans and certain foreign governments granting their citizens specific exemptions from Ottoman law, and their national consuls, European merchants congregated in sections of port cities while relying on intermediaries familiar with local languages and the region's commercial nuances. For their services, intermediaries were placed under the umbrella of a European consulate, according them low customs duties applicable to Europeans.

The Middle East became a destination for increased amounts of British goods during the Napoleonic Wars (1799–1815). Britain expanded its Middle Eastern presence and strengthened its control of the Mediterranean at the expense of France, which reasserted its position during the 1840s. European economic stagnation prompted entrepreneurs to search abroad for financial investments. In addition, improved transportation systems throughout the Middle East encouraged Europeans to expand their commercial penetration.

European governments supported their own merchants' commercial interests and exerted political pressure on their behalf. European-controlled commercial tribunals were established during the 1850s. The Ottoman Commercial Code (1850), based on French customs, was a response to European pressure to comply with Anglo-French commercial practices. Britain exerted military and political pressure on the Ottoman government in 1838 to reduce its monopolies, and the British renegotiated the Anglo-Turkish Commercial Convention (1820) to include a reduction of internal tariffs.

Following the Napoleonic Wars, the Ottomans attempted to reform their military along European lines. While such efforts in Turkey were meant to counter increasing European political and military intervention, in Egypt they were simultaneously directed toward achieving independence from Ottoman authority. In both cases, these reforms were financial burdens. Attempts to increase revenue by reasserting control over the countryside met mixed results and increased administrative costs.

The Ottoman government's failure to collect sufficient revenues forced it to issue short-term bonds. During the 1830s, the military received about 70 percent of revenues, yet many officers remained unpaid. Ottoman rulers concluded that a government loan was inevitable, yet the government's inability to secure adequate revenue cast doubts on its capability to repay the loan.

THE ROAD TO BANKRUPTCY IN TURKEY

The 1850s and 1860s brought a period of rapid economic expansion in Europe, where increased foreign trade corresponded with rising foreign investment. New institutions for mobilizing domestic savings developed in Europe; these were capable of drawing funds from a wider range of investors. These institutions adopted more aggressive investment policies to generate rapid returns to compete with traditional banks. The Middle East was a promising investment area due to increased trade and Ottoman efforts to create a European-style military, administration, and economy.

The development of transportation and irrigation systems proved enticing for European investors searching for new schemes following the end of the British and French railway construction boom. The most lucrative loans were government loans, which were easy to publicize and involved increasing sums of money with minimal flotation risks. Credit institutions created schemes to attract Ottoman investment and used gimmicks to convince the European investing public to purchase Oriental bonds.

Many European-controlled banks in the Middle East were instrumental in collecting revenue for Turkey and Egypt. Initially focused on Middle Eastern economic development, such banks concentrated on obtaining profits from state finance. A further stimulus was tensions between European powers eager to extend their Middle Eastern economic and political influence through financial and administrative schemes or through development projects.

Although in 1851 the Ottoman sultan rejected an agreement for a loan of 55 million French francs, it became apparent that the Ottoman financial situation was desperate. The sultan feared increased European interference, yet maintaining a modern military competent to defend Ottoman integrity was financially onerous. The government experimented unsuccessfully with short-term fiscal measures to balance its finances. With no alternative, the government pursued a policy of regular foreign borrowing.

Although the Ottomans paid high interest rates on the full amount of their loans, they never received the face value of the sum borrowed due to heavy flotation fees and discounting. The first loan, for £T3,300,000 (British pounds), was arranged in 1854 after the outbreak of the Crimean War (1853–1856). One year later, an agreement was signed for a loan from London's Rothschild bank. Britain and France, anxious for the Ottomans to continue warring against Russia, assisted in getting the Ottomans favorable terms. Over the next twenty years, the Ottomans obtained thirteen more loans from European banks, amassing a total debt of

£T242,000,000 and a large floating debt comprised of short-term bonds. As Ottoman debt mounted, terms of subsequent loans became less favorable.

The Ottomans used most of the sums received from loans for debt payments, leaving little for administrative and military costs. Consequently, economic development and public works projects received hardly any government funds. Attempts to increase tax revenues were hindered by administrative irregularities concerning collection methods, as well as numerous residents, including Europeans, who qualified for tax exemptions. Furthermore, the government failed to exploit new sources of revenue. As expenditure continued to surpass income, the Ottomans relied on short-term finance methods to make regular payments, resulting in additional small loans at high interest rates and the mass issuing of bonds. Attempts to liquidate bonds with further loans were unsuccessful due to the amount issued.

The Ottoman financial administrative system was inept at dealing with the crisis. The sultan's ministers jointly approved departmental budgets without the minister of finance's approval. The sultan's private expenditure was not restricted, and an auditing and accounting department did not exist until 1880. Financial control in rural areas was limited, and reform efforts, often posed to secure European funds, were unsuccessful. Furthermore, accessibility to European loans perpetuated a relationship of financial dependability.

On October 6, 1875, the Ottoman government announced its intention to pay half of the amount necessary to service its debt in cash, paying the rest in bonds. Europeans interpreted this as a declaration of bankruptcy. The Ottomans attempted to find alternative methods of payment and abandoned nearly all cash payments in 1876.

OTTOMAN PUBLIC DEBT ADMINISTRATION

From 1876 to 1881, the Ottoman government and its European creditors trudged toward a general financial agreement to restore financial stability and reinstate access to further loans. There was difficulty convincing creditors to agree to common terms, since each loan had been issued under different conditions. Furthermore, the Ottomans attempted to resist the further surrendering of their financial sovereignty to European powers coordinating their efforts on behalf of their nationals.

The Ottoman financial and political situation continued to deteriorate. A famine and die-off of livestock in 1873 and 1874 exacerbated matters. The empire lost vast amounts on military campaigns in the Balkans (1875–1876) and against Russia (1877–1878). The Ottoman need for soldiers for combat prompted the reduction of its military in the countryside, hindering attempts for more efficient tax collection. The Ottoman government lost some of its richest sections at the Berlin Congress of 1878, where bondholders lobbied for international support. In 1879 Britain sent warships to the Dardanelles, (a strait in Turkey), pressuring compliance with foreign demands.

The Ottoman Empire and its creditors reached an agreement in 1881. Published in the Decree of Muharram, the agreement resulted in the creation of a system of international financial control through the Ottoman Public Debt Administration (PDA), which eliminated Turkey's financial sovereignty. The PDA consisted of a council with representatives from the main groups of bondholders (British, Dutch, French, German, Austro-Hungarian, Italian, and Ottoman), although the Ottoman representative had no vote. The council's presidency rotated between members from Britain and France, which argued that they had the largest interests at stake.

The PDA received support from European embassies in Istanbul and from foreign-controlled banks. Britain and France were the powers initially interested in Turkey's financial situation, yet Germany soon took increased interest. While imperial rivalries existed among the powers, they cooperated within Turkey to protect the interests of those with shares in the Ottoman public debt and to further European economic penetration through the development of public works projects, as well as concessions for the production and export of mineral products. It was implied that Ottoman refusal to support such projects would prompt the revocation of European financial support. While this method of economic control fostered resentment, the empire's weakened political and economic condition made it impossible for it to be challenged.

The Ottomans attempted to develop the empire's economy on its own. However, inept administrators, limited financial resources, a weakened international position, and a growing technological gap between the Middle East and Europe hindered these efforts. The Ottomans realized that constructing a proper means of transportation throughout the empire was essential for economic progress. The cost of transportation by camel was expensive and restrictive, hindering trade and limiting agricultural production for export. Yet lack of finances was a constant problem, and the Ottomans were forced to rely on European funds and the PDA.

European assistance for construction of public works projects was a frequent liability to the Ottoman government. For example, the agreement for the construction of the Izmir to Aydin railway guaranteed an interest rate of 6 percent on construction costs set at 31 million francs. As the construction company encountered financial and engineering difficulties, the government agreed to increases in the sum guaranteed to 46 million francs in 1861 and to 48 million francs in 1863. The company did not amass profits until 1869, thereby involving an enormous outlay by the Ottoman government.

European railways, built primarily in the 1850s and 1860s, assisted the development of Middle Eastern export crops by improving their transportation and lowering costs. Yet the more extensive railway systems allowed European economic penetration of the interior. The value of land located by railways increased, and in 1867 Europeans pressed for a law to extend their rights to landed property so they could increase purchases and push inland.

The providing or withholding of money was used to pressure the Ottomans into accepting financial projects. Banks or credit institutions might agree to float a loan only in exchange for concessions for its nationals. At other times, a loan might not be offered unless used toward a particular development project or to purchase specific foreign imports. The PDA, banks and credit institutions, and entrepreneurs coordinated efforts to exploit the Ottoman Empire. An example of this alliance was the awarding of ancillary rights to foreign railway companies, including rights to mineral deposits located within 20 kilometers (about 12.5 miles) of either side of the railway. Another example of this alliance was the practice of granting railway companies an Ottoman guarantee for compensation for losses, provided a certain number of trains ran over a particular section of track.

Under the Decree of Muharram's terms, the PDA directly collected specified tax revenues for the payment of the external debt and its interest. The PDA expanded its functions to include duties reserved for the Ministry of Finance and the reservation of funds for the servicing of new loans, increasing Ottoman dependence on the PDA and foreign money, or for financial guarantees for public works and mineral-extraction projects.

The PDA provided security for European investments, which increased the value of shares in the public debt. The PDA also delivered regular debt payments. The Ottomans secured better terms for further loans, and the PDA assisted in underwriting the empire's credit. Yet the PDA's growing administrative staff added costs to the government, which incurred expenditures assisting the PDA in completing its functions, and the PDA's independent operations fostered resentment. The PDA nonetheless continued to expand its economic control by establishing more tax-collecting offices and extending the types of taxes it collected. Until 1903, the PDA could withhold collected revenues from the government, including amounts exceeding the fixed debt. An amendment called for division of surplus revenue between the

PDA and the government at the ratio of seventy-five to twenty-five.

The imbalance between Ottoman expenditure and income continued. From 1886 to 1914, the government received nearly thirty foreign loans totaling £T170,000,000. The European powers' economic and financial cooperation was not affected by conflicting interests until shortly before World War I (1914–1918), when increased nationalism fostered the tentative division of the Ottoman Empire into spheres of economic interest.

THE ROAD TO BANKRUPTCY IN EGYPT

The Egyptian ruler Muhammad Ali (1769–1849) initiated reforms in Egypt during the early 1800s, and he attempted to raise revenues through state monopolies of cash crops. Egypt briefly regained financial independence, but reliance on cotton exports proved disastrous when its declining price in the global market from 1836 to 1837 initiated a period of instability. Muhammad Ali also constructed European-style factories to realize Egypt's industrial potential. Initially producing military supplies, such factories soon produced manufactured goods, eliminating Egypt's reliance on foreign production. Egypt's limited market, lack of coal and workable iron, and lack of technological experience hindered Muhammad Ali's endeavors. Furthermore, the elimination of local industrial competition enabled European manufacturers to infiltrate the Middle Eastern market.

After Muhammad Ali, rulers attempted reforms and development programs surpassing Egypt's financial capabilities. Sa'id Pasha (1822–1863), who ruled from 1854 to 1862, sponsored numerous public works projects and attempted to develop Egypt's infrastructure through joint Egyptian-European companies. Several Europeans exploited Sa'id by befriending him and then manipulating him for personal gain. Foreign consuls, whose influence increased, extracted government indemnities for alleged losses of concessions. For example, in 1858 the bankrupt Nile Navigation Company persuaded Sa'id to purchase its investors' shares to prevent them from losing money.

The initial agreement between Ferdinand de Lesseps (1805–1894), a French diplomat and developer, and Sa'id for the construction of the Suez Canal disadvantaged the Egyptian government. The canal would eliminate revenues from the transport of mail and from passengers crossing from Alexandria to Suez. Egypt agreed to supply an annual corvée of 20,000 laborers, and the country abandoned its rights to territory along the main canal, as well as a second canal constructed to provide fresh water for workers. Egypt assumed responsibility for purchasing 64,000 of the initial issue of 400,000 (500-franc) shares. Subscriptions sold poorly when opened to the public in 1858, and Sa'id agreed to purchase most remaining subscriptions.

Upon advice from de Lesseps, Egypt issued treasury bonds and later used bonds to pay its employees. By 1859, there was over £2,000,000 of government paper in circulation. An additional £3,500,000 was issued to purchase Egypt's canal shares. In 1860 Sa'id secured a foreign private loan for 28 million francs. Under the agreement's conditions, Egypt was to stop issuing treasury bonds. However, the government continued issuing short-term paper under different guises to meet its financial obligations. Egypt's floating debt may have been as high as £11,000,000 by late 1861.

In 1863 Ismail Pasha (1830–1895) inherited a state in financial crisis. The government was required to pay 34,000,000 francs to shareholders of the bankrupt Medjidiah Company. Under the Convention of March 1863, Egypt reaffirmed its obligations to the Suez Canal Company and agreed to pay the remaining 200 francs per share, which totaled 35,000,000 francs. Ismail exacerbated matters by sponsoring ambitious public works projects and joint companies. He began borrowing from local banks, but hesitated from taking out foreign public loans, which required the sultan's formal approval. Such a situation became inevitable after the imposition of the arbitration terms negotiated by the French emperor Napoléon III (1808–1873). The arbitration terms resolved a dispute between Egypt and the Suez Canal Company, requiring Egypt to compensate the company for £84,000,000 over the return of some granted concessions.

Egypt secured its first pubic loan in September 1864 for £5,700,000. In the following years, Egypt arranged six additional loans for a total of £60,000,000. The terms for loans became increasingly onerous as Egypt's financial situation deteriorated. The government again resorted to issuing treasury bonds and other short-term paper to meet its obligations, amassing a floating debt of about £35,000,000 in 1873. In 1875 Egypt sold its canal shares to Britain for £4,000,000. In 1876 the government borrowed short-term loans at high interest rates to meet its obligations.

In April 1876 the Egyptian government announced its inability to honor the interest payments on its debt for three months. Egypt's creditors interpreted this as a declaration of bankruptcy. The government's weak international position placed it at a greater disadvantage than Turkey to negotiate a settlement with its creditors. Egypt's small size, semiautonomous status, and strategic position made it important to ambitious European powers, which saw the debt as a means to achieving political control and eagerly supported their national creditors. When Egypt challenged its creditors' terms,

foreign troops occupied the country, a fate Turkey avoided until the end of World War I.

CAISSE DE LA DETTE PUBLIQUE

From 1876 to 1880, Egypt's creditors devised several unsuccessful plans incorporating European control to regulate Egypt's financial situation. None of these plans reduced Egypt's debt or accurately estimated what Egypt could pay in interest and amortization. Such plans accompanied the establishing of a Caisse de la Dette Publique (Public Debt Fund) with directors from Britain, France, Italy, Austria-Hungary, and later Russia to collect revenues assigned for debt repayment.

In 1876 George Goschen (1831–1907) and Edmond Joubert, representatives of British and French stockholders, devised a plan that remained operational until 1880. They divided Egypt's debt into four categories: Ismail's private loans, to be paid from his personal revenue; shares of loans due for early repayment (those of 1864, 1866, 1867); preference debt established for holders of some government bonds issued for Egypt's remaining outstanding loans (those of 1862, 1868, 1873); and all remaining debts. As a whole, Egypt's debt was fixed at £89,309,000, with an annual interest charge of £6,000,000.

A series of events, including the low level of the Nile River in 1877 and the financial strain of the Ottoman war against Russia, worried Europeans, who feared a second Egyptian bankruptcy. In 1878 Anglo-French diplomatic pressure increased European control by allowing a commission of inquiry to complete a full examination of Egypt's finances and recommend better financial management methods. The commission's preliminary report called for the royal family's private estates to serve as security for a new loan, with some income set aside for extra budgetary support. Meanwhile, the government continued its payments using unofficial bank loans.

After the report, Ismail's cabinet received a British minister of finance and a French minister of public works. Ismail, attempting to limit increased foreign control, dismissed the European ministers in April 1879. Anglo-French control was soon reimposed, and in November one British controller-general to supervise government receipts and one French controller-general to oversee expenditure were appointed with seats in the Egyptian cabinet. Both were nominated by their governments under the understanding that neither could be dismissed without British and French consent. The commission of inquiry issued a second report in 1879 recommending the reduction of Egypt's annual interest charge and an increase in revenue through tax reforms.

Opposition to tax reforms resulted in a protest by large landholders and led to Ismail's overthrow.

The Law of Liquidation of 1880 created a second commission and served as the basis for the final settlement between Egypt and its creditors. Egypt's debt was fixed at £98,378,000, while the annual interest charge was lowered to 4 percent, or £4,243,000. The commission concluded that this fee was the maximum amount Egypt could afford based on Anglo-French experiences making debt payments during the initial years of occupation after the restructuring of Egypt's financial administration and revenue-collection system. The settlement called for expanding European control over Egypt's finances and stated explicitly the limits placed on Egypt's financial sovereignty. Britain regarded the law as having international treaty status, and its violation would be justification for direct foreign intervention.

Expanded European control led to an increase in the number of Europeans serving in Egypt's civil administration. In 1876 Europeans reorganized Egypt's Customs Office, Post Office, and Office of Public Accounts, placing them under the direction of Europeans receiving inflated salaries. These actions were justified through claims that such offices controlled sections of revenues reserved to service the public debt.

Egyptian resentment against Europeans mounted. The strain on Egypt to make regular payments to its creditors, along with anti-European sentiments, played a significant role in the National Movement of 1881 to 1882, led by Colonel Ahmed Urabi to restore the national integrity of Egypt by seizing control of the government to remove foreign control. Military reductions in terms of manpower and salary paved the way for Muhammad Sharif Pasha (1826–1887) and his successors to take control of Egypt and attempt to reclaim financial sovereignty.

British occupation of Egypt was regarded initially as a temporary situation for reestablishing foreign control. However, Britain repeatedly delayed its withdrawal and amended mechanisms of foreign control to strengthen British influence. Britain dissolved the "dual control" of Egypt between itself and France, replacing it in 1883 with the appointment of one British financial advisor to supervise all government financial decisions. In addition, an international conference amended the Law of Liquidation by increasing the limit for government expenditure and making a provision that revenues assigned to the Caisse de la Dette Publique exceeding the amount required to meet the annual interest and amortization payments would be split with the Egyptian government in a fifty-fifty ratio.

One last public loan was issued to fund the floating debt incurred during the first years of occupation, and also to fund works of economic development. As part of the 1904 Anglo-French entente, France agreed to remove the limit set for government expenditure and allowed the abolition of the international agencies established to control organizations whose revenues had been allocated to the Caisse de la Dette Publique. Following this agreement, Britain essentially gained control of Egypt's daily financial operations, even while subject to international obligations, such as servicing the public debt.

Once Egyptian occupation became permanent, Britain sought an economic policy enabling it to retain control at minimal cost to itself. British officials were concerned over Egypt's agricultural sector, believing an alliance with the landowning and peasant classes was essential to maintain imperial rule. British officials claimed their policies benefited Egypt economically, therefore justifying imperial control. The 1907 financial crisis and the disastrous 1909 cotton harvest countered British claims. Under British control, Egypt became dependent on a single crop and lost the ability to develop its own economy.

LEGACY OF FINANCIAL DEPENDENCE

By 1914, Middle Eastern elites generally believed that the region's political weakness resulted from its economic weakness, which was caused by dependence on foreign financial institutions and on agriculture rather than industry. Such elites reasoned that progress would result only if the state apparatus assumed a direct interventionist role and pursued a nationalist economic policy. Such a program became difficult to implement following World War I. The Ottoman Empire was divided into separate polities and zones of influence among European powers that continued to exploit the region before gradual withdrawal around the mid-twentieth century. Nationalist Egyptian elites had to rely on large landowners and foreign executives for political support, while the Turkish regime of Kemal Atatürk (1881–1938) remained dependent on foreign capital and enterprise.

SEE ALSO *Empire, Ottoman.*

BIBLIOGRAPHY

Blaisdell, Donald C. *European Financial Control in the Ottoman Empire: A Study of the Establishment, Activities, and Significance of the Administration of the Ottoman Public Debt.* New York, Columbia University Press, 1929. Reprint, New York: AMS, 1966.

Bonné, Alfred. *State and Economics in the Middle East: A Society in Transition,* 2nd ed. London: Routledge and Kegan Paul, 1955.

Cain, P. J. *Economic Foundations of British Overseas Expansion, 1815–1914.* London: Macmillan, 1980.

Coles, Paul. *The Ottoman Impact on Europe*. New York: Harcourt Brace, 1968.

Cook, M. A., ed. *Studies in the Economic History of the Middle East: From the Rise of Islam to the Present Day*. New York: Oxford University Press, 1970.

Farnie, D. A. *East and West of Suez: The Suez Canal in History, 1854–1956*. Oxford, U.K.: Clarendon, 1969.

Faroqhi, Suraiya, Bruce McGowan, Donald Quataert, and Sevket Pamuk. *An Economic and Social History of the Ottoman Empire*; Vol. 2: *1600–1914*. Cambridge, U.K.: Cambridge University Press, 1997.

Fromkin, David. *A Peace to End All Peace: The Fall of the Ottoman Empire and the Creation of the Modern Middle East*. New York: Henry Holt, 1989.

Gibb, Hamilton A. R., and Harold Bowen. *Islamic Society and the West: A Study of the Impact of Western Civilization on Moslem Culture in the Near East*. 2 vols. London: Oxford University Press, 1950–1957.

Gran, Peter. *Islamic Roots of Capitalism: Egypt, 1760–1840*. Austin: University of Texas Press, 1979.

Hansen, Bent, and Karim Nashashibi. *Foreign Trade, Regimes, and Economic Development*, Vol. 4: *Egypt*. New York: National Bureau of Economic Research, 1975.

Heller, Joseph. *British Policy Towards the Ottoman Empire, 1908–1914*. London: Frank Cass, 1983.

Hourani, Albert. *Europe and the Middle East*. Berkeley and Los Angeles: University of California Press, 1980.

Issawi, Charles, ed. *The Economic History of the Middle East, 1800–1914*. Chicago: University of Chicago Press, 1966.

Issawi, Charles, ed. *The Economic History of Turkey, 1800–1914*. Chicago: University of Chicago Press, 1980.

Kedourie, Elie. *England and the Middle East: The Destruction of the Ottoman Empire, 1914–1921*. London: Bowes and Bowes, 1956; 2nd ed., Hassocks, U.K.: Harvester, 1978.

Landes, D. S. *Bankers and Pashas: International Finance and Economic Imperialism in Egypt*. London: Heinemann, 1958.

Marlowe, John. *History of Modern Egypt and Anglo-Egyptian Relations, 1800–1956*, 2nd ed. Hamden, CT: Archon, 1965.

McCarthy, Justin. *The Arab World, Turkey, and the Balkans (1878–1914): A Handbook of Historical Statistics*. Boston: G. K. Hall, 1982.

Nevakivi, Jukka. *Britain, France, and the Arab Middle East, 1914–1920*. London: Athlone, 1969.

Owen, Roger. *Cotton and the Egyptian Economy, 1820–1914: A Study in Trade and Development*. Oxford, U.K.: Clarendon, 1969.

Owen, Roger. *The Middle East in the World Economy, 1800–1914*, 2nd ed. London: Methuen, 1993.

Pamuk, Sevket. *The Ottoman Empire and European Capitalism, 1820–1913: Trade, Investment, and Production*. Cambridge, U.K.: Cambridge University Press, 1987.

Polk, William R., and Richard L. Chambers, eds. *Beginnings of Modernization in the Middle East: The Nineteenth Century*. Chicago: University of Chicago Press, 1968.

Quataert, Donald. *Social Disintegration and Popular Resistance in the Ottoman Empire, 1881–1908: Reactions to European Economic Penetration*. New York: New York University Press, 1983.

Seddon, David. *A Political and Economic Dictionary of the Middle East*. London: Europa, 2004.

Tanenbaum, Jan K. *France and the Arab Middle East, 1914–1920*. Philadelphia: American Philosophical Society, 1978.

Tignor, Robert L. *Modernization and British Colonial Rule in Egypt, 1882–1914*. Princeton, NJ: Princeton University Press, 1966.

Wilson. Keith M., ed. *Imperialism and Nationalism in the Middle East: The Anglo-Egyptian Experience, 1882–1982*. London: Mansell, 1983.

Eric Martone

FRANCE'S AFRICAN COLONIES

Until the 1850s, the French position in Africa was a very marginal one. In 1659 France occupied two island bases: Saint-Louis in the mouth of the Senegal River and Gorée in what is now Senegal's Dakar harbor. Trading posts on the upper Senegal River, along the West African coast, and in Madagascar served as bases for French trade, mostly in slaves but also in gum, hides, and wax. When the slave trade ended in the early nineteenth century, various colonial governors sought a new trade in commodities.

In 1854 Major Louis Faidherbe (1818–1889) was appointed governor of Senegal. In wars with major Senegalese states, he established control of the Senegal River, opened up access to the Niger Valley, reduced customs paid to African states, and occupied some coastal areas. He also built schools, organized a bank, created a rudimentary civil administration, and began an accommodation with Islam.

France was forced to cut back its imperial ambitions by the Franco-Prussian War (1870–1871), but within a decade French soldiers, interested in seeing action and restoring France's military prestige, were promoting railroad construction in Senegal and between the Senegal and Niger rivers. The first, which connected Dakar and Saint-Louis, was built between 1882 and 1885. The second, connecting the Senegal and Niger rivers, necessitated a military effort if the line was to be protected. In 1879 Governor Brière de l'Isle (1827-1896) sent Colonel Joseph-Simon Gallieni (1849–1916) to investigate possible routes. The following year, French troops under Major Gustave Borgnis-Desbordes (1839-1900) began the conquest of the Sudan.

In Equatorial Africa, French interests were more limited, though there were several trading stations along the coast from the 1830s. The most important was Libreville (in modern Gabon), founded in 1849 for freed

Louis Faidherbe (1818–1889). *Faidherbe, the French governor of Senegal during parts of the 1850s and 1860s, was a leader in the establishment of the French Empire in Africa.* © CORBIS. REPRODUCED BY PERMISSION.

slaves. In 1875 France sent Pierre Savorgnan de Brazza (1852–1905) to explore the interior. His two explorations and treaties signed with African chiefs became the basis for French claims to land north of the Congo River when the European powers divided up Central Africa at Berlin in 1885. The Berlin Conference also set up the ground rules for the partition of Africa and began a race for control of Africa.

The Soudan (Sudan) became the fief of soldiers, who conquered it between 1883 and 1898, often ignoring civilian authority in the process. In Madagascar, French rule was not definitively established until the suppression of a Malgache revolt by Gallieni in 1896. French Guinea was created in 1893 by uniting various trading posts. In 1896 a small French force was able to take over the powerful kingdom of Futa Jallon (in present-day Guinea). Dahomey was conquered in 1894, and French rule was gradually extended further north. The colony of Côte d'Ivoire (Ivory Coast) was proclaimed in 1893, but was not securely under French control until the eve of World War I (1914–1918). In Mauritania, efforts at peaceful pacification failed when its architect, Xavier Coppolani (b. 1866), was assassinated in 1905, and the last resisters were not defeated until 1934.

After a brief period of rule through the governor of Senegal, decrees of 1902 and 1904 created two federal administrations with capitals in Dakar and Brazzaville (in present-day Republic of the Congo). Each had authority over law, administration, communication, health, public works, and agriculture. Boundaries between colonies were regulated and each was divided into *cercles* (administrative districts), which in turn, were divided into *cantons*.

Writers on colonialism have often compared French direct rule and British indirect rule. In some ways, this comparison is deceptive. The French did not preserve the trappings of the traditional state and were more likely to interfere with rules of succession and boundaries between traditional states. The French did, however, rule through chiefs, most of whom were chosen from traditional ruling families, and in areas like the Futa Jallon and the Mossi kingdoms (Burkina Faso), those traditional chiefs had a great deal of power. Colonial rule was thinnest in Saharan *cercles*, where tribal leaders were usually recognized, and in Equatorial Africa, where the regime gave large areas to concessionary companies.

Conquest brought peace and an end to slave-raiding and slave-trading. The regime was more timid in dealing with slavery. A 1905 law abolished any transactions in human beings. Administrators were also told they could no longer support the claims of masters to their slaves. Though many administrators hoped that slaves would not leave their masters, more than a million did so, often to return to earlier homes. Others remained where they were, but gradually asserted greater control over their work and family lives.

The major concern of the new colonial regimes was economic growth. The end of warfare and the construction of railroads opened large areas to trade and cash-crop production. The process was, however, often a harsh one. The French had obtained large areas, but with lower population densities and lower productivity than areas acquired by the British and Belgians. Colonies were expected to pay their own way, which led to taxes, which were coercive for peasants who worked the lands with hoes. Much of the infrastructure of the colonial state was created by the use of forced labor.

The French ideal of assimilation had a limited importance. The disestablishment of the Catholic Church during the early years of the twentieth century raised the cost of schools, which had been run by the missions. Those schools generally placed importance on the acquisition of French language, which in the long run produced an elite very much at home in French culture.

Politically, the rights of French citizens were given only to the inhabitants of the Four Communes of Senegal (Saint-Louis, Dakar, Rufisque, and Gorée).

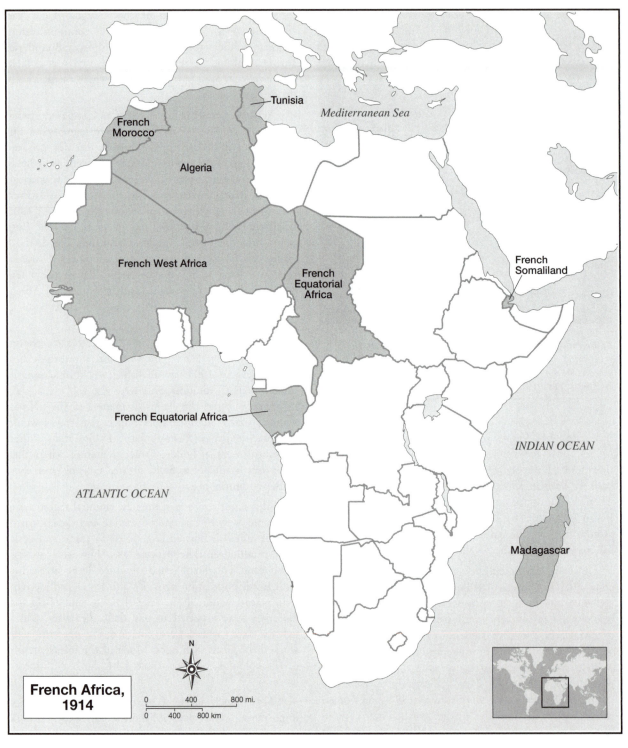

MAP BY XNR PRODUCTIONS. THE GALE GROUP.

These rights were poorly defined until World War I forced France to turn for help to African soldiers, and France gave Senegal's black deputy, Blaise Diagne (1872–1934), the leverage to demand confirmation of those rights. The idea of assimilation was most clearly articulated by the reforms that took place after World War II (1939–1945). All French colonies were given representation in the French Parliament.

This experiment contributed to the political education of a new elite, but it did not last long. Colonial voters recognized that they would always remain second-class citizens in the French Union. Leaders of wealthier colonies, most notably Felix Houphouet-Boigny (1905–1993) of the Ivory Coast, did not want their taxes used to support poorer colonies. The *loi-cadre* of 1956, which restructured French West Africa weakened federal authority and focused power more on the individual colonial governments. In 1958 the constitution of Charles de Gaulle's (1890–1970) Fifth Republic offered those colonies a much greater autonomy. Only the Guinea of Sekou Toure (1922–1984) rejected that offer and chose independence. Nevertheless, within two years, the leaders of all of France's African colonies had gone to Paris and been given independence. Formal French rule in West and Equatorial Africa was ended.

SEE ALSO *Empire, French; Scramble for Africa.*

BIBLIOGRAPHY

Cohen, William. *Rulers of Empire: The French Colonial Service in Africa.* Stanford, CA: Hoover Institution Press, 1971.

Conklin, Alice. *A Mission to Civilize: The Republican Idea of Empire in France and West Africa, 1895–1930.* Stanford, CA: Stanford University Press, 1997

Coquery-Vidrovitch, Catherine. "French Colonization in Africa to 1920: Administration and Economic Development." In *Colonialism in Africa, 1870–1960,* edited by Lewis H. Gann and Peter Duignan. Vol. 1: *The History and Politics of Colonialism, 1870–1914.* New York: Cambridge University Press, 1969.

Kanya-Forstner, A. S. *The Conquest of the Western Sudan: A Study in French Military Imperialism.* Cambridge, U.K.: Cambridge University Press, 1969.

Manning, Patrick. *Francophone Sub-Saharan Africa, 1880–1985,* 2nd ed. New York: Cambridge University Press, 1998.

Marseille, Jacques. *Empire colonial et capitalisme français: Histoire d'un divorce.* Paris: Albin Michel, 1984.

Suret-Canale, Jean. *French Colonialism in Tropical Africa, 1900–1945.* Translated by Till Gottheiner. New York: Pica, 1971.

Martin Klein

FREEBURGHERS, SOUTH AND SOUTHEAST ASIA

Alongside official crown or company servants, unbound European males called *freeburghers* shaped the character of Europe's early modern expansion to South and Southeast Asia. Generally, they settled in the European centers of the Asian trading world, made their living from interport trade or the supply of services, and were married to indigenous women. Portuguese *casados* and Dutch *vrijburghers* were the most important groups among the freeburghers.

For the numerous members of the Portuguese lower classes who reached Asia without contract onboard Portuguese ships, an existence as *soldado*—unmarried and only recruited in case of need by the Estado da India (the governmental organisation of Portuguese presence and commerce in Asia)—did not offer a sufficient income. Alternatively, a considerable number strove as private merchants and settled down with an indigenous wife, which was the only way for Europeans to establish a family in early modern Asia.

During the sixteenth and seventeenth centuries, *casados* lived in all Portuguese settlements as a constitutive part of the colonial society. In 1635 approximately 4,900 *casados* settled under the Estado's authority (which included 12,000 Portuguese overall), with their greatest communities in Macau in southern China (850) and Goa in western India (800).

The *casados* were generally divided into three major hierarchical categories. Those born of white parents were known as *reinois* (in Portugal) and *castiços* (in Asia). *Mestiços,* as descendants of a Portuguese father and his Asian or Eurasian wife, were less prestigious. *Casados pretos* (black casados), converted and acculturated native Asians, were not regarded as at all integrated into the *casado* community.

As free traders, the majority of the *casados* guaranteed close commercial ties between the different Portuguese settlements from East Africa to China, even when Dutch competition, as well as corruption and inefficiency, induced the decline of the Estado da India. Whereas the latter primarily controlled the main sea routes, the former used the offered advantages to fill trading gaps and to gain from their transcultural commercial networks, as well as from land ownership (especially in Goa). Thus, they were an indispensable pillar of the shrinking Portuguese presence in South and Southeast Asia.

From the beginning, the position of the Dutch *vrijburghers* was much more difficult. After primary plans to establish a colonial society by immigration of male and female Europeans failed early in the seventeenth century, the Dutch East India Company placed emphasis on cooperation with Asians and allowed their time-expired employees to settle down and to marry indigenous women. But the company's restrictive policy limited the attractiveness of this option. Individual settlement and marriage required a permit, and profitable trade with Indian and Moluccan spices, high-quality textiles from India and China, and raw materials like indigo or copper were strictly prohibited to private merchants.

Furthermore, the strong indigenous and Chinese competition in crafts and services interfered with the economic efforts of the *vrijburghers,* who, therefore, preferred economic niches. Tavern-keeping became the most popular occupation, and private merchants concentrated on supply functions for Dutch communities, trading foodstuff and European luxury goods. In the course of the eighteenth century, they penetrated increasingly typical Asian trades, including slaves and maritime products.

At the beginning of this century, endeavors to improve the Dutch East India Company and liberalize Asian trade achieved only slight success. Private capital and know-how proved to be insufficient, and the company's insistence on monopolies anticipated the expansion of a mercantile community. Thus, the number of *vrijburghers* was always low. In 1673 the largest community of *vrijburghers* (340 persons) lived in Batavia (present-day Jakarta). Smaller groups concentrated on the main Dutch port cities, such as Colombo, Cochin, Malacca, or Makassar. This colonial society remained small and, beyond Indonesia, disappeared during the early nineteenth century.

Nevertheless, in the core regions *casados* (Macau, Goa, Malacca) as well as *vrijburghers* (Indonesia, Ceylon) became the nucleus of new transcultural colonial societies. Their mestizo descendents perpetuated the families, which combined elements of both cultures. Luso-Asiatic communities have prevailed until the present, and the "Indische Culture" (Milone 1966/1967) offered recruitment potential for economic and administrative elites in colonial Indonesia.

SEE ALSO *Empire, Dutch; Empire, Portuguese.*

BIBLIOGRAPHY

Boxer, Charles R. *The Dutch Seaborne Empire, 1600–1800.* London: Hutchinson, 1965.

Boxer, Charles R. *The Portuguese Seaborne Empire, 1415–1825.* London: Hutchinson, 1969.

Milone, Pauline D. "Indische Culture and its Relationship to Urban Life." In *Comparative Studies in Society and History* 9 (1966/1967): 407–426.

Russell-Wood, A. J. R. *The Portuguese Empire, 1415–1808: A World of the Move.* Baltimore, MD: Johns Hopkins Press, 1992.

Subrahmanyam, Sanjay, and Luís Felipe F. R. Thomaz. "Evolution of Empire: The Portuguese in the Indian Ocean During the Sixteenth Century." In *The Political Economy of Merchant Empires,* edited by James D. Tracy. Cambridge, U.K.: Cambridge University Press, 1991.

Taylor, Jean Gelman. *The Social World of Batavia: European and Eurasian in Dutch Asia.* Madison: University of Wisconsin Press, 1983.

Veen, Ernst van. *Decay or Defeat? An Inquiry into the Portuguese Decline in Asia, 1580–1645.* Leiden, Netherlands: Research School CNWS, 2000.

Jürgen G. Nagel

FRENCH COLONIALISM, MIDDLE EAST

The Middle East and North Africa were central regions in the history of modern French colonialism. France's second colonial empire was founded in Algeria in 1830, after the loss of most of the first overseas empire in the Americas in the eighteenth century and the final defeat of Napoléon in Europe in 1815. France's "Islamic" empire was concentrated in North Africa, which remained the lynchpin both of a wider "French Africa" stretching far south of the Sahara, and of France's strategic position in the Mediterranean. However, the conquest of the Maghrib (Algeria, Tunisia, and Morocco) was preceded by involvement in Egypt that, beginning with the Napoleonic occupation of 1798 to 1801, also had long-term significance, and was followed by rule over Syria and Lebanon in the Mashriq (Levant) between 1920 and 1946. Formal French control at the height of the empire therefore extended to both major regions of the Arab world, with informal influence (through schools, commercial interests, and, especially in the nineteenth century, technical and military advisors) reaching more widely, for example, into Iran.

While French imperial interests and policies were frequently formulated in direct competition, and often in real or imagined conflict, with those of Britain, the rationales and practices of French colonial rule in the Middle East were similar to those of the British in many respects. Perceived French commercial and strategic interests dictated decisions about colonial expansion to a large extent; colonial administration was for the most part "indirect," operating through local intermediaries, and the French, like the British, attempted to secure long-term influence in their colonized territories after the departure of occupation troops and administrators. Unlike the British in the Middle East, however, the French, particularly in North Africa, engaged in large-scale colonization of land by European settlers, and many French imperialists considered their project as part of a specifically French vocation to promote a republican and humanist "civilization" worldwide. Perhaps most enduringly, French, like British, colonialism in the region created the context that shaped influential contemporary ideas about the societies and cultures of the Middle East and of Islam. These ideas were of great significance not only in the creation of dominant Western perceptions of "the Orient," but in the self-perception and political organization of the postcolonial Middle East itself.

EGYPT

Napoleon Bonaparte's invasion of Egypt in 1798, and the subsequent occupation of the country that was ended by British and Ottoman forces in 1801, has often been seen as the moment marking the beginning of the Middle East's "modern" history, a fact demonstrating the salience of imperialism in Europe-centered conceptions of history, and overlooking internal developments in the region as well as its connections with and beyond Europe in the eighteenth century. The occupation was important, however, in that it effectively separated Egypt from the Ottoman Empire, a significant moment in the long process of the empire's partition by European powers, and it demonstrates the importance of the broader social and cultural, as well as specifically political and strategic, aspects of imperialism that would continue to characterize the colonial relationship between France and the Middle East. As a strategic episode in France's revolutionary war against the monarchical powers of Europe, the Egyptian expedition was intended to attack Britain's communications with India. Coming in the wake of the French Revolution, it also marked the beginning of a newly asymmetrical relationship between post-Enlightenment, revolutionary, and "modern" France and an Arab-Muslim world imagined by French writers, travelers, soldiers, and politicians as backward, irrational, and fanatically superstitious. A major expression of the new, scientific understanding of the "backward" East by the "advanced" West was the *Description of Egypt*, an encyclopedia of discoveries in Egypt produced by the scholars who accompanied Napoleon's army.

The French occupation was resisted by the Egyptian population of Cairo, who rebelled in October 1798, and in the countryside. Napoleon himself remained in Egypt only a few months, and French troops were evacuated in September 1801. France retained great influence, however, as a political, economic, and cultural power, for the dynasty founded by the new ruler of Egypt, Muhammad Ali (or Mehmet Ali, r. 1805–1849), an Albanian soldier who arrived with the Ottoman army in 1801 and took effective control of the country in 1811. A series of Egyptian educational missions was sent to study in France from 1827 onward. Under the engineer Ferdinand de Lesseps, the Suez Canal project began in the 1850s as a primarily French undertaking. In 1876 France and Britain began exercising control of Egypt's finances, to guarantee payments on Egyptian debts to European creditors. Politically, France eventually gave way to

Britain, when British troops occupied Egypt in 1882, but both in the legal system and culturally, French influence remained significant. French tutors educated members of the royal family, and French remained a language of the Egyptian ruling class into the twentieth century. Egyptian law was (and remains) largely derived from the French model.

French troops returned to Egypt alongside British forces in the two powers' last colonial adventure in the Middle East, the Suez invasion of October 1956, when both governments, in collusion with Israel, attempted to overthrow Gamal 'Abd al-Nasser's Arab nationalist regime. At Suez, however, France was not primarily interested in Egypt, but in ending Egyptian support for the independence of France's last colonial territory in the region, Algeria.

NORTH AFRICA

The Napoleonic army that invaded Egypt in 1798 had been supplied with grain from Algeria during campaigns in Italy, and from the sixteenth through the eighteenth centuries, the rulers of Algiers dealt as diplomatic equals with European monarchs. The Ottoman Empire exercised a nominal suzerainty over the North African regencies of Algiers and Tunis, but a local dynasty was established in Tunis in 1705, and the rulers of Algiers in the seventeenth and eighteenth centuries were selected from among leading members of the city's military forces, governing notables, and corsair captains (privateers). The pursuit of corsairing by ships from Algiers, when European fleets had largely abandoned this form of warfare, was partly the result of European merchants' closing their markets to North African shipping at the end of the 1700s, but gave rise to the stereotype of "Barbary piracy" as "the scourge of Christendom." This image persisted through the colonial period. Debts on Algiers' grain shipments to revolutionary France remained unpaid by the Restoration government, and in 1827 a confrontation in which the ruler of Algiers, Husayn Dey, struck the French consul with a fly-whisk, escalated into a French naval blockade. In 1830, beset by domestic pressure, the government of Charles X (r. 1824–1830) launched an invasion that toppled the Ottoman establishment in Algiers. Charles X himself fell from power only weeks later in the 1830 revolution, and the new government inherited an indecisive military occupation of Algiers. As projects for both military and civilian colonization gained support, however, the conquest expanded in the east and west of the country, and southward toward the Sahara.

Resistance to the conquest emerged almost immediately, as Algerian leaders, sometimes in rivalry with each other, responded to the collapse of central authority.

In the west, the emir 'Abd al-Qādir (1808–1883), acting at first in the name of the Moroccan sultan, defeated his local rivals with French help and tried to come to terms with the French, to limit their occupation to coastal enclaves while establishing his own state inland. In the east, the city of Constantine fell in 1837 but its Ottoman governor, Ahmad Bey, led resistance in the Aurès Mountains until 1848. Local revolts broke out throughout the country, and French troops penetrated further inland and into the mountains in "pacification" campaigns, repressing resistance on the edge of the Sahara in 1849 and in the Djurdjura Mountains of Kabylia in 1857. 'Abd al-Qādir surrendered in 1847, and the last major revolt was crushed in Kabylia in 1871.

By 1872 Algeria had lost one-third of its 1830 population of about three million. To the colonial lobby, influenced by social Darwinist ideas, this was a sign of inevitable racial decline among the "natives," who were destined to be replaced by "industrious" European settlers. Later Algerian nationalist writers called it "genocide." The European population, however, never expanded significantly after the turn of the twentieth century, and instead of presiding over a demographic replacement of "natives" by colonists, colonial politics became obsessed by the demographic "threat" of a rapidly growing Algerian population (5 million in the 1920s, ca. 9 million by 1954), apparently set to overwhelm the Europeans (ca. 800,000 in the 1920s, ca. 900,000 in 1954). White minority rule was preserved by refusing full French citizenship to Algerian Muslims (indigenous Algerian Jews became citizens by decree in 1870), limiting or blocking the reform programs that began to be proposed after World War I, and repressing nationalist opposition from the late 1920s into the 1950s. By the time of the centenary celebrations of "French Algeria" in 1930, the country, considered as three *départements* of metropolitan France, was seen by officials, settlers, and travelers as an "integral part of France"—as, indeed, it had been designated in 1848.

Algeria's situation set it apart from other Middle Eastern colonial territories: It was ruled as part of France's "interior," its economy was entirely geared to French interests (especially the export of minerals, cereals, and wine), and its administration, public services, industry, infrastructure, and major landholdings were almost entirely controlled by a large and assertive European population. Algeria's precolonial social, political, and cultural institutions were either destroyed or subjected to pressures that were generally experienced with lower intensity in other parts of the region; much of what survived colonization was uprooted in the war of independence (1954–1962), which dislocated much of Algeria's rural society as well as finally precipitating the departure of the colonial European population.

By the later nineteenth century, this Algerian model of total conquest "by the sword and the plough" (war and settlement) gave way to supposedly more enlightened methods known as "peaceful penetration" and colonial development. The security of the Algerian frontier and the prospect of land and investments encouraged colonial soldiers and commercial lobbyists to press for the extension of French rule to Tunisia and Morocco. In Tunisia, the state-strengthening policies of Ahmed Bey (r. 1837–1855) and the promulgation of a constitution in 1861 were intended to prevent foreign domination. Funding the expansion of the state and its powers, however, led to unmanageable foreign debt and rural insurrection when taxation was increased to meet debt repayments. British, French, and Italian influence in Tunisia's politics and the economy increased, and in 1869 the regency was forced into bankruptcy, with an international financial commission set up to protect the interests of European creditors. On the pretext of securing the Algerian border against incursions by Tunisian tribes, a French military expedition occupied Tunisia in 1881. A protectorate was imposed, under which at first the management of Tunisia's defense and foreign relations, and then also domestic government and the economy, fell under the control of a French resident-general and his staff. Officially the resident-general was only chief advisor to the Tunisian monarch, the bey, but the beys quickly became almost powerless figureheads in whose name policy was enacted by French officials appointed by the foreign ministry in Paris. Beys who attempted to assert their own authority were threatened with military force, as in 1922, when Muhammad al-Nāsir Bey's palace was surrounded with troops to prevent his abdication in protest against French policy, or removed, as in 1943, when Munsif Bey, who opposed Vichy France's anti-Semitic laws and hoped to restore his own sovereignty, was deposed and exiled.

Control of land, towns, industry, and commerce passed largely into European hands. By 1914 European control of the country's productive resources had already almost reached its maximum extent—about one-fifth of the total cultivated land, and almost half of the richest land, was owned by just under five thousand Europeans. A European landholding averaged 250 hectares (618 acres), whereas the Tunisian rural population of about 480,000 families retained holdings averaging about 6 hectares (15 acres) each, or became tenants of landlords at increasing rates of rent. The tendency toward concentration of landholdings was marked throughout French North Africa, with small colonial farms as well as formerly private, collective, or tribal lands being absorbed into large, European-owned estates. In the fertile area around Tunis, by 1950 Europeans held between 30 and 50 percent of all cultivated land. The concentration of

Louis Lyautey with Sultan Moulay Youssef, Circa 1925. *Louis Hubert Gonzalve Lyautey, the French military leader and resident-general of Morocco from 1912 to 1925, dines with Moulay Youssef, sultan of Morocco.* © **HULTON-DEUTSCH COLLECTION/CORBIS. REPRODUCED BY PERMISSION.**

the best land in the hands of a small group of individual and corporate owners paralleled the increasing urbanization of both the European and indigenous populations. In Algeria, in the early 1870s almost half the European population lived on the land; only a quarter remained by 1936. And whereas in the 1890s the Europeans outnumbered the Muslims in major Algerian towns, by the mid-1930s the proportions of urban population were equal, and by 1954 there were almost twice as many Muslims as non-Muslims in the main urban centers. French political dominance was also threatened by rival European powers, especially in Tunisia, where in 1901 there were only 24,000 French, but over 71,000 Italian, citizen settlers. French predominance was ensured by naturalization campaigns, in which Europeans of Maltese, Italian, Spanish, Greek, and other origins, as well as indigenous Jewish families and the few Muslims who converted to Christianity, were encouraged to take French citizenship. In Tunisia, the French colony began to outnumber the Italians only in the 1930s. But among Algerian or Tunisian Muslims, only a small number, mainly

decorated war veterans, members of important families, or those with access to education and liberal professions, wished or were allowed to gain the full political rights that came with French citizenship.

Similar factors as those leading to the annexation of Tunisia were responsible for the gradual incorporation of Morocco, first under French economic and military influence, and finally, in 1912, into formal political control under a protectorate. The *Comité de l'Afrique française* (French Africa Committee), a lobby group of business and political interests set up in Paris in 1890, and military officers anxious both to secure Algeria's western borders and to extend and consolidate their African conquests, pushed for French dominance in Morocco against Spanish, Italian, German, and especially British rivals, all of whom had material or declared commercial and political interests in the country. Increasing European commercial and financial control over Moroccan products and markets increased local resentment and instability, undermining the credibility of the sultan. The ruling Alawi (or Filāli) dynasty had been established in the seventeenth century. The sultan was understood to be invested with authority by virtue of the recognition of Morocco's religious and political leaders that he would uphold the law, the integrity of the country, and the duty to defend it from foreign enemies. The increasing instability of the throne, however, largely caused by imperial penetration, contributed to the insecurity that European powers saw as anarchy threatening their interests, and hence to further pressure for direct imperial intervention. In 1907, when riots broke out in Casablanca, the French navy shelled the city and landed troops (some of whom joined in the rioting). When Moroccan tribes rose in revolt against the French occupation of Casablanca, they called on the sultan's brother to replace him, leading to civil war in 1907 to 1908. The new sultan, 'Abd al-*H*afiz, however, was financially dependent on France, which now controlled Morocco's internal revenue, banking, and remaining state-owned commerce. In 1910, a French military mission took over the organization of the Moroccan army. When unrest broke out again in 1911, French troops occupied the major cities, and the sultan had to accept the establishment of a protectorate. Most of the country fell under French control, while a Spanish protectorate was set up in the Rif Mountains of the north and in the coastal strip of desert to the south that became the Spanish Sahara (now Western Sahara). The city of Tangier, on the strait of Gibraltar, became an international zone.

The protectorate regime in Morocco was especially influenced by the work and ideas of Louis-Hubert Lyautey. France's first resident-general in Rabat, Lyautey was an army officer who served first in Indochina (Vietnam) as it fell under French control, and who played an important part in the gradual extension of French rule to Morocco after his arrival in the Sahara, on the border between Algeria and Morocco, in 1903. Lyautey ruled Morocco for thirteen years, and was buried there when he died in 1934. When his remains were transferred to Les Invalides in Paris in 1961, he was officially celebrated as the theorist of French imperialism at its most "humane." Lyautey's model of colonial conquest and rule was the antithesis of what had happened in Algeria. Instead of total conquest by force of arms, the destruction of indigenous institutions, and the takeover of land by thousands of colonial settlers, Lyautey proposed what he called "peaceful penetration" of territory and the "association" of local institutions and society with what he saw as the enlightening and modernizing influence of France. Peaceful penetration meant that armed force was to be used as a last resort; instead, the army should establish outposts providing security for travel and trade, medical assistance, and policing, and reach agreements with local leaders whose positions would be strengthened by the French, and through

whom French influence would spread. Association meant indirect rule, by a handful of European planners and administrators, through existing local institutions, which, like the law, customs, and way of life of the people, must be preserved, while their environment and economy would be modernized, rationalized, and made more productive.

The actual operation of colonial rule hardly worked as straightforwardly as the theory supposed. After 1913, when landownership began to be registered and traded on an open market, Moroccan peasants became landless cultivators or tenants on estates owned by local notables or by Europeans, and property transactions involving Europeans, as elsewhere in North Africa and the Middle East, were taken out of the jurisdiction of local courts and entrusted to French courts. The attempt to preserve and codify local custom provoked the beginning of mass nationalism in 1930, when a decree was passed placing civil law in Berber-speaking areas (much of rural Morocco) under Berber customary law, and criminal law under the jurisdiction of French administrators; the decree was seen as an attack on the country's Islamic law and customs, and as an attempt to divide Berber-speaking Moroccans from their Arabic-speaking Muslim compatriots. The careful preservation of Morocco's urban heritage in the great medieval cities of Fez and Marrakesh led to the creation of a kind of "urban apartheid," with the old cities' development frozen and new, effectively racially segregated European towns developing alongside, but distinct from, them. The European population, too, especially in the rapidly developing city of Casablanca, became numerous and relatively privileged, and when decolonization became imminent in the 1950s, European terrorist groups emerged to oppose it in Morocco (under the name *Présence française*, French Presence) as in Tunisia (*La Main rouge*, the Red Hand) and Algeria (*Organisation armée secrète*, Secret Armed Organization). As in Algeria and Tunisia, however, colonialism in Morocco also contained space for North Africans to challenge the system on its own terms. In 1934, Moroccan leaders called for a "real protectorate" that would work in the interests of Moroccans, just as Tunisian constitutionalist leaders in 1905 to 1907 called for a reformed protectorate to benefit Tunisians, and Algerian liberals from 1912 to 1936 made proposals for Algerians to gain full civil and political rights within French Algeria.

Despite Lyautey's theory, armed force remained integral to French colonialism in the Maghrib. After the occupation of Fez, messianic religious figures led resistance in the north and south of Morocco until 1918, and so-called pacification campaigns continued in the countryside until 1934. In the Rif Mountains of the north, French troops and air power were used in 1926 to 1927 to repress the resistance led by the emir 'Abd al-Krīm al-Khattābi, who set up an independent Republic of the Rif after defeating the Spanish army in 1921. Armed resistance to colonial rule reemerged in both Morocco and Tunisia in 1952, and in 1953 the sultan, Muhammad ben Yūsuf, was deposed at gunpoint by the French and forcibly removed into exile. But by 1955 the French government, faced with the end of one colonial war in Indochina (Vietnam), and the beginning of another in Algeria, opted for a negotiated transition to independence for the protectorates, in Morocco on March 2, and in Tunisia on March 20, 1956. In Algeria, however, the renunciation of French sovereignty was unthinkable, and decolonization came only through another long war, from November 1954 to March 1962.

THE LEVANT

Formal French rule in the eastern Mediterranean was more mitigated, and of shorter duration, than in the Maghrib. Nonetheless, here too French colonialism both drew on and departed from an earlier, longer-term historical relationship with the region. And in the Arab east as in North Africa, France's empire sought to imprint a durable cultural and social influence as well as expanding the metropole's political and strategic power.

France's relationship with the Ottoman Empire had been ambiguous, as part of the long struggle for dominance among the European powers. The Ottomans, as the world's most powerful Islamic state and the dominant power in the eastern Mediterranean and southeastern Europe, were important allies of the French monarchy against the Holy Roman Empire, dominated by the rival Habsburg dynasty, during the sixteenth century. From 1853 to 1856, French as well as British soldiers fought in alliance with the Ottomans to protect the empire against Russian expansion in the Crimean war. At the same time, French expeditions against Egypt, Algiers, and Tunis captured territory that had been under at least nominal Ottoman sovereignty, and French commercial and financial expansion in the nineteenth century played an active part in imperial Europe's penetration of the central Ottoman state. From 1890 to 1914, France was the largest investor in the Ottoman Empire, with double the investments of the nearest European rival, Germany. When the impossibility of servicing debt on state loans led to Ottoman bankruptcy in 1875, France was part of the international consortium managing the state's debt and the revenues appropriated to pay it, 63 percent of which was in French hands by 1913. After 1883 a French-owned agency controlled the production, processing, and tax revenue on tobacco in the empire. The port of Beirut, and the road and railway linking Beirut with Damascus, were constructed by French companies.

As in Morocco, economic interests became the prelude to political control when the Ottoman state, allied with Germany in World War I, collapsed following defeat in 1918, and its territories were partitioned. France's diplomacy at the end of World War I, which aimed at control of Syria and Lebanon as France's share of the former empire's provinces, was based on these material interests combined with longstanding cultural claims—especially the claim, originally made by Louis XIV in 1649, to protect the Maronite community in Lebanon (members of a Christian church linked to Roman Catholicism). French troops occupied the Lebanese coast and pushed inland, but an Arab government set up in Damascus in 1918 attempted to assert sovereignty over as much of historic Ottoman Syria (present-day Syria, Lebanon, Jordan, Israel, and Palestine) as could be preserved from European rule. Financially dependent on Britain, however, and faced with internal instability and French force, the Damascus government fell before French troops who occupied all of Lebanon and Syria in 1920, under a mandate from the League of Nations for the governance of the two countries. The mandate system devised after World War I changed the international rules under which colonialism operated, so that Syria and Lebanon were never "French" in the way protectorate Morocco and Tunisia were, much less annexed as Algeria had been. European rule was now supposed to guide the political and economic development of mandated territories until they were judged capable of self-government. If national independence was explicitly foreseen as the outcome of colonial rule, however, European powers hoped to create states in the mandated countries that would be locally effective and stable rulers while remaining firmly under imperial influence after formal independence was declared. The effects of imperial strategies intended to ensure this, however, turned out to be unpredictable.

The long-standing French relationship with the Maronites in Lebanon helped shape a Lebanese republic partitioned from Syria in such a way that the Maronite community became politically dominant, but in a "Greater Lebanon" that was made economically viable only by the addition of areas inhabited mainly by Sunni and Shia Muslims. The institutionalization of confessional communities as political units, and the country's changing demography, meant that the National Pact of 1943, which set the proportions of each community's political representation, was soon out of step with the country's social makeup. Divergent loyalties on local, regional, and international levels—to conservative and Christian Lebanese nationalism, radical and secular Arab nationalism, or, more recently, revolutionary and

Gunnery Instruction in Lebanon, Circa 1925. *Soldiers of the regular French Levant army instruct volunteer forces in the use of rifles in preparation for threatened attacks by Druzes and revolutionary Syrians.* © BETTMANN/CORBIS. REPRODUCED BY PERMISSION.

utopian transnational Islamism—later aggravated these tensions when the Lebanese state imploded in civil war in 1958 and again in 1975.

In Syria, French rule was imposed against widespread popular opposition and was faced with a major revolt in 1925 to 1927, repressed by massive military force. At the same time, Lyautey's Moroccan model of imperial administration was now orthodox doctrine for colonial officers and officials, and many aspects of the theory of rule recently applied to North Africa were adopted in the Levant. This included ideas about the Middle East's population being fundamentally characterized by division into separate, mutually hostile, ethnic or religious groups. French administrators arrived in Lebanon and Syria with ready-made assumptions that, like the divisions they believed to exist between Berbers and Arabs, cities and countryside, peasants and nomads, in North Africa, the Levant's people existed only as ethnic groups or sects, in anarchy among themselves and having known nothing but oppression by "despotic" Muslim rule under the Ottoman sultans. Developed and articulate political demands of Syrians

for unity and independence were ignored as agitation fomented against French rule—supposedly by the British. On this basis, colonial rule divided Syria into autonomous ethnic mini-states, and although this policy was subsequently revised, French administration continued to instrumentalize preconceived social fracture lines, attempting to find support in the countryside against the cities, where the most organized opposition to the mandate was located, and in Christian and other religious minority groups against the Sunni Muslim community and its dominant urban notables. The previously isolated and heterodox Alawi community, an offshoot of Shia Islam living mainly in the mountainous northwest of Syria, were heavily recruited into the military, giving them a new-found dominant role in Syria's armed forces after independence.

After the failure of negotiations with Syrian leaders for a treaty relationship in 1933, unrest and a general strike in 1936 forced concessions from the French and a Franco-Syrian treaty that provided for nominal independence and allowed elections to be held. But the *Kutla,* or National Bloc government that took office in November

1936, resigned three years later, after the French parliament failed to ratify the 1936 treaty and agreed to cede the partly Turkish-populated district of Alexandretta, in northwest Syria, to Turkey. Military rule was imposed and the parliaments dissolved in 1939, with the onset of World War II, and in 1941 British and Free French troops invaded Syria and Lebanon, removing the Vichy government's administration there. In 1943 the constitutions, suspended in both countries before the outbreak of the war, were restored and new elections held, giving majorities to nationalist governments who proclaimed independence from France. The French administration began to transfer civilian government functions to the nationalists, but attempted to maintain France's cultural and military presence in both countries. After mass protests and violent demonstrations in both Syria and Lebanon, France was forced by international pressure, particularly Anglo-American, and eventually from the U.N., as well as by massive popular demand, to evacuate its troops from Syria in April, and from Lebanon in December 1946.

LEGACY

The lasting influence of French colonialism on the shape of society, culture, and politics in France's former territories in the Middle East, and on their relationship to the former colonial power, was not always what the imperial planners had intended, but in several ways it continued to be important. The models of the colonial state, as a republic, in Lebanon, Syria, and Algeria, or the monarchy in Morocco, and its bureaucratic practices were largely taken over into the independent nation-states that followed. In Morocco, former officers of the colonial army became the mainstays of the armed forces and internal security when the sultan returned from exile as King Muhammad V, and the institution of the monarchy, through which the French had attempted to rule but that had become the central symbol of nationalism, inherited a stronger state than it had ever possessed before the protectorate. In Tunisia, Habib Bourguiba, the nationalist leader who had studied law in France, embarked on a rationally authoritarian, top-down "modernization" of law, the economy, and society, enabling important social liberalization, especially in the status of women, but never political democratization. The sectarian political divisions, and the class positions of dominant and subordinate social groups that they often expressed, continued to influence developments in Lebanon and Syria. Despite the rejection of French cultural preeminence, French educational models and institutions, especially French-language secondary schools in North Africa and Egypt, and higher education institutions, notably St. Joseph University in Lebanon, remained important in the education of new ruling

groups. France remains important in the commercial and political connections of social and cultural elites from its formerly colonial countries, and with the exception of Algeria and Syria, these territories (including Egypt) remain members of the intergovernmental "Francophonie" organization, a grouping of francophone countries, especially those formerly part of the French empire. French public space is a significant arena in cultural, political, and economic terms; in France, writers, students, filmmakers, human rights activists, and workers from North Africa and the Middle East publish books, attend university, show their work, lobby governments, and look for jobs. The connections between France and its former colonial territories in the region are also significant for migration, tourism, investment, and trade.

SEE ALSO *Algeria; Egypt; North Africa; North Africa, European Presence in.*

BIBLIOGRAPHY

Firro, Kais M. *Inventing Lebanon: Nationalism and the State under the Mandate.* London: Tauris, 2003.

Hourani, Albert. *A History of the Arab Peoples.* London: Faber and Faber, 1991.

Khoury, Philip S. *Syria and the French Mandate: The Politics of Arab Nationalism, 1920–1945.* Princeton, NJ: Princeton University Press, 1987.

Owen, Roger. "Egypt and Europe: From French Expedition to British Occupation." In *The Modern Middle East,* edited by Albert Hourani, Philip S. Khoury, and Mary C. Wilson. London: Tauris, 1993.

Pennell, C. R. *Morocco since 1830.* London: Hurst, 2000.

Perkins, Kenneth J. *A History of Tunisia.* Cambridge, U.K.: Cambridge University Press, 2004.

Ruedy, John. *Modern Algeria: The Origins and Development of a Nation.* Bloomington and Indianapolis: Indiana University Press, 1992.

Thompson, Elizabeth B. *Colonial Citizens: Republican Rights, Paternal Privilege, and Gender in French Syria and Lebanon.* New York: Columbia University Press, 2000.

Yapp, Malcolm E. *The Middle East since the First World War: A History to 1995.* 2d ed. London: Longman, 1996.

James McDougall

FRENCH EAST INDIA COMPANY

The European competition for the lucrative trade routes to India in the seventeenth and eighteenth centuries was played out amongst rival trading companies, of which the French were relative latecomers. It is somewhat of an historical misnomer to speak of the French East India Company as a single entity because it evolved from a variety of disparate predecessors rather than from a singular corporate entity. Hence, the history of the French East India Company is not the history of a continuous, unitary corporate body. Unlike the English and Dutch companies, moreover, the later French variants were more closely aligned to the state and more prone to the fiscal pressures and internal dynamics of official government policy. While the French saw themselves as rivals to the English East India Company, however, they preferred to emulate the federated structure of the Dutch East India Company.

In fact, historians are able to trace six different companies that were formed at various times. Although Henry IV issued the first patent in 1604 to grant the *Compagnie des mers Orientales* exclusive rights to trade in Asia and to establish colonies, this venture was largely a failure due to lack of funds and the opposition of the Dutch. Louis XIII granted a new patent in 1615 to form a company called *La Compagnie des Moluques,* which sent two ships to India, of which only one returned.

However, it is not until the influence of Cardinal Richelieu under Louis XIV that maritime endeavors received the attention of the French state. The formation of *La Compagnie d'Orient* in 1642 was the first company of colonization in the Indian Ocean area, founding the trading post of Fort Dauphin on the island of Madagascar as the strategic midway point between France, Africa, and the lucrative Asian trade. The establishment of *La Compagnie des Indes Orientales* in 1664 by Jean-Baptiste Colbert and the emerging importance of colonies such as the *Ile de France* (Mauritius) and the *Ile de Bourbon* (Réunion) saw a new era of direct competition with the Dutch and the English for the South Asian trade. Whereas *La Compagnie des Indes Occidentales* had a trading monopoly in North America and on the west coast of Africa, the former was given the French patent to trade from the Cape of Good Hope and throughout the Indian and Pacific Oceans and, hence, covered a vast area that included the southern and eastern coasts of Africa, India, Southeast Asia, China, Japan, and stretching as far as New Caledonia and Tahiti. In 1719 the company was amalgamated into the broader American and African operations under the umbrella organization *La Compagnie des Indes.*

The difficulty of establishing a base on Madagascar saw the French Company look further afield to India, which was the main object of European colonial ambition. First settling in Surat in 1666 and then founding the important center of Pondicherry in 1673, the French was the last European power to compete with the Indian trade on the subcontinent and were in direct competition with the English and the Dutch who were already established there. Under Benoît Dumas and Jean François Dupleix in the 1730s to 1750s, the French Company

developed a largely successful policy of forming subsidiary alliances with local rulers to gain commercial advantages and sought corporate control of Indian territory. This was a strategy that was later emulated by the British to their greater advantage.

The defeat of the French at the Battle of Wandiwash in 1760 and the intermittent capture of Pondicherry and other French settlements during the Anglo-French Wars meant that the company's operations in India were precarious. The French East India Company was liquidated in 1770 with the transfer of all assets and trading stations to the French government who took direct control of colonial affairs under the Marine Ministry. There were some attempts to revive purely commercial operations in 1785 when a new company was formed by Charles-Alexandre de Calonne, but these were thwarted by the events of the French Revolution and the emergence of the English East India Company as the paramount territorial sovereign power on the Indian subcontinent.

SEE ALSO *Dutch United East India Company; Dutch West India Company; English East India Company (EIC).*

BIBLIOGRAPHY

Barbier, J. "La compagnie française des Indes." *Revue historique de l'Inde française* 3 (1919): 5-96.

Boucher, P. *The Shaping of the French Colonial Empire: A Bio-Bibliography of the Careers of Richelieu, Fouquet and Colbert.* New York: Garland, 1985.

Lokke, C.L. *France and the Colonial Question: A Study of Contemporary French Public Opinion, 1763-1801.* New York: Columbia University Press, 1932.

Malleson, G.B. *History of the French in India.* London: W.H. Allen & Co., 1893.

Sen, S.P. *The French in India, 1763-1816.* Calcutta: Firma K.L. Mukhopadhyay, 1958.

Sen, S.P. *The French in India: First Establishment and Struggle.* Calcutta: University of Calcutta Press, 1947.

Subramanian, Lakshmi, ed. *French East India Company and the Trade of the Indian Ocean: A Collection of Essays by Indrani Chatterjee.* Delhi: Munshiram Publishers, 1999.

Adrian Carton

FRENCH INDOCHINA

Indochina is a French colony and four protectorates in Southeast Asia established between 1860 and 1904, and covering the present-day territories of Cambodia, Vietnam, and Laos. The five colonial components of Indochina became independent in 1954.

BEGINNINGS

French imperialism in Southeast Asia began almost accidentally in 1858, when a French fleet bombarded the Vietnamese port of Tourane (present-day Danang) to avenge the execution of Catholic missionaries by the Vietnamese regime. Hoping to gain commercial advantages and military renown, French troops occupied the southern city of Saigon (present-day Ho Chi Minh City) in 1860 and by 1867 France had expanded its colony—which it named Cochinchine (Cochin China)—over six adjoining provinces. The Vietnamese emperor in Hue, who had been taken completely by surprise, acceded reluctantly to these developments, signing a treaty with France in 1862.

In 1863, in order to protect the western frontiers of Cochin China, the French imposed a protectorate on the kingdom of Cambodia. They did so with the consent of the Cambodian monarch, Norodom (r. l863–1904), who feared that continuing pressure on his kingdom from Siam would jeopardize his freedom of maneuver. The French were drawn to Cambodia by illusory notions of commercial rewards that might accrue via the unmapped Mekong River. Because King Norodom acquiesced willingly to French protection and accepted what the French called their "civilizing mission" (*mission civilisatrice*), Cambodia soon became one of France's favorite possessions.

Between 1873 and 1885, the French expanded their empire by imposing separate protectorates over Annam (central Vietnam)—a region that included the imperial capital of Hue—and the northern provinces of Tonkin, where the important cities of Hanoi and Haiphong were located. France broke the Vietnamese empire, which had been unified by the Nguyen Emperor Gia Long (r. 1802–1820), into three pieces. Intentionally or not, they destroyed the old, Confucian-based administrative order, and created opportunities for the Vietnamese elite to imagine and devise new ways of governing their country. "Vietnam," in any case, had disappeared and as late as the 1940s the French forbade local people to use the word.

In 1904 three principalities east of the Mekong and north of Cambodia that the French named Laos came under French control, following over twenty years of French pressure and diplomatic maneuvering. The Lao princes were happy to exchange the patronage of the Siamese ruler in Bangkok for open-ended, relatively genteel French protection.

In 1907 France persuaded Siam to relinquish control over two provinces in western Cambodia annexed by Siam in the 1790s. Following the transfer of these provinces, one of which contained the ruins of Cambodia's medieval capital of Angkor, French Indochina assumed

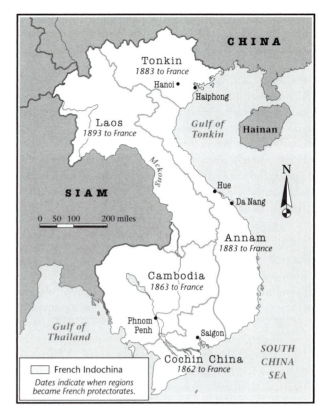

MAP BY XNR PRODUCTIONS. THE GALE GROUP.

the physical dimensions that it retained (save for a brief hiatus in World War II) until the end of the colonial era.

CHARACTERISTICS OF INDOCHINA

French policies and administrative styles differed over time and from place to place, responding in part to differences among the components of their empire. Cochin China was a colony and was subject to French law. Its French citizens elected a member to the National Assembly in Paris. The regime encouraged the Vietnamese elite to take up French citizenship. France used hundreds of local people in their administration, with a French governor as the supreme authority. The press was relatively free and people were better educated than elsewhere in Indochina. In the "protectorates," where local rulers supposedly retained authority, French citizenship was harder to obtain, educational institutions developed more slowly, and French controls over the press and political activity were more repressive.

The component parts of Indochina also differed demographically: the Red River Delta in Tonkin, bordering China, was one of the most densely populated regions in the world, whereas Annam, Cambodia, and Laos housed relatively few people. The parts differed culturally as well, as the name *Indochina* suggests. The national languages of Laos, Cambodia, and Vietnam were mutually unintelligible. The Lao and Cambodians were Theravada Buddhists with cultures influenced indirectly by India, whereas the Vietnamese were nominally Mahayana Buddhists, and had been deeply influenced by Chinese Confucian culture and administration for over two thousand years. Eating habits, writing systems, clothing styles, and domestic architecture differed between Laos and Cambodia on the one hand and Vietnam on the other. Finally, largely because of nineteenth-century events, the Khmer and the Lao were fearful of Vietnamese expansion, whereas the Vietnamese, in general, looked down on their "barbarian" neighbors to the west.

Under the French Governor General Paul Doumer (1897–1902), administrative distinctions in the region blurred as the overarching entity of "Indochina" was imposed onto its component parts. Doumer's reforms brought Indochina's accounts into balance, via the efficient collection of taxes. Government monopolies on the sale of opium, salt, and alcohol provided almost half of the total revenues. Local people (including the Lao, after 1904) were also heavily taxed. They now came under the jurisdiction of a French Governor General, resident in Hanoi. The French maintained the fiction that they governed on behalf of local rulers (except in Cochin China), but gave those rulers no authority.

ECONOMICS AND ADMINISTRATION

To rule over millions of people, the French needed local help. In Vietnam they could count on experienced administrators to collect taxes and to maintain law and order. In Laos and Cambodia, a career civil service was undeveloped but taxes were collected with the help of local elites.

In economic terms, Cochin China was the most prosperous part of Indochina. The benefits of French law, combined with profitable rice and rubber plantations (the latter controlled by French companies) and the entrepreneurial energy of Chinese and Sino-Vietnamese merchants, made Cochin China the liveliest, most prosperous, and most Francophile component of Indochina. Hundreds of wealthy Cochin Chinese were educated in France, and immigrants from southern China poured into the colony, where most of them engaged in commerce and petty manufacturing. Saigon and its Chinese suburb of Cholon were linked by trading networks to the outside world and functioned as powerful engines of free market capitalism.

By the 1920s, rich coal deposits in Tonkin and rubber plantations in Cambodia also produced revenue for French investors and spawned the beginnings of a proletariat, later drawn toward the Indo-China Communist Party

(or ICP; founded in 1930). Investments in Indochinese public works such as the Hanoi to Saigon railroad, which carried few passengers and very little freight, reaped large profits for shareholders in France, who constituted the Indochina lobby. At the same time, France was reluctant to encourage any manufacturing in Indochina that would compete with imported French goods. Local merchants grew rich in the import-export business and by buying up agricultural harvests, while local rice growers in Cambodia and the Mekong Delta (after the region had been drained by French engineers) became more prosperous as they expanded their subsistence-oriented holdings to produce crops for export. Marketing was assisted by a new network of roads, market towns, and railways in Vietnam and Cambodia. In the 1920s most of Indochina enjoyed an economic boom, spurred by international demands for rubber, rice, and other agricultural products.

THE MONOLOGUE OF COLONIALISM

The French expected to stay indefinitely in Indochina. In what the French scholar Paul Mus has called the "monologue of colonialism," they made no sustained effort to prepare local people for self-sufficiency, higher education, free trade, relations with other countries, political participation, or independence. Unlike the British in India, the French had no exit strategy. The process of domination involved infantilizing their colonial protégés. Quarantined in theory (and by the French police) from politics and drastic change, local people were forbidden to grow up, meaning that the civilizing mission could never be complete. In fact, widespread modernization took place throughout Vietnam, especially among the expanding reading public, after the French introduced a Roman alphabet (*quoc ngu*) for writing Vietnamese, replacing the Chinese ideograms that had been in use for two millennia. Thousands of Vietnamese readers happily absorbed new nonpolitical publications (including women's magazines, self-help manuals, and technical handbooks) as well as new literary forms, such as daily newspapers and the novel. In Laos and Cambodia, where literacy was less widespread and less prestigious, the psychological effects of what Benedict Anderson has called print capitalism, and has linked to nationalism, were much slower. At the same time, roads and railroads, market towns, automobiles, movies and radio, telecommunications, the expansion of education, and the growth of cities—developments in which the French participated but could not control—took place alongside the ongoing political repression that kept local people in check and has preoccupied so many writers.

French administrators—who enjoyed lower status at home than their British counterparts in India, and were more numerous—tried to preserve, as if in amber, supposedly "traditional" culture, class divisions, and patterns of land ownership. It was pleasing and inexpensive for them to do so. Traditional rulers had similarly sought to control and exploit local people, who had never had a voice in administration. In Cambodia, the French restored the medieval temple complex of Angkor and in effect presented the Khmer with the gift of a history that they had forgotten. The Vietnamese were less happy at being placed in a Confucian time warp, especially after Chinese elements of their culture and traditional government had been so severely undermined. The French made sure, in the meantime, that local people paid the costs of governing Indochina. Until the closing year of World War II, with rare exceptions, the system worked.

RESISTANCE TO THE FRENCH

Resistance to the French in Vietnam began in the 1860s and continued sporadically until the 1930s, reemerging during World War II and reaching a climax in September 1945 when the Vietnamese Communist leader Ho Chi Minh (l890–1969) declared Vietnam's independence. There was much less resistance to France in Cambodia and Laos. Because of the intensity of resistance in Vietnam and the eventual victory of anticolonial forces there, it is tempting to read Vietnamese history in terms of continuous and eventually triumphant resistance to foreign control. Many scholars have chosen to do so. Vietnam's victories over France and the United States, following centuries of resistance to China in precolonial times, provide a pleasing structure for Vietnamese historical writing, from the winners' point of view.

More recently, scholars have argued that multiple readings of the Indochinese past are preferable to unilinear ones. The resistance model, for example, does not clarify the histories of Laos or Cambodia, nor does it explain the thirty-year-long alliance between southern Vietnam and the United States. Scholars have also drawn attention to the complex social history of the region, where developments occurred without reference to the political interplay between the French and the Vietnamese. Print capitalism has been mentioned. Scholars have also singled out the sizeable contributions made by such historical "losers" as nonrevolutionary women, Catholics, Francophiles, members of religious sects, ethnic minorities, and the southern Vietnamese allied with the United States.

Nonetheless, in an article of this length, resistance has to occupy a prominent position. Without it, after all, the French might have stayed on much longer, or might even still be in command.

In the 1880s the "aid the king" (*can vuong*) movement mobilized thousands of patriots who sought

fruitlessly but with great courage to restore the *status quo ante*. They were crushed by French military force, but their patriotism inspired many later thinkers, including Ho Chi Minh.

In the early twentieth century, the prospects for turning the clock back dimmed. Vietnamese patriots like Phan Boi Chau (1867–1940) were impressed by developments in China and Japan, while opponents of France in the 1920s and 1930s, most notably Phan Chu Trinh (1871–1926), drew on European examples—including democracy and Communism—for their ideology. After 1900, few Vietnamese intellectuals sought refuge in the precolonial past.

Until the late 1940s, French repressive mechanisms in Indochina were sufficient to keep most resistance in check. When armed resistance broke out in 1930 to 1931 in northern and central Vietnam, partly in response to severe economic conditions, it was ruthlessly repressed. Hundreds of rebels were put to death. The ICP (founded by Ho Chi Minh) had been involved in the uprisings, and soon became the best organized of the clandestine groups opposed to French colonialism. As thousands of Vietnamese were arrested for political "crimes," the prisons became training schools for anti-French political cadre, especially Communists, many of whom were released under France's Popular Front government (l936–1939).

The most substantial resistance to France in Cambodia came in 1884 to 1886, when the French tried to abolish what they called "slavery" in the kingdom. Their move struck at the networks of patronage and clientship that allowed Cambodia to function in a premodern fashion. The revolt forced the French to slow down the pace of reform. Until the l940s, Cambodia was at peace. Historians looking for the roots of Cambodian nationalism have found them in the small Cambodian elite educated in the 1930s, and in the Cambodian language newspaper *Nagara Vatta* (*Angkor Wat*), which flourished between 1936 and 1942. Resistance to the French in Laos was also insignificant because the Lao population was scattered and apolitical, while the relatively benign Lao elite remained in place, supported by the French.

FRENCH INDOCHINA: THE FINAL PHASES

World War II was a turning point in Indochina. When it began in 1939, France was more firmly in control than ever. Six years later, thanks to the Japanese, all the components of Indochina declared their independence, and France had to fight its way back into the region.

France's defeat in Europe led Thailand (formerly known as Siam) to attack Cambodia and Laos so as to regain some of the territory that had been taken from it

Ban Me Thoot, May 1950. *General Jean de Lattre de Tassigny (right), commander of French troops in Indochina, and Bao Dai, the former emperor of Vietnam, visit in Ban Me Thoot with the Vietnamese Mois people, who were fighting the communist-dominated Vietminh forces.* **AFP/GETTY IMAGES. REPRODUCED BY PERMISSION.**

by France. In 1941 Japan reached an agreement with the French in Indochina whereby the Japanese stationed troops in the region while France retained administrative control. The arrangement suited both parties but displeased France's former European allies. Japan launched its invasion of the rest of mainland Southeast Asia from Indochinese bases in December 1941.

In the same year, Ho Chi Minh returned to Vietnam after forty years in exile, and established the Viet Minh ("Free Viet") independence movement as a united front (secretly led by the ICP). He was joined in the mountains by new recruits and by members of the ICP. Nationalists in Cambodia and Laos, drawn from the educated elite, also accelerated their anti-French activities, encouraged by Japan and by the Thai, but armed resistance to France failed to develop before 1945.

On March 9, 1945, fearing an Allied attack, the Japanese moved suddenly to sequester French military and civilian officials throughout Indochina. The French were taken by surprise. The Japanese then urged local rulers, who had been handpicked by the French, to declare independence. For the next few months Cambodia and Laos governed themselves, Vietnam was

briefly reunited, and the Viet Minh descended from their strongholds to take control over much of Tonkin. In September 1945 Bao Dai abdicated in favor of Ho Chi Minh, who proclaimed Vietnam's independence in Hanoi a day after Japan surrendered to the Allies.

After the surrender, under agreements reached at Potsdam in June 1945, British troops were sent to disarm the Japanese in southern Indochina, while Chinese Nationalist troops performed the same task in the north. British support for French colonialism (opposed by the United States) meant that several hundred French troops were able to reenter Cochin China and reassert control there and in Cambodia. They were unable to do so in the north, where they were forced to negotiate with Ho Chi Minh's new national government, known as the Democratic Republic of Vietnam (RDVN). In November 1946 fighting broke out between French and RDVN forces, first in northern Vietnam and later throughout the country. By 1950 the Vietnamese Communists had also come to dominate the poorly organized Lao and Cambodian independence movements. After the Communist victory in China in 1949, Chinese aid helped the Viet Minh to defeat the French, and all of Indochina became independent in 1954. Vietnam, however, was divided at the seventeenth parallel, and an anticommunist regime in southern Vietnam held out against North Vietnamese military pressure with American assistance until 1975, when RDVN forces occupied the south and reunited the country, which they renamed the Socialist Republic of Vietnam.

A BALANCE SHEET

Half a century after the collapse of the French empire in Indochina, and nearly thirty years after the end of the second Indochina War, we can assess the colonial era more objectively than would have been possible in the 1940s and 1950s, when independence movements throughout Southeast Asia, supported by large sections of global public opinion, swept out their colonial masters. The historian Nicholas Tarling has called colonialism in Southeast Asia a "fleeting, passing phase" and certainly France's brief time in Indochina has to be weighed against the thousands of years that came before and the half-century that has elapsed since France departed from the region. It is tempting to say that the colonial era in Indochina was unimportant. Nonetheless, while it is possible to imagine Vietnam modernizing itself without the intrusion of a colonial power, it is unlikely that Laos and Cambodia would have survived as independent states without French protection against their Southeast Asian neighbors.

A legacy of French town planning, official architecture, and design is still visible in Indochina, especially in the larger towns. Museums in Cambodia, Laos, and Vietnam were established by the French and flourish today, while in Cambodia the French still play an important role in the restoration and maintenance of Angkor. The major cities, especially Hanoi and Phnom Penh, still have a French "feel" about them, and whereas Vietnam and Laos now have Marxist-Leninist regimes, the government of Cambodia retains many organizational features inherited from the colonial era. Finally, while the many shortcomings of French rule must be firmly kept in mind, it is impossible to blame or praise the French for developments that have occurred in Indochina since the 1970s, after French influence had sharply diminished throughout the region.

SEE ALSO *Mekong River, Exploration of the.*

BIBLIOGRAPHY

Anderson, Benedict. *Imagined Communities: Reflections on the Origin and Spread of Nationalism.* Rev. ed. London: Verso, 1991.

Chandler, David. *A History of Cambodia.* 3d ed. Boulder, CO: Westview Press, 2000.

Duiker, William. *The Rise of Nationalism in Vietnam, 1900–1941.* Ithaca, NY: Cornell University Press, 1976.

Edwards, Penny. *"Cambodge": The Cultivation of a Nation, 1860–1945.* Honolulu: University of Hawaii Press, 2005.

Evans, Grant. *A Short History of Laos.* Crow's Nest, Australia: Allen and Unwin, 2002.

Marr, David. *Vietnamese Anticolonialism, 1885–1925.* Berkeley: University of California Press, 1971.

Marr, David. *Vietnamese Tradition on Trial, 1920–1945.* Berkeley: University of California Press, 1981.

Marr, David. *Vietnam 1945: The Quest for Power.* Berkeley: University of California Press, 1995.

McLeod, Mark. *The Vietnamese Response to French Intervention, 1862–1874.* New York: Praeger, 1991.

Murray, Martin J. *The Development of Capitalism in Colonial Indochina (1870–1940).* Berkeley: University of California Press, 1980.

Osborne, Milton. *The French Presence in Cochinchina and Cambodia: Rule and Response (1859–1905).* Ithaca, NY: Cornell University Press, 1969.

Stuart-Fox, Martin. *A History of Laos.* Cambridge, U.K.: Cambridge University Press, 1997.

Tarling, Nicholas. *Imperialism in Southeast Asia: "A Fleeting, Passing Phase."* London and New York: Routledge, 2001.

Tully, John. *France on the Mekong: A History of the Protectorate in Cambodia, 1863–1953.* Lanham, MD: University Press, 2002.

Woodside, Alexander. *Community and Revolution in Modern Vietnam.* Boston: Houghton Mifflin, 1976.

Zinoman, Peter. *The Colonial Bastille: A History of Imprisonment in Vietnam, 1862–1940.* Berkeley: University of California Press, 2002.

David Chandler

FRENCH POLYNESIA

French Polynesia is a group of islands in the South Pacific, including five archipelagos: the Austral Islands, the Gambier Islands, the Marquesas Islands, the Tuamotu Islands, and the Society Islands (Tahiti, Moorea, Tetiaroa, Raiatea, Tahoa, Huahine, Bora-Bora, and Maupiti).

The first European sailors to reach this part of the world were Spanish (Alvaro Mendaña de Neira [1541–1595] reached the Marquesas in 1595) and Portuguese (Pedro Fernandez de Quirós [1565–1615] reached Tuamotu in 1605), though neither initial ventures led to imperial control in these areas. The rekindling of important shipping expeditions in the Pacific over the eighteenth century (particularly Samuel Wallis [1728–1795] in 1767 and James Cook [1728–1779] between 1769 and 1777 for Britain; Louis-Antoine de Bougainville [1729–1811] in 1768 and Jean-François de La Pérouse [1741–1788] in

1786 for France) sharply increased interest in these areas, while also sharpening Anglo-French colonial rivalries.

Initially, Britain held the advantage, as English Protestant missionary groups gained favor with the Pomaré dynasty (1762–1880), which reigned over Tahiti and the surrounding islands of Mooréa, Tuamotu, Mehetia, Tubai, and Raivave. However, the London Missionary Society was never able to induce London to establish a British protectorate in the region.

In contrast, France's search for ports and prestige led to annexation of the Marquesas and the establishment of a protectorate in 1842. The same occurred in Tahiti at the request of the Queen Pomaré IV (1813–1877). A protectorate agreement by the French recognized the sovereignty of the Marquesas and Tahiti states and the authority of the local chiefs.

Although the British instigated local rebellions, French influence prevailed over the next six decades, leaving a lasting impact in the region. After the abdication of King Pomaré V (1839–1891) on June 29, 1880, France seized the opportunity to annex Tahiti, and then the Gambier Islands the following year, the "Islands-Under-the-Wind" (Raiatea, Tahoa, Huahine, Bora-Bora, and Maupiti) between 1888 and 1897, and the Austral Islands in 1902. These different archipelagos then took the name of "French Settlement of Oceania" until 1957, when they became French Polynesia.

As with many French colonies, inhabitants of these islands have expressed a desire for autonomy since World War II. In 1946, with the new French constitution, the islands became a French overseas territory. Since 2003, they have been an internally autonomous overseas collectivity.

SEE ALSO *Pacific, European Presence in.*

BIBLIOGRAPHY

Hough, Richard. *Captain James Cook.* London: Hodder & Stoughton, 1994.

Pollock, Nancy J., and Ron Crocombe, eds. *French Polynesia: A Book of Selected Readings.* Suva, Fiji: Institute of Pacific Studies of the University of the South Pacific, 1988.

Thompson, Virginia, and Richard Adloff. *The French Pacific Islands: French Polynesia and New Caledonia.* Berkeley: University of California Press, 1971.

Monique Milia-Marie-Luce

FUR AND SKIN TRADES IN THE AMERICAS

A robust exchange of North American furs for European metal goods combined with imperial ambitions in the sixteenth century to effect dramatic transformations in the lives of Amerindians. It was a harbinger of European colonization from the Atlantic to the Pacific. Annual expeditions by French fishermen trawling for cod off Newfoundland and what was then known as Acadia on the North Atlantic coast (from the Grand Banks to the Gulf of Saint Lawrence) bartered for furs with the indigenous inhabitants. In the 1570s, the fashion for wide-brimmed felt hats created a lucrative market for beaver pelts in Europe, giving momentum to this long-established commerce.

The North American fur trade served as a bridgehead for the pursuit of colonial expansion amid imperial competition between Spain, Portugal, England, France, and Holland. The motives for exploration of the Atlantic coast of North America were the search for an inland sea or a northwest passage to Cathay (China) and to find precious metals or spices.

In 1524 the Italian navigator Giovanni da Verrazano (ca. 1485–1528) explored the areas coterminous with present-day New York Harbor, Narragansett Bay, and the coast of Maine. He observed that a protocol already existed for trade between passing ships and the Amerindians of coastal Maine. In 1534 and 1535 Jacques Cartier (1491–1557), sailing out of Saint-Malo, France, explored the upper reaches of the Saint Lawrence River. He reported the Mi'kmaq (Micmac) Indians as offering furs for trade and saw extensive crops and orchards in the towns at Stadacona (near present-day Quebec) and Hochelaga.

When Samuel de Champlain (ca. 1570–1635) followed Cartier's route in 1603, he found Stadacona deserted, no trace of the orchards, and Mohawk war parties in the vicinity. However, the imperatives of competition required Europeans to align themselves with indigenous trading partners and therefore to become enmeshed in local rivalries. Thus, the Montagnais Indians became the main agents and beneficiaries of the French trade, but their Iroquois enemies were denied access to trade, and therefore subsequently aligned themselves with the Dutch.

The beginning of the seventeenth century saw the establishment of permanent settlements, after a series of failed attempts. The English-based Virginia Company founded Jamestown in 1607; Samuel de Champlain founded Quebec in 1608 on behalf of the New France Company; and the Dutch West Indies Company founded Fort Nassau at Albany in 1614 and New Amsterdam (New York) in 1624.

The French controlled the northern route from Quebec, with access to the course of the Saint Lawrence River, which led to the Great Lakes. The Dutch controlled the Hudson River to Albany and the route westward to Lake Ontario until 1644, when they surrendered

European and Indian Fur Traders. *A robust exchange of North American furs for European metal goods combined with imperial ambitions in the sixteenth century to effect dramatic transformations in the lives of Amerindians. This Native American offers beaver pelts to European traders.* HULTON ARCHIVE/GETTY IMAGES. REPRODUCED BY PERMISSION.

it to the English. French and English traders then began to compete for territorial as well as commercial advantage, drawing Amerindians into competing trading networks. The results were often costly. After 1624, the Iroquois obtained guns from the Dutch, in 1648 they attacked and destroyed Huronia, the Huron homelands which lay between Lake Simcoe and Georgian Bay, and from 1649 to 1651 they inflicted the same fate on the Hurons' dependent neighbors (the Tobacco and Neutral nations), as well as on the Nipissing Indians, the Cat nation, and the Erie Indians during the so-called Beaver Wars.

The advance of the fur trade frontier exacerbated existing rivalries among Amerindians now competing for access to the European trade, and warfare casualties increased with the deployment of European guns and metal weapons. However, the most catastrophic consequence of the fur trade was the introduction of European-borne diseases that devastated Amerindian populations. By 1611 the Abenaki, among the first Native Americans to ally themselves to the French, saw their number reduced from ten thousand to three

thousand after just one decade of sustained contact. Furthermore, the consumption of alcohol became entrenched as part of the trading ritual and caused much harm to the social fabric of Amerindian tribes and many drink-related deaths. Missionaries evangelizing among Amerindians ineffectually railed against the practice.

Mortality among European traders who settled in the region was also high in proportion to their number, due for the most part to scurvy and the rigors of the North American winter. None of these calamities diminished the European determination to pursue trade, nor Amerindian eagerness for European goods, most notably axes, guns, gunpowder, kettles, and knives, which replaced traditional stone, wood, and bone tools. These commodities were acquired in exchange for beaver and otter skins by the northeastern natives, and deerskin by those in the Southeast, where the Cherokee traded the astonishing figure of 1.25 million deerskins between 1739 and 1759.

The establishment of the Hudson's Bay Company in 1668 heralded a new era of expansion of the lucrative North American fur trade. The Hudson's Bay Company was to change the life of Amerindians heretofore untouched by the fur trade in significant and enduring ways, even though, for its first hundred years of existence, the company was content to erect trading posts at Hudson Bay and James Bay, allowing Indian entrepreneurs to conduct business inland. Access to trade most benefited those tribes acting as middlemen, in this case the Cree and Assiniboine.

French traders and explorers pushed out on to the Great Plains in the eighteenth century. The ensuing competition for trade affected prices, not least because of the French imperative to retain Amerindians as allies. French traders maintained a presence in the fur trade even after France lost Canada to Britain in 1763, at the close of the Seven Years' War (or French and Indian War). The French trading network was now taken over by the North West Company, a Canadian-based concern.

In 1793 Alexander Mackenzie (1764–1820), an explorer for the North West Company, crossed the Rocky Mountains to reach the Pacific Coast. Russians had been trading sea otter pelts along the Pacific coast since the 1740s, and James Cook had visited Nootka Sound in 1778. Exploitation of the Pacific fur trade gained impetus after the amalgamation of the North West Company and the Hudson's Bay Company in 1821, which strengthened the Canadian position against the inroads of American competitors.

However, the depletion of beaver populations and the decline of the European fur trade in the early nineteenth century—when silk hats superseded beaver—shifted the demand to buffalo (bison) robes. What began as a commercial interest in the buffalo to provide provisions for the Hudson's Bay Company and the Red River Colony, a Highland and Irish colony founded by Lord Selkirk in 1812 on lands to the south of Lake Manitoba and Lake Winnipeg, which developed into a strong market for robes in the 1840s until the demand shifted to hides after 1865.

European settlement accelerated, and the colonization of North America now extended from the Atlantic to the Pacific. This process was underwritten by violence and land dispossession, and culminated in the Great Plains and prairies with the destruction of the once extensive buffalo herds. By the 1880s, indiscriminate slaughter put an end to the prosperity gained through the fur trade by the indigenous tribes whose very existence depended on the buffalo. This ecological cataclysm was followed by famine and the confinement of native peoples to reservations. The fur trade continued, moving further northwards, and survives to this day, an ambivalent legacy of European colonization of North America.

SEE ALSO *Cacao; Company of New France; Cotton; Sugar Cultivation and Trade.*

BIBLIOGRAPHY

Axtell, James. *Beyond 1492: Encounters in Colonial North America.* Oxford, U.K.: Oxford University Press, 1992.

Calloway, Colin G. *First Peoples: A Documentary Survey of American Indian History*, 2nd ed. Boston: Bedford/ St. Martin's, 2004.

Eccles, William J. *France in America,* rev. ed. East Lansing: Michigan State University Press, 1990.

Fisher, Robin. "The Northwest from the Beginning of Trade with Europeans to the 1880s." In *Handbook of North American Indians*, edited by William C. Sturtevant; Vol. 4: *History of Indian-White Relations*, edited by Wilcomb E. Washburn. Washington, DC: Smithsonian Institution Press, 1988.

Morton, W. L., *The Kingdom of Canada: A General History from Earliest Times.* Toronto: McClelland and Stewart Limited, 1969.

Ray, Arthur J. "The Hudson Bay Company and Native People." In *Handbook of North American Indians*, edited by William C. Sturtevant; Vol. 4: *History of Indian-White Relations*, edited by Wilcomb E. Washburn. Washington, DC: Smithsonian Institution Press, 1988.

Simmons, R. C. *The American Colonies: From Settlement to Independence.* London: Longman, 1976.

Trigger, Bruce G., and William R. Swagerty. "Entertaining Strangers: North America in the Sixteenth Century." In *The Cambridge History of the Native Peoples of the Americas*; Vol. 1: *North America*, edited by Bruce G. Trigger and Wilcomb E. Washburn. Cambridge, U.K.: Cambridge University Press, 1996.

Wolf, Eric R. *Europe and the People Without History.* Berkeley: University of California Press, 1982.

Blanca Tovías

G

GAMA, VASCO DA
1469–1524

The Portuguese explorer Vasco da Gama discovered the sea route from Europe to India. Continuing the long-term Portuguese project of exploring the African coastline, he rounded the Cape of Good Hope and continued to Calicut, India, during a voyage that lasted from 1497 to 1499, "an open-sea excursion of unprecedented duration for a European navigator... a demonstration of audacity rather than ability" (Fernández-Armesto 2000a, p. 479).

Gama was a violent, ruthless, and ambitious man whose successes in forging a network of Portuguese footholds in Asia became, over the course of his lifetime and subsequent centuries, the stuff of Portuguese national legend. Portugal's national epic, *The Lusíads* (1572) by Luis Vaz de Camões (1524–1580), is based on Gama's activities, transforming a story of seamanship and poor diplomacy into one of endurance, adventure, and heroism in the face of seemingly insurmountable obstacles.

Vasco da Gama was a minor Portuguese noble born in the 1460s (probably 1469, argues Sanjay Subrahmanyam [1997] in the most authoritative and scholarly biography of Gama), possibly in the southern Portuguese coastal town of Sines. Much of what we know about Gama's background and life are based on conjecture from notoriously inclusive and fragmentary surviving documents. There are huge gaps in our knowledge and much disagreement among historians over many of the details.

It is far from certain why Gama was chosen as the leader of the expedition that made his name and career. He was a member of the Order of Santiago, one of the several military orders that played important political and social roles in medieval Portugal. In the 1490s the orders were particularly tied up with contests over court influence and the ends and means of overseas expansion.

Subrahmanyam argues that Manuel I (known as "the Fortunate," r. 1495–1521) gave Gama command of the modest expedition of four ships to the pepper emporium of Calicut in the hope that, should the expedition fail, some of the disrepute would rub off on the political faction with which Gama was associated. This group gathered around Dom Jorge (1481–1550), the illegitimate son of João II (r. 1481–1495), Manuel's predecessor on the throne. Dom Jorge's faction believed that the old enemy Castile, rather than India, should be the object of the state's imperial activity, although Gama himself pragmatically came to see the value of India once his own fortunes became tied to the success of Portugal's expeditions to the region.

Motivations for the "voyage of discovery" were mixed. As Gama acknowledged at the beginning of the narrative of his first voyage (probably written by his crewmember Álvaro Velho), "In the year 1497 King Dom Manuel, the first of that name in Portugal, dispatched four vessels to make discoveries and go in search of spices" (Ravenstein 1898, p. 1). Adventure, colonization, commerce, and religion combined to send Gama in search of the sea route to India.

Once in the Indian Ocean, Gama encountered polycentric networks of great religious and ethnic diversity—not a monolithic Islamic monopoly—a mix into which Gama's aggression and ambition cast a further complicating factor. In East Africa, Gama and his men at first

Vasco da Gama (ca. 1469–1524). The Portuguese explorer who in the 1490s rounded the Cape of Good Hope and discovered the sea route from Europe to India, in a 1572 woodcut portrait. © BETTMANN/CORBIS. REPRODUCED BY PERMISSION.

pretended to be Muslims out of fear of the locals. When this ruse was discovered, Gama's party was regarded with distrust and suspicion. Gama aggravated things by frequently taking hostages as part of negotiations. In March 1498, several months before reaching India, he bombarded the shores of Mozambique in order to demonstrate, as an anonymous onlooker recorded, "how much harm we could do them if we wanted." He continued his confrontational strategy in India, which contributed to souring relations with the rulers of Calicut, the main pepper market and the principal destination of his voyage.

Despite his preference for violence and confrontation over compromise and negotiation, Gama was not above taking advantage of local expertise or politics. During his first voyage, Gama used local pilots (although

not, as was thought, the great Ahmad Ibn Majid [1432–1500]) to cross the Indian Ocean, and exploited local political tensions to gain friends in Malindi in Africa and amongst the Saint Thomas Christians in Cochin in India. Yet he did so without compassion: One pilot was whipped after mistaking some islands for the mainland. Gama did not bring conflict single-handedly into the region, but rather intensified it by his ruthless tactics and by introducing new naval technology and a more systematic approach to warfare.

Upon his return to Lisbon in 1499, Gama was not received as the hero he felt himself to be. The Portuguese Crown awarded him a grant of land around Sines, but Gama was infuriated with what he perceived to be the meager nature of this prize. The turn of the century saw deep rivalry between other profoundly ambitious social climbers who sought patronage in Iberia for adventurous schemes of exploration and "discovery."

On the follow-up voyage to Gama's discovery of the sea route, in 1500 Pedro Álvares Cabral (ca. 1467–1520) happened upon the Brazilian littoral. Yet the failure of either Gama's or Cabral's voyages to yield tangible financial profits, considered in the light of news of the discoveries of Christopher Columbus (1451–1506) in the Indies to the west, put considerable pressure on Gama's second expedition (1502–1503). On this voyage Gama bore the Columbus-inspired title of Admiral of the Seas of Arabia, Persia, and India. He was just as confrontational in style on this voyage, which included an infamous and terrible incident in which he plundered, burned, and sank a passing ship, the *Mîrî,* thus ensuring the death by drowning of the 240 Muslim pilgrims it was carrying.

Such deeds have not prevented a long Portuguese history of elaborating and promoting Gama's legend. The image of Gama as national hero and icon grew out of his triumphant return to Lisbon from his second voyage in 1503, laden with gold and spices. Nevertheless, it was immediately followed by a lengthy period in the political wilderness from 1504 to 1523 because Gama did not share Manuel I's conception of a universal Portuguese empire in Asia that might link up with the realm of Prester John, a mythical ruler of a Christian empire thought to lie in Central Asia or Africa, and other local Christians to outflank and destroy Islam.

Profits from the spice trade were a secondary consideration. Gama—famously spendthrift and money-grubbing—thought colonial enterprises to be a waste of money that a kingdom with meager resources like Portugal could ill afford. Gama believed it would be better for private merchants to handle the spice trade and for the state to establish and service just a few trading posts in order to facilitate commerce. This allowed others to reap the financial and political rewards of voyages to

India, in particular one of Gama's rivals, Afonso de Albuquerque (1453–1515). The descendents and admirers of the two men perpetuated the two heroes' images and exploits in subsequent centuries, but Gama himself set about manipulating his growing legend during his period out of political favor precisely in order to ensure his own rehabilitation. That he did succeed in returning to a position of power and influence and that he died as a viceroy was testament to his vigorous social climbing and endurance.

Upon the death of Manuel I in 1521 and the arrival on the throne of João III (r. 1521–1557), Vasco da Gama became one of the king's advisors, arguing forcefully that Portugal should limit its position in India to Cochin and Goa. Faced with financial constraints and Dutch and Castilian threats to Portugal's imperial outposts, João sent Gama to India as viceroy and count of Vidigueira in 1524 to carry out a program of administrative and organizational reform and to remove Castilian infiltrators from the Moluccas. In the brief period in India that his poor health allowed him (less than a year), Gama once again revealed his characteristics as a stern disciplinarian, an avid fortune hunter, and an assiduous enemy of Muslims in Malabar. Overworked and unable to overcome the effects of the local climate on his weakened body, Gama died on December 24, 1524. He was buried with full honors in the Franciscan Church of San Antonio in Cochin.

Contemporaries did not all see Gama as a courageous hero. Some saw him as a "xenophobe improbably transplanted to the tropics" (Fernández-Armesto 2000b, p. 13). Certainly he was an arrogant and uncompromising leader who was resolutely focused on his own status and wealth (and that of his clientele). He was a merciless killer of opponents and unfortunates. Yet his legend continued apace, assured most notably by the success of Camões's *Lusíads*. In the late nineteenth century, the Portuguese state sponsored extravagant and drawn-out celebrations surrounding the reinterment in Lisbon of Gama's bones.

The Indian nationalist historian K. M. Panikkar (1959) dubbed the period of European imperialism in Asia from 1500 to 1945 as the "Vasco da Gama era." Gama's discovery of the sea route to India for Portugal was not the forceful heroism of one man but the culmination of decades of advances and incremental accumulation of knowledge. Gama's tactics in assuring the success of his explorative and commercial ventures were hardnosed, confrontational, aggressive, and often violent. His initial cultivation of the legend surrounding his heroism was pursued with equal vigor. Gama was the first to profit from the "actual financial, fiscal and material returns" (Subrahmanyam 1997, p. 361) of this legend, but he was by no means the last.

SEE ALSO *Empire, Portuguese; Goa, Colonial City of.*

BIBLIOGRAPHY

Fernández-Armesto, Felipe. *Civilizations.* Basingstoke and Oxford, U.K.: Macmillan, 2000a.

Fernández-Armesto, Felipe. "The Indian Ocean in World History." In *Vasco da Gama and the Linking of Europe and Asia,* edited by Anthony Disney and Emily Booth. New Delhi and New York: Oxford University Press, 2000b, pp. 11-29.

Panikkar, K. M. *Asia and Western Dominance: A Survey of the Vasco da Gama Epoch of Asian History, 1498–1945,* new ed. London: Allen & Unwin, 1959.

Ravenstein, E. G. *A Journal of the First Voyage of Vasco da Gama, 1497-99,* London: Hakluyt Society, 1898.

Subrahmanyam, Sanjay. *The Career and Legend of Vasco da Gama.* Cambridge, U.K.: Cambridge University Press, 1997.

Matthew Brown

GENTLEMEN XVII
SEE *Heeren XVII*

GERMANY AND THE MIDDLE EAST

Germany and the Middle East have experienced a number of significant physical and political transformations in history, and the terms *Germany* and *Middle East* harbor many meanings as a result. In 1830 Germany was a linguistic zone of Central Europe where people spoke primarily German, and it encompassed all of Prussia, Bavaria, Austria, Saxony, Hanover, Württemberg, and Baden, and part of Silesia, Bohemia, Denmark, and France. In 1871 Prussian Prime Minister Otto von Bismarck (1815–1898) brought together dozens of German-speaking kingdoms, free cities, duchies, and principalities to form a new sovereign nation-state called Germany, which did not include the German-speaking parts of Austria or Czechoslovakia. The political borders of this Germany changed again after its defeat in World War I (1914–1918), during and after the Nazi Third Reich, and after the reunification of East and West Germany in 1989.

The meaning of the term *Middle East* has been even more fluid. Western European geographers and historians after the Renaissance divided the Orient (the land east of Western Europe) into three regions: Near East (the region nearest Europe and extending from the eastern Mediterranean to the Persian Gulf); Middle East (the region from the Persian Gulf to Southeast Asia); and Far East (the region bordering the Pacific Ocean).

In English the designation of *Middle East* changed during World War II (1939–1945) when the term identified the British military command in Egypt, which consisted of the states or territories of Turkey, Cyprus, Syria, Lebanon, Iraq, Iran, Palestine (now Israel), Jordan, Egypt, Sudan, Libya, and the Arabian Peninsula. This designation parallels current scholarly convention that identifies the Middle East as a region that includes Turkey in the northwest, Egypt in the southwest, the Arabian Peninsula in the southeast, and Persia (Iran) in the northeast. Greece is sometimes included in definitions of the Middle East because a problem for the European Great Powers called the Eastern question first arose when the Greeks fought for their independence from the Ottoman Empire in 1821. This Eastern question provides a natural focus for scholarly discussions of Germany and the Middle East, which concentrate on German relations with the Ottoman Empire in the period from 1880 to 1918 and particularly on German imperial ambitions in the Ottoman sphere of influence during that period—a sphere of influence that corresponds very closely to the current scholarly definition of the Middle East.

PRUSSIA/GERMANY AND THE EASTERN QUESTION IN THE NINETEENTH CENTURY

In 1853 the Russian Tsar Nicholas I (1796–1855) described the Ottoman Empire as the "sick man" of Europe, vocalizing the underlying assumption of the Eastern question that a once great and powerful empire was diseased and dying. Indeed, the Eastern question was one of the major geopolitical problems facing Great Britain, France, Russia, Prussia, and Austria in the nineteenth and early twentieth centuries. The slow disintegration of the Ottoman Empire in the eastern Mediterranean threatened to upset the equilibrium established at the Congress of Vienna between the European Great Powers after the defeat of Napoléon Bonaparte (1769–1821) in 1815. Most of the Great Powers in this self-styled Concert of Europe constantly probed Ottoman weakness to expand their imperial holdings in the Balkans and Middle East. Austria and Russia coveted Ottoman lands on their borders and the British in India desired control of neighboring Persia in the Ottoman sphere of influence.

The Eastern question attained volatile intensity during the Greek War of Independence (1821–1832), the Crimean War (1853–1856), the Balkan crisis between 1875 and 1878, the Bosnian crisis of 1908, the Balkan Wars of 1912 and 1913, and World War I. France and Britain preemptively intervened on the side of the Greeks against the Turks in the 1820s to foil longstanding Russian designs on controlling the Bosphorus region

leading from the Black Sea to the Mediterranean Sea, and they united again in the Crimean War against the Russians when Russia defeated the Ottoman navy and invaded a part of the Ottoman Empire (Moldavia and Wallachia) that is now Romania. In the peace treaty ending the war, all the Great Powers guaranteed the integrity of the Ottoman Empire, the Bosphorus remained closed to warships, and Moldavia and Wallachia remained under Turkish suzerainty. Austria mediated the conflict, whereas Prussia remained aloof.

Prussian aloofness to the Eastern question ended when Prussia fought and won wars against Austria in 1866 and France in 1870 and 1871 to unify Germany as a sovereign nation-state. As the leader of a new but satisfied Power, the Prussian/German Prime Minister Bismarck saw his task as maintaining peace among the Great Powers. Prussian victories had upset the old balance of power in the heart of Europe and had unsettled old alliances. Bismarck identified the Balkans—that hotbed of the Eastern question where the continued disintegration of the Ottoman Empire could easily lead to conflict between Austria and Russia—and France, which desired revenge for its defeat in 1871 and its loss of Alsace-Lorraine to Germany, as destabilizing forces. Ever wary of the violent potential present in the Eastern question and observing no German economic or political interest in the region per se, Bismarck quipped in 1876 that the solution to the Eastern question was not worth the bones of a single Pomeranian grenadier (i.e., German soldier). He crafted the Three Emperors' League with Russia and Austria in 1873 to prevent their alliance with France, but it collapsed when rebellion broke out in the Ottomans' Balkan provinces and Russia declared war on the Turks in 1877.

When Russia forced the Ottomans to cede extensive territory in the Treaty of San Stefano, Bismarck called for an international conference to reconsider the treaty. To maintain Great Power balance in regards to the Eastern question, Bismarck brokered a deal whereby the Russians accepted more modest territorial gains in the Balkans at the Congress of Berlin in 1878; Serbia, Montenegro, and Romania gained independence from the Ottomans, and Austria achieved temporary administrative rights to Bosnia-Herzegovina, which were still legally Ottoman territories. Bismarck next negotiated an alliance with Austria in 1879, which he repeatedly used to prevent Austria from going to war with Russia over Ottoman territories. He reluctantly extended Germany's influence to the Middle East in 1882 when he agreed that the German Empire would replace France as the military adviser to the Ottoman army.

Germany's military mission began a more active political and economic engagement with the Ottoman

Empire and the Eastern question. Nicknamed *Drang nach Osten* (Drive to the East) and promoted by the German ambassador to the Ottomans in the early 1880s, the new policy advocated German cultural and economic penetration of the Ottoman realm to achieve imperial parity with France and Britain there. The Ottoman Sultan Abdülhamid II (1842–1918), who ruled from 1876 to 1909, turned to the Germans as a counterbalance to the British after the British occupied the Ottoman territories of Cyprus and Egypt and became involved in administering the Ottoman public debt.

After 1885 Germany's military mission was responsible for instituting a network of military preparatory schools, reorganizing the Ottoman officer corps on the Prussian model, creating a market for arms shipments from Germany, and initiating concessions for construction of a railroad. Because the German Empire arrived late as a European overseas imperial power, especially in Africa and the Middle East, the Ottomans regarded the Germans as free from the taint of snatching land from Turkish rule. The same could not be said of the French (who seized Algeria in 1830 and Tunis in 1881) or the British (who occupied Cyprus in 1878 and Egypt in 1882). Also pleasing to the Turks was Bismarck's stated policy of preserving what remained of the Ottoman Empire as a bulwark against Russian expansion into the Balkans and Middle East. Finally, the growing importance of the Middle East to Germany can also be seen in the founding of the Seminar for Oriental Languages in Berlin in 1887 to train Orientalist scholars.

German involvement with the Ottoman Empire and the Middle East quickened after Bismarck's departure in 1890. Kaiser (emperor) Wilhelm II (1859–1941), who ruled from 1888 to 1918, proposed a new course, which he officially proclaimed in 1896 and 1897, that called for expanded German influence overseas. The resulting *Weltpolitik*, or drive for global power, produced the direct competition with the other Great Powers that Bismarck tried to avoid. The construction of a new German high seas battle fleet antagonized Britain, and both Britain and Russia felt threatened by the expanding German military and economic influence in the Ottoman Empire.

GERMANY AND THE MIDDLE EAST, 1896–1907

From 1880 to 1918 German Middle Eastern policy centered on the Ottoman Empire. As part of its new relationship with the Turkish state, Germany supported the Ottomans in the Turkish-Greek War over Crete in 1897, much to the irritation of the British. Especially disturbing to the British was Germany's promotion of pan-Islamic politics. Pan-Islamism was an anti-European Ottoman doctrine that proclaimed that the sultan in his

role as caliph (successor to Muhammad) was the spiritual leader of the world's Muslims. The doctrine called on Muslims everywhere to defend the Ottoman Empire and caliphate against infidels (i.e., European imperialists). In a widely publicized speech during a state visit to the Ottoman Empire in late 1898, the kaiser proclaimed himself the protector of the world's 300 million Muslims allying the German Empire with a Pan-Islamism that he believed would inspire revolts against Britain's global empire by the 96 million Muslims living within it.

Sultan Abdülhamid II and the Turks appreciated Wilhelm's words and in December 1899 awarded Deutsche Bank and German industrial firms the concession to build a railroad from Ankara to Baghdad. The deal was officially signed in 1903. The potential value of the railroad was obvious to the Germans and the British. When completed it would link Istanbul, the Ottoman capital, with Baghdad and the Persian Gulf, and the Germans planned to run the line all the way to Berlin. The intended Berlin-to-Baghdad railroad became a potent and much used symbol of German penetration of the Ottoman realm. The railway would allow Germany easy economic access to Mesopotamia, Persia, and the Gulf region (and British India) and the Germans were granted mineral (oil) rights along the route, a development that alarmed the British.

In 1903 the same German businesses received a concession to construct the Hijaz railway from Damascus to Mecca. German-Turkish financial ties were further strengthened with the founding of the German-Palestine Bank in 1903 in Jerusalem and the German Orient Bank in Cairo in 1906. In 1906 the Hamburg-Amerika line began competing with British ships for Persian Gulf traffic. Germany's ambassadors to Turkey—Marschall von Bieberstein (1842–1912), who held office from 1897 until his death, and Hans von Wangenheim (1859–1915), who took over from 1912 to 1915—worked tirelessly to open markets for German products. By 1914 Germany's share in the Ottoman public debt reached 22 percent (it had been 4.7 percent in 1888), Germans had a 67.5 percent share in Ottoman railway investment, and German banks played an important role in the Turkish economy.

In the two decades before World War I, Germany replaced France and Russia as Britain's main rival in the Middle East, the territory occupied by the Ottoman Empire. Germany rebuffed British overtures for an alliance in 1899 and 1900 and instead engaged in a major naval arms race with Britain that encouraged Britain to settle its colonial differences with France and Russia in the Middle East and create Bismarck's nightmare, a Germany encircled by a hostile Great Power alliance. The British agreement with France in 1904 was a severe blow to German diplomacy in the Middle East, which had exploited Anglo-French tensions over the British occupation of Egypt to wring colonial concessions from Britain. Britain and Russia solved issues on the eastern edge of the Ottoman Empire by reaching an understanding on Persia and Afghanistan in 1907.

GERMANY, THE EASTERN QUESTION, WORLD WAR I, AND AFTER

In July 1908 an army revolt placed nationalists called Young Turks in key positions of power in the Ottoman Empire. They intended to put an end to the Eastern question by making the Ottoman Empire a modern, parliamentary, centralized, industrial state along European lines. During the chaos caused by the army revolt, however, Austria annexed Bosnia-Herzegovina in October 1908 and Bulgaria declared its complete independence, further reducing Ottoman territories and resurrecting the Eastern question in its full force. Official Russian and Serbian reactions to Austria's move were belligerent and the Bosnian crisis nearly led to a European-wide war. The Eastern question was still simmering and four years later the Turks suffered a crushing defeat in the first Balkan War (1912–1913) with Serbia, Greece, and Bulgaria, which cost the Ottomans four-fifths of their European territories. A coup in January 1913 gave the pro-German faction of the Young Turks complete power and in November 1913 the Germans dispatched General Otto Liman von Sanders (1855–1929) to become inspector-general of the Turkish Army. His mission was to reorganize and modernize the Turkish army to block Russian designs on the Bosphorus and the Middle East. The glowing embers of the Eastern question sparked a renewed crisis in the Balkans in July 1914 involving Austria, Serbia, and Russia in the wake of the continued diminution of Ottoman power, and they soon ignited a world war.

Just as the Great Powers were declaring war on each other, the pro-German faction of the Turkish government signed a secret alliance with Germany on August 2, 1914, reflecting the strong German influence in the army faction headed by Enver Pasa (1881–1922), the minister of war, as well as centuries-long enmity with Russia. As part of the pact, the Germans promised to protect the territorial integrity of the Ottoman Empire while the war aims memorandum of German Prime Minister Theobald von Bethmann-Hollweg (1856–1921), written in September 1914, called for the establishment of German economic domination of the Balkans and the Turkish Middle East after the war. The Ottomans remained officially neutral until November 1914 when early German victories against the French and the

Russians, and a huge loan from Germany, led to an open alliance with the Germans.

The German Empire assisted the Ottomans militarily in World War I, especially in the defense of Gallipoli (1915–1916) against British and Australian forces, and hoped to incite rebellion among Britain's Muslim subjects in Egypt and India and to inflame anti-British fervor in the Middle East as a whole, thereby weakening the British war effort in Europe. The Germans persuaded the new sultan-caliph Mehmed V (1844–1918) to declare a holy war (jihad) against Britain, France, and Russia in late 1914 as part of a military strategy to defeat the Allies, but the agitation among Arabs fell on deaf ears and the Germans were completely unprepared to organize indigenous revolts. In addition, the Young Turk rulers disliked German involvement in pan-Islamic and Ottoman affairs because it threatened Turkish sovereignty and foreign political interests and they were not interested in granting more political autonomy to the Arabs.

In the end, German leaders did not contest Turkish sensibilities regarding national minorities in the Ottoman Empire because the Germans intended to use the empire as a base for future economic and political expansion in the Middle East. Such a decision prevented any genuine German support of Arab nationalism. Ironically, harsh Ottoman treatment of Arabs and persecution of Arab nationalists led to a British-inspired revolt of the Arabs against Turkish rule in June 1916, which helped end Turkish rule in Arab lands by 1918. Also, German authorities rarely objected, and then only mildly, to the massacre of over a million Armenians beginning in April 1915 because the Germans wanted to maintain good relations with the Turks and accepted Turkish claims that the Armenians were traitors who were subverting Turkish military campaigns against the Russians.

The German-Turkish military alliance failed to prevail, however. Two major Turkish-German attacks on the Suez Canal, February 1915 and August 1916, were unsuccessful but they caused the British to keep large numbers of troops in Egypt. Advancing British and Arab forces from Egypt and Mesopotamia eventually won the desert campaigns against the Turks and Germans, whose problems included insufficient troops, weapons, and food, differences over military priorities, and the diversion of troops and supplies by the Turks to the Caucasus. The war ended in November 1918 and the last German forces left Turkey in January 1919. For the first time since 1835, when Prussia sent a small permanent military mission to Istanbul, there was no German military presence in Turkey. Germany's once formidable position in the Ottoman Empire disappeared. The Treaty of Versailles (June 1919) made German losses permanent and official: Articles 147–155 and 434 liquidated its investments in the former Ottoman Empire and Egypt.

During the 1920s the Middle East was virtually absent in the foreign policy of the German Weimar Republic. With its investments and trade destroyed and no military presence to exert political influence, the area became peripheral to German national interests. Once again those interests focused on the European continent and particularly the revision of the war guilt and reparation clauses of the Versailles treaty. Serious German interest in the Middle East ended with the Wilhelmine Empire. It was not resurrected by the Third Reich of Adolf Hitler (1889–1945), who ruled Germany from 1933 to 1945, which had no steady policy toward the Middle East.

Nazis gave early support to the Zionist movement as a way to rid Germany of Jews, but after 1937, when it was recognized that a Jewish sovereign state in the Middle East was possible and it might serve as a base of activity against the Nazi genocidal state, Hitler opposed Jewish emigration to Palestine. The German *Afrikakorps* under General Erwin Rommel (1891–1944) fought an unwanted war (1941–1943) in North Africa to keep the Germans' Italian allies in Libya from being routed by the British and to forestall an Allied invasion of Italy. Germans were not attacking British Egypt in a repeat of the economic and political Drive to the East, which animated the kaiser's imperialism. The focus of Nazi imperialism, expansionist *lebensraum* (living space), was Soviet Russia, not the Middle East, to which Hitler refused to give much thought until the mammoth and time-consuming undertaking of conquering and pacifying Soviet Russia was completed. Haphazard and belated arms shipments by the Nazis to anti-British governments in Iraq, Syria, and Iran in the early 1940s did not forestall British victories in those countries.

From the early 1880s until 1918, the Ottoman Empire was Germany's bridge to the strategic and economic resources of the Middle East and the object of its political and economic expansion in the region. With the collapse of the Ottoman Empire, the Eastern question—as far as it concerned the question of which European Great Power or Powers would take the place of the Ottoman Empire and fill the vacuum created by its disappearance—ceased to exist. With it went German ambitions but, in a broader sense, as an international question that dealt with the conflicting interests and rivalries of the Great Powers in the political and economic fields in the Middle East, the Eastern question has by no means been settled. As the German experience in the Middle East revealed, it became a question with global implications.

SEE ALSO *Ottoman Empire: France and Austria-Hungary.*

BIBLIOGRAPHY

Bentley, Jerry and Herbert Zeiger. "Territorial Losses of the Ottoman Empire, 1800–1914." In *Traditions & Encounters: A Global Perspective on the Past.* Boston: McGraw Hill, 2003.

Chubin, Shahram, ed. *Germany and the Middle East: Patterns and Prospects.* New York: St. Martin's Press, 1992.

McKale, Donald M. *War by Revolution: Germany and Great Britain in the Middle East in the Era of World War I.* Kent, OH: The Kent State University Press, 1998.

Schwanitz, Wolfgang G., ed. *Germany and the Middle East, 1871–1945.* Princeton, NJ: Markus Wiener, 2004.

Alexander M. Zukas

GERMANY'S AFRICAN COLONIES

The unification of Germany in 1871 constituted a watershed in Germany's imperial agenda of acquiring colonies in Africa. A number of lobbying groups formed after the unification, including the West German Society for Colonization and Export (1881) and the Central Association for Commercial Geography and the Promotion of German Interests Abroad (1878). These groups exerted pressure on the government to acquire colonies abroad, especially in Africa, by arguing that Germany needed the territories to maintain its economic preeminence. The result was the founding of the German Colonial Association in 1882. The expansion of German industry and the growth of German maritime interests facilitated a more aggressive colonial program. Chancellor Otto von Bismarck (1815–1898) was initially not a colonial expansionist, but he changed and signed on to the demands of the lobbying groups for a more proactive role in the race for colonies.

Bismarck became convinced that it was imperative for Germany to move quickly if the country was to protect its trade and economic interests because of the emerging protectionist policies that would come with colonialism. This position was best articulated by the Hamburg Chamber of Commerce in 1884 when it asserted that if Germany were not to forever renounce colonial possessions in Africa, especially the Cameroon coast, then it had to act swiftly by acquiring the territory.

Annexation of territory was a significant feature of the emerging protectionist imperial world order of the late nineteenth century. In addition, the prevailing international situation strengthened Bismarck's resolve to acquire territories in Africa. The British occupation of Egypt in 1882 and imperial incursions by France into Africa and Asia combined to make the issue of colonies a national necessity that had to be embraced by Germany because of its preeminent role in continental European diplomacy and politics. Being the skillful politician he was, Bismarck also envisioned the politics of German colonies serving as a stabling force in domestic politics by emphasizing nationalism and the greatness of Germany internationally. Bismarck was a pragmatist and his drive to acquire colonies in Africa was largely a function of economic considerations, both real and potential, in the emerging imperial world order, European diplomacy, and domestic politics as well.

The Berlin Conference of 1884 to 1885, hosted by Bismarck, was a turning point because it not only recognized European colonial claims in Africa but also hastened the process of partition. The European powers agreed that those nations claiming parts of Africa had to physically occupy them in order to legitimize those claims. Germany annexed South West Africa (present-day Namibia) in 1884 after negotiations with Great Britain. In the same year Germany annexed a strip of coastline on the Gulf of Guinea, which was later expanded into the territory of German Cameroon. The acquisition of Togo completed German annexation of territory in West Africa. Germany acquired German East Africa (present-day mainland Tanzania, Rwanda, and Burundi) in 1885, and a formal protectorate was declared in 1890. However, formal boundaries were not concluded until the late 1890s.

Germany used concessionary companies during the infancy stages of establishing a colonial presence in the annexed territories. The companies were granted charters to administer the colonies on behalf of the German government. The concessionary firms were supported on the grounds that they would mobilize private capital for the purpose of investment in the colonies. The argument was that private enterprise would be less costly, both to the government and taxpayers, since the latter two would be spared the burden of financing the empire.

In South West Africa, German imperial interests were advanced by the German South-West Africa Company and in East Africa by the Imperial German East Africa Company. The companies failed to perform as expected because of two main factors. First, the companies lacked a strong capital base to undertake the various governmental functions, including constructing the infrastructure required for colonial control. Second, the companies were ill-equipped to contain uprisings during the initial stages of establishing imperial control. By the end of the 1890s, direct governmental control had supplanted administration by concessionary companies.

Germany developed a reputation for ruthlessness in dealing with uprisings in its colonies. The Herero Uprising of 1904 was ruthlessly suppressed, resulting in the deaths of nearly sixty thousand out of a population of eighty thousand. The Germans not only shot the victims but also poisoned the water holes from which survivors could have drawn water, resulting in the deaths of thousands more. Those who survived were forced into work camps and became the subject of various medical experiments and examinations.

In German East Africa, the Abushiri Revolt was ruthlessly suppressed in 1889. The same fate befell the Hehe community following an uprising in 1893 when their leader, Mkwawa, was arrested and hanged. The 1905 to 1907 Maji Maji Rebellion in southern German East Africa was equally stamped out when Germans resorted to a "scorched earth" policy that resulted in killings, as well as a massive destruction of crops. The Duala resistance in Cameroon was brutally suppressed. In Togo, the Dagomba fiercely resisted German intrusion, but were overwhelmed. The colonization of African territories by Germany was to a large extent achieved through forceful means, which included overt military campaigns, economic coercion, and land seizure and expropriation.

After the colonial wars of pacification, Germany proceeded to institutionalize political and economic control by putting in place an administrative structure. The colony was headed by a governor. The commanders of the armed forces in the colony, although answerable to the governor, retained a lot of power because they were subject to the High Command in Berlin. The military performed the vital function of maintaining power relations in the colony. A number of the officers also doubled as regional administrators. African chiefs were appointed and made subject to the authority of the local German officials, who were invariably few. The chiefs were supposed to undertake such functions as collecting taxes, conscripting labor for colonial projects, and enforcing government policy. The Germans established a colonial administration that embraced both direct and indirect rule that varied from one colony to another, and on occasions even within the same colonial territory.

The administration of justice in the German colonies was anything but impartial. Its function was to maintain the status quo on the erroneous premise that Africans were inferior, which led to the degrading practice of corporal punishment as well as the frequent arbitrary executions in the colonies. The Germans developed public hospitals as well as educational institutions. But even in these two areas, the facilities were inadequate to cope with the large number of people who desired health and educational services.

The German colonial government encouraged the participation of missionary societies in the provision of these services. The situation in the German colonies was hardly dissimilar from that in other European colonies in

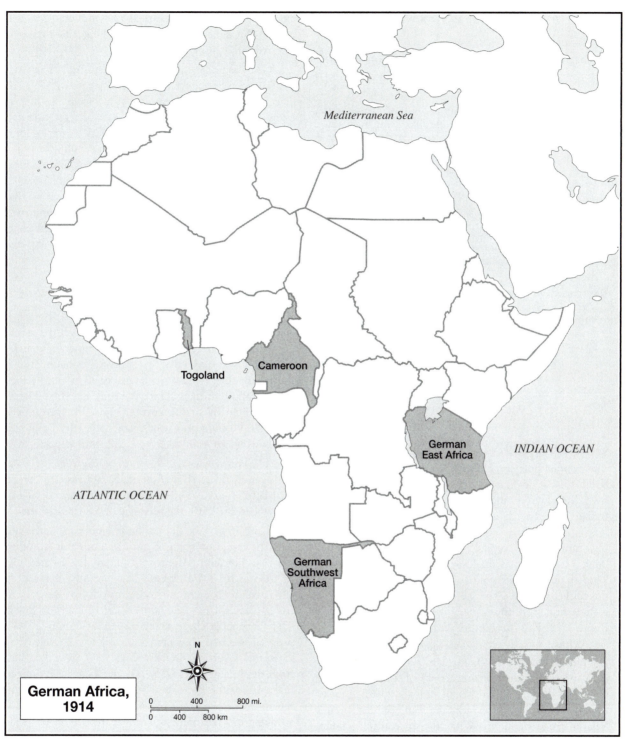

Togoland

Cameroon

German
East Africa

INDIAN OCEAN

ATLANTIC OCEAN

German
Southwest
Africa

Mediterranean Sea

**German Africa,
1914**

N

0   400   800 mi.
0   400   800 km

MAP BY XNR PRODUCTIONS. THE GALE GROUP.

Africa. German colonial rule was still evolving by the time World War I broke out. Africans were conscripted to fight on various warfronts in defense of German imperial interests. However, the end of the war in 1918 proved disastrous for Germany's imperial ambitions in Africa. Germany was defeated and forced to surrender all its colonies, which were subsequently taken over by the other European imperial powers—Britain, France,

Belgium, and in the context of South West Africa, South Africa.

SEE ALSO *Berlin Conference; Maji Maji Revolt, Africa.*

BIBLIOGRAPHY

Baer, H. M. *Carl Peters and German Colonialism: A Study in the Ideas and Actions of Imperialism.* PhD diss., Stanford University, 1968.

Boahen, A. Adu, ed. *Africa Under Colonial Domination, 1880–1935.* Berkeley: University of California Press, 1985. Abridged ed., 1990.

Smith, W. D. "The Ideology of German Colonialism, 1840–1906." *Journal of Modern History* 46 (1974): 641–663.

Stoecker, Helmut, ed. *German Imperialism in Africa: From the Beginnings Until the Second World War.* Translated by Bernd Zöllner. Atlantic Highlands, NJ: Humanities Press International, 1986.

Wesseling, H. L. *Divide and Rule: The Partition of Africa, 1880–1914.* Translated by Arnold J. Pomerans. Westport, CT: Preager, 1996.

George O. Ndege

GOA, COLONIAL CITY OF

The colonial port city of Goa corresponds to present-day Velha Goa (Old Goa), located on the left bank of the river Mandovi in the Tiswadi Taluka district of the Indian state known as Goa. Situated about 400 kilometers (249 miles) south of Bombay, the city of Goa was formerly the capital of Portuguese India, whose limits extended from the Cape of Good Hope to Japan. Though the fabulous wealth of this city once earned for it the epithet Golden Goa, and its elegant and magnificent ecclesiastical institutions made it worthy of being called Rome of the East, for centuries it has been a city in ruins.

When Afonso d'Albuquerque (ca. 1460–1515) conquered Goa in 1510, the city was known as Ela. Ela's prosperity before the arrival of the Portuguese depended largely upon wealth from trade in horses brought from Arabia to meet the war needs of India's Vijayanagara kingdom. With the increase in trade, diverse merchant groups left Gopakapattanam (present-day Goa Velha), located on the banks of the Zuari River, and settled down in Ela by the mid-fourteenth century, leading to its emergence as an important port city in south Konkan. Eventually the city passed from the domain of the Vijayanagara rulers to the control of Muslim rulers, first into the hands of the Bahmani sultans in 1471 and then into the hands of the Bijapuri ruler Yusuf Adil Shah (d. 1510) in 1498. From this port city

alone the Bijapuri ruler earned one million *pardaos* (a type of Portuguese coin) annually in the first decade of the sixteenth century.

Goa was under the control of Yusuf Adil Shah when the Portuguese conquered the city on February 17, 1510. The Portuguese conquerors benefited from the help of many who wanted to reestablish Vijayanagara rule over the territory, including such personalities as the Hindu chief Thimmaya. The conditions prevailing in Goa favored an invasion. Yusuf Adil Shah was busy fighting the king of Vijayanagara, Narasimha (r. 1505-1509) in order to consolidate his recent conquest, and he had entrusted the governance of Goa to Yusuf Gurgi, who with his Turkish soldiers was mistreating the local population. This mistreatment antagonized the locals, who welcomed the invading Portuguese.

THE INITIAL STAGE: 1510–1540

By taking control of Goa, the Portuguese hoped to establish their grip over Asian trade through the implementation and furtherance of their commercial policies. Thimayya was appointed by Afonso d'Albuquerque to the post of chief *thanadar* (captain) of all of Goa's people on the condition that Thimayya would pay 60,000 gold *pardaos* annually to the government. Albuquerque also established a mint and struck new gold, silver, and copper coins worth 480, 40.5, and 2.25 *reals* respectively.

The Portuguese were forced to retreat from Goa when the Bijapuri ruler, Yusuf Adil Shah, laid siege to the city on May 23, 1510. The Portuguese reconquered Goa on November 25, 1510, the feast day of Saint Catherine.

Until 1543, Goa did not have significant hinterlands, with the exception of the chain of islands that surrounds the city. However, Afonso d'Albuquerque favored Goa to Cochin for a Portuguese base in India because the latter was too close to territory controlled by the *zamorin* (ruler) of Calicut, the main enemy of the Portuguese. The Portuguese chose to base their operations in Goa primarily because it remained outside of the range of the *zamorin*'s recurring attacks. Goa was also equidistant from the Indian states of Kerala and Gujarat, a position that enabled the Portuguese to disrupt the trade of both regions. Moreover, Goa provided the Portuguese with an advantageous position from which they could block the flow of commodities to the ports of the Red Sea.

Afonso d'Albuquerque embellished the city with new edifices, including a chapel in honor of Saint Catherine and an adjacent hospital. He transformed Goa's old Palace of the Sabaio into the governor's palace, formed a municipal government on the model of Lisbon, and retained the region's prevailing system of agricultural communities (the *communidade* system). The mint for coining Portuguese money was reestablished, and marriages between Portuguese men and indigenous women were fostered. In 1517 the first Franciscan monastery was set up in Goa with nine members; in 1583 it became the seat of the Franciscan province of Saint Thomas of the East Indies.

Meanwhile, Goa's population had reached two thousand, and the number of public and private edifices in Goa increased so much that during the tenure of Lope Soares de Albergaria (1515–1519) land for new construction became scarce. As a result, the limits of the city were extended by filling a large trench encircling the city wall, and new buildings were erected.

In 1530 the capital of the Portuguese seaborne empire was transferred from Cochin to Goa. The entire empire, with Goa as the metropolitan capital, was subject to the Portuguese viceroy (or governor), whose residence was in the city of Old Goa till 1696, when it was relocated to Panelim, a suburb of Goa, following epidemics in the city. Under the supervision of the viceroy were five governors, who ruled over Mozambique, Malacca, Ormuz, Muscat, and Ceylon. They were supported by captains of fortresses, with civil and military authority. The viceroy's tenure was generally limited to three years, but his powers were almost absolute and extended to all branches of the administration

In 1534 Goa was elevated to the status of an Episcopal see (the seat of a diocese), and Bishop João d'Albuquerque (1478-1553) took charge of the Goa cathedral and diocese in 1538. Previously, the ecclesiastical administration of Goa was run by the Funchal diocese, from whence vicar generals were sent periodically to attend to the people's spiritual needs. The last vicar general was Father Miguel Vaz, who continued to work in Goa in the 1540s, even after the establishment of the bishopric and the arrival of the first bishop. The jurisdiction of the diocese of Goa extended from the Cape of Good Hope to the extreme east.

EXPANSION OF THE CITY: 1540–1600

In 1543 Viceroy Martim Afonso (ca. 1500–1564) obtained from Adil Shah the perpetual donation of Salcete and Bardez to the Portuguese Crown. Salcete and Bardez were two agriculturally important territories adjacent to Goa. The possession of these provinces gave the Portuguese access to wealth from agricultural production. A portion of this wealth and a sizeable share of the trade surplus accrued from intra-Asian trade carried out by Portuguese *casado* traders were used to beautify the city of Goa and to build churches and civic structures. By 1548, there were fourteen churches and chapels in the city and surrounding area, most of them built after 1540.

The first group of Jesuits reached Goa under the leadership of Francis Xavier (1506–1552) on May 6,

1542. For about ten years, Xavier undertook a long chain of travels preaching the gospel mostly in the peripheral areas of the empire and in places outside of Portuguese control. The initial base of the Jesuits in the city of Goa was the seminary of Santa Fé, which later became the famed College of Saint Paul, where native boys were trained to become priests, interpreters, catechists, and missionaries. The Jesuits were responsible for evangelizing the newly obtained territory of Salcete, while the Franciscans were responsible for Bardez; both orders attempted to erase the remnants of Hinduism in these areas.

These religious institutions also provided the platforms for the introduction of European cultural elements into Goa. In 1553 the Jesuits brought the first printing press to the city, and its first leaflet, the *Conclusões publicas,* and first book, a catechism by Xavier (1557), were printed at the College of Saint Paul. In 1553 the body of Xavier, who had died on the island of Sancian off the coast of China on December 3, 1552, was brought to Goa, where it remains the focus of religious devotion even today.

In 1557 Goa's ecclesiastical status was raised to archdiocese, with Cochin and Malacca as subordinates. With this move, Goa's cathedral, which was the only parochial church in the city until 1542, became the archiepiscopal metropolitan church in India. Church-centered urban growth had already evolved in Goa by this time. The Dominicans started building a monastery in 1550, completed in 1564, at the foot of a hillock named Monte. This structure became the headquarters of the Dominicans in the East. The Augustinians, who came to Goa in 1572, founded their monastery on Holy Hill and erected a Renaissance-style church called Our Lady of Grace. Adjacent to it was the Convent of Santa Monica, built by Dom Alexis de Menezes in 1606 as the only convent for women in the East.

Most of Goa's churches, monasteries, and civic structures were built between 1570 and 1600, a period when trade was liberalized by the Portuguese king Sebastian (1554–1578). The Indo-European trade, which until then was conducted from Goa as a royal monopoly, was handed over on a contract basis to German, Italian, and Portuguese private traders. Gabriel Holzschuher representing Konrad Rott of Augsburg (1579–1585), Ferdinand Cron representing the Fuggers and the Welsers of Germany (1586–1592), Filippo Sassetti representing Giovanni Rovallesca of Milan (1580–1592), and the Ximenes brothers representing the New Christian Portuguese traders of Lisbon (1592–1598) were the principal commercial agents who organized Indo-European trade to and from Goa between 1570 and 1600.

The Convent of Saint Monica. *Goa's Convent of Saint Monica, a three-story laterite structure, was built in the early 1600s by Dom Alexis de Menezes.* © BARNABAS BOSSHART/CORBIS. REPRODUCED BY PERMISSION.

Following this development, the intra-Asian trade passed into the hands of *casados*, who established their own commercial networks for commodity movement in the Indian Ocean with a base in Goa. The increase in Goa's private trade is also attested by the dramatic changes in the rate of customs (taxes on imports and exports) in Goa between 1540 and 1600. Collection of duties on spices in the 1540s amounted to 1350 *pardaos*; by the 1590s the duty on spices added up to 7755 Portuguese *xerafins* (a type of coin), suggesting a more than 500 percent increase in the private trade in spices in Goa during this period. Meanwhile, food grains brought in 2,500 *pardaos* in the 1540s, and 11,630 *xerafins* in the 1590s, indicating a more than 450 percent increase in the rice trade of Goa.

During the period of contract trade, when there was a favorable commercial atmosphere for private enterprise, a sizeable number of merchant capitalists from the Portuguese *casados* and the private traders began to emerge. This period also corresponds with increasing attempts by Portuguese private traders to build churches and elegant living quarters. A considerable share of the trade surplus from the *casados* and the wealth of the *fidalgos* (noblemen) was diverted for construction projects in Old Goa. The main structures built with this financing were the monastic houses of the Dominicans and the Augustinians, as well as Bom Jesus Basilica, Se Cathedral, and the College of Saint Paul. New epithets like "Rome of the East" were applied to Goa to give legitimacy to this building process and to mobilize support for it.

The hilly slopes of Old Goa were crowned with elegant edifices, and the ground below was dotted with magnificent palatial buildings and private houses surrounded by gardens and orchards. According to Pedro Barreto de Resende, there were 3,500 Portuguese houses in the city of Goa; 800 of them were made of stone and lime. Goa's Portuguese houses had beautiful windows and balconies, were covered with tiles, and featured alluring frontages that bordered the street with beautiful symmetry. Goa's population at the beginning of the seventeenth century was about 225,000. The most beautiful street in the city was *Rua Direita* (Straight Road), which was lined on both sides by lapidaries, goldsmiths, the homes of the wealthy, and the better merchants and craftsmen. Each class of artisans and traders resided together in Goa's localities.

The city of Goa extended hospitality to such eminent personalities as the Portuguese writer Luis Vaz de Camões (1524–1580), author of *The Lusiads*; Garcia da Orta (ca. 1500–1568), whose book *Colloquios dos simples e drogas da India* was published from Goa in 1563; and the Dutch traveler and historian Jan Huygen van

Linschoten (1563–1611), who as the private secretary of the archbishop of Goa remained in the city from September 1583 to November 1588 and passed on information to the Dutch about the maritime route to the East through his work *Itinerario*.

In 1597 Goa's aldermen hung a portrait of Vasco da Gama in the sessions hall of the Camara de Goa or city council of Goa and later built an arch over the gate through which people entered the city. A large marble statue of Gama was placed on top of the arch. Around 1598 an official archives was established in Goa with the name *Torre do Tombo* (Tower of the Cartulary), and Diogo do Couto was appointed as its chief custodian.

THE CITY IN CRISIS: 1600–1750

The seventeenth century presented a series of problems for Goa, the most serious being recurring Dutch attacks on the navigational lines of Goa's *casado* traders and the frequent epidemics resulting from water contamination. In 1603 the Dutch, having been expelled from Amboina, blockaded Goa for the first time but were compelled to raise the siege a month later. Though the Twelve Years Truce of Antwerp (1609–1621) provided interim relief, Goa was blockaded again by the English and Dutch for two months in 1623. Against this backdrop, in 1629 the new viceroy, Miguel de Noronha (1629–1635), count of Linhares, fortified Goa and Bardez and commenced work across the salt marshes on the long Panjim-Ribandar Bridge, often called the Ponte de Linhares.

To revive the Europe-oriented trade of Goa, the Portuguese authorities established in 1628 the Portuguese India Company with headquarters in Goa and a branch in Cochin on the model of other European commercial companies. However, this company was liquidated in 1634 after a great deal of money was wasted on the duplicated arrangements made for the company. The various ranks and grades of Portuguese officials instituted earlier for looking after trade and political affairs continued to exist, even after the appointment of separate officials for attending to the administrative and routine affairs of the Company, which led to duplication of arrangements. Moreover, the company had to make separate arrangements for transportation of commodities, which meant additional shipping expenses besides the normal ones involved in the routine navigational activities of the crown. The major portion of the extra expenses were to be paid by the crown, who promoted the idea of the company. On realizing this fact the crown liquidated the company.

During this period, new religious structures were also built in Goa, by the Carmelites in 1630, the Theatines in 1640, and the Oratorians in 1683. Joseph Vaz (1651–1711), a priest born near Goa in Sancoale,

joined the Oratorians in 1685 and is now regarded as the patron saint of Sri Lanka because of his evangelization work there.

In 1639 a serious epidemic struck Goa, laying low Viceroy Pedro da Silva himself. Things became worse with the repeated Dutch attacks on the city from 1637 to 1643. Trade to and from Goa declined drastically, and the loss of the Portuguese possessions of Coromandel and Malabar to the Dutch by 1663 deprived Goa of access to aid in times of emergency. This problem became acute when the Marathas from west-central India began attacking Goa in 1668. This attack by Shivaji (1630–1680), a Maratha prince, followed by an attack of Shambaji, the Maratha leader who succeeded Shivaji and controlled the affairs of Konkan and Maratha territory, in 1683, convinced the Portuguese authorities of the weakness of Goa's defense system.

In order to avoid further Maratha invasions and to escape from the frequent outbreak of epidemics, Viceroy Francisco de Tavora (1681–1686) decided to transfer the capital to Mormugao, which only hastened the decline of the city of Goa. Many wealthy families had already moved to the suburbs and to such cities as Batim (Guadalupe), San Lourenco, Naroa, and Chorao. The private edifices that had adorned Goa began to crumble. In 1693 Viceroy Pedro Antonio de Noronha (1661–1731) arrived in India with an order to expedite the Mormugao works and even move the ecclesiastical and civil offices from the city of Goa to the new capital. But he found it difficult to execute the order, and located his own residence in Panelim. The archbishop of Goa and most of the nobility followed his example.

Until the first decade of the eighteenth century, repeated orders were issued from Portugal to demolish the public structures of the old city of Goa and use the material to construct new structures in Mormugao, where the viceroy was directed to move his residence. Under various pretexts, however, the viceroy did not move. At this stage the state set aside 160,000 *xerafins* for the purpose of constructing a new capital in Mormugao. The capture of Bassein by the Marathas in 1739 had a major impact on the many personalities and institutions of the city of Goa, including the Convent of Santa Monica, that had direct and indirect involvement in the trade of Bassein. These developments drained the remaining economic vitality from the city of Goa.

THE PHASE OF TERRITORIAL EXPANSION AND SOCIOECONOMIC CHANGES: 1750–1961

By 1750 the city of Goa had entered a phase of deurbanization due to the mass exodus of people and the decline in trade. The city lost its privileged position as the seat of political and ecclesiastical life in Portuguese India.

Portuguese authorities tried to compensate for the loss incurred by the decline in trade by occupying additional cultivable space, which led to the conquest of new territories.

This effort began with the conquest of Ponda from the Marathas in 1763, followed by the occupation in 1764 of Sanguem, Quepem, and Canacona from the rulers of Sonda, who had sought asylum from the Portuguese at the time of the invasion of the Mysorean ruler Hyder Ali (1722–1782). Pernem, Sattari, and Bicholim were captured from the Bhonsles of Sawantwadi between 1781 and 1788. These newly acquired territories later came to be called the New Conquests, while the earlier possessions (Tiswadi, Bardez, and Salcete) were known as the Old Conquests. The New Conquests were twice the size of the Old Conquests and were chiefly Hindu, whereas the populations of the Old Conquests were predominantly Christian.

In the Old Conquests, the traditional system of *gauncaria* or *communidade*, which implied communitarian ownership of land, was continued with necessary modifications to suit Portuguese colonial designs. *Communidade* formed the principal rural institution around which the society and economy of Goa revolved. According to this system, proprietorship rested with the descendants or representatives of those by whom the village was, at some remote period, conquered or reclaimed from waste. About 12 percent of the land of Goa was under the possession of various *communidades*. Control of the village land, village economy, and village socioreligious life rested with the *communidades*.

The New Conquests, in contrast, maintained a system of *dessaidos*, whereby feudatory chiefs were allowed possession of individual property along with the duty to collect taxes, imposts, and other contributions. This system paved the way for the dilution of the *communidade* system and the emergence of private landownership in the New Conquests. The *dessais,* or feudal chiefs, controlled about 2,650 hectares (about 10.23 square miles) of land in this region. They raised annual revenues of about 110,000 *xerafins* during the nineteenth century. Between 1750 and 1800, a significant portion of the wasteland and low-lying areas of Goa were reclaimed and converted into cultivable land. A department of agriculture was established (1776–1834) to bolster agricultural production. Though the department tried to introduce new cash crops in Goa and bring more areas under cultivation with a view to solving the region's cereal deficit, success was only partial. These efforts in no way helped to infuse vitality into the old city of Goa, which the authorities in Panelim had completely forsaken.

Meanwhile, the Society of Jesus was expelled from Portugal and its colonies, including Goa, in 1759 by the Marquês de Pombal (1699–1782). The Jesuits were expelled from Portugal and its colonies as they formed a strong lobby interfering even in the administrative affairs of the State in their capacity as "Confessors"(hearers of Confession) to the ruler. The Jesuit houses in the city of Old Goa were converted into military storehouses and were thereafter little attended to, a development that sped up the process of decay in the city. However, the landed estates of the Jesuits were distributed among private proprietors and enterprising people, which increased the number of private holdings in the Old Conquests. After the expulsion of the Jesuits, the practice started of publicly exhibiting the body of Saint Francis Xavier periodically in the city of Old Goa, at first primarily to demonstrate to the Goan people that the Jesuits had not taken the body of the saint out of Goa.

Between 1760 and 1850 Goa's trade was revived by private traders, who developed larger mercantile networks for long-distance commodity movement to Macao, Mozambique, Bahia, and Lisbon. The wealth accumulated from this trade went largely into the making of the city of Panjim, which soon became the new capital of the *Estado da India*. In 1835 the senate chambers were moved to Panjim, and by 1843 the transfer of governmental institutions to the new city was more or less complete.

Meanwhile, the city of Old Goa was neglected and increasingly falling into ruin. The roof of the viceroy's palace collapsed in 1812, and the remainder of the palace was demolished in 1830. The final blow to Goa's remaining urban institutions came in 1835, when all the Portuguese religious orders were suppressed and their property confiscated following the establishment of a constitutional liberal government in Portugal under Queen Maria II (1819–1853). With this move, members of Goa's religious orders were forced into exile and the monasteries, as well as the religious houses of Old Goa, became lifeless buildings. These structures were left unattended for ninety-one years, when some of them were reintroduced in 1926 by António Salazar (1889–1970), who later became prime minister of Portugal.

The gap of ninety-one years without maintenance and care was enough to erase many structures altogether from Old Goa. Both churches and civic structures started collapsing, one after another. Some were even demolished on the orders of the viceroy. In 1829 the building that housed the Jesuit College of Saint Paul was destroyed by the government. The Church of Saint Thomas was demolished in 1831. Similarly, the Dominican monastery in Old Goa was destroyed in 1841 on the order of Governor Lopes de Lima. The vault of the Augustinian monastery and the church attached to it collapsed in 1842. The Augustinian college in the old city of Goa was demolished in 1846.

Another impact of the suppression of religious orders was that the New Conquests, which the Portuguese had obtained in the second half of the eighteenth century, remained primarily Hindu, a development that emerged out of the paucity of missionaries and religious people to do evangelization work there. This situation eventually led to a cultural demarcation on the basis of religion between the Old Conquests (predominantly Christian) and the New Conquests (predominantly Hindu).

The constitutional liberal government established in Portugal under Maria II appointed for the first time a Goan, Bernardo Peres da Silva, to be prefect of Goa, a post equivalent to the office of the governor, in 1834. But soon he had to step down because the Portuguese army officers rebelled, as they did not want to serve under a Goan. The general economic condition of Goa also started to deteriorate, particularly after the 1840s. Trade declined drastically. With outdated technology and antiquated methods of production, a major share of the cultivable land was underutilized and the returns from the agricultural sector dropped sharply. The price of essential commodities, including food, increased three- to fourfold, while wage increases were minimal.

All these problems prompted Goans to emigrate to such places as Mozambique, Karachi, Bombay, Madras, and Calcutta. The railway line constructed by the English to connect Mormugao with Bombay in 1881 as a follow-up action of the Anglo-Portuguese Treaty of 1878 was the major carrier of Goan emigrants to British India. By 1910, more than 63,000 Goans had emigrated to the various cities of British India in search of jobs. The annual value of remittances dispatched by Goan emigrants from around the world from 1905 and 1914 amounted to 1,253,318 reis.

Meanwhile, the exodus of working-class Goans to the cities of British India and East Africa created a dearth of able-bodied people to work on farms and rice fields in Goa. Consequently, there was a rise in wages and a decrease in production, followed by an increase in the importation of food materials. Eventually Goa, which was initially sustained by commerce and later by agriculture, had to rely increasingly on foreign remittances to balance the rising foreign deficit caused by the import of cereals.

Salazar's totalitarian regime, characterized by a reign of terror and poor economic growth, coupled with inspiration from the independence movement in British India, generated among the Goans a strong desire to free Goa from the yoke of foreign dominance. However, Salazar viewed Goa as an integral part of Portugal, as a result of which he refused to hand it over to India, even after the British granted freedom to India. When diplomacy failed to resolve these issues, the Indian army

entered Goa and "liberated" it from the Portuguese in 1961, incurring as few causalities as possible.

This incident strained for some time the relationship between Portugal and India. However, Goa benefited from its integration into India, initially as a union territory and later as a state. Its economy got a boost with diversification of production activities and special encouragement to mining and shipping. Infrastructural facilities, including bridges across the Mandovi and Zuari rivers, railway lines, an airport, and roads linking Goa with the rest of India, facilitated movement of commodities and people.

However, the old city of Goa remained in ruins. In 1964 the Archaeological Survey of India came forward to preserve Goa's heritage sites, and many of the old buildings are now maintained by the Archaeological Survey and several Portuguese foundations, including Fundação Oriente and Fundação Calouste Gulbenkian in Lisbon.

SEE ALSO *Albuquerque, Afonso de; Colonial Port Cities and Towns, South and Southeast Asia; Empire, Portuguese; Malabar, Europeans and the Maritime Trade of.*

BIBLIOGRAPHY

Borges, Charles J., Oscar G. Pereira, and Hannes Stubbe, eds. *Goa and Portugal: History and Development.* New Delhi: Concept Publishing, 2000.

Cottineau de Kloguen, Denis L. *An Historical Sketch of Goa.* New Delhi: Laurier Books, 1995.

da Silva Gracias, Fatima. *Beyond the Self: Santa Casa da Misericordia de Goa.* Panjim, India: Surya Publications, 2000.

Gomes, Olivinho. *Village Goa: A Study of Goan Social Structure and Change.* New Delhi: S. Chand and Company, 1987.

Malekandathil, Pius. "The Impact of Indian Ocean Trade on the Economy and Politics of Early Medieval Goa." *Deccan Studies* II (1) (2004): 3-22.

Pearson, M.N. *Coastal Western India: Studies from the Portuguese Records.* New Delhi: Concept, 1981.

Pinto, Celsa. *Trade and Finance in Portuguese India: A Study of the Portuguese Country Trade, 1770-1840.* New Delhi: South Asia Books, 1994.

Pius Malekandathil

GOVERNMENT, COLONIAL, IN BRITISH AMERICA

There were three main forms of government tried in the American colonies: government by company; by proprietor(s); and by the Crown. Most of the earliest colonies were settled by companies, groups of powerful individuals in England who obtained a charter from the king granting them a right to settle. Modelled on the great English trading companies such as the Muscovy Company and the East India Company, the Virginia Company pioneered American colonization by founding Jamestown in 1607. Although the Virginia Company had a disastrous history and eventually lost its royal charter in 1624, the leading English politicians retained their faith in the company model of settlement, chartering, for instance, the Massachusetts Bay Company in 1629. But whereas the Virginia Company, based in London, had found it difficult to direct colonization in America from such a distance, the Puritan merchants who founded the Massachusetts Bay Company actually went to America themselves, and took their charter with them.

After 1630 the Crown no longer granted colonization rights in America to companies, preferring to deal with individuals, or groups of individuals, it termed proprietors. Between 1634 and 1681 almost every new English settlement in the Americas was a proprietory colony. Leading English Catholic Lord Baltimore (1605–1675) was made proprietor of Maryland in 1634; a number of English nobles and adventurers became proprietors of Carolina in 1663 and of the Bahamas in 1670; James, duke of York, (1633–1701) became proprietor of New York in 1664; and Quaker William Penn (1644–1718) became proprietor of Pennsylvania in 1681. The proprietors were granted enormous, royal-like, powers over their territories, and all came into conflict with settlers about the role that representative assemblies would play in the government of the colony. Virginia had been granted a House of Burgess by the Virginia Company in 1619, Bermuda by the Somers Isles Company in 1620, and the Massachusetts General Court was formed soon after the first settlement in Boston in 1630. English settlers elsewhere in America agitated for representative assemblies, and most proprietors eventually granted some form of representative democracy in their territories. The proprietory government of Barbados and the Leeward Islands, for instance, permitted the creation of assemblies on most islands between 1639 and 1670. Franchises were often more open than in England because property qualifications were met more easily in land-rich colonies such as Virginia, though in Massachusetts the franchise was limited to full church members and therefore excluded significant numbers not in communion with the Congregational church. All colonies enjoyed a degree of latitude from English control and were able to pass laws that did not conform to English common law, though the Crown was not above intervening when it thought necessary, for instance, to end the persecution of Quakers in Massachusetts in 1660.

Many colonists found common cause with their English cousins following the accession of James II in 1685 (1633–1701). James's reluctance to create an assembly in New York was regarded as typical of his attitude toward representative government by many colonists, and when he instituted whole-scale reforms of the colonial system in the 1680s it triggered a rebellion. The individual charters of the New England colonies were revoked, and the separate territories were merged, together with New York, into the Dominion of New England. James appointed his staunch supporter, Edmund Andros (1637–1714) as governor of the new Dominion, and rode roughshod over the objections of elected assemblies and officials in America. When James's absolutist tendencies led to his overthrow in England and the accession of William of Orange (1650–1702), rebellions quickly followed in Massachusetts, New York, and Maryland. Those seen as pro-Catholic or pro-James were ousted, and popular sovereignty was restored.

While the charters of most individual colonies in New England were returned, they had been altered in one significant respect. William gradually began to abolish the system of proprietory colonies and replace them with royal colonies. Virginia and a number of the West Indian islands had been royal colonies since the 1620s, but now most New England colonies, New York, and Bermuda also came under the direct control of the Crown. Each colony was granted a form of representative government, but with an appointed colonial council and a governor who was ultimately answerable to government officials in London, especially those in the newly created Board of Trade. Only Connecticut and Rhode Island retained the right to choose their own governors.

However, the extension of royal control over the American colonies did not lead to greater interference from London in the day-to-day affairs of colonial government. William was far too distracted with European wars, and the Hanoverians who acceded in 1715 showed little initial interest in America. Apart from the regulation of trade, the American colonial governments were left to develop as they pleased, and this period of "salutory neglect" has often been credited with encouraging an American sense of independent government. Governors were often dependent on their assemblies for their salaries, a situation that tended to make most governors cooperate with, rather than obstruct, the elected chamber. Therefore, although nominal control rested with the governor, in reality colonial government rested with the elected assemblies. Certainly with the North American continent secure following the defeat of France in the French and Indian War (1756–1763) in 1763, the attempt by British ministers to re-exert some form of control over the colonies was fiercely resisted by colonial governments used to making these sorts of

King James II of England (1633–1701). *James administered colonies in Africa and New York before being crowned king in 1685.* **LIBRARY OF CONGRESS.**

inalienable, and indeed had been safeguarded by the Glorious Revolution (1688) and the Bill of Rights; the assemblies in America considered themselves sister institutions to those in England. In Britain many politicians considered that these rights were only applicable against royal or absolutist power, and not against an elected body such as Parliament. The American assemblies were seen as secondary bodies under the control of the supreme imperial assembly in Westminster. These very different conceptions of the relationship between Britain and its colonies were to prove irreconcilable and to end in the American War of Independence (1776–1783).

SEE ALSO *Native Americans and Europeans.*

BIBLIOGRAPHY
Breen, Tim. *The Character of the Good Ruler: A Study of Puritan Political Ideals in New England, 1630–1730.* New Haven, CT: Yale University Press, 1970.

Jordan, David. *Foundations of Representative Government in Maryland, 1632–1715.* Cambridge, U.K.; New York: Cambridge University Press, 1987.

Labaree, Leonard. *Royal Government in America; a Study of the British Colonial System Before 1783.* New York: Frederick Ungar, 1958.

Lovejoy, David. *The Glorious Revolution in America.* Middletown, CT: Wesleyan University Press, 1987.

Pole, Jack. *Political Representation in England and the Origins of the American Republic.* New York: St. Martin's Press, 1966.

Tim Lockley

decisions alone. Well-established, popularly elected colonial, such as those in Virginia and Massachusetts, felt justified in defending their autonomy. It is noticeable that in the newer colonies such as Georgia, Quebec, and East and West Florida, where representative democracy was in its infancy, or non-existent, opposition to British tactics was much more muted. The position of the West Indian islands is harder to explain. Democratic institutions had been long established on most islands, but the ruling white elite was numerically small and closely modelled on the English aristocracy. Children were educated in British schools and universities and each generation reaffirmed cultural ties to Britain in ways that mainland colonies simply did not. Moreover, elite colonists were well aware of their reliance on the British navy for defense against the French and against possible slave uprisings. For the Caribbean colonies, the advantages of ties to Britain clearly outweighed the disadvantages.

The robust response by several elected governments in mainland America to attempts by successive British administrations to tax them revolved around the historic rights of Englishmen regarding representative government. In America such rights were regarded as

GOVERNMENT, COLONIAL, IN PORTUGUESE AMERICA

Portuguese colonial government was far less centralized than the Spanish model, but it did not grant the local autonomy of the British North American colonies. Unlike the Spanish or British, the Portuguese did not have a large domestic population with which it could populate colonies; therefore, successive monarchs experimented with several systems, and ultimately instituted a system based on a viceroys and colonial governors.

EARLY TRADING POSTS

The first Portuguese settlements in Brazil were trading posts. These posts were fortified but only had a small number of Portuguese inhabitants, who were supported by indigenous allies. Portuguese merchants sought brazilwood, which was commonly used as a source of dye at the time. Beginning in 1500, the crown offered leases for Brazilian territory to merchant groups, but a lack of interest led the king to place the area under direct royal

João VI of Portugal, circa 1810. In 1815 Brazil was granted the status of a kingdom and a dual monarchy under Dom João, who became João VI. HULTON ARCHIVE/GETTY IMAGES. REPRODUCED BY PERMISSION.

control. The king retained title to land, but licenses were granted to individuals and companies to trade specific goods (those items not subject to royal monopolies). In 1511 natives were placed under the protection of the crown, although local officials were granted the authority to differentiate between peaceful natives who could be converted, and those judged irredeemable and therefore allowed to be enslaved.

The first major effort to develop the area occurred in the 1530s in response to French incursions. King João III (1502–1557) tried to encourage interest in the region through a unique system of royal land grants, known as captaincies or *donatarios*. The *donatarios* were about 241 kilometers (150 miles) in length and extended into the interior to the border created by the Treaty of Tordesillas (1494), which divided the world between Portugal and Spain.

João created fifteen *donatarios,* which were distributed to courtiers known as *donees*. Each *donee* was responsible for the costs of settling his territory and attracting settlers. In order to defray the costs of the colony, the *donees* were allowed to issue smaller grants. Few of the *donees* were actually interested in relocation to Brazil, and most of the grants failed. However, two *donatarios*

succeeded very well and led to the establishment of São Vicente and São Paulo. The successful *donatarios* were able to forge alliances with local tribes to obtain labor and allies to fight hostile tribes. They also took advantage of a boom in sugarcane production.

Sugarcane quickly became the chief economic export of the colonies and led to a renewal of royal interest in Brazil when one of the *donatarios*, Pernambuco, came to have greater economic output than Lisbon. In the 1540s the crown decided to reassert royal control over the failed *donatarios*. In 1549 royal authority was further enhanced through the appointment of a governor-general to oversee all of Brazil. The first governor-general, Tomé de Sousa (d. 1573), founded the colonial capital, Salvador, and worked with the Jesuits to establish missions in the interior of the country. The Jesuits eventually developed a series of significant settlements and challenged the authority of local colonial officials (especially when those officials endeavored to enslave natives who were under the protection of the order following their conversion). In 1759 the Jesuits were expelled from Brazil, thereby ending any potential challenge to the colonial establishment.

THE DUAL MONARCHY AND NEW WEALTH

The union of the Portuguese and Spanish thrones (1580–1640) had a dramatic impact on colonial administration. Because of the Dutch insurrection against Spain, the Brazilian colonies were forbidden from trading with Dutch merchants (the Dutch had previously been the primary trade partners with the Brazilian colonies). After being shut off from the lucrative sugar trade, the Dutch launched a series of attacks on the Brazilian colonies and captured the colonial capital of Salvador and the wealthy Pernambuco province.

Many colonists supported Dutch rule, while others opposed the commercial restrictions and heavy economic debts they found themselves under. The Dutch were eventually driven out in 1654 by a coalition of Brazilian planters, Creoles, and merchants. One result of the conflict was a period of significant economic decline that was exacerbated by the emergence of rival sugar plantation economies in the English and French islands in the Caribbean. The decline was only reversed by the discovery of gold in 1693.

The resultant gold rush in the region that became known as Minas Gerais ignited new tensions between established colonial families and the adventurers who arrived to take advantage of the newfound wealth, while also populating a previously neglected area of the interior. In addition, the capital was moved from Salvador to Rio de Janeiro to be closer to the gold mines in 1763. Colonial officials found it difficult to keep control, as gold prospectors moved deeper into the interior and beyond the ability of authorities to collect taxes or enforce law. Armed conflict broke out between the original settlers and Creoles on one side and the newcomers on the other. In response, the crown enacted new policies to bring the region under control.

By the 1750s gold production began to decline and the colony moved toward development of a more diversified economy that included ranching. This diversification was aided by reforms undertaken by Portugal's prime minister, the marquis de Pombal (José de Carvalho e Melo, 1699–1782), who ended concessions enjoyed by foreign merchants and reformed the sugar and gold trade. Portugal's efforts to exert closer control over its colonial subjects did not go unchallenged, however, and resentment against royal authority resulted in the Minas Conspiracy of 1789, in which the activities of colonial elites and even local officials foreshadowed later independence movements.

THE DUAL KINGDOM AND INDEPENDENCE

The most dramatic shift in colonial government occurred in 1807 when the regent, Dom João (1769–1826), moved the monarchy to Brazil in order to escape the invasion of Napoléon Bonaparte (1769–1821). In order to support its Portuguese allies, the British transferred some fifteen thousand courtiers and officials from Portugal to Brazil and lent the relocated government some $3 million.

Dom João recreated many of the components of royal government in Brazil, including a supreme military council, a high court, and various boards to oversee trade and commerce. In 1815 Brazil was granted the status of a kingdom and a dual monarchy under Dom João, who became João VI. However, discontent with Portuguese rule led to the Pernambuco Revolution in 1817. The rebellion encouraged army officers in Portugal to rebel, which in turn forced João and the court to return to Lisbon in 1820. João's son, Dom Pedro (1798–1834), remained in Brazil and led a movement for independence in 1822. He was subsequently crowned Emperor Pedro I, inaugurating a new phase in the history of the state in Brazil as an independent constitutional monarchy.

SEE ALSO *Empire in the Americas, Portuguese; Empire, Portuguese; Minas Gerais, Conspiracy of.*

BIBLIOGRAPHY

Alden, Dauril, ed. *Colonial Roots of Modern Brazil: Papers of the Newberry Library Conference.* Berkeley: University of California Press, 1973.

Boxer, C. R. *Race Relations in the Colonial Portuguese Empire, 1415–1825.* Oxford, U.K.: Clarendon Press, 1963.

Hemming, John. *Red Gold: The Conquest of the Brazilian Indians.* Cambridge, MA: Harvard University Press, 1978. Rev. ed., London: Papermac, 1995.

Kieman, Mathias C. *The Indian Policy of Portugal in the Amazon Region, 1614–1693.* Washington, DC: Catholic University of America Press, 1954.

Maxwell, Kenneth. *Conflicts and Conspiracies: Brazil and Portugal, 1750–1808.* Cambridge, U.K.: Cambridge University Press, 1973.

Russell-Wood, A. J. *A World on the Move: The Portuguese in Africa, Asia, and America, 1415–1808.* New York: St. Martin's, 1992.

Schultz, Kirsten. *Tropical Versailles: Empire, Monarchy, and the Portuguese Royal Court in Rio de Janeiro, 1808–1821.* New York: Routledge, 2001.

Schwartz, Stuart B. *Sovereignty and Society in Colonial Brazil: The High Court of Bahia and its Judges, 1609–1751.* Berkeley, University of California Press, 1973.

Tom Lansford

GOVERNMENT, COLONIAL, IN SPANISH AMERICA

In the Capitulations of Santa Fe (1492), the Spanish monarchs named Christopher Columbus (1451–1506) as viceroy of the "discovered lands" and granted him extensive powers to govern in the new lands and to benefit from the wealth they created. But it was not long before the crown sought to take back control of the discovery and colonization of America, effectively suspending Columbus's authority. A decade later, the monarchs appointed Nicolás de Ovando (ca. 1451–1511) as governor of Hispaniola (the island that now comprises Haiti and the Dominican Republic) and began to assert their authority over subjects of Spain who went to the New World and the indigenous peoples whom they found there.

As the Spanish Crown became aware of the rich potential of the Indies, it soon started to build institutions for government on both shores of the Atlantic. In 1503 the crown founded the Casa de Contratación (Chamber of Commerce) at Seville to ensure Castille's control of all aspects of trade with America. The Casa de Contratación had multiple functions. It supervised the movement of passengers and the shipments of goods from Spain to America and received products brought back from America (gold, cotton, sugar, silver, cacao, medicinal plants, etc.). It also enforced regulation of all aspects of the transatlantic trade (taxation, security in business and voyages, insurance and contracts, and the maintenance of the state's presence in all operations), and it compiled information on the trade and trade routes of the Indies.

From 1546 the Casa de Contratación was given certain legal functions. In 1524 the crown further reinforced its command over the Americas by establishing the Consejo Real y Supremo de las Indias (Royal and Supreme Council of the Indies), which served to oversee colonial affairs, to advise the king on such matters, and to act as the supreme court for legal issues arising in the Indies. Its influence was far-reaching, since it also compiled and published the laws for America, laws that were collected in 1681 under the title *Recopilación de leyes de los reinos de Indias* (Code of Laws of the Kingdoms of the Indies).

Early in the sixteenth century, the monarchy also began to build structures of royal government on the other side of the Atlantic Ocean. When Ovando arrived in Hispaniola in 1502, he was accompanied by a number of other officials (a comptroller, a treasurer, an inspector, and others), all of whom were responsible to the crown. To ensure that its command was respected in the lands that conquistadors brought under Spanish sovereignty, the crown created a new system of government that placed a governor in charge of each new province, with administrative, legal, and, at times, military powers.

With the advance of Spanish influence in the new lands, the crown established institutions that directly represented the person and power of the king, and were staffed by high-ranking officials chosen from the nobility. The first such institutions were the *audiencias*—bodies responsible for administering justice—of which ten were established in the course of the sixteenth century, at Santo Domingo (1511), Mexico (1527), Panama (1538), Lima (1543), Guatemala (1543), Guadalajara (1548), Santa Fe de Bogotá (1548), Charcas (1559), Quito (1563), and Chile (1565); others were added in the eighteenth century at Buenos Aires (1776), Caracas (1786), and Cuzco (1787).

During the first half of the sixteenth century, the crown also introduced another, maximum authority into its new territories: the viceroys. Appointed from among members of the nobility or the clergy, the viceroy was the chief representative of the king and held political, military, administrative, and minor legal powers. The first viceroyalties were those of New Spain (1535) and Peru (1543); two new viceroyalties were added in the eighteenth century at New Granada (1717) and Río de la Plata (1776).

In addition to these institutions, the crown created another tier of government for dealing with revenues raised by royal taxes. Treasury officials were appointed to supervise the collection of all kinds of taxation, from the tributes paid by Indians to the sales taxes and customs duties derived from trade, and the *quintos*, or royal fifth, that was levied on all products of mining.

At the local level, the viceroyalties and *audiencias* were subdivided into smaller units that were in closer contact with the king's subjects. These were the *gobernaciones* (provincial governorships); the *corregimientos* (known as *alcaldías mayores* or mayoralties in New Spain), and the *corregimientos de indios* who, as their name suggests, were responsible for supervising Indian governance outside the Spanish towns. In the towns and cities where the white population was grouped together, the *cabildos* provided municipal government. Their magistrates and councilors enforced law and order, and supervised matters of common interest, such as food distribution, cleanliness, craft statutes, prices and salaries, and the handling of public goods.

This framework of government was largely in place by about 1570, although it continued to expand as new territories were brought under Spanish rule, as the business of government grew, and, with the growth of revenues from mining and trade, as the crown was able to pay an increasing number of salaried officials. One special feature of the system of government was the overlapping jurisdictions of institutions, a system designed to prevent the concentration of power in a single office and to ensure that officials such as the viceroy and the *audiencia* judges acted as a check on the authority of the other. If this structure aimed to prevent institutions distant from Spain from becoming too independent, it also allowed royal officials some space for autonomous action, so that they could ensure that the application of laws was appropriate to local circumstances. Another special feature of the system of colonial government introduced by the Habsburg kings of Spain was the use of special commissioners who undertook investigations into colonial officials through the *residencia* (legal investigation of civil servants) and the *visita* (inspection of bodies or authorities).

Over the course of the seventeenth century, royal power began to be replaced by local power as a consequence of the loosening of relations with the metropolis and of the growing influence of Creoles in the colonial bureaucracy. This situation was brought on by changes in the economy and the administration of the empire. With the fall in transatlantic traffic after about 1620, due to the wars in Europe, piracy, and contraband, many regions became more self-sufficient and depended less on Spain for their economic prosperity. The chronic fiscal problems of the state further contributed to the loss of power for two reasons: (1) because official posts were increasingly acquired through the exercise of personal influence, a situation in which even the viceroys took part,

Building Saint Augustine's Roads. *Colonists in the Spanish settlement of Saint Augustine, founded in 1565 in what is now Florida, work together to construct roads. They take measurements with string and dig with shovels and pickaxes.* © CORBIS. REPRODUCED BY PERMISSION.

practicing nepotism and clientelism; and (2) because the financial needs of the crown led to the sale of public offices on an increasingly large scale.

Creoles gradually took over the governing posts in their cities and came to dominate the *cabildos*. These posts generated benefits that were both economic (bribes and access to public revenue) and social (honor, influence, and local power). After around 1630, governmental, military, and treasury offices were also sold off, so that Creoles penetrated areas of the royal bureaucracy that had previously been reserved for Spaniards. At the end of the century, the Peruvian viceroyalty was virtually

up for sale. The result was that large sectors of administration were placed in the hands of the rich Creole elites, and colonial government had become "Americanized."

The eighteenth century began with the inauguration of a new dynasty—that of the Bourbons—on the Spanish throne, and successive kings sought to reverse the trend toward decentralization that had marked the rule of their Habsburg predecessors. The new dynasty opted for an administrative continuity during the first part of the century, while making some changes aimed at tightening control over the administration of the colonies. By mid-century, however, the need for reform was increasingly accepted, and, after Spain's humiliating defeat by the British in the Seven Years War (1756–1763), the ministers of King Carlos III (1716–1788) introduced reforms designed to reassert royal authority and harness colonial resources for the benefit of Spain and its monarchy. The reform program started in Cuba in 1764, and was then extended to Mexico by José Gálvez (1720–1787), who acted as inspector-general of New Spain from 1766. Gálvez pursued reform with such vigor that he was promoted to the powerful post of minister of the Indies in 1776.

At the same time, the crown sought to exert its authority over the Catholic Church, ordering the expulsion of the Jesuits from all Spanish territories, including the American colonies, in 1767. As minister of the Indies, Gálvez unleashed a wave of reforms that affected the whole range of political, economic, and military relations between Spain and its colonies. His aim was to ensure that the colonies contributed more to the Spanish treasury and economy, while reducing Creole participation in American government. To these ends, a new viceroyalty was established in the River Plate region in 1776 with its capital at Buenos Aires, and general inspectors were sent to Peru, New Granada, and Chile to overhaul their governments.

Gálvez then introduced the system of *intendancies* throughout America (1782–1790; Cuba in 1764), and thus implanted a new body of government officials, the *intendants*, who were responsible directly to the crown and exercised a wide range of political, military, fiscal, and economic powers. Trade between the Spanish ports and America was also liberalized by the 1778 decree of *comercio libre* (free trade) within the empire, designed to increase colonial commerce with the metropolis.

While these reforms brought the growth of colonial commerce and increases in the yields of taxation, they also provoked colonial antagonism and triggered major rebellions. The most formidable rebellions broke out in Peru and New Granada in 1780 to 1781 in opposition to fiscal and administrative reform. The greatest of these was the rebellion of Túpac Amaru, which spread throughout Southern Peru and Upper Peru as native populations seized the opportunity to protest against the various forms of exploitation to which they were subject. Another major regional revolt broke out in New Granada, where a large rebel force known as the *comuneros* demanded the reversal of fiscal and political reforms. In New Granada, rebellion ended peacefully through negotiation; in Peru, the outcome was considerably more violent and many lives were lost before the crown fully restored its authority.

Although Spain's colonial governments survived these challenges, new threats arose at the end of the century when Creole political adventurers inspired by the American and French revolutions sought to stir uprisings against Spain in the name of freedom and independence. They did not attract any substantial support in the colonies, but changes in the international situation gradually weakened Spain's position in the Americas and were eventually to give Creole revolutionists their chance to break away. Spain sided with France in almost continuous war with Britain from 1796 to 1808, and bonds with America were substantially weakened during this prolonged conflict.

The system of colonial government remained intact, but the foundations of the empire, strained by continuous international war, were finally undermined when in 1808 Napoléon Bonaparte (1769–1821) invaded Spain, seized the throne, and precipitated a crisis of imperial authority. In 1810 the great edifice of colonial government, built by the Habsburgs and renovated by the Bourbons, began to fall apart.

In Spain, meanwhile, an emergency government resisted the French and sought to build a new constitutional monarchy, embodied in the Constitution of Cádiz (1812) created by the Cortes (parliament) set up at Cádiz in 1810. However, pleas for unity and concessions to the colonies were insufficient to save Spanish rule because, in leading cities throughout the Americas, Creoles asserted a right to autonomy and began to set up their own governments, beginning a secession that would eventually lead to the emancipation of most of Spain's American territories by 1824.

SEE ALSO *Conquests and Colonization; Túpac Amaru, Rebellion of.*

BIBLIOGRAPHY

Brading, David A. *The First America: The Spanish Monarchy, Creole Patriots, and the Liberal State, 1492–1867.* Cambridge, U.K.: Cambridge University Press: 1991.

Céspedes del Castillo, Guillermo. *América Hispánica (1492–1898).* Barcelona: Labor, 1984.

Domínguez Ortiz, Antonio. *Descubrimiento, colonización, y emancipación de América.* Barcelona: Planeta, 1990.

Lynch, John. "The Institutional Framework of Colonial Spanish America." *Journal of Latin American Studies* 24 (1992): 69–81.

Navarro García, Luis, ed. *Historia de las Américas.* 4 vols. Madrid: Alhambra-Longman, 1991.

Zaragoza, Gonzalo. *América latina: Época colonial.* Madrid: Anaya, 2004.

Donato Gómez-Díaz

GREAT TREK

Afrikaners left the Cape Colony (in present-day South Africa) in large numbers during the second half of the 1830s, an act that became known as the "Great Trek" and that helped define white South Africans' ethnic, cultural, and political identity. In line with Afrikaners' belief in a separate existence, developing tensions between these settlers, British authorities, and African communities drove the "Boers" to quit the Cape and found their own exclusive republics. It was not unheard of for the Boers to leave the Cape in search of an existence far removed from an administration that they perceived as oppressive. This leave-taking stretched back to the period before Britain's initial arrival in 1795. After its arrival in 1652, the Dutch East India Company (Verenigde Oost-Indische Compagnie, or VOC) had attempted to force its employees and those to whom it had granted landholdings to do business solely with the company. Officials also expected settlers to willingly pay taxes supporting company operations. Many people refused, deciding instead to relocate beyond the VOC's grasp.

British authorities were more efficient at tax collection, thereby appearing more domineering than the VOC. Moreover, when Britain assumed de facto control of the Cape in 1806, administrators replaced the Dutch system with their own. The British also slowly replaced locally known authorities with their officials, thereby severing the Boers' (farmers') link with the administration.

With politics in flux, settlers and Africans were increasingly at odds over territory, as evidenced by the string of Xhosa wars that began in 1779. British administrators had no qualms about supporting African states when appropriate. Although they were not wedded to African rights, officials certainly did not want to encourage free movement across the land that could fuel still more trouble between settlers and the African communities.

Boer anger grew in 1815 when the British hanged five Afrikaner settlers for starting a rebellion. The rebels claimed that the British favored African rights over those of Afrikaners when officials attempted to arrest a man for beating his African servant. The fact that British missionaries had lobbied the government to protect African rights was a cultural insult to the neo-Calvinist Boers and their beliefs in a divinely chosen society built upon racial and religious purity.

When the British government outlawed slavery in the British Empire in 1833, it promised to compensate former owners, but only at one-third the assessed value of the slaves. Claimants had to travel to London in order to petition for compensation. It was the efficient British administration, the clash of cultures, and the division of Europeans over African policies that helped cement Afrikaners' decision once again to move beyond the grasp of the Cape-based government.

Piet Retief (1780–1838) published a manifesto in the *Grahamstown Journal* appealing to those Afrikaners who had suffered long enough in the Cape. Following the Voortrekkers who, in 1835, had left the Cape to scout for ideal territory, families began moving north to the highveld (part of the central South African plateau) in 1836, crossing the Orange River and even the Vaal River still farther to the north. Disagreements over a proper government and the best areas in which to settle led some of the trekkers to push east across the Drakensberg range into modern Natal. In both cases trekkers came into contact with African states, and competition for land ensued. In October 1836, Ndebele led by Mzilikazi (1795?–1868) launched an attack near Vegkop, killing livestock but not overrunning the Boers' defensive *laager* (a protected camp). The Boers countered in 1837, and by the end of the year had driven the Ndebele north over the Limpopo River.

In Natal, Zulu King Dingane (1795–1840) wiped out a party of Boers under Piet Retief. Afrikaner reinforcements arrived from the Cape and the highveld, meeting the Zulu at the Ncome River on December 16, 1838. The river ran with African blood as the Zulu attack withered under the sustained Boer fire. Blood River Day would go on to become a significant holiday on the Afrikaner calendar. With the defeat came civil war among the Zulu, finally enabling the Boers to begin implementing their own administration. They established the Natal Republic, with six thousand people settling in the fertile valleys around the Tugela River.

Although the Boers successfully implanted themselves in the areas that would become the Orange Free State and the Transvaal republics, their good fortune did not last in Natal. Britain would not accept potentially hostile settlers with a market savviness controlling coastal ports. Moreover, the Boers' racial policies had the potential to cause trouble among the rising African population. If the British intended to control trade, they would have to control Natal. In 1843 the British government annexed the territory, thereby driving many of the settlers back over the Drakensberg mountains.

The Great Trek enhanced the developing Afrikaner mythology. By 1854 the Boers had successfully established two republics north of the Cape Colony, thus legitimating efforts to separate themselves from an oppressive higher authority. With its images of a dedicated spiritual people working to establish a society based solely upon their beliefs, it is no wonder that the event was celebrated and recreated a century later.

The Great Trek. *Years of chaffing under British rule led Afrikaners in the Cape Colony to begin a mass exodus in the mid-1830s. The trekkers moved north to the highveld, eventually crossing the Orange River and even the Vaal River still farther to the north.* **THE GRANGER COLLECTION, NEW YORK. REPRODUCED BY PERMISSION.**

As in other nations in the 1930s, South Africa suffered from the effects of economic depression. In unstable times, the Afrikaners sought to reaffirm their existence. This was made easier by the centennial celebration of the Great Trek. Families joined in a recreation of the trek and a number of celebrations highlighting Afrikaner culture. The Ossewabrandwag (Ox-Wagon Guard), a cultural organization created in 1939, also exploited the image of a people trekking to their homeland in the struggle to be free.

When apartheid was under threat of collapse in the 1980s, the mythology of the Great Trek resurfaced again with the creation of new commando organizations designed to protect the state against a growing African nationalist insurgency. Groups such as the *Afrikanerweerstandbeweging* (Afrikaner Resistance Movement) also harkened back to the days of racial purity and struggle against an oppressive foe. As the Great Trek symbolized the life of the Afrikaner, it also symbolized the purely idealistic efforts to create a separate neo-Calvinist state. This was impossible in a nation dependent upon African labor and a relationship with the outside world. Especially as colonialism ended, bringing independence to African states, it became painfully

obvious that such visions of racial purity and exclusivity were unrealistic.

SEE ALSO *Afrikaner; Apartheid; Boer Wars; Cape Colony and Cape Town; Dutch United East India Company.*

BIBLIOGRAPHY

Fisher, John. *Paul Kruger: His Life and Times.* London: Secker and Warburg, 1974.

Shillington, Kevin. *History of Southern Africa.* Harlow, U.K.: Longman, 1987.

Thompson, Leonard. *A History of South Africa,* 3rd ed. New Haven, CT: Yale University Press, 2001.

Jeffrey Lee Meriwether

GUANGZHOU

Guangzhou, known as the city of the rams (*yangcheng*) and the city of flowers (*huacheng*), is the capital city of Guangdong province and one of the foremost metropolises and international ports in China. Guangzhou, approximately 161 kilometers (100 miles) away from the South China Sea, is located in the northern part of

Canton Harbor. *This Chinese painting depicts the harbor of Canton (Guangzhou) as it looked in the early 1800s. Ships from many nations fill the harbor, which is lined with foreign factories and trading stations.* © BETTMANN/CORBIS. REPRODUCED BY PERMISSION.

the Pearl River Delta, at the confluence of the West, North, and East Rivers. River channels link Guangzhou to the former British colony of Hong Kong, and to Macau, the former Portuguese colony. Besides Hong Kong and Macau, neighboring areas are the provinces of Hunan, Jiangxi, Fujian, and Hainan, as well as the Guangxi Zhuang autonomous region.

Guangzhou is situated on the plains, backed by mountainous land to the north. Located in the subtropical and monsoon zone, Guangzhou has a year-round average temperature of 20° to 22° C (68°–70° F), with 79 percent average humidity. Guangzhou's annual precipitation is about 2,200 mm (87 inches). Warmth, humidity, and fertile delta soil provides for flowering trees, subtropical flowers, and abundant fruits (such as banana, citrus, lichee, and pineapple).

Since early in its history, Guangzhou has been the key center of the *lingnan* (south of the mountain range) region in progressive South China as well as the hub of

domestic and international trade. A large number of its population has emigrated to Southeast Asia, North and South America, as well as to other parts of the world, and this provides Guangzhou and South China with a significant link to overseas Chinese and the outside world.

Municipal Guangzhou has a population of about 6 million and covers an area of 7,434 square meters (8,891 square yards). The indigenous residents of Guangzhou were the Nanyue who were absorbed by the Han Chinese during the Tang dynasty (618–906). Today, the primary ethnic group living in Guangzhou is Han, with small numbers of Li, Yao, Zhuang, Miao, Hui, and Manchu. Cantonese, one of the major seven dialects in China, is the native tongue of Guangzhou. Cantonese cuisine, Yue opera, folk music, including *bubugao* and *xiyangyang*, are distinctive to the region and influential in China and overseas.

As the starting point of the Silk Road on the sea, Guangzhou had established trade relationship in silk with

Rome already in 116 C.E.. Other trading partners were India, Ceylon, Syria, Persia, and Arabia. In the eighth century, a regular foreign trade market was founded with the *Shibo Si* (Bureau of Sea Trade) to manage foreign trade. Buddhism and Islam were introduced into Guangzhou with the arrival of Indian and Arab merchants.

The coming of the Portuguese to Guangzhou in 1517, followed by the Spaniards in 1575 and English in 1636, ushered in a new era of colonialist penetration of China, in which the Arabs lost their dominant position. In 1685 the Manchu Qing regime lifted the ban on the entry of foreign vessels, thus facilitating foreign trade. The British East India Company, from 1715, then signing a favorable trade agreement with the Guangdong customs, to the first Opium War (1839–1842), was the dominant foreign trading power in Guangzhou. In 1720, the *cohong* system was instituted by the Qing government authorizing certain Cantonese merchants, known as Thirteen Hongs (guilds), to conduct business with the English, Dutch, French, Americans, Swedes, Danes, Spaniards, and other foreigners who maintained their factories in the designated areas of Guangzhou. In 1757 all foreign trade was restricted solely to Guangzhou.

Frictions occurred when the foreigners found the *cohong* system manipulative and inconvenient, whereas the Qing authority did not allow foreigners to trade freely or to establish diplomatic relations with China. Unable to sell well manufactured goods in the China market, British merchants began smuggling Indian opium into China to make up for their trade deficit. In response to the Qing government's crackdown on opium traffic, Britain went to war with China in 1840, and in 1842, they forced the defeated Qing regime to sign the Treaty of Nanjing. This treaty opened up five ports, including Guangzhou, to foreigners, and conceded Hong Kong to Britain.

Guangzhou has played a key role in Chinese revolutions. After the demise of the Qing government in 1912, Guangzhou became the headquarters of the Nationalist Party (Guomindang, GMD) and the base, shared by the GMD and the Chinese Communist Party (CCP), of the anti-warlord and anti-imperialist Nationalist Revolution.

Since the opening of China in 1979, Guangzhou has again emerged as a prominent city of commerce and has been at the forefront in China's domestic economic reforms and China's interactions with the outside world. Along with Shanghai, Guangzhou's labor force is one of the most productive in China. Guangzhou's economic, political, and social influence in contemporary China is further reinforced by its geographical closeness to Hong Kong, and to the two special economic zones of Shenzhen and Zhuhai.

SEE ALSO *China, After 1945; China, First Opium War to 1945; China, Foreign Trade; Chinese Revolutions; Empire, British, in Asia and Pacific; Hong Kong, from World War II; Hong Kong, to World War II; Opium; Opium Wars.*

BIBLIOGRAPHY

Johnson, Graham E. *Historical Dictionary of Guangzhou (Canton) and Guangdong.* Lanham, MD: The Scarecrow Press, Inc., 1999.

Lee, Edward Bing-Shuey. *Modern Canton.* Shanghai: The Mercury Press, 1936.

Ng, Yong Sang. *Canton, City of the Rams: A General Description and a Brief Historical Survey.* Canton: M.S. Cheung, 1936.

Vogel, Ezra F. *Canton Under Communism: Programs and Politics in a Provincial Capita, 1949–1968.* Cambridge, MA: Harvard University Press, 1969.

"China Tourist and Travel Guide for Guangzhou City, China." Travelnet Ltd. Available from http://www.orientaltravel.com.hk/China/Guangzhou.htm.

"Guangzhou Travel Guide: Hotel, Map, Climate, Pictures, and Tour." Available from http://www.travelguide.com/cityguides/guangzhou.htm.

Dong Wang

H

HACIENDAS IN SPANISH AMERICA

The hacienda, or large estate in Latin America, is traced back to the sixteenth century. The Spaniards who risked life and limb in the invasion, conquest, and exploration of the "New World" expected rewards for their efforts. Those early on the scene received a share of the plunder and *encomiendas*. But the accumulated gold and silver of the native societies did not last long and there were never enough *encomiendas* to meet the demand of people who, sincerely or not, claimed that they had served the crown and deserved one.

As the Spanish population increased, the native population succumbed to disease, overwork, and harsh treatment. Others fled contact with the Europeans. By mid-century, some Spaniards without rewards had become troublesome vagabonds in native communities and Spanish cities alike. Demand was increasing for labor and foodstuffs, especially grapes (for wine), wheat (for bread), and olives (for oil). Vast amounts of land became available as the native population fell or fled. Therefore, the Crown began a policy of founding new Spanish towns or *villas* as farming centers. Individuals with some capital could apply for citizenship in these new cities.

Those selected were rewarded with a house site (*solar*), a garden plot (*huerta*) in the suburbs, and a larger land grant (*merced*) in the surrounding countryside. The size of the land grant varied by the status of the individual grantee and the available resources. The first settlers usually did not have the capital to plant all the land granted to them, but, over time, successful farmers did and even expanded their land holdings through a combination of purchase, donation, marriage into a landed family, or usurpation. The latter usually was at the expense of surrounding native communities.

By the seventeenth century, three types of large estates existed. The first was a ranch. Cattle raising required relatively little capital for equipment and minimal labor. In many areas, native shepherds cared for large flocks of sheep or herds of cattle, which grazed on pastures, officially considered common and open to all, as they were in Spain. In the eighteenth century, these common pasture lands were divided and sold to users by a Spanish government intent on increasing the flow of revenue to the peninsula. It was then that many ranches, like those of Northern Mexico, officially became estates measured in leagues rather than the more common and smaller land units.

The second type of large estate was known as a hacienda or mixed farm. It produced foodstuffs and animals for a regional market. This type required more capital (for equipment and infrastructure), more labor for cultivation, and became the stereotypical estate throughout the Spanish Americas. The third and last type was the specialized farm. Most of these produced cash crops, like sugar or cacao for a distant, sometimes overseas, market. In some areas, sugar estates became known as *trapiches*, *molinos*, *ingenios*, or *haciendas y trapiches*. They required the largest infusions of capital for specialized mills and processing facilities. High demand for both skilled and unskilled labor was filled by seasonally-employed laborers and black slaves.

The owners of these estates often became the most powerful group in the area. The owners were entrepreneurs who oversaw operations and marketed their

Hacendados. *The owners of haciendas in Spanish America were entrepreneurs who oversaw operations and marketed their products. In good times, profits allowed them to acquire a lifestyle that was the envy of society.* LIBRARY OF CONGRESS. REPRODUCED BY PERMISSION.

products. In good times, profits allowed them to acquire a lifestyle that was the envy of society. They purchased seats on the town council, which they passed on to their male heirs for generations, giving them and their families inordinate influence in local politics. They endowed chapels and other pious works and gave their sons access to higher education. They also invested in other activities, serving, for example, as local financiers. Wealthy Spanish immigrants and creoles joined the landed elite by investing in land or marrying into landed families. By the late seventeenth and early eighteenth century, the hacendados often had multiple roles—serving simultaneously as landowner, miner, bureaucrat, or merchant—with observable economic and political power and influence in the colonies. The institutional exception was the church, which either became a direct holder of many large estates or indirectly benefitted from mortgages on them.

The hacienda was not a static institution. It tended to become bigger over time. But it was susceptible to more general economic fluctuations. Though profits from these landed estates were usually lower than those from mining and commerce, the wealthy continued to buy because yields tended to be more predictable and stable than those of other investments and landowning brought social prestige that added lasting luster to family names and houses. In sum, the hacienda, or great estate,

became the American counterpart of the Spanish estate, established to meet European and American conditions and the need for creating and holding wealth and power.

SEE ALSO *Empire in the Americas, Spanish; Encomienda.*

BIBLIOGRAPHY

Brading, David A. *Haciendas and Ranchos in the Mexican Bajio: Leon, 1700–1860.* Cambridge, MA; New York: Cambridge University Press, 1978.

Burga, Manuel. *De la encomienda a la hacienda capitalista.* Lima, Peru: Instiudo de Estudios Peruanos, 1976.

Chevalier, Francois. *Land and Society in Colonial Mexico; the Great Hacienda.* Translated by Alvin Eustis. Berkeley, CA: University of California Press, 1963.

Cushner, Nicolas. *Lords of the Land: Sugar, Wine, and Jesuit Estates of Coastal Peru, 1600–1767.* Albany: State University of New York Press, 1980.

Konrad, Herman W. *A Jesuit Hacienda in Colonial Mexico: Santa Lucia, 1576–1767.* Stanford, CA: Stanford University Press,1980.

Morner, Magnus. "The Spanish American Hacienda: A Survey of Recent Research and Debate." *Hispanic American Historical Review* 53, no. 2 (May 1973), 183–216.

Ramirez, Susan E. *Provincial Patriarchs: Land Tenure and the Economics of Power in Colonial Peru.* Albuquerque, NM: University of New Mexico Press 1986.

Susan Elizabeth Ramírez

HAITIAN REVOLUTION

It is not easy to pinpoint precisely when the Haitian Revolution began. Historians have located its beginnings at different points between 1789 and 1804, the year St. Domingue was transformed, amidst rebellion and war, from a French colony into the independent state of Haiti. However, the roots of the rebellion, which transformed St. Domingue are undoubtedly found in the revolutionary turmoil that convulsed France itself following the fall of the Bastille and the abolition of slavery in 1794. These events had a highly disruptive impact on a slave-based society that was already experiencing serious social tensions after a period of rapid growth.

During the previous decade, St. Domingue had become the most prosperous colony in the Caribbean. In the 1780s, it produced nearly half of all the sugar and coffee consumed in Europe and the Americas, and, as the source of two-fifths of France's colonial trade, two-thirds of its ocean-going shipping tonnage, and a third of its seamen, had become the most valuable of French colonial possessions. This growth had been very rapid and had been achieved through a massive annual importation of African slaves, mostly young males, that averaged about

40,000 per year in the 1780s. By 1789 there were close to half a million slaves in St. Domingue, greatly outnumbering the white population of about 40,000, and the 28,000 free coloreds (blacks and mulattos) who occupied an intermediate position in this slave society. A relatively small percentage of French and free colored owned most of the plantations and slaves. If the presence of large numbers of slaves fresh from Africa made this an unusually volatile society, so too did the aspirations of free coloreds, some of whom had fought in French forces in the American War of Independence and were in the 1780s already aspiring to equality with whites. But it was the great political crisis in France that threw St. Domingue into turmoil, by generating conflicts at all levels of society and undermining French government and sovereignty on the island.

Political upheaval started among the whites, who came into conflict over the great political questions that also divided the French at home. While the rich planters and their allies sought to maintain their command of colonial society, poor whites backed those who attacked the wealthy, privileged elites and overturned the monarchical authorities whose power had been weakened by the overthrow of the old regime in France. The free coloreds, inspired by the 1789 Declaration of the Rights of Man, were also quickly drawn into politics, with the encouragement of the Société des Amis des Noirs (Society of Friends of Blacks), which campaigned for the abolition of the slave trade and for equal rights for free coloreds. When rebuffed, some free coloreds decided on armed rebellion. Vincent Ogé, a mulatto who had been active on behalf of free colored rights in revolutionary Paris, led a revolt of mulattos in favor of civil equality for freed coloreds in 1790. He refused to recruit slaves to his rebellion and was soon defeated, but Ogé's execution triggered a scandal in France and persuaded the National Assembly to legislate legal equality for free coloreds born of free parents. This produced, in turn, a backlash from whites, who although divided over the French Revolution, were generally united in wanting to maintain slavery in the colony, to preserve its plantation society and to defend its racial hierarchy.

Conflict among and between whites, and between whites and free coloreds, had thus come close to civil war and it was in these tense circumstances that political factionalism among the minorities was suddenly overtaken by the greatest slave rebellion yet seen in the Americas. In 1791 fieldworkers in northern St. Domingue rose up, claiming that they had already been emancipated by the French king. Slaves met to coordinate an uprising of slaves in Le Cap and the nearby countryside. The political decision was sanctified in a voodoo ceremony in which two hundred slaves drank the blood of a pig sacrificed by a priestess and swore

***Portrait of Jean-Baptiste Belley* (1797) by Anne-Louis Girodet de Roucy-Trioson.** *Senegalese-born Belley, a leader of the Haitian revolution, became a representative to the French National Assembly from Saint-Domingue. In his portrait, he leans against a bust of Abbé Raynal, an eighteenth-century French critic of slavery.* CHATEAU DE VERSAILLES, FRANCE/ GIRAUDON/BRIDGEMAN ART LIBRARY. REPRODUCED BY PERMISSION.

obedience to Boukman Dutty, leader of the planned revolt. Dutty chose as his lieutenants Georges Biassou, Jeannot Bullet, and François Papillon. They planned to kill the French elite in Le Cap and set about destroying plantations and killing whites over a wide area, sometimes in alliance with free coloreds, sometimes against the joint resistance of whites and free coloreds.

Many historians see the slave rebellions that began in 1791 as the start of the revolution in St. Domingue because they involved the mass mobilization of slaves and forced France to introduce a significant political change. In order to curb violent upheaval that spread to all the main regions of the colony, France conceded full citizenship to free persons in April 1792. This brought a significant change in the position of mulattos. They now held full legal rights and were allowed to hold office and promptly sought to consolidate their gains by entering into alliances with white planters to defeat the slave rebels, whom they saw as a threat to their property and position. The French Revolution had ended white supremacy but preserved slavery, and when three French civil commissioners charged with preserving order arrived in St. Domingue in September 1792, the free coloreds sided with them. This development promised a return to stability under French revolutionary government, which favored the free coloreds over whites who were often suspected of royalism, but the intervention of foreign powers against the French regime in St. Domingue led to another, more destructive cycle of wars.

War against Britain and Spain changed the position not only of free coloreds but also of blacks. When the French king was overthrown in 1793, the commissioners from France, particularly Léger Félicité Sonthonax and Etienne Polverel, moved against royalists, deported large numbers of whites, and promoted free coloreds in their place. When war broke out, they moved closer to the blacks by recruiting slaves to fight royalist white colonists and the forces of Spain and England, which invaded St. Domingue in 1793. Sonthonax decreed that slaves in St. Domingue's northern province would be free as of August 29, 1793, a date often cited as the beginning of the Haitian Revolution. The commissioners in the two other areas of St. Domingue followed suit. This presented the French National Convention with a *fait accompli*, and on February 4, 1794 (16 *pluviôse*, year II), slavery was abolished by the Convention in all the colonies. St. Domingue's slaves had won emancipation for themselves and (temporarily) for French slaves everywhere. Though the British and Spanish had been attempting to preserve plantations and slavery, they had produced the opposite effect by persuading the French authorities that the only way to save French power in St. Domingue was to abolish slavery and so win the rebellious slaves for France. This had an immediate effect on the balance of power within the colony, as slave leaders emerged to challenge the privileges of both whites and free coloreds.

The Convention's law abolishing slavery attracted the free black General Toussaint L'Ouverture (born François-Dominique Toussaint), who switched from supporting Spanish troops to fighting on the side of the French government in 1794. This is another moment regarded as the beginning of the Haitian Revolution, because the black troops of Toussaint L'Ouverture now were free and looked to a Haitian as their ruler. It was certainly a turning point in that Toussaint L'Ouverture's army and military genius played decisive roles in defeating foreign invaders and slave-owners, forcing the Spanish and British to withdraw, a move that freed slaves in the west in 1798. French rule was saved, but at the cost of promoting the power of Toussaint L'Ouverture.

Toussaint L'Ouverture moved to establish his rule over all of St. Domingue, from his position of strength in the North and Port-au-Prince, and sent the French commissioners back to France. He fought a civil and race war against the mulatto André Rigaud, who controlled the southern part of St. Domingue, where many mulattos owned plantations. Known to Haitians as the War of the Knives, this struggle was complicated by the fact that mulatto officers served with Toussaint L'Ouverture, while black troops fought on both sides. By mid-1800, Toussaint L'Ouverture dominated all of St. Domingue. He then moved to occupy Spanish-speaking Santo Domingo even though it was under French rule. An angry Napoleon, who had seized power in France in 1799, decided to invade St. Domingue to restore French rule. Toussaint L'Ouverture's constitution of 1801, promulgated against the wishes of Napoleon Bonaparte, made Toussaint L'Ouverture a governor for life with all power concentrated in his hands. The French could no longer claim to rule St. Domingue, and St. Domingans were no longer colonial subjects. Some historians therefore choose 1801 as the date when St. Domingue became self-governing and the Haitian Revolution began.

Another key phase of the Haitian Revolution is the period from 1802 to 1804 when Napoleon's brother-in-law Victor Emmanuel Leclerc led a French army of invasion into St. Domingue, and sought to reestablish the old slave regime. Toussaint L'Ouverture and his generals fought a guerrilla war against the French, then surrendered and retired to their plantations. Two of Toussaint L'Ouverture's main generals—Jean-Jacques Dessalines and Henri Christophe—turned him in for plotting rebellion and a year later, in 1803, he died as a prisoner in France. But the situation on the ground changed dramatically when it was learned in July 1803 that France had reinstated slavery. Mulattos and blacks now united against the French under mulatto officers Dessalines and Alexandre Pétion and the black Christophe. The success of these insurgents, the death of General Leclerc, and the renewed war with the British that starved French forces of supplies and reinforcements, led to French defeat and evacuation of St. Domingue in November 1803. The race war was renewed, this time against the white French, and around 3,000 were massacred on orders of Dessalines in 1804. On January 1, 1804, *de jure* independence was proclaimed by Dessalines and the name "Haïti," from the Indian Arawak language, was substituted for Saint Domingue.

What began as a civil war among the whites who had split into factions (*petits blancs* against *grands blancs*, planters versus merchants, colonists against French administrators, and creoles against absentee planters), thus became a race war (blacks against mulattos, whites against mulattos, blacks and mulattos against whites), and ended in a revolutionary war when the blacks rose up as an independent group and struck for independence from France, in 1802 to 1804.

There are diverse explanations for why the blacks won: Toussaint L'Ouverture and some of his lieutenants were exceptional leaders, tropical diseases felled European troops, the colonists were divided, the whites and mulattos were outnumbered, and the slaves knew how to fight. John Thornton emphasizes that the majority of slaves in St. Domingue were African-born, and had arrived within ten years of 1791. They came principally from two areas that were sites of warfare: the Lower Guinea coast (comprised of present-day Benin, Togo, and Nigeria) and the Angolan coast. Most of the slaves sold to Europeans were prisoners of war from these engagements and had military experience. Familiar with European muskets, lances, axes, shields, and swords, they also knew African military organization and tactics such as guerrilla warfare by platoons and large engagements in columns. Thornton surmises that mulattos and European deserters used the artillery noted in rebel armies, and that horsemen were largely creoles, mulattos, and Africans from Oyo and Senegal. New armies under creole and mulatto leadership adopted European military tactics and fought alongside African leaders using African tactics. African religious practices fortified the soldiers. All rebel armies relied on African soldiers who were veterans as well as agricultural workers. More than any other factor this could explain why the Haitian slave revolt succeeded.

The significance of the Haitian Revolution extended far beyond the island. It was the first great reversal of slavery in the world of European colonialism, achieved by an extraordinary slave resistance against the French planter class and the armies of the three great colonial powers, France, Spain, and Britain. In addition, it contributed to the end of colonial empire by becoming the second colony in the Americas after the United States to achieve independence. The Haitian Revolution also blocked Britain's ambitions to extend its empire in the Caribbean. As such, it served as a symbol for both abolitionists and proponents of slavery, colonialists and anticolonialists. Alexandre Pétion gave military and financial assistance to the Miranda expedition to free Venezuela from Spain in 1806, and to Simón Bolívar, who sought refuge in Haiti in 1815, on the condition that the latter promise to abolish slavery in the lands he liberated. There is little evidence that Haitians stirred up slave populations elsewhere, however, although slaves and freemen throughout the Americas knew that the Haitians had freed themselves and this served as inspiration, along with many other factors, in slave revolts in Venezuela (1795), Havana (1812), and Charleston, South Carolina (1822). The Haitians invaded neighboring Santo Domingo under Toussaint L'Ouverture, and again in 1822 when they stamped out slavery, although it was later resumed by the Spanish. Haiti never again prospered, and after the assassination of Dessalines in 1807, it became divided between Pétion's oligarchic republic of small landholders in the south, and Christophe's authoritarian black kingdom of plantations in the north. Toussaint L'Ouverture, and later Dessalines and Christophe, had insisted on plantations and forced labor in order to make coffee and sugar cane profitable. Toussaint L'Ouverture compelled labor on plantations to earn foreign exchange to buy arms, build fortifications, and make preparations for a French invasion. In the long run, the ex-slaves rejected involuntary servitude and plantations, and Haiti became a nation of small farms and free labor.

Rather, the greatest impact of the Haitian Revolution seems to have been its refugees, whites, free blacks, mulattos, and slaves who fled to the United States, France, Jamaica, Cuba, and other Caribbean islands. Their skills and knowledge led to the establishment of businesses, but most of all contributed to the growth of sugarcane plantations and slavery. Cuba became the most prosperous sugarcane island after 1800. Due to Napoleon's occupation of Spain, Haitian refugees were expelled from Cuba in 1808, and many immigrated to Louisiana, where they helped stimulate and maintain the French culture that preceded Anglo settlement. Initially these refugees were welcomed in the United States and given funds by the U.S. Congress, Pennsylvania, Virginia, New York, and South Carolina, and cities such as Philadelphia, New York, Charleston, and Baltimore. Many private citizens also responded to pleas for charitable contributions. The U.S. Congress exempted St. Domingans from the new 1807 law forbidding the importation of slaves into the United Sates. Many who brought in slaves could hire them out or use them as slaves on their own plantations. Immigrants doubled the free black population of New Orleans. The mulattos came to occupy a special status between whites and free blacks, giving New Orleans a special Creole flavor.

On the other hand, the Haitian Revolution had a negative impact in the South by hardening the attitudes of whites. Beginning in 1792, South Carolina and other states restricted immigration of slaves, freedmen, and mulattos from Haiti to protect their slaves and freedmen from any "contagion." Louisiana, under Spanish rule since 1763, discouraged refugees from seeking asylum in the 1790s. The New Orleans *cabildo* banned slaves and free blacks from landing. France regained control of Louisiana from 1801-1803, but Napoleon's rule remained nominal due to the failure of the French expedition to St. Domingue. After the United States took possession of Louisiana in 1803, the number of refugees from St. Domingue increased. They arrived primarily from Jamaica and Cuba. The New Orleans *cabildo* prohibited the landing of free blacks. The fear of "another Haiti" moved the U.S. Congress to end the importation of slaves after 1807, but an exception was made for slaves brought to Louisiana by French refugees.

Thomas Jefferson found himself supporting Toussaint L'Ouverture in Haiti, because the defeat of the British and French armies allowed Americans to trade directly with Haiti. In addition, the defeat of the French motivated Napoleon to sell Louisiana to the United States, a transfer that greatly furthered American attempts to expand to the west. Federalists wanting to discredit the French and open commerce with the West Indies praised Toussaint L'Ouverture. Southerners admired his reimposition of plantations using forced labor and his control over Haitian blacks. They credited him with defeating radical ideology deriving from the French Revolution. Likewise, the British signed a commercial treaty with Toussaint Louverture, and kept the sea-lanes open for trade. But it was not until France recognized Haitian independence in 1825, after Haiti agreed to pay huge reparations to the colonial exiles, that other countries formally recognized Haiti. And it was only when the U.S. Civil War ended slavery that full diplomatic relations were established between the United States and Haiti. By then Haiti was no longer considered a threat.

SEE ALSO *Abolition of Colonial Slavery; Revolutions in the Americas.*

BIBLIOGRAPHY

Baur, John E. "International Repercussions of the Haitian Revolution." *Americas* 26, no. 4 (1970): 394–418.

Cauna, Jacques. "The Singularity of the Saint-Domingue Revolution: *Marronage*, Voodoo, and the Color Question." *Plantation Society in the Americas* 3, no. 3 (summer 1966): 321–345.

Fick, Carolyn E. *The Making of Haiti: The Saint Domingue Revolution from Below.* Knoxville: University of Tennessee Press, 1990.

Garrigus, John D. "White Jacobins/Black Jacobins: Bringing the Haitian and French Revolutions Together in the Classroom." *French Historical Studies* 23, no. 2 (spring 2000): 259–275.

Geggus, David P. "The French and Haitian Revolutions, and Resistance to Slavery in the Americas: An Overview." *Revue française d'histoire d'Outre-Mer* 76, nos. 1–2 (1989): 107–124.

Geggus, David P. *Haitian Revolutionary Studies.* Bloomington: Indiana University Press, 2002.

Geggus, David P. *The Impact of the Haitian Revolution in the Atlantic World.* Columbia: University Of south Carolina Press, 2001.

Hunt, Alfred N. *Haiti's Influence on Antebellum America.* Baton Rouge: Louisiana State Press, 1988.

Munford, Clarence J., and Michael Zeuske. "Black Slavery, Class Struggle, Fear, and Revolution in St. Domingue and Cuba, 1785–1795." *The Journal of Negro History* 73, nos. 1–4 (winter–autumn 1988): 12–32.

Thornton, John K. "African Soldiers in the Haitian Revolution." *The Journal of Caribbean History* 25, nos. 1–2 (1991): 58–80.

Virginia W. Leonard

HAKLUYT, RICHARD
1552–1616

Richard Hakluyt (pronounced HACK-loot) was an English geographer, historian, editor, and a leading promoter of English colonial expansion in North America. He was known as "Richard Hakluyt of Oxford" to distinguish him from his older cousin, Richard Hakluyt of the Middle Temple, who was a lawyer and also an advocate of English colonization.

Richard Hakluyt of Oxford was born in London in 1552 and was educated at Christ Church, a college of Oxford University. He later taught at Oxford, was ordained as a priest in the Church of England, and pursued a career as both a scholar and clergyman. He was well connected to many of the leading political figures of Elizabethan and Jacobean England, including Sir Walter Raleigh (ca. 1554–1618).

Hakluyt's earliest writings on English overseas expansion included plans for establishing a colony on the Strait of Magellan at the southern tip of South America. He soon abandoned this plan, however, in favor of English settlement of the Atlantic coast of North America.

In 1584 Hakluyt completed one of his major works, titled *Discourse of Western Planting*, which was presented to Queen Elizabeth I (1533–1603) in manuscript but was not actually printed until almost three hundred years later. This text established English legal claims to North America (based in part on the writings of John Dee [1527–1608]) and discussed in depth the benefits of English settlement, including the commercial and strategic advantages that England stood to gain from colonizing the region. Although Elizabeth was in agreement with the sentiments of this manuscript, England was engaged in a rivalry with Spain and unable to finance the colonial project that Hakluyt proposed, though Hakluyt's writing probably had an influence on the formation of the unsuccessful colony established in 1585 on Roanoke Island, off the coast of present-day North Carolina.

Hakluyt's next great work, *The Principal Navigations, Voyages, and Discoveries of the English Nation*, published in 1589 (with later editions published under a slightly different title), was a compilation of reports and documents pertaining to English voyages of exploration to America, the Arctic, Russia, Asia, and Africa. Unlike earlier compilations of this kind, Hakluyt's text was based on original documents and explorers' reports, and on his own translations of foreign texts. *The Principal Navigations* narrates the history of English exploration, and also constitutes a kind of prose epic of the heroic exploits of the English. This work was hugely influential in stimulating English interest in establishing colonies in North America, especially because it was published only one year after England's defeat of the invading Spanish Armada in 1588. Spain's defeat gave the English a freer hand in exploring and colonizing North America north of Florida and allowed for the rise of English imperialism more generally.

Hakluyt died in 1616 and was buried in Westminster Abbey in London. Many of the unpublished documents he left at the time of his death were later edited and published by Samuel Purchas (ca. 1577–1626) in *Purchas His Pilgrimes*, which continued Hakluyt's project of documenting English exploration. The London-based Hakluyt Society, founded in the nineteenth century and named after him, continues to publish important documents in the history of exploration.

SEE ALSO *Empire, British; European Explorations in North America.*

BIBLIOGRAPHY

Hakluyt, Richard. *Voyages and Discoveries: Principal Navigations, Voyages, Traffiques, and Discoveries of the English Nation.* Edited and abridged by Jack Beeching. London: Penguin, 1972.

Hakluyt, Richard. *Discourse of Western Planting.* London: Hakluyt Society, 1993.

Taylor, E. G. R. *Late Tudor and Early Stuart Geography, 1583–1650.* London: Methuen, 1934.

Michael Pretes

HARKIS

Harkis were indigenous Muslim soldiers in Algeria who, organized into units called *harkas,* served in the French army during the colonial period in Algeria (1830–1962). By extension, all Algerians who favored to some degree the French presence in Algeria—as opposed to the movements for independence whose supporters called for total withdrawal—came to be called *harkis.*

According to a 1962 report presented to the United Nations by Christian de Saint-Salvy, the general controller of the French army, 230,000 indigenous Algerians were engaged on the French side during the Algerian war of independence (1954–1962), including 60,000 active-duty soldiers; 153,000 civilian employees; and 50,000 Francophile public servants. The Algerian National Liberation Front (*Front de libération nationale,* or FLN) called them all *harkis.* The word thus became a pejorative term signifying submission to the colonial power and symmetrical betrayal of the aspiration of nationalist Algerians.

The harkis and their families added up to about one million indigenous Muslim Algerians (of a total population of eight million) sympathetic to France. From the point of view of the independence movements, all these people were guilty of collaboration with the colonial oppressor, hence of treason to the fatherland. At a deeper, cultural level, they were accused of treason to their Algerian identity as they colluded with a European power to impose a Western model on Algeria. This view was reinforced by the French state's attempt to count Algeria as a French province (*département*), rather than a colony. Both of these interpretations made the harkis subject to the scorn of the FLN and other Algerian nationalist forces.

In spite of their loyalty to France, the Accords of Evian, signed by French president Charles de Gaulle (1890–1970) on March 19, 1962, which put an end to the war and recognized the independence of Algeria, left the harkis and their families at the mercy of the FLN. As French armed forces left Algeria and the *pieds noirs* (literally, "black feet," a term used to refer to French citizens who had settled in Algeria) were evacuated, the harkis were disarmed and abandoned.

Although the Accords of Evian paid lip service to national reconciliation and amnesty, the retribution was swift and cruel. A low estimate puts the number of harkis massacred in the immediate aftermath of Algerian independence at tens of thousands. Harkis associations cite much higher figures. The charges of treason brought against them often combined with accusations of violence committed on behalf of France against their fellow Algerians. Harkis were therefore despised and executed both as political offenders (i.e., traitors to the country and to Algerian national identity as defined by the FLN) and as bloodthirsty criminals.

This massive collective punishment was typically executed without trials and without any right to defense. It is therefore difficult to determine if and to what extent the harkis committed crimes. The widespread view of most survivors is that harkis became the victims of revenge killings and also of political settling of scores. The killings were particularly gruesome. Eyewitnesses and official documents catalog a long list of refined forms of torture. The extreme suffering and humiliations had

Harkis Soldiers in Paris. *Soldiers of the special Harkis regiment from Algiers march past the Arc de Triomphe and down the Champs Elysées on July 14, 1957, during the annual Bastille Day parade in Paris.* **HULTON ARCHIVE/GETTY IMAGES. REPRODUCED BY PERMISSION.**

the pedagogical purpose of convincing the majority of Algerians of the evils of collaboration with the French and of the usefulness of pledging full allegiance to the new authorities.

Some harkis managed to escape Algeria and enter France, where they encountered a chilling welcome. More often than not they were arrested and returned to Algeria to face torture, imprisonment, and death. Many individual French officers tried to help their former allies. In doing so, they disobeyed the orders of the high command, which considered such actions as infractions of the military code, carrying various punishments. A note from the minister of the French army, Louis Joxe (1901–1991), dated May 12, 1962, threatened further sanctions against French military personnel engaged in helping the flight of harkis towards France, and decreed that all harkis caught on French territory would be returned to Algeria.

By the end of 1962, however, 20,000 harkis had been processed in special transit camps which served to facilitate their integration into French society. These camps were organized in former military bases such as Larzac,

Bourg Lastic, and Rivesaltes. 3,200 harkis joined the regular French army. Eventually, 91,000 harkis and their families were permitted to relocate to France. This did not, however, mean that they had been given the opportunity to start new lives. Most harkis spent many years in camps akin to ghettos, during which time their children were not allowed to attend local schools. They were educated in special camp schools, which further perpetuated the stigma of their harkis identity and made their integration into French society even more difficult. Algerian legislation still bars the harkis from visiting their homeland.

Caught between the deadly revenge of fellow Algerians and the sudden abandonment of the French authorities, the harkis who managed to settle in France have long been the object of contempt from all sides. Algerian official discourse continues to present them as criminal collaborators, while anticolonial opinion in France depicts them as traitors to the aspirations of their own people. Until recently, the official position of the French government was assiduous indifference, sometimes combined with the exasperation of having to deal

LAW OF FEBRUARY 23, 2005

The law of February 23, 2005, is a declaration of the gratitude of the French state for the service of the *harkis* in Algeria, up to the independence of Algeria (1962). In addition to official recognition of past service to France, the law establishes monetary compensation to the tune of 2,800 euros a year or a lump sum of 30,000 euros. The law also guarantees protection against insults and defamation and other efforts to deny the tragedy of the *harkis*, although it stops short of admitting the responsibility of the French state.

The law has been the subject of heated debate among historians, especially because the *pieds noirs* (former French colonists in Algeria) were included among the categories of individuals entitled to both recognition and compensation. But the most sustained criticism was provoked by article 4, which calls on history programs and textbooks to give more space to the history of the French presence in Northern Africa, and also recommends that such programs and textbooks underline the "positive role" of the French presence in that part of the world. Furthermore, the law recommends that the sacrifices of North Africans who fought in the French army be taught in schools. In response to the law of February 23, 2005, an open letter signed by dozens of historians was sent to the French parliament, deploring both the tendency to embellish France's colonial past and the attempt of the government to control the teaching of history. A great debate followed in the press over the various ways the colonial period is remembered, over the interface between memory and history, and over the lack of consensus on the way in which this particular facet of French history should be addressed.

with an embarrassing relic from the past at a time when French authorities were looking for a fresh start in the country's relation with former colonies.

Since the end of the Algerian war harkis organizations in France have fought an uphill battle to restore the honor of these former French allies. The second generation of harkis has especially worked for recognition of and respect for the service the harkis performed for France. Much effort has gone towards exposing the opportunistic abandonment of the harkis by the French state, a betrayal akin to criminal neglect, considering that French authorities were fully aware of the fate awaiting their hitherto allies. A number of community associations keep alive the memory of the tragedy of the harkis, and they work towards rehabilitation of the community, both in Algeria and in France.

While the harkis are still outcast in Algeria, in France a number of books have gradually made the public aware of the plight of the harkis, as well as the way the French state treated this segment of the Algerian population. These efforts at rehabilitation culminated with a law passed on February 23, 2005, by the French Parliament. The law expresses France's gratitude towards the harkis and establishes monetary compensation for the sons and daughters of former French allies in Algeria in the form of an *allocation de reconnaissance* (gratitude grant) of 2,800 euros per year or a lump sum of 30,000 euros. The law also guarantees protection against insults and defamation and other efforts of denying the tragedy of the harkis, although the law stops short of admitting the responsibility of the French state in this tragedy.

SEE ALSO *Algeria; French Colonialism, Middle East.*

BIBLIOGRAPHY

Azni, Boussad. *Harkis, crime d'état: Généalogie d'un abandon.* Paris: J'ai lu, 2002.

Besnaci-Lancou, Fatima. *Fille de Harki.* Paris: Editions de l'Atelier, 2003.

Méliani, Abd-El-Aziz. *Le drame des Harkis.* Paris: Perrin, 2001.

Doina Pasca Harsanyi

HAVANA

In 1514 Diego de Velazquez (1465–1524), the conqueror of Cuba, incorporated *San Cristobal de la Habana* as one of the initial seven villas of the island. Originally sited on the southern coast near the anchorage of Batabano, in 1519 officials moved Havana to its present location on the north coast where the enormous deep water bay and proximity to the Bahamas channel confirmed its strategic importance. French, Dutch, and English incursions prompted construction of elaborate fortifications, the most emblematic being the Morro castle at the harbor mouth. The city became the political and military capital of the colony in 1553, while the Bishop of Santiago de Cuba habitually resided in Havana until 1789 when an independent see was created.

Until the early nineteenth century Havana possessed a diverse economy. Foodstuffs, with an early emphasis on cattle ranching and leather exports, occupied the hinterlands and confirmed the city as the agricultural service center for the western half of the island. The royal tobacco monopoly was established in 1717. The Havana Company, founded in 1740, promoted the island's produce, especially sugar. The bay constantly hosted the transatlantic treasure fleets, whereas the city furnished maintenance and provisioning. Complementing the expanding shipyard, which constructed the world's largest wooden vessels in the eighteenth century, were a canon and anchor foundry.

Following the British capture and occupation of Havana in 1762, Spain introduced numerous reforms—taxation with consent of the *habaneros*, a monthly transatlantic mail service, and massive new fortification construction with free and prisoner labor. The Free Trade Act of 1765 opened Havana to nine Spanish ports, while an act passed in 1778 opened additional American ports. The creation of white, mulatto, and black militia companies provided new, wider reaching opportunities. Havana ranked as the "key to the New World."

The quickening rise of the sugar oligarchy at the end of the eighteenth century coincided with the destruction of the neighboring island of Saint Domingue (later Haiti), stimulating monoculture. The loss of Spanish colonies in the early nineteenth century diminished Havana's turntable function, but increased free trade, especially in sugar and tobacco, and confirmed a new, prosperous economy.

SEE ALSO *Caribbean.*

BIBLIOGRAPHY

Johnson, Sherry. *The Social Transformation of Eighteenth-Century Cuba.* Gainesville, FL: University of Florida Press, 2001.

Kuethe, Allan. *Cuba, 1753–1815: Crown, Military, and Society.* Knoxville, TN: University of Tennessee Press, 1986.

Marrero, Levi. *Cuba: Economía y sociedad.* Río Piedras, Pueto Rico, and Madrid: Editorial San Juan and Editorial Playor, 1972–1992.

Martín Zequeira, María Elena, and Rodríguez Fernández, Eduardo Luis. *La Habana, guía de arquitectura.* Madrid: Agencia Española de Cooperación Internacional, 1998.

Segre, Roberto, Mario Coyula, and Joseph L. Scarpaci. *Havana: Two Faces of the Antillean Metropolis.* Chichester, U.K.: John Wiley & Sons Ltd., 1997.

Wright, Irene A. *The Early History of Cuba, 1492–1586.* New York: Macmillan, 1916.

G. Douglas Inglis

HAWAI'I

The geologically recent Hawaiian Island chain is the most remote archipelago in the Pacific Ocean. Native Hawaiians are descendants of long-distance Polynesian ocean voyagers. Population estimates for the late eighteenth century range from 110,000 to 1 million. Although Spanish explorers visited earlier, a British naval expedition led by Captain James Cook (1728–1779) initiated the first sustained European contact in 1778. In 1810 the smaller Hawaiian monarchies were unified by King Kamehameha I (1758–1819), who ruled from 1795 to 1819. The British provided protection until 1816. The United States extended diplomatic recognition to the Kingdom of Hawai'i in 1826. The two countries signed five treaties during the next sixty-one years.

In the Kingdom's evolution as a parliamentary monarchy, successive constitutions limited the power of the monarch. In a harbinger of future dependency, sovereignty was interrupted by five months of British rule in 1843. By 1850, foreigners could purchase land legally. And migrations of Protestant missionaries, capitalists from the United States, and farm workers from Asia and elsewhere began transforming Hawai'i into an export-oriented agricultural colonial settler-state. Sugar plantations became central to the economy.

Signed under duress, the Bayonet Constitution of 1887 severely reduced the monarch's dwindling powers. Non-Hawaiians were members of the cabinet. By 1890, the Native Hawaiian population fell to 40,622, or 45 percent of the total population. Fearing the independent spirit of Lili'uokalani (1838–1917), queen of the Hawaiian Islands from 1891 to 1893, sugar plantation owners formed the Annexation Club and a committee of safety. Backed by a contingent of U.S. Marines, they arrested the Queen on January 17, 1893. Having overthrown a weakened constitutional monarchy, they established the rebel Republic of Hawai'i (1893–1898). At the outset of his second nonconsecutive term, U.S. President Grover Cleveland (1893-1897) refused to recognize the Republic. Although Cleveland did not support annexation, he and like-minded political leaders could not convince Congress to endorse restoration of the monarchy.

Native Hawaiians did not acquiesce. Thousands of Hawaiian women were among those resisting nonviolently. In 1897, as the Caucasian oligarchy renewed plans to facilitate annexation, Native Hawaiians signed the *Ku'e* (Resist) petition, organizing a massive campaign to secure signatures. According to Hawaiian-language documents from the National Archives of the United States, a majority of Native Hawaiian adults signed the petition. The extraordinary outpouring of opposition caused the annexation treaty to fail. Colonization stalled, but only for a few years.

Ceremony Marking the Annexation of Hawaii, August 13, 1898. *American sailors from the* USS Boston *form an honor guard in front of Iolani Palace in Honolulu during ceremonies marking the annexation of the Hawaiian Islands as a U.S. territory.* © CORBIS. **REPRODUCED BY PERMISSION.**

Despite misgivings expressed by individual members of Congress, the United States ultimately ignored Hawaiians' protests. During the Spanish-American War (1898), the Congressional Newlands Resolution of July 7, 1898, asserted U.S. administrative control over the islands. Also, Congress promised to enact special laws for the management and disposition of 1.8 million acres of ceded Crown lands. Under the U.S. Constitution, a two-thirds vote by the Senate is required to ratify treaties. Because the Newlands Resolution ostensibly was not an agreement between two sovereign states, it needed a simple majority in both houses of Congress. More curiously, the Newlands Resolution acknowledged "treaties of the Hawaiian Islands with foreign nations." Although the Newlands Resolution was formally not a treaty, unsurprisingly the rebel Republic ratified it.

The Territory of Hawai'i was established in 1900. Ceded lands (Crown lands) were transferred to the Territory and, later, to the state of Hawaii. In the 1930s and especially with the United States entrance into World War II (1941–1945), Hawai'i became increasingly militarized. Fifty years of U.S. bombing of Kaho'olawe Island by the U.S. Navy began under President Franklin D. Roosevelt (1882–1945), who held office between 1933 and 1945. After World War II (1939–1945), Hawai'i was listed as a non-self-governing territory under Article 73 of the United Nations (UN) Charter. During and after the Cold War (1946–1991), Hawai'i served as a venue for the U.S. Army, Navy, Air Force, and Marine Corps basing areas, live-fire training areas, and storage areas for nuclear and other weapons.

On June 27, 1959, voters in Hawai'i participated in a referendum to determine their future political status. However, the referendum ballot denied voters two options: free association (a form of self-governing autonomy) and independence. With choices limited to continued territorial status, statehood, and abstaining altogether, a majority opted for statehood. Effective August 20, 1959, the U.S. Congress admitted Hawai'i as the fiftieth state. In response, the UN General Assembly removed Hawai'i from the list of "Non Self Governing Trust Territories." In 1960 UN General Assembly Resolution 1541 recommended that plebiscites in "Non Self Governing Trust Territories" let voters choose from all three alternatives to colonialism. However, that decision did not overturn statehood for Hawai'i.

In the 1960s and 1970s, the Hawaiian Sovereignty Movement reopened the decolonization debate. Political protests against the continued bombing of Kaho'olawe included a series of illegal occupations in the late 1970s. The Constitutional Convention of 1978 established an Office of Hawaiian Affairs (OHA). In 1991 naval bombardment of Kaho'olawe ended during President George H. W. Bush's 1989 to 1993 term. Between January 17 and January 21, 1993, a four-day centennial memorial of the overthrow stimulated a large pro-Hawaiian sovereignty protest demonstration in Honolulu. Ten months later, the 103rd Congress passed Joint Resolution 19 (Public Law 103–150). Signed by William J. Clinton (b. 1946), U.S. president from 1993 to 2001, this resolution apologized for the American role in overthrowing the Hawaiian monarchy. Challenged by efforts to classify Hawaiians as a race, the apology's full legal impact remained contentious for more than a decade.

In its *Rice v. Cayetano* decision (2000), the U.S. Supreme Court struck down the Hawaiian-only voter eligibility requirements for OHA elections as unconstitutional. That decision catalyzed reflection on goals and tactics by the Hawaiian Sovereignty Movement. In reaction to the Supreme Court's decision, a succession of bills were introduced in Congress by Senator Daniel J. Akaka (b. 1924) and colleagues. Although Hawaiians are neither a tribe nor Native Americans, the purpose of the proposed legislation was to invest them with political status similar to Native American tribes.

Reflecting continued militarization in 2000, armed forces personnel and families accounted for 16 percent of Hawai'i residents. Continuing another trend, 17.9 percent of Hawai'i residents were born outside the United States. Local births and immigration from Asia, the Pacific, and the continental United States led population increases to 1.2 million. Hawaiians and part-Hawaiians were less than 25 percent of the population. In early 2005 control of Ceded Lands remained in dispute.

SEE ALSO *Empire, United States.*

BIBLIOGRAPHY

Fuchs, Lawrence H. *Hawai'iPono: A Social History*. San Diego, CA: Harcourt Brace Jovanovich, 1983.

Lili'uokalani, Lydia. *Hawai'i's Story*. Boston: Lee, Lothrop and Shepard, 1898.

Pollard, Vincent Kelly. "Joint Resolution." In *Encyclopedia of the United States Congress*, edited by Robert E. Dewhirst. New York: Facts on File, Inc., 2005.

Silva, Noenoe K. *Aloha Betrayed: Native Hawaiian Resistance to American Colonialism*. Durham, NC: Duke University Press, 2004.

Trask, Haunani-Kay. *From A Native Daughter: Colonialism and Sovereignty in Hawai'i*, revised edition. Honolulu: University of Hawai'i Press, 1999.

United States, 103rd Congress, 1st Session. "Resolution of Apology" (Public Law 103–150/Senate Joint Resolution 19). *Congressional Record—Senate* 139 (18) (October 27, 1993): 26423–26430.

Vincent Kelly Pollard

HEEREN XVII

Heeren XVII or Gentlemen Seventeen was the name for the board of directors of the Dutch United East India Company (VOC), founded in 1602. This central executive body consisted of representatives from the VOC's six constituent chambers, located in cities where previously separate "pre-companies" had been established: Eight were from Amsterdam, four from Middelburg (Zeeland), and one each from the four smaller chambers—Rotterdam, Delft, Hoorn, and Enkhuizen. The seventeenth member was appointed in turn by Zeeland or one of the smaller chambers. In theory, Amsterdam could be outvoted, but in practice the power of this large chamber over the smaller ones was such that it could usually get its way. The Gentlemen Seventeen met two or three times a year in the presiding chamber, either Amsterdam (six years in succession) or Middelburg (two years in succession). The timing of these meetings, which usually lasted four to five weeks, coincided with the rhythms of the shipping traffic between the Dutch Republic and Asia. New directors were to be appointed by the provincial assemblies, the states of Holland and Zeeland, from a short list prepared by the acting directors. This power, however, was soon usurped by the town councils of the respective chambers. Partly as a result of the appointment policy close ties were formed between the ruling oligarchy of regents, members of the town councils, and the company directors.

The founding charter of 1602 permitted the VOC to build forts, appoint governors, maintain soldiers and fleets, wage war, and conclude treaties with foreign powers in Asia in the name of the States General of the Dutch Republic. Instructions to governors had to be approved by the States General, and the top VOC officials had to swear an oath of allegiance in the presence of the States General. In addition, commanders of homeward-bound fleets had to report on conditions in Asia. From a legal perspective, the VOC can be considered an executive instrument of the States General with a restricted mandate. In practice, however, the States General had little effective control and rules were soon ignored. Close informal contacts existed between the government and the company because the directors came from the same ruling regent class, but official control was minimal until the late eighteenth century. The financial report submitted to a committee from the States General every four years was a mere formality. When the company's charter had to be extended, the occasion was seen primarily as a suitable opportunity to extract money from the directors.

Several committees advised the meetings of the Gentlemen Seventeen or carried out preparatory work. There was a committee for checking the bookkeeping, one for preparing the annual balance, another for attending and supervising the company auctions, a wartime committee dealing with secret routes and signals, and one for dealing with correspondence with the High Government and other company servants in Asia. The latter committee met in the company lodge in The Hague and was therefore called the *Haags Besogne*. It was formed by ten directors: four from Amsterdam, two from Zeeland, and one from each of the smaller chambers.

An important VOC official was the company's advocate, the secretary to the board of directors. He attended both the meetings of the Gentlemen Seventeen and the Haags Besogne and drafted the resolutions of these bodies. In addition, he participated in the deliberations of the Amsterdam chamber, and carried out numerous other tasks for the directors. The advocate was the only permanent official at the highest level and could sometimes exert a great deal of influence on company policy. Pieter van Dam, for example, occupied this post for more than fifty years from 1652 until his death in 1706. Van Dam wrote his multivolume *Beschryvinge van de Oostindische Compagnie* (Description of the East India Company) at the request of the Gentlemen Seventeen. The work, describing the history and organization of the VOC, was intended to act as an internal reference and policy guide for the directors. Today it serves as an invaluable source of information on the Dutch East India Company in the seventeenth century.

Some controversy exists over the alleged inadequacy of company bookkeeping and the declining quality of management in the eighteenth century. Though bookkeeping in the Dutch Republic could be quite problematical and balances reported by the individual chambers did not provide a complete picture, the Gentlemen Seventeen had inside access to the figures from Asia and additional financial details. At crucial points, the process of decision-making was institutionalized and rational. To compare the company with a modern multinational corporation, however, would be to ignore the restricted technological means available and the different mentality of the seventeenth and eighteenth centuries. The slowness and uncertainty of overseas communications inevitably formed a weak link in the system. Patronage and personal preferences played a decisive part in the appointment of directors and other senior officials. It was accepted at all levels that, to a certain extent, one could enrich oneself through and at the cost of the VOC. Finally, management was not always of consistent quality. Against periods characterized by an active, inspiring, and innovative policy on the part of the directors must be set others in which routine, inertia, and lethargy were dominant.

SEE ALSO *Batavia; Empire, Dutch; Moluccas.*

BIBLIOGRAPHY

Bruijn, J. R., F. S. Gaastra, and I. Schöffer, eds. *Dutch-Asiatic Shipping in the Seventeenth and Eighteenth Centuries.* Rijksgeschiedkundige Publicatiën, Grote Serie, 165, 166, and 167. 3 vols. The Hague, Netherlands: M. Nijhoff, 1979–1987.

Dam, Pieter van. *Beschryvinge van de Oostindische Compagnie*, Vol. 1, Pt. 1. Edited by F. W. Stapel and C. W. Th. van Boetzelaer. Rijksgeschiedkundige Publicatiën, Grote Serie 63. The Hague, Netherlands: M. Nijhoff, 1927.

Gaastra, Femme S. *Bewind en Beleid bij de VOC: De Financiële en Commerciële Politiek van de Bewindhebbers, 1672–1702.* Zutphen, Netherlands: Walburg Pers, 1989.

Gaastra, Femme S. *The Dutch East India Company: Expansion and Decline.* Zutphen, Netherlands: Walburg Pers, 2003.

Korte, J. P. de. *The Annual Accounting in the VOC, Dutch East India Company.* Amsterdam: NEHA, 2000.

Meilink-Roelofsz, M. A. P. "The Structures of Trade in Asia in the Sixteenth and Seventeenth Centuries." *Mare Luso-Indicum* 4 (1980): 1–43.

Somers, J. A. *De VOC als Volkenrechtelijke Actor.* Gouda, Netherlands: Quint, 2001.

Steensgaard, Niels. "The Dutch East India Company as an Institutional Innovation." In *Dutch Capitalism and World Capitalism*, edited by Maurice Aymard. Cambridge: Cambridge University Press, 1982.

Markus Vink

HEGEMON AND HEGEMONY

A hegemon is a country with the economic, political, and military power to set and enforce the prevailing rules of the international system. Unlike an empire, the hegemon does not have to exert formal control over other states or powers in the global arena; instead, it exercises a degree of informal control known as hegemony. The power and influence of the United States on world affairs in the twentieth century is often cited as an example of hegemony.

ROLE AND FUNCTIONS OF THE HEGEMON

Hegemons work to maintain the status quo in international affairs because their hegemony is the result of the current global order. Consequently, hegemons serve to discourage major wars, although minor conflicts have been common during periods of hegemonic stability. When states violate the explicit or implicit rules of the international system, the hegemon punishes those transgressions. The hegemon also rewards states for their compliance by ensuring that those states receive a share in the global economic markets or trade.

Individual states usually either join with the hegemon, or seek to displace it. The balance of power politics in the past has often attempted to prevent the rise or triumph of hegemonies as the coalitions against Napoleonic France and Nazi Germany demonstrated. States that align with the hegemon receive protection and access to economic rewards, whereas states that balance against the hegemon face various forms of retaliation, including military attack. A successful, mature hegemony results in a great degree of stability in the international system because the major powers tend to align with it to enjoy the rewards provided by the global leader. A hegemon need not be a global hegemon. A powerful country may be a regional hegemon that dominates a specific area, even though there are more powerful nations elsewhere.

RISE AND FALL OF HEGEMONS

With the rise of the modern nation state and its high levels of military and economic cohesion, it became increasingly unlikely that any single empire could conquer the entire world. Instead, the world witnessed the rise of hegemonic powers that dominated certain historic periods and certain regions without achieving global conquest. Scholars point to the Hapsburg Empire of the fifteenth century, the Dutch in the sixteenth century, and the British Empire in the nineteenth century as examples of past hegemons.

Periods of hegemony are cyclical and can be divided into four distinct phases. The first phase occurs as a rising state endeavors to gain advantage over other international powers. This period is often characterized by major wars and may be accompanied by the decline of an existent hegemon. The second phase begins when a new state gains hegemony and begins to impose its rules and influence on the system. The third phase is marked by stability within the international system and the maturation of hegemonic leadership. The fourth and final phase is the fall of the hegemony because of domestic decline, or the rise of a new hegemony. This period is often marked by system-wide war.

Historians have demonstrated that periods of prolonged hegemony were less common before the Industrial Revolution. The growth of industry and global trade that occurred with the Industrial Revolution allowed certain states to gain material advantages in production and technology and, consequently, use that advantage to drive for hegemony. The British Empire and the United States are examples of this trend. In the case of the British Empire, the competition for markets and access to resources spurred colonialism and the development of global empires in the nineteenth century. The United States, by contrast, sought to dismantle formal colonialism as it gained global hegemony at the end of World War II (1939–1945). It wanted to expand its commercial interaction with the newly independent states and to replace colonial interests with American values and ideals.

U.S. HEGEMONY

During the first half of the twentieth century, the United States rose to replace the British Empire. World War I (1914–1918) marked the ascent of the United States as a hegemon and the decline of British hegemony. At the end of World War II, the United States began to impose its rules and preferences on the world as it gained hegemony. The United States avoided colonization and was instead able to impose its will on other states through less formal means of control, including economic and military incentives. The post–World War II era was characterized by the mature American hegemony. Even though the United States was challenged by the Soviet Union and its bloc during the Cold War, it dominated the world to a degree far greater than past hegemons.

In 1945 the United States had a clear preponderance of economic and military power. Although Soviet military power grew to match that of the United States, the Soviets were unable to match U.S. economic power. Global institutions such as the United Nations, the World Bank, and the North Atlantic Treaty Organization (NATO) reflected American preferences for world order and helped promote American interests. Despite a range of small wars, the Cold War era was remarkably stable in terms of economic growth and the absence of system-wide war. The end of the Cold War

Japanese Locals in Okinawa. *Two Japanese young people pose for a photograph on a busy street in Okinawa, Japan, on April 17, 1997. The long-standing presence of the U.S. military in Okinawa was responsible for the gradual Americanization of this Japanese island prefecture.* **ANDRES HERNANDEZ/LIAISON/GETTY IMAGES. REPRODUCED BY PERMISSION.**

can be seen as the triumph of U.S. hegemony over its rivals. However, the Cold War also witnessed the decline of American economic power in relative terms. The United States produced almost half of the world's economic output in 1945. By the 1970s that figure declined to 25 percent, where it has more or less remained through the early twenty-first century.

The end of the Cold War may also mean the decline of U.S. hegemony. While the United States once again has a clear preponderance of military power, other incentive to align with the country has decreased. Like any hegemon as its economic power declines, more countries are willing to challenge the United States. The willingness of states to refute American leadership during the second Iraq war demonstrated an increased tendency to

balance against, instead of align with, the United States. In addition, regional economic hegemons such as the European Union or China are increasingly willing to challenge American economic leadership.

SEE ALSO *Empire, United States.*

BIBLIOGRAPHY

Calleo, David P. *Beyond American Hegemony: The Future of the Western Alliance.* New York: Basic Books, 1987.

Hardt, Michael, and Antonio Negri. *Empire.* Cambridge, MA: Harvard University Press, 2000.

Kennedy, Paul. *The Rise and Fall of the Great Powers: Economic Change and Military Conflict from 1500 to 2000.* New York: Random House, 1987.

Keohane, Robert O. *After Hegemony: Cooperation and Discord in the World Political Economy.* Princeton, NJ: Princeton University, 1984.

Ruggie, John G., ed. *Multilateralism Matters: The Theory and Praxis of an Institutional Form.* New York: Columbia University, 1993.

Walt, Stephen M. *The Origins of Alliances.* Ithaca, NY: Cornell University, 1987.

Tom Lansford

HENRY THE NAVIGATOR
1394–1460

Prince Henry (1394–1460), properly Infante Dom Henrique, was the third surviving son of Portugal's King João I and Philippa of Lancaster. Though labeled "the Navigator" by nineteenth-century Europeans looking approvingly on the roots of Western expansion, he was in fact neither seaman nor shipbuilder, but rather an avid religious crusader and patron of early Atlantic exploration.

Fate and upbringing helped point Henry toward his achievements. At his birth, astrologers saw in his zodiac a destiny to make "great and noble conquests" and uncover "secrets previously hidden from men," and Henry's parents selected as his patron saint the French crusader-king St. Louis. Personal ambition joined these portents to make crusading and exploration—along with acquiring fame and wealth—his life interests.

Henry's efforts need to be viewed in the context of his time and place. Since the expulsion of the Moors from Portugal in 1249, Portuguese seamen had been expanding their commercial range. Once it was apparent that Venice controlled the eastern Mediterranean and Muslims blocked access to products from sub-Saharan Africa, sailors, merchants, and bankers from Genoa and Florence brought their skills to Spain and Portugal,

Prince Henry of Portugal (1394–1460). *Prince Henry, known as "Henry the Navigator," is pictured circa 1440 in battle gear near the port of Ceuta in North Africa.* HULTON ARCHIVE/GETTY IMAGES. REPRODUCED BY PERMISSION.

Sierra Leone, 2,000 miles from Europe. The move down the Atlantic coast did not end with Henry, of course: in 1497 Vasco da Gama would sail around Africa's southern tip and reach India, opening East Africa and the Indian Ocean to Portuguese imperial designs.

Henry, thus, was not an explorer himself, but the major patron of the early fifteenth-century Atlantic explorers and colonizers who showed how newfound lands could be exploited, and who brought back information to help subsequent European mariners. Henry's greatest importance may be in sponsoring those who answered the age-old question of how to return to Europe after sailing down West Africa's Atlantic coast: by making a long westward tack to pick up prevailing winds. This permitted European sailing into the south Atlantic and, soon, all the seas of the world.

SEE ALSO *Empire, Portuguese.*

BIBLIOGRAPHY

Boxer, Charles. *The Portuguese Seaborne Empire, 1415–1825.* New York: Random House, 1969.

Russell, Peter. *Prince Henry "the Navigator": A Life.* New Haven, CT: Yale University Press, 2000.

Donald R. Wright

hoping to find support for their plan to outflank Venetians and Muslims and thus gain access to Asian spices and African gold. Henry, who had gone crusading in 1415 and had helped capture Ceuta, the Muslim stronghold in Morocco, gained control of funds for "worthy ventures" in 1420 when the pope appointed him administrator of the military Order of Christ. From then on, he would use his own and the order's wealth primarily to organize and sponsor exploration and colonization.

An expedition Henry sent in 1424 to colonize Grand Canary failed, but mariners he sponsored discovered the uninhabited Madeiras, and colonization of these islands paid off in production of wheat, grapes, and sugar. Henry also oversaw colonization of the Azores, due west of Portugal, in the 1440s, but the Atlantic, leading south down Africa's western edge, was the main focus of his attention. He sponsored Gil Eannes to pass Cape Bojador, eight hundred miles south of Portugal and previously a psychological barrier to travel, in 1434, and subsequent mariners he sent reached Cape Verde, Africa's westernmost point, in 1445. At Henry's death in 1460, Portuguese-financed sailors were approaching

HONG KONG, TO WORLD WAR II

Unlike many other colonies, Hong Kong was annexed by Britain not for the purposes of settlement, acquisition of natural resources, or the spreading of Western civilization, but for trade in the Far East. The first hundred years of colonial rule in Hong Kong were essentially shaped by trade imperatives.

Long before the site was established as a colony, Hong Kong Island and its adjacent peninsula were part of the larger Canton (Guangzhou) delta region in southern China, which had been a center of transnational trade between China, Southeast Asia, and the West. Hong Kong's strategic location, its possession of a natural deep-water harbor, and its easy access from both inland China and the open sea soon caught the attention of Britain when the latter was looking for a trading base on the China coast.

When European trade with China expanded, the balance of trade became more and more unfavorable to Britain as Chinese tea and raw silk were exported to Britain in exchange for silver. In response, Britain exported opium produced in British India to China, thereby reversing the balance of trade. Alarmed by the

Signing of the Treaty of Nanjing. *Chinese Mandarins met with British representatives onboard the* HMS Cornwallis *on August 29, 1842, to sign the Treaty of Nanjing, which ended the First Opium War. The scene is depicted in this 1842 picture from The Illustrated London News.* HULTON ARCHIVE/GETTY IMAGES. REPRODUCED BY PERMISSION.

drain of silver from the country and the increasing number of addicts in China, the Qing authorities banned the drug trade and in 1839 confiscated and destroyed opium stocks from British traders. This led to a series of armed conflicts between Britain and China in the so-called First Opium War (1839–1842). During the war, British forces took control of Hong Kong Island in 1841 and threatened to attack other Chinese cities. The Qing government yielded and signed the Treaty of Nanking in 1842, which ceded Hong Kong Island permanently to Britain. Before long, Britain and France attacked a number of ports and cities including Beijing during the Second Opium War (1856-1860), forcing the Qing court to sign the Convention of Peking in 1860, which ceded Kowloon Peninsula and nearby Stonecutters Island to Britain. In 1898 Britain gained possession of the area north of the Kowloon Peninsula on a ninety-nine-year lease from the Qing authorities, due to expire on June 30, 1997. The area was renamed the New Territories. Together with Hong Kong Island and the Kowloon Peninsula, these areas became the British colony of Hong Kong. The colony remained under British control (except for a short period during World War II when Hong Kong fell into Japanese hands) until it was handed over to the People's Republic of China in 1997.

Hong Kong was declared a free port as soon as the colony was officially under British possession. The intention was to turn Hong Kong into a trading post. In fact, the entire colonial administration was designed and set up to facilitate trade. Taking advantage of its strategic position and the extensive Chinese trading networks in East and Southeast Asia, Hong Kong became the regional trade center for British manufactures and traditional Chinese products such as silk, tea, and porcelain. In the early years, the colony also played a key role in the opium and coolie trade. Some Chinese merchants in the colony obtained their first tank of gold after becoming involved in the highly exploitative coolie trade under which tens of thousands of poor peasants were shipped to Southeast Asia and North America as contracted labor.

The primacy given to trade in the colony was reinforced by an imperial policy of discouraging colonial industrialization for fear of competing with British industries. When local industries sprouted in Hong Kong in the 1930s, the colonial government looked at these industries with great skepticism and refused to offer any protection or promotion. In fact, during the first hundred years of British rule, there was little attempt to invest in the colony because of a lack of confidence over the political future of Hong Kong. Economic planning and industrial investment in what the British saw as a borrowed place living on borrowed time were considered politically undesirable. The Communist takeover of China in 1949 and the Communist government's refusal to recognize the three "unequal" treaties reinforced Britain's belief that minimal investment in the colony was the right policy.

However, this policy did not imply that Britain simply adopted a hands-off attitude in its rule. On the contrary, the subsequent development of Hong Kong was crafted out of complex interactions between the colonial rulers, British business interests, indigenous inhabitants, and the Chinese migrants who came to the colony either to take advantage of the economic opportunity or to seek refuge from political turbulence in mainland China.

From the outset, the colony faced both cooperation and resistance from its Chinese inhabitants. On the one hand, Britain's acquisition of Hong Kong depended not only on military strength but also on the indispensable help of Chinese contractors, compradors, and other merchants in providing essential supplies during the Opium War. After the occupation, British businesses relied on preexisting Chinese trading networks to penetrate other Asian markets. In exchange for their collaboration, British authorities rewarded the native Chinese in Hong Kong with social and economic privileges, so that these collaborators became the first generation of Chinese bourgeoisie in the colony.

On the other hand, colonial rule also met with resistance from Hong Kong's indigenous inhabitants, especially those from the New Territories. Such resistance resulted in harsh military suppression from the colonial authorities. And as soon as order was secured, the colonial government implemented measures to pacify potential anticolonial hostilities. The landownership system in rural areas was reformed to limit the power of the pro-China landholding elite. The criminal justice system was established not only to secure law and order, but also to police the Chinese inhabitants and to secure easy convictions of suspected members of the populace.

In subsequent years, the colonial government selectively co-opted business elites (mostly British but also some prominent Chinese merchants) into policy-making bodies. It sponsored urban and rural associations to preempt anticolonial influence. It also backed one local faction against another to create social support. In addition,

Hong Kong's colonial government manipulated ethnic and dialectal differences among the Chinese inhabitants and migrants to exercise divide and rule. In return, different social groups also made use of colonial state power to mediate relations among themselves in the creation of relationships of domination and subordination.

SEE ALSO *China, First Opium War to 1945; China, Foreign Trade; Chinese Diaspora; East Asia, European Presence in; Empire, British, in Asia and Pacific; Opium; Opium Wars.*

BIBLIOGRAPHY

Miners, Norman. *Hong Kong Under Imperial Rule, 1912–1941.* Hong Kong: Oxford University Press, 1987.

Ngo, Tak-Wing, ed. *Hong Kong's History: State and Society Under Colonial Rule.* London: Routledge, 1999.

Tsai, Jung-fang. *Hong Kong in Chinese History: Community and Social Unrest in the British Colony, 1842–1913.* New York: Columbia University Press, 1993.

Tak-Wing Ngo

HONG KONG, FROM WORLD WAR II

Hong Kong was colonized by the British in three phases. The island of Hong Kong was occupied by the British in 1841 and was later made a British colony under the Nanking Treaty in 1842. Subsequently, its territory was extended by the cession of the Kowloon Peninsula in 1860 and the lease of the New Territories for ninety-nine years dating from July 1, 1898.

The British colonial regime, with an interruption from 1941 to 1945 when the colony was under Japanese occupation, was brought to an end when Hong Kong was returned to China on July 1, 1997. Because of the ninety-nine-year lease of the New Territories, post–World War II Hong Kong was described as a "borrowed place" living on "borrowed time" (Hughes 1976), being a British colony in the neighborhood of Communist China, which had never given up its sovereignty over the region. The status quo of Hong Kong prior to the 1997 handover hinged upon a delicate balance and compromise in terms of interests and power among the governments of China, Britain, and Hong Kong.

Contrary to the expectations of General Chiang Kai-shek (Jiang Jieshi, 1887–1975), when the Pacific war came to an end in 1945, the British government was determined to accept the Japanese surrender in Hong Kong. After Harry Truman replaced Franklin D. Roosevelt as the president of the United States, Chiang Kai-shek lost his support from Washington. This, along with the

Britain Returns the Sovereignty of Hong Kong to the People's Republic of China. *When Hong Kong reverted to Chinese sovereignty on July 1, 1997, leaders from both nations attended the flag-raising ceremony. In the foreground (left to right) are Tung Chee-hwa, Zhang Wan Nian, Qian Qichen, Li Peng, Jiang Zemin, Prince Charles, Tony Blair, Robin Cook, Chris Patten, and Brian Dutton.* © REUTERS/CORBIS. REPRODUCED BY PERMISSION.

imminent Communist threat in China, forced Chiang to accept the compromise of having Cecil Harcourt (1892–1959), the British commander, receive the surrender from the Japanese. Hong Kong thus resumed its status as a colony of the British Empire after World War II.

For much of its history, colonial Hong Kong was an arena of political struggle that had spilled over from mainland China. During the civil war in China and in the decades after Chiang Kai-shek's Nationalist government moved to Taiwan in 1949, Hong Kong continued to serve as a stage for the political rivalry between the Communists and the Nationalists.

At the same time, because of the Communist victory in China and the outbreak of the Korean War in 1950, Hong Kong, then regarded as the "Berlin of the East," played its part in the Cold War. The United States perceived Hong Kong as a strategic location in its overall

project of containing Communism. Hong Kong was "a rest and recreation oasis [for the American military] during the Korean and Vietnam wars" (Tucker 1994, p. 211). It was also a "window into the communist heartland" (Tucker 1994, p. 213), and a base for intelligence activity on China.

For China, Hong Kong played a role in the grander political struggle expressed in the Chinese ideological line "Patriotism and Anti-imperialism." The Soviet Union's approach to Hong Kong was inconsistent. Sometimes driven by ideological concerns, the Soviets denied Hong Kong's colonial status. At other times, the Soviet Union was driven by economic interests to try to capitalize, though far from successfully, on Hong Kong's growing economy.

The civil war in China and the subsequent Communist victory in 1949 brought Hong Kong a massive influx of refugees from the mainland. The opening of economic opportunities driven by the new international division of labor in the 1950s and 1960s, together with the arrival of capitalists (who brought with them both capital and know-how) and refugees (constituting a supply of cheap labor) from the mainland, launched Hong Kong toward export-oriented industrialization in the 1950s, when the city's *entrepôt* trade was brought to an end as a result of the trade embargo, imposed by the United Nations for sanctioning the shipment of arms and war materials in response to China's participation in the Korean War, against the People's Republic of China.

Paradoxically, Hong Kong's economic success was both a source of embarrassment to Communist China (Hong Kong, perceived by many as a place of economic and political freedom, was the destination of illegal migrants coming out of China) and an important "window" that allowed China to maintain limited contact with the outside world. When China launched its "Four Modernization" program (in agriculture, industry, national defense, and science and technology) in 1978, Hong Kong was conceived as an important agent in the facilitation of socialist economic reform.

Economic success did not bring colonial Hong Kong the expected political democratization, despite a rising demand since the 1970s from the people of Hong Kong for accountable governance and political participation. Gradual and cautious steps towards partial democratization were triggered by diplomatic talks between China and Britain about Hong Kong's political future in the 1980s. The process of democratization was, however, compromised when China insisted on an institutional convergence to its design of "One Country, Two Systems."

The idea of "One Country, Two Systems" was a product of political pragmatism. At a time when capitalist Hong Kong was prosperous and Communist China was eager to reform its economy, the Chinese government made a promise to the people of Hong Kong. In order to ease their fear of a Communist takeover, China promised Hong Kong that, as stated in the Basic Law of the Hong Kong Special Administrative Region, its existing way of life would "remain unchanged for fifty years," from 1997 onwards. That is, Hong Kong would become a "special administrative region," would remain a capitalist system, and would continue to be "stable and prosperous" despite its return to China.

During the 1990s and early 2000s, with China deepening its market reform and experiencing rapid economic growth, along with Hong Kong's massive relocation of its manufacturing activity to the mainland, the tension between capitalism and socialism eased. But the economic recession after the Asian financial crisis and rising social and political discontent since 1997 (dramatically expressed in a major protest with reportedly 500,000 people joining an anti-government demonstration on July 1, 2003, the sixth anniversary of Hong Kong's return to China) did point to one problem—partial democratization had hugely undermined the legitimacy of the government. Problems in Hong Kong after 1997 were not about contradictions between the systems of capitalism and socialism. Rather, they had their roots in politics, particularly in the tension between China's authoritarian approach to Hong Kong and the Hong Kong people's demand for democracy.

SEE ALSO *China After 1945; Chinese Diaspora; East Asia, European Presence in; Empire, British, in Asia and Pacific; Opium; Opium Wars.*

BIBLIOGRAPHY

Chiu, Wing Kai, and Tai-lok Lui, eds. *The Dynamics of Social Movement in Hong Kong.* Hong Kong: Hong Kong University Press, 2000.

Hughes, Richard. *Borrowed Place, Borrowed Time: Hong Kong and Its Many Faces*, 2nd ed. London: Deutsch, 1976.

Share, Michael. "The Soviet Union, Hong Kong, and the Cold War, 1945–1970." The Cold War International History Project Working Paper Series. Woodrow Wilson International Center for Scholars. Available from http://wwics.si.edu/.

Tucker, Nancy Bernkopf. *Taiwan, Hong Kong, and the United States, 1945–1992: Uncertain Friendships.* New York: Twayne, 1994.

Tai-lok Lui

HOWLAND ISLAND

SEE *Pacific, American Presence in*

HUMAN RIGHTS

Human rights abuses and protests against them have been a major issue in European overseas expansion from its inception. The abuses themselves indicate a significant aspect of the nature of colonialism: its tendency to treat non-European peoples as alien "others" and thus subject them to various forms of exploitation and suppression. The protests voiced by both Europeans and colonized populations against such abuses were sometimes used as attacks against the very idea of colonialism. However, these criticisms have also served to justify and inspire many new forms of colonialism as well as their continuation into the postcolonial era.

In tracing the historical links between colonialism and human rights, one must review a rather complicated series of events, motivations, and responses. The abuses that resulted from efforts to extract wealth from Asia, Africa, and the Americas often occurred at the hands of perpetrators who attempted to rationalize their actions by references to the inhumane practices of the indigenous societies in these regions. However, even the protesters against such European atrocities as the Atlantic slave trade often proposed in their place new colonial regimes devoted to human rights-based "trusteeship" rather than exploitation. Colonialism thus developed, alongside its political economy, a moral economy driven by human rights concerns.

This article examines five major cases of colonial human rights abuse with the resulting protests and the way such protests could produce new forms of colonialism. A more complete catalog of the abuses themselves can be found in the compendium *Le livre noir du colonialisme* (The Black Book of Colonialism, 2002).

In considering claims to associate colonialism with human rights, we first have to consider how this concern for overseas territories may also have served—or even been determined by—more self-interested economic or political motives. However, the moral economy of colonialism had a life of its own. In almost all instances such human rights campaigns were immediately justified as a response to very real social problems in various parts of the world. Often these problems resulted from a prior European colonial presence, although the targets could also be indigenous practices. Within Western society these efforts were further driven by the need to validate Europe's religious heritage, its secular Enlightenment humanitarianism, or the moral consciences of modern individuals.

SPAIN AND AMERICAN INDIANS

The sufferings of Native American populations during the first centuries of Spanish trans-Atlantic expansion are among the best known episodes of colonial human rights abuse. Just in terms of population, Mexico alone lost somewhere between 25 and 50 percent of its population between 1500 and 1600. During the same period almost all of the indigenous inhabitants of the Caribbean islands of Hispaniola (present-day Haiti and the Dominican Republic), Cuba, Puerto Rico, and Jamaica also disappeared.

The main cause of this demographic catastrophe was not intentional Spanish action but rather the introduction of new diseases, especially smallpox, into a region with no previous exposure to such illnesses. However, the violent attacks upon local peoples by early Spanish explorers and conquistadors, eager to find gold and other sources of quick wealth, also contributed to population decline. Even more significant was the postconquest mistreatment of Indians who were forced to work for the Spaniards under a system known as *encomienda,* which required many natives to pay tribute in money or labor to conquerors or other powerful settlers.

These abuses became known throughout Europe because one of these Spanish colonizers, the missionary friar Bartolomé de Las Casas, wrote about them in a widely circulated work, *A Brief Account of the Destruction of the Indies* (1552). Even before his book came out, Las Casas and other Spanish clergy had publicized the plight of Spain's Native American subjects and debated publicly with other priests, who claimed that the Indians deserved punishment for their barbarous customs of human sacrifice and refusal of conversion to Christianity. The defenders of the Indians reformed and tamed the *encomienda* and officially abolished slavery in 1542. It was ultimately in the material and political interest of the Spanish Crown to preserve its newly acquired subjects and maintain some control over European settlers in the New World, whose *encomiendas* at first provided a kind of feudal autonomy. However, such reforms proved difficult to enforce overseas and were challenged many times by colonial interests in Spain.

Las Casas is justifiably recognized as one of history's greatest champions of human rights and his *Brief Account* challenged the basic legitimacy of a colonial regime responsible for such massive atrocities. At the same time he continued to search for a more humane way to continue the colonial project and tried to understand Native American culture as a stage on the way to Christianity. Moreover the moral and ultimately economic crisis of the brutal Spanish attempts to exploit New World Indians produced other forms of colonialism that raised their own human rights issues. The quick translation of Las Casas's book into a number of European languages created the *Leyenda negra* (Black Legend) of Spanish colonialism and thus provided propaganda for rival powers, most notably Britain, France, and the Netherlands, to launch their own initiatives in overseas regions claimed by Spain. In the Caribbean these new settlements completed the near annihilation of the indigenous population. Las Casas at first recognized that if Indians should not be enslaved, Africans could easily replace them. He later recanted this judgment.

SLAVE TRADE AND COLONIALISM IN THE ATLANTIC

The Atlantic slave trade ranks among the greatest atrocities of European colonialism. Over three and one-half centuries (1500–1870) it brought somewhere between 11 and 12 million involuntary migrants from Africa to the New World. Approximately 15 percent of the Africans forced upon slaving ships died under the horrendous conditions of the "Middle Passage" across the Atlantic. Many more lost their lives in wars and raids within Africa and on the often lengthy foot journeys from the interior to the coast. As workers in the New World, particularly on the Caribbean and Brazilian sugar plantations, which were their most common destination, slaves had low life expectancies, bore few children (two-thirds of those purchased were males), and thus had to be replaced constantly.

Detailed information about the Atlantic slave trade (including a digitalized database) exists because sophisticated European entrepreneurs conducted the entire enterprise as a highly organized business. They purchased the vast majority of slaves under peaceful market conditions from African middlemen who either captured slaves themselves or bought them from other Africans. The high demand for such labor in the New World and competition among various European buyers meant that the prices offered to African suppliers rose steadily throughout the history of the trade. However, most of the profit went to Europeans who controlled the oceanic shipping as well as the production, processing, and sale of valuable plantation goods.

African societies subject to slave trading found various means of resisting or at least evading such horrors, although their efforts appear, at best, to have diverted and extended the routes used by their captors. Historians like John Thornton have argued that, in its earliest stages, when the scale of European demand was still modest, this commerce fit easily into African economic conceptions, which centered upon "wealth in people"; that is, the accumulation of human dependents and supporters rather than control over land. Whether or not one accepts such an explanation, once the slave trade reached the high numbers of its last two centuries (1650 and later) the competition among Africans for European goods (now needed to retain any significant body of supporters) and firearms (required for defense as well as aggression) made it difficult to drop out of this commerce. African oral tradition contains a strong version of what historians understand to be a human rights critique of the slave trade: Those ancestors who delivered people to the overseas servitude are depicted as witches who drew their wealth from killing others or transforming them into zombies.

The termination of the slave trade (and eventually plantation slavery) came about in the nineteenth century as the result of actions in the larger Atlantic world. One important force was resistance by captured Africans themselves. Whether still aboard ships or installed in the New World, slaves frequently fled or revolted against their conditions. However, given the profitability of the plantation system, until the 1790s European authorities were able to mobilize the necessary resources to overcome such threats.

At the end of the eighteenth century two new factors contributed to the demise of the slave trade: the growth of an abolitionist movement within Europe and the 1791 slave revolt in the very rich French colony of St. Domingue (which became, in 1804, the independent Republic of Haiti). These two developments cannot be entirely separated, because the Haitian revolt occurred in the turbulent context of the French Revolution, which embraced abolition along with other radical reforms. Haiti encouraged further revolts among New World slaves but also strengthened the resolve in some places, such as the United States and Cuba, to maintain strict controls of their still highly productive servile laborers. Moreover, post-emancipation society within Haiti proved to be anything but a model of human rights. The initiative in antislavery thus remained with the citizens of those nations that had organized and prospered from the Atlantic plantation complex.

Historians often view the abolitionist movement as the first international human rights campaign. Its secular ideology drew upon the same Enlightenment beliefs as the French Revolution. However, the major base of antislavery was in Britain, where it also found support among new, invigorated Christian churches—first Quakers and evangelical sects but later more established Protestant denominations and eventually Roman Catholics (including churches in continental Europe). During the nineteenth-century heyday of abolitionism Britain was the center of the wealthiest and most extensive empire in the world. Thus British sponsorship of such a crusade has raised a number of questions about the relationship between human rights and colonialism.

For many proponents and opponents, antislavery involved a major sacrifice of colonial interests and for this reason was resisted not only by British planters but also by broader interest groups in France, Portugal, Spain, and the United States. Others saw slavery as economically outdated because of its incompatibility with the free trade and free labor values of a new industrial order, which also had little need of colonies. Finally, in the overseas spaces of slavery and the slave trade, abolition required active intervention by human rights proponents, resulting in strengthened and even expanded colonial responsibilities.

The debate about the costs of colonialism and its compatibility with industrial capitalism has centered around the writings of Eric Williams, both a major historian and leading figure in the decolonization of his native Trinidad. Arguing against a long tradition of extolling British self-sacrifice, Williams asserted that the Atlantic triangle had made critical contributions to British industrialization but was then jettisoned when sugar colonies became unprofitable and industrial interests saw them as an obstacle to the development of new global markets. While there is still considerable debate among scholars about how important colonial trade was to Britain in the eighteenth century, few historians would support Williams's view that plantation slavery was economically moribund in the first half of the nineteenth century. The booming export of slave produce from Brazil, Cuba, and the southern United States made this clear. Even liberal economists of the time recognized that in regions with low ratios of population to land (including tropical Africa) some kind of constraint over people was necessary in order to provide affordable labor to large agricultural enterprises.

The outlawing of the slave trade (1808) and then slavery itself (1834–38) did, in fact, cost Britain significant sums of money. Plantation production in British colonies was hampered, ex-slave owners received generous compensation payments, domestic consumers were required to pay extra import duties on slave-grown foreign sugar, and the Royal Navy was mobilized to enforce prohibitions against the slave trade, thus also undermining British commercial domination over the rich territory of Brazil. However, Williams was not entirely wrong, since the British could now afford such a price given both their great prosperity as the first industrial power and the much smaller role that the plantations system now played in their economy. The bottom line seems to be that changes in the economic valuation of colonies only permitted, rather than drove, the antislavery movement so that human rights concerns remain a significant force in this change.

It is possible to see an ideological link between the needs of an industrial society and antislavery. Industrialization was accompanied by great displacement and often severe hardship for the working classes of Britain and the image of slaves, still worse off than they were, might have reconciled them to their situation as legally free laborers. Contemporary observers like the novelist Charles Dickens sometimes caricatured antislavery advocates as people more concerned with sufferings in distant "Borrioboola-Gha" than the situations immediately around them. However, to be fair to Victorian reformers, they did intervene in domestic as well as foreign matters. Moreover, the British working class appropriated antislavery rhetoric to emphasize the hardships rather than the freedom of their own conditions.

There are other domestic purposes served by human rights campaigns, particularly in maintaining the relevance of religious institutions that might otherwise be seen as out of touch with the modern world. The stress created from the breaking up of families as the primary evil of slavery (as depicted by Eliza fleeing across the ice with her baby in the global bestseller *Uncle Tom's Cabin* by Harriet Beecher Stowe's) also reinforced the "cult of

domesticity," a major mainstay of Victorian middle-class morality. Victorian domesticity meant that women whose husbands could afford to support them should focus their energies upon creating a proper home. However, antislavery was one of the causes that allowed middle-class European and American women to move from their homes out into public life and thus laid the groundwork for women's rights efforts.

In the case of antislavery, colonies were not abandoned but rather given new attention. The same evangelical and dissenting Scots churches that played a leading role in antislavery agitation at home also sent missionaries out into the Caribbean colonies as well as regions of Africa that were not yet colonized. Under the motto of "Christianity, Civilization, and Commerce" such efforts combined evangelization with efforts to promote economic enterprise that might provide a positive alterative to slave trading and slavery.

In the New World plantation colonies, the urge to convert the local working force did not necessarily spring from abolitionist sentiments. In Catholic colonies, slaves had always been made into at least nominal Christians without any thought of freeing them. In the British Caribbean, however, the earliest Methodist and Baptist missionaries arrived only late in the eighteenth century. Although these groups took no public stand against slavery, they had close links to abolitionists at home and were always under suspicion by planters. As a result they found themselves caught between the politics of strengthened colonialism and anticolonialism. To fend off the attacks from local whites, who enjoyed considerable autonomous rule through their own assemblies, the missionaries allied themselves with official colonial authorities. At the same time the teachings of the missionaries encouraged slaves and the small number of free blacks to demand greater rights and even to establish their own churches, which became the organizing centers for revolts in the last decades before emancipation.

After emancipation missionaries played a more overt and direct secular role in helping ex-slaves establish farms and villages independent of their former plantations. But planters again opposed them by blocking access to land, and in 1865 another major revolt broke out in Jamaica, for which missionaries, as before, were blamed. The British government now had the option of loosening its control over this and other islands, as had already been done with white settlement colonies such as Canada. However, this would have meant either leaving whites in charge and inducing further violence or enfranchising a significant part of the black majority, which Britain was then unwilling to do. The choice instead was to take away existing self-government privileges and impose a more authoritarian colonial regime on most of the

The Torturing of Native Americans by Spanish Explorers. *This mid-sixteenth-century print by Theodor de Bry illustrates reports of the torture of Native Americans in Florida by the Spanish explorer Hernando de Soto and his men.* **HULTON ARCHIVE/GETTY IMAGES. REPRODUCED BY PERMISSION.**

Caribbean islands. Here the cost of human rights (for both local subjects and the British government, which now had little economic interest in the Caribbean) was trusteeship, with decolonization postponed for almost a century.

During the era of the slave trade, tropical Africa had not been colonized beyond a few small territories around European trading posts. During the nineteenth century new exports (mainly vegetable oils) were found to sustain trade with the outside world, but none had the strategic importance of slaves. Some European nations like Holland and Denmark thus abandoned their African holdings. The British, however, not only retained their old positions but found a new naval and diplomatic mission in policing both the Atlantic and Indian Oceans against slave trading. Three new colonies, Sierra Leone (British), Gabon (French), and Liberia (United States),

were founded to accommodate either Africans rescued from illegal slaving vessels or freed slaves from North America.

Meanwhile missionaries and explorers, usually motivated to some degree by antislavery, brought an entirely new European presence to large portions of Africa. The most famous of these figures, David Livingstone, both a missionary and explorer, carried on relentless propaganda against the slave trade whether practiced by yet-unreformed Europeans (Afrikaners in South Africa, the Portuguese in Angola and Mozambique) or a new non-European target, Muslim Arabs and Swahilis in East and Central Africa.

In retrospect, all the antislavery efforts of the earlier 1800s appear like a prelude to the abrupt colonial partition of tropical Africa at the end of the century. The immediate reasons for these moves must be sought in the Great Power political rivalries and domestic European economic and social anxieties. However, antislavery initiatives provided bases for claims to particular territories and an additional justification at home for such heavy commitment to territories of little or no proven commercial worth.

Once colonies were established mission societies greatly expanded their activities in tropical Africa, combining efforts to win converts with social services, especially education and medical care. In this sense they provided a kind of humanitarian justification for colonialism. However, the missions also took responsibility for exposing human rights abuses, sometimes within African societies (such as female genital cutting in Kenya) but more publicly by colonial regimes, most notably the Belgian Congo, the Portuguese territories, and British Kenya. Even more than in the Caribbean, such interventions aimed less at the removal of colonial rule than at shifting power from private European entrepreneurs to government officials, presumed to be more committed to trusteeship than exploitation. The model for such a moral colonial regime first emerged at the same time as the antislavery movement, in British India.

INDIA AS THE "WHITE MAN'S BURDEN"

The end of the 1700s witnessed a kind of "moral turn" throughout the European colonial world. Not only did plantation interests in the Atlantic have to contend with abolitionism, but the administration of the British East India Company (EIC) went through a radical reform. In the case of India, the field for human rights intervention was not an established colonial order but rather one that had sprung up, even more sensationally than in Africa a century later.

The British EIC was one of the most important players in the British economy of the early and mid-eighteenth century but at that time controlled only a few coastal enclaves in India itself. Between 1750 and 1765 it suddenly became the territorial ruler of Bengal, the richest state within India, and engaged in local warfare that would eventually give it dominion over the entire South Asian subcontinent. This transformation at first provided a great boost to the EIC's revenues, but the company soon fell into bankruptcy, due to corruption and high military costs. As a result, its affairs came under the direct supervision of the British Parliament.

In the ensuing British debates about Indian reform, human rights issues played a major role, since the EIC servants had clearly abused both their employer and its Indian subjects in order to amass great personal fortunes. The solution imposed upon the EIC by the Cornwallis Reforms of 1787–93 created a civil service entirely independent of the Company's commercial functions but whose senior ranks were restricted to British, as opposed to Indian, membership. The new civil servants were required to sign covenants guaranteeing their probity and received sufficiently high salaries and benefits so as to dissuade them from the temptations and risks of corruption. Because of the attention stirred by Indian issues in Britain, many of these officials were recruited from the same Evangelical circles as those of the antislavery movement. Thomas Babington Macaulay, the great British historian, also served in the Indian administration and was the son of the first governor of the Sierra Leone colony. The ethos of the early Indian Civil Services has thus been described by historian Francis Hutchins, in terms very similar to the antislavery movement, as "an atonement for original sin" (Hutchins 1967, p. 5).

In the first stage of their rule in India the British did not attempt to impose their own ideas of human rights upon anyone but British administrators themselves. Instead they tried to understand the indigenous Sanskrit and imported Muslim culture that had been used to govern the subcontinent previously. Although these "Orientalist" researchers provided the basis for modern scholarship on India, contemporary historians claim that they froze tradition in such a way as to make institutions like caste discrimination, communal (Hindu-Muslim) division, and *sati* (widow burning) more abusive than they had been in the past.

From the early 1800s until the uprising of 1857, men from an Evangelical and Utilitarian background, who wanted to propagate British culture and its values more directly, dominated Indian administration. As stated in Macaulay's famous minute on educational reform, the object was to produce "a class of persons, Indian in blood and colour, but English in taste, in opinions, in morals and in intellect." In this period *sati* was abolished and a school system was established, both of which eventually created the basis for what Macaulay called "the proudest day in British history" (Stokes, 1959, pp. 45-46) when Indians would be prepared to take over their own governance.

Even for Macaulay, however, such a day was seen as very distant, and it was postponed still further by the great Indian uprising of 1857. On the side of both Indian rebels and British avengers, the rebellion involved horrendous atrocities against civilian populations. Colonial authorities responded to these events by strengthening their political control over India, but did so with less intervention into local culture, which they presumed to be one of the causes of the uprising. The initiative in human rights advocacy thus shifted to Western-educated Indians. The major demand among these elites was self-rule, but under the leadership of Mahatma Gandhi both the methods and goals of nationalism came to be associated with nonviolence, concern for the poor, and the building of bridges across divisions of caste and religion.

When Indian independence was finally achieved in 1947, it fell far short of these standards. The partition of the former British Raj, along Hindu-Muslim lines, into India and Pakistan produced massive population displacements accompanied by killings that cost between 500,000 and 1 million lives. Gandhi was assassinated the following year by a Hindu fundamentalist. However, his example continues to inspire human rights activism in India and has been a major influence on efforts against oppression in other parts of the world, most notably the civil rights movement in the United States.

MAX HAVELAAR: OPPRESSION AND REFORM IN DUTCH INDONESIA

Examples of colonial moral economy have concentrated upon the British Empire for two reasons: British overseas possessions far outstripped those of other European countries through most of the modern era and religiously inspired moral reform played a greater role in metropolitan British life during this period than for the other major colonial powers, the Netherlands and France. The Netherlands is a particularly interesting comparison, since the country shared a good deal of the Protestant culture and commercial orientation of Britain and also transformed its East India Company into the ruler of a large Asian territory, in this case the future Indonesia.

During the late 1700s and early 1800s, human rights discourse played little role in Dutch colonial affairs. Slavery was not abolished in the Dutch West Indies until 1863 and the far richer East Indies (Indonesia) was very profitably exploited as a kind of state plantation under the notorious *cultuurstelsel* (cultivation system). Some protests began to emerge in the 1850s against the excessive demands made upon Javanese peasants but it was only in 1860, with the publication of Multatuli's (Eduard Douwes Dekker) novel, *Max Havelaar*, that the issue really drew wide public attention. In a rare case for Dutch literature, *Max Havelaar* was translated into all major European languages and became perhaps the most widely read work on colonialism in the nineteenth century. Like *Uncle Tom's Cabin*, to which it is often compared, it uses very romantic and sentimental literary devices to depict the plight of its victims, in this case Javanese peasants.

In the wake of such bad publicity, the cultivation system was abolished in 1870. However, the new economic regime that replaced it still relied upon European-run plantations, as opposed to the more independent peasant farming advocated by most humanitarian critics in the Caribbean and tropical Africa. At the end of the 1890s the Dutch announced their conversion to an "Ethical Policy" in the East Indies, meaning a greater investment in indigenous welfare. However, the colony continued to be seen and operated as a major economic asset of the mother country. The Dutch showed little tolerance for nationalist movements and only departed after the violence of Japanese occupation and a brief but bitter war for independence.

FRANCE AND THE STRUGGLE OVER ALGERIA

France was the center of Enlightenment thought and its revolution produced the first formal Declaration of Human Rights in 1789. However, such ideas were not extended to the colonies under the succeeding Napoleonic regime and the restored monarchies of the nineteenth century. By this time France had few overseas possessions left after losing a long series of world wars to Britain. Moreover, political authorities and the Catholic Church associated abolitionism, the main project of colonial humanitarianism at the time, with the radical excesses of the French Revolution and the continuing British threat. Slavery in the French sugar islands of the Caribbean and Indian Ocean was only abolished in 1848, during the brief Second Republic interlude between the monarchy and the Second Empire of Louis Napoleon.

The monarchy had, however, bequeathed to France a new colonial realm, Algeria, which raised its own set of human rights issues. French colonialism in Algeria followed a pattern similar to that of South Africa: Much of the land and most government resources were devoted to white settlers but the already large indigenous Arab and Berber population did not fade away, as in much of the Americas and Australasia, but instead grew in size and discontentment.

France's most liberal solution to colonial problems was not, as in the British case, to grant local self-government with loose membership in the empire-commonwealth, but rather to assimilate colonies to the mother country. Thus the entire population of the old plantation colonies became French citizens, with representation in the Paris National Assembly. These policies could not be fully applied to tropical Africa or Indochina, regions that thus gained eventual independence; the former mostly peacefully, the latter after a violent but distant war. In Algeria the white settlers (as well as native Jews) were granted full citizenship rights by 1870. However, the majority Muslim population could only attain such privileges by accepting French civil regulations of their personal status; since this amounted to abandoning Islam, only a tiny number undertook it.

The initial imposition of French rule in Algeria, as well as later concessions to settlers, had produced many episodes of violent confrontation with the local population. But these clashes only came to be viewed as a major human rights issue during the 1954–62 war for Algerian independence, which cost somewhere between 350,00 and 1 million lives. Violence took the form of terrorism against civilian settler populations and native collaborators on the part of Algerian nationalists, and counterterror, including bombing and torture, by the large number of French troops sent to enforce European rule.

The Algerian forces never won a military victory, but the war created a disastrous divide among the French. On one side were metropolitan leftists and liberals, appalled at the moral costs of repression; opposing them were Algerian settlers and right-wing elements within the army, who joined in a rebellion that overthrew the Fourth Republic. The man brought in to establish a new regime in France, Charles de Gaulle, first appeared to represent those monarchical and imperial traditions that favored national interests over human rights. But after assessing the forces at work in Algeria, De Gaulle shifted toward granting independence. This move unleashed a last wave of right-wing terror in both Algeria and the Métropole, but at the end France finally disengaged from its North African colony.

Algeria, like Haiti before it and many other former European colonies, experienced horrendous violations of human rights in the decades after its independence. There is clearly some historical connection between the colonial heritage and abuses of postcolonial regimes against their citizens and various ethnic and religious groups against one another. However, with very few exceptions, most notably Iraq in the 2000s (where human rights was not presented as the main basis for an American-led invasion) Western powers have not returned to impose their own regimes. Instead it is the human rights movement, based in various religious and secular non-governmental organizations (NGOS), that mounts protest and offers various kinds of social and material aid. These bodies are the heirs to the moral mission of Bartolomé Las Casas, the Enlightenment, and the anti-slavery campaign. Whether such efforts are the basis for a more just and egalitarian world order or an ethnocentric continuation of colonialism remains open to debate.

SEE ALSO *Abolition of Colonial Slavery; Empire in the Americas, Spanish; Encomienda; Haitian Revolution; Mandela, Nelson; Slave Trade, Atlantic.*

BIBLIOGRAPHY

Austen, Ralph A. "The Moral Economy of Witchcraft: An Essay in Comparative History." J. and J. L. Comaroff, eds. *Modernity and its Malcontents.* Chicago: University of Chicago Press, 1993.

Boyle, Elizabeth Heger. *Female Genital Cutting Cultural Conflict in the Global Community.* Baltimore: Johns Hopkins University Press, 2002.

Davis, David Brion. *The Problem of Slavery in Western Culture.* Ithaca: Cornell University Press, 1966.

Diouf, Sylviane A., ed. *Fighting the Slave Trade: West African Strategies.* Athens: Ohio University Press, 2003.

Ferro, Marc, ed. *Le livre noir du colonialisme: XVIe-XXIe siècle, de l'extermination à la repentance.* Paris: Laffont, 2003.

Horne, Alistair. *A Savage War of Peace: Algeria, 1954-1962.* New York: Viking Press, 1978.

Hutchins, Francis G. *The Illusion of Permanence: British Imperialism in India.* Princeton: Princeton University Press, 1967.

Las Casas, Bartolomé de. *A Short Account of the Destruction of the Indies* (edited and translated by Nigel Griffin). London: Penguin Books, 1992.

Mutua, Makau. *Human Rights: A Political and Cultural Critique.* Philadelphia: University of Pennsylvania, 2002.

Multatuli, Eduard Douwes Dekker. *Max Havelaar or the Coffee Sales of the Netherlands Trading Company.* (1860). London: Penguin, 1987.

Ruedy, John. *Modern Algeria: The Origins and Development of a Nation.* Bloomington: Indiana University Press, 1992.

Stokes, Eric. *The English Utilitarians in India.* Oxford, U.K.: Clarendon, 1978.

Thornton, John. *Africa and Africans in the Making of the Atlantic World, 1400-1800.* Cambridge: Cambridge University Press, 1998.

Todorov, Tzetvan. *The Conquest of America: The Question of the Other.* New York: Harper & Row, 1983.

Williams, Eric. *Capitalism & Slavery.* Chapel Hill: University of North Carolina Press, 1944.

Ralph A. Austen

I

IDEOLOGY, POLITICAL, MIDDLE EAST

European colonialism elicited in the Middle East a wide range of ideological reactions, both at the official and unofficial levels. These reactions ranged from outright rejection or defiance to a gradual acceptance of the inevitability of instituting reforms or overhauling entire political and economic systems. In the nineteenth century, these reactions were largely couched in religious terms and suffused with references to indigenous cultural traditions. However, as the century wore on a new ideological vocabulary began to be adopted. Such a vocabulary was soon to develop into an all-encompassing discourse embracing ideologies as disparate as liberalism, nationalism, socialism, and Marxism. Nevertheless, the seeds of such a discourse were first planted in the nineteenth century, despite its dominant religious overtones.

ADMINISTERING CHANGE: THE NINETEENTH CENTURY

The nineteenth century witnessed the steady and large-scale intrusion of Western colonial powers in the Middle East. These intrusions took the form of either outright military conquest or repeated attempts to open local markets to Western goods and industrial commodities. These twin movements were also supposed to allow Western powers to obtain inexpensive primary sources and agricultural products for their own markets and industries. The end result of such policies was to create a wide gap between an advanced Western set of institutions and structures and other societies increasingly perceiving themselves to be falling behind in the realms of

nation building, sound economic development, and cultural progress. In other words, the indigenous articulation of new ideas and ideological responses was in large measure conditioned by the inexorable advance of European colonialism as an all-pervading movement. Ottoman officials and bureaucrats, as representatives of the most prominent and powerful Middle Eastern state, put forward one of the earliest ideas designed to halt the decline of the Ottoman Empire, on the one hand, and check the colonial encroachments of European powers, on the other.

The first ideological articulations were initially confined to military and administrative measures. The defeat of Ottoman forces by European armies on numerous occasions could be said to have dictated such an initial diagnosis. It was thus thought that European supremacy resided in the production and acquisition of better armaments and as a result of a coherent set of rules capable of creating efficient systems of organization. What the Ottoman state needed to do was simply acquire such military equipment, and hire Western experts to acquaint local soldiers with their mode of operation and deployment, in addition to mastering the art of administering institutions closely connected with enforcing law, order, and security.

This line of reasoning gained widespread support under Sultan Selim III (r. 1789–1807) and his successor Mahmud II (r. 1808–1839), as well as the autonomous governor of Egypt, Muhammad 'Ali (r. 1805–1848). As these military and administrative reforms did not succeed in halting either the decline of the empire or the increasing presence of European influence, it was now thought that more radical reforms had to be implemented in order to create viable political structures and revive the old spirit of military efficiency. This meant the introduction of a number of new ideas that broached for the first time the question of nationality, political identity, and the rights of citizens, albeit citizens who were at the same time loyal subjects of their emperor. Hence such a political program, proclaimed toward the end of the 1830s, constituted a revolutionary intellectual rupture, heralding thereby far-reaching repercussions in the development of modern Middle Eastern culture and theoretical debates.

So it was that hitherto purely communal, local, or tribal affiliations were to be transcended and linked to the notion of equality based on the presumption of sharing a common national identity, to be later elaborated as Ottomanism. Moreover, individuals, rather than communities, were henceforth to be equal subjects of one single state, governed by a uniform set of standard rules and laws, irrespective of race, religion, or language. The idea of a common fatherland *(watan)* was consequently highlighted as an essential prerequisite for building a modern state capable of meeting the challenges of Western domination.

Because those who articulated such arguments belonged to the official stratum of state representatives, their reforms were restricted to what became known as the twin concepts of modernization and centralization. Such an attitude excluded the possibility of introducing universal suffrage or the idea of democratic participation as part of the rights and duties of citizenship. More importantly, these reforms were deemed to derive from Islam itself as a religion based on rationalism and the notion of self-renewal. It was in this context that those who wished to widen the scope of these reforms, or render them more coherent practically and theoretically, reached back for the same Islamic traditions to put forth the case for a new vision.

ISLAMIC REFORMISM, 1839–1900

Launched in its systematic formulations by a group dubbed the Young Ottomans, organized in 1865, this trend developed in direct response to the officially inspired movement known as the Tanzimat, or reorganization, which had by now embraced the central Ottoman establishment, Egypt, Tunisia, and Iran to a lesser degree. These Young Ottomans, or their counterparts in various Middle Eastern and North African countries, represented a new intelligentsia whose members were products of modern institutions and networks introduced by the first generation of reformers. Being educated in secular schools and largely familiar with Western ideas, while at the same time deprived of the opportunity to influence the decision-making process of their states, they began to articulate a counter-ideology based on a rigorous theoretical approach. Although the adherents of this approach represented diverse groups and sometimes divergent political attitudes, they shared a number of common ideas that have been given the label of *Islamic reformism*. Moreover, their ideas roamed far and wide, embracing in their sphere of operation not only religion or politics, but literature, the arts, theatre, poetry, journalism, and translation of foreign works, particularly French and English.

By and large, this new trend accorded Islam a more prominent position as an ideological system, deeming it capable of meeting the demands of modernity and its institutions, while keeping its original message intact. The reformers did so by reinterpreting certain traditions, practices, and Qur'anic injunctions in such a way as to make them in complete harmony with the notions of constitutionalism, parliamentary systems of government, and the rights of nationality.

Although some religious leaders, such as the fiery Persian-born militant and intellectual Jamal al-Din al-Afghani (1839–1897) and his disciple the Egyptian reformer Muhammad 'Abduh (1849–1905), came out in favor of such novel interpretations, the *ulema* (the body of Muslim scholars and officials) as a professional group were largely opposed to such innovations for theoretical reasons or as a result of pragmatic calculations. It was during the second half of the nineteenth century that this modern, Western-educated intelligentsia began to replace the religious leaders in various realms and fields relating to education, justice, and the promulgation of new laws, or by simply articulating the grievances of their communities.

As a political force, Islamic reformism scored a number of practical victories when various Ottoman provinces introduced quasiparliamentary institutions in Tunisia (1860) and Egypt (1866), culminating in the promulgation and endorsement of an Ottoman constitution in 1876 that provided for an elected chamber. However, these experiments were short-lived either because of constant colonial interventions, as in Tunisia and Egypt, or as a result of combined internal and external pressures, as in the case of the Ottoman Sultan 'Abdülhamid II (r. 1876–1909) proroguing the Parliament and suspending the constitution until 1908. By this time, new ideas and ideologies were being entertained to counter both internal tyranny and external interference.

NATIONALISM AND LIBERALISM, 1900–1979

By the turn of the twentieth century the question of national identity came to the fore in ideological debates of the members of the Middle East intelligentsia. In the central Ottoman establishment it was taken up by military officers, college teachers, journalists, and lawyers as an exercise in discovering the best means of balancing purely Turkish interests with those of other nationalities in the empire, mainly Arabs, Armenians, Kurds, and Albanians. Whereas Ottomanism was the preferred option of a previous generation, the Young Turks, who restored the Ottoman constitution of 1876 in the wake of the 1908 revolution, began to favor a program of tighter central control. This program, while not aiming at relinquishing the idea of the unity of imperial domains, envisaged the Turks as the central community charged with preserving its integrity. The era of constructing national identities had begun.

The other Middle Eastern nationalities were at the same time rediscovering their own identities in a more systematic and persistent fashion. It was now assumed that each ethnic or linguistic community possessed its own distinct history, language, and territory, and was therefore entitled to form its own nation-state. However, Arab intellectuals in particular did not at first argue the case for outright separatism, aiming instead at some form of decentralization whereby both Turks and Arabs would enjoy equal rights. Nevertheless, the outbreak of World War I put an end to such schemes. On the other hand, European Zionist organizations had by this time set their eyes on Palestine as the future site of the dispersed Jews of the world. More importantly, since its inception Zionism sought the backing of major Western powers as a prerequisite condition for its success.

The idea of building a modern nation-state, based on a combination of distinct factors or ingredients, was to a large extent inspired by a number of European or Western examples, ranging from England and France to Italy and Germany. Although the new imperialist fever, which, at this stage, gripped various Western states, did not escape their notice, most Middle Eastern thinkers and writers married their nationalist aspirations to a liberal model of state and government, echoing the general themes of the Enlightenment, as well as those of the American and French revolutions.

More importantly, local political alliances were largely dictated by the disposition of European powers and their particular strategies. Thus the period between 1900 and 1950 was essentially characterized by the struggle for independence from the tutelage or occupation of one European power or another. It was intellectually dominated by ideological options revolving around the best way of constructing national identities and the problem of adopting an appropriate system of governance in the wake of liberation. It was also in this period that the rights of women became a controversial issue, either supported or rejected by various members of the intelligentsia.

Broadly speaking, the disintegration of the Ottoman Empire allowed Turkey to emerge as a fairly homogenous nation-state under the leadership of its nationalist hero, Kemal Atatürk (1881–1938). Adopting a program of

sweeping changes, Atatürk discarded all the remaining religious symbols of the old empire and opted for a secular system of government, unabashedly modeled on European lines. However, having experimented with its failed liberal phase earlier than other Middle Eastern states, the new Turkey introduced authoritarianism as the most efficient instrument of development and national renewal. It was only in the second half of the twentieth century that democratic politics or pluralism began to take hold in Turkish public life.

In Iran, a similar pattern of intellectual debates and ideological allegiances emerged from 1900 onwards. Reacting to commercial and financial concessions granted to Western interests and companies, Iranian intellectuals and enlightened religious leaders published tracts, pamphlets, and newspaper articles praising the benefits of constitutional government and parliamentary elections. Iran's 1906 revolution represented the culmination of these ideological debates and ushered in a brief period of liberalism in state institutions. However, the shah, Muhammad Ali (1907–1909), with the aid of Russia, was able to put an end to such an experiment within a few years.

A new generation of Iranian writers, journalists, and historians emerged in the 1920s and 1930s as the advocates of a new type of Iranian nationalism that emphasized the pre-Islamic glories and culture of Persia, thereby rediscovering or resurrecting at the same time its Aryan identity. This tended to marginalize, at least at the state level and its institutions, the religious discourse and its representatives. Such a state of affairs continued to manifest itself under various forms until the Iranian Revolution of 1979, led by Ayatollah Khomeini (1900–1989).

In the Arab world, both liberalism and nationalism were at first embraced as two concomitant concepts, equally validated by religion, reason, and the example of Western states in their positive domestic achievements, as opposed to their negative foreign policies. Liberalism was, for example, enthusiastically acclaimed by large sections of the Egyptian, Moroccan, and Syrian educated elites between 1900 and 1952, before they became disillusioned with its efficacy either in regenerating political participation or achieving national independence. Some Egyptian leaders and writers, such as Ahmad Lutfi al-Sayyid (1872–1963), introduced to the Arab reading public the ideas of the British philosopher and economist John Stuart Mill (1806–1873) and his brand of liberalism, while one of the most popular Egyptian nationalists, Mustafa Kamil (1874–1908), insisted on the twin goals of complete independence and the establishment of a parliamentary system of government.

Moreover, nationalism in the Arab world was both local, centering on a particular Arab state, and general, embracing all the Arab lands. The first trend was particularly pronounced in North African countries and Lebanon—but tended to lose its local peculiarities by the second half of the twentieth century. It was then that Arab nationalism came into its own as a dominant ideology, particularly under the leadership of the Egyptian president, Gamal Abdel Nasser (1918–1970).

Arab nationalism was represented by three closely related ideological currents: Nasserism, named after the Egyptian president; Baathism, deriving from the pan-Arab political party, the Arab Socialist Baath Party, set up in Damascus in 1947; and the Movement of Arab Nationalists, founded by Palestinian, Syrian, and Kuwaiti former students of the American University of Beirut in 1952. They all called for the liberation of Arab lands from colonialist domination or control, considered Zionism as an alien movement allied to the ultimate aims of colonial powers, and sought to chart an independent socialist path of economic development as the only viable solution to dependency and backwardness.

COMMUNISM AND ISLAMISM IN THE TWENTIETH CENTURY

However, prior to the ideological hegemony of Arab, Turkish, and Iranian nationalisms, two other trends made their appearance in the 1920s and 1930s as part of the intellectual and political landscape. The first trend was represented by communism in its Soviet version, while the other was embodied in Islamist organizations seeking to turn Islam into a political system. Communist parties in the Middle East were established, after the triumph of the Bolshevik Revolution in 1917, in Turkey, Iran, Syria/Lebanon, Palestine, and Egypt.

By the 1940s there were communist parties in almost every Middle Eastern state. The parties that made the most enduring impact were those of Iran, Syria/Lebanon, Iraq, and the Sudan, particularly after World War II. These parties adopted ideological and political attitudes that were in line with those of the Soviet Communist Party, preaching a message of anti-imperialism and championing the cause of the working classes, broadly interpreted to include peasants and civil servants. Moreover, Marxism, in its Chinese, Vietnamese, and Cuban varieties, enjoyed for a brief moment after 1967 a noticeable ideological ascendancy in Iran, Turkey, and the Arab world, serving in the process to inject its theoretical concepts and units of analysis (such as class struggle and the characteristics of imperialism) into the intellectual discourse of purely nationalistic movements.

On the other hand, Islamist movements, such as the Muslim Brotherhood in Egypt (founded in 1928) and its subsequent expansion into other Arab countries, Fedayeen of Islam in Iran (founded in 1942), and other groups, were initially anti-colonialist organizations opposed to British, French, and Western interests in the region, with particular emphasis on their rejection of the harmful effects of these cultures and their permissible moral values. However, by the mid-1950s and the onset of the Cold War, political Islam became more identified with the struggle against communism rather than imperialism in its American incarnation. Such a state of affairs persisted until 1975 in some countries, and well beyond that in other countries. This was particularly the case in Afghanistan when Islamist fighters from all over the Arab world joined the United States, Saudi Arabia, and Pakistan in their efforts to resist the Soviet invasion of 1979. The final split between Islamism, in its Sunni varieties, and American policies in the Middle East did not occur until after the liberation of Kuwait in 1991.

The defeat of the Arab armies by Israel in 1967, the death of Nasser in 1970, the sudden rise in oil revenues after 1973, the growing repression in Iran of the regime of Shah Muhammad Reza Pahlavi (r.1941–1979), the intensification of the Soviet–American rivalry, and the demographic explosion in all Middle Eastern countries, coupled with the subsequent collapse of the Soviet Union—all these factors combined to herald new ideological configurations across the region. The most noteworthy feature was the fierce assault on radical movements associated with what came to be known as the ideology of secularism. In this sense, secularism was used by its critics to denote and identify a set of ideas associated with Western culture and values. Thus, liberalism, nationalism, and socialism were all condemned and considered to have caused irreparable harm to the inner and authentic dynamics of Arab and Muslim civilizations.

This assault coincided with a new wave of democratization that swept across Eastern Europe, Latin America, and some Afro-Asian countries. It was in this context that the region seemed to be polarized between two currents of thought and practice. One current, initially classified under the controversial rubric of *fundamentalism*, received its most spectacular vindication with the triumph of the 1979 Iranian Revolution. The other current grew amongst circles of writers, intellectuals, and professional groups formerly associated with authoritarian ideologies that favored one-party rule and excluded pluralist democracy as a reactionary ideology linked to the interests of particular social groups and their colonial masters. Such a line of argument was suddenly dropped in favor of a new discourse born out of what came to be known as the necessity of conducting intellectual self-criticism as a prelude to regaining the initiative in the face of new dangers emanating either from within or from Western powers.

Arab authoritarian regimes, facing the twin challenges of fundamentalist politics and democratic arguments, coupled with external pressures and mounting economic problems, responded by introducing reforms of liberalization and privatization. However, these reforms have so far failed to yield concrete and enduring results owing to their haphazard application, or to the reluctance of the leaders of these regimes to accept the full implications of democratic participation. Turkey and Iran have faired better as they both embrace pluralistic politics, with the former approaching a Western-type democracy and the latter restricting participation to a limited number of vetted candidates.

SEE ALSO *Abdülhamid II; Afghāni, Jamal ad-Din al-; Empire, Ottoman; Empire, Russian and the Middle East; Islamic Modernism.*

BIBLIOGRAPHY

Barakat, Halim Isber. *The Arab World: Society, Culture, and the State.* Berkeley: University of California Press, 1993.

Berkes, Niyazi. *The Development of Secularism in Turkey.* Montreal: McGill University Press, 1964. Reprint, London and New York: Routledge, 1998.

Brown, L. Carl. *Religion and State: The Muslim Approach to Politics.* New York: Columbia University Press, 2000.

Choueiri, Youssef. *Arab Nationalism: A History.* Oxford and Malden, Mass.: Blackwell, 2000.

Choueiri, Youssef. *Islamic Fundamentalism*, rev. ed. London and Washington, DC: Pinter, 1997.

Cronin, Stephanie, ed. *Reformers and Revolutionaries in Modern Iran: New Perspectives on the Iranian Left.* London: Routledge Curzon, 2004.

Esposito, John L. *Islam and Politics,* 4th ed. Syracuse, NY: Syracuse University Press, 1998.

Humphreys, R. Stephen. *Between Memory and Desire: The Middle East in a Troubled Age,* 2nd ed. Berkeley: University of California Press, 2005.

Jones, Clive, and Emma Murphy. *Israel: Challenges to Identity, Democracy, and the State.* London and New York: Routledge, 2002.

Khalidi, Rashid. *Resurrecting Empire: Western Footprints and America's Perilous Path in the Middle East.* Boston: Beacon, 2004.

Dr. Youssef M. Choueiri

IGBO WOMEN'S WAR

The 1929 Igbo Women's War, referred to as *Ogu Umunwanyi* in Igbo or the Aba Women's Riot by the British colonial authority in Nigeria, was one of the most significant protest movements in the former British Empire. The protest was organized and led by rural women, and once the war started, it spread like wildfire in southeastern Nigeria among the Igbo and Ibibio of Owerri and Calabar provinces, covering a total area of over 15,550 square kilometers (about 6,000 square miles) and involving a population of two million people.

HISTORICAL BACKGROUND

By the mid-nineteenth century, formal British policy in what later became Nigeria was designed to protect British interests in the expanding trade activity in the Nigerian hinterland. By 1861, British administration was formally established in the colony of Lagos and the Niger Delta region. Through a series of treaties and military expeditions designed to end internal slavery and facilitate trade in such commodities as palm oil and kernel (palm produce), present-day Nigeria came under effective British control by the beginning of the twentieth century.

The women's protest arose in the palm-oil belt of Southern Nigeria. The Igbo and Ibibio lived largely in mini-states where men and women exercised varying degrees of political power. Meetings of the village council involved adult males and were held in the common cultural center and the abode of the community's earth-goddess. Important laws of the village council were ritualized with the earth-goddess and given a sacerdotal sanction. Their violation was seen as an act of sacrilege that needed ritual purification to restore the moral equilibrium of the society and save humans from infertility, famine, and other calamities.

Women had their own sociopolitical organization. They held weekly meetings on the market day of their community, and made and enforced laws that were of common interest to them. But British colonialism brought fundamental changes that eliminated women's political roles in precolonial Igbo and Ibibio societies. Women, however, saw themselves as the moral guardians and defenders of the taboos of the earth-goddess, believing that they naturally embodied its productive forces. The cosmology of the women, and the moral outrage they expressed over the intense economic and social changes that occurred during colonialism, are helpful in understanding not only the roots of the Igbo Women's War, but the unusual solidarity and frenzy the women displayed during the crisis.

The initial protest was sparked off in Oloko in Bende Division of Owerri province, where in 1926 the colonial government had counted the number of men without indicating that the figures would be used in taxing them in 1928. Thus, when on November 18, 1929, the British-appointed Warrant Chief Okugo asked a teacher to count his people in keeping with the directive of the British district officer, women who feared that they would be taxed began to protest against the census.

The women dispatched palm fronds to other women in Bende Division, summoning them to Oloko. The meaning of the palm fronds vary according to circumstances, but in this case palm fronds signified a call to an emergency meeting, and people were forbidden to harm those who bore the fronds. Within a short period, thousands of them had assembled in the compound of Okugo, "sitting on him" (Warrant Chief Okugo), a traditional practice involving chanting war songs and dancing around a man, making life miserable for him until the women's demands were met, and demanding his resignation and imprisonment for allegedly assaulting some of them.

Fearing that the situation might get out of hand, especially as the protests spread to Umuahia, where factories and government offices were located, the British district officer acceded to the women's demands, and jailed Okugo for two years. Generally, the protest in Bende Division ended peacefully, and the district officer effectively used the leaders of the women to contain the protests.

The Women's War, however, took on a more violent form in Aba Division of Owerri province, and it was from there that the protests spread to parts of Owerri, Ikot Ekpene, and Abak divisions. The protest began in Owerrinta after the enumerator (census taker) of Warrant Chief Njoku Alaribe knocked down a pregnant woman during a scuffle, leading to the eventual termination of her pregnancy. The news of her assault shocked local women, who on December 9, 1929, protested against what they regarded as an "act of abomination." The women massed in Njoku's compound, and during an encounter with armed police, two women were killed and many others were wounded. Their leader was whisked off to the city of Aba, where she was detained in prison.

Owerrinta women then summoned a general assembly of all Ngwa women at Eke Akpara on December 11, 1929, to recount their sad experiences. The meeting attracted about ten thousand women, including those from neighboring Igbo areas. They resolved to carry their protests to Aba.

As the women arrived on Factory Road in Aba, a British medical officer driving the same accidentally injured two of the women, who eventually died. The other women, in anger, raided the nearby Barclays Bank and the prison to release their leader. They also destroyed the native court building, European factories, and other establishments. No one knows how many women died in Aba, but according to T. Obinkaram Echewa's compilation of oral accounts of women participating in the war, about one hundred women were killed by soldiers and policemen.

The Women's War then spread to Ikot Ekpene and Abak divisions in Calabar province, taking a violent and deadly turn at Utu-Etim-Ekpo, where government buildings were burned on December 14 and a factory was looted, leaving some eighteen women dead and nineteen wounded. More casualties were recorded at Ikot Abasi near Opobo, also in Calabar province, where on December 16 thirty-one women and one man were reportedly killed, and thirty-one others wounded.

CAUSES

Diverse views have been offered to explain the causes of the Women's War. Some colonial apologists described the war as "riots" carried out by African women who failed to appreciate the "blessings" of British rule. Colonial apologists also forwarded spurious theories of female biopsychology to justify their views, arguing that the "riots" were rooted in "irrational mass hysteria" resulting from "a sudden flow of premenstrual or postpartum hormones"(Echewa 1993, p. 39).

Another school of thought that emerged during the decolonization period of Nigerian history offered a conflicting analysis and blamed the Women's War on the warrant chief system the British imposed on the peoples of southeastern Nigeria. Although the warrant chief system contributed to the Women's War, a more holistic analysis of the war's underlying causes is necessary, and a more fundamental issue must be considered: an economic one.

The imposition of direct taxation and the economic upheaval of the global depression of the 1920s saw a drastic fall in the price of palm produce and a high cost of basic food stuff and imported items. Thus the women's protest was precipitated, in part, by the global depression. The protests occurred when the income women derived from palm produce dropped, while the costs of the imported goods sold in their local markets rose sharply. For example, from December 28, 1928, to December 29, 1929, the prices of palm oil and kernel in Aba fell by 17 percent and 21 percent, respectively, while duties on imported goods like tobacco, cigarettes, and gray baft, a form of cloth used to make dresses, increased 33 percent, 33 percent, and 100 percent, respectively. The deteriorating terms of trade led to the impoverishment of women, and once the rumor spread that they would be taxed, the Women's War started.

Another important cause of the protest was rooted in the political transformation resulting from the British indirect-rule policy. According to some historians, the Women's War stems from the military occupation of the Igbo area by the British in the early 1900s and the "warrant chiefs" they appointed to administer the various communities. The society's traditional authority holders, who feared that they would be punished for resisting the invaders, did not come forward to receive the "certificates" or "warrants" the British issued to appointed chiefs. As a result, the majority of warrant chiefs were young men who were not the legitimate authority-holders in the indigenous political system. The appointment of warrant chiefs as representatives of the local people was contrary to the political ideology and republican ethos of the Igbo people.

The appointment of warrant chiefs intensified conflicts in the society, as evidenced by the Native Courts Proclamation of 1901, which conferred exclusive judicial functions on the new chiefs in their communities. The village councils were denied their traditional functions, and worse still, cases involving abominations were punished without the ritual propitiations and sacrifices necessary for "cleansing the earth" and restoring moral equilibrium. Women were particularly upset by the desacralization of laws, and during the protests they called for the restoration of the old order.

The British-appointed warrant chiefs also abused their offices to enrich themselves, in part because they were paid meager allowances that could not sustain their newly acquired prestige and lifestyle. Virtually all of them established private courts in their compounds, where they settled disputes. They also used their headman to collect fines and levies, thus alienating members of their community.

Similarly, the executive functions the warrant chiefs performed for the British government, including the recruitment of men for forced labor to build railways, roads, and government guest houses, heightened their unpopularity. During the protests, women complained about forced labor, claiming that it increased their workload by depriving them of the services they received from their husbands in farming and the production of palm produce. Women were also concerned about the emerging urban centers, which had become hubs for those engaged in prostitution and other vices that the women believed polluted the land.

CONSEQUENCES

The British government authorized civil and military officers to suppress the disturbances, and district officers were granted the right to impose fines in the disaffected areas as compensation for damages to property and as a deterrent against future riots. On January 2, 1930, the government also appointed a commission of inquiry to investigate the roots of the disturbances in Calabar province.

The commission submitted a short report on January 27, 1930, but due to the report's limited scope, the government appointed a second commission on February 7, 1930, to cover Owerri and Calabar provinces. The commission began its work at Aba on March 10, 1930, and submitted its report on July 21. The report convinced the government to carry out many administrative reforms, including the abolition of the warrant chief system, a reorganization of the native courts to include women members, and the creation of village-group councils whose decisions were enforced by group courts.

The achievements of the Women's War are remarkable, and an analysis of the roots of the protests indicate that the women were concerned about the abuses of the warrant chief system, the rapid pace of social change, and the fear that they would be taxed. Their solidarity was reinforced by their common religious ideas and values and the moral revulsion they expressed over acts of sacrilege.

Although the government suppressed the protests ruthlessly to avoid future disturbances, Igbo women mounted similar protests during the 1930s and 1940s against the introduction of oil mills and the mechanization of palm production, which undermined their economic interests. A discussion of the Igbo Women's War provides a broad picture of British colonialism in Africa, the difficulties involved in imposing a foreign administration on indigenous peoples, and the crucial role women played in a primary resistance movement before the emergence of modern Nigerian nationalism.

SEE ALSO *Empire, British; Warrant Chiefs, Africa.*

BIBLIOGRAPHY

Afigbo, Adiele E. *The Warrant Chiefs: Indirect Rule in Southeastern Nigeria, 1891–1929.* London: Longman, 1972.

Allen, Judith V. "'Aba Riots' or Igbo 'Women's War'?" In *Women in Africa: Studies in Social and Economic Change,* edited by Nancy Hafkin and Edna Bay, 59–85. Stanford, CA: Stanford University Press, 1976.

Allen, Judith V. "'Sitting on a Man': Colonialism and the Lost Political Institutions of Igbo Women." *Canadian Journal of African Studies* 6 (2) (1972): 165–181.

Echewa, T. Obinkaram. *I Saw the Sky Catch Fire.* New York: Penguin, 1993.

Gailey, Harry. *The Road to Aba: A Study of British Administrative Policy in Eastern Nigeria.* New York: New York University Press, 1970.

Ifeka-Moller, Caroline. "Female Militancy and Colonial Revolt: The Women's War of 1929, Eastern Nigeria." In *Perceiving Women,* edited by Shirley Ardener, 127–154. New York: Wiley, 1975.

Leith-Ross, Sylvia. *African Women: A Study of the Ibo of Nigeria.* London: Faber and Faber, 1939; Reprint, New York: Praeger, 1965.

Martin, Susan M. *Palm Oil and Protest: An Economic History of the Ngwa Region, South-Eastern Nigeria, 1800–1980.* New York: Cambridge University Press, 1988.

Oriji, John N. "Igbo Women From 1929–1960." *West African Review* 2 (1) (2000). Available from http://westafricareview.com/vol2.1/oriji.html/.

John N. Oriji

IMPERIALISM, CULTURAL

Cultural imperialism is the effort by powerful states to force their culture and societal systems upon subjugated, or less powerful, people. These formal and informal efforts are often based on ethnocentrism and were exemplified by the social Darwinist movement of the late nineteenth century. Cultural imperialism is responsible for the spread of some positive values, including democracy and equal rights, but it also brought about the demise of many indigenous cultures and languages and provided a justification for colonialism. During the early period of Western colonialism, cultural imperialism was marked by efforts to forcibly spread Christianity and European economic values to indigenous societies. The onset of the new imperialism of the nineteenth century saw the maturation of this trend as imperial states sought to replicate their legal, political, and educational systems within their colonies. With the rise of the United States as a global power in the twentieth century, American culture came to dominate the world through an informal and tacit form of cultural imperialism.

THE GOALS OF CULTURAL IMPERIALISM

Usually two divergent cultures that come into contact tend to influence each other. There is a give-and-take that often results in a new, hybrid culture. Societies have historically adopted and integrated different languages, political or legal systems, religions, and traditions into their own cultural identity. Only rarely are such cultural interactions mainly unidirectional. However, cultural imperialism distorts normal societal exchanges. Instead, the dominant power seeks to suppress and, in some cases, eradicate other cultures. Although a dominant culture may incorporate specific products into its mainstream, as the Europeans did with corn, sugar, and potatoes, through cultural imperialism, there is a range of actions taken to destroy indigenous ways of life. The suppression of native religions and their replacement by outside faiths is one example of this trend. In addition, societal attributes, including language, legal traditions, and family patterns, also are often forcibly changed through new legal codes and colonial policies.

During the initial period of European colonization, the imperial powers sought two things from their overseas territories, and both of these imperatives often led to efforts to completely eradicate native cultures. First,

under the prevailing mercantile system of the period, the European states tried to maximize the economic potential of their colonies. They wanted colonies that would be economically profitable and provide resources that were unavailable, or in limited quantities, in Europe. In much of North America, the Caribbean, and Africa, this often meant replacing the existing agrarian and hunting cultures with European economic systems based on resource extraction and large-scale agriculture. Second, the colonial powers endeavored to minimize the costs of their empires. One way to ensure that colonies did not become profitably expensive was to ensure that those territories remained politically subservient to the mother country. Replicating European political culture provided one method of maintaining submissive colonies. This was especially important to the European colonizers in those areas, such as the Aztec Empire in Mexico, in which there was an existent, strong, and stable political system that could provide leadership for anti-colonial insurgencies. In such cases, one immediate goal for the colonial powers was to exterminate, or co-opt in some cases, the indigenous political leadership.

During the late imperial era of the nineteenth century, colonization also increasingly came to be based on strategic considerations. Imperial states no longer only sought colonies simply for profit, they also wanted territory for political and military reasons, including naval bases for refueling and refitting; buffer areas to protect wealthy colonies; and to deny rival empires territory. In addition, public sentiment in many imperial powers, especially Great Britain and France, opposed the wholesale eradication of indigenous cultures and people. This combination of factors resulted in less overtly brutal methods of suppressing native cultures. This imperial period was marked by efforts among several of the leading colonial powers to integrate their possessions into their broader culture and traditions. A common theme was that it was the duty of the imperial power to uplift the people who came under its suzerainty. This idea would later be modified and embraced by the United States and its allies in the twentieth century as America sought to promote its ideals and values in the post–World War II era, but often dismissed local culture and tradition, even if it was compatible with the goals of U.S. policy.

Not all of the negative impacts of cultural imperialism are deliberate. In some cases, actions taken by colonial governments and settlers had disastrous impacts on indigenous lifestyles. Colonialism disrupted societies by elevating some groups, while disenfranchising others from positions of power or status. Colonial powers often removed or eradicated those groups that held political or economic power within a new acquired territory. The colonists then elevated other groups within societies to elite status as a means to bind those groups to the colonial power, and then exploited them to maintain control. Such actions exacerbated existing ethnic rivalries or initiated long-lasting intra-societal conflicts. In addition, the artificial borders created during the colonial period disrupted societies and broke apart ethnic and religious groups, further contributing to the demise of many cultures.

The economic consequences of colonialism also eroded cultures. The introduction of new agricultural systems by imperial powers led to the demise of hunter-gathering cultures. For instance, the spread of ranching and farming in the American Midwest resulted in the decline of indigenous cultures such as those of the Native Americans of the Plains region. In the later imperial era, the introduction of European manufactured products destroyed local economic systems. In the twentieth century, the spread of American culture through the globalization of the entertainment industry undermined regional literature and arts.

EARLY CULTURAL IMPERIALISM AND WESTERN COLONIALISM

Cultural imperialism did not begin with the period of modern European colonization. Ancient empires such as the Greeks and the Romans spread their ideals, values, and language to conquered areas. During the Middle Ages, successive English monarchs attempted to subjugate the Welsh and Scottish cultures, whereas the 1453 fall of Constantinople to the Ottoman Turks resulted in the demise of the Byzantine culture and society, and the policies of imperial Russia resulted in the suppression of non-Russian cultures on the periphery of the empire.

What initially differentiated colonization after 1400 from earlier periods was the effort to justify the acquisition of new territory. Europeans initially asserted that the new areas were unoccupied and claimed possession based on the principle of first discovery. However, as it became clear that the areas had resident populations, European states struggled to develop a legal justification for conquest. Most governments asserted that they had the right to exercise dominion over native people to spread the gospel, uplift them, and improve their barbaric way of life. In an argument advanced initially by Spanish Dominicans, and adopted thereafter by most of the colonial powers, indigenous people were declared barbarians based on a range of criteria that included religion, family and marriage customs, language (especially the lack of a written language), legal systems, and political arrangements. The colonists also would contend that native cultures did not encourage people to make maximum use of land and other resources. The colonial powers argued that they should have dominion over these new

areas to make them more productive. These arguments would be utilized by colonial powers in such diverse settings as the Spanish in America and the British in Ireland. Hence, the theoretical underpinnings of colonialism came to be based on the assumption that the cultures of native people were inferior to those of the Europeans and that the colonial states had a duty to transmit their customs and norms to these populations.

The first Portuguese colonies in Africa were established to extract resources and establish trading posts. As a result there was only minor cultural penetration, mainly in the form of economic interaction. Even as the Spanish and Portuguese conquered the Canary Islands and Sao Tome, there was little effort made to integrate the inhabitants into the European culture. Native people did increasingly learn European languages to facilitate commerce and the slave trade. As long as the trading posts remained on the periphery of Africa and other areas, European culture initially made little impact on indigenous societies.

This changed as the Spanish established colonies in the Americas. To gain ascendancy over the area, the Spanish had to destroy two major indigenous empires (the Aztec and Inca) and replace their cultural influence. This marked the first major step in the spread of cultural imperialism in the Western Hemisphere. The destruction of major native political bodies also would occur in North America with the destruction or subjugation of groups such as the Powhattan Confederacy.

A second major step toward the goal of eradicating native cultures and imposing European norms and values outside of Europe came as efforts to evangelize and spread Christianity became increasingly intertwined with colonialism itself. Following Pope Alexander VI's (1431–1503) 1493 papal bull, which divided the new world between Spain and Portugal, and the subsequent Treaty of Tordesillas (1494), which reaffirmed the bull, both states pursued colonies to accumulate wealth, but did so under the justification of the need to spread Christianity. The Protestant Reformation would further accelerate these efforts, as Catholic and Protestant missionaries competed to replace native religions with their denominations of Christianity. For instance, even though the Dutch empire was based almost exclusively on trade, missionaries were dispatched to Dutch colonies to ensure that native peoples were converted to Protestantism as opposed to Catholicism.

Those areas with long-recognized cultures, or with the military might to prevent European incursions, received very different treatment from the colonial states. For instance, in India, the various colonial powers often sought to gain trade and other concessions through treaty instead of conquest. One result was the survival of many

Indian Tennis Party. *A group of Indian men meet to enjoy tennis, a game imported by the British, at Kapurthala during the British colonial period.* HULTON ARCHIVE/GETTY IMAGES. REPRODUCED BY PERMISSION.

cultural traditions on the Indian subcontinent. It would only be in the later imperial period that the British began to seriously erode Indian culture. In contrast, when efforts to spread Christianity, or otherwise suppress native cultures, met with failure, the colonial states often resorted to strategies of displacing native people, or exterminating whole groups of them. For instance, after the 1622 native rebellion in Virginia, the colonists engaged in widespread reprisals and a broad effort to force the native tribes from their land.

THE NEW AGE OF IMPERIALISM

While the initial period of European colonialism after 1400 was characterized by efforts to completely eradicate or suppress native cultures, the new imperial era of the late nineteenth century was usually marked by less brutal efforts to spread dominant, colonial cultures. This period marked the height of European imperialism and the maturation of colonial systems. This era also marked the formalization of the self-perceived civilizing mission

by colonial powers in areas of Africa and Asia and the prevalence of institutionalized racism.

The development of new technologies during the nineteenth century not only accelerated the drive for imperialism, it also further undermined indigenous cultures. The imperial powers actively embraced new technologies, including military weapons, the telegraph, steamboats, and the railroad. These technological advances reinforced the attractiveness of European culture among native people. This included perceptions of superiority among both the colonizers and the people colonized. Many native rulers who were not under the dominance of imperial powers often hired European military and economic advisers to tacitly, or overtly, spread colonial cultures.

In addition, many native leaders sent their children to European schools, a custom that the British in India, and the French in North Africa, particularly encouraged. The imperial powers also developed a series of colonial schools, including universities in some cases, to educate the native population and the colonial elites. At colonial schools, native students were taught the history, culture, and traditions of the imperial state, while their own culture was denigrated.

As new colonies were added to empires for strategic reasons, there was increasing pressure on colonial governments to lessen the costs of empire. One method to accomplish this goal was to integrate local groups into the colonial hierarchy. In British colonies, such as Canada, Australia, and the Caribbean islands, this was accomplished through colonial settlers who brought with them the main elements of British culture. In other areas, the British and other colonial powers endeavored to use local populations as soldiers, government officials, and bureaucrats to lessen the costs of empire. One result of these methods was the consolidation of areas populated by small, decentralized groups or tribes under colonial powers.

In binding groups to the colonial establishment, there was a range of efforts undertaken to supplant indigenous cultures with colonial or European ones. These efforts included ongoing drives to spread Christianity, European-style education and training, and inter-colonial policies that pitted favored groups against others. One result of these efforts was the emergence of native-colonial elites who adopted the main aspects of the imperial cultures, including the hierarchical class system of the dominant imperial powers. These elites increasingly formed the core of the colonial civil service and military.

Even as new economic imperatives for imperialism emerged, including the discovery of diamonds in South Africa in 1867 or the rise of the ivory trade in the Belgian Congo, colonial tactics remained constant. In pursuing their economic interests, colonial powers often specifically targeted cultures to undermine existing political entities. For instance, the British promoted the use of opium to undermine Chinese culture and gain economic concessions in the 1840s.

The contemporary popular notion of social Darwinism, which argued that different ethnic groups were at different stages of intellectual and physical development, was often used as a justification for imperialism. Pro-imperial politicians and officials would even use social Darwinism to contend that the imperial states had a duty to civilize the less-developed regions of the world by spreading European culture. Such sentiments were presented in contemporary newspapers and literature that reinforced public support for imperialism. Social Darwinism was also used to justify the elevation of some groups and the suppression of others. For example, many British and French colonial officials believed that people from the India subcontinent or Asia were superior to Africans and, therefore, transported people from these regions to Africa where they often became part of the colonial elite.

POSTCOLONIALISM AND CULTURAL IMPERIALISM

During the independence movements, the colonial powers sought to bind their possessions through economic, political, military, and cultural ties. Great Britain formed the Commonwealth of Nations and France formed the Francophone Association to perpetuate their influence in the former colonies. However, many colonial powers found that the Western-educated elites formed the core of independence movements. In colonies such as India, Burma, or Indonesia, these native elites endeavored to combine positive aspects of Western culture with their own indigenous traditions. This helped revive native culture in many areas, even as Western-style governments and economic systems remained prevalent.

European culture continued to exert an enormous influence in terms of language, educational systems, and religion; nonetheless, it would be the United States, not the former colonial powers, that would ultimately have the greatest cultural impact in the post–World War II era. The economic preponderance of the United States at the end of World War II (1939–1945) allowed the nation to export a range of products and to gain access to emerging markets as states became independent. Products such as Coca-Cola, Levi's jeans, and General Motors vehicles came to be regarded as synonymous with the United States. This American economic expansion would evolve into cultural imperialism as the world embraced U.S. products. In addition, the rise of the American entertainment industry helped expand the cultural influence of the United States. During the Cold War, the rivalry between the United States and the Soviet Union limited the global reach of American culture. With the end of the Cold War, these constraints were lifted. The result was a dramatic period of American cultural dominance.

The opening of a McDonald's restaurant in Moscow in 1990 was followed by a round of global expansion that resulted in 24,500 restaurants in 115 nations. In addition, American films, media, and music came to dominant the global entertainment industry. The Cable News Network (CNN) is broadcast in 120 countries while the world's top-selling author is America's Stephen King. In 1992 Disney even opened a theme park near Paris. American cultural expansion has been aided by the revolution in telecommunications and the widespread use of English. For instance, approximately 90 percent of the content on the Internet is in English.

As American products continue to find new markets and cultural icons such as Spiderman or Superman replace local heroes, many local customs will give way to a global cultural uniformity dominated by the United States. The prominence of U.S. culture has even led foreign companies to utilize American symbols in advertising. A range of foreign corporations use cowboys or American icons to advertise a variety of products such as cigarettes, alcohol, and clothing. Critics of these trends have decried what they perceive to be a second century of American cultural homogeneity.

While many aspects of American culture have positive connotations, including the ideals of gender and racial equality, and political and economic freedom, the violence and materialism that many perceive is inherent in the United States has produced a backlash. States such as France have imposed limitations on American media products, including films and music (the French government briefly tried to prevent the American film *Jurassic Park* from being released in France). On a broader level, opponents of globalization have increasingly targeted American firms such as Starbucks as symbols of what is wrong with the contemporary world market. Finally, radical anti-Western extremist groups have defined themselves by their opposition to the main features of American culture.

SEE ALSO *Anti-Americanism; Assimilation.*

BIBLIOGRAPHY

Armitage, David, ed. *Theories of Empire: 1450–1800.* Aldershot, U.K.: Ashgate, 1998.

Cannadine, David. *Ornamentalism: How the British Saw Their Empire.* Oxford; New York: Oxford University Press, 2001.

Diamond, Jared. *Guns, Germs, and Steel: The Fates of Human Societies.* New York: Norton, 1997.

Dirks, Nicholas, ed. *Colonialism and Culture.* Ann Arbor: University of Michigan Press, 1992.

Hardt, Michael, and Antonio Negri. *Empire.* Cambridge, MA: Harvard University Press, 2000.

Headrick, Daniel R. *The Tools of Empire: Technology and European Imperialism in the Nineteenth Century.* New York: Oxford University Press, 1981.

Kuisel, Richard. *Seducing the French: The Dilemma of Americanization.* Berkeley: University of California, 1993.

Nandy, Ashis. *The Intimate Enemy: Loss and Recovery of Self Under Colonialism.* Delhi, India: Oxford University Press, 1983.

Pakenham, Thomas. *The Scramble for Africa, 1876–1912.* New York: Random House, 1991.

Prakash, Gyan, ed. *After Colonialism: Imperial Histories and Postcolonial Displacements.* Princeton, NJ: Princeton University Press, 1995.

Sowell, Thomas. *Conquests and Culture: An International History.* New York: Basic Books, 1998

Tomlinson, John. *Cultural Imperialism: A Critical Introduction.* London: Pinter, 1991.

Tom Lansford

IMPERIALISM, FREE TRADE

Free trade imperialism was a nineteenth-century English political movement that advocated a primary focus on commercial domination, rather than formal colonization and territorial expansion. Over time, the phrase came to refer to the use of military and diplomatic power to force underdeveloped, or militarily weaker, countries to grant access to their markets to more powerful states. The result of this policy was the rise of an informal economic control that stopped short of outright colonization, but significantly curtailed the sovereignty of weaker countries. Free trade imperialism was practiced by many colonial states, but was primarily associated with British policies, especially in Latin America and Asia. As economic expansion became increasingly intertwined with empire, critics of imperialism, including Karl Marx and his later adherents, focused on the economic implications and motivations of imperialism and neocolonialism.

LITTLE ENGLANDERS

The advocates of free trade imperialism, who were initially referred to as "Little Englanders," rejected broader arguments in favor of imperialism that were based on the supposed strategic or cultural advantages associated with the acquisition of new areas. The increasing emphasis on accruing national economic benefits on the part of leading figures such as Richard Cobden resulted in the growth of the "informal" empire, and caused both pro- and anti-colonial factions to support commercial expansion into underdeveloped regions of the world.

During the late 1700s and early 1800s, the older, less formal era of British colonialism came to an end with the loss of North American colonies and the subsequent acquisition of new colonies and territories as a result of the Napoleonic Wars. Concurrently, mercantilism, the dominant economic theory of the early imperial period, also gave way to a greater emphasis on free trade and laissez-faire economics. Adam Smith's concept that markets could regulate themselves through competitive equilibrium, combined with the lessons of the post–American Revolution period, led to a shift in British policy. When England continued to dominate trade with the new United States and to control markets following the loss of the North American colonies, many English supporters of anticolonial free trade pointed out that England continued to reap many of the economic benefits it had previously enjoyed, but without the costs of administering and defending the colonies. Pro–free trade factions also allied themselves with the antislavery Whig faction in Parliament to promote the eradication of slavery and the slave trade. With the abolition of the slave trade within the British Empire in 1807, free traders argued that the ban needed to be applied universally in order to ensure that other countries did not gain an advantage over British goods because of lower labor costs. Similar arguments were used against the institution of slavery itself (namely that it resulted in unfair labor costs) and in 1834 Britain abolished slavery outright, although various forms of indentured servitude continued.

There was, however, a strategic dimension that linked colonialism and free trade. From the early formation of the empire onward, Britain sought colonies as a means to protect other colonies. For instance, the acquisition of Cape Colony was motivated by a desire to control sea-lanes around the bottom of Africa and thus ensure that goods from India would flow freely. Expansion of the empire within the Indian subcontinent (including conquest of Indian territories and the later expeditions in Afghanistan) was viewed as a means to protect the profitable coastal colonies.

The nexus between free trade and imperialism became highly apparent toward the end of the 1830s. By this time, the British and other European powers had developed commercial interests in China. A particularly profitable trade for British merchants was the importation and sale of opium. The British East India Company cultivated opium in India, shipped the drug to China, and then traded it for highly sought-after goods, such as silk or tea. In 1839 a new Chinese customs official sought to enforce his government's ban on the import of opium (a ban that corrupt officials had previously been bribed to ignore). In response, England used naval power in 1840 to forcefully open Chinese ports. The Chinese eventually bowed to British pressure and in 1842 signed the Treaty of Nanking, which granted England most-favored-nation trade status, opened new ports to British merchants, and granted extraterritoriality to the British, making Britishers accused of crimes in China subject not to Chinese but to British law and courts.

From the 1840s through the 1870s, the so-called Manchester school of free trade advocates held political and economic sway in England. Supported by factory owners, as well as many in the working class, adherents to this style of free trade emphasized the importance of exports and the need for the government to undertake action to remove foreign impediments to British products. Free trade was seen both as a means to enhance the nation and as a mechanism to promote universal values (in this case, British values). However, while the Manchesterites believed it was the government's role to champion free trade, they sought to limit government expenditures on the military or on colonial administration, as they considered such expenditures to be a diversionary use of resources.

One of the early leaders of the free trade movement was Richard Cobden (1804–1865). Cobden earned a fortune early in life through trade and became a staunch advocate of imperial retrenchment and commercial expansion. *Cobdenism* was a strong belief in the market and opposition to state intervention in the economy. Cobden himself believed that free trade would promote peace and provide the best means to improve the social conditions of England's poor. With John Bright (1811–1889), Cobden led the Anti-Corn Law League, an anti-tariff organization that was able to force a repeal of England's strict agricultural protectionist laws in 1846. As British markets were opened to foreign competition, London increasingly pursued policies designed to force other states to adopt reciprocal trade policies. Cobden was also an early campaigner for arms reductions and international arbitration as an alternative to war (Cobden and his supporters believed that war was an unnecessary waste of resources and manpower). Cobden's opposition to armed conflict and his sense of ethics led him to join Bright and other liberals of the time in opposing British military action during the Second Opium War in 1857, and he worked with other parliamentarians to bring down the government of Lord Russell over the conflict. Cobden made several visits to France to argue in favor of free trade and against tariffs and is generally credited with fostering reforms in French economic policy during the period. In 1860 Cobden negotiated a major tariff-reduction treaty with France. Cobden was a vocal supporter of the Union during the American Civil War, but died of bronchitis in 1865 before the war had ended.

By the 1840s the free trade movement could claim credit for several significant accomplishments. The repeal of major protectionist legislation within England spurred the expansion of the popularity of free trade principles. By 1860 some tariffs on around four hundred items had been removed. Income from tariffs fell from 25.3 percent of government revenues in 1846 to 11.5 percent in 1865 and 5.3 percent in 1900. The lower tariffs led to reduced consumer prices for the growing British middle class, as well as for the working class. The result was widespread political support for free trade. Victorian voters embraced Cobdenism and supported the efforts of successive governments to open markets to British goods and products. However, whereas Cobden supported means that would promote international peace, other British politicians believed that free trade could be spread through military and diplomatic coercion. In addition, British governments mainly supported only those free trade policies that benefited England and the empire.

FREE TRADE AND IMPERIALISM

The costs of empire constrained British expansion from the 1840s through the 1860s. Though new territory was added, successive governments sought to exercise control through informal means rather than outright colonization. Nonetheless, the 1840s saw significant growth in both the formal and informal empires. During the period, the British expanded into, or took some degree of control over, areas such as Hong Kong, the Gold Coast, Natal, New Zealand, the Punjab, and Sierra Leone. The return of Lord Palmerston as foreign secretary in 1846 marked an increasingly assertive British foreign policy in regards to trade issues. Palmerston sent a British fleet to Portugal to pressure the Portuguese government during a trade dispute, and the British used military intervention in Borneo and Africa to open markets. More significantly, in 1848 Palmerston issued a clear endorsement of free trade imperialism when, in a diplomatic note, he declared that Britain would use diplomatic and political pressure to protect "investments" if it deemed that the loss of those investments threatened the stability or security of England. Cobden and his supporters in Parliament sought to limit Palmerston's aggressive policies by reducing the government's military expenditures, but successive bills were rejected in Parliament. Instead, Britain's formal and informal empires began a period of sustained growth.

In 1848 British traders seized a port in Nicaragua and ultimately forced the Nicaraguan government to sign an advantageous commercial treaty. That same year, British troops occupied the Boer area of Natal and seized Natal's main port after British merchants began cultivating cotton on formerly Natalese territory that had been annexed into the Cape Colony in 1847. In 1843 James Brooke created a personal fiefdom in Sarawak in the north of Burma. Meanwhile, throughout Africa and Asia, British merchants began negotiating and signing a series of trade treaties with local leaders. In some cases, charter companies led the commercial expansion. In addition to the well-known British East India Company, a range of smaller, but in many cases just as successful, companies such as the Royal Niger Company or the Royal South Africa Company, were able to expand British commercial hegemony.

In order to protect commercial interests, the British undertook military action to either prevent encroachments from neighboring powers or expand access to resources. Often conflicts were initiated in remote areas, and London responded by sending troops to suppress native populations. On a grand scale, the 1857 Sepoy Revolt and the subsequent dissolution of the East India Company by an imperial administration is demonstrative of this trend in which minor disagreements were used by colonial officials, merchants, and so-called adventurers to expand the formal empire. Indeed, the economist John Galbraith's "man-on-the-spot" thesis asserts that individuals were responsible for much of the expansion of the

empire, because they initiated colonial agreements or conflicts that London would have avoided.

NEW MARKETS

From the 1840s through the 1860s, British governments attempted to sign free trade agreements with their European counterparts and to gain most-favored-nation trade status with states on the continent. This effort was initially successful and British merchants increased their market share in a range of European states. However, the depression of 1870 led a number of European countries to reinstate tariffs. This closed markets to the British. Indeed, the British began to develop a trade deficit in the 1870s, but nonetheless continued to vigorously support the principle of free trade throughout the period. One result of the closure of European markets was a rise in support for imperialism. Merchants began to publicly endorse imperialism because they hoped that the acquisition of new territories would provide new markets to offset the loss of revenues caused by the new round of European tariffs. Concurrently, the "scramble" for colonies in Africa and Asia added a new strategic emphasis as imperial governments sought territory in order to protect their commercial interests. By the early 1900s, almost 60 percent of British manufacturing was directed toward the empire or dependent on the colonies for raw materials. The British also benefited from imperialism in general, as 40 percent of the world's products and services were transported by British ships.

Consequently, from the 1870s onward, the expansion of both the formal and informal empires accelerated. Between 1870 and 1914, there was a dramatic increase in the amount of surplus economic capital in Great Britain. By this time, London had firmly established itself as the commercial and financial center of the world and British firms dominated the global shipping, insurance, and manufacturing markets. British promotion of free trade was perceived by both the public and elites as a means to further enhance the nation's wealth. As other European states developed their colonial empires, and often shut British merchants out of trade in the colonized regions, commercial leaders in Britain lobbied various governments to support increased access to new markets and materials. Other states emulated British tactics. For instance, after the first Opium War, the United States and France used the threat of military force to gain concessions from China that were similar to those granted to Great Britain under the Treaty of Nanking.

During these years there was still considerable debate over the cost and benefits of formal colonization. For instance, the financial and manpower costs of the 1879 Afghan War led to the fall of the government of the proexpansionist Benjamin Disraeli. However, his successor, economic expansion influenced several of the most significant scholars of the nineteenth and twentieth centuries, including Karl Marx (1818–1883). Marx tied imperialism to the rise of a global capitalist economic system. He believed that the capitalist system would lead to a worker's revolution and then a utopian socialist society. In 1902 the British political philosopher J. A. Hobson, a follower of Marx, published *Imperialism: A Study*, in which he argued that the financial sector was the only area of the economy that actually benefited from imperialism. In other areas, the military and administrative costs of empire outweighed any financial gains. Hence, Hobson contended that imperialism only benefited a small group of elites and did not provide long-range economic gains for the lower and working classes.

Hobson significantly influenced Vladimir Lenin, whose 1917 work *Imperialism: The Highest Stage of Capitalism* attempted to explain the causes of World War I by portraying the conflict as a logical outcome of ongoing imperial competition. Lenin asserted that capitalist states had delayed Marx's worker's revolution through imperialism. Through imperialism, capitalist powers were able to establish new markets and to gain access to cheap labor and raw materials. In this fashion, the developed imperial nations managed to create dependencies among their colonies, as these territories were never able to keep more than a small portion of the wealth created by their resources and labor (instead, much of the wealth and resources were transferred to the colonizing state). This led to a pattern of underdevelopment in most colonies.

In many ways, these early Marxist critics were reacting to shifts in the philosophy of imperialism. The heyday of free trade imperialism was the period between 1840 and 1870. During this era, the Little Englanders broadly supported disengagement from the empire as a means to lower public expenditures. However, the new wave of imperialism of the 1880s, combined with increased economic competition from Europe and the United States, led many in the British business class, who had previously been Little Englanders, to reassess their stance toward empire. As a result, there was an increasing degree of support for some level of continued engagement and even expansion of the empire. One method to lower expenditures while retaining imperial ties was home rule through dominion status and varying degrees of self-government. In 1867 Canada was granted dominion status, followed by Australia (1901), New Zealand (1907), and South Africa (1910). Once the period of decolonization began, other means, including the Commonwealth system, were developed to maintain economic, political, and military ties between the former colonies and Great Britain. Other imperial powers used

The Waters of Free Trade. *This cartoon, published in England on August 21, 1852, ridiculed the trepidation of British politicians toward the economist Richard Cobden's philosophy of free trade.* HULTON ARCHIVE/GETTY IMAGES. REPRODUCED BY PERMISSION.

William Gladstone, also found himself dragged into colonial wars such as the First Anglo-Boer War. One compromise solution was the creation of protectorates that minimized British financial outlays for administration or defense, but secured for the British commercial advantages. British agents had chiefs sign protection treaties in which the local leader surrendered sovereignty in exchange for British diplomatic or military protection. The treaties were inevitably written in London (and in English) and local leaders often did not understand the implications of the agreements. Examples of such treaties include the 1884 Treaty of Protection with the Itsekiri in present-day Benin.

FREE TRADE IMPERIALISM AND THE MARXIST TRADITION

The importance of trade in spurring the drive for new colonies led many scholars and philosophers to assert that trade was the overriding factor in imperialism. At the core of the argument was the assertion that powerful states naturally sought outlets for their investments and products. The role of surplus capital and the drive for similar tactics, including the French Francophone system.

Such overt and tacit efforts to maintain economic suzerainty in the former colonies led many Marxist scholars to contend that the decolonization period simply marked a transition to a different form of imperialism: neocolonialism or neoimperialism. For instance, dependency theorists asserted that even after the formal colonial institutions departed, foreign actors were able to maintain control over resources and exploit local populations, with the assistance of pliable local regimes. These regimes, in turn, grew wealthy through bribes or through manipulation of contracts and enjoyed military support from foreign powers. A range of former imperial powers, including Great Britain, France, and Italy, engaged in neoimperialism, as did emerging world economic powers such as the United States, Japan, and Germany.

Neoimperialism, furthermore, was not really even "new"; instead, it was simply a more sophisticated manifestation of free trade imperialism. The tactics and strategies employed by the postcolonial powers mirrored the tactics utilized by the British during the latter half of the nineteenth century in areas such as Latin America. For instance, by 1913 the British had almost one billion pounds invested in Latin America (about one-quarter of total British overseas investments), despite having scarcely any formal colonial presence in the region. The British also used political and military intervention to support client regimes, as happened in Guatemala and Colombia in the 1870s. The British were also able to gain commercial concessions by linking recognition of colonies with trade agreements. Consequently, British recognition of new colonies in Africa resulted in commercial clauses that opened markets to British merchants in such treaties as the Anglo-Congo Arrangement (1885) or the Anglo-German Agreement on East Africa (1886). The informal methods of empire advocated by the free trade imperialists of the mid-1800s continue to be utilized and remain a major component of the ongoing debate over the causes and results of imperialism.

SEE ALSO *Commonwealth System; Neocolonialism.*

BIBLIOGRAPHY

Armitage, David, ed. *Theories of Empire: 1400–1800.* Aldershot, U.K.: Ashgate, 1998.

Cannadine, David. *Ornamentalism: How the British Saw Their Empire.* New York: Oxford University Press, 2001.

Diamond, Jared. *Guns, Germs, and Steel: The Fates of Human Societies.* New York: Norton, 1997.

Dumett, Raymond E., ed. *Gentlemanly Capitalism and British Imperialism: The New Debate on Empire.* Harlow, U.K.: Longman, 1999.

Fieldhouse, David K. *The West and the Third World: Trade, Colonialism, Dependence, and Development.* Oxford: Oxford University Press, 1999.

Hardt, Michael, and Antonio Negri. *Empire.* New York and Cambridge, MA: Harvard University Press, 2000.

Headrick, Daniel R. *The Tools of Empire: Technology and European Imperialism in the Nineteenth Century.* New York: Oxford University Press, 1981.

Kaufmann, W. W. *British Policy and the Independence of Latin America, 1804–1828.* New Haven, CT: Yale University Press, 1951.

Pakenham, Thomas. *The Scramble for Africa: White Man's Conquest of the Dark Continent from 1876 to 1912.* New York: Random House, 1991.

Prakash, Gyan, ed. *After Colonialism: Imperial Histories and Postcolonial Displacements.* Princeton, NJ: Princeton University Press, 1995.

Wallerstein, Immanuel. *The Capitalist World-Economy.* Cambridge, U.K.: Cambridge University Press, 1979.

Tom Lansford

IMPERIALISM, GENDER AND

The recovery of women's lives and the analysis of the impact of women in history has been a fruitful exercise that, alongside other categories of postmodern analysis, has led historians and others to critically reexamine not only past lives but also the contemporary world. The result has been a deconstruction of what has too often been understood as "natural" in order to understand how all levels of human relations are both consciously and unconsciously constructed in ways that reinforce power structures, most often in order to protect those in power against resistance from those outside power frameworks.

Beginning in the 1960s, increasing numbers of imperial and colonial historians have used gender as a category of analysis, applying it alongside analysis of race and ethnicity, and class. The resulting scholarship has included a recovery of women's stories—stories of women who up to then had languished on the margins of history, and that exercise has value in itself. However, beyond that, the analysis of women's past contributions, a consideration of ways in which their actions were constrained and why, and an analysis of why women's lives have been underrepresented in imperial historiography has resulted in a fundamental shift in imperial historiography.

As in other areas of historical scholarship, some of the most exciting literature on modern empires is that which has employed a gendered lens. It has honed analysis of accepted historical narratives, and in doing so it has contributed to the reconfiguration of the European "us" and the colonial "other." It is impossible to properly analyze modern imperial relations without serious consideration of gender.

HISTORIOGRAPHY

The earliest accounts of modern European empires were written by and about imperial personnel, both domestically and those posted abroad. Scholarly literature analyzed both types of accounts for an "in the field" understanding of empire, and it analyzed the domestic political and diplomatic machinations behind the creation and maintenance of imperial connections. As has been well documented regarding such episodes as the late nineteenth-century "scramble for Africa," imperial actions and the resultant effect on colonial territories could in fact have more to do with domestic politics and inter-European diplomatic relations than with European relations with the rest of the world, and this is as true in understanding the gender order as with other realities.

In each case—the colonial memoir and the imperial apologia—it tended to be men who dominated both the action and the writing of that action. Because of elaborate gendered religious, social, and legal ideologies and the resulting realities of early modern and modern European society, women's roles in empire tended to be as supportive rather than as active independent agents, and their choices were often prescribed. Furthermore, even though gendered realities were often much more complicated than a simple gendered division of roles, what was often recorded was the ideal rather than the reality.

Thus women tended to be excluded from writing about empires for two stereotypical reasons: either because of their exceptionality they did not "fit," or because of their conformity—as wives, sisters, and daughters of the male administrators; the nurse as opposed to the doctor; the teacher as opposed to the preacher—they were deemed less necessary to remember. This is true both of women from the sending societies, and of women from the cultures with which European nations interacted as part of their imperial ventures. Thus in understanding the role of women and gender in imperialism, it is imperative to understand gender relations in European society, as well as the gendered realities of the societies with which Europeans came into contact, and thus the way in which gendered expectations shaped the interactions between them.

Despite the fact that women were active agents in European imperial ventures from first contact, they did not "count" as equivalent to their male counterparts. Furthermore, when women were written about, accounts either romanticized or vilified the roles they assumed in empire. The writing of women travelers and missionaries tended to present a view of empire in which the "plucky"

European woman successfully made her way in the world. These memoirs spent little time seriously dealing with indigenous reality or the writer's perspective of the imperial encounter; instead, they emphasized the danger and adventure of distant lands, surmountable through a mixture of gendered national characteristics and individual uplift through education. On the other hand, writing about female travelers had much more room for negative stereotypes, such as the "memsahib" wives of colonial administrators who sought to reproduce Britain, the missionary prude seeking to reform life and hearth alongside conversion to a modern Western variant of Christianity, and the teachers and workers for social reform who joined the imperial venture in ever-greater numbers in the late nineteenth and early twentieth centuries.

Women's increasing access to professional education resulted in more and more Western women with the will and ability to join the imperial venture, their aim being the "uplift" of women in cultures deemed inferior to their own, but in these roles they were simultaneously appreciated and pilloried. Nowhere in the literature does yet another "other" women appear—women of the barracks by whose labor as nurses, cooks, and seamstresses the imperial armies functioned, and with whom sometimes a succession of soldiers partnered as they traveled, fought, and died over long tours of duty in a succession of unhealthy climates. Neither these women, nor others, had the privilege to follow a middle-class ideal of womanhood, but the reality of ladies who worked to support themselves—in small street-front businesses selling goods and themselves on the streets—did not appear as subjects themselves in the analyses of modern empires until the 1970s.

Similarly celebrated and censured were the women in indigenous societies. Even when celebrated, women in indigenous societies across the globe had what was their complicated reality romanticized, and more often than not as a negative dressed up as a positive. Foreign women were exotically "other"—either desirable but studiously unavailable due to traditions of class and belief, or too readily available for official or unofficial consumption, but dangerously so.

A well-developed literature now analyzes how women from South Asia to southern Africa to the Americas acted as cultural go-betweens in empire. In these encounters, women were consumed as a valuable commodity: in encounters of a variety of sorts—military, economic, and sociocultural—they served as a medium of barter and exchange. Their worth lay in access to powerful men and in their knowledge of language, culture, and material reality. They also served as companions and provided offspring to European men destined to spend long periods of time, if not their entire lives, away from "home." Given the length of time it took to travel the globe, this was true in particular during the period of early modern empires; it remained the case well into the modern era of empires, given the length of both civil and military postings due to the expense of travel and the value of continuous service. Despite this, long-term interracial liaisons became less acceptable overall across the nineteenth century both because of the increasing ease of travel and because of the rise of scientific racism. This development is not wholly to be blamed on the increased presence of European women, as has been suggested.

WOMEN'S CONTRIBUTION TO MERCANTILE EMPIRES AND GENDERED CONSTRUCTIONS OF CULTURE

There is a wealth of evidence about these encounters in locales as diverse as South and East Asia, the African continent, the Middle East, and the Americas. Some of the most interesting and telling research regarding gender in imperial relations focuses on the role of women in the North American fur trade. This literature offers examples of the recovery of women's lives and agency, and also extricates the role of gender constructs in culture as societies entered into modern economic and political world systems. It further challenges what has been an accepted narrative of the economic development of North American resources from early European contact. In the case of Canada, it demands a re-creation of what has been posited as a historically calm and unproblematic multicultural national identity.

That a Canadian national identity is firmly entrenched in an amorphous spiritual-historical tie to "the land" is well documented. This is a tendentious claim—in the first place because of the very variety of geography contained in the large landmass that makes up the modern nation-state, and second because the harsh climate necessitated that European newcomers learn a lifestyle of survival. From Charles II's (1630–1685) granting of a trade monopoly to the Hudson's Bay Company in 1670 to collect and profit from the national resources found in the drainage system of Hudson Bay, "Canadians" came to see themselves as a conglomerate of immigrant peoples that carved a home out of an empty wilderness, husbanding resources of fish, fur, trees, minerals, and water in order to create the capital to build the modern infrastructure necessary to support a commercial economy.

The folk-identity of this historic Canada is strongly gendered, from the male *voyageur* or *coureur de bois* (employees of the Hudson's Bay Company and the North West Company who paddled canoes through the river systems of the north to trade European manufactured goods in exchange for animal pelts that were processed for European consumption), to the cowboy culture of western Canadian oil companies in the twentieth century. This identity also has a strong ethnoracial element—it is largely northwestern European and is reflected in Canada's political and legal structure, in its economic development, and in its cultural identity.

That this identity as "Canada and Canadian" is problematic began to be argued systematically from the 1960s, both by Canadians concerned about the civil rights of newcomers and aboriginal peoples, and by historians examining these issues. For example, Sylvia Van Kirk (1980) inspired a generation of scholars with her deconstruction of the origins of a strongly male-dominated, resource-based Canadian economy and identity. She argued that the entire fur trade was in fact dependent in large part on the presence, knowledge, and support of female native and mixed-blood partners, and in particular the "country wives" of fur traders who, from the late eighteenth century and for roughly a century thereafter, supplied a knowledge of native society and customs, the know-how to survive in a harsh climate and cross foreign terrain, fit and active labor, and companionship to the European traders who came to work in the fur industry. Evidence from the 1820s suggests that it was these women who prepared the furs for export; made clothing, including footwear and winter gear (moccasins and snowshoes); gardened, fished, and prepared food for long-term storage (as pemmican); and served as language and cultural interpreters. However, they also—despite the myth of the strong and able male teams of *coureurs de bois* leaving civilization for trade between the spring melt and autumn frost, and despite Hudson's Bay Company injunctions against the practice—at times traveled in canoes with their partners and worked with them, work that seems to have included paddling.

Although evidence suggests that traders did not often record the work of these women in their journals, this is because this form of writing was not intended as a record of their doings and thoughts for private reflection, but was instead a corporate document produced for the very company that had forbidden the presence of women in the canoes. There are, however, journals that not only record the presence of women, but also praise native women as being "as useful as men."

Thus it is clear that the labor of these women was of both immediate and indirect use to individual traders, to the companies, and to the fur-supported colonial society as it developed what would become western Canada. These women also contributed to the industrial and commercial growth of western European nations that was necessary for the spread of modern empires.

British Missionary Women in India. *One of the significant areas in which European women could participate in modern empires as active and respectable agents was as Christian missionaries. In this late nineteenth-century photograph, a missionary woman from England poses with teachers and students at a new mission school in India.* © **TOPHAM PICTUREPOINT/THE IMAGE WORKS. REPRODUCED BY PERMISSION.**

Despite this, the role of such women has been long undervalued, as is true of women in similar situations elsewhere in modern empires, and such women could actually be devalued because of their role "in between" existing and newcomer societies.

Partnerships between indigenous women and traders resulted in mixed-blood offspring (called *métis* in French fur-trade society) who by the first half of the nineteenth century made up a cadre of workers who were both born into and were educated to become the next generation of workers in the fur trade. Until roughly midcentury, fur trade society contained elements of both its constitutive parts, and indigenous women played an important part in their "in-between" role. However, as the century progressed, their position became increasing tenuous for a variety of reasons. Increasing numbers of educated middle-class "gentlemen" were hired by the Hudson's Bay Company to work for their operations across the

Canadian west. These men arrived with increasingly strict middle-class Victorian attitudes regarding the importance of wife and family in establishing a professionally successful identity and lifestyle that left little room for liaisons with local women. Dating from roughly the 1870s, changes in business practices underscored these attitudes, and from the 1880s quicker and easier travel meant that increasing numbers of European women could functionally replace their indigenous predecessors. At times, this occurred in reality—some British women arrived to find they had literally replaced a previous indigenous "country" wife—but overall this turnaround happened gradually.

In either case, by the turn of the century a mixed-blood marriage would have been unacceptable in respectable society. The immediate result was that aboriginal and mixed-blood women were marginalized. The long-term result was that their important role in the early economic and social development of Canadian society has also been marginalized due to hardening gender and ethnoracial expectations in the modern imperial era. From 1867, the newly created nation of Canada had little room for diversity of cultural expression. Late twentieth-century Canadians struggled to recognize the historic roots of relative privilege and inequity that is the real legacy of Canada's colonial past.

WOMEN IN MISSIONS

One of the significant areas in which women could participate in modern empires as active and respectable agents was as Christian missionaries. Organizations created to promote mission activity were established in most western European nations from the late eighteenth century, and were a product of the evangelical awakening. Evangelicalism was of increasing importance in popularizing and democratizing the Christian message both domestically and abroad as Western Christian missions joined the commercial, military, and administrative arms of colonial and imperial ventures, and as the "civilizing message" that became linked to the evangelical imperative came to influence foreign policy across the nineteenth century.

The mission field serves as a clear example of the way gender functioned elsewhere in modern empire. Women supported missions both at home and abroad as the wives and female relatives of missionary men, and by raising much of the money channeled to foreign missions through the nineteenth century. Their early roles were constrained because the first missionaries were ordained ministers and no church organization would allow women access to either education or ordination. It was not until later in the century that mission societies began to hire lay workers, and it was during the period 1865 to 1910 that the number of women in the mission field grew exponentially, and lay workers, both male and female, came to outnumber the ordained clerics who had dominated missions throughout the nineteenth century.

However, the male workers, and often those who were ordained, continued to dominate mission administration throughout this period, as is demonstrated by their strong presence in mission records. Despite this, women in particular brought specific skills to missions. They expanded the notion of what constituted valid mission labor from primarily exhortation to include the provision of education and primary healthcare and the care of widows and orphans. In so doing, women changed the concept of mission professionalism. Women's very emotive participation in British evangelical revivals, coupled with their successes in communicating with mission supporters, gradually influenced their male colleagues to consider as less marginal and more central to mission work and church work in general the type of activities women had previously engaged in on a volunteer basis.

One unpublished study of women's professional motivation and opportunity in late nineteenth-century Britain underlines how important it is for historians to keep religious belief in mind when considering why women entered professions and chose an imperial career. Rather than simply providing a romantic portrayal of fulfilled professional freedom, the history of professions emphasizes that women's labor in empire, and in missions in particular, remained undervalued in terms of both remuneration and administrative advancement until well into the twentieth century.

CONCLUSION

The study of gender in missions and of the contribution of aboriginal women to the fur trade adds to the growing body of work that deals with the contribution women made to empire in general. Gendered analysis has focused attention on the personal and professional opportunities afforded to women as European influence spread across the globe. The rhetoric of women's work for women opened opportunities for Western females and highlighted the necessity for women's professional development, but women were also constrained by the very expectations contained in the slogan.

Advocates for women's increased role in missions and empire more broadly argued that it was only distinctly feminine characteristics that could "save the heathen," not only spiritually (evangelism) but also physically (social welfare). Reform campaigners gained public support for women's rights, specifically for widened access to further education and increased public roles, by promoting the idea that it was only Western women who could help their foreign counterparts. These secular campaigners underlined the specific needs of foreign women for their own interests. However, research has also indicated that neither the number of British women working in the empire nor the professional opportunities afforded to them by doing so should be overstated, and it is clear that this rhetoric also emphasized a false rhetoric of sisterhood that in fact hardened ethnoracial tensions that remain in the feminist movement today.

SEE ALSO *Sex and Sexuality.*

BIBLIOGRAPHY

Allman, Jean, Susan Geiger, and Nakanyike Musisi, eds. *Women in African Colonial Histories.* Bloomington: Indiana University Press, 2002.

Bowie, Fiona, Deborah Kirkwood, and Shirley Ardener, eds. *Women and Missions, Past and Present: Anthropological and Historical Perceptions.* Providence, RI: Berg, 1993.

Burton, Antoinette. *Burdens of History: British Feminists, Indian Women, and Imperial Culture, 1865–1915*. Chapel Hill: University of North Carolina Press, 1994.

Chaudhuri, Nupur, and Margaret Strobel, eds. *Western Women and Imperialism: Complicity and Resistance*. Bloomington: Indiana University Press, 1992.

Clancy-Smith, Julia, and Francis Gouda, eds. *Domesticating the Empire: Race, Gender, and Family Life in French and Dutch Colonialism*. Charlottesville: University Press of Virginia, 1998.

Foley, Timothy P., ed. *Gender and Colonialism*. Galway, Ireland: Galway University Press, 1995.

Foucault, Michel. *The History of Sexuality: An Introduction*. Translated by Robert Hurley. New York: Vintage, 1990.

Friend, Elizabeth. "Professional Women and the British Empire, 1880–1940." PhD diss., University of Lancaster, U.K., 1998.

Grimshaw, Patricia. *Paths of Duty: American Missionary Wives in Nineteenth-Century Hawaii*. Honolulu: University of Hawaii Press, 1989.

Huber, Mary Taylor, and Nancy C. Lutkehouse, eds. *Gendered Missions: Women and Men in Missionary Discourse and Practice*. Ann Arbor: University of Michigan Press, 1999.

Hunt, Tamara, and Micheline R. Lessard, eds. *Women and the Colonial Gaze*. New York: New York University Press, 2002.

Levine, Philippa, ed. *Gender and Empire*. Oxford: Oxford University Press, 2004.

Levine, Philippa. *Prostitution, Race, and Politics: Policing Venereal Disease in the British Empire*. London and New York: Routledge, 2005.

McClintock, Anne. *Imperial Leather: Race, Gender, and Sexuality in the Colonial Contest*. New York: Routledge, 1995.

Midgley, Clare, ed. *Gender and Imperialism*. Manchester, U.K.: Manchester University Press, 1998.

Pickles, Katie, and Myra Rutherdale, eds. *Contact Zones: Aboriginal and Settler Women in Canada's Colonial Past*. Vancouver: University of British Columbia Press, 2005.

Prochaska, Frank. *Women and Philanthropy in Nineteenth-Century England*. Oxford: Oxford University Press, 1980.

Said, Edward. *Orientalism*. New York: Vintage, 1979.

Semple, Rhonda. *Missionary Women: Gender, Professionalism, and the Victorian Idea of Christian Mission*. Woodbridge, U.K.: Boydell & Brewer, 2003.

Stoler, Ann Laura. *Race and the Education of Desire: Foucault's History of Sexuality and the Colonial Order of Things*. Durham, NC: Duke University Press, 1995.

Strobel, Margaret. *European Women and the Second British Empire*. Bloomington: University of Indiana Press, 1991.

Van Kirk, Sylvia. *Many Tender Ties: Women in Fur Trade Society, 1670–1870*. Norman: University of Oklahoma Press, 1980.

Ware, Vron. *Beyond the Pale: White Women, Racism, and History*. London: Verso, 1991.

Wilson, Kathleen. *The Island Race: Englishness, Empire, and Gender in the Eighteenth Century*. London and New York: Routledge, 2003.

Wilson, Kathleen, ed. *A New Imperial History: Culture, Identity, and Modernity in Britain and the Empire, 1660–1840*. Cambridge, U.K.: Cambridge University Press, 2004.

Rhonda A. Semple

IMPERIALISM, LIBERAL THEORIES OF

Liberal philosophy grew out of the Enlightenment's preoccupation with freedom, which led to intense efforts to find the right balance between the social need for order and the individual's natural liberties. Enlightenment philosophers unanimously excoriated all elements of the corporate society, which was ruled by landed elites wedded to the feudal ethos of conquest and the subsequent hoarding of resources.

The foundations of liberalism were laid by the science of political economy, developed in the eighteenth century on the new assumption that reason and enlightened self-interest guided a humanity recently arrived at the Age of Reason, after centuries of blinding prejudices. To the feudal order based on landed wealth, mercantile economics, and aggressive policies of conquest, eighteenth-century liberals opposed trade-generated wealth, free-market economics, and peaceful commercial relations between all nations.

The nineteenth-century disciples of the classical political economists went one step further and theorized that rational self-interest provided the maximum of individual freedom and the best guarantee of social peace at the same time. From here there was only one step, which many liberal theorists took, to concluding that a society based on free-market economics and individual freedoms represented the highest stage in the progress of humanity from darkness to freedom. Accordingly, liberal thinkers reflected on empires, and on the very concept of imperialism, from the perspective of the perceived links between trade-generated wealth, freedom, and progress.

Economic liberalism, built on the key concept of free trade, came mainly as a challenge to the doctrine of mercantilism, the dominant economic thinking of previous centuries, which considered the accumulation of wealth a zero-sum game: the more one nation enriches itself, the more another one would become impoverished. Consequently, mercantile economists advocated protectionism, high levels of exports but low levels of imports, state intervention, and the hoarding of bullion. Conquest and the subsequent exploitation of new land was part of the system, as the new possessions, the colonies, could be included in trade circuits that essentially exchanged the colonies' raw materials for the mother country's manufactured goods. Mercantilist economists rarely theorized on imperialism; still, a theory of imperialism emerged from their writings. Based on the assumption that, in a world of limited resources, one nation's gains depended generally on the losses of another, they pushed for a favorable balance of trade between the metropolis (mother country) and the colonies. Colonial monopoly was, in this view, a legitimate way of maintaining or improving current national levels of wealth and power, a matter of what in the French political tradition was called "reason of state."

Liberals opposed these views on economic grounds and argued that protectionism and state intervention distorted the market. Any gains to the metropolis depended on the fortunes of conquest, which meant that any change in the military balance of power put economic profits at risk. By contrast, the mutually profitable engagement of commercial partners in the marketplace assured long-term profits, which did not depend on the fortunes of war.

The doctrine of free trade was best expressed by the French phrase "*laissez-faire, laissez-passer*," meaning "let [commerce] follow its course, let [merchandise] pass," coined in France in the mid-1700s by a group of economic theorists called *physiocrats*. The physiocrats still put agriculture at the center of the ideal economic system, but adamantly opposed trade barriers. Freedom of trade, in their view, was bound to increase the wealth of the nation, because capital and goods were allowed to move freely as the state gave up its interventionist habits.

Less openly expressed, but well understood by the audience of enlightened salons and academies who listened to the physiocrats, was the belief that the freedom of individuals would derive naturally from the freedom of the markets. Considering that France was an absolutist monarchy, a highly centralized state with an established mercantile economic system, the physiocrats' call for free trade was subversive on several levels. It challenged an economic system that was supposed to maintain France's supremacy and grandeur; it challenged the complicated web of privileges that maintained the existing social hierarchy along with the corporate sources of influence and power; it challenged the aristocratic ethos by extolling the virtues of commerce, which had no use for the traditional feudal notions of honor and lineage. Finally, free trade also implied the equality of all individuals as participants in the market, regardless of birth.

The notion that commerce had the ability to subvert aristocratic aggressive impulses and replace them with peaceful cooperation was further corroborated by the very respected Baron de Montesquieu (1689–1755), who regarded "le doux commerce," or peaceable commerce, as an excellent device for converting irrational aggressive passions into rational—and thus peaceful—

interests. The philosopher Voltaire (1694–1778) concurred in "Letters Concerning the English Nation" (1732), where he described approvingly how the desire for profits compelled people of diverse backgrounds to cooperate at the London stock exchange in the belief that they could all win by taking part in trade rather than wasting their time dwelling on ancient hierarchies. Commerce, in conclusion, could turn greed, a negative passion, into a positive force working toward social harmony, an unsentimental, yet optimistic belief that remained central to the liberal philosophy well into the twentieth century.

The explicit link between commerce and freedom explains why commerce was held in high esteem by many French philosophers of the Enlightenment age and became one of the main components of the revolutionary discourse. Expanded to the level of international relations, such beliefs logically led to the repudiation of imperialism on grounds that what was true within a given country was true for relations between nations: each nation had something that another needed, and each could potentially benefit from trade. Hence, free trade made the very rationale for conquest and domination disappear.

An economic liberal argument against colonial monopoly and imperialism, seen as outcomes of mercantilism, emerged in this way. It must be stressed, however, that Montesquieu and Voltaire, as well as the physiocrats, tended to emphasize the subversive capabilities of free trade more than the English economists, who lived in a system with fewer political and economic restrictions. In England, the economic argument against imperialism only marginally addressed the issue of freedom. Individual freedom, for metropolitan and colonial citizens alike, came as a positive consequence of freedom of trade, but was not the main objective of classical political economists. If mercantilism posited the predominance of politics over economics, liberalism strove to make economics an autonomous field, in the belief, however, that economic reason contained an intrinsic moral reason.

LIBERAL ECONOMIC THEORIES OF IMPERIALISM

The landmark work that brought brilliantly together laissez-faire economics and the faith in the liberating potential of commerce was *The Wealth of Nations* (fully, *An Inquiry into the Nature and Causes of the Wealth of Nations*) by the Scottish economist Adam Smith (1723–1790), published in 1776. Smith accepted and developed many of the arguments of the physiocrats, including, albeit with qualifications, the high esteem they had for agriculture. In discussing the movements of capital, Smith believed that capital was more profitably invested in domestic commerce than in overseas trade, given the

Adam Smith. *Smith's* Wealth of Nations *(1769) was a landmark work that brought together laissez-faire economics and the faith in the liberating potential of commerce.* **HULTON ARCHIVE/GETTY IMAGES. REPRODUCED BY PERMISSION.**

overhead expenses of long-distance trade and the fact that such trade often supported the labor of other nations more than it helped the labor market at home.

Moreover, the cost of supporting the colonies outweighed whatever benefits the metropolis could extract. Smith had little sympathy for the rebellious American colonies, especially when it came to taxation. "It is not contrary to justice," Smith wrote, "that...America should contribute towards the discharge of the public debt of Great Britain.... a government to which several of the colonies of America owe their present charters, and consequently their present constitution; and to which all the colonies of America owe the liberty, security, and property which they have ever since enjoyed" (Smith 1776, bk. 5, chap. 3). That said, Smith believed that the cost of governing the colonies, and putting down the "disturbances," was simply more trouble than it was worth. Empire, in his view, was more of a fanciful ambition, a matter of grandstanding rather than a practical, wealth-producing endeavor:

The rulers of Great Britain have...amused the people with the imagination that they possessed a great empire on the west side of the Atlantic. This empire, however, has hitherto existed in imagination only. It has hitherto been, not an empire, but the project of an empire; not a gold mine, but the project of a gold mine; a project which has cost, which continues to cost, and which, if pursued in the same way as it has been hitherto, is likely to cost, immense expense, without being likely to bring any profit. (Smith 1776, bk. 5, chap. 3)

The reason for this assessment was simple: the colonies were supposed to function as British provinces, integrated into the domestic market; once it was clear that this was not the case, common sense dictated that they should be treated as what they were—foreign markets and trade partners, which is why Smith recommended granting the colonies their independence, the sooner the better.

Observing the enthusiasm for investment in overseas trade and the very advantages that Britain could reap by the opening of new markets, Smith argued for abandoning the imperial system in favor of a vast free market. England would benefit much more from trading with the Americans than wasting time and money trying to keep them into the fold. Remarkably, this argument remained confined to the economic level, with no regard for the soaring rhetoric of freedom coming from the "west side of the Atlantic."

This argument was brought to its logical conclusions by the economist Josiah Tucker (1712–1799), who demonstrated in a work published in 1776 that Britain would profit more from letting the American colonies go and trusting in their need for British products than from maintaining the colonies and thus continuing to be obliged to buy American raw materials instead of cheaper, similar products from other places. However, Tucker confined this argument to the specific situation of the American colonies. In an earlier debate with the Scottish philosopher David Hume (1711–1776), Tucker had still argued in favor of tariff protections for poor countries, in order to keep the poor nations from being swallowed by the rich, a phenomenon apt to encourage rich countries to make colonies out of the poor countries and thus render meaningless the very principle of free trade.

THE INTERNATIONAL DIVISION OF LABOR

The obligation of buying the products of the colonies, even at a disadvantage, could seem a small price to pay if offset by the opening of secure markets for the metropolis's industrial products. The problem of a glut of capital, production, and even people could easily find its solution in the large privileged markets the colonies provided, all the more if, as Josiah Tucker demonstrated, colonies were poor countries unable to compete on the free market.

Classical economists suggested alternative solutions that they deemed more reliable in the long term because the solutions were rooted in free-trade mechanisms, independent of unpredictable political changes. In *Commerce Defended* (1806), a reply to an English disciple of the physiocrats (William Spence) who warned against overproduction in an industrial system, the Scottish philosopher and economist James Mill (1773–1836) introduced the theory of the international division of labor.

This theory was further developed by the economist David Ricardo (1772–1823) in *Principles of Economy and Taxation* (1817), a work that pleaded for the mutual benefits of such a system, insisting that free trade did not disadvantage any country, since each had the opportunity to sell its own surplus and buy what it lacked. Ricardo's examples demonstrated the uselessness of maintaining imperial administrative control over the international system of trade. If England, Ricardo argued, manufactured better quality cloth at a cheaper cost than Portugal, while Portugal was able to produce wine with cheaper labor, and hence at a lesser price than England, then England would find it to its advantage to import the wine and export the cloth. This comparative advantage will endure, Ricardo argued, if both countries agreed to maintain their relative dependence on each other, for technical improvements could induce a certain country to produce all the products it consumes, which would in the end lead to rising prices in both countries. Ricardo argued that:

> Under a system of perfectly free commerce, each country naturally devotes its capital and labour to such employments as are most beneficial to each. This pursuit of individual advantage is admirably connected with the universal good of the whole. By stimulating industry, by regarding ingenuity, and by using most efficaciously the peculiar powers bestowed by nature, it distributes labour most effectively and most economically: while, by increasing the general mass of productions, it diffuses general benefit, and binds together by one common tie of interest and intercourse, the universal society of nations throughout the civilized world. It is this principle which determines that wine shall be made in France and Portugal, that corn shall be grown in America and Poland, and that hardware and other goods shall be manufactured in England. (Ricardo 1821, chap. 7, p. 11)

On the subject of colonial trade, Ricardo agreed essentially with Adam Smith that free trade was a better option than colonial monopoly for the "mother country" and for the colonies alike, because trade barriers and regulations inevitably brought about price distortions with far-reaching consequences:

> Foreign trade, then, whether fettered, encouraged, or free, will always continue, whatever may be the comparative difficulty of production in different countries; but it can only be regulated by altering the natural price, not the natural value, at which commodities can be produced in those countries, and that is effected by altering the distribution of the precious metals. This explanation confirms the opinion which I have elsewhere given, that there is not a tax, a bounty, or a prohibition, on the importation or exportation of commodities, which does not occasion a different distribution of the precious metals, and which does not, therefore, every where alter both the natural and the market price of commodities. (Ricardo 1821, chap. 25, p. 12)

Classical economists then opted, more often than not, for free trade against the trade monopoly brought about by imperial commercial requirements, arguing that free trade in the end benefited all parties, poor and rich participants alike, more than any taxes, barriers, and other protections could. While keen on keeping economics autonomous from politics, liberal economists were not oblivious to the political, social, and cultural implications of imperialism.

James Mill offered the most brilliant example of merging economic theory with reflections on the meaning and mission of empire. A proponent of free trade himself, Mill became so interested in British–Indian relations and the activities of the English East India Company that he spent twelve years on the subject. In his massive *History of India*, published in 1817, Mill argued that there was a certain hierarchy between countries according to their greater or lesser degree of adherence to the principles of reason and individual freedom cherished by all members of the Scottish Enlightenment, of which he was a member. India, in his thinking, had to be seen as a nation just emerging out of its barbarian stage, while England, as a more advanced country with respect to freedom and self-government, had a civilizing mission to fulfill. Mill later famously complained that the British Empire had become "a vast system of outdoor relief for the upper classes," nonetheless what he criticized were the failures of England's mission to civilize less advanced nations, not the principle that some countries have the duty to civilize others.

In an effort to reconcile free trade with the hierarchy of civilizations between nations, Mill criticized the trade monopoly of the East India Company and argued that all companies—British companies, that is—should be able to compete on the Indian market; yet he defended the rule of a revamped East India Company as a better solution than direct government control over India, a solution that corresponded with his strict noninterventionist beliefs. He did recommend that officials of the East India Company familiarize themselves with the customs and culture of India, and he suggested a number of reforms, but ultimately Mill accepted imperialism. He argued for what he understood to be an enlightened, civilizing imperialism, advantageous to both England and India, with India benefiting especially from the spread of English values via commercial relations.

Mill thus put elements of the theory of free trade, which on the whole weighed against imperialism, in the service of a social and political argument in favor of imperialism. In this respect he followed the method of British utilitarian philosopher Jeremy Bentham (1748–1832) of judging all human actions, imperial enterprises included, according to their degree of utility or lack of utility to the nation, but also to humanity in general.

LIBERAL SOCIAL THEORIES OF IMPERIALISM

Social liberals were concerned with the balance of freedoms as much or more than with the balance of trade. International commerce and imperial expansion were to be judged according to their ability, or lack thereof, to expand freedom. The classical economists reasoned that the freedom of the market implied the freedom of the individuals, as free trade implied freedom from the controlling and regulating hand of the state in favor of the "invisible hand" of the market. The argument was often invoked by philosophers who battled feudal social hierarchies and the feudal ethos of conquest and domination, in keeping with Montesquieu's thesis that commercial societies were more conducive to social equity and peaceful coexistence than feudal societies.

Extended to the relations between nations, this thinking led to the conclusion that industrial and commercial nations, where the utilitarian ethos prevailed, should lead the nations that still clung to traditional, that is, in European terms, feudal values. This sort of international tutoring in political progress contributed to global peace and justified a sort of temporary imperialism, even though most liberals remained faithful to Adam Smith's thesis that the colonies failed to bring any long-term advantages to the mother countries.

Jeremy Bentham encouraged both the English and the French to get rid of the colonies and thus spare themselves the manifold danger of wars, corruption, and continuous useless litigation, benefits that came to reinforce the advantages of free trade. However, even Bentham admitted that some colonies were riper than others for independence; in his view the American

colonies, the West Indies included, were ready, which is why he advised France to grant them independence, while India was not.

Similarly, in his *History of India* James Mill stipulated that the Indians would be happier under British rule than under their own despotic kings, because they would be able to profit from the freedom and progress the British imparted to them. The universality of the principles of Enlightenment and the malleability of human nature made the civilizing of India possible and desirable. Moreover, once the Indians became civilized, that is, once notions such as practical reason, individual freedom, and constitutional government became the organizing principles of the Indian society, India would be in a position to lead the rest of Asia on the same road.

Far from making gains, the British economy was bound to lose in the process, on account of the high cost of running an empire, as Adam Smith and Jeremy Bentham had so clearly proved. However, the benefits to the Indians, whose path toward progress was sped up, outweighed those losses. Most importantly, ancient reasons for war were eliminated, as peaceful interactions based on trade replaced relations based on conquest and domination. The utility of imperialism, in Mill's and Bentham's view, derived from its contribution to the formation of a peaceful liberal global order.

It must be stressed that Mill makes it clear that what makes Britain more advanced than India are its ideas, freedoms, and spirit of enterprise, not a racial superiority of any kind. In principle, it was just as desirable that India rule Britain if by chance the Indians became more advanced in terms of freedoms and government. As the situation stood in his time, Mill believed that it was desirable and useful to both sides for Britain to rule, that is, to guide India, on the condition that Britain would let go as soon as India reached the desired stage of political maturity.

French liberals who admired the British system approved of British imperialism on the grounds that it spread liberty. Thus French author Madame de Staël (1766–1817) defended British imperialism, although she, along with her friend and fellow liberal Benjamin Constant (1767–1830) reproved French imperialism as practiced by Napoléon Bonaparte (1769–1821). "England," wrote Madame de Staël, "has adopted the principle of governing the inhabitants of the country according to their own laws. It may be hoped that the example of the English will sufficiently form these people so that they may one day claim independence. All enlightened men in England would approve the loss of India through the very benefits the government has bestowed there" (Staël 1964, p. 358). And, taking a leaf from Adam Smith's book, she continued:

This Oriental empire is virtually a luxury; it contributes more to splendor than to real strength. England has lost its American colony and trade has been increased by it. If the colonies still remaining to them declared themselves independent, it would still maintain its naval and commercial superiority, because it has within itself a source of action, progress, and endurance that always puts it above circumstances. (Staël 1964, p. 358)

By contrast, Napoleonic imperialism was inhibiting the emancipation of the conquered peoples, which is why Madame de Staël and her circle opposed it forcefully.

In conclusion, classic liberals theorized that free trade was the preferred option for international relations, rather then imperialism, with its built-in governmental controls and trade monopolies. They also believed that trade rather than imperial domination would bring about global peace. However, they agreed that in order to spread the vision of a global liberal world, functioning according to the virtues of liberty, autonomous individualism, property, and peaceful commerce, empire was the best available tool for making these values accepted around the world. In ideal terms, then, classical liberal theory sees empire as a short-term economic anomaly, the utility of which is to be measured by the spread of liberal values around the world and the subsequent formation of a global liberal order.

While, in this view, there was no doubt that European, and especially British, political and social norms were superior to those of the colonies, there was no hint of racial superiority in the writings of the classic liberals. Later, during the nineteenth century, however, as European racial superiority became part of the discourse on empire, the goal of spreading liberal values became the British author Rudyard Kipling's (1865–1936) famed "white man's burden," which, resting on the illiberal hypothesis of racial superiority, entirely changed the substance of the discussion.

Assumptions of ethnic or racial superiority/inferiority subsequently gave cover to aggressive policies of brutal conquest and all manner of ill-treatment of the native populations. The focus on superior/inferior races made even luminaries of liberalism lapse into illiberal calls for domination. Thus the French historian and philosopher Alexis de Tocqueville (1805–1859), while decrying the dismal record of the French administration in Algeria, still concluded that power should remain in French hands, by force if necessary, on account of the inferior capabilities of the Algerians to rule themselves properly.

Awareness of the exploitative and oppressive imperial policies of the British government led the philosopher Herbert Spencer (1820–1903) to restate the terms of liberal theory on imperialism. Spencer continued to advocate the fundamentally beneficial role of laissez-faire trade and individual competition, in the belief that the free market was the best organizer of social life, because it demanded and then rewarded with the greatest precision services and contributions to the general good. On the subject of imperialism, Spencer abhorred state-sponsored, militaristic imperialism, which resulted in oppression, injustice, and brutality, all topped by market distortions, a system that could not but push both the colonized and the colonizers into barbarism. However, he considered that individual groups settling in far-off lands, on the model of the Puritans settling in America, ran none of the risks of state colonization.

Spencer's work, continued by economist J. A. Hobson (1858–1940), saw in the nineteenth-century imperialism that merged high finance and military might a form of neomercantilism, with all its ills, economic, social, and moral. The more this new imperialism departed from the liberal ethos, the more vicious, militaristic, and unjust it became, in addition to benefiting nobody other than the upper classes, who were the only ones to benefit from the trade protections and interventionist policies of imperial governments.

The liberal theories of imperialism encountered opposition from several corners soon after they were elaborated. National economists emphasized the need for trade protections and exploitation of colonies as the interests of the mother country dictated. In the second half of the nineteenth century, Marxist theorists pointed to the exploitation of the colonies and deemed liberal ideals a fig leaf barely hiding naked domination and pillaging of weaker countries by the powerful ones. The supposedly good intention of advancing freedom was in fact bringing nothing but despoliation and inequality, with the result of making indigenous populations into a vast global proletarian class. This view of imperialism, already sketched out by the German philosopher Immanuel Kant (1724–1804), became the major and most fertile critique of liberal theories of imperialism. These arguments articulate, to this day, the dominant critical discourse on imperialism.

Finally, with the rise of cultural anthropology in the second half of the twentieth century, the very goal of spreading a certain set of political values, be they admirable in themselves, fell into disrepute among historians and other observers of imperialism. Liberal views on imperialism are currently criticized for advocating the adoption of particular political and social values over the cultural codes and system of values of the colonized peoples, in short for pursuing a racist agenda under the guise of spreading progress, itself viewed as a questionable endeavor.

THE PHYSIOCRATS

During the mid-1700s, a group of French economic theorists known as the physiocrats played an instrumental role in the growth of economic science. Also known as "the sect" or "the economists," the physiocrats coined the phrase "laissez-faire, laissez-passer," which means, "let [commerce] follow its course, let [merchandise] pass." They put agriculture at the center of the ideal economic system, believed that land was the root of all wealth, advocated a single land tax, and adamantly opposed trade barriers. Freedom of trade, in their view, was bound to increase the wealth of the nation, because capital and goods were allowed to move freely as the state gave up its interventionist habits.

François Quesnay (1694–1774) was the founder and leader of physiocracy, which means "rule of nature." It was he who argued that land and agriculture served as the basis of all wealth. While he did not condemn industry, Quesnay argued that only agriculture could produce a surplus, which he called *produit net* (net product), and that a nation could not prosper economically if it did not completely support agriculture. This axiom was the very

nucleus of physiocracy. Victor Riqueti, Marquis de Mirabeau (1715–1789), a French soldier and devoted follower of Quesnay's, was the main author of the physiocratic doctrine calling for a single land tax. According to some, his 1763 work *La philosophie rurale* is among the best statements of early physiocracy.

Expanding upon the contributions of both Quesnay and Mirabeau were Paul Pierre le Mercier de la Rivière (1720–1794) and Pierre-Samuel du Pont de Nemours (1739–1817). It was le Mercier de la Rivière who promoted the concept of "nature's plan" in relation to the state. A businessman and adventurer, du Pont de Nemours founded and published *Journal de l'Agriculture, des Arts et des Finances* until 1766. He also coedited the journal *Ephémèrides du Citoyen* with fellow physiocrat Abbé Nicholas Baudeau (1730–1792).

Other physiocrats included the French economist Anne-Robert-Jacques Turgot (1727–1781), who modified physiocratic theories and had a major impact on Scottish economist Adam Smith, author of *Inquiry into the Nature and Causes of the Wealth of Nations* (1776).

The classical liberal vision on imperialism was intimately connected to Enlightenment notions of freedom, utility, and progress. It certainly sinned by overoptimism in the possibility and, indeed, the need to create a global free market as a prerequisite for global peace. It also postulated the universality of liberal values and counted on the malleability of human nature, with no regard for the strength and endurance of local customs and cultural practices. Liberals also often failed to properly recognize the scale of dismal pillage and inhumane exploitation that imperial policies carried out, frequently hiding behind an ossified liberal discourse.

Liberal theories on imperialism are nowadays relegated to the history of ideas, and rarely, if ever, invoked for any lessons individuals in the twenty-first century might be able to learn or emulate. However, the continuous drive toward globalization and global markets under free-trade agreements, the oft-repeated belief that trade and not aid is what will help poor countries develop, and trade arrangements such as the North American Free Trade Agreement (NAFTA) and the Central American Free Trade Agreement (CAFTA) all echo the basic assumptions of classic liberalism. Finally, the great success of Niall

Ferguson's six-part television series *Empire* on the British Empire airing on the BBC in 2003, which integrates many points of the classical social liberal theories, demonstrates a certain renewed interest in liberal views on empire.

SEE ALSO *Enlightenment Thought; Imperialism, Free Trade; Imperialism, Marxist Theories of; Neocolonialism.*

BIBLIOGRAPHY

Armitage, David. *Theories of Empire, 1450–1800.* New York: Columbia University Press, 1998.

Hirschman, Albert O. *The Passions and the Interests: Political Arguments for Capitalism Before its Triumph.* Princeton, NJ: Princeton University Press, 1977.

Pitts, Jennifer. *The Rise of Imperial Liberalism in England and France.* Princeton, NJ: Princeton University Press, 2005.

Ricardo, David. *On the Principles of Political Economy and Taxation,* 3rd ed. London: John Murray, 1821. Available from the Library of Economics and Liberty at http://www.econlib.org/library/Ricardo/ricP1.html/.

Semmel, Bernard. *The Liberal Ideal and the Demons of Empire: Theories of Imperialism from Adam Smith to Lenin.* Baltimore, MD: Johns Hopkins University Press, 1993.

Smith, Adam. *An Inquiry into the Nature and Causes of the Wealth of Nations* (1776). Available from the Adam Smith Institute at http://www.adamsmith.org/smith/won-index.htm/.

Staël, Madame de. *Madame de Staël on Politics, Literature, and the National Character.* Translated and edited by Morroe Berger. Garden City, NY: Doubleday, 1964.

Doina Pasca Harsanyi

IMPERIALISM, MARXIST THEORIES OF

In the spring of 1845, a young German philosopher and journalist scribbled eleven epigrams on the back of a piece of paper. They were published some forty years later by the executor of his estate. The last of these pithy comments has become one of the world's best known one-liners: "Philosophers have only interpreted the world in various ways, the point, however, is to change it." With uncharacteristic clarity, Karl Marx (1818–1883) had set the agenda for thousands of his contemporaries and hundreds of millions of people in subsequent generations.

Changing the world is what Marxism is all about, and yet neither Karl Marx nor his life-long colleague and executor Friedrich Engels (1820–1895) ever developed a theory of imperialism. Instead, their theoretical work focused on explaining how capitalism's complex development creates the necessary preconditions for socialism. As young revolutionaries they were committed to the radical wing of a largely liberal-nationalist reform movement that would rise up to challenge the legitimacy of governments from London to Vienna in the spring and summer of 1848. In this context, Marx and Engels considered the most urgent question to be the struggle of the emerging working class against the industrial bourgeoisie. In contrast, imperialism, by then centuries old, appeared outmoded and in decline. After all, just in their short lifetimes, all the mainland Spanish colonies in America achieved independence, while the only new empire had resulted from the French conquest of Algeria.

In the wake of the defeat of the revolutions of 1848, Marx and Engels emigrated to England, where from 1852 to 1863 they regularly wrote articles on world affairs for the *New York Daily Tribune*. These commentaries on current events cover a remarkably wide range of topics and include their only published work that directly relates to imperialism. These articles are critical syntheses of European press coverage of the major issues of the day, supplemented by their own background reading and research. The main imperial topics treated include Ireland, the renewal of the Honourable East India Company's charter in 1853, the "Eastern Question" as it degenerated into the Crimean War (1853–1856), the Anglo-Persian War of 1856, the Second Opium War (1856–1860), the Indian "Mutiny" of 1857 to 1858, and the Spanish invasion of Morocco (1858–1860).

At best, these articles offer occasional theoretical insights scattered amidst denunciations of "Oriental despotism" fueled by an abidingly Eurocentric humanist questioning: "Can mankind fulfill its destiny without a fundamental revolution in the social state of Asia?" (Marx 1853/1979, vol. 12, p. 132). On the whole, the image conveyed is how the destructive creativity of capitalism forces needed change, but for the wrong reasons. The historical significance of this for their primary concern of revolutionary action in Europe was summarized in a letter that Engels sent Marx in October 1858: "the English proletariat is actually becoming more and more bourgeois, so that the ultimate aim of this most bourgeois of all nations would appear to be the possession, *alongside* the bourgeoisie, of a bourgeois aristocracy and a bourgeois proletariat. In the case of a nation which exploits the entire world this is, of course, justified to some extent" (Engels 1958/1983, vol. 40, p. 344).

A century later, out of this eclectic body of journalism, the Institute of Marxism-Leninism of the Central Committee of the Communist Party of the Soviet Union would compile collections on topical questions of theory: *On Wars of Independence, On India, On Colonialism, On the Irish Question,* and so on. These collections posit an ahistorical theoretical coherency that neither author would have recognized, and that the articles cannot support. When Marxist theories of imperialism did develop, it would not be through journalism, but by direct engagements in anti-imperialist struggles. Despite their serious flaws, the *Daily Tribune* articles remain historically interesting. Nuanced, contextualized, yet differing, critical analyses of them have been written by the historian V. G. Kiernan (1974) and the literary critic Aijaz Ahmad (1992).

The absence of a sustained theoretical engagement with imperialism by the cofounders of Marxism does not mean that their work offers little of interest. Indeed, some of the most important theoretical work on imperialism is in the Marxist tradition, precisely because it can build on concepts and processes first articulated by Marx and Engels. Four of their ideas have proven to be of particular relevance to subsequent theoretical debates on imperialism.

The first relevant idea is their recognition of the primacy of town–country relations: "the whole economic history of society is summed up in the movement of this antithesis" (Marx 1867/1967, vol. 1, p. 352). The second relevant idea is also spatial. Marx argued that in the transition to capitalism, capital reaches out to reinforce or even introduce older forms of labor mobilization and discipline. From the seventeenth-century imposition of serfdom upon eastern European peasants, as the estates they worked became supply regions for western grain markets, to the rapid expansion of slave plantations in the American South producing cotton for the textile industry in Manchester, England, capitalist expansion was the enemy of freedom.

Third, Marx drew a distinction between *merchant capital* and *industrial capital*. Merchants accumulate capital by exploiting differences in the sale price that are temporal, usually seasonal, or spatial, usually between markets. Industrialists accumulate capital through the appropriation of surplus value—the value created by labor but not paid out in wages. So merchant capital is in the realm of circulation, while industrial capital is in production. As long as the commodity being bought or sold by the merchant is not an industrial product, and in the early history of capitalism it rarely was, merchant capital is engaged in what Marx called *primitive accumulation*.

The systematic transfer of wealth generated by the trades in precious metals, slaves, and opium were examples of primitive accumulation. Merchants are accumulating at the expense of noncapitalist societies. When, however, the merchant sells an industrial commodity, this fuels a systemic contradiction within capitalist society itself, because the merchant is appropriating some of the surplus value created in industry. In the nineteenth century, these tensions often took the form of industrial producers criticizing "unproductive" merchants and the banks they controlled.

The fourth relevant Marxist concept builds on the analytical primacy accorded to the capital goods sector within industrial society. For Marx, the simple application of machine tools to the production of consumer goods did not mean that a society had entered the era of modern industry. He defined a mature capitalist economy as one where machine tools were used to produce machines. Marx argued that in mature capitalism the capital goods sector appropriates from the consumer goods sector a substantial part of the value added in the manufacture of commodities. This transfer occurs through the high prices charged for capital goods. This systemic constraint leaves the consumer goods sector only two options: either cut costs or reduce competition and raise prices.

With the rapid growth of colonial empires following the Berlin Conference (1884–1885) that sanctioned a European division of Africa, imperialism became for many Marxists a question of colonial policy. Should socialists support colonial expansion as a necessary step in historical evolution? Generally, Marxists considered that social revolution in Europe was the necessary precondition for socialism elsewhere. This assumption

followed logically from the revolutionary primacy Marxism accords to the industrial working class, but it also reflected contemporary racial and cultural prejudices. As Engels put it in 1894 when discussing whether the communal basis of Russian peasant agriculture might permit Russia to bypass capitalism:

> Only when the capitalist economy has been relegated to the history books in its homeland and in the countries were it flourished, only when the backward countries see from this example "how it's done," how the productive forces of modern industry are placed in the service of all as social property—only then can they tackle this shortened process of development. (Engels 1894/ 1990, vol. 27, p. 426)

In this context, two divergent intellectual contributions stand out. The first is the struggle by the German social democratic leader Karl Kautsky (1854–1938) to convince his comrades that the rise of corporate concentration in the form of cartels and trusts, militarism, and the export of capital to colonial and semicolonial regions of the world, which was the hallmark of the new colonialism, were all the result of the low wages paid to European and American workers. In *Socialism and Colonial Policy* (1907), Kautsky argued that the limited market for consumer goods caused by these low wages meant that continued growth under capitalism required the imposition of monopolistic pricing policies, unproductive investments in a suicidal arms race, and new forms of superexploitation in the colonial world. Thus, opposing colonialism was an integral part of the struggle for socialism and against war.

The second highly original contribution was *Accumulation of Capital* (1913) by Rosa Luxemburg (1870–1919), who was born and educated in Polish Russia but was politically active in Germany. Luxemburg was caustically critical of the underconsumption theory used by Kautsky. She argued that the central problem lay elsewhere. The question that needed answering for her was why capitalist societies continue to grow despite the internal contradictions between sectors and types of capital. She concluded that Marx's analysis of capital was fundamentally flawed. The accumulation of capital and so the continued growth of the system rested on the continual subordination of new areas of the world to capitalist domination. Thus, capitalist growth requires intensified globalization. Militant internationalism was, therefore, the only correct revolutionary strategy, while the mass strike was its most effective tactic.

As influential as these theorists were, they were soon overshadowed by the publication of a slim volume by Vladimir Ilyich Ulyanov, better known as Lenin (1870–1924): *Imperialism, The Highest Stage of Capitalism*

(1917). Although this work is a significant contribution to Marxism, there can be little doubt that its impact was as great as it was because its author would within the year lead the Bolshevik Revolution in Russia.

Lenin's characterization of this new stage of capitalism incorporated numerous elements of earlier work. Key ideas had already been developed by Nikolai Bukharin (1888–1938) in his *Imperialism and World Economy*, for which Lenin wrote an introduction in 1915. Lenin's *Imperialism* represented nonetheless a significant break with the treatment of imperialism as simply a question of colonial policy. Indeed, Lenin's theory of imperialism does not require there to be colonies at all. His theory deals primarily with changes in the socioeconomic structures of the leading capitalist powers.

For Lenin, imperialism had a number of characteristic features. Taking a term from a major analysis of Austrian banking published in 1910 by the social democrat Rudolf Hilferding (1877–1941), Lenin argued that imperialism meant the dominance of *finance capital*. Unlike Hilferding, for whom this meant banks controlling industry, Lenin argued that finance capital represented a synthesis of merchant and industrial capital. This was only possible, he argued, because of the rise of monopolies in industry, utilities, and transportation. These firms required not only privileged access to capital markets, but were large enough to create cartels to fix prices and divvy up the world economy amongst themselves. Consolidating control of the world meant that the export of capital, rather than the export of industrially produced commodities, increasingly characterized international trade.

These fundamental changes in the economic relations that had characterized capitalism in its competitive stage meant new social groups emerged. In the centers of finance capital, new bourgeois oligarchies developed that controlled the commanding heights of their respective economies, while an aristocracy of labor emerged within the working class that supported imperial policies. Lenin considered the social democratic leaders, like Kautsky, who supported their respective government's efforts in World War I (1914–1918), to have their social and political basis amongst this strata of the working class. This historic "betrayal" of proletarian class interests made them the particular target of Bolshevik attacks both during and after the war.

In colonial and semicolonial countries, Lenin argued that capital exports created a division within the bourgeoisie between those who were beholden to imperial interests and those who favored a more autonomous economic development and so were opposed to finance capital. This distinction between a comprador bourgeoisie and a national bourgeoisie, and the relationships that

revolutionary forces should maintain with these differing factions, was at the heart of Marxist strategic debates in the 1920s.

At the Second Congress of the Third International (Communist International, or Comintern) in Moscow in July 1920, Lenin advanced the position that in colonial and semicolonial countries the revolutionary struggle had first to carry out a bourgeois democratic revolution before moving to social revolution. This position was challenged by Manabendra Nath Roy (1887–1954), founder of both the Mexican and Indian Communist parties. Roy defended a Luxemburgist antinationalist line, arguing that the toiling masses of workers and peasants were the only consequential revolutionary force in Asia and had no need to align themselves with bourgeois nationalist movements. Although his position was adopted as a supplementary thesis to Lenin's own position paper and Roy would occupy prominent positions in the Communist International until being purged in 1929, the main thrust of Comintern policy stressed the importance of a two-stage revolution and considered, in the counterrevolutionary climate of the 1920s, the struggle against British and French imperial interests to be primary. This was clearest in the debates over revolutionary strategy in China.

Under the leadership of the Kuomintang (KMT, also known as the Guomindong or Nationalist Party), a bourgeois nationalist alliance led first by Sun Yat-Sen (Sun Zhongshan, 1866–1925) and then Chiang Kai-Shek (Jiang Jieshi, 1887–1975), a strong anti-imperialist mass movement had developed in southern China. The fledgling Chinese Communist Party (CCP) was directed by the Comintern to enter into a strategic alliance with the KMT. This subordination of the class struggle to anti-imperialism was facilitated by a theory of Li Dazhao (1888–1927), cofounder of the CCP and a historian and librarian at Beijing University, that imperialism had "proletarianized" China. The implication of this analysis, which strongly influenced Mao Zedong's (1893–1976) thinking, was that a multiclass alliance might seamlessly pass from a bourgeois democratic, anti-imperialist stage to one of social revolution. In April 1927 this alliance collapsed when the KMT massacred an estimated six thousand Communists in the streets of Shanghai.

Speaking to the First Latin American Communist Conference in June 1929, José Carlos Mariátegui (1894–1930), the leading Peruvian revolutionary of his generation, observed: "The betrayal by the Chinese bourgeoisie and the failure of the Kuomintang have not yet been understood in their full magnitude. Their capitalist style of nationalism (one not related to social justice or theory) demonstrates how little we can trust the revolutionary nationalist sentiments of the bourgeoisie, even in countries like China" (Mariátegui 1929/1996).

Mariátegui went on to argue that this experience highlights the importance of concretely examining the history and politics of each specific country, so that what was an appropriate strategy in Central America, where patriotic feelings were shaped by the numerous American invasions, was not at all appropriate for a country like Argentina, with its large landholders and extensive bourgeoisie. In the case of Peru, specifically, and the Andean countries more generally, Mariátegui argued in his *Seven Essays of Interpretation of Peruvian Reality* (1928) that a revolutionary movement that does not recognize the rights of indigenous peoples is doomed to failure. Furthermore, he argued that communal institutions within indigenous societies offered a template for the development of socialism. There was no suggestion here of the need to wait for the Europeans to show "how it's done."

But old attitudes died hard. In 1936, at the Sixth Congress of the Comintern in Moscow, there was a chance encounter between Maurice Thorez (1900–1964), the leader of the French Communist Party, and Nguyen Ai Quoc, better known as Ho Chi Minh (1890–1969), the Vietnamese revolutionary. Thorez assured Ho that after the revolution in France, everything would be so much better in the Indo-Chinese colonies. Ho responded: "I hope you don't mind if we don't wait."

Long years in a fascist prison allowed Antonio Gramsci (1891–1937), cofounder and early leader of the Italian Communist Party, to deepen his understanding of why one of the most militant workers' movements in Europe had failed to stop fascism. Gramsci argued that the most advanced form of capitalism was not finance capitalism, but *Fordism*, named after the type of mass production pioneered by American automobile manufacturer Henry Ford (1863–1947). This phenomenon, then uniquely American, combined assembly lines and mass consumerism and was based on a cultural dominance that made modern, individualist, bourgeois values appear to be common sense. According to Gramsci, this universalizing and invasive Western cultural hegemony, with its related political economy, contrasted sharply with the nature of finance capital in France, where it rested on an alliance with small proprietors, and in Italy, where it relied on extensive parasitical classes "with no essential function in the world of production" (Gramsci 1971, p. 281).

This remarkable contribution to contemporary Marxism went largely unheeded at the time. Instead, at their 1936 Congress, the Comintern formally defined fascism as the "open dictatorship of finance capital." This effectively denied any qualitative difference between bourgeois democracies and fascist regimes, so when war broke out in September 1939 it was classified as an "imperialist" war. Only when Germany invaded the Soviet Union in June of 1941 did defense of the "socialist motherland" justify a Communist reengagement in the antifascist struggle.

Such was not the case, however, in China, where a more voluntarist form of Marxism was developing in the isolated Communist bastion of Yenan. In the 1930s and 1940s, Mao considered there to be "two big mountains lying like dead weight on the Chinese people: imperialism and feudalism" (Mao Zedong 1956, vol. 4, p. 317). They were to be removed through a national front that resisted the Japanese invasion, while simultaneously carrying out land reform. Thus, the social dimensions of this anti-imperialist struggle were not conceived as part of a struggle against capitalism, but rather as part of a necessary first stage that would build a people's democracy. Indeed, the CCP would not formally enter into the second stage, that of the building of socialism, until the Great Leap Forward in 1958.

Ironically, in the increasingly polarized world of the Cold War, it was this Chinese rearticulation of Lenin's two stages that provided the basis for a third way, when in April 1955, in the words of the American author Richard Wright (1908–1960), "the despised, the insulted, the hurt, the dispossessed—in short, the underdogs of the human race" met in Bandung, Indonesia (Wright 1956, p. 12). Although the nonaligned movement would not formally be created until 1961, this early meeting of Asian and African leaders consecrated the idea of a "third world" where a national democratic struggle against imperialism and indigenous forces of reaction was the principal revolutionary task.

This rejection of the primacy of class struggle against the bourgeoisie had a direct impact on revolutionary movements in Asia's most populous countries. In India, where the world's first democratically elected Communist government took office in Kerala in 1957, it contributed to the extraordinarily divisive nature of Marxist politics. In Indonesia, which had the third largest Communist Party in the world, support for President Sukarno (1901–1970) ended brutally in April 1967 with the slaughter of an estimated one million Communists by the military led by General Suharto (b. 1921), operating in close cooperation with the American government.

Despite these failures, the extreme bitterness of the Sino-Soviet dispute led the CCP to equate the Soviet Union with the United States as a hegemonic superpower. In the foreign policy of the "three worlds," first articulated by Deng Xiaoping (1904–1997), who went on to become China's "paramount leader," anti-imperialism came to mean opposing any Soviet-supported movement in a third world country. The effects of this policy were disastrous, nowhere more so than in the former Portuguese colonies in Africa, where it fuelled protracted civil wars that claimed the lives of millions.

Since the 1960s, Marxist theories of imperialism have developed primarily outside organized movements for social change. Academics, in particular historians, economists, and sociologists, have been prominent in this new theoretical work. This is a historically significant change, for as Marxist theories of imperialism have gained in precision, focus, and historical complexity, they have lost in political influence and indeed relevance. Three intellectual clusters will serve to illustrate the richness and diversity of this neo-Marxist literature: the development of underdevelopment and world-systems approaches; the *Monthly Review*; and the work on *Unequal Exchange*.

Influenced by Paul Baran's *The Political Economy of Growth* (1957), in the mid-1960s André Gunder Frank (1929–2005) pioneered the concept of the development of *underdevelopment* to critique prevailing economic aid policies to Latin America. Those policies distinguished between developed and undeveloped economies and largely argued that by following the development path taken by wealthy countries the undeveloped could catch up. Frank said there are no undeveloped economies, there are only developed and underdeveloped ones. Both are intimately related through century-old processes whereby the developed economies expanded by actively underdeveloping the rest of the world. His analysis stressed the importance of trade and challenged the legitimacy of a specifically national focus to deal with what he argued was clearly an international process of global restructuring. Walter Rodney (1942–1980) significantly expanded the analysis with his 1972 book, *How Europe Underdeveloped Africa*.

This much more historical understanding of imperialism was consistent with the theoretical framework of the *longue durée* (long duration) developed by Fernand Braudel (1902–1985), editor of the most influential European history journal, *Les Annales* (The Annals). Braudel stressed the significance of the very long geographic time and the multiple generations of social time over the fleeting moments of individuals' lives or events. Immanuel Wallerstein (b. 1930), a historical sociologist, in his three-volume *Modern World-System* (1974–1988) developed Braudel's concepts and adapted the Marxist distinction between town and country, to his explanation of how differing, internally coherent, parts of the world interacted. He argued between 1500 and 1800 a spatial hierarchy of core economies emerged that controlled resource-producing peripheral areas.

Since the 1970s, there has been a sustained and active debate within the social sciences and humanities of advanced capitalist academe on the merits of this world-systems approach. Suffice it to say here that most participants in this debate do not draw any clear distinction between capitalism and imperialism, which they think of as largely coterminous, while only a minority would consider their work a contribution to Marxism.

Such is certainly not the case for the group of scholars and activists associated with *Monthly Review*. Since its founding by the noted economist Paul Sweezy (1910–2004) and popular historian Leo Huberman (1903–1968) in 1949, the *Monthly Review* collective has set itself the task of analyzing in accessible prose anti-imperialist struggles around the world. For as Sweezy and Baran explained in their *Monopoly Capital: An Essay on the American Economic and Social Order* (1966), which was dedicated to the Latin American revolutionary leader Che Guevara (1928–1967), the primary struggle has shifted from the class struggle within advanced capitalism to the third world's struggle against imperialism.

This third worldism soon became the most widely shared position among nonaligned Marxists in the advanced capitalist world. In their analysis of imperialism, Sweezy and his colleagues stressed the significance of transnational corporations. Their analysis of the systemic need for unproductive military investments and planned obsolescence in consumer goods, although evocative of older theories of underconsumption, has permitted the development of an innovative and articulate environmental critique.

The failure of so many newly independent countries to redress the economic disparities with their former colonial powers led in the 1960s and 1970s to a profound critical reassessment of the nature of international trade and the difference between growth and development. Central to this work was Arghiri Emmanuel's (1911–2001) study of the imperialism of trade, *L'échange inégal* (Unequal Exchange, 1969), which showed how contemporary capitalism inverts the assumptions underlying David Ricardo's (1772-1823) law of comparative advantage. As a result, increased trade simultaneously creates poverty and generates wealth, but in differing parts of the world.

The African economist Samir Amin (b. 1931) has structurally analyzed this unequal development (*Le développement inégal,* 1973) of peripheral societies. According to Amin, subsequent globalization has done nothing to reduce this core-peripheral divide. Indeed, it has permitted its consolidation, through the emergence of monopolies over technology, military hardware, communications and culture, finance, and institutions of international governance. These monopolies systemically favor advanced capitalist countries.

Since 1999, the ecological and human cost of neoliberal globalization has given rise to an opposition movement around the world. This challenge to a particularly virulent form of imperialism is the first in more than a century not to draw explicitly on the Marxist tradition. This disjuncture speaks eloquently to the ethical and political failure of Marxist attempts to build socialist societies in the twentieth century. One can well understand why a new generation who believes a better world is possible would want to distance themselves from such a tragic legacy. Yet to achieve a better world requires a critical understanding of how power relationships work in this world and so this new struggle will require many of the analytical tools first developed as Marxist theories of imperialism.

SEE ALSO *Imperialism, Liberal Theories of; Modern World-System Analysis.*

BIBLIOGRAPHY

Ahmad, Aijaz. *In Theory: Classes, Nations, and Literatures.* London: Verso, 1992.

Amin, Samir. *Le développement inégal: Essai sur les formations sociales du captialisme périphérique.* Paris: Éditions de minuit, 1973. Translated by Brian Pearce as *Unequal Development: An Essay on the Social Formations of Peripheral Capitalism.* New York: Monthly Review Press, 1976.

Bukharin, Nicolai. *Imperialism and World Economy* (1915). New York: Monthly Review Press, 1972.

Emmanuel, Arghiri. *L'échange inégal: Essai sur les antagonismes dans les rapports économiques internationaux.* Paris: François Maspero, 1969. Translated by Brian Pearce as *Unequal Exchange: A Study of the Imperialism of Trade.* New York: Monthly Review Press, 1972.

Engels, Friedrich. "Afterward" (1894) to "On Social Relations in Russia." In *Marx-Engels: Collected Works* (1970–1992), vol. 27. New York: International Publishers, 1990. Available from http://www.marxists.org/archive/marx/works/1894/01/russia.htm/.

Engels, Friedrich. "Letter: Engels to Marx in London." October 7, 1958. In *Marx-Engels: Collected Works* (1970–1992), vol. 40. New York: International Publishers, 1983. Available from http://www.marxists.org/archive/marx/works/1858/letters/58_10_07.htm/.

Gramsci, Antonio. "Americanism and Fordism." In *Selections from the Prison Notebooks of Antonio Gramsci (1926–1935),* edited and translated by Quintin Hoare and Geoffrey Nowell Smith, 277–318. New York: International Publishers, 1971.

Kiernan, V. G. *Marxism and Imperialism: Studies.* London: Edward Arnold, 1974.

Lenin, V. I. *Imperialism, The Highest Stage of Capitalism* (1917). Moscow: Foreign Language Press, 1952.

Luxemburg, Rosa. *The Accumulation of Capital* (1913). Translated by Agnes Schwarzchild. New York: Monthly Review Press, 1968.

Mao Zedong. "How Yu Kung Removed the Mountains." (1945) In *Selected Works, vol. 4,* 316–319. New York: International Publishers, 1956.

Mariátegui, José Carlos. "Anti-Imperialist Viewpoint." Presented to the First Latin American Communist Conference, June 1929. Translated by Michael Pearlman, 1996. Available from http://www.marxists.org/archive/mariateg/works/1929-ai.htm/.

Marx, Karl. *Capital, A Critique of Political Economy. Volume 1: The Process of Capitalist Production* (1867). Translated from the Third German Edition by Samuel Moore and Edward Aveling. Edited by Frederick Engels. New York: International Publishers, 1967.

Marx, Karl. "The British Rule in India" (1853). In *Marx-Engels: Collected Works* (1970–1992), vol. 12. New York: International Publishers, 1979. Available from http://www.marxists.org/archive/marx/works/1853/06/25.htm/.

Marx, Karl, and Frederick Engels. *Marx-Engels: Collected Works* (1835–1895). 45 vols. New York: International Publishers, 1970–1992. Available from http://www.marxists.org/archive/marx/works/cw/.

Marxist.org Internet Archives. Available from http://www.marxists.org/.

Sweezy, Paul, and Paul Baran. *Monopoly Capital: An Essay on the American Economic and Social Order.* New York: Monthly Review Press, 1966.

Wright, Richard. *The Color Curtain: A Report on the Bandung Conference.* Cleveland, OH: World Publishing, 1956.

Robert C. H. Sweeny

INCA EMPIRE

The origins of the Inca civilization lie in the Cuzco region of modern-day Peru, though some archaeologists maintain that its beginnings are also to be found in the region previously dominated by the Huari and in Tiahuanaco. In any case, among the various groups who constituted small kingdoms in the region of Cuzco during the thirteenth century, only the Incas managed to establish cultural hegemony. The Incas gradually consolidated a kingdom thanks to the military conquest of neighboring populations and by around 1400 had created a state. The most powerful rival they had to overcome were the Chancas, who occupied the Pampas River valley and formed a powerful coalition with other groups in order to stop the Incas' economic and military onslaught. After the victorious battle of 1440 against the Chancas, the Sapa Inca Pachacuti, considered by most historians to be a key figure in Inca expansionism, changed his name to *Pachacútec Inca Yupanqui*, meaning "reformer of the world" or "savior of the Earth."

By around 1450 the Inca army dominated the territory of the Colla people; following this, they reached Arequipa on the southern coast. In the north, they

MAP BY XNR PRODUCTIONS. THE GALE GROUP.

arrived at the city of Cajamarca, after which the Chimú capital was defeated and the march toward the north was completed with the conquest of Quito, which was annexed along with the lands of other tribes from present-day Ecuador. In 1471, after Inca troops had returned to Cuzco, Pachacútec Inca Yupanqui was succeeded by his son, Túpac Yupanqui, who extended Inca conquests in the southern Andes into regions encompassing present-day Chile, Bolivia, and Argentina. Túpac's son, Huayna Cápac, sent numerous expeditions to the north, to put an end to the uprisings of various tribes reluctant to accept Inca authority. Such revolts were nearly continuous and highlight the difficulty of controlling and administrating a far-flung empire made up of populations with so many different languages and ethnic origins.

CHARACTERISTICS OF THE INCA EMPIRE

Politically, the Inca Empire was a mixture of absolute monarchy, theocratic power, and agrarian collectivism, organized around a centralized bureaucratic state at the service of the ruling class. The Inca king (the *Sapa Inca* or "Unique Inca") was treated as a divine being whose authority was above any law. The Incas themselves called their empire *Tahuantinsuyu* or "The four parts together."

Each part of the Tahuantinsuyu was governed by an *apo*, a close relative of the Sapa Inca, who served as a viceroy, while also being a member of the council of state and an advisor on imperial affairs. The organization of the Inca Empire rested on certain key elements: a theocratic concept of power; the organization of tribute from subject peoples, taken in labor services; and the tripartite division of land into the lands of the Sapa Inca, the lands of the Sun (the priests' lands), and the lands of subject peoples collectively called the *ayllu*.

The *ayllu* formed the base of Andean and Inca social organization. It was a clan based on ties of kinship, and a community bonded by shared landholding and religious beliefs, under leaders whose power varied with the size and number of *ayllus* under their authority. For the Incas, the *ayllu* was a vital building block of social organization, because it served as the entity that could satisfy the work tribute required by the Sapa Inca, which it delivered through the *mita*, or work draft.

Andean societies were territorially integrated units but often took the form of what have been called *vertical archipelagos*, a term referring to the practice of establishing settlements at high altitudes in the mountainous environment. These vertical archipelagos comprised the *ayllus'* ancestral homeland—the core of tribal identity—and also served as outlying agrarian settlements where farmers specialized in raising various types of produce for distribution and exchange among the dispersed branches of the tribe. The Incas took their tribute from the lands of the *ayllus*, which they set aside for this purpose, and then "gave back" to the community in return for the goods its labor produced on these lands. In this way, the Incas used a notion of redistribution common in the Andean world, where the organization of production and exchange was based on the cooperation of kinship groups. This enabled the Incas to represent their exploitation of others as simply an extension of the family obligations on which Andean peasant communities were built. The bulk of tribute goods collected from the peasants went toward provisioning the army, the bureaucracy, and other branches of the imperial state, but a portion was kept back in storehouses and released in times of famine.

The Incas were able to dominate their neighbors thanks to their organizing capabilities and their ability to assimilate different cultures. One example of this would be the integration of the *curacas* or tribal lords through the establishment of personal relationships with the Sapa Inca, symbolized in the exchange of presents. Many of the treaties that linked ethnic groups with the government in Cuzco were not the fruit of conquests but of offers of special prerogatives for joining the Empire, combined with the threat of force. Should any group

Atahualpa as the Prisoner of the Spaniards. *Francisco Pizarro's forces captured the Inca leader Atahualpa in 1532 and held him for ransom. Although the Incas paid the ransom in gold and silver, Pizarro had Atahualpa executed.* THE ART ARCHIVE/ARCHAEOLOGICAL MUSEUM LIMA/DAGLI ORTI. REPRODUCED BY PERMISSION.

refuse, they would be attacked by the Inca army. Hence, it is clear that the Inca Empire had a fragile equilibrium, constantly threatened by the possibility of a refusal that would require military intervention.

One of the main strategies for maintaining the cohesion of such a vast territory was the imposition of a common language—Quechua, the language of the political and administrative elite—which subject populations were obliged to use alongside their own local languages. Another strategy was the *mitmaq* or forced migration, through which whole communities, sometimes numbering thousands of families, were sent to distant and already colonized regions so that they could be assimilated into the dominant culture and become less resistant to Inca power. The census of subject populations was another potent tool for controlling conquered peoples, as was the very efficient network of roadways used by the *chasquis* or imperial messengers to link all major urban

centers and provinces. In the absence of the wheel, transportation depended on manpower, though Andean societies found in the llama, a cameloid, an animal well suited to carrying light cargoes, as well as supplying meat and wool. The Incas also sought to use religious practice as a force for binding the empire. The conquered populations were obliged to convert to the official cult, devoted to Inti, the Sun. But this could coexist with the continuation of cults based around local divinities. All conquered populations had to convert to the main religion of the empire, that is, the adoration of Inti. But this could coexist with preexisting cults based around local divinities. Similarly, the conquered populations had to learn and use the Inca language, Quechua, but they were also allowed to preserve their local dialects. The Incas thereby gained the conquered populations' gratitude and attachment while ultimately controlling them. But the Incas insisted on veneration of the Sapa Inca, the highest religious and political authority.

The Inca nobles shared in the Sapa Inca's power and in the legitimacy conferred by religion because their lineages were connected by blood ties to the royal dynasty. The business of government was turned into a dynastic monopoly based on privileged knowledge, as the absence of a system of writing restricted important information to a close oligarchy, who had access to the records kept on knotted cords or *quipus*. So long as the belief in the divine origin of the Inca dynasty and in its right to extensive privileges could be upheld, the edifice of the state would remain in place.

DEFEAT BY THE SPANISH

The arrival of the Spanish was preceded by the diffusion of smallpox, which had spread from areas of Spanish settlement in the Caribbean region and weakened the population, even killing the Sapa Inca Huayna Cápac in 1525. His death, and that of his immediate heir, led to a political crisis within the empire, in the form of a fratricidal fight for succession between the two descendants of the deceased Inca: Huáscar and Atahualpa. To strike a balance, Huáscar was offered the throne in Cuzco and Atahualpa was offered Quito, the second city of the empire. But this division of power did not prevent conflict and a concomitant weakening of Inca power at a time when a new and unimagined threat had arrived from outside the empire.

In 1532 Francisco Pizarro arrived in Peru with around 170 soldiers and sought to make contact with the Incas. To do so, he and his men headed toward the Inca town at Cajamarca where Atahualpa's army was resting during their march southward to take control of Cuzco. Pizarro took advantage of Atahualpa's misplaced confidence in Inca superiority to capture him, and then exploited divisions among the Incas and subject peoples to overthrow the Inca kingdom. The Spanish entered Cajamarca without resistance because they were small in number and were expected to pose no danger. Once there, they captured Atahualpa, after killing most of the population of the city, and accepted his offer of a fabulous treasure in exchange for his life. This did not prevent his assassination, however, and having executed Atahualpa, the Spaniards then turned to his relatives for allies, placing them on the Inca throne as puppet kings, while making alliances with ethnic leaders who saw Spanish rule as preferable to that of the Incas. The conquest of the Inca Empire was, therefore, a multilateral war, between and among the Incas, their subject populations, and the European invaders. The war effectively ended the Tahuantinsuyu, though for some years the Spaniards sought to maintain a façade of Inca leadership in order to strengthen their own authority.

SEE ALSO *Peru Under Spanish Rule; Pizarro, Francisco.*

BIBLIOGRAPHY

Alcina Franch, José. *Los Incas: El reino del Sol.* Madrid: Anaya, 1988.

Andrien, Kenneth J., and Rolena Adorno, eds. *Transatlantic Encounters: Europeans and Andeans in the Sixteenth Century.* Berkeley: University of California Press, 1991.

Bravo, Concepción. *El Tiempo de los Incas.* Madrid: Alhambra, 1986.

Craig, Morris, and Adriana von Hagen. *The Inka Empire and its Andean Origins.* New York: Abbeville, 1993.

D'Altroy, Terence N. *The Incas.* Malden, MA: Blackwell, 2002.

Davies, Nigel. *The Incas.* Niwot: University Press of Colorado, 1995.

Longhena, María, and Walter Alva. *The Incas and Other Andean Civilizations.* San Diego, CA: Thunder Bay, 1999.

Means, Philip Ainsworth. *Fall of the Inca Empire and the Spanish Rule in Peru, 1530–1780.* Revised edition. New York: Gordian, 1964.

Vega, Inca Garcilaso de la Vega. *Comentarios Reales de los Incas.* Edited by Carlos Araníbar. Lima: Fondo de Cultura Económica, 1991; reprint, Mexico: Fondo de Cultura Económica, 2004.

Cristina Blanco Sío-López

INDEPENDENCE AND DECOLONIZATION, MIDDLE EAST

In the decades immediately following the conclusion of World War II, European formal empires in the Middle East began to unravel. France retreated from Syria and Lebanon in 1946 after numerous catastrophic engagements with local peoples. The British withdrew from Palestine in 1948, leaving behind the new state of Israel, which was carved out of a large portion of Palestine; from most of the rest was created Jordan. A series of treaties and agreements led to British withdrawal from Egypt and Iraq; as a result of one of these agreements, Sudan also gained independence. While the formal empires of European countries seemingly disintegrated in the 1950s, the former colonial powers, now joined by the United States, continued to maintain a presence in the region. Britain and the United States focused on controlling the production of oil. Such interests now had the added dimension of being pursued within the larger framework of geopolitical tensions created by the Cold War between the United States and the Soviet Union. Indeed, the independence process has been very complex in the Middle East. According to historian Albert Hourani, "It would be better . . . to see the history of this period as that of a complex interaction: of the will of ancient and stable societies to reconstitute themselves, preserving what they had of their own while making the necessary changes in order to survive in the modern world increasingly organized on other principles, and where the centers of world power have lain for long, and still lie, outside the Middle East" (Hourani, Khoury, and Wilson 2004, p. 4).

To understand the form the processes of independence and decolonization took in the Middle East, one has to begin in the nineteenth century. The British, the French, and the Ottomans had varying degrees of control in different parts of the region; throughout the region, a strong nationalist sentiment opposed this foreign control. During the second half of the nineteenth century, the ideal of autonomy was disseminated by such organizations as the National Party in Egypt, the Young Ottomans and then the Young Turks in the Ottoman Empire, secret Arab societies in Beirut and Damascus, and the Young Tunisians. During the late nineteenth and early twentieth centuries, such groups began to organize nationalist demonstrations; some directly challenged the imperial rule of the British, the French, and even the Ottoman Turks. The organizations' ideological leadership gave direction to these direct challenges to imperial presence. Arab nationalism became popular among intellectuals in Greater Syria; Turkish nationalism also grew, with its own ideas about how national communities ought to be formed. In Iran, different currents of nationalism imagined different futures for the country.

Throughout the region, the relationship between colony and metropole (the colonizing power) deeply affected the intellectual, ideological, and material development of both. For example, the more the French sought to gain materially from Algeria, the more resistance developed among the Algerians. Over time, this resistance coalesced into a sense of nationalism that was completely at odds with the political reality of being colonized, that is, existing only for the betterment of the colonizer. Feelings of political identity, economic identity, geographic identity, and religious identity coalesced into a powerful force. This force, on the one hand, forged powerful bonds, and on the other hand, made Middle Easterners see themselves as distinctly different from Europeans.

Some of the earliest attempts to achieve independence, or at least self-determination, occurred in the context of World War I. In 1916 the British promised independence to Hussein ibn Ali, the emir of Mecca and sharif of the Hashemite family, if he would help them against the Ottomans. In the same year Britain also signed the secret Sykes-Picot Agreement with France, which called for an independent Arab State or a confederation of states, although it was calculatedly ambiguous on the question of how much of a role each of these powers would play in this "independent" state. According to the agreement, postwar Middle East was to be divided among the allies, with France and Britain "prepared to recognize and protect an independent Arab state or a confederation of states . . . under the suzerainty of an Arab chief." Portions of present-day Turkey, Syria, Transjordan, Palestine, and Iraq were to constitute this so-called independent state. At the conclusion of the war, Britain and France divided various portions of the Middle East into new territories called mandates, with the ostensible rationale of mentoring these mandates as they progressed toward independence. In reality, they used their powerful position as a way to advance their own interests, thus earning the resentment of Arabs. For much of the nineteenth century the various nationalist groups mentioned above, and others like them, organized and in some cases fought against imperial rule—not only against the British and the French, but also against the Ottoman Turks. In the Arab countries, nationalism, which originated among educated elites, spread increasingly to all sectors of society as the promised self-determination failed to appear and occupation and colonial control continued. In Turkey and Iran, nationalist movements began gaining strength in the late nineteenth century and modern states began to emerge in the 1910s. Over the course of the twentieth century, decolonization took varying forms in these disparate areas, as did the new states and societies that emerged.

THE DEVELOPMENT OF ARAB NATIONALISM

Arab nationalism continues to be a powerful force in today's world. The term *Arab* is fraught with historical difficulties; today it usually refers to a person whose language is Arabic. Equally difficult is the phrase *Arab nationalism*; this can be used both as an equivalent to *Pan-Arabism* and more specifically to refer to independence struggles in Arabic-speaking countries. The 1850s and 1860s witnessed a growing sense of Arab identity. This was manifest in the renewed study of the 'Abbasīd period (ca. 750 to ca. 1258), and, in turn, accounts of 'Abbasīd grandeur, wealth, and intellectual pursuits served to inspire Arab pride and solidarity. By the close of the nineteenth century and into the early part of the twentieth century, in Baghdad, Cairo, and Damascus, a new literate class developed that began advocating the notion of Arab "nations." This growing intelligentsia advocated not only a sense of national solidarity, but also a method of societal organization and plans for independent development. Arabs had to at once break loose from the Ottoman Empire's historical control and keep the European nation-states at bay. World War I led to a decrease in the power of the Ottomans, but there was a simultaneous, if short-lived, increase of British and French domination of the Arab world's socioeconomic development.

In 1913, the Arab National Congress demanded governmental autonomy for the Arab provinces of the ailing and loosely consolidated Ottoman Empire. Calls for greater autonomy were also directed at the British and French, whose influence and control were well established, but deeply resented by the Arabs. With the advent of World War I in 1914, Arab demands began to threaten Britain's position in the region, particularly as the Germans took advantage of the situation to promote anti-British sentiment. The Germans made contact with Hussein, the Sherif of Mecca, who had considerable influence on regional Muslim populations. Hussein continued to assist the Germans until June 1915. Another valuable contact for the Germans was Ibn Saud, who was quite powerful in the Arabian Peninsula, and exercised considerable influence in the region up to the Persian Gulf to the east; all of this land was exclusively under British authority. In the latter part of 1915, Hussein resumed friendly relations with the British, whose assistance he sought in negotiations aimed at winning Arab freedom from Ottoman control. In 1916, despite offering their assistance and support for an "Arab Confederation," the British signed the Sykes-Picot agreement with the French, the details of which were to be kept a secret from the Arabs. These details were nonetheless made public by Bolshevik Russia; as news spread, the various Arab nationalist organizations became alarmed, as sovereignty appeared to be slipping away rather than coming closer.

The year 1917 was witness to an event that has had a lasting impact on the geopolitics of the Middle East. The Balfour Declaration, made in November of that year, left a legacy that the Middle East and the rest of the world continue to confront into the twenty-first century. In a published letter to Lord Rothschild, a prominent leader of the British Jewish community, the British secretary of foreign affairs, Arthur James Balfour, stated that Britain favored the establishment of a homeland for the Jewish people in Palestine. Balfour added that such a homeland was to be established with the understanding that nothing would be done to compromise the civil and religious rights of the other inhabitants of Palestine. That Palestine continues to be occupied and the state of Israel continues to contest its borders belies the initial intent of creating a Jewish homeland there.

The Arab Revolt against the Ottomans that started in 1916 came to an end in 1918 with Palestine and Syria free of Ottoman control. However, in place of the older empire came British control; it was an unforeseen consequence of seeking British help in ousting the Ottomans. Arabs expected the British to grant them independence at the end of World War I. Instead they got the 1919 arrangements between the French and British to divide the Middle East between themselves—Britain gained control of Mesopotamia (Iraq), Palestine, and present-day Jordan, and the French were to control Syria and Lebanon. Only the remote desert areas were free of British-French control. As mentioned above, these new territories were officially considered mandates, and were registered as such with the recently formed League of Nations. From the 1920s to about the 1960s, Arab nationalism matured into a force that was ever more difficult to contend with for the British and French. The most powerful example of this maturation was the formation of the League of Arab States, which was set up by Egypt, Lebanon, Iraq, Syria, Transjordan, Yemen, and Saudi Arabia; it demonstrated Arab unity and cooperation in creating a future for Middle Eastern peoples. As one after another nation-state was formed, each with a distinct identity, a new era emerged in the western and southwestern reaches of Asia.

THE EMERGENCE OF MODERN NATION-STATES

The section that follows will consist of a country-by-country consideration of decolonization and modernization in the Middle East; because the region comprises so many nation-states, the attention paid to individual countries will necessarily be brief. Turkey and Iran have been included here because they fall within some definitions of the Middle East and are clearly part of the regional geopolitical mix; barring Egypt, North African states are not discussed. A notable factor affecting all countries in the region was the discovery of oil in the 1920s and 1930s. Oil production had a tremendous impact on Middle Eastern economies, of course, but by

the 1950s it also was affecting the entire global economy. This inevitably led to a shift in the geopolitical processes at work in the region.

BAHRAIN

Located on the Persian Gulf, and comprised of thirty-three islands, Bahrain historically has had contact with several other peoples and nations, mostly through trade. Additionally, it has been occupied by several of them, namely the Persians, the Omanis, the Portuguese, and the British. Between 1861 and 1971 Bahrain was a British protectorate. The ruling family of Bahrain, the Al Khalifa family, arrived in the area in the mid-eighteenth century, and had to contend with successive occupiers. It was one of the Al Khalifas, 'Isā ibn Salmān Al Khalifā, who effected the transfer of Bahrain from the British to its own people in 1971. Termination of British control was not necessarily the result of pressure from the local people. Perceptions of Britain's changed position in the world were largely responsible for its receding from the Gulf regions. Britain's withdrawal of troops from the Gulf region in 1968 led to Emir al Khalifa declaring independent in 1971. Bahrain signed a treaty of friendship with Britain, thus concluding Britain's status as a protectorate. Eventually Bahrain joined the United Nations and the Arab League. Bahrain is a constitutional monarchy, and the reins of government are passed by the emir to his eldest son. Bahrain was one of the first Gulf states to reap oil profits following the discovery of oil in 1932. Its citizens enjoy these benefits today in the form of high-quality education and health care; however, unemployment continues to be a problem. Tensions between Bahrain's rulers and the country's poor Shi'ites also give cause for concern. Bahrain has cordial relations with its Gulf neighbors, other Arab nations, and several Western nations, including Britain and the United States. Because its economy is well diversified, the economic future of this small kingdom is bright.

EGYPT

France and Britain had equal interest in managing Egypt's future; this sharing of power was called *caise de la dette* (dual control). Their dual partnership of commercial and then eventually political interests started at the turn of the nineteenth century and continued until 1882. 'Urābī Pasha Al-Misrī, an officer in the Egyptian army and a nationalist, resented the presence of Turkish ad Circassion officers. He led a revolt against them in 1881 and became a national hero with his slogan, "*Misr li'l Misriyīn*" (Egypt for Egyptians). The ruler of Egypt, concerned about 'Urābī's increasing popularity, asked for British and French assistance in curbing it. Eager to oblige, Britain and France orchestrated a naval demonstration at Alexandria. Riots followed in the city, which the British then bombarded. ʿUrābī led the Egyptian army against the foreigners; he was defeated, which cleared the way for Britain's domination over Egypt.

Egypt, which was acquired by Britain as a protectorate in 1914, formally became an independent state in 1936, though it remained a monarchy until 1953. Arab nationalism and anti-imperialism, which were at times militant, were strong in Egypt as long as British rule, direct and indirect, continued to emanate from Cairo.

Egyptian nationalism was evident throughout the early decades of the twentieth century. Britain declared war against the Ottomans in November 1914 and a month later pronounced Egypt its protectorate. At this point nationalism was a response to local concerns; the masses suffered due to the demands of World War I on Egypt. British occupation, with the declaration of martial law, damaged nationalist expressions of the intellectuals. In 1917 Ahmad Fuʿād became the sultan. In the days following the conclusion of the Great War, three Egyptian politicians led by Saʿd Zaghlūl demanded autonomy for Egypt; they decided to take a delegation (in Arabic, *Wafd*) to England.

The British government took two actions that accelerated the spread of the nationalist movement. First it refused the delegation, and then it arrested Zaghlūl. Egypt erupted in revolt. The representatives in Britain negotiated a calm with the nationalists; Zaghlūl was released and the *Wafd* began to dominate Egyptian politics. It pressured the British to negotiate an "independence," which ended Egypt's protectorate status, but the British government reserved authority in matters of defense, foreign interests, imperial communications, and the Sudan.

Fuʿād became the king of Egypt in 1922, heading a constitutional monarchy. The *Wafd*, the most popular nationalist party led by Zaghlūl, continued its demands for true national independence. In the 1930s King Farouk (who succeeded Fuʿād) was considerably popular, but the *Wafd* rapidly lost its place as the beacon of Egyptian nationalism when its leadership elected to assist the British in the war effort.

At the end of World War II, Egyptian politics were in complete disarray. The *Wafd* almost disappeared from the scene; the torch of nationalism passed to the Muslim brotherhood, a militant organization that had mass appeal. Through the 1940s, Cairo witnessed demonstrations that at times were violent. During the same decade, when Egypt played a crucial role in the formation of the Arab League and when Israel was created, Egypt's nationalism reached new heights. Political instability became the order of the day until 1952, when waves of nationalism changed the course of Egypt's destiny.

On January 26, 1952, anti-British demonstrations that proved pivotal to the Egyptian nationalist movement broke out, leading to extensive damage to symbols of British presence in Cairo, such as hotels, a travel agency, and the airline offices. Seventeen Britons were also killed in what has since been named the Black Saturday riots.

On July 23, 1952, a coup d'état overthrew King Farouk, who was by now widely considered a puppet of the British. Planned by a group of military officers called the Free Officers' Executive Committee, the coup was almost bloodless and Farouk went into exile. The president of the Free Officers' Executive Committee, Gamal Abdul Nasser, became Egypt's new leader. About a year later, Egypt was proclaimed a republic. Nasser quickly introduced social and land reforms, ultimately developing a reform program that came to be called *Arab Socialism*. Even with Nasser in power, Egypt continued to have ties—albeit uneasy ones—with the British and the Americans. Egypt became a leader among other Arab nations, and Nasser an Arab hero. Nasser demanded international recognition of Arab dignity and the right of Arab nations to cooperate in building their own futures. However, there were several roadblocks along Egypt's path to decolonization. Western countries were not willing to offer loans without attaching unreasonable terms, leading Nasser to dub such loans "imperialism without soldiers." By 1961, however, Nasser had developed a better relationship with Britain and the United States; both nations established full diplomatic ties with Egypt. A powerful challenge to Egypt's future stability was the unresolved issue of the Occupied Territories of Palestine, also known as the state of Israel. Another challenge to Nasser's government from within Egypt's borders came from the Islamist lobby known as the Muslim Brotherhood. Nasser and his successor, Anwar Sadat, began a modernization process in Egypt that was met with resistance from Islamic conservatives, many of whom were jailed. Sadat paid with his life in 1981 when he was assassinated by Islamist extremists.

In the last years of the twentieth century there were several difficulties confronting Egypt, particularly economic ones. While oil and cotton continued to be the country's primary exports, most Egyptians—who constituted the fastest growing population in the Arab world— did not benefit from these exports. This led to increasing disaffection among some segments of the population, which turned increasingly to fundamentalist Islamist groups. The country's leader, Hosni Mubarak, attempted to improve Egypt's image in the Arab world—in recent decades Egypt had been perceived by many Arabs as being too close to the United States and Israel—while maintaining cordial relations with Western powers and Israel.

Habib Bourguiba, March 23, 1956. *Triumphant Tunisians carry nationalist leader Habib Bourguiba upon his return from Paris after the signing of the Franco-Tunisian Protocol proclaiming the independence of the protectorate. Bourguiba was elected president of independent Tunisia in 1957.* © BETTMANN/CORBIS. REPRODUCED BY PERMISSION.

IRAN

Since the beginning of the twentieth century, this Middle Eastern nation, currently known as the Islamic Republic of Iran, has undergone revolutionary political and ideological changes. The Qājār dynasty had ruled Iran from 1796 to 1925, but in 1925 Reza Khan established himself as Reza Shah of the Pahlavi dynasty; his heirs had the right of succession to the throne. European presence and influence had grown throughout the nineteenth century, and by the end of the century there was considerable popular and religious antipathy because of the lavish lifestyle of the shahs and the resources expended to keep the Europeans pleased. In the popular unrest against the shah, merchants and Shī'ite clergy (*ūlāma*) combined their efforts. During the early part of the twentieth century they were joined by the landlords as well. A simultaneous movement started that was grounded in the ideologies learned through contact with the West, one that called for democratic reforms.

With World War I the Russians withdrew from northern Iran, leaving the British as the sole European presence. Bowing to international pressures, Britain withdrew in 1921. In the same year an Iranian army officer, Reza Khan, staged a coup, taking over control of all the armed forces. As the war minister for the last Qājār ruler, Reza Khan built a strong army and brought political stability to a land that was in administrative upheaval. In 1925 he deposed the ruler, and with the approval of the ūlāmā he was crowned as the shah.

Reza Shah's central government began to assert its authority in every aspect of the people's lives. In 1935 the name of the country was changed from Persia to Iran. In the 1960s and 1970s the Shah of Iran began a concerted effort to turn Iran into a modernized and westernized state, utilizing the wealth gained from oil for this purpose. The Shah launched the "White Revolution," by which suffrage was extended to women, and limited land reforms were made. However, the wealth from the massive reserves of oil and natural gas was unequally distributed, causing internal strife and dissent on a rather large scale; opposition came most prominently from Islamic officials, particularly Ayatollah Ruhollah Khomeini. In an effort to control the dissent from within and maintain good relations with Western nations, the Shah became more repressive. At the same time, to silence his critics at home he promised that his government would observe Islamic tenets, extend support to Palestinians, and stop the export of oil to Israel and South Africa. He did not make good on those promises, and for this and a host of other reasons he was unable to prevent a revolution. In January 1979, after his own army refused to continue firing on the people, the Shah was forced to leave Iran.

Weeks after, Ayatollah Khomeini flew in from Paris and set off an Islamic revolution that led to the creation of the Islamic Republic of Iran. The Republic is a theocratic state, with an elected president and a unicameral Islamic Consultative Assembly. From 1980 to 1988 Iran and Iraq fought a bitter war after Iraqi leader Saddam Hussein sent his troops to invade Iran. Despite the vast amounts of oil production from its nationalized oilfields, Iran continues to have economic problems as it has not diversified its economy or encouraged foreign investment. Iran remains a loner among the nations of the Middle East, as it does not have cordial relations with most of its Arab neighbors and also has not maintained congenial contacts with Western nations.

IRAQ

As mentioned earlier, Iraq became a formal mandate of Britain in 1919. British presence in the region predated the formal assignation of mandate status, however, and was already a source of resentment; the mandate system only made matters worse. The system was reworked when Iraqi revolts against the British started in the 1920s; in its place was formed a provisional government controlled by the British. Arab resistance to being colonized grew apace. In June 1930 an Anglo-Iraqi treaty formally conferred independence to Iraq, with the caveat that Iraq would have "full and frank consultations with Great Britain on all matters of foreign policy." In this manner, Britain retained control over Iraq's future relations with its neighbors (of which the most important for Britain was Iran). Furthermore, with the Hashemite monarchy in power, pro-British civilians governed Iraq well into the 1950s. A military coup d'état in 1958 displaced the Hashemites, after which Iraq aligned with Egypt. As the process of decolonization took a more militant turn, Iraq suffered much unrest, until 1963 when a new socialist government formed by a coalition of nationalist army officers and members of the Ba'ath Party took power. After 1968 the Ba'athists were the sole ruling authority of Iraq. Saddam Hussein, who had played a powerful role from the wings, became the president of Iraq in 1979 and stayed in power until 2003, when he was ousted by the coalition forces of the United

States and United Kingdom. While the exports of this oil-rich country could have made for a modern state, the benefits of oil wealth did not accrue to Iraq's people. This resulted in deteriorating infrastructure, periodic rebellions on the part of Kurdish and Shi'ite populations, economic sanctions from the United Nations, and involvement in wars with Iran, Kuwait, and the United States. These problems led in turn to a depletion of Iraq's national resources, financial bankruptcy, and a dramatic drop in standards of living. In March of 2003 the United States invaded Iraq, which as of 2006 it continues to occupy, with no end to the occupation in sight, despite a violent and protracted insurgency aimed at driving it from the country.

JORDAN

Like most nations of the Arab world, Jordan seeks to preserve its ancient history alongside modern developments. Because Jordan (formerly known as Transjordan) is surrounded by numerous other, arguably more powerful, Arab states (and Israel), it has had to delicately balance its affairs and relations with other countries.

The territory that is now Jordan was formerly part of Syria and under Ottoman control. After World War I the Ottoman Empire collapsed and in 1922 the League of Nations split up the former Syria into modern-day Syria, which became a French mandate, and Palestine and Transjordan, which became British mandates. Transjordan's independence was achieved in two stages. First, in December 1922 the British, while retaining the country's mandate status, recognized its constitutional independence under Emir Abdullah, son of Sherif Hussein. It was not until March 1946 that full independence was granted; Transjordan became a constitutional monarchy and Emir Abdullah was proclaimed king. In 1949 the country was renamed the Hashemite Kingdom of Jordan, an entity Abdullah hoped would eventually include Palestine. Other Arab nations, particularly Egypt, objected to the idea of incorporating Palestine, and in 1951 Abdullah was assassinated in Jerusalem's al-Aqsā Mosque by a Palestinian youth who opposed his expansionist ideas. The throne passed to his son, who was quickly deposed because of his problems with mental illness. In 1952 British-educated Prince Hussein, then only seventeen, became the ruler. King Hussein is perhaps the best known of Jordan's rulers, because of his untiring efforts to achieve a stable balance of power in the Middle East. He was assisted in his efforts by the United States, which, in pursuance of the Eisenhower Doctrine, sought to replace Britain as the primary Western power in the region. King Hussein maintained good relations with several Arab nations as well, notably Egypt and Saudi Arabia. As a small country with limited resources,

Jordan has had to contend with chronic debt, poverty, unemployment, and water shortages. Following the Israeli occupation of the West Bank in 1967, Jordan lost almost half of its arable land, causing further economic hardship. Arab refugees from Palestine make up about a third of the population of Jordan and have been given citizenship; however, they remain largely unintegrated and discontent. Despite these problems, Jordan's educational and medical systems are among the best in the Middle East. Since 1999 the country has been led by King Abdullah II.

KUWAIT

Much like other Gulf regions, Kuwait was initially a British protectorate, in its case from 1899 until 1961. Another small country on the Persian Gulf, Kuwait derives its wealth from oil production; like Jordan, it has to carefully balance its relations with neighboring states. Sheikh Abdullāh al-Salem al-Sabāh was the first emir of independent Kuwait. It was on Kuwait's instigation that the relationship with Britain was terminated in 1961, even though the British maintained an influential presence for another decade. Kuwait had been established by members of the Bāni Utūb clan in the middle of the eighteenth century after they moved to the region from the central part of the Arabian peninsula. Almost immediately, Kuwait's independence was threatened by the military rulers of Iraq. Iraq's expansionist aims in 1961 were thwarted first by British military assistance, then firmly denied when an Arab League force from Jordan, Saudi Arabia, Sudan, and the United Arab Republic pushed Iraq's army back to its borders. In 1990 Iraq invaded Kuwait yet again, which led to an expensive war to liberate Kuwait, the Persian Gulf War, led by the United States. Today, Iraq and Kuwait continue to observe an uneasy truce. In order to rebuild its infrastructure after the war, Kuwait spent more than $160 billion.

Kuwait is an oil-rich nation nominally governed by a constitutional monarchy; in reality, the parliament is essentially an advisory body and the emirs, who come from the Al-Sabāh family, exercise exclusive authority. Like most Gulf states, Kuwait has a multicultural society as a result of its large number of expatriate workers, who in fact outnumber native Kuwaitis. The citizens of Kuwait enjoy a very high standard of living, as Kuwait's rulers spend a large percent of oil profits on public services, healthcare, education, and municipal services. Kuwait is a member of the Gulf Co-operation Council (GCC), a loose six-state alliance devoted to ensuring regional stability and promoting economic development. Kuwait's allies include Western nations as well as its Arab neighbors.

LEBANON

Lebanon is perhaps the most cosmopolitan of Middle Eastern states. As a territory mandated to the French, it had a difficult relationship with its European ruler, at best. At the onset of World War II, Lebanon demanded the end of French domination and suzerainty. In 1943, putting aside their differences, both Christian and Muslim political groups signed the National Pact, a clear declaration of Lebanon's intent to establish autonomous self-rule. Lebanese nationalists then drew up a constitution that recognized and promoted Lebanon's religious diversity. It divided up political responsibilities in the following way: a Maronite would hold the presidency, a Sunni Muslim the premiership, parliament's speaker of the house was to be a Shi'ite Muslim, the chief of staff of armed forces was to be a Druze, and the parliament's seats would be divided in a six-to-five ratio between Christians and Muslims. In a bold statement of autonomy, the new constitution eliminated all existing statutes and provisions that could potentially compromise Lebanon's independence. The French, unhappy with these actions, arrested the president and suspended the constitution. But the tide had already turned. The United States, Britain, and other Arab states came to Lebanon's support, leaving the French no option but to recognize Lebanon's sovereignty, which they did in December 1943. In the next few decades, Lebanon's stability created an environment conducive to economic growth and social progress. This initial phase, so full of promise, came to an end in 1975, however. A civil war, followed by Syrian occupation, and continued violence and attacks lasting until 1991 took their toll on Lebanon. The country's infrastructure is seriously damaged, relationships between Christians and Muslims are tense, and there has been uncontrolled growth of debt. However, Syria has since withdrawn from Lebanon.

OMAN

Of all the Middle Eastern states, Oman has the singular distinction of having achieved independence prior to the twentieth century. It was in the mid-seventeenth century that Omani tribes expelled the Portuguese from the region. Because of its favorable location, Oman grew to be a valuable trading partner with various European countries. This commerce brought Oman considerable wealth even prior to the discovery of oil. However, it is important to note that the British did exercise considerable influence in the region during the nineteenth and twentieth centuries. The British became allies of the Omani rulers in disputes over land ownership—for example, British forces assisted in reestablishing Oman's sovereignty over the Būraimī area, which Saudi Arabia also claimed—and this led to a quid-pro-quo relationship

The Signing of the Pact of the League of Arab States, March 1945. *Saudi Arabian sheikh Youssek Yassin (center), the acting minister for foreign affairs, signs the League of Arab States charter in Cairo, Egypt.* © **HULTON-DEUTSCH COLLECTION/CORBIS.** **REPRODUCED BY PERMISSION.**

between the two. Oman is ruled, as it has been for centuries, by a sultan who acts simultaneously as the head of state, prime minister, and minister of foreign affairs, finance, and defense. A consultative body called the *majlis al-shūra* assists him in making all decisions and policies. Oman has only recently decided to embark on a path of modernization. Indeed, the sultan's refusal to modernize and liberalize the country had previously been so unbending that in 1964 it prompted an uprising on the part of the Jibali hill tribespeople. The economy of the country is entirely government-controlled, and public utilities, education, trade, commerce, and employment have all been closely regulated. Sultan Qaboos bin Said Al bū Said, however, has introduced new modernizing policies and promises an open and bright future for this strategically situated nation-state.

QATAR

A tiny state whose ruler is a member of the ath-Thānī family, Qatar is currently home to the popular television station Al-Jazeera. The history of this little country is similar to that of the other countries that were British mandates, that is, from the mid-1800s to the twentieth century, Qatar was a British protectorate. In 1971 Qatar became an independent state. In 1968 Britain had announced its intention to withdraw from the Gulf region. The ath-Thānī family negotiated with the sheikhs of neighboring areas (which were soon to become the United Arab Emirates). Qatar declared independence from the British, though it continued relations with them through the formal signature of the Treaty of Friendship. In 1971 Qatar joined the Arab League and the United Nations. Qatar's economy is heavily dependent on oil and natural gas. It has been more liberal than many of its Arab neighbors, and has a close relationship with the United States even though its identity is strongly Arab. Qatar plays a small but vital role in the deliberations of the GCC countries.

SAUDI ARABIA

Saudi Arabia is arguably the leading kingdom in the Middle East. It fought for and regained its autonomy first from the Ottomans in 1902 and then from Hussein, the Sherif of Mecca, in 1924 when Ibn Saud and his Wahhābi tribesmen warriors invaded the Hejāz and captured Mecca. Prior to 1924, the British had made some unsuccessful attempts to reconcile Ibn Saud with the Hashemite Hussein. In 1933 the Ibn Saud family became the uncontested rulers of the Kingdom of Saudi Arabia; today, the country is still a hereditary monarchy and the Ibn Saud family is still in power. King Fahd bin Abd al-Az al-Saud (r. 1982–2005) transformed Saudi Arabia into the greatest economic power in the Middle East. Following Fahd's death in 2005, his half-brother Abdallah became king.

Western powers have had varying degrees of influence and presence in Saudi Arabia, but throughout the twentieth century the country was, largely, an independent, powerful, sovereign kingdom. Saudi Arabia's leading role in the Middle East, and indeed globally, is guaranteed by its reserves of oil, which are the largest in the world, its leadership in OPEC, and its spiritual and religious importance as the keeper of Mecca and Medina, the two holy cities of Islam.

SYRIA

As mentioned above, Syria was originally a part of the Ottoman Empire. In 1920 the independent Arab Kingdom of Syria was established, under Feisal, the commander of the Arab forces and the third son of the Sherif of Mecca. Feisal only ruled for a few months, however, before Syria was attacked and then occupied by French forces. In 1922 Syria became a French mandate. The French faced a series of uprisings from 1925 to 1927. Syria declared its independence in 1941 and achieved recognition as an independent republic in 1944, but didn't win real independence until 1946, when France pulled its troops out of the country. The newly independent country adopted a republican form of government; its constitution required that the president be a Muslim. Since 1963 Syria has been ruled by a succession of Ba'ath Party military governments, who have been suspicious of Western nations, leading to some tensions. Syria is a heterogeneous society with Muslims, Christians, Druze, Alawites, and a small minority of Jews. The economy of Syria is dependent on textiles and handicrafts; the infrastructure of this new country in an ancient land needs immediate improvement if the economy is to grow and provide sustainable livelihoods for Syria's many inhabitants.

TURKEY

The Republic of Turkey was proclaimed in 1923, after a War of Independence in which Turkey ousted the Greeks, who had occupied the formerly Ottoman territory between 1918 and 1922. During World War I there were a number of wartime agreements made between the European powers intended to carve up the Ottoman Empire into their spheres of influence; some of these included the Istanbul Agreements; Sykes-Picot Agreement, London Agreement, and the Balfour Declaration. Postwar conditions reopened negotiations on territorial claims. A tripartite agreement between Britain, France, and Italy would have defined Turkey as a French and Italian area of control. However, it was abrogated by the Treaty of Lausanne in 1923, as a result of resolute resistance of Mustafa Kemal whose singular aim was total independence for Turkey. In October 1923, Turkey was declared a republic, and Mustafa Kemal Atatürk was its first president. The Ottoman caliphate was abolished the following year; all members of the family were banished from the country. A republican constitution was adopted in 1924, which retained Islam as the state religion. But in 1928 the state religion clause was dropped, converting Turkey into a secular republic.

Under the leadership of Mustafa Kemal Atatürk, Turkey underwent a sweeping program of modernization based on progressive and secular ideas. Turkey is a republican parliamentary democracy and its constitution is founded on six basic principles: republicanism, Turkish nationalism, populism, secularism, statism (close state control of the economy), and revolutionism. The growth of the Turkish economy has been erratic, as the country has been disrupted by political scandals, internal strife, and conflicts with other nations. The long-range picture for Turkey's economy is, perhaps, relatively positive, however. Turkey is currently seeking alliances and trading partnerships with European nations; it hopes to become a member of the European Union (EU) on the basis that Turkey already has considerable economic trade with the EU. However, Islamist resistance at home and questions about Turkey's human rights record from abroad have stalled all EU membership discussions.

THE UNITED ARAB EMIRATES

One of the more unusual nations of the Persian Gulf, the United Arab Emirates (UAE) was under the control of the British from 1853 until 1971, when it declared its independence. During the years of the British mandate, the region was known as the Trucial States. The Trucial States were essentially sheikhdoms, that is, they each were ruled by a family whose leader was the emir (ruler).

The trucial state system was itself an emendation of an earlier arrangement. In 1820 the emirates Abu Dhabi, Dubai, Sharjah, Ajman, Ras al-Khaimah, Umm al-Quwain, and Fujairah were forced to sign agreements with Britain, which sought to protect its naval and merchant carriers in the Persian Gulf and Indian Ocean. However, even after the treaty signing, various uprisings continued to cause the British some concern. In 1853, after a truce was brokered between Britain and the emirates, the trucial state system—a relationship that allowed Britain to exert influence in the emirates' foreign affairs—was established. This arrangement was maintained until 1971, when Sheikh Zāyed bin al-Nahyān and Sheikh Rāshid bin al-Maktoum created the present independent federation. This federation has a federal government, but each of the emirates also has some of its own powers. A president, currently Sheikh Khalīfa bin Zāyed al-Nahyān since Sheikh Zāyed's death in November 2004, is elected head of the federation by the Supreme Council of Rulers, which is the highest body in the country. The cabinet's posts are divided among members of different emirates; the current minister for economy is a woman, Sheikhā Lubnā al Qasimi.

The UAE is a progressive and modern Islamic nation. Its remarkable features include a high standard of living, modern infrastructure and housing, a diversified economy, a stress on education, good healthcare, public utilities, and amicable relationships with both Western nations and the UAE's Arab neighbors. The UAE is perhaps the most multicultural society in the Middle East, which has led to its nickname, "the crossroads of continents."

CONCLUSION

The various peoples and nations of the Middle East have all experienced different decolonization and independence processes. While Islam is a common factor that binds together these peoples and nations, there are many regional cultural differences as well. Each of these nations follows different paths toward development, modernization, social change, and economic growth. The issue of Occupied Palestine remains a contentious and unresolved matter that has made lasting peace in the region impossible. Arab nations are bound together by the politics of Arab identity, but this can be a nebulous connection at times. For their part, Iran and Turkey have national identities that are remarkably different from those of Arab nations. As far as relations between the Middle East and the rest of the world are concerned, the countries and peoples of the region see themselves as part of a larger whole, yet wish to remain independent and to develop at their own pace and in their own way.

SEE ALSO *Anticolonialism, Middle East and North Africa; British Colonialism, Middle East; French Colonialism, Middle East; Secular Nationalisms, Middle East.*

BIBLIOGRAPHY

Gettleman, Marvin E. and Stuart Schaar, eds. *The Middle East and Islamic World Reader.* New York: Grove Press, 2003.

Hourani, Albert, Philip S. Khoury, and Mary C. Wilson. *The Modern Middle East.* Rev. ed. London: Tauris, 2004.

McCoy, Lisa. *Modern Middle East Nations and Their Strategic Place in the World: Facts and Figures about the Middle East.* Stockton, NJ: Mason Crest, 2004.

Ovendale, Ritchie. *The Middle East since 1914.* 2nd ed. New York: Addison, Wesley, Longman, 1998.

Sayyid-Marsot, Afaf Lutfi al-. *A Short History of Modern Egypt.* Cambridge, U.K.: Cambridge University Press, 1985.

Sicker, Martin. *The Middle East in the Twentieth Century.* Westport, CT: Praeger, 2001.

Jyoti K. Grewal

INDIA, IMPERIAL

British influence in India came to a head with the transfer of power from the English East India Company (EIC) into the hands of the British government in 1773 as the British Government extended political, social, and economic influence in the region. Thus began the period referred to as the "British Raj" when the government created a British state on the Indian subcontinent by subjugating the princes of smaller states around the region.

India was known as "the jewel in the crown" of the British Empire because of its rich natural resources and long-established trading posts. Although Queen Victoria (1819–1901) promised equality to India according to British law, the circumstances leading up to the Indian Revolt of 1857 (the Sepoy Rebellion) brought to the foreground a distrust of the British in the Indian consciousness.

Prior to the end of EIC rule, Indian industrialists were required to pay extremely high taxes and to sell their goods only to the EIC at low fixed prices. British manufacturers, beneficiaries of the Industrial Revolution, began to produce and export textiles for the vast Indian market. Indian manufacturers, excessively taxed and regulated, were unable to compete with the new industries in Manchester and Birmingham and were squeezed out of business. By 1867 India imported £21 million (British pounds) of goods from Britain (by comparison, Australia imported £8 million that same year). The collapse of the Indian middle class and the increasing unemployment of skilled artisans and textile workers spread discontent among more and more Indians. New British institutions for administration and planning were met with suspicion by many Indians as further means of controlling and subverting the native social order. The

James Andrew Broun Ramsay, the Marquis of Dalhousie.
The British statesman and governor-general of India from 1847 to 1856, in an engraving after a painting (ca. 1847) by J. W. Gordon. LIBRARY OF CONGRESS.

isolation of peasants in their already isolated rural communities, in addition to the British ignoring the concerns of Indian soldiers who served them, fostered an environment conducive to mass resistance.

The 1857 revolt of Indian soldiers known as *sepoys* is referred to as the First War of Indian Independence in South Asia because it marked the solidification of resentment against British socioeconomic policies. The rebellion was sparked when the Indian soldiers, who were vegetarians by religion, objected to the use of animal fat to grease the shells of gun cartridges. The issues surrounding the gun cartridges were one example of how *sepoys* felt the British were ignoring Muslim or Hindu custom. This, in addition to poor pay and the rise of British presence against local princes, increased the tension between the two groups. Through a series of political maneuverings in which the British obtained the territories of princes who did not have male heirs, the British Crown solidified its power and presence in the subcontinent. The harsh policies of Governor-General James Ramsay Dalhousie (1812–1860) would prove symptomatic of many of the viceroys and British authorities intervening in India. Their heavy-handed tactics

resulted in violence, which would spark a nationalist consciousness among Indians and lead to the promotion of self-governance.

Native states and territories were quickly overcome by the British strategies to divide and rule. In the case of the Mughal Empire, the British strategically pitted local interests against one another, and ensured that princes were focused on their particular provinces rather than larger regional influences. In the state of Mysore, for example, the British capitalized on internal civil strife to gain complete control. The reduction of provinces into British territories rankled Indian nationalists, who felt that many European practices, including Christianity, were eroding traditional Indian culture. The British wrote laws to counter cultural practices that were seen as Westernizing movements against Indian culture. Child marriage, sati, and female infanticide were all practices with which the British became intrusive social reformers, which in turn increased the resentment against imperial presence and fears of cultural erosion.

The introduction of the Indian Civil Service (1886) was a strategy by the British to ensure domination through control of those serving in political and professional positions in India. The ICS was also a means of managing the vast empire. The government in Calcutta housed the viceroy and governor-generals, who supervised local officials. The most coveted positions, salaries, and opportunities were reserved for British-born officials, causing many to view India as a place to establish and further their careers. Ironically, it was a former member of the Indian civil service, the Scotsman Allan Octavian Hume (1829–1912), who in 1885 established the Indian National Congress, a political party that led the movement for independence.

By 1861, small measures ensured that Indians gained a presence in the electoral process, as well as access to the viceroy. These changes would prove significant when the question of independence was addressed directly. However, in 1877 Queen Victoria was named empress of India, underscoring British reluctance to entirely relinquish control of India. The Morley-Minto Reforms, also known as the Government of India Act of 1909, granted Indians the right to fill elected positions in government. Although few Indians were elected, the opportunity to be voted into office and the ability to influence the legislative process helped the Indian population establish a level of comfort with parliamentary action.

Education also proved to be a key element in preparing a class of bureaucrats and officials to govern the country. Government-established colleges and universities allowed the upper-middle class access to European thought and culture. Through the education and promotion of a native class of bureaucrats, the impression that

The Viceroy of India with Officials. *Thomas George Baring, Earl of Northbrook (center front) and viceroy of India, poses with British and Indian officials at Simla, circa 1875.* **HULTON ARCHIVE/GETTY IMAGES. REPRODUCED BY PERMISSION.**

sovereignty would eventually be granted became commonplace among Indians, even though most British rejected this notion. Increasingly at the local level the number of Indians interested in politics exceeded that of the officially selected representatives, but without an eye for the interplay between the elite upper-class elected officials and the much larger number of constituents, the British Raj was not interested in representation in Indian politics. Decisions continued to be made in the London-based Parliament and through British-appointed viceroys in order to ensure the interests of the Crown over that of the population.

The partition of Bengal, which lasted from 1905 to 1911, established two important precedents that would become central in India's struggle for freedom. First, the establishment of East Bengal was opposed by much of the population and helped arouse a collective national consciousness. Second, the Muslim majority that was created in East Bengal would later mimic the division within the independence movement, eventually causing many to advocate the creation of a separate Muslim state.

Britain granted more concessions when India proved to be a valuable contributor to Britain's effort during World War I (1914–1918). As the war continued, nationalist sentiment within India grew. Indian soldiers, specifically Sikhs and Gurkhas, distinguished themselves in service during the war, and they expected the

furtherance of their requests for autonomy after the war ended. Assurances were given with the Montagu Declaration (1917) and later in the Montagu-Chelmsford Report (1918) that Indian self-rule was a possibility.

With the Government of India Act of 1919, Indians were legally incorporated into every aspect of government at the provincial level. These partial concessions continued to encourage confidence among Indians in their ability to rule themselves. Yet their aspirations remained unfulfilled because the viceroy and other British officials were still beholden only to London, a situation that would continue to rankle until the fight for freedom began in earnest.

The passing of the Rowlett Act in 1919 ensured that the British could deal with freedom fighters as they saw fit, a development that proved pivotal in generating nationalist sentiment. In April 1919, 379 people were killed and 1,200 injured when police fired 1,650 rounds of ammunition into an unarmed crowd of approximately ten thousand people who had gathered in Amritsar, a park in Jalianwala Bagh, to peaceably protest the Rowlett Act. The event became a symbol for the nation of British willingness to abuse power and of the injustice of colonial rule.

The 1930s saw much debate in England in both the houses of Parliament over the status of India and its potential liberation; formal meetings were held from 1930 to 1932 to discuss the issue of Indian self-rule. These meetings comprised the three roundtables called by the British government to examine the formation of an Indian constitution. The first, which began in 1930, had 73 representatives from all states and parties but for the Indian National Congress party, which was in the midst of the civil disobedience movement. The second roundtable had Ghandi as the representative of the Congress party but no consensus was reached on any of the issues. The third roundtable in 1932 was the least successful and shortest; neither the British Labour party nor the Indian National Congress attended. The outcome of the three conferences, however, resulted in the Government of India Act of 1935. This act legalized creation of provincial governments where locals created policies. Additionally Indians were allowed to be elected to national legislative offices in Delhi. This was the last pre-independence act of the British government. With its passing India was being prepared for dominion rule, which was thought to satisfy Indians as well as the conservatives in Britain.

Jawaharlal Nehru (1889–1964) and Mohandas Gandhi (1869–1948) emerged as the first elected leaders in 1937. Muhammad Ali Jinnah (1876–1948), who would later provide leadership for the Muslim minority in the pursuit of a sovereign Muslim state, also emerged at this time. The rise of nationalism and the road to independence occurred as the British attempted to exert more power and influence over the subcontinent, while increasingly depending upon Indians for commerce, trade, and the army.

SEE ALSO *Indian Revolt of 1857; Sepoy.*

BIBLIOGRAPHY

Blyth, Robert J. *The Empire of the Raj: India, Eastern Africa, and the Middle East, 1858–1947.* Basingstoke, U.K., and New York: Palgrave Macmillan, 2003.

Buettner, Elizabeth. *Empire Families: Britons and Late Imperial India.* Oxford and New York: Oxford University Press, 2004.

Chandavarkar, Rajnarayan. *Imperial Power and Popular Politics: Class Resistance and the State in India, c. 1850–1950.* New York: Cambridge University Press, 1998.

Mohanalakshmi Rajakumar

INDIAN ARMY

The British Indian Army was one of the strongest armed forces in nineteenth-century Asia. Its origins lay in the consolidation of three forces—the Bengal, Bombay, and Madras Armies—created in the eighteenth century, when the English East India Company recruited soldiers to fight wars against local powers. The Bengal Army was among the first to coalesce into an impressive unit, with recruits coming mostly from Awadh (present-day Uttar Pradesh), the great nursery for the armies of British India. The concentration of Hindu upper-caste recruits from this area invested the Bengal Native Army with a sense of fraternity and it was not entirely coincidental that the Bengal Army played such a key role in the Revolt of 1857.

The Indian troops in the English East India Company's service were almost entirely infantrymen and were commanded almost exclusively by European officers. Each presidency, or territorial unit corresponding to each of the English East India Company's headquarters, had a number of European units—infantry and gunners who represented the core of its military strength. Between 1763 and 1805, the increase in the number of troops was substantial—the Bengal army grew from 6,680 to 64,000 men, the Madras army from 9,000 to 64,000, and the Bombay army from 2,550 to 26,500. Each presidency army had a commanding officer, and the officer who commanded the Bengal army was the commander in chief.

In terms of the command structure, what distinguished the Indian army throughout the eighteenth and early-nineteenth centuries was that the officer corps remained exclusively European. In 1895, the three armies were amalgamated and reorganized. The basic chain of command started with the European captain at the top, followed by subaltern sergeant majors (also European), under whom were *subedars, jamedars,* and *havildar-naiks (recruiting agents).* The sepoys (native soldiers) in each battalion were divided into ten companies that comprised one *subedar,* three *jamedars,* four *naiks,* two drummers, one trumpeter, and seventy sepoys. The formation of sepoys into regular battalions represented the first serious attempt to introduce a European-style organization in the sepoy army. The formation of sepoy battalions diluted the authority of the sepoy leaders, for the *subedar* was now subject to the command structure of the battalion. Whereas earlier the *subedar* had commanded an independent company, now his company became one among nine or ten that made up a battalion.

The British army for the greater part of the eighteenth century and the first quarter of the nineteenth century fought against indigenous powers—Awadh, Mysore, Marthas, and subsequently the Sikhs of the Punjab. In all of these encounters, the sepoys bore the brunt of casualties and their performance was by the end of the eighteenth century above reproach, as they learned to handle formidable opposition. Subsequently, however, the army was geared to launch expeditions along the frontiers against the Afghans as well as the Burmese, leading to the Burmese wars of 1825 to 1826 and the British Afghan Wars of 1838 to 1842. In the course of the Burmese campaigns, Indian troops suffered more than 15,000 fatalities and it was only their sheer superiority in numbers that enabled the British to sustain the campaign through two successive rainy seasons. The Afghan wars, on the other hand, were disastrous, forcing the British to stage tactical retreats.

It was the combination of these distant expeditions with the defective organization of the army that produced deep-seated resentment among its ranks long before the great revolt of 1857. The poor quality of the army's regimental subalterns, and the incompetence and senility of its senior officers, coupled with the constant poaching from regiments of talented officers for general staff and political posts, severely impaired its leadership. Added to this was the discontent and indiscipline among its native ranks, as a result of the system of promotion by seniority and of the pressures of distant and hazardous expeditions without adequate compensation in the form of increased pay or prestigious rank.

The rebellion of 1857 began within the sepoys of the British Army. By this time, the widespread resentment, largely concentrated in Awadh, interfaced with larger rural dissatisfaction that British expansion and rule engendered. The modernizing imperatives of British rule produced social fears of losing caste and religion. Consequently, many of the new institutions associated with the modernizing imperatives of empire-law courts, government offices, and Christian missionaries were targeted for attack.

The core area of the mutiny was the area surrounded by Delhi in the west and Ghazipur in the east, with the Jamuna acting as the southern boundary, where native regiments were stationed in Kanpur, Meerut, and Delhi. Other areas where native regiments mutinied were clustered around this core in central India. The mutinies started in Meerat on May 10, 1857, and thereafter spread within a couple of months to Delhi, Aligrah, Etawah, and Lucknow, where they interfaced with rural insurrection. Groups whose interests had been adversely affected by the New British Revenue Settlements joined the revolt providing leadership to the sepoys.

The Revolt of 1857 failed, but not without threatening the foundations of British rule in India. The British Empire faced its first formidable challenge, in that the authorities had to consider army reorganization in a manner that would ensure loyal and active service to the British Empire. Broadly speaking, three perspectives emerged. The first advocated a heterogeneous pattern of recruitment that would cut across all sections of society. The second position stressed the need to eliminate certain castes and classes altogether and to even consider

recruiting Christians from Southeast Asia and Latin America. A third intermediate position argued that no class on principle should be excluded and that an attempt should be made to balance different ethnic groups. The third position seems to have prevailed and British recruitment policy in the 1860s was to divide the Indian army into four main elements, which were recruited from different areas. The army was composed of mixed groups and castes but not so consciously as to prevent the development of pan-Indian nationalism. The military commissions more than anything else, evaded the task of specifying in detail the composition of the army and concentrated more on organizational details.

Until the Burma War of 1887 to 1889, the Indian Army was seen primarily as an instrument of internal security. As a result, official policy following the recommendations of the Peel Commission of 1859, and subsequently of the Eden Commission of 1879, was informed by the sole consideration of making the army reliable. This meant that distinctive regiments were to be created and that recruitment was to be restricted to a specific territory. It was only after the Burmese wars and with the growing possibility of external conflicts that new notions of military security took precedence over considerations of balance and of the social composition of the military.

In 1895 the Army was thoroughly reorganized. In line with contemporary military thinking, four regional commands were created, each under a Lieutenant General: these were Punjab, west of the Yamuna River, commanding the Frontier Force as well; a truncated Bengal command; Madras (with Burma); and Bombay with Sind, Quetta, and an extension in Aden.

In 1902 to 1903 Lord Kitchener streamlined the system, making changes that finally resulted in the reforms of 1908 to 1909. He eliminated the military member of council interposed between the commander in chief and the political executive. What emerged from this decade-long turmoil was an expanded army headquarters, with a general staff branch and a director-general ordnance branch being added to the existing adjutant general and quartermaster general branches. Two territorial commands were created—the Northern and Southern—and the field army was subdivided into a field force and a group of internal security troops, totaling 152,000 (nine divisions and eight cavalry brigades) and 82,000, respectively.

Alongside this reorganization, there were major changes in recruitment patterns. Caste once more became an organizing principle in recruitment; the distinction between class regiments and class company regiments became a factor. Class regiments were composed entirely of the same ethnic or caste group, while class company regiments were mixed. Promotion of Indians to commissioned posts varied in the two types of regiments; in class regiments, promotion was based on a general seniority list encompassing all companies, but in class company regiments, promotion was made from the rolls of the particular class in which a vacancy occurred. No Indian officer of one class was allowed to command troops of another; this guaranteed that the link between a sepoy and his British commander would be an Indian commissioned officer of the same class as the sepoy was.

The second feature was the growing presence in the army of recruits from the Punjab. From 1892 to 1914, Punjabi troops increased rapidly in number, edging out other groups like Mahars, Brahmins, Gujars, and Ahirs. The emphasis was on homogeneity; particular units not only recruited, for example, solely Punjabi Muslims or Rajputs, but also recruited them only from a particular clan. This shift in recruitment is generally explained in terms of the resurgent *martial race* ideology—the belief that Indians from certain regions were more inherently militaristic—that held sway over certain sections of the policy-making class.

The British Indian Army, while possessing a highly competent officer corps, was adequate only for brief probing expeditions and as a line of defense for internal security. Its vulnerability was tied up with British recruiting procedures and with the fact that the high command was exclusively British, which meant that troops under their command were often more loyal to regional elites than to them. Further, the system was not receptive to technological innovations.

The Indian Army's combat strength at the commencement of World War I was 155,423, and swelled to 573,484 by the time the war neared its completion. During World War I the weakness of the Indian army came to the surface. The war effort exposed the obsolete state of technology and equipment as well as the narrowness of the recruitment base, and forced the authorities to try new classes as recruits. This new policy entered the debates that followed in nationalist circles about the need to Indianize the army. In 1919 to 1920, ten vacancies were reserved for "suitable" Indians at the Royal Military Academy, Sandhurst. Indian political demands also impelled the British to set up the Indian Military Academy at Dehra Dun on October 1, 1932. World War II exposed the weakness of the army even more acutely; not a single unit of the Indian Army was mechanized to respectable standards. Motorization was selective, and the availability of standard and updated weapons was far from satisfactory. The Indian Army's contribution to the war effort came in the form of personnel, and the number of men that India gave to the Allied cause was impressive. The Army had 189,000 soldiers in its ranks in 1939, a number that rose to 2,644,323 in 1945, when the army was at peak strength.

SEE ALSO *Empire, British; India, Imperial; Indian Revolt of 1857.*

BIBLIOGRAPHY

Barat, Amiya. *The Bengal Native Infantry: Its Organisation and Discipline, 1796–1852.* Calcutta: K. L. Mukhopadhyay, 1962.

Omissi, David. *The Sepoy and the Raj: The Indian Army, 1860–1940.* Houndsmills, U.K.: Macmillan, 1994.

Ray, Kaushik. "Recruitment Doctrines of the Colonial Indian Army: 1859–1913." *Indian Economic and Social History Review* 34, no. 3 (1997): 321–354.

Wickremesekera, Channa. *"Best Black Troops in the World": British Perceptions and the Making of the Sepoy, 1746–1805.* New Delhi: Manohar, 2002.

Lakshmi Subramanian

INDIAN NATIONAL MOVEMENT

India's movement toward independence occurred in stages prompted by the inflexibility of the British and, in many instances, their violent responses to peaceful protests. Many attribute the Indian Revolt of 1857 (known by the British as the Sepoy Mutiny) as the first battle in the struggle for Indian independence.

The 1857 Indian Revolt revealed the miscalculations of the British in understanding the social and cultural issues important to Indians. Indian soldiers called *sepoys* (from the Hindi *sipahi*) grew increasingly uncomfortable with the British encroachment on India's states and provinces as the English East India Company expanded its influence in the region. In addition, poor wages and harsh policies made nationals increasingly tired of the British presence in India.

Moreover, many of army's regulations were perceived by Indians as attempts to Christianize the Hindu, Sikh, and Muslim sepoys. Tensions came to a head when the British began using animal fat (from pigs and cows) to coat cartridge shells. Although steps were taken to correct the situation, distrust grew between the sepoys, who were vegetarians by religion, and the British, culminating in 1857 in the sepoy revolt.

In 1885, the Indian National Union was formed, which became the Indian National Congress and had as its goal the moderate position of seeing more locals in political representation. The Indian National Congress (INC) was created to help ease the tensions in the British relationship with Indians after the Sepoy Mutiny. In the beginning, the INC did not contradict British rule, but

Indian National Congress Meeting, 1922. *Mohandas Gandhi (center, with white hat) meets with members of the Indian National Congress in 1922, shortly before Gandhi was taken into custody by the British.* © BETTMANN/CORBIS. REPRODUCED BY PERMISSION.

in the face of increasingly egregious acts by the government, the INC came to identify with the independence movement. The INC would dominate Indian politics and house many of the early leaders of the independence movement including Gopal Krishna Gokhale, leading those in favor of dominion status and Bal Gangadhar Tilak, leading those who saw self rule as the only option. Throughout the impendence movement leaders emerged from among the Congress' membership including Mahatma Ghandi, the leader of the non-violence movement, as well as Jawaharlal Nehru, the first prime minister of the new nation.

The INC is the oldest political party in India. Originally the organization was made up of upper middle-class, often Western-educated men, who represented a political class of Indian civil servants invested in the interests of India. Although the first female prime minister of India, Indira Ghandi (1917–1984), came from the Congress party, women's participation in the independence movement was not in formal party membership but rather by support of campaigns led by the party such as the move to make and wear homespun cloth rather than buying imported fabric. The Indian National Congress began to clamor against British economic

policies and demand independence in exchange for support of the British during both World Wars. Prior to entering World War II (1939–1945), the Congress attempted to negotiate postwar independence as precursor to Indian involvement. They were denied, the party outlawed, and its members jailed. After World War II the demand for self rule became especially strong because the prospect of dominion status no longer appealed to those who thought India had earned the right to self rule by troop support in both international wars.

Two factions developed within the INC that were defined by their stance on British rule in India: a moderate one that hoped to attain rights through negotiation and talks, and a revolutionary one in favor of agitating for rights through physical, and if necessary, armed resistance. The split deepened over time as the revolutionary faction led by Subhash Chandra Bose (1897–1945), one of the leaders of the leftist wing of the Congress party and president of the Congress from 1938–1939, argued that military action was the only way to ensure freedom. The other faction, led by future Indian Prime Minister Jawaharlal Nehru (1889–1964), felt that socialism was a necessary element in the forward movement of a national identity. Bose wanted the INC to push for immediate

Women's Protest in Bombay, 1930. *Independence-minded Indian women argue with police during a protest over the right to hold a meeting of the Indian National Congress on the Esplanade Maidan in Bombay.* © HULTON-DEUTSCH COLLECTION/CORBIS. REPRODUCED BY PERMISSION.

British withdrawal from India, an idea opposed by moderates within the organization. His insistence on extreme measures resulted in his stepping down from office and a ban on his further election. Bose later organized a countermovement in the Indian army when, without consulting Indian leaders, the British declared India to be a warring state during World War II.

The INC served as a clearinghouse for all who supported independence from Britain before various splinter groups and factions formed. Although the INC was founded to include all Indians, the organization came to be seen as representative of Hindu rights, and Muslim Indians broke away to establish a new political organization, the All India Muslim League, in 1906. In later independence discussions, the fears of underrepresentation by Muslims led to pleas to protect Muslim rights, and eventually to create the nation of Pakistan.

The split in the INC was eased under the influence of Mohandas Karamchand Gandhi (1869–1948) in 1920 when he became party leader. Gandhi, a lawyer by training, had been educated in London and had worked in

South Africa, where he used nonviolence and noncooperation strategies to resist British rule. The British refusal to acknowledge him as a full citizen in South Africa contributed to the development of an anticolonial identity in Gandhi before his return to India in 1914. In a climate steeped in tradition, spirituality, and symbolism, Gandhi was an ideal figure around whom the political drive toward independence could congeal.

In the Indian National Congress, Gandhi turned to his previous experience in South Africa to establish the ground rules for the movement toward Indian independence. Other important INC figures included Jawaharlal Nehru, who became India's first prime minister in 1947 and served in that office for eighteen years. Nehru's father, Motilal Nehru (1861–1931), also became a leader in the INC and the independence movement after he was educated in England and returned to India to practice law.

The push for independence occurred in three interconnected stages: the noncooperative movement, the civil disobedience movement, and finally the "Quit India" movement. None of these stages were rigidly defined; they naturally flowed into one another as a result of contemporary events. The foundational principles of the noncooperative movement included resisting the British by not buying imported goods, refusing to pay taxes, and not working for the British, rather than violence as a means of gaining independence.

A major turning point occurred in March 1930 with the Dandi March, which sparked the civil disobedience movement. In what many consider a stroke of political savvy, Gandhi chose the British taxes and regulations on salt as the issue around which to stage a protest. Every Indian, whether aristocrat or peasant, knew the value of salt, which was used as a preservative. Gandhi's highlighting of the British monopoly on salt production helped showcase the issue of native choice in daily life. In a strategic move, Gandhi and seventy-eight supporters undertook a twenty-three-day journey by foot to Dandi, a coastal region where salt was abundant. Upon their arrival, Gandhi made natural salt, thus violating the British law that only imported salt could be used or purchased. Illegal salt was being made all over the country, and many Indians, including Gandhi, were being imprisoned for doing so. Salt thus became a symbol for the injustice and oppression of the British Empire. After the Dandi March, the entire nation became more aware of the fight for sovereignty from British rule.

In 1942 Gandhi announced the "Quit India" campaign. Backed by the INC, all thoughts turned toward eliminating the British presence in India and establishing self-governance. The issuance of the declaration resulted in the British government outlawing the Indian National Congress and in the subsequent arrests of INC leaders, including Gandhi. The public fray between the INC and the British brought the Quit India campaign into prominence across the country, and resistance grew.

When the British conceded independence to India, it came with such swiftness that many of the unresolved tensions were swept aside, only to come bursting forth later. Lord Louis Mountbatten (1900–1979), the last viceroy of British India, who was in good standing with Nehru, granted the demands of the Muslim League to create a separate state, Pakistan, for Muslims. Increasingly uncomfortable in Hindu-dominated India, many in the Muslim League had agitated for the formation of a separate Muslim state. At the time of his assassination in 1948, Gandhi opposed the partitioning of India, but the speed of independence overshadowed such concerns. Violence ensued as Hindus attempted to cross newly created borders into India, while Muslims fled to Pakistan, resulting in many deaths and clouding India's long-awaited freedom from the British Raj.

SEE ALSO *Empire, British; India, Imperial; Indian Army; Indian Revolt of 1857; Sepoy.*

BIBLIOGRAPHY

Chandra, Bipan. *India's Struggle for Independence, 1857–1947.* New Delhi: Viking, 1988.

Coward, Harold, ed. *Indian Critiques of Gandhi.* Albany: State University of New York Press, 2003.

Low, D. A., ed. *Congress and the Raj: Facets of the Indian Struggle, 1917–47.* London: Heinemann, 1977; 2nd ed., New Delhi and Oxford: Oxford University Press, 2004.

Moore, Robin James. *The Crisis of Indian Unity, 1917–1940.* Oxford: Clarendon Press, 1974.

Mohanalakshmi Rajakumar

INDIAN OCEAN TRADE

Trade in the Indian Ocean dates back to the time of classical antiquity, if not earlier. Though there are archaeological records attesting to the fact that Indian Ocean societies had merchants shuttling between them before the time of Christ, one of the first reliable written records is the Periplus of the Erythrean Sea, a geographic primer written by a Greek in Egypt in the first century C.E. Arab geographers wrote copiously about trade movements in the precolonial age, and Ibn Battuta, a Moroccan jurist, left a detailed record of his own Indian Ocean wanderings on the wings of regional commerce in the early fourteenth century. By the early fifteenth century, a Chinese traveler, Zheng He, was also traversing this ocean, only at the head of a huge treasure fleet sent by a curious Ming emperor, Zheng. He brought a giraffe from East Africa back to China on one of his ships; this augured the more concerted and rigorous economic exchanges that would commence with the dawn of the colonial age in the following century.

SOUTHEAST ASIA

The Southeast Asian littoral of the Indian Ocean underwent a wide variety of transitions during and after the sixteenth century that were directly caused by the collision of European and indigenous worlds. The ongoing results of this interface, however, were gradual in nature: hegemony did not arrive with the first Portuguese ships at Melaka in 1511, nor did European political and commercial power begin to truly build in much of the region until nearly 350 years later. Set against this mosaic of intrusion were local patterns of action, agency, and response. Heightened royal absolutism in the early years of contact, marked by indigenous territorial expansion, administrative centralization, and the commercial monopolies of ruling classes, gradually gave way to subsumation and finally incorporation as the European presence

The First English Trading Station in India. *This illustration from the 1727 edition of* The Voyages of Mandelslo *by Johann Albrecht von Mandelslo shows the first English trading station in India, established at Surat in 1613.* © **BETTMANN/CORBIS. REPRODUCED BY PERMISSION.**

solidified. Yet what remains to be explained in the unfolding of these processes is the actual place of Western trade as a stimulus for systemic historical change. What were the long-term results of contact, from economic, political, and modes-of-production vantages?

In the early modern age, Southeast Asia's population of 20 million traded heavily amongst themselves, mostly in the larger bulk items of commerce such as rice, dried fish, and salt. Foreign goods that entered the nexus of trade in the early European contact period fit into local systems of culture and exchange, with alcohol circulating alongside native *arrack,* tobacco alongside betel, and with Chinese porcelain being incorporated into existing dowry and burial rituals throughout much of Southeast Asia. The arrival of European ships accelerated the incorporation of a range of other goods into the region, however, such as textiles and metals.

Most pre–industrial age households in Southeast Asia aimed to be at least partially self-sufficient in cloth

production, but with increased shipments of textiles from the Coromandel coasts of Southeastern India (via East India Company and country-trade ships) and still higher exports later from British India, foreign cloth became the largest item of luxury expenditure in the region. This was generally true from Sumatra to what is now Malaysia, from Siam up into Burma. Extensive cloth imports had enormous repercussions on Southeast Asian textile industries, which on the much smaller village-scale could produce only on commissioned orders as hedges against inadequate food supply.

The increased importation of metals also brought about widespread change, as substances like iron and bronze—used first for war, and second for agriculture—penetrated local communities in large quantities for the first time. Such a trade, however, was also a double-edged sword for Europeans: fantastic in its potential for profit, but also deadly if turned against Westerners themselves. This indeed eventually happened throughout Southeast

Asia's Indian Ocean rim: in Burma (in the 1820s, 1850s, and 1880s), on the Malay Peninsula throughout the nineteenth century, and particularly in Sumatra, as the Dutch began their slow crawl up that enormous island culminating in the Aceh War of 1873. Commerce could phase into resistance in this way, and this certainly happened in parts of Southeast Asia throughout the nineteenth century.

THE INDIAN SUBCONTINENT

In South Asia, many of these patterns were echoed and were also different at the same time. The sixteenth century, which older historiographical literature has portrayed as a cataclysmic epoch of Portuguese arrival (with the consequent fire and sword), is in modern times interpreted by scholars to have been much less than that. Though the Iberians were certainly aggressive after appearing off the coasts of Western India in 1498, overall patterns of India's trade and the mechanisms therein did not universally change during this century. While the Portuguese erected their *cartaz* (pass) system the cost to local traders was sometimes minimal. While many Indians did pay the passage fees, those in areas under weaker Portuguese surveillance and policing simply avoided it altogether. The Zamorins of Calicut and the Rajas of Cochin, Cannanore, and Quilon (all on the Malabar coast), for example, continued to trade effectively, incorporating themselves under the umbrella of Portuguese protection when they had to, but they also ignored the Portuguese at other times and in other places.

It was only with the arrival of the seventeenth century, and the far more organized Dutch and British concerns, that the balance of Indian commerce began to change. Yet even here such change often benefited Indian trade instead of crippling it, as *banians* and other brokers took advantage of new opportunities. Though historians need to be mindful of the available sources, the records actually seem to indicate that the arrival of Northern Europeans initially served as a boon for indigenous commerce, providing new capital, shipping, navigational technology, and marketing, all for Indians to use. Thus Gujarati trade extended across the Indian Ocean as far away as Manila in the 1660s, using British ships and navigation routes while Gujarati capital funded the voyages. The diversity of trade and its actors stood out in this period—by region, religion, and linguistic group—as well as by occupation, as when English pilots sailed Tamil and Bengali ships.

The eighteenth century pushed change in a new direction, which from the standpoint of Indian choices was a negative one. Although European trade did not initially hurt most Indian merchants, Indian shippers suffered a different fate: as more and more of the carrying trade was monopolized by foreign vessels, India's fleets dwindled, shrinking in competition with the new so-called "country traders." It was this special-interest bloc, diverse in its own right, that pushed the once grand Gujarati fleets off the international trade routes, and into the more minor, subsidiary role of small coastal carriers. Yet it was also these Anglo/Indian country traders—some of whom worked for the East India Company, others of whom were free agents—who began to radically alter what the great Indian historian Ashin Das Gupta has called the "strange Mughal mix of despotism, traditional rights, and equally-traditional freedoms" that was the prevailing system of trade and production in the rural Indian countryside. This involved a system of relationships that transited from port merchants to brokers, from subbrokers to headmen, and from weavers to growers throughout rural South Asia. The Industrial Revolution, with its Dickensian factories and the new importance of steam-powered engines, brought the Indian Ocean closer to Europe than it had ever been before. The numbers and carrying capacities of European ships heading south to this arena to trade rose year after year. By the nineteenth century, this entire system was under stress by the tectonic pressures of Immanel Wallerstein's burgeoning world system.

THE EAST AFRICAN LITTORAL

East Africa's coast was an important site of growing Western influence on Indian Ocean trade and production during the colonial age. Here, the salient issues were analogous to patterns elsewhere along the Indian Ocean Rim: change in the coastal population centers such as Kilwa, Mombasa, Malindi, and Mogadishu; the incorporation of increasingly important hinterlands; and the movements of local peoples, whether these were merchants, *banians,* or slaves.

Several major trends can be identified as being of primary importance among these phenomena for the East African case, however. Perhaps first and foremost was the rise of Zanzibar, which became an Omani outpost at the end of the seventeenth century and gradually developed into a commercial empire on its own accord. This vault to prominence was achieved by mercantilist means, but the Zanzibari "empire," once established, underwent fundamental structural changes over the course of the eighteenth and nineteenth centuries. This process, as related both by indigenous accounts such as the Ancient History of Dar es-Salaam, and period English documents, was inherently linked to Zanzibar's relations with British India. In greater perspective, these developments were also tied to the evolving world of global capitalism in general, and to the changing institution of slavery in particular.

FORT JESUS

In 1593 the Portuguese began construction of Fort Jesus to guard the Old Port of Mombasa, Kenya, a critical outpost securing their trade route to India and their territories in East Africa. Built on the Island of Mombasa, Fort Jesus was designed by the Italian architect Jao Batisto Cairato and, when viewed from the air, resembles the shape of a man. Now housing a museum, the fort is considered one of the finest remaining examples of Portuguese colonial fortifications. Prior to Fort Jesus, the Portuguese based their East African coastal operations at Malindi, north of Mombasa. Following several attacks by the Turks, however, the Portuguese decided to move their primary coastal trading center south to Mombasa Island, which provided a better natural defense. While the site proved ideal for a fortress, control of Fort Jesus nonetheless changed hands nine times between 1631 and 1875, with the Portuguese and various Arab sultans vying for control. In 1875 the British took control of the fort; they kept possession of the outpost, which they used as a prison, until Kenyan independence in 1963.

The long, extended coastline of East Africa was an arena of constant warfare and turmoil in the sixteenth and seventeenth centuries. More than elsewhere along the rim of the Indian Ocean, the Portuguese presence here proved to be not only fundamentally destabilizing, but part of a century-long pattern of violence and reprisal as different actors warred for the riches of coastal trade. Omani Arabs were involved in this contest, as were the Portuguese themselves and African communities on the coast. Initially, Fort Jesus at Mombasa was the focal point of these struggles, and good contemporary records (both eyewitness accounts and archaeological remains) attest to the ferocity of assaults on this structure from all parties. Yet by 1698–1699, it was the unobtrusive Omani station at Zanzibar that was emerging as an important new factor in regional trade and diplomacy. The small port town's influence steadily grew as the seventeenth folded into the eighteenth century only a year later.

As Zanzibar became more economically and politically incorporated into Indian Ocean circuits of exchange, its basic productive and social relations changed to accommodate new international realities. Instead of trading on its own behalf, the Zanzibari polity became a "conveyor belt" between African goods and markets and the industrializing West. Dhows and caravans that had once been utilized for predominantly mercantilist purposes were now directed toward different ends: the purchase of slaves, for instance, to populate clove and food-production plantations under Zanzibari rule, and the transit of ivory, which fetched high prices in Europe and America.

Such changes in the nature of the empire, of course, also had their reverberations on the peoples of the mainland, as weaker polities were depopulated and stronger ones were reoriented to provide desired primary materials, such as ivory and gum copal. Yet even in the metropole itself (which in this case was Zanzibar) vis-à-vis its own East African hinterland, changes rearranged the existing social fabric such that new hierarchies developed. Indians, for example, who were important traders under the old mercantilist state, were given vast new advantages by their British associations, clearly to the detriment of ethnically Arab merchants.

By the mid-nineteenth century, the Omani rulers of Zanzibar were so dependent on the British military to maintain tribal stability in Oman itself, as well as on the capital that British Indians brought from the Raj, that they could do little to preclude these changes from happening. In 1862 Oman and Zanzibar were formally split in order that Britain might better control both, and in 1890 Zanzibar was named a British Protectorate.

Trade in the Indian Ocean in the early twentieth century, the twilight of European rule, evinced certain continuities and cleavages with this *longue duree* past. Commodities and the merchants who moved them continued to circulate around the rim of the ocean, often in far greater quantities (for cloves and ivory, for example) than in the past. Other lines of commerce, such as the slave trade, were discontinued in the previous century but continued in altered forms with the movement of huge numbers of indentured laborers, often from India to East Africa and Southeast Asia. The rise of independent nation-states all along the shores of the Indian Ocean, after two World Wars and a great depression, gave impetus to age-old patterns of trade to be continued, only now under the auspices of indigenous rule. In some ways, this brought the history of commerce in this great maritime space, centuries if not millennia old, full circle after the passing of the colonial age.

SEE ALSO *Bullion Trade, South and Southeast Asia; Cities and Towns in the Americas; India, Imperial; Malaysia, British, 1874–1957.*

BIBLIOGRAPHY

Alpers, Edward A. *Ivory and Slaves: Changing Pattern of International Trade in East Central Africa to the Later Nineteenth Century.* Berkeley: University of California Press, 1975.

Chaudhuri, K. N. *Trade and Civilization in the Indian Ocean: An Economic History from the Rise of Islam to 1750*. New York: Cambridge University Press, 1985.

Das Gupta, Ashin. *Merchants of Maritime India, 1500–1800*. Brookfield, VT: Ashgate, 1994.

Hall, Richard. *Empires of the Monsoon: A History of the Indian Ocean*. London: HarperCollins, 1996.

Keay, John. *The Honourable Company: A History of the English East India Company* . New York: Macmillan, 1991.

Matthew, K. S. *Trade in the Indian Ocean During the Sixteenth Century and the Portuguese*. Studies in Maritime History series. Pondicherry: Pondicherry University, 1990.

McPherson, Kenneth. *The Indian Ocean: A History of People and the Sea*. New York: Oxford University Press, 1993.

Pearson, Michael. *Port Cities and Intruders: The Swahili Coast, India, and Portugal in the Early Modern Era*. Baltimore: Johns Hopkins University Press, 1998.

Pearson, Michael. *The Indian Ocean*. London: Routledge, 2003.

Prakash, Om. *Precious Metals and Commerce: The Dutch East India Company in the Indian Ocean Trade*. Brookfield, VT: Variorum, 1994.

Ray, Indrani, ed., *The French East India Company and the Trade of the Indian Ocean*. Calcutta: Munshiram, 1999.

Reid, Anthony. *Southeast Asia in the Age of Commerce: The Lands Beneath the Winds*. New Haven, CT: Yale University Press, 1993.

Eric Tagliacozzo

INDIAN REVOLT OF 1857

The Indian revolt of 1857 was a widespread Indian rebellion against British rule. The mutiny-rebellion has been the topic of fierce historical controversy. Whereas some see it as being caused by the insensitivity of the British military to the religion of its high-caste Hindu sepoys, others see it as an inevitable reaction to the British policy of annexation of heirless native states, the annexation of the province of Awadh in 1856, and the introduction of a revenue policy that disadvantaged India's landed classes. It began in Meerut city as a mutiny in the army of the English East India Company. In that year the Indian soldiers (sepoys) of the Bengal Army recruited by the English East India Company mutinied. The Company ruled India as a sovereign power until 1857. The Indian component of its army was the mainstay of its power. Thus it felt threatened as the mutinous sepoys spread the fire of protest to civilian areas. As rural India rallied around the sepoys a civil rebellion engulfed British India. The British crushed the rebellion in 1858. The Parliament did not renew the charter of the English East India Company as a result of its failure to prevent the rebellion. The Company lost its sovereign status in India. A fresh Act of parliament passed in August 1858 made the British Queen Victoria the sovereign of British India. Indians thus came directly under the rule of the British crown.

Social histories of the mutinous Bengal Army argue that the military and civil causes cannot be separated because the English East India Company had assiduously built a military culture that sustained a range of Indian traditions in its regiments. The Bengal Army included, for example, high-caste regiments, the cavalry regiments of Rohilla-Afghan freebooters, and the Gurkha regiments. This was in sharp contrast to the Madras and Bengal Armies also maintained by the English Company. These did not have such a wide-ranging cultural mix. This variety ensured a careful balancing between the army, polity, and society, and it stabilized East India Company rule in northern India.

From the 1820s, the status that sepoys and their families derived from this heterogeneous military culture began to be threatened. This was an age of financial strain for the English East India Company. Because most parts of north India were in its control, the company began to reduce its military establishment. This caused disaffection in military ranks. The already disgruntled sepoys were outraged when rumors spread that the new greased cartridges used in the Enfield rifle were made of cow and pig fat. This hurt the religious sentiments of Hindu and Muslim Sepoys. Their religion forbade them to kill and eat these animals, respectively. The introduction of greased cartridges in 1857 was merely the spark that ignited these larger resentments. The disgruntled soldiers made common cause with the Indian landed magnates and princes of the regions from which the soldiers had came.

It was the soldiers of Meerut that set the ball of mutiny rolling. On May 10, 1857, three infantry regiments of the city killed British officers and other Europeans. They burnt their bungalows and set off towards Delhi. Mutinies followed in eastern Uttar Pradesh and western Bihar, which were the major recruiting sites of the Bengal Army. In the Bundelkhand region, rebels in Jhansi took the lead. Rebelling soldiers from Jhansi then marched to Kanpur and Delhi, which became the center of much action.

In each of these regions the most striking change preceding the revolt was the sudden displacement of the English East India Company as the chief employer by the patrons of the rebel leaders, who began to offer the sepoys the material, political, and ritual inducements that the company had hitherto monopolized. In this context, the actions of rebel leaders like Kunwar Singh in the Shahbad district of Bihar, the *rani* (princess) of Jhansi in Bundelkhand, and Nana Sahib of Bithoor were reminiscent of the East India Company's efforts to project a Hindu image for the army so as to garner sepoy support.

The Battle of Lucknow. *Indian sepoys engage British troops in 1857 at Lucknow, where some of the most intense fighting of the Indian Revolt occurred.* KEAN COLLECTION/HULTON ARCHIVE/GETTY IMAGES. REPRODUCED BY PERMISSION.

Whereas, in Delhi, very much like the promises of Mughal status that the company offered to its cavalry regiments recruited from this area, leaders like Bakht Khan furthered their military ambition by their promise to restore the Mughal emperor to the throne of Delhi.

The British suppressed the mutiny by use of force. The British sack of Delhi that followed was retribution for British casualties. Many mutiny leaders were killed in encounters with the British. The mutinous soldiers were subjected to court martial and publicly executed after being charged guilty. A transfer of power from the East India Company to the British Crown followed the revolt. The East India Company ceased to be the sovereign of India as a result of an act of parliament enacted on August 2, 1858. The new sovereign of British India was Queen Victoria. The inauguration of a new era of British rule had begun.

Nationalist historians see the 1857 rebellion as a full-blown nationalist movement that united all classes in India, but the historiography of 1857 does not substantiate this view. The consensus now is that the motivations of the rebels were both general and local, and riveted by class, caste, and family politics.

SEE ALSO *English East India Company (EIC); Indian Army; Sepoy.*

BIBLIOGRAPHY

Alavi, Seema. *The Sepoys and the Company: Tradition and Transition in Northern India, 1770–1839.* New Delhi and New York: Oxford University Press, 1995.

Roy, Tapti. *The Politics of a Popular Uprising: Bundelkhand in 1857.* New Delhi and New York: Oxford University Press, 1994.

Taylor, P. J. O., ed. *A Companion to the Indian Mutiny of 1857.* New Delhi and New York: Oxford University Press, 1996.

Seema Alavi

INDIGENOUS ECONOMIES, MIDDLE EAST

The spread of the Islamic state out of Arabia in the seventh century C.E. led within just a few decades to a large empire that covered the Fertile Crescent, North

Africa, Spain, Persia, and parts of India and Central Asia. The new state afforded its newly acquired domains a centralized administration, a unified territory, and secure conditions, all of which were highly conducive to the development of agriculture, industry, and trade. Some of the institutions that structured this economic expansion were continued from earlier times and adapted to the injunctions of Islamic law, while others were developed by Muslim jurists to accommodate the needs of business and production.

The discussion below first considers the major institutions that structured the economy of the Middle East—land tenure, guilds and markets, financial and production structures, and taxation—and then briefly surveys the historical development of Middle Eastern economies.

LAND TENURE

Land tenure and land taxation in the Middle East varied according to time and place as their form depended on both Islamic and state law, but a few overarching principles can be identified. Islamic law considers that land belongs to the Creator and is gifted by Him to His creatures. Thus land ultimately belongs to the community, a principle that in turn allows a community's members to hold land privately, and also grants the rights of usufruct, sale, and inheritance. The state, then, as the representative of the community, has the right to tax land (as it is rented from the community at large), as well as to confiscate it if left unproductive. Productive land then may be acquired through purchase or inheritance or by reclaiming wasteland, after which the normal rules of private property and taxation apply to it; agricultural land may be held and worked individually (or through hired labor) or collectively by villages that then divide the produce into individual shares. Two categories of land fall outside this general scheme: *mulk*, that is, inalienable and nontaxable property that is used for private dwellings (mainly houses and small orchards) and to which all the principles of private ownership apply; and *waqf*, that is, any property (*mulk* or otherwise) deeded by its owner to serve as a foundation or endowment for a segment of the community—such as students or jurists—or an institution with a public purpose, such as a mosque, school, or hospital. A *waqf* is inalienable; it cannot be sold or purchased, nor can its original purpose be changed. Whatever income it generates can be spent only on the specified purpose and any related administrative costs.

In practice, though the broad lines of Islamic law were followed, the state could and did implement its own rules regardless of the jurists' views. From the second half of the eighth century, during the early Abbassid period, the state arrogated to itself the right to grant large estates from its vast holdings to powerful figures whom the

caliph wanted to reward or reconcile with, though Islamic rules of inheritance provided for their eventual subdivision. Under the Ottomans (1450–1921), land that was neither *mulk* nor *waqf* was categorized as state land (*miri*); new regulations were introduced, establishing the principle that cultivators owned only the usufruct, so that the land could not be sold or parceled out among heirs (who would have to own it collectively). Though village agricultural land was often held in this way, traditional patterns of landholding remained generally in force throughout the Middle East.

GUILDS AND MARKETS

By the nineteenth century, craftsmen and artisans throughout the Middle East were organized in guilds, which were patterned after the *waqf* structure found in Islamic law schools. A master craftsman headed the guild, flanked by associate artisans who supervised the apprentices. The guilds regulated the prices of finished products as well as the wages and employment of artisans; the system was strictly controlled in order to maintain income protection and product quality. Traders were similarly organized, though it was often the case that merchants also owned factories and controlled part of the production process. Crafts and industry developed mainly in the cities, which were the primary markets for the adjoining countryside. A *muhtasib* was in charge of ensuring that the city was properly supplied; he also supervised the market, ensuring honesty in the calculation of weights and measurements and watching for hoarding or abusive monopoly practices that would cause price instability.

FINANCIAL AND PRODUCTION STRUCTURES

Throughout the Middle East, taxes on land often consisted of a percentage of the harvest, but most transactions, and especially trade, used currency, which was minted and controlled by the state from the very beginning of the Umayyad dynasty (661–750). Indeed, for several centuries gold and silver coins minted in the Middle East were international instruments of payment (except in China, which for a while required the use of its paper currency). To facilitate international trade, money was deposited with banks that issued local orders of payment (*hawāla*), as well as bills of exchange (*suftāja*), throughout the trade routes. The letters of credit on which trade agents drew could be issued by their employers or the employer's bank.

Islamic law provided for a number of instruments intended to promote production and trade. Land partnerships (*muzāra'a* and *musāqāt*) allowed for the maximization of production by bringing together land, capital, and labor. Business partnership could be of two kinds: proprietary (*sharikat al mulk*) or commercial (i.e., contractual) (*sharikat al 'aqd*). The first implied joint ownership of capital, whereas the second covered labor, capital (*mudāraba*), and credit (*wujūh*) partnerships. Although some jurists allowed some forms of unlimited partnerships (under stringent rules), most partnerships were of the limited kind (*'inān*). The latter category included labor partnerships that were used in agriculture and crafts; capital partnership (which would eventually be introduced into Europe through Italian traders as the *commenda*) could also be used in those fields, though it was mostly used in trade. The terms of partnerships and the distribution of profits and losses according to specified shares were strictly governed by the law to ensure that contracts would not become usurious. Contracts required witnesses to be valid but were not always recorded in writing.

TAXATION

Taxes were levied on the basis of Islamic law, but the state could and did add as many new taxes as it wished (despite occasional objections from the jurists). Besides the *zakāt* (levied upon Muslims) and the *jizya* (levied upon non-Muslims), state land was subject to either the *kharāj* (which could consist of up to 50 percent of the produce) or the *'ushr* (10 percent of the produce). Crafts and industries were generally taxed around 10 percent of their production and various taxes and customs regulated trade profit. Taxes and methods of collection varied widely according to time and locale. Whereas early on the central government received taxes directly through its governors, the eventual weakening of the state forced it to delegate the right to collect taxes to the semi-independent emirates that divided the empire and gave only formal allegiance to the Abbassid caliph in Baghdad.

THE EARLY DEVELOPMENT OF THE ECONOMIES OF THE MIDDLE EAST

Agriculture, the basis of the economy in the pre-Islamic Middle East, flourished with the Islamic expansion. A large variety of cereals, vegetables, and fruits became available as traders brought back new species to their native land. Revolutionary changes in irrigation techniques and soil management, helped by new advances in physics and chemistry and the blossoming of sciences in general, brought much more land under cultivation and made land more productive than previously possible. This, in turn, led to a sizable population increase and the development of two primary industries, textiles and sugar refining, which in turn led to expanded agricultural production of cotton, flax, and sugarcane. This expansion and experimentation with new plants also led to the development of various new medicines, cosmetics,

perfumes, and so on. A variety of other new products and techniques were developed or introduced as well, including types of pottery, glass, bookbinding, leather goods, paper (brought back from China), ships, armaments, tools, and so on. Three main trade routes (the Silk Road through Persia and Central Asia, the Persian Gulf route, and the Red Sea route) linked the Middle East to the Far East, which remained its most important trade partner for several centuries. Textiles, sugar, glass, medicine, and agricultural products were exported and silk, spices, precious stones, and paper (at first) were imported.

Political developments were to somewhat hamper these achievements, however. The flourishing economy of the early centuries, though maintained at first despite the fragmentation of the empire into small emirates, could not sustain the blows dealt by successive foreign invasions that were facilitated by the emirates' intense political and sectarian infighting. The disruptive effect of the Crusades, which started in 1095 and lasted for almost two centuries, was compounded by the Mongol attacks that culminated in the sack of Baghdad in 1258. Indeed, these attacks would have devastated the Muslim world had the Crusaders and a faction of Isma'īlīs (a small sect whose members governed Fatimid Egypt and parts of Syria) been successful in their attempts to establish an alliance with the Mongols. It was not until the region was united again under the control of the Sunnī rulers Nūr al Dīn (d. 1174) and Saladin (d. 1193) that both Crusaders and Mongols were repulsed and the economy could grow again.

The descendants of Saladin did not rule for long, however, as Syria and Egypt were soon overtaken by the powerful Mamluk military dynasty (1250–1517). But the return of security, the unification of Central Asia under the Golden Horde, and the subsequent Mongol conversion to Islam (starting with the Il-Khans who controlled Iraq and Persia) paved the way for another great expansion in industry and trade, which lasted throughout the thirteenth century. The state, whose tax revenues increased when trade flourished, provided protection to merchants by taxing their competitors, ensuring the security of their ships, and jealously guarding access to the trade routes. The great expansion in trade gave rise to an oligarchy of powerful merchants in Egypt, known as the Karīmī merchants, many of whom were also factory and ship owners. However, while the Mamluks encouraged industry and trade, they also formed a ruling class that to some extent interfered in the production process. They provided their own dynastic members the right to collect taxes from agricultural districts while not paying any on their own factories, and to impose the *corvée* (forced labor) on their estates. The state became an economic agent with monopolistic tendencies that slowed down competition and production.

DECLINE AND STAGNATION

The main cause of the economy's decline arose from natural factors, however. The expansion of the thirteenth century came to an abrupt halt with the spread from the East of the Black Death (1347–1350); Syria and Egypt were ravaged and lost almost half of their population. In Egypt, local industries were taken over by the state and became state monopolies. The weakened rulers found themselves bereft of revenue and vulnerable to the incursions of Tamerlane (d. 1405) throughout the fourteenth century. As a result, exploitative taxes that made economic conditions even worse were imposed on the peasants. Bad administration and lack of competition lowered the level and quality of the state-owned monopolized industries. In addition, the circumnavigation of Africa allowed European traders to bypass the Middle East and break its monopoly over trade routes.

The resulting political and economic weakness of the region allowed the rising Ottoman state, which had already spread throughout Anatolia, to expand southward in the fifteenth century and to incorporate Syria and Egypt under its rule. The return of security and of a centralized government that provided protection along trade routes, repaired irrigation systems, organized taxation, and removed trade barriers, allowed for an economic renewal in Syria and Egypt during the sixteenth century (though most of Iraq remained a battleground between the Safavids of Persia and the Ottomans until it finally fell to the latter in 1638). Villages that had been abandoned were occupied again and the population seems to have increased by as much as 40 percent. Despite increased competition from Europe, industry and crafts found local markets and niches in the international market; thus, when the Portuguese monopolized the spice trade, merchants shifted to another highly sought commodity, coffee, which originated from Yemen.

But the sixteenth-century expansion did not generate the steadily accelerating growth that was occurring in Europe. While local production did not decline over the next two centuries (as evidenced by the sustained tax receipts collected by the Ottomans), it did not grow either. A number of factors contributed to this stagnancy. One of the main problems was the renewed onset of the plague, which struck several times in Cairo and Syria in the seventeenth and eighteenth centuries, leading to a stagnant or even declining population (in contrast with European population growth). Competition from cheaper European finished goods, a slow recovery from plague epidemics, the need for immediate income, and

the increasing European demand for raw materials drew the peasants into a reliance on cash crops and led to a corresponding stagnation in crafts and industry. The guilds were unprepared to meet this challenge, as their structure did not encourage competition: guilds restricted and controlled entry into given professions, prohibited the merging of different crafts, and supervised finished products and their prices. The situation was made worse by a devaluation of the currency due to the import of cheap silver from America.

However, the main reason for the stagnation of the economy resides in the taxation system, which varied according to political conditions. In Anatolia and Syria, the Ottomans had instituted the *timar* system, which guaranteed to the state a certain part of the taxes collected by the *sipahis* (Ottoman cavalrymen), with the rest going to fund local administration as well as a local army that could be enlisted when needed. In Egypt, an Ottoman governor was appointed to collect taxes directly and there was no attempt at creating a local army. However, continued warfare and the need to keep up with European military advances and innovations forced the Ottoman state to create a standing army and to increase its military expenditures. The *timar* and *ziamet* systems were discontinued in favor of a system based on the sale of "tax farms" (*iltizām*), in which the tax farmer collected taxes over specific agricultural areas or urban crafts and industries. These tax farms were then auctioned off to local elites. Such sales raised immediate funds—and in effect resulted in deficit financing. The assigning of lucrative *iltizāms* led to social reorganization: the Mamluk upper class that had been shunted aside reasserted itself in Egypt and a class of *a'yān* (notables) arose in Syria. It also led to conflict and sometimes bitter feuding; in Syria, local military men, Ottoman Janissaries, merchants, *'ulamā'* (Muslim scholars), and owners of large estates all competed with each other to acquire *iltizāms*, while in Egypt the competition was between the great Mamluk houses. The assignment of *iltizāms* was initially temporary, but as this led to abusive taxation of the peasants, the tax farm was eventually given for life and then on a hereditary basis (*malikane*), with the hope that the tax farmer would seek to protect his source of income by refraining from unduly disrupting peasant farming. But the *multazims* (holders of *iltizām*) did often disrupt the production process: by cultivating large estates, by first providing credit to farmers who could not keep up with taxes, and then eventually seizing their property, or by purchasing the entire crop of a region and hoarding it in order to manipulate prices. There was as a result a considerable increase in *waqf ahlī*, private property that could not be bought or sold and was set up solely for the use of the descendants of the owner, who avoided in this way seizure of the land by creditors.

Thus the attempt at creating a new economic system faltered mainly because of the formation of an elite class that could not rule and whose only interest was to maximize its revenues. Whereas in the past, the state used part of its tax revenues for reinvestment in the agricultural system and provided security, public repairs, and legal protection, the new class now used their revenues only for consumption and power consolidation, and extorted and imposed illegal taxes on the peasants. And while it was true that customary law, which protected the individual, did not allow actual enserfment of the peasants, who resisted the extortions by fleeing, revolting, or seeking the protection of nomadic tribes, the political conditions were such that the peasants could be abused. The result was that more than two thirds of their produce was taken away from them, and agricultural production could not develop and be maximized.

REVIVAL

During the nineteenth century, the economy expanded again as the plague disappeared and the population increased at a very high rate. In turn, this growth led to more agricultural production, exports of raw materials, and expansion in the local industries. However, the political conditions did not allow for industrial growth. In Egypt, the extortions of the elite led to social instability, urban revolts, and the flight of peasants from their villages. This chaotic situation allowed Muhammad 'Alī, who had been sent by the Ottomans with a garrison in the wake of the French invasion of 1798, to seize power and become governor of Egypt. Suppressing the old Mamluk elite, 'Alī embarked on an ambitious program of economic reform, Westernization of the educational system, and cadre formation. Land was expropriated and administered directly by the state, as was trade. Agriculture improved, irrigation was expanded, and new crops (especially a new breed of cotton that proved very successful) led to some trade growth. But the economy had become primarily a state venture and all entrepreneurial possibilities were eliminated. Furthermore, Muhammad 'Alī's relative success in forming a new army led him to challenge the Ottoman state and invade Syria, prompting intervention by France and Great Britain to stop him.

Following this European intervention, Syria reverted to Ottoman rule, but the Ottoman state, overwhelmed with internal problems, was not able to maintain effective control. The old system of *iltizām* was restored and the struggle between the tax farmers and the peasantry resumed. Further penetration by Western goods, aided by Western governments who obtained low tariffs on their merchandise and imposed high customs on imports, made industrial production sluggish. And though trade (mostly, the importing of finished goods and the

exporting of raw materials) improved generally, the Capitulations, agreements the Ottoman state was forced to make with Western powers, provided special privileges for Western traders and their protégés, Christian and Jewish minorities. The latter found themselves prospering and attracting popular anger and resentment.

In Egypt, the downside of Muhammad 'Alī's creation of a state economy came to a head when prices for cotton fell worldwide. Centralized and inefficient administration and lack of an entrepreneurial class prevented industry from adjusting to these circumstances. The state resorted to hoarding, which in turn pushed its trading partners into bankruptcy; the resulting lack of revenues and the high cost of administration forced Muhammad 'Alī to redistribute large tracts of land to family members and associates in return for upfront tax payment. His descendants made things worse by taking on public works projects financed with foreign loans, often made at terms unfavorable to the state. This led to further borrowing from European powers, paving the way for ultimate bankruptcy and, as a result of the ensuing popular unrest, colonization by Great Britain. As for the Ottoman state, the same policy of borrowing, pursued in order to finance the military it needed to defend itself, led to its eventual financial and military demise and allowed Western colonial powers to seize Syria and Iraq at the conclusion of World War I.

SEE ALSO *Capitulations, Middle East; International Trade in the Pre-Modern Period, Middle East.*

BIBLIOGRAPHY

Abu-Lughod, Janet. *Before European Hegemony: The World System, A.D. 1250–1350.* New York: Oxford University Press, 1989.

Owen, Roger. *The Middle East in the World Economy, 1800–1914.* Rev. ed. London: I. B. Tauris, 1993.

Udovitch, A. L., ed. *The Islamic Middle East, 700–1900: Studies in Economic and Social History.* Princeton, NJ: Darwin Press, 1981.

Maysam J. al Faruqi

INDIGENOUS RESPONSES, EAST ASIA

To analyze the historical experience of East Asia and its interaction with the West, including the United States, it is necessary to recognize that such indigenous responses were initiated by major trends radiating out of Western Europe. These trends include the expansion of European industrial-capitalist modernization because of inter-European rivalry, Protestant as well as Catholic

Christian evangelization, and the rise of imperialistic colonialism across the world in the sixteenth through nineteenth centuries. When the United States initially interacted with East Asian civilizations in the early 1800s, it did so as a third-tier Western power, often piggybacking on the much more extensive and intrusive activities of Europeans. East Asian nations did not clearly distinguish between European and American culture until the United States rose in the twentieth century to world-power status.

In the long historical period prior to the arrival of Westerners in East Asia, the region was influenced primarily by the ancient Chinese civilization and secondarily by subcontinental Indian religion and culture. Asians were accustomed to political and cultural influences, negative and positive, coming to them over land from the west via the Silk Road (an ancient trade route), by ship on the Indian Ocean, or on horseback from the northern steppes. The arrival of Western Europeans in south Chinese seaports in the 1500s on trading ships— later followed by military flotillas—was a new phenomenon that was not viewed as a major threat by the great and small peoples of East Asia. However, in the 1800s the superior firepower held by the Western traders enabled the East Asian region and peoples to be systematically absorbed into a colonial empire system with radically different religious, technological, political, commercial, and social elements from the indigenous Asian societies. The resulting psychological shock followed by backlash strongly contributed to the rise of modern nationalism in East Asia in the twentieth century.

Imperial China during the Ming (1368–1644) and Qing (1644–1911) dynasties, an empire of different cultures and peoples, thought of itself as the natural leader of Asia. It was ill-equipped to deal with the arrival of Westerners, especially the British, whose own industrialization depended upon the opening up of new markets and the search for more raw materials. When China was reluctant to, and even hostile toward, trade for Western goods, European merchants blamed local Chinese bureaucrats and regulations. The British in two Opium Wars (1839–1842 and 1856–1860) humbled the Chinese military and forced China to permit westerners to establish zones for trade and residence in major Chinese coastal cities. Such Western European economic imperialism was explained away by the West as bringing civilization and modernization to the barbaric Asian world.

For the Chinese to be thought of and treated by Westerners as unequal inferiors, particularly as codified in the unequal treaties, was unbearable. It was considered shameful for the Manchu Chinese officials in Peking (modern Beijing) and in the treaty ports to be revealed as powerless to stop foreign encroachment. This identity crisis intensified as the Western foreign powers (Britain, Russia, Germany, France, and Belgium) moved north into China, carving out large territories in which Chinese people were barred and local laws were not Chinese but Western.

In response to such treatment and feelings of both inferiority and anger, local antiforeigner movements mushroomed. The two most famous violent responses were the Taiping Rebellion (1851–1864) and the Boxer Rebellion (1899–1901). Also, there was an intellectual self-strengthening movement within the Chinese government and intelligentsia after the 1840s to study "Western learning." Despite some success, this movement ultimately failed because Chinese officials could not abandon their old Confucian bureaucratic mentality. The United States, which did not have any concessions, in 1899 declared an "open-door" policy to protect China from total dismemberment, and this action made a strong favorable impression on the Chinese people.

With the fading of Chinese influence in Asia in the 1800s, the Western powers took over the peripheral Southeast Asian states that had acknowledged Chinese suzerainty. France colonized Vietnam and established a protectorate over Cambodia. Britain moved into Burma (Myanmar) from subcontinental India and built up the colony of Hong Kong. The Dutch took over the Muslim island chain of Indonesia. The United States, feeling locked out of China, turned its attention to Japan, which had an isolationist Tokugawa government that only permitted one Western trading ship a year to land at its southern city of Nagasaki.

In 1853 U.S. Admiral Matthew Perry (1794–1858) led a small flotilla, known as the Black Ships, into today's Tokyo Bay to force the Japanese to abandon their isolationist policies. The Japanese response to the shock of the arrival of American and other Western armed trading vessels was seen twelve years later in the Meiji Restoration (1868). For the next thirty years, Japan embraced Western technology and successfully modernized the military and domestic industrial sector. The success of this modernization was revealed clearly in the early 1900s when Japan defeated both the Czarist Russian and the Chinese navies, and became a colonial power in China, Taiwan, and Korea. The May Fourth Movement of 1919 was a Chinese backlash to this Japanese militarism, but imperial Japanese aggression continued to expand throughout Asia until open conflict with the United States and Britain broke out during World War II (1939–1945).

Despite the loss of the Russo-Japanese War, Russia's centuries-long push into Asia continued across Siberia to the Pacific and then down into Mongolia. The Mongols, who had been allies of the Manchus during the Qing period, lost much territory during the dynasty to the Chinese in southern Inner Mongolia, and were in danger of total incorporation. When in 1911 the Qing dynasty was overthrown and the Chinese Republic was founded, Mongolia found support for its independence from the Bolshevik Russian government newly installed in Moscow. Mongolia became a communist republic in 1924 and remained a Soviet satellite—independent but strongly influenced by the Russians—until there was a peaceful democratic revolution in 1990.

Asian indigenous reactions toward the United States as distinct from the European West generally did not become pronounced throughout the region until after World War II. After the United States defeated and occupied Japan, it attained superpower status and vied with the Soviet Union for influence in East Asia in conflicts in Korea and Vietnam. Japan was drawn into the American orbit, while other Asian nations achieved independence by rejecting their Western occupiers. Often nationalist movements among the indigenous peoples became mixed with communist peasant movements, particularly in China, Vietnam, Laos, and Cambodia.

With the end of the Cold War period in the 1990s and the new economic global integration, the triumph of liberal democratic market systems is now labeled (or criticized) as "American" rather than "Western." Yet such East Asian reactions are intertwined intimately with nationalistic responses to the forced economic, social, cultural, and military changes inflicted by Western nations over centuries in successive waves upon historic, indigenous East Asian societies.

SEE ALSO *Assimilation, East Asia and Pacific; Boxer Uprising; China, First Opium War to 1945; China, to the First Opium War; Chinese Revolutions; Empire, Japanese; Korea, from World War II; Korea, to World War II; Self-Strengthening Movements, East Asia and the Pacific; Taiping Rebellion; Treaties, East Asia and the Pacific.*

BIBLIOGRAPHY

Chow Tse-tsung (Zhou Cezong). *The May Fourth Movement: Intellectual Revolution in Modern China.* Cambridge, MA: Harvard University Press, 1960.

Iriye, Akira. *Across the Pacific: An Inner History of American–East Asian Relations.* Rev. ed. Chicago: Imprint, 1992.

Jansen, Marius B. *Sakamoto Ryōma and the Meiji Restoration.* Princeton, NJ: Princeton University Press, 1961.

Mackerras, Colin, ed. *East and Southeast Asia: A Multidisciplinary Survey.* Boulder, CO: Lynne Rienner, 1995.

McGrew, Anthony, and Christopher Brook, eds. *Asia-Pacific in the New World Order.* New York: Routledge, 1998.

McWilliams, Wayne C., and Harry Piotrowski. *The World Since 1945: A History of International Relations*, 6th ed. Boulder, CO: Lynne Rienner, 2005.

Preston, P. W. *Pacific Asia in the Global System: An Introduction.* Oxford and Malden, MA: Blackwell, 1998.

Wright, Mary, ed. *China in Revolution: The First Phase, 1900–1913.* New Haven, CT: Yale University Press, 1968.

Alicia Campi

INDIGENOUS RESPONSES, THE PACIFIC

Some three millennia ago, the ancestors of the indigenous people of Oceania began migrating from Asia across the vast stretches of ocean between the island groups that today constitute Micronesia, Melanesia, and Polynesia. What prompted this migration has been a matter of great conjecture, but at some point the migrations out of Asia became inconsequential and Oceania entered into a long period of isolation from the rest of the world. Although there were significant movements of populations across the region that periodically reshaped the cultures of particular islands or island groups, cultural influences from outside the region remained negligible.

So, when European explorers first began crossing the Pacific in the sixteenth century, the indigenous people of the region were truly dismayed at the sudden appearance of a very different race of men with strange customs and very dangerous armaments. Although the explorers were sometimes keen to demonstrate the firepower of their vessels and crews, they generally attempted to establish amicable relations with the indigenous people. Unfortunately, the early seamen's tales of tropical paradises populated by hospitable, handsome, and sexually uninhibited natives attracted equally large numbers of unscrupulous adventurers and zealous missionaries. Both groups undermined the customs and traditions that had for millennia governed the behavior of the indigenous people. The adventurers disregarded the codes of responsibility that governed the seemingly unconstrained behavior of natives, and the missionaries condemned the indigenous culture as degenerate and wished to eradicate it, to replace native beliefs and mores with Christian doctrines and principles.

Ironically, because representatives of European governments, religions, and commercial enterprises all wished to enter into favorable and uncomplicated agreements with the indigenous people, they essentially superimposed authoritarian indigenous regimes on societies that had traditionally stressed local autonomy, systems of shared authority, and complex customs governing relations between communities. Thus, at the point where

European culture was poised to overwhelm the indigenous cultures, the resistance of the indigenous people was undermined by tensions between the supporters of the new authoritarian regimes and those natives who resisted such regimes in the name of indigenous traditions.

Like indigenous people in other regions of the world, the Pacific islanders had no resistance to many communicable diseases introduced by Europeans, and as their social institutions were undermined, they seemed especially susceptible to such consequences of personal degradation and communal decline as alcoholism and venereal disease. Furthermore, as Europeans sought to exploit the natural resources of the islands, they attempted alternately to recruit or to conscript indigenous laborers. Unused to such heavy, regimented work and weakened further by the effects of poor arrangements for accommodating large concentrations of workers, the indigenous population suffered additional dramatic declines. As a result, European colonials began to import large numbers of Indian and Chinese laborers, in much the same way as enslaved Africans were brought to the West Indies to offset the devastation of Native American populations. Although most groups of Pacific islanders never disappeared as completely as the Ciboney, Arawak, and Carib, they sometimes became minority populations in their own homelands.

In the nineteenth century, the European powers formally defined their spheres of influence across the Pacific, much as they did in Africa and Asia. Despite the relative brevity of the formal colonial rule, the British and French, in particular, left an enduring cultural legacy. In many places across Oceania, British or French influence continues to define the local culture more pointedly than indigenous practices and traditions. The American victory in the Spanish-American War (1898) and the German defeat in World War I (1914–1918) combined to make the United States and the Japanese Empire the emergent powers in the region during the interwar period. The awesome scale of the military operations in the Pacific during World War II brought many of the trends during the colonial period to a terrible climax. The indigenous populations experienced extensive and extended dislocations. The tremendous numbers of men and amounts of material introduced into the region permanently changed the face and pace of life in the islands. What had previously been imported only at great cost was now available in surplus—as war surplus.

After the surrender of Japan, the Pacific region did not experience the same convulsive movement toward independence as many of the other former territories within the European colonial empires. The indigenous populations were simply not concentrated or cohesive

enough for revolution. In fact, as American influence spread throughout the region, the islands increasingly became welfare states, dependent on U.S. foreign aid for their very survival. It was not until the 1970s that some of the island groups became autonomous territories and then, politically, fully independent states. Still, most remained economically dependent states. The increasing economic reliance on tourism and the increasing emphasis on material culture has created environmental issues that threaten to become a crisis. Most pointedly, there is simply not enough space to dispose of burgeoning amounts of waste in conventional ways. The very coral reefs that have for millennia protected many of the islands from storms have, in the space of several decades, created toxic lagoons in which industrial and human waste have ruined the colonies of fish that once sustained the islanders by providing their primary source of protein.

SEE ALSO *China, After 1945; China, First Opium War to 1945; China, to the First Opium War; Chinese Revolutions; Compradorial System; Empire, Japanese; Korea, from World War II; Korea, to World War II; Self-Strengthening Movements, East Asia and the Pacific.*

BIBLIOGRAPHY

Edmond, Rod. *Representing the South Pacific: Colonial Discourse from Cook to Gauguin.* Cambridge, U.K.: Cambridge University Press, 1997.

Fischer, Steven R. *A History of the Pacific Islands.* New York: Palgrave Macmillan, 2002.

Frost, Alan. *The Global Reach of Empire: Britain's Maritime Expansion in the Indian and Pacific Oceans, 1764–1815.* Carlton, Victoria: Miegunyah Press, 2003.

Lawson, Stephanie. *Tradition versus Democracy in the South Pacific: Fiji, Tonga, and Western Samoa.* Cambridge, U.K. and New York: Cambridge University Press, 1996.

Price, A. Grenfell. *The Western Invasions of the Pacific and Its Continents: A Study of Moving Frontiers and Changing Landscapes, 1513–1958.* Westport, CT: Greenwood Press, 1980.

Martin Kich

INDIRECT RULE, AFRICA

Although the historiography of indirect rule in Africa is abundant, the subject is still generally misunderstood, misunderstood in its origins, meaning, operation, and significance.

Historically, imperialist regimes generally controlled conquered peoples through the agency of the local ruling elite. They did so for practical reasons. While the elite were allowed to reign according to their local laws, customs, and political institutions, they were required to acknowledge the overlordship of the conqueror and to respect it. Failure to do so resulted in their deposition and replacement with those willing to accept the new dispensation. This is *indirect rule* broadly defined.

There was a degree of cooperation between the colonizer and the colonized, and it exhibited various manifestations to suit prevailing circumstances. Indirect rule was not, therefore, a concept invented by the British colonial administrator Frederick Lugard (1858–1945) as the proper system for governing the Islamic emirates of northern Nigeria. Even in Nigeria, such a system was already in place in the south before Lugard conquered the emirates. In addition, a "warrant chief" system, which was devised for societies where no centrally recognized authority existed, was in operation in southern Nigeria by 1891.

Nevertheless, it was Lugard who modified and popularized indirect rule, elevating it to the status of a doctrine. A passage in his *Political Memoranda* (1906), a set of official instructions to his colonial administrative officers in northern Nigeria, states: "There are not two sets of rulers—British and Native—working either separately or in cooperation, but a single Government in which native Chiefs have well-defined duties and an acknowledged status equally with the British Officers. Their duties should never conflict and should overlap as little as possible" (Bello 1962, p.73). The chiefs, in short, were not subordinates or inferiors to the officers but were agents who cooperated with them in the great civilizing mission.

Later, Donald Cameron, former colonial governor of Tanganyika and Nigeria, respectively (1872–1948), and a "Lugardian," explained that it was vital that African institutions, which the chiefs "have inherited, molded or modified as they may do on the advice of British officers," should "develop in a constitutional manner" (Karugire 1980, p. 116). The contradictions inherent in both passages are clear and need no further explanation. The bottom line is that native chiefs were not independent actors but rather junior partners in the colonial enterprise who could be dispensed with at will by the senior partner. Lugardian indirect rule, whether of the emirate or warrant chief variety, was a paternalist concept, replete with irreconcilable contradictions, and indeed, a convenient fiction necessary for the justification of colonialism. It did not take long to realize that Lugardism could not be applied in practice without undermining colonialism.

In 1922 Lugard published his famous *The Dual Mandate in British Tropical Africa*, ostensibly a reiteration and elaboration, but actually a rationalization of a doctrine that was clearly in trouble. Curiously, the book made Lugard an international celebrity in the interwar years. Indirect rule became a sort of occult science, the quintessential bible for governing colonial peoples. The British government adopted it for most of its African colonies, except in those colonies where the existence of prefabricated white colonial collaborators made it superfluous. The League of Nations also appointed Lugard as its advisor regarding the proper governance of colonial peoples. France, Portugal, and Belgium joined the bandwagon, perhaps against their better judgment, and adopted modified forms of indirect rule.

Indirect rule was considered necessary for practical, economic, and climatic reasons. It functioned within "Native Councils" and minor courts, which were responsible for local administration. The councils, which comprised traditional rulers, made bylaws, regulated matters of local interest, tried minor cases, enforced the construction of community access roads and buildings with no monetary compensation for the workers, and performed other functions dictated by the colonial officials.

For the most part, this flawed system functioned better in societies where, prior to colonization, government was centralized; in the noncentralized societies it was less successful. In either case, the chiefs generally were unaware of their powers, obligations, and rights; their place was not properly defined; they were under the thumb of colonial officers; and the exclusion of the Western-educated elite from participation in local administration caused the system to come under sustained attack by the emerging nationalists in the post-1930 period, primarily because the system was an impediment to the rise of nationalism, the establishment of democracy, and the regaining of independence.

SEE ALSO *Indirect Rule, Africa; Lugard, Frederick John Dealtry.*

BIBLIOGRAPHY

Afigbo, A. E. *The Warrant Chiefs: Indirect Rule in Southeastern Nigeria, 1891–1929.* New York: Humanities Press, 1972.

Akpan, Ntieyong U. *Epitaph to Indirect Rule: A Discourse on Local Government in Africa.* London: Cassell, 1956. Reprint, London: Cass, 1967.

Atanda, Joseph A. "Indirect Rule in Yorubaland." *Tarikh* 3, no. 3 (1970), 16–24.

Bello, Ahmadu. *My Life.* Cambridge, U.K.: Cambridge University Press, 1962.

Igbape, Philip A. "Indirect Rule in Benin." *Tarikh* 3, no. 3 (1970), 29–40.

Ikime, Obaro. "The Establishment of Indirect Rule in Northern Nigeria." *Tarikh* 3, no. 3 (1970), 1-15.

Lugard, Frederick D. *Political Memoranda* (1906). London: Cass, 1965a.

Lugard, Frederick D. *The Dual Mandate in British Tropical Africa* (1922). London: Cass, 1965b.

Karugire, S.R. *A Political History of Uganda*. London: Heinemann, 1980.

G. N. Uzoigwe

INDONESIAN INDEPENDENCE, STRUGGLE FOR

The Indonesian Revolution took place immediately after the Japanese surrender in World War II on August 15, 1945, lasted until the end of that year, and was in part political and in part social. The revolution had been in the making for years. Before the war the expanding colonial state not only educated a modern Indonesian elite that started to strive for a more democratic colonial government, it also modernized Indonesian society, which undermined the power and influence of traditional aristocratic rulers who used to be the most important allies of the colonial state. However, in response to the wishes of the modern Indonesian elite, the Dutch colonial government only halfheartedly introduced a few semidemocratic institutions and stuck to its traditional allies. The leaders of the Indonesian nationalist movement were, with a few exceptions, imprisoned or banned to a small number of peripheral places in the archipelago.

World War II shook the already weakened foundations of the Dutch colonial state. The ease with which the Japanese army defeated Dutch colonial forces and occupied the Dutch East Indies fundamentally altered the way Indonesians perceived Dutch power in the archipelago. The prestige upon which colonial rule rested had disappeared. Second, during the Japanese occupation, Dutch officials and civilians were interned in prison camps and virtually disappeared in Indonesian society. Third, and most importantly, Japanese authorities mobilized the Indonesian population on Java. The most influential nationalist leader, Soekarno (1901–1970), was brought out of internment to Java and was allowed to address the Javanese people. Javanese youth were trained in a semimilitary fashion and organized in paramilitary organizations.

As the war progressed, the Javanese *pemuda* (youth) increasingly took a radical and independent position toward the Japanese and also toward the issue of Indonesian independence. In response, Japanese authorities promised Indonesia a degree of independence. They created the Badan Penjelidik Oesaha-Oesaha Persiapan Kemerdekaan (Committee to Investigate Independence),

Achmed Sukarno (1902–1970). The Indonesian nationalist leader, statesman, and president, photographed on January 4, 1949. HULTON ARCHIVE/GETTY IMAGES. REPRODUCED BY PERMISSION.

which came together for the first time in Jakarta in May 1945. During the meetings of this committee, Sukarno formulated his doctrine of *Pancasila* (Five Principles), the state ideology of independent Indonesia: nationalism, humaneness, democracy, social justice, and belief in one God. However, it took until August 7, 1945, before the Japanese authorities allowed the establishment of the Panitia Persiapan Kemerdekaan Indonesia, the committee to prepare actual Indonesian independence.

This meant that on the day of Japan's surrender in 1945, nothing was arranged with regard to a possible independence of Indonesia. The main nationalist leaders, Sukarno and Mohammad Hatta (1902–1980), were very much surprised by the sudden collapse of the Japanese Empire and had no clear ideas on how to proceed further. However, for many Indonesian *pemuda* it was obvious that the time had come for Indonesia to declare itself fully independent on its own terms. When Sukarno and Hatta reacted with hesitancy, they were kidnapped by angry *pemuda* and brought to army barracks east of Jakarta. The *pemuda* expected an uprising by the population of the capital, but when this uprising did not materialize, they returned Sukarno and Hatta to the city. There, the Japanese admiral Tadashi Maeda promised not to interfere when Sukarno and Hatta proclaimed the independence of Indonesia.

Under pressure from the *pemuda* and with the assurances of the Japanese authorities in Jakarta, Sukarno and Hatta wrote a short declaration of independence, which on August 17, 1945, Sukarno read in front of his house at the Jalan Pegangsaan Timur: "We, the people of Indonesia, declare the independence of Indonesia. All matters regarding the transition of power will be dealt with in an orderly fashion and as soon as possible." A day later, a makeshift parliament adopted a constitution and elected Sukarno to be the first president of the Republic of Indonesia and Hatta to be the first vice president. However, at that moment, the Republic of Indonesia existed only on paper, without an effective bureaucracy or powerful police and security forces.

In the meantime, the old colonial power, the Netherlands, had no means to respond to the events in Indonesia. The Dutch not only lacked military forces in the region, formal power on Sumatra and Java was in the hands of the British supreme commander in Southeast Asia, Admiral Lord Louis Mountbatten (1900–1979). Mountbatten was convinced that Asian nationalism was a force to be reckoned with. Therefore, he left the countryside to the Republic of Indonesia and deployed his forces only in a few important cities along the coast, with the aim of transporting Japanese forces out of the country and of helping imprisoned and interned European military and civilians. As August progressed, this project became more and more difficult due to a rising revolutionary fever among the Indonesian people. When Dutch Lieutenant Governor-general H. J. van Mook (1894–1965) returned to Batavia—as he knew Jakarta—on October 2, 1945, he had to conclude that the situation for the Dutch was much worse than he had expected.

From the start of October onward, the Indonesian Revolution became a chaotic and bloody affair. The disappearance of the Japanese, the arrival of Allied forces, and the return of some of the Dutch from imprisonment or internment to their houses, resulted in attacks on Dutch civilians and property. Dutch houses were searched, and Dutch and Indo-European citizens were executed under the cry *siaaap!* (be prepared). The period became known as the Bersiap period.

The situation for the Dutch became even more difficult when Indonesians started an economic boycott against them on October 13. However, most frightening for the Dutch were the radical *pemuda*, who roamed the streets, raped women, and killed as they pleased. They not only targeted the Dutch, but also Chinese citizens who did not join the anti-Dutch economic boycott. In addition, Indonesians who cooperated with the Dutch, such as Ambonese and Menadonese members of the Dutch colonial army, were also attacked, resulting in bloody revenge from their side. It is not known how many people died during the Bersiap period. An estimated 3,500 Dutch were killed, but many others went missing.

In the Javanese countryside, the rage of the *pemuda* was directed against the members of the aristocratic elite who before the war had cooperated with the Dutch colonial rulers. In western Java, a revolutionary council took power and jailed the old elite. In central Java, in particular in the regency of Pekalongan, the same happened during the so-called Tiga Daerah Affair—or "Three Regencies Affair". Village chiefs, districts leaders, police officers, Chinese, and Indo-Europeans were attacked, kidnapped, imprisoned, or murdered. Elsewhere on Java and Sumatra, similar events occurred. It all resulted in chaos and the weakening of the position of the traditional indigenous elite.

The revolution made a return to colonial rule more and more unlikely because it undermined directly the foundations of the old colonial state. But the disorder also made the position of the government of the Republic of Indonesia more difficult. In order to counter the chaos on Java and Sumatra, Sukarno and Hatta founded on October 5, 1945, a national army, the Tentara Keamenan Rakjat (TKR), and named the thirty-year-old Sudirman (1915–1950) *panglima besar*, or supreme commander. However, the new government only slowly managed to establish order in the revolutionary chaos. To protect Dutch and Indo-European civilians, it established approximately 220 "protection camps" on Java, where more than 35,000 persons found refuge.

One of the worst episodes of the Indonesian Revolution took place in Surabaya. In the middle of October, approximately six thousand British soldiers entered the town, only to be welcomed by hostile revolutionary gangs that were supported by the Scottish-born American artist Muriel Pearson (1899–1997)—nicknamed Surabaya Sue, but better known as K'tut Tantri. The Indonesian government barely managed to keep order. The fragile order collapsed when British Brigadier General A. W. S. Mallaby was killed on October 30. The British decided to attack Surabaya; the "Battle of Surabaya" started on November 10 (a date later commemorated as Hari Pahlawan—or "National Heroes Day" in Indonesia) and lasted until November 26, after which the British controlled the city.

The Netherlands Recognizes Indonesia's Independence. *On December 27, 1949, Queen Juliana of the Netherlands met in Amsterdam with Indonesian prime minister Mohammed Hatta (left of the queen), Dutch prime minister Willem Drees (right), and others to sign the agreement formally recognizing Indonesia's independence.* **HULTON ARCHIVE/GETTY IMAGES. REPRODUCED BY PERMISSION.**

After the Battle of Surabaya, the government of Indonesia slowly took full control of the countryside. The independence of Indonesia had come in a revolutionary way. *Pemuda* had forced the nationalist leaders Sukarno and Hatta to proclaim the independence of Indonesia, while revolutionary gangs made clear that there was no future for Dutch or Indo-European citizens in the new Indonesia. The Indonesian Revolution also aimed at the traditional aristocratic elites who had cooperated with the Dutch. Their position in society was undermined, which made a return to colonial rule even more unlikely. However, a full social revolution never materialized, since it was in the interest of the government of the Republic of Indonesia to restore stability in order to win international support.

In the years that followed, the Republic of Indonesia combined the strategy of *diplomasi* (diplomacy) and *perjuangan* (struggle) against the Dutch. Through *diplomasi*, Indonesia became more and more acceptable to the Western powers, thereby slowly isolating the Dutch, who demonstrated their failure to come to terms with Indonesian independence when the Dutch Parliament rejected the original 1946 Linggadjati Agreement, in which the government of the Republic of Indonesia and a commission representing the Dutch government agreed to establish a sovereign federal Indonesian state connected with the Netherlands through a "Dutch-Indonesian Union". However, the majority of the Dutch parliament and the Dutch government wanted to establish a Dutch-dominated sovereign "Dutch-Indonesian Union" in which the Republic of Indonesia would play only a minor role. While the Republic of Indonesia was prepared to compromise as long as a sovereign Indonesian state would be established, the Dutch sought a continuation of their dominating role in the archipelago. These fundamentally different visions of the future inevitably led to military conflict. In the end, the Dutch tried to defeat the Republic of Indonesia in two military actions, to which the Indonesian army responded by waging guerrilla warfare, which kept Dutch forces too thinly spread over the country to gain control of Indonesia. The military actions also led to intervention by the United Nations, which sent a special United States–led committee to Indonesia to facilitate negotiations between the Netherlands and the Republic of Indonesia.

In 1948 in Madiun, a communist-led attempt to initiate a full social revolution within the Republic of Indonesia occurred. The Indonesian government was quick to suppress this revolt. Before the revolt the United States had remained more or less neutral, but having seen the Indonesian government acting with force against communism, the American government pressured the Dutch to give up their fight against the Republic of Indonesia. Finally, the Dutch accepted the independence of Indonesia on December 27, 1949. In order to appease conservative members of the Dutch parliament—which had to agree with the transfer of sovereignty with a two-thirds majority—Irian Jaya was not included in the agreement, but remained a Dutch colony until 1962. The Indonesian revolution brought Indonesia independence, but without a social revolution more radical nationalists had envisioned. In the early years of the Cold War, it was better to avoid such a revolution in order to achieve revolutionary results.

SEE ALSO *Dutch-Indonesian Wars.*

BIBLIOGRAPHY

Anderson, Benedict Richard O'Gorman. *Java in a Time of Revolution: Occupation and Resistance, 1944–1946.* Ithaca, NY: Cornell University Press, 1972.

Cribb, Robert. *Gangsters and Revolutionaries: The Jakarta People's Militia and the Indonesian Revolution, 1945–1949.* Honolulu: University of Hawaii Press, 1991.

Doel, H. W. van den. *Afscheid van Indië: De val van het Nederlandse imperium in Azië.* Amsterdam: Prometheus, 2000.

Frederick, William H. *Visions and Heat: The Making of the Indonesian Revolution.* Athens: Ohio University Press, 1989.

Kahin, George McTurnan. *Nationalism and Revolution in Indonesia.* Ithaca, NY: Cornell University Press, 1952.

Klooster, H. A. J. *Bibliography of the Indonesian Revolution: Publications from 1942 to 1994.* Leiden, Netherlands: KITLV Press, 1997.

Lucas, Anton. *One Soul One Struggle: Region and Revolution in Indonesia.* Sydney: Asian Studies Association of Australia, Allen and Unwin, 1991.

Reid, Anthony. *The Indonesian National Revolution, 1945–1950.* Hawthorn, Victoria: Longman, 1974.

Wim van den Doel

INTERNATIONAL TRADE IN THE PRE-MODERN PERIOD, MIDDLE EAST

Before the discovery of the Americas at the end of the fifteenth century, the Middle East (the area between Egypt and Iran) played an important role in world trade, especially in the high-value west–east and east–west trade. Between the eleventh and thirteenth centuries, the main west–east axis, the Silk Road, ran across the region from Aleppo to Baghdad, Rayy, Nishapur, Marv, and Samarkand, and through Kashgar to the T'ang capital, Chang'an (Xi'an). In the Indian Ocean, fleets traded from East Africa to the Red Sea, the Gulf, and the Indian subcontinent, and Muslim emporia in India traded with the southern Arabian Peninsula and with ports in Malaya and Indonesia, where Islam had arrived at the end of the thirteenth century. In Africa, trade routes followed the northern coasts, while there was a lively trans-Saharan trade, both north–south, from Fez and Sijilmassa to Timbuktu and Gao, and south–west and north–east, from the latter two towns and Kumbi Saleh and Walata across the desert to Alexandria and Cairo through Ghat, Zawila, Ajila, and Siwa. Mediterranean trade between the Middle East and North Africa and Europe in the twelfth through fourteenth centuries was conducted largely by the Italian maritime republics: Venice and its dependencies Zara, Ragusa (Dubrovnik), Salonika, and Crete; Pisa and Amalfi; and Genoa and its dependencies Palermo, Alméria, and Malaga.

The major components of the east to west exchanges were silk, porcelain, and spices, with dates, textiles, and horses going in the opposite direction. Slaves and gold from sub-Saharan Africa were brought across the desert in exchange for textiles and salt, and slaves were brought from East Africa to Egypt and to the Indian subcontinent in return for spices and textiles. Grain and salt were imported into Anatolia and further east from northern Europe; dates formed a major export to Europe from the Arab world, as did ivory and gold from sub-Saharan Africa. In general, therefore, there was a lively and continuous series of exchanges both around the Mediterranean and between the worlds of the Mediterranean and of the Indian Ocean. This was promoted, to an imported extent, by the continuous vibrancy of the urban life of the Islamic world, in cities such as Seville, Fez, Mahdiyya, Cairo, Damascus, Aleppo, Baghdad Basra, Hamadan, Shiraz, Marv, and Samarkand.

From the fourteenth century onward, close commercial relations existed between the Ottoman Empire and many western states, even in times of war. The sultan granted guarantees for residence, travel, and trade to "nations" or individuals trading with the Levant, in return for a kind of pledge of allegiance or friendship from those involved. These capitulations or *'ahdnames* were supposed to function reciprocally, and from the fifteenth century onward there were Ottoman merchant colonies in Ancona, Lvov, and Venice. To some extent, these agreements functioned as treaties of alliance, so that, for example, the terms of Ottoman-Venetian capitulatory agreements generally included clauses preventing the Venetians from hiring out their navy to the Papacy to enable it to fight against the Ottomans.

Capitulatory agreements were enacted with France in 1569—after which France took over from Venice as the leading trading nation in the Levant—and later with England and the Netherlands. Especially after the foundation of the Levant Company in 1581, which followed the capitulatory agreement of 1580, England came to dominate trade in the Eastern Mediterranean, typically sending goods overland to Turkey via Poland, Hungary, and Rumania—bringing gunpowder, tin, lead, woolen cloth, and probably most importantly, gold and silver coins. These commodities could be exchanged for raw silk (originally from Iran), which could then itself be traded for wine, currants, or olive oil from the Venetian-ruled Greek islands, or for cotton, carpets, and gallnuts (used in dyeing) from Anatolia, or for spices, drugs, and dyes from India or Indonesia. The Dutch Republic, which was favored because of its hostility to the Ottomans' enemies the Habsburgs, had long traded with the Ottomans, and formalized the relationship in 1612.

Similar arrangements existed in Iran, although Shah Ismāʿīl, the founder of the Safavid dynasty, was not strong enough to resist the establishment in 1507 of a Portuguese trading post that remained on Hormuz Island for more than a century. Under Shah ʿAbbās (1587–1629) the Portuguese were eclipsed both by the English East India Company (founded in 1600) and by the Dutch East India Company (founded in 1602), the latter of which established a trading counter at Bandar Abbas in 1622. Both states had capitulatory agreements with the Safavids, and both trading companies were substantially financed by the bankers of Surat.

Unfortunately, very little is known about Ottoman merchants, both Muslim and non-Muslim, before the nineteenth century, particularly whether individuals were regularly involved in large-scale trading operations in the same way as they were in India. We know that a fairly small number of Egyptian merchants controlled the coffee trade from Yemen to Europe via Egypt in the seventeenth and eighteenth centuries. Evidently, there were also substantial entrepreneurs in the Balkans, notably the Gümüşgerdan family of Plovdiv, whose members were engaged in woolen cloth manufacture, later

branching out into banking and money lending, and the Panayoti-Politi family from the Peloponnese, who were major ship-owners in the latter part of the eighteenth century.

In general terms, the capitulations continued in some form until the rise of the Turkish Republic (they were formally abolished under the Treaty of Montreux in 1936), but the position of the Ottoman Empire in international trade changed very greatly in the late eighteenth and nineteenth centuries. In the first place, the British navy's defeat of the French in Egypt in 1798 began a period of virtual British monopoly of Ottoman trade, and in 1838 the first of a series of highly unequal international trade treaties was concluded between Britain and the Ottoman Empire (the Treaty of Balta Liman). This treaty and its successors with other European states initiated a commercial regime under which the Europeans paid virtually no customs dues on the goods they or their local protégés imported into the Empire, while these privileges were not reciprocated for Ottoman subjects trading with Europe, unless, of course, they had acquired European nationality or protection. Amongst other important consequences, the treaties initiated a period of constantly unfavorable trade balances for the Empire, which were a major factor in bringing about the bankruptcy of the Ottoman state in 1875.

SEE ALSO *Dutch United East India Company; Dutch West India Company; Empire, Ottoman.*

BIBLIOGRAPHY

Abu-Lughod, Janet. *Before European Hegemony: The World System, A.D. 1250–1350.* New York and Oxford: Oxford University Press, 1989.

Chaudhuri, K. N. *Asia before Europe: Economy and Civilisation of the Indian Ocean from the Rise of Islam to 1750.* Cambridge, U.K.: Cambridge University Press, 1990.

İnalcık, Halil, with Donald Quataert, eds. *An Economic and Social History of the Ottoman Empire, 1300–1914.* 2 vols. Cambridge, U.K.: Cambridge University Press, 1994.

Lombard, Maurice. *The Golden Age of Islam.* Translated by Joan Spencer. Amsterdam and Oxford: North-Holland, 1975.

Lopez, Robert S., and Irving W. Raymond. *Medieval Trade in the Mediterranean World: Illustrative Documents Translated with Introductions and Notes.* New York: Columbia University Press, 1955; reprint, 1990.

Todorov, Nikolai. *The Balkan City, 1400–1900.* Seattle and London: University of Washington Press, 1983.

Walz, Terence. *Trade between Egypt and Bilād as-Sūdān, 1700–1820.* Cairo: Institut français d'archéologie orientale du Caire, 1978.

Peter Sluglett

IRAN

While it is convenient to organize Iranian political history in dynastic terms, this does an injustice to the complexity of forces that have shaped modern Iran. Alongside this dynastic history it is important to note that changes in Iran's economy and political culture did not always coincide with this neat organization but influenced it decisively. When Reza Shah seized power from the Qajar Dynasty, he had to appeal to tradition but also a new constitutional order. The traditions he appropriated—Twelver Shi'ism, the very sense of Iran's territorial extent—stretched not back to ancient past, but to a political and religious order established by the Safavid Dynasty in the sixteenth century.

THE SAFAVID DYNASTY (1501–1722)

The Safavid dynasty is mainly important for two reasons. First, as the Ottoman Empire did elsewhere in the Middle East, Iran's Safavid dynasty consolidated and defined traditional forms of administration and high culture. Second, the Safavid dynasty gave shape to two ideas that have endured as part of modern Iranian society: the dominance of Twelver Shi'ism in Iran and the very concept of where the territory of Iran is "naturally" or historically located. The boundaries of the Safavid Empire—from southern Iraq to the borders of Herat in modern Afghanistan, from Baku in present-day Azerbaijan to Kandahar in Afghanistan, and from the Caspian Sea to Bahrain—have come to define where Iran is (or ought to be) in the contemporary Iranian national imagination.

The Safavids began as a Sunni Muslim mystical order founded by Sheikh Safi al-Din of Ardabil (1252–1334) and evolved into a radical Shiite mystical order even as the Safavid family intermarried with the Sunni Aq-qoyyunlu dynasty. When Turkish tribal supporters of the Safavids, known collectively as the *qizilbash* ("redheads," for the color of their headgear), helped Esma'il I (d. 1524) defeat his Aq-qoyyunlu rivals for supremacy in northwestern Iran in 1501, a new chapter in both Iranian and Safavid history was inaugurated.

Shah Esma'il suppressed his own mystical order in favor of orthodox Twelver Shi'ism and forcibly converted the majority Sunni population of his expanding empire to Twelver Shi'ism. Twelver Shi'ites follow the example of twelve Imams whom, in contrast to Sunni Muslims, they view as the only legitimate leaders of the Islamic community since the death of the prophet Muhammad in 632 C.E. They await the return of the Twelfth Imam, Muhammad al-Mahdi, who went into a state of occultation in the Tenth Century until the return of the hidden Imam, Twelver Shi'ites invest religious leadership in the persons of ranking members of the clerical establishment,

recongnized as Marja' al-taqlid ("sources of imitation"). Suppression of the mystical order, paired with a policy of establishing a slave military with its paramount loyalty to the shah (or at least his money) created an enduring tension with the old *qizilbash* tribes, who remained the indispensable core of Safavid military power until the reign of Shah 'Abbas I ("the Great," r. 1587–1629). It was under 'Abbas I that the Safavid Empire reached its greatest extent, successfully engaging the growing European hegemony over world trade and achieving a fairly durable peace with its chief regional rival, the Ottoman Empire.

The social and institutional strength of Si'ism in the Safavid Empire was achieved through state-sponsored popular preaching, patronage of schools and shrines, and the development of a government-supervised clerical hierarchy, the apex of which was the office of *mollah-bashi* (head mullah). The office was created in the reign of the last Safavid shah, Soltan Hosayn (r. 1694–1722), and occupied by Mohammad Baqer Majlesi (d. 1698). Majlesi worked to extend clerical influence over court policy and supervised the *Bihar al-Anwar* ("Oceans of Light") collection of Twelver Shi'ite hadith (accounts of the sayings and actions of the prophet Muhammad and, in this case, the Imams).

THE CONFLICT BETWEEN THE AFSHARS, ZANDS, AND QAJARS, 1722–1997

It was the heavy-handed rule of Soltan Hosayn's governors in Qandahar that eventually provoked a rebellion among Afghan Sunni tribes in Kandahar, which resulted, ultimately, in an Afghan invasion of Iran. Much of the Safavid royal family was captured after the battle of Golanabad in 1722 and subsequently massacred in the capital, Isfahan. This set the stage for the rivalry of three *qizilbash* tribes, the members of which had more or less stood by as mercenary troops failed the Safavids at Golanabad, to attempt a restoration of the Safavid Empire.

These three tribes—the Afshars, the Zands, and the Qajars—each championed a different Safavid pretender to the throne as the Afghan tribes were pushed out of Iran. The chief of the Afshars, Nader (d. 1747), was the most successful initially. His restoration of many former territories of the Safavid Empire emboldened him to depose his puppet Safavid leader, Tahmasp II (r. 1722–1732), in favor of the young 'Abbas III in 1732. Nader claimed the Iranian throne for himself as Nader Shah in 1736 when 'Abbas III died. Nader later had Tahmasp II and his remaining sons executed.

Nader fueled his military ambitions with the wealth of the Mughal court when he invaded India in 1738 and sacked Delhi in 1739. He negotiated with the Ottomans for a marriage alliance and a reconciliation of Sunni and

© MARYLAND CARTOGRAPHICS. REPRODUCED BY PERMISSION.

Twelver Shiʿism, but these efforts collapsed when Nader Shah was assassinated in 1747. The contest among Afsharid tribal factions to claim Nader Shah's throne provided an opening for Karim Khan Zand (d. 1779) to assert his control over central Iran by 1760 in the name of yet another Safavid pretender, Esma ʿil III (d. 1773).

Karim Khan never styled himself as shah, selecting the title *vakil al-raʿeya* (representative of the [king's] subjects). His death caused similar factional fighting among the Zands, and this provided an opportunity for the Qajar tribe, with whom the Zand tribe had been vying for control of Iran since the collapse of the Afsharids.

The Qajars had managed to survive the previous decades as masters of Gilan and Mazandaran provinces;

their own factional strife was quashed by the brutal chieftain, Agha Mohammad Khan. After destroying the remnants of the Zand tribe (in 1794) and Afsharid power, Agha Mohammad was crowned shah in 1796. His assassination in 1797 might have spelled a quick end to the Qajar Empire because Agha Mohammad Shah, castrated as a young man while in the captivity of an Afghan warlord, had no heirs. However, Agha Mohammad had consolidated his power over the Qajar tribe, in part by arranging for his younger brother's son, crowned Fath ʿAli Shah (1797–1834), to succeed him.

Another important consequence of the interregnum that preceded the hegemony of the Qajars was a wave of Iranian Shiʿite clerics that emigrated to Najaf and

Karbala in Iraq. The surplus of clerical talent aggravated the ideological dispute between "traditionalist" *(akhbari)* clerics and "fundamentalist" *(osuli)* clerics, with the latter coming to dominate the shrine and religious school economies in southern Iraq. As Iranian clerics continued to train in Iraq and return to Iran once the relative stability of the Qajar period was established, the *osuli* dominance of Shi'ism in Iran was assured as well.

THE QAJAR PERIOD, 1797–1925

The Qajars had the daunting task of establishing their own legitimacy without disavowing certain crucial and useful aspects of the Safavid legacy: Twelver Shi'ism and Safavid administrative practices. The Qajar kings and aristocrats sponsored the renovation of Shiite shrines in Iran and Iraq and encouraged the production of *ta'ziyeh* (passion play) performances commemorating the martyrdom of Imam Husayn, the grandson of the Prophet Muhammad, at Karbala in 680. But in maintaining their political and religious legitimacy, the Qajars faced two challenges. From the outside, the pace of European "balance-of-power" politics would bring semicolonial domination of Iran by Great Britain and Russia, making the preservation of the Qajar Empire's borders a difficult challenge, to say nothing of expanding them (though the Qajars tried throughout the nineteenth century to do so). Internally, the Qajars would be rocked by a religious rebellion: the Babi/Baha'i movement. These combined pressures forced questions of reform and modernization on the Qajars as it had on the neighboring Ottoman Empire.

Fath 'Ali Shah was successful in consolidating Qajar control over the Iranian plateau, but he failed to reestablish Iranian control over the Caucasus and lost control of Azerbaijan north of the Aras River in two disastrous wars with the Russian Empire (1804–1812 and 1826–1828). The treaties that concluded these wars (Golestan, 1813, and Turcomanchai, 1828) formalized the unequal relationship between the Qajars and their northern neighbors.

Russian gains in Iran gave further impetus for Great Britain to strengthen its presence there also. As various princes vied to succeed the present king or sought to secure their positions in Iran's provincial capitals, the aid of Russia and Great Britain was sought by all. From 1828 onward, no Qajar king or politician could simply ignore the wishes of Moscow or London, with the best strategy often being to play the two "Great Game" rivals off of one another.

Another strategy, which did not bear much fruit, was the cultivation of better relations with other Western countries (France, Prussia, Austria, and, ironically, the United States). The relationship with the United States,

in fact, produced another challenge to the religious legitimacy of the Qajars in that American Christian missionaries had an expanding presence in Iran over the course of the nineteenth century. At the same time, Russia became Iran's main trading partner, insisting on the sort of favorable trade terms it had exacted from the Ottoman Empire. Other European countries (or their colonies, such as British India) also secured terms of trade akin to that of Russia. These limits on import taxes and accompanying privileges of legal "extraterritoriality" for European subjects and their clients further eroded Iranian sovereignty.

The Qajars inherited an administrative system that was largely a Safavid creation—a military patronage state in which the Qajar tribe was only first among tribal equals. The unreliability of tribal levies in times of war or internal crisis was the primary spur to reform. Indeed, the inadequacy of its military, its bureaucracy, and its education system was brought home to the Qajars by the difficult encounters with Russia and Great Britain. As early as 1815, Iranians were being sent abroad to receive training in military and medical arts. The Ottoman Empire also served as a model for Qajar modernization.

The first Qajar military and administrative reforms under Crown Prince 'Abbas Mirza (d. 1833) were called *nezam-e jadid* (new order). Under Naser al-Din Shah (1831–1896), several top-down reforms were initiated. Before he fell out of favor with Naser al-Din Shah, the prime minister, Mirza Taqi Khan Amir Kabir (d. 1852), had created a state technical school (the Dar al-Fonun) and the beginnings of a state media. Subsequent modernization efforts sought to expand the effective administrative control of the government and to fund the education of modern military officers and bureaucrats for the state.

Later modernization efforts, with Ottoman-inspired names such as *tanzimat-e hasaneh* (the good reordering), advanced in fits and starts. These efforts generally languished due to lack of funding. No matter how forward-looking the planning, the Qajar state presided over a medieval, agricultural economy. Money could not be raised to support the modernization of Iran's transportation and communication infrastructure, let alone the industrialization of the agricultural or manufacturing sectors of the Iranian economy.

The Qajars resorted to development concessions (such as the aborted De Reuter concession of 1872 and the much narrower tobacco concession of 1890) to attract foreign capital for Iran's development schemes. Owing to a mix of local opposition and rivalry between Great Britain and Russia for winning such concessions, the more ambitious concession schemes failed. The Iranian government under Naser al-Din Shah began to go into debt and to hand over key government functions, such as the collection of customs and the creation of a reliable unit of the military (the Persian Cossack Brigade), to foreign companies or foreign governments.

The Anglo–Russian rivalry in Iran had complex effects on the modernization of Iran's infrastructure. British concern over imperial communication with India undoubtedly helped the development of telegraph communications in Iran. On the other hand, the Iranian government was forced to postpone the development of rail transportation throughout the nineteenth century because the British and Russians could not come to an accord about how such development contracts would be shared between them.

In 1896 Naser al-Din Shah was assassinated near the Shah 'Abd al-'Azim cemetery by Reza Khan Kermani (d. 1897). In Kermani's desperate act can be found strands of two important movements: the religious movement of Baha'ism and the more amorphous cultural movement known, mainly in retrospect, as the *tajaddod* (renewal) movement. Baha'ism began as the Shi'ite heresy of Babism when its founder, Mohammad 'Ali Shirazi (d. 1850), proclaimed himself to be the Bab, or "gate," facilitating the arrival of the *mahdi* ("The Guided One") and later serving as the gateway to new divine revelation. It was mainly during the reign of Naser al-Din Shah that the Qajars examined and finally condemned Shirazi as a heretic and engaged in a civil war to suppress the movement, driving its leaders underground or overseas.

In exile in the Ottoman Empire in 1866, one of the followers of the Bab, Hosayn 'Ali Nuri Baha'ollah (d. 1892), declared himself to be the true heir of the Bab for leadership of the Babi community. This led to a split between the majority Baha'is, who accepted the teachings of Baha'ollah, and the Azali Babis, who considered themselves to be correct followers of the teaching of the Bab under the leadership of Baha'ollah's younger half-brother, Mirza Yahya Nuri (Sobh-e Azal, d. 1912).

Many Iranian followers of Babism and Baha'ism proved receptive to the ideals of renewalism. These ideals were advanced in the writings of Mirza Fath 'Ali Akhundzadeh (d. 1878, an atheist), Mirza Malkam Khan (d. 1908, an Armenian convert to Islam and disgruntled member of the Qajar bureaucracy), and Mirza Aqa Khan Kermani. These writers expressed a desire to restore a pristine Iranian national character through the modernization of education, social reforms, and the democratization of politics.

Renewalist writings also expressed a resentment of Western hegemony and suspicion of religious tradition. Nonetheless, Iranian renewalists forged relationships with other activists, such as the pan-Islamist Jalal al-Din Asadabadi ("Al-Afghani," 1838–1897). The Qajar court

had also flirted with Al-Afghani, but Naser al-Din Shah fell out with him over the tobacco concession of 1890, expelling him from Iran in 1891. Once outside Iran, Al-Afghani was quoted in Mirza Malkom Khan's London-based newspaper *Qanun* (The Law) on many issues, including opposition to the tobacco concession. In the end, renewalist intellectuals, the traditional clergy, and elite merchants forged an alliance and sustained a nationwide protest (facilitated, ironically, by the British-built telegraph network and the inviolate nature of the diplomatic post, which allowed *Qanun* and other expatriate Iranian newspapers to be smuggled past Qajar censors) that forced the cancellation of the tobacco concession in 1892.

The consequences of all these connections were visited upon Naser al-Din Shah in 1896. His assassin was a disciple of Al-Afghani and implicated Mirza Aqa Khan Kermani as well. Both men were in the Ottoman Empire at the time of the assassination. Al-Afghani was under house arrest, dying of cancer, but Kermani was extradited and ultimately executed along with Mirza Reza Khan Kermani in 1896. The reign of Mozaffar al-Din Shah (1896–1907) continued the trend of political suppression, top-down reforms, and development concessions (most notably, the d'Arcy concession of 1901 that led to the formation of the Anglo-Persian Oil Company in 1909, the first oil company in the Middle East) that simultaneously deepened Iran's financial problems and trained a westernized elite increasingly drawn to the democratic strands of renewalism. Economic disruptions caused by the Russo-Japanese War of 1905 and resentment over heavy-handed government tactics to prevent hoarding by merchants sparked a new alliance of intellectuals, merchants, and ranking clergy against the monarchy.

Politicians with renewalist sympathies channeled the protest toward the creation of a Parliament (Majles) and a constitution over the course of 1906 to 1907. But no sooner was constitutional order established than disputes broke out over the nature of democracy in Iran. Some religious clerics felt that Islamic law was being flouted by the constitution and efforts to draft supplementary articles to the constitution failed to win the conservatives back. When Mohammad 'Ali Shah (1872–1925) ascended the throne in 1907, it was with a mind toward using this conservative reaction (and Russian support) to restore the autocratic rule his father lost.

In 1908 the Parliament was bombarded by the Persian Cossack Brigade, and civil war broke out throughout the country. Constitutionalist forces gained the upper hand in 1909, and Mohammad 'Ali Shah was deposed in favor his young son, Soltan Ahmad (r. 1909–1925). Parliamentary leaders quickly moved to bolster their positions with the creation of the Swedish-officered gendarmes as a counterweight to the Persian Cossack Brigade.

In 1911 Russia invaded Iran again over the employment of American Morgan C. Shuster as a financial adviser. Much to the chagrin of some British intellectuals and politicians who formed the Persia Committee to lobby against the British foreign policy (led by Cambridge Persianist and chronicler of the constitutional revolution E. G. Browne [1862–1926]), Great Britain offered no effective support for Iran's fledgling democracy, choosing to remain bound instead by a 1907 agreement with Russia to divide Iran into "spheres of influence."

The British attitude toward Russian involvement in Iran changed over the course of World War I (1914–1918) and the Bolshevik Revolution of 1917. Russian, British, German, and Ottoman agents and forces all violated Iran's official neutrality during the war, leaving both the central government and the promise of parliamentary rule in tatters. In addition to consolidating its colonial gains in the Middle East, the fiercely anti-Bolshevik policy of Great Britain led it to attempt the creation of an Anglo-Persian protectorate in 1919. This was foiled by parliamentary opposition. The British then tried another tactic. They cultivated Colonel Reza Khan (1878–1944) of the Persian Cossack Brigade, and in February 1921 Reza Khan and the pro-British journalist Sayyed Ziya' al-Din Tabataba'i (d. 1969) organized a coup. The coup supporters were ostensibly loyal to the Qajar court, but many prominent Qajar aristocrats found themselves in jail for a time.

Initially securing the portfolio of the minister of war and the title *sardar sepah* (commander of the army), Reza Khan moved quickly to displace Tabataba'i, and by 1923 had secured the position of prime minister. Reza Khan combined a ruthless military campaign against an array of separatist movements (e.g., Kurds under Isma'il Simko and the Jangali movement of Mirza Kuchek Khan of Gilan) and autonomous provincial and tribal leaders with the shrewd cultivation of parliamentary politicians.

Early political factions, such as the Social Democrats and others, had developed into more ideologically coherent parties by the end of World War I in 1918. Despite the passage of universal male suffrage in 1913, these parties did not represent large organized constituencies and still depended on the personalities and patronage networks of their leaders. The Socialist Party, for example, was led by a Qajar prince. Reza Khan developed especially close relations with the nationalist Tajaddod (Renewal) Party, which had influential press organs both inside and outside Iran and appealed to frustrated supporters of the constitution, who were increasingly interested in strong central leadership of the state to force through modernization programs.

Nonetheless, Reza Khan's first attempt to remove the Qajars backfired badly when a proposal to turn Iran into a Turkish-style republic was met with clerical, popular, and parliamentary opposition in 1924. He quickly regrouped and pressured the Parliament into deposing Ahmad Shah (1898–1930), who hardly helped himself by refusing to return to Iran from an extended European holiday, and into proclaiming Reza Khan's Pahlavi family as the new dynasty of constitutional monarchs on December 15, 1925. The parliamentary vote to end the Qajar dynasty prolonged the institution of the monarchy, but also cemented the role of an elected legislature in Iranian politics.

Even the Islamic Republic of Iran could not completely dispense with the institution of parliament, as it did with the monarchy in 1979. The Qajar-era constitution (1906–1907) had guaranteed clerical oversight of the legislative process, but neither parliamentary politicians nor the Pahlavis enforced that guarantee. Such religious oversight became a central principle of the constitution of the Islamic Republic in 1980.

SEE ALSO *Khomeini, Ayatollah Ruhollah; Tobacco Protest, Iran.*

BIBLIOGRAPHY

Amanat, Abbas. *Pivot of the Universe: Nasir al-Din Shah Qajar and the Iranian Monarchy, 1831–1896.* Berkeley: University of Californian Press, 1997.

Babayan, Kathryn. *Mystics, Monarchs and Messiahs: Cultural Landscapes of Early Modern Iran.* Cambridge, MA: Distributed by the Center for Middle Eastern Studies of Harvard by Harvard University Press, 2002.

Bakhash, Shaul. *Iran: Monarchy, Bureaucracy and Reform Under the Qajars, 1858–1896.* London: I. B. Tauris, 1978.

The Cambridge History of Iran. Volume 6: The Timurid and Safavid Periods. Edited by Peter Jackson and Lawrence Lockhart. Cambridge, U.K.: Cambridge University Press, 1986.

The Cambridge History of Iran. Volume 7: From Nadir Shah to the Islamic Republic. Edited by Peter Avery, Gavin Hambly and Charles Melville. Cambridge, U.K.: Cambridge University Press, 1991.

Melville, C. P. *Safavid Persia: The History and Politics of an Islamic Society.* London: I.B. Tauris, 1996.

Savory, Roger. M. *Iran Under the Safavids.* Cambridge, U.K.: Cambridge University Press, 1980.

Tucker, Ernest. *Nadir Shah's Quest for Legitimacy in Post-Safavid Iran.* Gainesville: University Press of Florida, 2006.

Camron Amin

IRAQ

Iraq's entry into the colonial period is closely connected to its entry into statehood. Iraq as a separate territory with state borders is a product of World War I (1914–1918), officially a creation of the League of Nations, but in fact a result of the expansion of Great Britain's influence in the Middle East. This does not mean, however, that Iraq was merely a Western design, assuming that the population was unprepared for statehood. In fact, the territory of Iraq had long been part of the Ottoman Empire and, to different degrees during different periods of history, its formidable system of state administration.

OTTOMAN IRAQ BEFORE 1914

Iraq was formed out of three former Ottoman provinces with Basra as a capital in the South, Baghdad in the center, and Mosul in the North. The provinces were first submitted under Ottoman rule in the sixteenth century, but remained a frontier land between the Ottomans and the Iranian Safavid Empire. Mesopotamia was of strategic and symbolic importance for both. The Euphrates and Tigris were important waterways and Basra, controlling the access to the Persian Gulf, was an important hub of Indian Ocean trade. Moreover, the country hosted the most important shrines of Shia Islam in the towns of Najaf, Kerbala, and others. The struggle between the Sunni Ottomans and the Shiite Safavids over Mesopotamia lasted until 1639 when the provinces fell, finally, into Ottoman hands. Iraq, however, remained a frontier region. The complex Ottoman system of central control and local autonomy was bound to give way to local forces. In the eighteenth century, the Ottoman provinces of Iraq became virtually independent under the rule of local dynasties, the most important being Georgian Mamluks, a military elite of slaves that managed to take over governorship in Baghdad and Basra. They officially acknowledged Ottoman suzerainty, but coexisted with local elites in a complex system of checks and balances that guaranteed mutual interests.

In the early nineteenth century, the growing threat of European imperialism prompted reform efforts in the Ottoman Empire that would strengthen the state apparatus. In 1831 Ottoman troops started to reassert Istanbul's control over the Mesopotamian provinces ousting the Mamluk pashas. Efforts to integrate Iraq into a reformed and more centralized Ottoman state system were only partially successful against local resistance, though. The elite of Ottoman bureaucrats, therefore, had to enter arrangements with urban notable families and the tribal leaders. Increasing numbers of influential people in the provinces started to accept a state-centered system of power sharing and running political and economic affairs within a patronage system overseen by state authorities.

During this period colonial penetration affected Mesopotamia in the framework of the empire as a whole. In the nineteenth century, British merchants became a serious competition for local tradesmen. In 1861 the Ottoman government gave out a license to a British steamship company on the Tigris. It supported British interests in neighboring Iran in competition with tsarist Russia, and created a link to the British strongholds in the Persian Gulf. In the so-called Baghdad-Bahn project the German Empire convinced Istanbul in 1902 to grant a license for building a railway line that would link Berlin and the European railway network with Baghdad. This project was part of a wider German strategy to enter an alliance with the Ottoman Empire. Even though it was never fully realized, it stirred a lot of British anxiety about competition in the Middle Eastern region. This is the background of the decision to send British Indian troops to Basra almost immediately after the outbreak of World War I in August 1914.

FROM MILITARY RULE TO THE MANDATE: 1914–1921

Basra was already under British control in November 1914. After a severe setback in 1916 at Kut, a town southeast of Baghdad where an entire British army surrendered to the Ottomans, the British captured Baghdad in 1917. Kirkuk in Northern Iraq fell in 1918, and British troops occupied Mosul after the armistice of Mudros in October 1918. After the war, both U.S. President Woodrow Wilson's (1856–1924) plans for the provinces of the Ottoman Empire and the secretly negotiated Sykes-Picot agreement of 1916 between Great Britain and France envisaged a partition of the territory into smaller nation-states. The mandate system designed at the Paris peace conferences was, however, a means to reconcile colonial interest with the Wilsonian idea of self-determination. Iraq was already under British military rule when Great Britain was assigned the mandate over it. Now, it was responsible for preparing the country to become independent with viable institutions.

The creation of Iraq as a separate entity was not compelling, though. The Mesopotamian provinces of Basra and Baghdad constituted a separate geographical entity oriented toward the Persian Gulf, but Mosul had traditionally closer links with Syria than with Baghdad and Basra. Turkey put a claim on Northern Iraq, too, which promised the future discovery of oil fields. It took until 1926 and the mediation of the League of Nations until Turkey acknowledged Mosul and Kirkuk as part of Iraq.

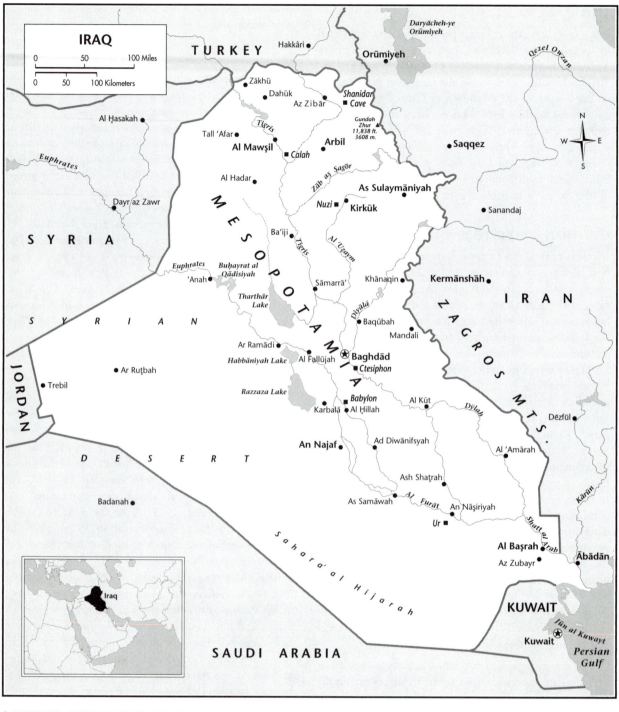

© MARYLAND CARTOGRAPHICS. REPRODUCED BY PERMISSION.

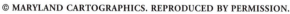

British-controlled territories in the Middle East did not follow one stringent line of policy. Palestine had been occupied by the British command in Cairo, which was in close touch with the government in London, whereas the Iraqi occupation had been in the hands of British India. Delhi was less attuned to the new anticolonial atmosphere in international politics. The first years of British rule in Iraq therefore saw a competition between British Indian promoters of direct colonial rule and those who favored indirect rule more in accordance with the rules of the mandate. At the same time this would help to uphold British interests with minimal expenses, because it was nearly impossible to justify a costly commitment in Mesopotamia to the parliament in London. After a large

642   ENCYCLOPEDIA OF WESTERN COLONIALISM SINCE 1450

countrywide revolt in 1920 had absorbed a large number of troops and financial resources until it was suppressed, the option of indirect rule prevailed.

Other than usual, the British efforts in Mesopotamia had not been sufficiently prepared by intelligence work. Information about social circumstances and power structures were therefore scarce and rested to some extent on prejudices. British administrators believed that there was a clear-cut division between the urban and the rural spheres. The real Arabs were the tribes controlling the countryside, whereas the city dwellers, they assumed, were corrupt, unreliable, and under the influence of centuries of Ottoman Oriental Despotism. The rise of mostly Shiite tribes during the revolt of 1920 proved that the actions of Iraqis were less predictable. The Cairo Conference of 1921 therefore drafted a plan for the constitutional future of a self-administered Iraqi monarchy under British supervision.

THE MANDATE SYSTEM: 1921–1932

There was as little dynastic tradition in Iraq as there was a cohesive national territory and identity. London put Prince Faisal (1885–1933) on the throne, who was the son of Sherif Husayn ibn 'Ali (1854–1931) of Mecca and military leader of the Arab revolt of World War I. After his troops had captured Damascus in 1918, Faisal had ruled Syria. When the French removed him in 1920, it was a matter of disappointment for all Arab nationalists that British arrangements with Paris from the Sykes-Picot agreement weighed heavier than their commitment to support Faisal as an Arab leader. The throne of Iraq was meant to make up for this. Moreover, London believed that Faisal's family origin as a descendant of the Prophet would give him authority among the diverse groups of the country. Faisal, however, was aware that he was entirely dependent on British support, and while the urban notability acquiesced to the new state structures soon, the tribal realm of Iraq did not comply. Other than the constitutional structures imposed on the state suggested, the new government needed British military force necessarily to coerce the tribes into obedience. Aid troops recruited among Assyrian Christians that had fled from Eastern Anatolia into Iraq, and the British Royal Air Force took on this task. Tribes were bombed into paying taxes, whereas London was reluctant to give in to demands of the Iraqi government to form an Iraqi conscript army. Conscription would have aroused even more opposition from the tribes.

London wanted to get rid of the mandate duties as quickly as possible in order to reduce the burden on the British treasury. In order to do this they had to fulfill contradictory tasks: convince the League of Nations that Iraq was fit to govern itself democratically, and at the same time bind the existing power elites—tribes, notables, Ottoman administrative elites—to a state that was dominated by a foreign king together with a military elite that had no stake in the traditional patronage networks of the country. These so-called Sherifian Officers of Iraqi origin had fought under Faisal's command during the Arab revolt and formed his entourage in Syria. Later they joined him in Iraq and entered high government posts. In order to make Iraq presentable to the League of Nations, the British tried to strengthen the state by a mixture of coercive power and support of the state elite. Effectively, the old and new elites of the country joined interests as one landholding class. The Sherifian Officers dominated this process through the legislative processes in the new state, creating possibilities to acquire large portions of former Ottoman state domain land, for example. The organic law of 1924 gave the overwhelming power to the executive, and in a society that lacked a developed public sphere, elections to the parliament could be easily manipulated. An abstract institutional power of constitutional structures therefore never emerged.

The treaty of independence between Iraq and Great Britain was signed in 1930 and became effective with Iraq's entry into the League of Nations in 1932. The treaty remained contentious, though, because it provided for a continued British military presence in the country. Two air bases were maintained, and Britain had the right to use Iraqi communication and transport lines in the case of war. Furthermore, Great Britain remained the exclusive supplier of military hardware and took responsibility for military training. On top of that, a large number of British advisers stayed in Iraqi ministries. The British ambassador remained highly influential, and Britain virtually controlled the Iraqi economy.

IRAQ IN THE 1930s

Nevertheless, Iraqi politicians had a wide leeway after 1932, even in foreign policy, which became the most contentious issue of the British–Iraqi relationship in the 1930s. The treaty remained a major concern of the Iraqi opposition, which ranged from pan-Arab nationalists and moderate socialists to the nascent communist movement. Ideological concerns were overshadowed by personal competition inside the existing patronage system. The Sherifian Officers and members of the old elites had all built their own power bases. After the unexpected death of King Faisal in 1933, the rivalries broke open and initiated a period of political turmoil and violence. Members of the opposition instigated tribal uprisings in order to put pressure on the frequently changing governments. The contradiction between the official statements of politicians and their pragmatic reliance on British support when they were in power led to growing frustration and political extremism among a younger generation of graduates from high schools, universities, and military academies.

The most important challenge to the authority of the pro-British Sherifian regime was the Iraqi army. It adopted British military tactics of coercion against tribal disobedience and applied them with brutal force against the Assyrian Levies and their families, who were stripped of their task in independent Iraq. In 1932 many were massacred by Iraqi military units after they had unsuccessfully pledged for autonomy. This created an international outcry, but no action followed. General Bakr Sidqi (1890–1937), a former Ottoman officer of Kurdish origin, gained a lot of authority in the army from his vital role in this and other internal military campaigns against rebellious tribes. In 1936 he staged the first military coup of Iraq, but in 1937 he was assassinated and his anti-Arab nationalist and moderately socialist government removed in a further military coup. During the following years, a clique of younger military officers with a strong Arab nationalist commitment dominated Iraqi affairs in a series of putsches. They represented a section of the younger generation that was highly critical of Iraq's close association with Great Britain

WORLD WAR II AND THE NATIONALIST CHALLENGE

The British did not interfere directly during these tumultuous years. Even during the period of military coups, the civilian governments would not put into question the Anglo-Iraqi treaty. Only with rising tension in Europe toward the outbreak of World War II (1939–1945) did London perceive political and ideological conflicts in Iraq differently. The young intelligentsia of Iraq used the nascent public sphere in newspapers and political clubs to challenge the Iraqi alliance with Great Britain. Many still supported a close relationship with London, but British officials reported with growing frenzy about a potential alignment of Iraq with Nazi Germany. This anxiety grew when German armies defeated France and pushed into the Mediterranean during 1940.

The new situation with a British Empire on the defense created two camps in Iraq: The throne and Nuri as-Said (1888–1958), a Sherifian officer and leader of the pro-British faction, demanded unconditional support for Britain, whereas a second camp in the officer corps, especially a group of four younger officers, the so-called Golden Square, demanded that Iraq should at least remain neutral, if not take sides with a victorious Germany. In April 1941 the Golden Square organized a military coup that ousted the pro-British regent Abdullah (1882–1951)who ruled on behalf of the minor Faisal II

(1935–1958), and Nuri as-Said. Rashid Ali al-Gaylani (1892–1965) became prime minister of a government of national defense. In London, Winston Churchill (1874–1965) decided that it was time to act. Insisting on the provisions of the Anglo-Iraqi treaty, he demanded rights of passage for large British Indian military contingents. Hostilities broke out on May 2. The British forces defeated the Iraqi army within one month. German and Italian air support arrived too late and had no impact. On May 31, Baghdad surrendered and submitted the country to the second British occupation.

THE DEMISE OF THE SEMICOLONIAL STATE: 1941–1958

The British occupation prompted a restoration of the monarchical state, its patronage system, and the dominance of the Sherifian paradigm. Nuri became the guarantor of the status quo and a close alliance with Britain. Iraq after World War II was a different country, however. Expanding state education, the military service established in 1934, beginning industrialization, and urbanization had turned the state from a closed elite affair into a daily reality for even the remotest places of the country. The growth of an urban proletariat accompanied the emergence of a mass society. Young men of underprivileged communities, such as the Shiites, demanded access to the state resources. It became more and more difficult to uphold a patronage system and legitimize the Sunni dominance in the inner government circles. Illegal parties such as the Iraqi Communists and later the Baath Party gained in influence among the masses. In this context, Iraq's economic and military dependence on Great Britain became the dominant symbol for the corruption of the old regime. Mass protests made the government revoke the Portsmouth treaty in 1948, which would have ended the British military presence in Iraq, but would have bound military planning, training, and expenditures to Great Britain for another twenty-five years.

During the period, semicolonial dependence became increasingly intertwined with Cold War issues. After the Egyptian revolution in 1952, the people of the Arab world had won an idol in Egypt's President Gamal 'Abd an-Nasir (1918–1970). His nonalignment policy and inclination toward the communist camp challenged Nuri as-Said's clear pro-British and pro-Western commitment. Nuri presented himself as an Arab nationalist, but under the condition of the regional dominance of the Iraqi monarchy and the internal status quo. The Baghdad Pact of regional cooperation between Great Britain, Iraq, Turkey, Iran, and Pakistan signed in 1955 was a clear sign of alienation between Iraq and revolutionary Arab nationalist regimes such as the ones in Syria and Egypt.

By joining the pact, the Iraqi regime underlined its self-perception as more of a regional player than as a forerunner of an Arab unification. Furthermore, the pact underlined Britain's role in Iraq's foreign policy.

The Iraqi monarchy fell in 1958, when important sections of the Iraqi officer corps had lost confidence in the regime. It was outdated, a product of the colonial past that had given way to the new Cold War world order. In that, a conspiratorial group of Free Officers, inspired by the Egyptian revolution of 1952 and the creation of the United Arab Republic between Egypt and Syria early in 1958, staged a coup on July 14. Many of the officers had a vivid memory of the 1941 war against Great Britain and the following suppression of pan-Arab tendencies in the Iraqi army, which they considered a humiliation. Politically, however, the officers entered the center stage unprepared and without a clear ideological commitment. The revolution of 1958, therefore, brought an end to Iraq's close association with Great Britain, but it also started a period of turmoil, dictatorship, and unprecedented violence that has still not come to an end even with the demise of Saddam Hussein in 2003 (b. 1937).

GREAT BRITAIN AND IRAQI OIL

Even after the 1958 revolution, the Iraqi oil industry remained largely under international control until it was nationalized in 1972. The dictatorial regimes of the following decades depended on the regular revenue guaranteed by state licenses given to the Iraq Petroleum Company (IPC).

Already prior to World War I, the Ottoman government had granted the first licenses to explore Iraqi oil fields to the Turkish Petroleum Company (TPC), an international consortium. After the Ottoman defeat, British companies dominated the consortium, and the British government held a substantial part of the shares. The precarious financial situation of the Iraqi state made it easy for the TPC, from 1929 named IPC, to exert pressure. Oil was discovered in 1927 only, and exporting did not start until 1934. After independence, the Iraqi government began to issue limited concessions for further exploration to other companies, such as the British Oil Development Company (BOD), with a major Italian interest.

After 1936 the German government wanted to combine an investment in the BOD with a concession over a large railway construction project to be shared with France. It would have linked the northern oil fields via Mosul to the railway network of French Syria and its Mediterranean ports. However, the British convinced Italy to cede the majority of BOD shares to the IPC in exchange for oil supply during the Second Italo-Abyssinian War (1935–1936). The Iraqi government chose a southern railway option, which should link Iraq to Palestinian ports; therefore, British control over Iraqi oil remained unchallenged. After the war, oil royalties became the most important component of Iraqi state revenues, but IPC control over oil production underlined the public impression that Iraq remained dependent on the former mandate power.

IRAQI JEWS AND ZIONISM

When Iraq was founded as a state in 1921, Jews entered many state offices because they were better prepared than others to serve in the new administration. The Iraqi Jewish community had been one of the most intellectually and economically successful Jewish communities in the Arab world. Jewish schools were the first to offer modern education starting from the 1860s.

After World War I, Iraqi Jews were very skeptical about Zionism that struck roots in Palestine. They considered themselves Iraqi patriots, faithful to the Iraqi state. During the late 1920s and the 1930s, however, Arab nationalist rhetoric identified the Zionist project more and more with British imperialist policy in the Arab lands and no longer made a clear distinction between Jews and Zionists. After the downfall of the Gaylani government in 1941, between 100 and 200 Jews fell victim to a pogrom mostly committed by youth bands in Baghdad. The situation of Jews in Iraq improved slightly under the restored old regime, but it became increasingly unbearable after the foundation of the state of Israel in 1948, when the Arab–Israeli conflict became a propagandistic device of Arab governments in general. The majority of Iraqi Jews left for Israel in 1951.

SEE ALSO *Mandate Rule; Mandate System; Oil.*

BIBLIOGRAPHY

Batatu, Hanna. *The Old Social Classes and the Revolutionary Movements of Iraq: A Study of Iraq's Old Landed and Commercial Classes and of its Communists, Ba'thists and Free Officers.* Princeton, NJ: Princeton University Press, 1978.

Cleveland, William L. *The Making of an Arab Nationalist: Ottomanism and Arabism in the Life and Thought of Sati' al-Husri.* Princeton, NJ: Princeton University Press, 1971.

Cohen, Hayyim J. "The Anti-Jewish Farhûd in Baghdad, 1941." *Middle Eastern Studies* 3 (1) (1966): 2–17.

Dodge, Toby. *Inventing Iraq: The Failure of Nation-Building and A History Denied.* New York: Columbia University Press, 2003.

Eppel, Michael. *The Palestine Conflict in the History of Modern Iraq: the Dynamics of Involvement, 1928–1948.* London and Portland, OR: Cass, 1994.

Fernea, Robert A., and W. Roger Louis, eds. *The Iraqi Revolution of 1958: the Old Social Classes Revisited.* London and New York: I.B. Tauris, 1991.

Gat, Moshe. *The Jewish Exodus from Iraq, 1948–1951*. London and Portland, OR: Cass, 1997.

Güçlü, Yücel. "The Role of the Ottoman-Trained Officers in Independent Iraq." *Oriente Moderno* 21 (2) (2002): 441–458.

Haim, Sylvia G. "Aspects of Jewish Life in Baghdad under the Monarchy." *Middle Eastern Studies* 12 (1976): 188–208.

Haj, Samira. *The Making of Iraq, 1900–1963: Capital, Power, and Ideology*. Albany: State University of New York Press, 1997.

Hopwood, Derek, Habib Ishow, and Thomas Koszinowski, eds. *Iraq: Power and Society*. Reading, U.K., and Oxford: Ithaca Press, 1993.

Kedourie, Elie. "The Break between Muslims and Jews in Iraq." In *Jews among Arabs: Contacts and Boundaries*, edited by Mark R. Cohen and Abraham L. Udovitch. Princeton, NJ: Darwin Press, 1989.

Kelidar, Abbas, ed. *The Integration of Modern Iraq*. London: Croom Helm, 1979.

Luizard, Pierre-Jean. "Mémoires d'Irakiens: à la découverte d'une société vaincue." *Monde arabe: Maghreb Machrek* 163 (1999): 5–23.

Lukitz, Liora. *Iraq: the Search for National Identity*. London and Portland, OR: Cass, 1995.

Marr, Phebe. *The Modern History of Iraq*, 2nd ed. Boulder, CO: Westview Press, 2004.

Mejcher, Helmut. *Die Politik und das Öl im Nahen Osten*. Stuttgart: Klett-Cotta, 1990.

Nakash, Yitzhak. *The Shi'is of Iraq*. Princeton, NJ: Princeton University Press, 1994.

Rodrigue, Aron. *French Jews, Turkish Jews: The Alliance Israélite Universelle and the Politics of Jewish Schooling in Turkey, 1860–1925*. Bloomington: Indiana University Press, 1990.

Shikara, Ahmad Abdul Razzaq. *Iraqi Politics, 1921–41: the Interaction between Domestic Politics and Foreign Policy*. London: LAAM, 1987.

Simon, Reeva S. *Iraq Between the Two World Wars: The Creation and Implementation of a Nationalist Ideology*. New York: Columbia University Press, 1986.

Simon, Reeva S., and Eleanor H. Tejirian, eds. *The Creation of Iraq, 1914–1921*. New York: Columbia University Press, 2004.

Sluglett, Peter. *Britain in Iraq: 1914–1932*. London: Ithaca Press, 1976.

Tarbush, Mohammad A. *The Role of the Military in Politics: A Case Study of Iraq to 1941*, 2nd ed. London: Ithaca Press, 1983.

Tripp, Charles. *A History of Iraq*, 2nd ed. Cambridge, U.K.: Cambridge University Press, 2002.

Wien, Peter. "Discipline and Sacrifice: Authoritarian, Totalitarian, and Pro-Fascist Inclinations in Iraqi Arab Nationalism, 1932–1941." Ph.D. thesis, Rheinische Friedrich-Wilhelms-Universität Bonn, 2003.

Wien, Peter. "'Watan' and 'Rujula': The Emergence of a New Model of Youth in Interwar Iraq." In *Youth and Youth Culture in the Contemporary Middle East*, edited by Jørgen Bæk Simonsen. Aarhus: Aarhus University Press, 2005.

Zubaida, Sami. "Contested Nations: Iraq and the Assyrians." *Nations and Nationalism* 6 (2000): 363–382.

Peter Wien

IRELAND, ENGLISH COLONIZATION

The histories of the islands and communities of the British Isles have always been closely intertwined. However, the arrival from England into Ireland of the Normans in 1167 marked the commencement of a new incursion and settlement that, although piecemeal, localized, and with a fluctuating frontier between Gaelic Irish and Norman areas, created the basis for a more comprehensive conquest of Ireland and a reconfiguration of its settlement in the late fifteenth and sixteenth centuries.

The English presence in Ireland at the end of the fifteenth century was centered in a small number of areas, focused upon the eastern and southern seaboards and parts of the southwest and southeast. These areas, governed from Dublin at the heart of the Pale in the east, bore allegiance to the reigning English monarch as lord of Ireland. This English lordship did not extend to the majority of the country, which remained under the control of the Gaelic lordships. Political instability in England during the Hundred Years' War and the Wars of the Roses ensured that a coherent policy toward Ireland had to await the advent of the Tudor Dynasty under Henry VII in 1485. A more focused and sustained policy began to emerge in response to support given in Ireland to a number of pretenders to the English throne in the 1490s. The appointment of an Englishman, Sir Edward Poynings, as chief governor in Ireland in 1494 represented the first Tudor attempt at establishing a more permanent English presence in Ireland by means of military conquest and constitutional reform. Poynings's endeavors failed militarily, though the enactment in the Irish Parliament in 1494 to 1495 of an Act known as Poynings's Law, which defined the relationship between the Irish legislature and the Irish and English executive arms of government, was to serve as the cornerstone of the Irish constitutional framework until the late eighteenth century.

In the reign of Henry VIII (1509–1547), fitful engagement with reform gave way to purposeful action under the guidance of Thomas Cromwell. Although early endeavors were interrupted in 1534 by the Kildare rebellion, that uprising's successful suppression created the opportunity for further reform, first within the areas of the English lordship, and then eventually throughout the country. However, the lack of a single, coherent policy for this undertaking resulted in the pursuit at different times of contrasting strategies of coercion and conciliation. Thus haphazard punitive raids into Gaelic areas were followed by systematic diplomatic missions aimed at a gradual establishment of English government through peaceful methods. Two key aspects of this latter strategy were the Act for the Kingly Title of 1541 and the concurrent program of Surrender and Re-Grant. The Act for the Kingly Title made all inhabitants of Ireland subjects of the English monarch, though as a sovereign entity distinct from that of the kingdom of England. Surrender and Re-Grant required that the leaders of these new Gaelic Irish subjects agree to participate in this new polity and to recognize the supremacy of the English monarch in church and state, in return for receiving English titles and re-grants of their lands under English law.

Concurrent with the creation of the kingdom of Ireland, a new church came into being following the Henrician break with Rome. The resultant confiscations of religious lands facilitated a further incursion from England and new settlements. However, the Protestant Reformation failed to take hold in Ireland, and this led in time to the creation of a new divide within Ireland between Catholics and Protestants. The pre-Reformation settlers who remained Catholic became known as the Old English, while the newer Protestant arrivals became known as the New English. Thus, the latter stages of the establishment of English rule throughout Ireland became entangled with the religious divisions and power struggles of the New and Old English, while the majority of the Gaelic Irish, who also continued to adhere to Catholicism, became marginalized and alienated.

Central to this next phase was a policy of plantation aimed at introducing English settlements into Gaelic areas as a means of establishing English law and control. The first substantive attempt at plantation was undertaken in the eastern province of Leinster in the 1550s in Counties Laois and Offaly. By the 1580s the policy had been extended into the southern province of Munster following the suppression of the Desmond rebellion. The first attempts at plantation in Ulster in the early 1590s helped to provoke a violent backlash that resulted in the Nine Years' War, which eventually spread throughout Ireland. However, the end of the war in 1603 marked the successful conclusion of the Tudor conquest of Ireland and the establishment of English rule throughout the country.

The "flight of the earls" in 1607 and the revolt of Sir Cahir O'Dogherty in 1608 facilitated the undertaking of the most comprehensive plantation yet, implemented in six of the nine counties of Ulster. Thereafter, the unresolved power struggle between the Old and New English was played out in a series of crises that were defined

"English Soldier Raised for Service in Ireland." This satirical drawing, published circa 1540, depicts the typical English soldier in Ireland as an unabashed plunderer. **HULTON ARCHIVE/GETTY IMAGES. REPRODUCED BY PERMISSION.**

ultimately by religious allegiance, with the rewards to the victors being signified in political power and a monopoly on landownership. A lengthy battle was fought and lost by the Old English and the Gaelic Irish, with the Cromwellian land confiscation and transplantation of the 1650s and the Williamite confiscation of the 1690s completing the transference of land on confessional lines. By the early eighteenth century, Ireland was both a sister kingdom of England populated by a Protestant elite and a colonized country populated by a predominantly landless and powerless Catholic majority.

The English incursion, settlement, and conquest in Ireland had created a hybrid polity, which bore the trappings of both a kingdom and a colony. This hybrid polity has led to ongoing debate and controversy, exemplified by the arguments put forward in 1698 by the Protestant MP for Trinity College, William Molyneux, in *The Case*

Tyrone's False Submission. In 1603 the Irish national hero and rebel leader Hugh O'Neill (ca. 1540–1616), the Earl of Tyrone, was forced to surrender to the English after the suppression of his Irish rebellion, an event pictured in this seventeenth-century engraving. HULTON ARCHIVE/GETTY IMAGES. REPRODUCED BY PERMISSION.

of Ireland's being bound by Acts of Parliament in England, stated. Debate has revolved around issues such as whether the spread of English government and law throughout Ireland was achieved primarily through coercion or conciliation; the importance of institutional forms and patterns of government; the interaction of communities and their sense of identity and separateness; the extent to which religious divisions distorted or altered the nature of incursion, settlement, and conquest; and the place and role of Ireland in the British Empire.

Debate also continues with regard to the extent to which English colonization and plantation in Ireland influenced English activity in North America and the West Indies. Though there was clearly some degree of transfer of ideas and practices from one arena of colonization to the next, it is also the case that English and, in particular, Scottish involvement in Ireland retarded aspects of British colonial activity in America. Likewise, while the Irish plantations of the late sixteenth and early seventeenth centuries evidently provided Englishmen with at least a term—that of plantation instead of colony—that they initially used to describe their settlements in North America and the West Indies, the original models for English colonial expansion in Ireland and beyond were ultimately the classical and medieval colonies within Europe, including those established in England itself.

SEE ALSO *Empire in the Americas, British.*

BIBLIOGRAPHY

Bradshaw, Brendan. *The Irish Constitutional Revolution of the Sixteenth Century.* Cambridge, U.K.: Cambridge University Press, 1979.

Brady, Ciaran. *The Chief Governors: The Rise and Fall of Reform Government in Tudor Ireland, 1536–1588.* Cambridge, U.K.: Cambridge University Press, 1994.

Brady, Ciaran, and Raymond Gillespie, eds. *Natives and Newcomers: Essays on the Making of Irish Colonial Society, 1534–1641.* Dublin: Irish Academic Press, 1986.

Canny, Nicholas, ed. *The Oxford History of the British Empire,* Vol. I: *The Origins of Empire.* Oxford, U.K.: Oxford University Press, 1998.

Canny, Nicholas. *Making Ireland British, 1580–1650.* Oxford, U.K: Oxford University Press, 2001.

Ellis, Steven G. *Tudor Frontiers and Noble Power: The Making of the British State.* Oxford, U.K.: Oxford University Press, 1995.

Ellis, Steven G. *Ireland in the Age of the Tudors, 1447–1603: English Expansion and the End of Gaelic Rule.* London: Longman, 1998.

Lennon, Colm. *Sixteenth-Century Ireland: The Incomplete Conquest.* Dublin: Gill and Macmillan, 1994.

Charles Ivar McGrath

IRISH NATIONALIST MOVEMENT SINCE 1800

During the nineteenth century, Ireland evolved to take a unique position in the colonial world. Ireland was an integral part of the United Kingdom, but unlike England, Scotland, and Wales, it had a colonial administration that answered to Britain's Colonial Office well after Ireland had achieved Catholic emancipation, that is, after the Catholic Relief Act of 1829, which permitted Catholics to sit in the British Parliament. Thus, politically, Ireland largely ceased to be a colony, while it simultaneously retained a colonial economic structure and the culture and symbols of a colonial people.

This hybrid of political, economic, and cultural structures engendered two corresponding Irish nationalist traditions. Parliamentary representation produced a constitutional tradition that became state-conscious and largely defined Irish independence as self-government, a goal that advocates held could be achieved through parliamentary or constitutional means. The continuation of a colonial economic structure, on the other hand, combined with Irish cultural nationalism to sustain a revolutionary, or republican, tradition throughout the twentieth century. This tradition sought an independent Irish republic, which supporters believed could only be achieved through physical force.

In the wake of the 1798 rebellion, in which the United Irishmen attempted to establish an independent Irish republic, Britain responded with the Act of Union (1800), placing Ireland within the United Kingdom but without the promised Catholic emancipation. In 1823 Daniel O'Connell's (1775–1847) Catholic Association began political agitation for emancipation. In doing so, the Catholic Association created Ireland's first mass movement and initiated a constitutional nationalism that served as an alternative to physical-force republicanism. Achieving emancipation in 1829, O'Connell, who was known as "the Liberator," shifted his agitation toward repealing the Act of Union and returning self-government to Ireland.

O'Connell's National Repeal Association organized "Monster Meetings," which were attended by hundreds of thousands of people and were to culminate in a national rally at Clontarf, near Dublin, in 1843. The government, however, proscribed the Clontarf rally, and O'Connell, the constitutionalist, complied. His retreat from Clontarf and the Great Irish Famine of the 1840s destroyed O'Connell's movement. With the limits of constitutional nationalism exposed, some of O'Connell's followers organized into the Young Ireland movement, which rejected constitutionalism and launched a futile uprising in 1848.

The Great Famine killed one million Irish and forced another million to emigrate. Many of the emigrants viewed themselves as exiles, adding a transatlantic dimension to Irish nationalism. In 1858 revolutionary nationalists established the Irish Republican Brotherhood (IRB) simultaneously in New York and Dublin. The IRB, or the Fenian movement, committed itself to a democratic Irish republic through force of arms. By the time the Fenians rebelled in 1867, the government had fully infiltrated their ranks and their insurrection was little more than a gesture. The IRB, however, survived the Fenian uprising and continued to influence the nationalist movement, principally through Irish-American organizations and their financial contributions.

Until 1879, neither constitutional nor revolutionary nationalists had attached their nationalism to the land question, that is, addressed the central Irish socioeconomic issue that a small minority of protestant and Anglo-Irish landlords owned the overwhelming majority of land in Ireland and leased the land to the Irish Catholic majority. This changed when Fenian Michael Davitt (1846–1906) established the Land League, which physically resisted the practice of landlords evicting their tenants and agitated for peasant proprietorship. Charles Stewart Parnell (1846–1891), an Irish member of Parliament dedicated to home rule (i.e., Irish self-government by means of an act of Parliament), became the Land League's president. The IRB, in a "New Departure," agreed to join the campaign, producing an alliance between revolutionary and constitutional nationalists. The league's agitation, known as the Land War (1879–1882), centered on ostracizing those who broke its code of conduct, as happened to Captain Charles Boycott (1832–1897), whose name became synonymous with the tactic. Britain responded to the agitation, which often included underground violence, with a Land Act (1881) that granted tenants' rights but fell short of the league's objectives.

Parnell moved away from agrarian agitation and directed the league's mass movement toward home rule, building a party that soon held the balance of power in the House of Commons. Parnell threw his nationalist

O'Connell Arrives at Parliament. *This cartoon, printed in 1829, shows the Irish politician Daniel O'Connell (center) arriving to take his seat in the British Parliament after the passage of the Catholic Emancipation Act in April 1829.* **HULTON ARCHIVE/ GETTY IMAGES. REPRODUCED BY PERMISSION.**

party's support to the Liberal Party, led by William Gladstone (1809–1898), which introduced a Home Rule Bill (1886), only to have the Conservative Party and Liberal defectors defeat it. The Conservatives, now in power, attempted to "kill Home Rule with kindness," by enacting a series of land acts that bought out landlords and created a peasant proprietorship.

Gladstone eventually passed a Home Rule Bill (1893) in the House of Commons but Britain's House of Lords rejected it. Parnell, however, did not live to see this happen. He was destroyed politically and his party split when an 1890 divorce case revealed that he had committed adultery; he died the following year.

After the fall of Parnell, "Ireland's uncrowned king," nationalist aspirations were increasingly expressed through cultural nationalism. In 1893 the Gaelic League was established to revive the Irish language and culture, and although its founders saw the league as nonpolitical, it eventually came under IRB control. The Gaelic Athletic Association was formed in 1884 to

prevent the spread of English games in Ireland. Fenians dominated the Gaelic Athletic Association from its inception, as was evident by its rules, which excluded those who were members of the police or military. In addition, a number of nationalist literary groups emerged whose members based their work on Gaelic literature and folklore, a movement that culminated in 1904 with the establishment of the Abbey Theatre in Dublin.

In 1905 the Sinn Féin ("ourselves") Party, founded by Arthur Griffith (1872–1922), emerged as a political alterative to Home Rule nationalism. Sinn Féin advocated a dual monarchy under the English Crown through a passive resistance in which Irish members of Parliament would withdraw from the British Parliament and form an Irish assembly.

When the Liberals passed the third Home Rule Bill (1912), the reformed House of Lords could only delay it for two years. Facing such a reality, the Protestant minority in Ireland, who were known as Unionists, formed the Ulster Volunteers and threatened armed resistance if the government implemented home rule. Nationalists

Anti–Home Rule Demonstration in Derry City, September 1912. *Unionist leaders (left to right: Hugh Barrie, Edward Carson, and Frederick Smith) are greeted by supporters at a demonstration against home rule in Londonderry.* **HULTON ARCHIVE/GETTY IMAGES. REPRODUCED BY PERMISSION.**

responded by forming the Irish Volunteers to safeguard home rule. Elements within the British Army asserted that they would not impose home rule (i.e., as an act of Parliament), and as such, Britain confronted a major constitutional crisis and the prospect of civil war. This did not happen; World War I permitted Britain to suspend home rule for duration of the war.

Britain's inconsistency, however, was not lost on Irish nationalists. When nationalists had sought independence though physical force, Britain crushed their efforts and encouraged them to proceed with constitutional means. When they achieved home rule through constitutional means, the government permitted it to be blocked by threats of physical force.

Most of the Irish Volunteers went off to fight in World War I, but a minority remained in Ireland, ostensibly to defend the achieved home rule. Unknown to most Irish volunteers, the secret oath bound by IRB had infiltrated the organization's leadership and was now preparing it for a rebellion. In 1916 Patrick Pearse (1879–1916) led the Irish Volunteers in a rebellion that began on Easter Monday. The smaller Irish Citizens Army, led by revolutionary socialist James Connolly (1868–1916), joined them. Pearse and Connolly proclaimed an Irish Republic and seized the Dublin city center. It took the British Army a week to crush the Easter Rising. Britain later executed its leaders.

Although Griffith had nothing to do with the Easter Rising, the British termed it "the Sinn Féin Rebellion," as Sinn Féin had become a pejorative term to describe all nationalists who rejected home rule. In 1917 a new "Republican Sinn Féin" emerged, led by Eamon de Valera (1882–1975), the highest-ranking Irish Volunteer to survive the Easter Rising and the subsequent executions. Although the party was republican dominated, Sinn Féin developed into a coalition that included constitutional nationalists, such as Griffith. Nonetheless, Sinn Féin contested the 1918 election on the proclaimed

Irish Republic of Easter 1916 and won seventy-three out of seventy-nine nationalist seats in the British Parliament.

In 1919 the elected Sinn Féin members of Parliament abstained from Westminster, that is, boycotted the British Parliament and formed themselves as Dáil Éireann (assembly of Ireland). Simultaneously, the Irish Volunteers, now calling themselves the Irish Republican Army (IRA), launched a sustained guerrilla war against British forces in Ireland. Britain responded with a counterinsurgency against the IRA, while working to separate the constitutional nationalists from the revolutionary republicans within Sinn Féin and the Dáil.

In 1921 a ceasefire led to negotiations that produced the Anglo-Irish Treaty. The treaty partitioned Ireland into two states: Twenty-six counties were given some powers of self-government as a dominion within the British empire, while six counties in Ulster (Northern Ireland) remained part of the United Kingdom—much more than home rule, far less than an Irish republic. The Dáil accepted the treaty by a vote of sixty-four to fifty-seven, and its supporters, led by Griffith and Michael Collins (1890–1922), the IRA's director of intelligence, formed the Irish Free State. Three-quarters of the IRA, however, rejected the treaty, leading to the Irish Civil War (1922–1923). The Free State Army, supported by Britain, defeated the IRA, but the IRA leadership ordered its units to place their weapons in secret arms depots and to disperse without surrender.

The defeated republicans, embodied in the self-described "semiconstitutional" political party Fianna Fáil ("soldiers of destiny") and with IRA electoral support, gained control of the Irish Free State in the 1932 election. Led by de Valera, however, Fianna Fáil did not declare an independent republic; their opponents, a five-party coalition government led by fine Gael ("kindred of the Irish"), did that in 1948 when they briefly won power.

Britain responded by reasserting its sovereignty over Northern Ireland, where in the late 1960s revolutionary nationalism returned. In the thirty-year conflict that followed, both the IRA and Sinn Féin reemerged. The most recent phase of "the troubles" ended with the IRA ceasefire in 1994 and the 1998 Good Friday Agreement that committed Sinn Féin to constitutional politics. To further the peace process in Northern Ireland, the IRA announced an end to its armed campaign in 2005. It reasserted its commitment "to building the republic outlined in the 1916 proclamation," but to do so through peaceful means.

Although often cited as England's first colony, scholars continue to debate the extent to which Ireland was a colony. Revisionist historians have challenged nationalist histories, arguing that the British–Irish connection was far more complex than a simple colonial relationship and that partition reflected that there were always two nations within Ireland. Given that such revisionism emerged during the resumption of physical-force nationalism in Northern Ireland, its opponents argue that it is a conservative, perhaps even Unionist, ideology designed to confront change in Ireland and that it serves as little more than an apology for British colonialism. More recently, literary and cultural studies have developed postcolonial theories that locate Ireland firmly within the third world experience, essentially viewing Ireland's colonial past and resistance to British imperialism within the same framework as, for example, India or Ghana.

SEE ALSO *Ireland, English Colonization.*

BIBLIOGRAPHY

Bell, J. Bower. *The Secret Army: The IRA*, 3rd rev. ed. London and New Brunswick, NJ: Transaction, 1997.

Boyce, David George. *Nationalism in Ireland*, 3rd ed. New York and London: Routledge, 1995.

Brady, Ciaran, ed. *Interpreting Irish History: The Debate on Historical Revisionism, 1938–1994.* Dublin: Irish Academic Press, 1994.

Garvin, Tom. *Evolution of Irish Nationalist Politics.* New York: Holmes & Meier, 1981.

Garvin, Tom. *Nationalist Revolutionaries in Ireland, 1858–1928.* Oxford: Oxford University Press, 1988.

Hachey, Thomas E., and Lawrence J. McCaffery, eds. *Perspectives on Irish Nationalism.* Lexington: University Press of Kentucky, 1989.

Laffan, Michael. *The Resurrection of Ireland: The Sinn Fein Party, 1916–1923.* Cambridge, U.K.: Cambridge University Press, 1999.

Mitchell, Arthur. *Revolutionary Government in Ireland: Dáil Éireann, 1919–1921.* Dublin: Gill and Macmillan, 1995.

Timothy M. O'Neil

ISLAM, COLONIAL RULE, SUB-SAHARAN AFRICA

The story of Islam under the colonial canopy in sub-Saharan Africa is complex because of the various types of Islam, directions of infiltration, varieties of local appropriation, and differing colonial, pragmatic policies driven by exigencies. Prominent is the interplay between local, Islamic, and Western cultures as patterns of African responses conditioned the religious landscape that emerged.

West African Islam originated from the Maghrib during the trans-Saharan trade in salt, gold, and slaves. Islam relied on the patronage of the older African indigenous traditions, acclimatized, acquired local coloring, and meshed into the indigenous cultural fabric naturally and unhurriedly; traders and scholars moved from a quarantine process of maintaining Muslim space, through mixing or crossing boundaries patronized by rulers, before jihadists reasserted orthodoxy or created Islamic states. Coincidentally, the colonial forces emerged at the tail end of the nine jihads in West Africa, hindered some, and left the wrong impression that many jihads were anticolonialist. The French colonized two-thirds of West Africa, but the British colonies had a larger population while the Germans held a few until World War I (1914–1918). Portugal was confined to Portuguese Guinea and some islands.

The Islam of eastern and central Africa came from Persian adventurers and Omani Arabs from the southern Arabian peninsula who established hegemony over Swahili Muslim communities on the coast. In the crusade spirit, the Portuguese brutalized Muslims and collected tributes. Fort Jesus, built in 1593, represents Iberian coastal imperialism; its loss in 1698 to Ottoman Turks reestablished Muslim power in the zone north of Cape Delgado. From 1840 the Omani Arabs established a cultural imperialism that forayed inland from Zanzibar while the Portuguese secured Mozambique for Portuguese East Africa. The eastern African coast was also known as *Estado da India* because of trading relationships with Indians whose Muslim population remained visible and were resented because of their exclusiveness and conspicuous prosperity. The partition of Africa heralded a territorial imperialism as rival Portuguese, French, Italians, Belgians, Germans, and British consolidated territories that absorbed Islamic communities at the expense of Ottoman Turks.

COLONIAL POLICIES

Colonial policies differed, shared many similarities, and changed through time. Prominent was a combination of evolutionary and positivist ideas that profiled Islam as midway between paganism and higher civilizations; therefore, suitable for Africans, and preferable to paganism. Yet suspicion survived based on a clash of civilizations, secularist ideology, the separation of church and state, and enlightenment worldview that bred an antireligious diatribe. Missionaries exacerbated the alarm that Islam would dominate Africa. Colonialism feeds on monopoly, control, order, and cultural domination to sustain capitalism. These traits determined policy. European-Muslim encounters in Maghrib confirmed that Islam is a competing religion and civilization, posing as a superior, universal, comprehensive way of life, endowed with an inherent power of resistance, and now capable of indigenizing into a variety dubbed as "Black Islam."

Colonial policies gyrated between hostility and accommodation based on the political realities, the intellectual fad at home, and caprices of a governor. All except Britain shared a policy of direct rule; Portugal and France assimilated colonies as parts of the metropolis. In practice, racism redefined citizenship and denied full rights to the *indigenat* or "native" (in Portuguese, *nao indigenas*) except when acculturated through education. Colonial incursion coincided with some jihads and compelled hostile responses.

Western instruments against Islam included superior technology, administrative and legal structures, education, economic transformations, and charitable and welfare institutions. Military power and negotiated agreements pacified rulers and secured colonial regimes that remained insecure until the end. But the administrative structure removed the powers from local competing nodes after the jihads had disintegrated many communities; a few chiefs were pensioned off. The new *chefs de canton* became the new power elite. When the Moro Naba of Mossi accepted French control, he was allowed to retain symbolical, moral, social, and religious authority without political power.

Local exigencies confounded colonial policies: sometimes the government aided pilgrimage, constructed mosques, and patronized Islamic education. But it would restrain contact with Maghrib Muslims and compromise Muslim education by insisting on communicating through European language and culture because of the need for an indigenous workforce. Marabouts frightened the colonialists, sufi brotherhoods were profiled as dangerous secret societies, while the ubiquitous Dyula traders (the strongest evangelists) appeared harmless.

Vibrant Western influence in the coastal and urban areas created *evolues* who would challenge traditional rulers, Islamic values, and ironically spearhead the nationalist movement. The *umma* would split among supporters for tradition, advocates of adaptation to modernity (Islam with democracy) and secularist attack on medieval Islamic structures. Colonial rule delinked political from religious power and caused an internal debate about appropriate responses: *hijra* withdrawal could not suffice; military *jihad* was countered; *taqiyya*, jihad of the mind that feigned accommodation while waiting for a more appropriate opportunity appeared as the only option based on *mulawat*, accommodation in the name of overriding interest (*maslaha*). This required the consolidation of Muslim space, piety, and learning, to ensure protection and freedom of religion.

Colonialism disrupted the social structures built on Islamic values. Posing as liberators of slaves, the abolition of serfdom (*captifs de case*) created the clientele system in many places or estate system in northern Nigeria. Colonialism catalyzed social mobility, and created new class structures and ethnicity. Cash crop economy and new commerce created new wealth, and consumption habits; old towns decayed as railways, roads, and motor and sea transports changed trade routes. Rural-urban

Grand Mosque in Djenne, Mali. *The Grand Mosque of Djenne in Mali was built with mud bricks from 1905 to 1907. The original Djenne mosque was destroyed by a fire in 1830.* © **CHARLES & JOSETTE LENARS/CORBIS. REPRODUCED BY PERMISSION.**

migration intensified though village associations, family and marriage systems preserved old values.

Islamic social structures are tenacious, survive against the forces induced by Western material culture, and thrive in urban settings. Ironically, Islam grew under the colonial canopy than many jihads could accomplish. It utilized colonial resources to spread into the hinterland. Many ethnic groups in Senegambia that had avoided Islam converted in large numbers; there are cases of mass conversion. Islam grew through trade, marriages, the evangelical ardor inspired by the Da'wah call, and the activities of various brotherhoods that sprouted to consolidate the spirituality. Some sufi brotherhoods as the Muridiyya had local provenance, ancient ones as the Quadriyya spanned the continent, while others like the Tiyaniyya, led by Ibrahim Niass, developed a network that linked the rest of West Africa to the Maghrib. Talisman, prayers, and rituals provided solace and anchor amidst rapid social change. The spasmodic harassment and exile of sufi leaders betrayed the discordant vestiges of Madhist expectations that contacts during pilgrimages intensified.

RESULTS OF ASSIMILATION

Assimilation policy created two cultural worlds and juxtaposed the incompatible worlds of modern medicine and magical-religious methods. Colonial policies sought to create detribalized, individualized "new men," protected from Arabic cultural centers; it invented Hamitic languages and lineages and ethnic distinctions that differentiated the Orientals from Africans and sought to counter Islamic community and total submission of all aspects of life to Allah, and the wall against Western ideals. By 1911, *le péril de l'Islam*, the old fears that the Muslims may serve as lightning rods conducting German attacks, resurfaced and encouraged repressive policies including the promotion of indigenous religions and cultures to counter Islam.

In practice, assimilation policy was never purist but resembled the British indirect rule policy because both faced manpower shortage, tense geopolitics, international turmoil, and portending world war. The British protected Islam, consolidated the Fulani hegemony in northern Nigeria, sponsored Islamic education, restrained missionary incursion into emirates, and granted local authority to effective, loyal Muslim rulers. In reality, it rested political power in the British administrator and limited the purview of *sharia* laws, allowing autonomy only in the law of personal status. But *sharia* ceased to be universal as in the ancient sultanate. Colonialism consolidated Western civilization through schools that combined Islamic and Western literacy and recruited educated Muslims into the civil service. One consequence was that custodianship of Islam passed gradually from the ruling hierarchy (the sultan, *qadis*, and *imams*) into the hands of *sufi turuq*, devotional, mystical, thaumaturgic leaders. These made it difficult for Islam to adjust to insurgent Western presence. Muslim groups, as the Ahmadiyya from India, imbibed Western education as a survival strategy against intramural demonization.

Nigeria serves as an example of the changes that followed in Anglophone Africa: by the 1920s, the protection was eased to permit missionary activities in the northern region, especially as these controlled social service infrastructures. World War I nationalism, security considerations, and changing administrative structures brought the Islamic communities closer to others and created new challenges. For instance, the amalgamation of the northern and southern provinces into one nation, Nigeria, brought diverse ethnic groups together, betrayed the gap in education, differences in religions, and catalyzed a virulent competition for power. The artificiality of colonial boundaries became palpable. In Ghana, the Muslims formed a protective association in 1932 in response. Though the southerners decried the protection of Islam, the Muslims chafed under the defeat by colonialists.

In eastern and central Africa, neither the British nor the Germans practiced indirect rule; both left the Muslims to practice their religions and concentrated in competitive pursuit of gold, glory, and serving God. The German folk (*volk*) ideology made them more sensitive to indigenous religion of colonized peoples, and this affected policy toward Islam that had developed a Swahili Islamic culture long before colonialism. This culture permeated inland after 1880 when Omani Arab penetrated the Lake Victoria region, spreading Islam among the Yaos of Malawi, the Congo, and Buganda. They traded in ivory and slaves, and resisted colonial and Christian missions enterprises. It was their rebellion against the African Lakes Company in 1887 that broke their backs. All colonial powers responded violently against rebellion. The Belgians were strongly Roman Catholic and hostile to the spread of Swahili Islam that the *sufi shaykhs* nurtured in the 1930s. On the whole, Islam in Eastern Africa remained strong along a coastal strip and weak in the hinterland.

The Islam in South Africa originated from neighboring Mozambique despite the hostility of Dutch Afrikaans; then came Indian Muslims linked to Ismaili Muslims of East Africa, followers of Agha Khan. These exclusivist Muslims neither mixed with the "Malays" or Cape Colored or the faintly Islamized Balemba and Lemba ethnic groups. Despite their investment in mosques and social services, they were deeply resented. Ironically, apartheid forced Muslim intellectuals to exegete the Koran to support the liberation of the oppressed in the mid-1900s.

World War II (1939–1945) questioned the capacity to maintain colonial policies. Nationalists forced broken France to abolish the *indigenat* status in 1946 and open citizenship to the colonized without accepting French personal laws or discarding Islamic heritage. *Assimilation* was abandoned for *association* policy that would permit indigenous people to govern their affairs and associate closely with French interests. In 1956 the devolution continued with universal adult suffrage, single electoral college, territorial assemblies, executive councils, and Africanization of the local administrations, which enlarged indigenous political rule by transferring the powers reserved to the French Parliament. The negritude movement and participation in European ideological parties signaled the rise of the *evolues* and Africanist ideology that contested the pillars of colonialism.

In Ghana, the Convention Peoples Party sought to ally with the Muslim Association Party (formed in 1939) rather than ignore them. In Nigeria, the new political realities at the end of colonial canopy frightened the aristocratic elite: they formed a political party that they could control, essayed to mobilize the whole northern region under an Islamic identity. They wove patronizing contacts with Arabic states. The Wahabbis in Saudi Arabia funded the Islamic project in Nigeria. This initiated a process that would expose African Islam to international, radical Islamic influences in the future. But the educated, clerics, and masses formed a counter party that would liberate the masses, building an Islamic constitutional modern state adapted to modern conditions. Many of the un-Islamized communities mobilized with their own party and linked themselves to larger ethnic groups to escape from Habe/Fulani hegemony. The collapse of the imperial structures created an enigma for Islam: how to survive in a postcolonial world imbued with predominantly Western values.

SEE ALSO *Muslim Brotherhood; Sub-Saharan Africa, European Presence in.*

BIBLIOGRAPHY

Hiskett, Mervyn. *The Course of Islam in Africa.* Edinburgh: Edinburgh University Press, 1994.

Levtzion, Nehemia, and Randall L. Pouwels, eds *The History of Islam in Africa.* Athens: Ohio University Press, 2000.

Robinson, David. *Muslim Societies in African History.* New York: Cambridge University Press, 2004.

Trimingham, J. Spencer. *Islam in West Africa.* Oxford: Clarendon Press, 1959.

Ogbu Kalu

ISLAMIC MODERNISM

A term associated with Muslim religious intellectuals who have appropriated modern Western point(s) of view and sought to reform Islamic institutions of learning, law, and politics in the light of Western ideas and values. The modernist trend flourished in many parts of the Muslim world in the heyday of colonialism, between the 1860s and World War I. Its proponents argued for the compatibility of Islam with Western concepts of (instrumental) rationality, science, and progress, and advocated constitutionalism and women's rights. In the course of the twentieth century, Islamic modernism gave way to one or the other of the two trends it had originally attempted to bridge: secularized modernism, most notably of the nationalist type, and the fundamentalist Salafiyya. Reflecting changes in notions of modernity in the West, later modernist thinkers put forth Islamic notions of democracy, equality, and civil liberties. The impact of Islamic modernism was generally confined to cultural elites, though in some cases it gave birth to political and socioreligious movements.

Islamic modernism is often merged with the modern Salafiyya, which also emerged in the second half of the nineteenth century in response to the Western challenge. Yet despite mutual influences, partial overlapping, and occasional crossovers, it is analytically important to distinguish between the two trends. The Salafi discourse draws legitimacy from the Islamic past, most notably the medieval thinker Ibn Taymiyya and his premodern followers: the ultraorthodox Wahhabis and the Yemeni jurist Shawkani. Following in their footsteps, the Salafis professed to revive the legacy of the forefathers of Islam (*al-salaf*), while downplaying their borrowings from Western models. This construction made the Salafiyya the prototype of Islamic fundamentalism and enabled it to gain a large following among the Muslim masses and be involved in politics, which modernism could never accomplish.

Islamic modernism has never been a monolithic trend. There has been wide divergence of opinion among its protagonists concerning what is to be adapted from the West, what of Muslim tradition is to be set aside, and what attitude is to be taken toward the colonial and postcolonial powers. Such divergence reflects both variations in the intellectual background and social standing of modernists—who range from traditionally trained mid-level *ulama* (religious scholars) to middle-class laymen—and the differing circumstances of time and place. The boundaries of Islamic modernism are likewise imprecise, and scholars often disagree as to whether one figure or another belongs to it or crossed the lines to secular modernism or Islamic fundamentalism. However, there are certain core concerns that at least to some extent all Islamic modernists share, and that give this trend a measure of unity.

The intensification of the colonial enterprise from the 1850s onward brought home to many Muslims the painful realization that their countries had become backward compared with the West. Subjected to either direct European rule or Westernizing regimes, they felt that the Muslim world had fallen into a state of cultural decline. The distinctive feature of the Islamic modernist project within this wider religious perception lay in its fuller internalization of the Orientalist vision of Islam as the inferior Other, and in the conviction that to regain its place in the world Islam must adapt not merely Western science and technology, but also many of its institutions and customs. Modernists accordingly advocated reforming the traditional educational system by introducing secular sciences into the school curriculum and by building modern schools beside the old *madrasas* (seminaries). They were also among the first religionists to have recourse to the new medium of the periodical press; they likewise adopted novel literary forms and simple language in an effort to reach out to the expanding literate populations.

In common with the Salafis, modernists put the blame for the degeneration of Islam on its latter-day religious leaders. According to this construction, the *ulamas* resorted to the practice of blind imitation (*taqlid*) within their legal and theological schools and thus stifled all original thinking, while the Sufis deviated from the right path in their irrational teachings and popular practices. Purporting to revive the "true" principles of Islam, modernists and Salafis alike turned to the legal practice of *ijtihad*, which in their hands was transformed from a technical term, meaning an authorized "effort" to find a ruling in the sources, into rational deliberation. Similarly, not being averse to Sufism as such—many of them had a Sufi background—they sought to set it on a sounder rational-moral basis. Still, whereas the Salafis grounded their reasoning in a literal interpretation of the Qur'an and *sunna* (the Prophet's example), the modernists made rationality and science the measuring stick for a continuous reinterpretation of the scriptures.

In the political sphere, modernists living under Muslim rule generally favored a constitutional form of government. Aware of the importance of the state in effecting the reforms they desired, they regarded constitutionalism as both a guarantee of civil rights and freedoms and a check on the state's drift to *Westernization*, the wholesale adoption of Western values without regard to Islamic law (*Sharia*). Islamic modernists living in colonized countries tended to accommodate themselves to their foreign rulers, and at times even accepted their self-proclaimed "civilizing mission," in the belief that the

Outdoor Lesson in Punjab. *A teacher for an Islamic school holds class outdoors in May 1933 in Taxila, Punjab.* © BETTMANN/
CORBIS. REPRODUCED BY PERMISSION.

process of shaping the Muslim personality must precede
the collective goal of independence. In the postindependence era modernists expounded their liberal ideals
against both Westernized authoritarian regimes and radi-
calized fundamentalist oppositions. In the social sphere,
Islamic modernists were committed to the promotion of
women's rights. They backed girls' education and raised
for public debate issues such as polygamy, divorce, the
veil, work outside the home, and suffrage.

Islamic modernists employed various discursive strategies to justify, for themselves and for their coreligionists, the far-reaching adaptation they favored. For one,
in their interpretation of the scriptures they made a
distinction between basic commands, which pertain to
religion proper, and contingent social and political rules
that were given for their time and place and are therefore
liable to amendment according to changing circumstances. Another strategy, taken from the Islamic philosophical tradition that modernists sought to revive, was
to postulate that knowledge attained from revelation
necessarily conforms to knowledge acquired by reason.

Finally, modernists adopted the apologetic line that
European science had been built on the foundations of
classical Islamic scholarship, and that by acquiring it
Muslims were merely reclaiming their own heritage.

Representatives of the Islamic modernist trend
appeared in practically every region of the Muslim world.
Its earliest centers were established in the 1860s and
1870s in India, the Ottoman Empire, and Egypt. In
the following decades modernist ideas radiated to other
Arab countries, Russia's Muslim territories, Afghanistan,
Indonesia, and elsewhere. Shi'i modernism spread mainly
in the twentieth century, reaching its peak in the 1960s
and 1970s.

In India, the early modernist trend is primarily associated with the name of Sir Sayyid Ahmad Khan (1817–
1898). He opposed the Great Revolt of 1857, and in its
aftermath devoted his energies to bringing about a rap-
prochement between British rulers and Muslim subjects.
Khan was deeply troubled by the perceived backwardness
of the Muslim community in India, and tried to persuade
his coreligionists to adopt Western ideals and standards.

He rejected tradition and reduced the essence of Islam to the Qur'an, which was reinterpreted in the light of modern reason and science. Social practices that did not conform to liberal standards, like aggressive war, slavery, and subjection of women, were similarly rejected. Khan established his own journal, *Tahdhib al-Akhlaq* (Refinement of Morals), and later on the Muhammadan Anglo-Oriental College at Aligarh, which, modeled on Oxford and Cambridge, was designed to train Muslims for service in the colonial administration.

Subsequent Indian modernists argued that Islam actually contained the Western values of the time. The theologian and historian Shibli al-Nu' mani (1857–1914), a long-time teacher of Arabic at Aligarh, drew on the Mu'tazilite rationalist school of early Islam to restate received theological positions in light of the contemporary Western scientific worldview. The Bengali jurist Sayyid Amir 'Ali (d. 1928) contended that Islam was inherently a civilizing and progressive religion, drawing evidence from the life and teachings of the Prophet Muhammad and from the intellectual achievements of Islamic civilization in its formative phase.

With the advent of the Indian nationalist demand for self-rule during and after World War I, the modernist project assumed a political dimension. Its proponents were thereby divided into two camps in regard to the struggle's objectives: one group stood for cooperation with the Congress for the sake of a unified Indian nation, the other lent its support to the Muslim League's demand for the creation of Pakistan. The major spokesman of the first group was Abu al-Kalam Azad (1888–1958), a journalist who distinguished himself at the time of the Khilafat movement and was later elected president of the All-India National Congress and appointed India's minister of education. Azad maintained that all faiths are one in their essence and advocated universal humanism. The second group was led by the poet-philosopher Muhammad Iqbal (1877–1938), the foremost intellectual figure in Muslim India in the interwar period, who had studied philosophy and law in England and Germany. Iqbal postulated the essential harmony of religion and science, and called for the use of *ijtihad* to create a strong Muslim personality and a progressive Muslim society.

The representatives of early Islamic modernism in the Ottoman Empire are generally known as the Young Ottomans. This was a group of religious-minded civil officials and journalists from Istanbul, who supported the state program of modernization (*Tanzimat*), but objected to the Westernizing turn it took under the high-handed direction of the Sublime Porte after the Reform Edict of 1856. The Young Ottomans arose in 1865 as a secret society, and often lived in exile in the provinces or in the West. They promoted their ideology of constitutional monarchy and patriotism through the press and the theater. They justified their resorting to Western notions of freedom and fatherland by the claim that these were part of Islam. Namik Kemal (1840–1888), their foremost writer, reinterpreted the Islamic concepts of *shura* (consultation) and *bay'a* (oath of allegiance) to mean parliament and popular sovereignty. The Young Ottomans helped bring about the first Ottoman Constitution in 1876, but were suppressed under the autocratic regime of Sultan Abdülhamid II and gave way to the secularized movement of the Young Turks.

Early Islamic modernism in Egypt was inspired by two forerunners: the education official Rifa'a Rafi' al-Tahtawi and the Iranian-born activist Jamal al-Din al-Afghani. Tahtawi (1801–1873) acquired a firsthand knowledge of Europe when he served between 1826 and 1831 as imam of the first student mission sent to Paris by Muhammad 'Ali. Subsequently he was appointed head of the Translation Bureau and editor of the official paper, and in the 1860s he took part in planning Egypt's new educational system. Tahtawi believed that modernization could be achieved through cooperation between an enlightened monarch and progressive *ulamas* bent on adapting Islamic law to modern conditions. He had recourse to the Islamic philosophical tradition to justify the study of modern sciences, and called for universal primary education for both boys and girls to develop their personality and inculcate in them patriotic feelings.

As a Shi'i by origin, Jamal al-Din al-Afghani (1838–1897) was acquainted with the Islamic philosophical tradition and with the methodology of *ijtihad*, both largely rejected in latter-day Sunnism but flourishing in Iran. Around 1857 he moved to India, where he learned of modern Western science but also developed strong anti-imperialist feelings, primarily against Britain. Afghani spent the rest of his life seeking to influence Muslim rulers to modernize and unite in the face of European domination (making him part of a current termed *pan-Islamic*). Afghani arrived in Egypt in 1871, after a sojourn in Istanbul, and became the guide of a group of young admirers, mostly from al-Azhar. Expelled by the Khedive, in 1884 he established in Paris the short-lived but influential journal *al-'Urwa al-Wuthqa* (The Firm Bond). Afghani ended his life in Istanbul, a virtual prisoner at the court of Sultan Abdülhamid II.

The foremost exponent of Islamic modernism in Egypt was Muhammad 'Abduh (1849–1905). 'Abduh was a disciple of Afghani, who encouraged him to study philosophy and engage in journalism. Exiled for his role in the resistance to the British occupation, he cooperated

Maulama Abul Kalam Azad (1888–1958). *The scholar and independence leader Maulama Abul Kalam Azad addresses a crowd in India, circa 1935.* © **BETTMANN/CORBIS. REPRODUCED BY PERMISSION.**

with the master in publishing *al-ʾUrwa al-Wuthqa*, but after that the two parted ways. ʿAbduh moved to Beirut, where he interacted with the Syrian Salafis, before being allowed to return to Egypt. There he accommodated himself to British rule and was appointed chief mufti and rector of al-Azhar, with the mission of promoting reform in the educational system and in the application of Islamic law. ʿAbduh was troubled by the division of society between Westernizers and conservatives. To bridge the gap he sought to prove that Islam accords with reason and science, and that it is capable of providing the moral basis and guiding principles for adapting to modernity. In his Qurʾanic exegesis ʿAbduh made a distinction between specific rules relating to worship and general principles concerning worldly affairs, the latter leaving wide scope for *ijtihad* as rational deliberation based on public interest and a synthesis among the four legal schools. Possibly under Salafi influence, ʿAbduh also emphasized the need to return to the "true" religion of the forefathers.

Contemporaries of ʿAbduh advocated modernist ideas in other regions of the Arab world. In Tunisia, the reformist Prime Minister Khayr al-Din al-Tunisi (1810–1889) established the Sadiqiyya college, which taught foreign languages and modern sciences along with Islamic subjects. For him, the road to integration in the modern world lay in the adoption of a responsible parliamentary government and in freedom of the person and the press. In Tripoli, Husayn al-Jisr (1845–1909) founded on similar lines the National Islamic School. More conservative in his outlook, he reformulated the Muslim doctrine in simplified language and in relation to modern sciences. In Damascus, Tahir al-Jazaʾiri (1852–1920), who had been influenced by the ideas of the Young Ottomans and cooperated with the reformist governor Midhat Pasha, established the Zahiriyya library, the core of Syria's national library, and worked for the revival of the Arab heritage.

The next generation of Arab reformers drifted away to either secular modernist and nationalist ideologies or to the fundamentalist cause. Prominent among the fundamentalists was the Syrian Muhammad Rashid Rida (1865–1935), who is commonly regarded as ʿAbduh's foremost disciple and a major proponent of the Salafiyya. At the other end of the spectrum was ʿAli ʿAbd al-Raziq (1888–1966), who justified the abolition of the caliphate by the Turkish National Assembly in 1924 and called for the separation of religion and state. ʿAbduh's efforts to reform al-Azhar were continued by the rectors Mustafa al-Maraghi (1881–1945) and Mahmud Shaltut (1893–1963).

Among the Muslim peoples of the Russian Empire, Islamic modernism was generally known as Jadidism. It was initiated by intellectuals from Crimea and the Caucasus and spread to the Volga region, Turkistan, and Central Asia. Beginning as a project of reform of the traditional educational system, Jadidism enlarged its focus to include most aspects of Islamic society. Its proponents accepted the ideas of progress and women's empowerment, and called for the adoption of modern science and technology to meet the Western challenge. The Jadidis were a diverse group in terms of ethnic, social, and intellectual background, and differed widely on the desirable balance between Islam and modernity. Their most articulate exponent was the Crimean Tatar Ismail Bey Gasprinski (1851–1914), editor of the influential newspaper *Tercüman* (The Interpreter). At the beginning of the twentieth century efforts were made to organize Jadidism as a political faction and empire-wide congresses were convened, but the Bolshevik Revolution brought these efforts to an end.

Islamic modernism in Afghanistan went hand in hand with the monarchy. The leading figure in the

QABD AL-KARIM SOROUSH

Born in 1945, Islamic scholar and revisionist thinker 'Abd al-Karim Soroush has been described as the "house intellectual" of Iran's democratic reform movement by *Boston Globe* writer Laura Secor, and as "the Martin Luther of Islam" by the *Los Angeles Times*'s Robin Wright, who called him "a man whose ideas on religion and democracy could bridge the chasm between Muslim societies and the outside world" ("Islamist's Theory of Relativity," January 27, 1995).

Soroush's philosophical beliefs began forming when, as a student in London, he studied both philosophy and science. Soroush developed the position that humankind's changing and evolving understanding of nature and metaphysics should extend to religion, and that these different perspectives should be considered together.

Active in the Muslim Youth Association during Iran's prerevolutionary years, Soroush returned to Iran during the revolution and became a member of the Culture Revolution Council. He was charged with combating the Marxist thought that had infiltrated Iranian politics. After the country's universities were closed, in order to establish fundamental reforms, Soroush was appointed by Ayatollah Khomeini to reopen them and restructure their syllabi.

Soroush ultimately questioned the rigid interpretation of Islam endorsed by Khomeini and challenged the establishment's use of religion to further its political and economic agendas. Soroush has never sought political office; indeed, his position is that Islamic religious leaders should not also be the leaders of governments—in other words, he advocates a separation of church and state.

During his career, Soroush has served as director of the Islamic Culture Group at Tehran's Teacher Training College, researcher at the Institute for Cultural Studies, professor of ethics at the Tehran Academy of Philosophy, lecturer at the Imam Sadeq Mosque in Tehran, and as an instructor at Tehran University. Soroush, whose talks in Iran are often disrupted by hard-line opponents, began lecturing abroad in 2000, and has served as a visiting professor at such leading institutions as Harvard Divinity School, Yale University, and Princeton University.

movement was Mahmud Tarzi (1865–1933), who had spent his youth in the Ottoman Empire and established contacts with reformers in the Levant. Tarzi propagated the ideas of an enlightened and constitutional Afghan nation-state and of pan-Islamism in his journal *Siraj al-Akhbar* (Torch of News), and supplied the ideological underpinning for the modernization project of King Amanullah until the monarch's downfall in 1928.

In Indonesia, Islamic modernism combined the call to adapt to modernity with rejection of the animist and Hindu traditions characteristic of indigenous Islam. It was stimulated by enhanced contacts with reformists of the Middle East, and secured a substantial base among the middle classes. The largest modernist movement in Indonesia is the Muhammadiyya, founded in 1912 in Java by Ahmad Dahlan (1868–1923), who was influenced by 'Abduh during his studies in Egypt. Shunning politics under Dutch colonial rule as well as after independence, the movement established hundreds of branches with millions of members. These support a network of schools, for both boys and girls, which combine religious education and modern sciences, as well as missionary societies, economic and welfare organizations, and newspapers and magazines.

Shi'i modernism was largely confined in its initial phase to the heterodox Babi and Baha'i faiths. Baha'ullah (1817–1892) advocated Western ideas such as separation of religion and state, constitutionalism, women's emancipation, and international peace. Within mainstream Shi'ism, modernism emerged as a response to the autocratic secular modernization of the Pahlavis in the 1930s and became popular in the years leading to the Islamic revolution of 1978 to 1979. In 1961 Mehdi Bazargan (1907–1995), an engineer who had studied in Paris, and the populist Ayatollah Mahmud Taleqani (1910–1979) founded the Liberation Movement of Iran, which called for an end to foreign domination and restoration of constitutional rights. The two played an active role in the revolution that toppled the Shah, trying to provide a bridge between Khumeini's fundamentalist followers and the secular nationalist opposition. Bazargan was appointed prime minister, but was soon forced to resign and the modernists were relegated to the margins of Iranian politics. Modern Western ideas—particularly of the Marxist type—are also apparent in the teachings of 'Ali Shari'ati (1933–1977), the chief ideologue of the Islamic revolution, who called for a rational and humanistic reinterpretation of Shi'ism to fight subjugation and injustice.

Despite its weakening during the twentieth century, Islamic modernism has never ceased to be cherished in religious-minded intellectual circles, and it attracts much sympathy in the West. Among its recent prominent proponents are the Pakistani scholar Fazlur Rahman, the Syrian civil engineer Muhammad Shahrur, and the Iranian thinker 'Abd al-Karim Soroush. Rahman (1919–1988) studied Islamic philosophy at Oxford and taught at Western universities. He called for a reformulation of Islamic theology and educational reform, though his attempt to effect them in Pakistan during the 1960s ended in failure. Shahrur (b. 1938) emphasizes the need to reinterpret the Qur'an in light of contemporary social and moral concerns, and advocates "creative interaction" with non-Muslim philosophies and women's equality. Soroush (b. 1945) developed an evolutionary approach to the human understanding of religion that makes room for modern sciences. Initially a member of the Cultural Revolutionary Council, his deepening criticism of the Islamic regime eventually obliged him to leave Iran and settle in the West.

SEE ALSO *Afghānī, Jamal ad-Dīn al-*.

BIBLIOGRAPHY

Ahmad, Aziz. *Islamic Modernism in India and Pakistan, 1857–1964*. London: Oxford University Press, 1967.

Chehabi, H. E. *Iranian Politics and Religious Modernism: The Liberation Movement of Iran under the Shah and Khomeini*. Ithaca, NY: Cornell University Press, 1990.

Commins, David Dean. *Islamic Reform: Politics and Social Change in Late Ottoman Syria*. New York: Oxford University Press, 1990.

Enayat, Hamid. *Modern Islamic Political Thought*. London: Macmillan, 1982.

Escovitz, Joseph H. " 'He was the Muhammad 'Abduh of Syria': A Study of Tahir al-Jaza?iri and His Influence." *International Journal of Middle East Studies* 18 (1986): 293–310.

Gibb, H. A. R. *Modern Trends in Islam*. Chicago: University of Chicago Press, 1947.

Hourani, Albert H. *Arabic Thought in the Liberal Age, 1798–1939*. Oxford: Oxford University Press, 1962. Reprint, Cambridge, U.K.: Cambridge University Press, 1983.

Jahanbakhsh, Forough. *Islam, Democracy, and Religious Modernism in Iran (1953–2000)*. Leiden, Netherlands: Brill, 2003.

Keddie, Nikki R. *An Islamic Response to Imperialism: Political and Religious Writings of Sayyid Jamal al-Din "Al-Afghani."* Berkeley: University of California Press, 1968.

Kerr, Malcolm H. *Islamic Reform: The Political and Legal Theories of Muhammad 'Abduh and Rashid Rida*. Berkeley: University of California Press, 1966.

Khalid, Adeeb. *The Politics of Muslim Cultural Reform: Jadidism in Central Asia*. Berkeley: University of California Press, 1998.

Kurzman, Charles, ed. *Modernist Islam, 1840–1940: A Sourcebook*. New York: Oxford University Press, 2002.

Lazzerini, Edward J. "Beyond Renewal: The Jadid Response to the Pressure of Change in the Modern Age." In *Muslims in Central Asia: Expressions of Identity and Change*, edited by Jo-Ann Gross, 151–166. Durham, NC: Duke University Press, 1992.

Mardin, Şerif. *The Genesis of Young Ottoman Thought: A Study in the Modernization of Turkish Political Ideas*. Princeton, NJ: Princeton University Press, 1962.

Nasr, Seyyed Vali Reza. "Religious Modernism in the Arab World, India, and Iran: The Perils and Prospects of a Discourse." *The Muslim World* 83, no. 1 (1993): 20–47.

Noer, Deliar. *The Modernist Muslim Movement in Indonesia, 1900–1942*. London: Oxford University Press, 1973.

Rahman, Fazlur. *Islam and Modernity: Transformation of an Intellectual Tradition*. Chicago: University of Chicago Press, 1982.

Weismann, Itzchak. *Taste of Modernity: Sufism, Salafiyya, and Arabism in Late Ottoman Damascus*. Leiden, Netherlands: Brill, 2001.

Itzchak Weismann

J

JAPAN, COLONIZED

Japan was not formally colonized by Western powers, but was a colonizer itself. It has, however, experienced formal semicolonial situations, and modern Japan was profoundly influenced by Western colonialism in wide-ranging ways.

Japan's first encounter with Western colonialism was with Portugal in the mid-sixteenth century. The Portuguese brought Catholicism and the new technology of gun and gunpowder into Japan. The latter changed the way *samurai* rulers fought wars, and accelerated the process of national unification. In the following era, national rulers came increasingly to regard Catholicism as a serious threat to their authority. The Tokugawa shogunate (1603–1868) eventually banned Christianity nationwide in 1613, and persecuted its followers during the 1620s. This experience contributed to the formation of the *sakoku* (closed nation) policy (fully implemented in 1641 and ending in 1854). *Sakoku* was a Tokugawa response to the advance of Western colonialism, although its major objective was to consolidate the new regime. It banned Japanese overseas travel and contact with foreigners, and gave the government a monopoly over foreign trade. The only European power that was allowed to trade with Japan was a new Protestant power, Holland, which was strictly confined to the port of Nagasaki in Kyushu. Yet through the study of Dutch materials, the Japanese were exposed to the latest European knowledge in fields such as medicine, botany, astronomy, and geography.

Colonial powers did not challenge the *sakoku* policy until the late eighteenth century. This challenge first came from Russia, and then from Britain and the United States. In 1825 the Japanese government began pursuing a hard-line policy, by attacking foreign ships other than those operated by the Dutch and Chinese, and by persecuting those who argued for *kaikoku*, or the opening up of the country to foreign trade. Britain's victory over China in the Opium War (1839–1842) deepened Japan's fear of colonization, and a debate erupted among concerned *samurais* in Japan over how to react to the encroachments of industrialized Western powers in search of markets and raw materials. Although the government acted quickly to strengthen Japan by acquiring the technology and skills of these powers, especially armaments and military strategies, the opening up of the country was now imminent.

Kaikoku, however, did not result from a government policy change, but was forced on Japan by the military might of the new Pacific power, the United States. While Britain was engaged in the Crimean War, the Tokugawa shogunate government gave in to the pressure of Commodore Matthew Perry and his East Indian U.S. Navy Fleet, and concluded the U.S.-Japan Friendship Treaty in 1854. As a result, the ports of Shimoda and Hakodate were opened. The government further concluded a bilateral trade treaty with the United States in 1858 (followed by similar treaties with the Netherlands, Russia, Britain, and France). This incident intensified an already bubbling anti-shogunate movement, as it revealed the shogunate's incompetence and eroded its legitimacy. Anger over the treaties eventually culminated in the fall of the shogunate and the Meiji Restoration of 1868.

Many who opposed the shogunate's handling of Western powers were alarmed and outraged by two clauses included in each of the above-mentioned treaties of 1858, clauses they believed gave Japan a semicolonial status. The first denied the Japanese the right to impose tariffs, which damaged the Japanese economy greatly. The second concerned consular jurisdiction. The treaties expanded the number of open ports to include Kanagawa (soon changed to Yokohama), Nagasaki, Niigata, and Kobe, and established settlement areas (*kyoryūchi*) near the ports for foreigners who belonged to the treaty nations. While their activities were limited to these areas, foreigners were not under Japanese jurisdiction, but under the jurisdiction of their respective consulates. This arrangement had, therefore, a similar effect to extraterritoriality, and created a formal semicolonial space within Japan.

Xenophobia and a wave of violent physical attacks on Westerners characterized the initial Japanese reaction to Western powers in this new era. Many leaders, however, learned quickly that this was not a viable approach, and switched to a pragmatic policy of friendly cooperation. The policy known as *kaikoku washin* (calling for an open country and friendly diplomatic relations) became the diplomatic orthodoxy of the new Meiji government. This orthodoxy, however, demonstrated the contradictions that were inherent in the international order of the time and intrinsic to Western colonialism. On the one hand, Japanese adaptation of this orthodoxy meant the country's integration into what some scholars now call an "international society," in which common diplomatic codes of conduct were shared and international laws were respected. The policy also marked a new and positive perception of the West—not as barbaric, but as sophisticated, civilized, and modern, a superior model to emulate. The Meiji government employed foreign advisers and imported Western systems, while intellectuals absorbed ideas and customs from the West and spread them to enthusiastic readers. On the other hand, the Meiji elite realized that this "international society" was based on the military and economic might of member countries. They saw the task of enriching the nation and strengthening the military as an absolute imperative for the new state in order to be a member of this community. Yet, the treaties of 1858 demonstrated that Meiji Japan was still not an equal member.

This unequal relationship with the West was manifested at the treaty ports, such as Kobe and Yokohama. Westerners who lived in the foreign settlement at these port cities (the largest group was British, followed by Americans and then continental Europeans) were mainly business people. Although they were restricted in their movements, they were beyond the Japanese laws. They enjoyed great advantages in business dealings and lived materially privileged lives. Non-Western foreigners, namely the Chinese, played a crucial role as mediators in this semicolonial relationship. While China did not have a formal treaty with Japan until 1871, many

Western business people came to Japanese ports from China, and brought Chinese servants, foremen, and compradors (business mediators). Soon, independent Chinese traders and workers of various types began arriving at the port cities, in such numbers that the Chinese quickly became the biggest foreign group in these cities. Significantly, it was Chinese tailors, artisans, and carpenters who initially introduced European clothing and European houses to Japan. The disputes in these foreign settlements, therefore, often involved Chinese mediators, who came to dominate day-to-day business. Significantly, it is various Chinatowns, as much as the few remaining Western buildings, that remind contemporary Japanese of the port cities' semicolonial experiences.

Repealing the two problematic clauses in the 1858 trade treaties was a major goal for the new Meiji government. Their quest was to overturn Japan's semicolonial status and make the country an equal of the Western powers. The Meiji government embarked on radical domestic reforms designed to make Japan a strong, civilized, and modern nation-state. Among their goals, the establishment of a modern legal system was a top priority. Yet, while persistent negotiations, drastic reforms, and rapid economic development were significant in the process of achieving a repeal of the two clauses, the demonstration of Japan's military might and its increased prestige as an empire were probably most significant. After the Japanese victory over China in 1895, Japan succeeded in repealing consulate jurisdiction in 1899. And after Japan's defeat of Russia (1905) and annexation of Korea (1910), it recovered tariff rights in 1911. The year 1911 not only marked the end of Japan's semicolonial phase, it also saw the consolidation of the Japanese empire in East Asia.

Western colonialism's influence on Japan was profound and wide-ranging, and modern Japan was shaped through a constant negotiation with this influence. This was evident not only in relation to the nation's key infrastructure and institutions, such as the legal system, the constitution, the Diet, the bureaucracy, the educational system, the police, transportation, the army, and the navy. It was also profoundly manifested in countless aspects of everyday life, including literature, arts, religion, architecture, music, food, hairstyle, clothing, customs, and even the standard of beauty. The implications of this were complex. Although the concepts of liberty, human rights, democracy, and socialism were introduced through the literature of Western powers, so too were the concepts of imperialism, Social Darwinism, and German-style statism. For many Japanese, these Western systems, institutions, technologies, ideas, and customs were superior to Japanese ones, whereas others saw them as detrimental to Japan. The division between these two camps was far less clear than is often assumed, and both sides were motivated by their own political agenda. Nevertheless, this binary understanding of the world often influenced the way major issues were framed in modern Japan. During the Pacific War, for example, Japanese propaganda painted the Japanese empire as a moral force fighting against the evil empires of the West, and liberating Asia from Western colonialism.

After 1945 the United States emerged as the most dominant foreign power for Japan, and its impact was and still is wide-ranging and profound. The U.S.-led occupation after the Pacific War also marked the first formal foreign rule of the nation. The desire to challenge the legitimacy of this occupation, however, was found only among an extremist minority. Many Japanese embraced U.S.-imposed democratization and demilitarization, and the new constitution of 1946, especially its pacifist clause, came to define the ideals of Japan's postwar democracy. Over time, however, progressives became increasingly concerned about an antidemocratic turn in U.S. policy, resulting from Washington's determination to keep Japan firmly in the anticommunist camp. Even after Japan regained independence in 1952, some continued to decry "U.S. imperialism," particularly in relation to the U.S. military bases spread across Japan and the U.S. occupation of Okinawa (not returned to Japan until 1972). The U.S. ambassador to Japan in the early 1960s, Edwin Reischauer, later called Okinawa "the only 'semi-colonial' territory created in Asia since the war." While American bases at Okinawa paid most dearly for Japanese militarism, experiences at American bases in other Japanese cities have also added a significant layer to the Japanese memory of Western colonialism.

SEE ALSO *East Asia, American Presence in; East Asia, European Presence in; Empire, Japanese; Japan, Opening of; Occupations, East Asia; Occupations, the Pacific; Perry, Matthew Calbraith.*

BIBLIOGRAPHY

Beauchamp, Edward, and Akira Iriye, eds. *Foreign Employees in Nineteenth-century Japan.* Boulder, CO: Westview Press, 1990.

Conroy, Hilary, Sandra T. W. Davis, and Wayne Patterson, eds. *Japan in Transition: Thought and Action in the Meiji Era, 1868–1912.* Rutherford: Fairleigh Dickinson University Press, 1984.

Dower, John, "Peace and Democracy in Two Systems: External Policy and Internal Conflict." In *Postwar Japan as History,* edited by Andrew Gordon, 3–33. Berkeley: University of California Press, 1993.

Kamachi, Noriko, "The Chinese in Meiji Japan: Their Interactions with the Japanese before the Sino-Japanese War." In *The Chinese and the Japanese: Essays in Political and Cultural Interactions,* edited by Akira Iriye, 58–73. Princeton, N.J.: Princeton University Press, 1980.

McOmie, William. *The Opening of Japan, 1853–1855.* Honolulu: University of Hawaii Press, 2004.

Miyoshi, Masao and H. D.Harootunian, eds. *Japan in the World.* Durham, NC: Duke University Press, 1993.

Tomoko Akami

JAPAN, FROM WORLD WAR II

Postwar Japan was officially in the hands of the United States, Great Britain, the Soviet Union, and China. However, aside from a small British contingent, only the United States provided occupation troops, and though the other powers were consulted, the United States made almost all of the decisions for occupied Japan.

The primary man in charge was General Douglas MacArthur (1880–1964), who, as supreme commander for the Allied powers, directed the rebuilding and restructuring of postwar Japan. The first order of business was dealing with the immediate aftermath of the war. What remained of the Japanese military was disbanded, and, as with Germany, some Japanese leaders were tried for war crimes. Thousands of these trials were held in areas such as Japan, Singapore, Philippines, and Hong Kong, but trials for those accused of the worst crimes were held in Japan. Twenty-five people were put on trial for the most severe crimes, deemed Class A. All were found guilty of at least some of the charges. Seven of them, including General Hideki Tojo (1884–1948), head of the army and prime minister throughout much of the war, and former Prime Minister Koki Hirota (1878–1948), were executed.

The focus then shifted to rebuilding and restructuring Japan. Almost all of Japan's major cities were destroyed, along with the country's infrastructure; this had to be rebuilt if Japan's economy could return to strength. It was also decided that many of the large corporations (*zaibatsu*) that had controlled the prewar economy were to be dissolved. This decision was not made primarily for economic reasons, but because these large entities had opposed democracy, the implementation of which was a primary goal of the occupation.

Japanese society also faced reforms, primarily intended to foster a new democratic ideal. A primary concern for the Americans was the Japanese education system. If democracy was to take hold in a country that for so long had been governed by different ideals, it must be fostered among the youth of Japan. The reforms included a careful monitoring of textbooks, the adoption of the American system of progression through the years, and the decentralizing of the entire education system.

MacArthur and Hirohito in Tokyo. *General Douglas MacArthur stands with Hirohito, Japan's wartime emperor, in the U.S. Embassy in Tokyo on September 27, 1945. Hirohito found a great ally in MacArthur, who believed that the retention of Hirohito himself, and not merely the office of emperor, was essential for the successful rebuilding of Japan.* © BETTMANN/ CORBIS. REPRODUCED BY PERMISSION.

The Japanese concept of Shinto was declared a religion, and was separated from the state. Following the tenants of state Shinto, the Japanese saw it as a duty to revere what they believed was their divine emperor. The question of what to do with the emperor was the most difficult for the Americans. Most in the American government wanted Japan to retain the office of emperor, but without the divine status that the position held before the war. The main reason given for retaining the emperor was that he could bring stability to Japan, which the Americans believed would help prevent the spread of communism to Japan.

As for Hirohito (1901–1989), Japan's wartime emperor, more than a few Americans in high office believed he should be removed or even put on trial for war crimes. But Hirohito found a great ally in MacArthur, who consistently told his superiors that the retention of Hirohito himself, and not merely the office

of emperor, was essential for the successful occupation and rebuilding of Japan.

The most significant of the reforms put into place was Japan's new constitution, which remains virtually unaltered to this day. The constitution, agreed upon in early 1946, guaranteed specific freedoms, civil liberties, and a democratic government; the constitution also officially ended Shinto as the state religion, and established a new role for the emperor. However, the most noticed, and later the most controversial, part of the constitution was Article IX. With this article Japan declared that it would never again go to war and that as a state it had no right to belligerent actions. Hence, Japan would be allowed no military forces.

The end of the occupation of Japan was initiated with the signing of the San Francisco Peace Treaty on September 8, 1951, and became official on April 28, 1952. Though the official occupation was ended, U.S. troops have remained in Japan for decades. This occurred, in part, because of Cold War considerations, but also because of Japan's new constitution—without its own military forces, Japan would have to be protected.

In Japan's government, party politics quickly became dominated by the Liberal Democratic Party. Japanese culture also began to find its way to different parts of the world, thanks in part to returning American soldiers who brought with them stories and small physical reminders from Japan. The post–occupation period coincided with a significant growth in world interest in Japanese movies, cartoons, comic books, and, to lesser degree, martial arts.

As the decades passed, Japan continued to experience unprecedented economic growth. Consumer products, especially electronics and automobiles, soon became the staple of Japan's economy. The 1980s and the 1990s established Japan as an economic powerhouse. However, some believed that this growth occurred in part because Japan had an unfair advantage. Though Japan created a self-defense force after the occupation, it still relied primarily on the United States for protection. Thus, Japan expended less of its gross domestic product for defense than almost any other industrialized country. Most experts believe the lack of this economic burden was a contributing factor to Japan's success.

SEE ALSO *Empire, Japanese; Japan, Colonized; Occupations, East Asia; Occupations, the Pacific.*

BIBLIOGRAPHY

Dower, John. *Embracing Defeat: Japan in the Wake of World War II.* New York: Norton, 1999.

Schonberger, Howard B. *Aftermath of War: Americans and the Remaking of Japan, 1945–1952.* Kent, OH: Kent State University Press, 1990.

Brian Stokes

JAPAN, OPENING OF

The final wave of European naval exploration reached Japan's shores in 1543 when a group of Portuguese traders landed on the island of Tanegashima, south of Kyushu. Merchants and missionaries from across Europe followed soon after. Eminent among Japan's early visitors was the Spanish Jesuit missionary Francis Xavier (1506–1552), who began a mission that resulted in the conversion of thousands of Japanese. An incalculable mixture of piety and desire for foreign commerce even led some *daimyo* (domain lords) to convert; the most famous, Omura Sumitada (1533–1587), opened the port of Nagasaki to foreign trade in 1571. By the end of the sixteenth century, Dutch, Spanish, Italian, Portuguese, and English traders and missionaries were common sights in the port towns and harbor cities of Japan; they were known as "red hairs" or "southern barbarians."

For those ambitious warlords who sought to reunify Japan during this tumultuous "Warring States" period, however, the Christian faith was a threat to be eradicated. The general Toyotomi Hideyoshi (1536–1598) sowed the first seed of Japan's "closed country" *(sakoku)* policy when he ordered the Jesuits to leave the country in 1587; although he did not enforce this edict, Hideyoshi made up for laxity a decade later with the ordered execution of twenty-six martyrs.

TOKUGAWA PERIOD

In the years surrounding the reunification of Japan under the Tokugawa shogunate in 1600, a series of edicts were announced that served to drastically reduce Japan's connection to the world beyond its shores. Relations with any country unwilling to separate missionary from merchant activity were severed (Spain, Portugal); Japanese were forbidden from traveling and trading abroad, or from building seafaring ships; and all contact between foreign countries and the daimyo domains was prohibited, thus establishing a shogunate monopoly on foreign relations.

In the end, only the Dutch and the Chinese were allowed to maintain their trading bases in Nagasaki. The former were quarantined on the small artificial island of Dejima, while the latter were similarly sequestered on shore (the Dutch trade paled in comparison to that of China: 700 Dutch ships made port during the entire Tokugawa era,

while the Chinese trade brought in 5,500 ships in that same period). While Japanese society was in many ways self-contained for most of the Tokugawa period (1603–1868), there existed opportunities for the Japanese to sate their curiosity for foreign knowledge. In fact, prospective students of such "Dutch studies" as Western medicine, shipbuilding, astronomy, chemistry, geography, mathematics, physics, ballistics, metallurgy, gunnery, botany, and so forth flocked to Nagasaki as that city's reputation as an information hub spread.

The late eighteenth century marked a gradual turning point with regard to Japan's seclusion policy. As the global power of the Dutch faded, other counties that had benefited from the industrial and bourgeoisie revolutions of the eighteenth and nineteenth centuries rose to take their place on the high seas. In the 1790s the Russians attempted to expand into northern Japan, while in the years that followed European whale- and gun-ships appeared in the southern harbors of Kyushu. Furthermore, whaling vessels sailing from the east coast of the United States had been entering Japanese waters since the early part of the nineteenth century, and after the acquisition of the California and Oregon territories in the 1840s (and the subsequent discovery of gold in 1848 to 1849), the country was determined to push westward toward the Pacific.

COMMODORE PERRY AND THE "BLACK SHIPS"

In 1853 a naval fleet under the command of Commodore Matthew Perry (1794–1858) was dispatched from Norfolk, Virginia, by the American government to request that Japan provide for the safety of shipwrecked sailors, as well as to allow the establishment of coaling and watering stations for American ships in the Pacific. Though unstated, the primary impetus for the Perry mission was to explore Japan's possibilities as a market for excess American industrial manufactures.

Upon his arrival in Japan in July 1853, Perry delivered a letter from President Millard Fillmore (1800–1874) to the Japanese government requesting first, the right to protect shipwrecked Americans who might possibly wash up on Japanese shores, and second, the right of American ships to stop in Japan to refuel (coal) and acquire provisions. After delivering the letter Perry announced that he and his party would return the following spring with a much larger force, if necessary, to receive an answer to Fillmore's request.

The head of the shogun's Council of Elders (effectively the head of the national government, as the shogun himself was a cipher) consequently ordered the coastal defenses around Edo (now Tokyo) Bay to be built up, and quickly moved to act on the requests of the Perry letter. Domestic opinion in Japan on the matter ran hot

Commodore Perry Meets the Japanese Royal Commissioner. *Commodore Matthew Perry of the U.S. Navy meets the royal commissioner at Yokohama, Japan, in 1853. Perry concluded the United States-Japan Friendly Treaty in 1854, ending Japan's longstanding isolationist policy and giving the United States preferential status as a trading partner.* © BETTMANN/CORBIS. REPRODUCED BY PERMISSION.

in both directions; some felt that the country was overdue to open itself to the West, while several influential hard-line traditionalists advocated attacking the "black ships" upon their return. Within the upper echelons of government, opinion was also very divided, and the death of the twelfth shogun Ieyoshi in late 1853—coupled with the ensuing succession debate—did not help in the matter. The Council of Elders therefore recommended that Perry's demands be accepted.

TRADE TREATIES AND OPEN PORTS

Perry returned on February 14, 1854, with double the squadron of the previous year. After several weeks of negotiations, a treaty was signed on March 31, 1854. Titled the "Treaty of Peace, Amity, and Commerce," the treaty allowed for American ships to dock at the ports of Shimoda and Hakodate, and for Americans to travel into Japan's interior up to a distance of 29 kilometers (18

miles) from each. It also promised humane treatment of shipwrecks, and accepted the eventual posting of an American consul in Shimoda.

The Treaty of Kanagawa, as it came commonly to be known, was soon extended to France, Great Britain, the Netherlands, and Russia. In 1856 U.S. consul general Townsend Harris (1804–1878) established residence in Shimoda and began negotiations on a commercial treaty with the shogunate. Harris's labors paid off in the signing of a treaty, and by 1858 trade relations between Japan and the Western powers were firmly established. The year 1859 witnessed the foundation of the "treaty port" of Yokohama for foreigners to reside and conduct business, and within a few years several other ports (including Nagasaki, Kobe, and eventually even Edo) were opened. Japan's "closed country" period, such as it was, had officially ended.

SEE ALSO *Empire, Japanese; Japan, Colonized.*

BIBLIOGRAPHY

Jansen, Marius B. *The Making of Modern Japan.* Cambridge, MA: Belknap, 2000.

Pyle, Kenneth B. *The Making of Modern Japan,* 2nd ed. Lexington, MA: Heath, 1996.

Todd S. Munson

BIBLIOGRAPHY

Blake, Robert. *Jardine Matheson: Traders of the Far East.* London: Weidenfeld & Nicholson, 1999.

Keswick, Maggie, ed. *The Thistle and the Jade: A Celebration of 150 Years of Jardine, Matheson & Company.* London: Octopus Books, 1982.

Anne Reinhardt

JARDINE, MATHESON & COMPANY

The firm of Jardine, Matheson & Company was founded in 1832 by William Jardine (1784–1843) and James Matheson (1796–1878), two Scottish participants in the private "country trade" between India and Canton (Guangzhou) during the last years of the British East India Company's monopoly. By the time of the monopoly's repeal in 1834, Jardine Matheson was the most prominent trading house in China, dealing in opium, teas, and textiles.

In addition to pioneering the extension of the opium trade along China's east coast, the firm's partners were active in the politics of the China trade in Britain, lobbying the British government to adopt more aggressive policies toward eliminating Chinese trade restrictions. In the 1870s, when the Suez Canal, steamship lines, and telegraph connections sped communications between China and Europe, the China trade became increasingly competitive, and Jardine Matheson diversified its import-export business into shipping, insurance, and banking and withdrew from the opium trade in 1872. After 1895, the firm established industrial enterprises in China's treaty ports that included cotton mills, a silk filature, and a brewery. In 1898 it formed the British and Chinese Corporation in partnership with the Hong Kong and Shanghai Bank in order to advance railway loans and equipment to the Chinese government.

From the 1830s through the 1950s, Jardine Matheson was the largest foreign concern in China, with headquarters in Hong Kong and Shanghai, and branch offices throughout China and in Yokohama, Japan. The firm survived significant disruptions during World War II, but was compelled to leave mainland China in 1954 by the government of the People's Republic. For the next several decades, Jardine Matheson operated from its Hong Kong headquarters, establishing transportation, hotel, and supermarket businesses in Southeast Asia and Australia. Following economic reform in the People's Republic of China, the firm reestablished its presence in mainland China and continues to be involved in business there.

SEE ALSO *China, Foreign Trade.*

JARVIS ISLAND

SEE *Pacific, American Presence in*

JAVA, CULTIVATION SYSTEM

After the Napoleonic Wars, Java and other posts in the East Indian archipelago were returned to the Kingdom of the Netherlands in 1816. The Dutch East India Company (Verenigde Oostindische Compagnie or VOC) had governed these lands in the eighteenth century. It had extracted products from them—coffee and pepper from Java, spices and tin from the other islands—that were shipped to Europe and sold there at a profit. Coffee was grown in the highlands of West Java under a tribute arrangement known as the Preanger System, which Mason Hoadley has termed a "feudal mode of production." It had become very profitable in the eighteenth century. The VOC was ended in 1800, but the wish to profit from its possessions remained.

The Dutch government hoped in 1816 to apply modern economic concepts to the governance of Java, instead of the outdated mercantile policies of the old trading company. The VOC had obtained products for export by placing itself in the position of the traditional Javanese rulers and by obtaining the desired products in the form of tribute that had previously gone to the rulers. This pattern of indirect rule left Javanese society much as it had been, a hierarchical patriarchal system from top to bottom. The peasantry at the bottom was subject to unlimited corvée (unpaid labor). The European trading company agents were few in number and dealt almost exclusively with the Javanese district heads, called *regents*, upon whom they imposed quotas of products to be delivered at fixed, low prices. The regents, in turn, were left to their own devices in governing their districts.

This system of control was to be replaced by new liberal concepts of open markets, free trade, private ownership, individual liberty, and responsible bureaucracy. Already before 1816 the Javanese and European administration had been reformed and salaried, and the forced deliveries of products had been replaced by a tax on land, known as *landrent*. Accepting these changes, the restored Dutch government in Java set about advancing the social and economic life of the Javanese population in the direction of greater personal freedom and economic liberalism. The years from 1816 to 1829 witnessed a variety of problems and missteps in the effort to achieve this goal. Initially, coffee from West Java, where the Preanger System remained unchanged, was the main source of colonial revenue. But when world coffee prices fell after 1820, revenues no longer covered the costs of ruling Java. Efforts to expand production of coffee, indigo, pepper, and sugar into the government lands of Central and East Java, where landrent was being applied, had only limited success because they left the production of these products in the hands of the Javanese, as the new policies dictated. The Javanese villagers showed little interest in growing these export crops, preferring instead to grow their staple food, rice.

ORIGINS OF THE CULTIVATION SYSTEM

By 1829 King William I of the Netherlands was in desperate financial straits. His possession of Java was costing large amounts of money, and conditions at home were reaching crisis proportions. He was therefore highly receptive to the ideas of an innovative socioeconomic thinker, Dr. Johannes van den Bosch. Van den Bosch contended that the products of Java produced under a liberal economic system would never be competitive with similar products produced in the West Indies and South America under a slave economy. The King decided to allow Van den Bosch to try his scheme; he made him governor general and sent him to Java in 1830. Van den Bosch's plan was admittedly a return to some aspects of earlier East India Company control, but with the incorporation of later changes such as tax on land (landrent) and a reformed bureaucracy.

THE SYSTEM IN OPERATION

Van den Bosch's system proposed setting aside one-fifth of village land subject to landrent for growing an export crop to be designated by the government. On the remaining four-fifths of its land a village was free to grow whatever crops it wished and to sell them on the open market. The value of the designated export crop would more than cover the amount of the landrent owed by the village. When ripe, this designated export crop would be delivered to government warehouses, or, in the case of sugarcane and indigo, to processing centers. In 1832 coffee became one of the designated crops and soon its production in Central and East Java rivaled the amount produced in West Java under the Preanger System.

The plan then called for the government to export the products so obtained to Europe using the recently established (1824) Netherlands Trading Company and to sell the products on the world markets for a profit. The Javanese administrative hierarchy was strengthened to assist in managing this scheme. Over the life of the system, sugar production became the greatest source of profit. Sugar was produced under contract with European and Chinese entrepreneurs who processed the cane in mills built with government loans. These loans were to be repaid in processed sugar. Such sugar contracts became the source of individual wealth for the entrepreneurs. Indigo production fell off as aniline dyes were developed, and coffee suffered a serious blight in the 1880s and dropped out of production. Overall, however, the Van den Bosch system seemed like a win–win situation.

Not surprisingly the plan did not work as neatly and simply as described here. It was soon apparent that more compulsion was needed to induce the villagers to plant the designated crops. Some crops, especially indigo, not only weakened the soil for later rice-planting but also produced insufficient revenue to cover the landrent. In some cases more than the allotted amount of land was taken for government crops; indeed, in some areas favorable to sugar production, almost all village lands were taken and much of the population conscripted for work in the mill. Robert Elson (1984) has detailed the impact of such development in one East Java district. Crop failures were often not taken into account as the system mandated they should be, and where they occurred little remedial action was taken. Administrators, both European and Javanese, were awarded extra pay calculated on a percentage of the value of the crops produced in their districts. Some of them imposed extra burdens and harsh penalties on the defenseless peasantry in an effort to achieve greater personal gain. These abuses and shortcomings were highlighted in the writing of liberals in Europe opposed to a system of closed government control. Clive Day's book is the English language account reflecting this viewpoint. Van den Bosch's system was, however, highly successful in providing profits for the government of the Netherlands. Its success rather than its shortcomings brought about its end. Liberals gained control of the Dutch parliament and in 1870 passed an agrarian and land reform law that opened Java to free economic enterprise with limited property rights to land. This in effect ended the system, though remnants lingered on into the twentieth century.

ASSESSMENT OF THE SYSTEM

Judgments of Van den Bosch's system by twentieth-century historians are less severe than the liberal accounts of the nineteenth century. The classic study of J. S. Furnivall already displays this trend. The most balanced and probably best account of the system is that of Cornelis Fasseur. It seems fair to say that the success of the system enhanced its dark reputation as the prototype of colonial exploitation. The wealth it brought to Europe and the capital infrastructure it created in Java laid the groundwork for future development. Its impact on Javanese society is difficult to assess, however. Clifford Geertz has written of the involution of the Javanese village, leading to "shared poverty"—though this view is now generally discounted. During and after the system, the Javanese village served as the vehicle for adapting Javanese socioeconomic life to the realities of changing market conditions and labor requirements. The peace and organization that the system brought to Java resulted in a rapid population growth that altered the nexus between land and labor that made liberal economic development possible. Robert Elson (1997) sees the stronger state control, growing capitalization, and production for international markets that the system introduced as the start of a trend that would ultimately destroy the small peasant producer.

SEE ALSO *Dutch United East India Company.*

BIBLIOGRAPHY

Day, Clive. *The Policy and Administration of the Dutch in Java.* New York: Macmillan, 1904.

Elson, Robert E. *Javanese Peasants and the Colonial Sugar Industry: Impact and Change in an East Java Residency, 1830–1940.* Oxford: Oxford University Press, 1984.

Elson, Robert E. *The End of the Peasantry in Southeast Asia: A Social and Economic History of Peasant Livelihood, 1800–1990s.* New York: St. Martin's, 1997.

Fasseur, Cornelis. *The Politics of Colonial Exploitation: Java, the Dutch, and the Cultivation System.* Ithaca, NY: Cornell Southeast Asia Program, 1992.

Furnivall, J. S. *Netherlands India: A Study of Plural Economy.* Cambridge, U.K.: Cambridge University Press, 1939.

Geertz, Clifford. *Agricultural Involution: The Process of Ecological Change in Indonesia.* Berkeley and Los Angeles: University of California Press, 1963.

Hoadley, Mason C. *Towards a Feudal Mode of Production: West Java, 1680–1800.* Singapore: Institute of Southeast Asian Studies, 1994.

Van Niel, Robert. *Java under the Cultivation System.* Leiden, Netherlands: KITLV Press, 1992.

Van Niel, Robert. *Java's Northeast Coast, 1740–1840: A Study in Colonial Encroachment and Dominance.* Leiden, Netherlands: University Center for Non-Western Studies, 2005.

Robert Van Niel

JAVA WAR (1825–1830)

The struggle waged by Prince Diponegoro (1785–1855) of Yogyakarta, a city in central Java (now part of Indonesia), from 1825 to 1830 was one of the most important turning points in the political history of nineteenth-century Java, and of Javanese history as a whole. The Java War, also known as the Diponegoro War, determined the increasing glory of Java's colonial government and the inevitable retrenchment of local powers.

From the Javanese perspective, the Diponegoro War was the end of the Javanese effort to combat colonial intervention and restore the greatness of Java, a greatness tattered since the coming of the Verenigde Oost-Indische Compagnie (VOC, or Dutch East India Company). Thereafter, the Javanese struggle was sporadically disconnected from the activities in its center of power.

The war can also be seen as the first major war against the Dutch involving Javanese leaders who were motivated by social and economic reasons, rather than the usual dynastic reasons that had caused earlier conflicts in Java. After the Diponegoro War, the kingdom and society of Java become a highly dependent subject of the colonial realm, not only politically, but also socially, economically, and culturally. The defeat of Diponegoro placed the Javanese solely and definitively under colonial control, forming one of the bases of the *Pax Neerlandica*. This situation placed the Dutch in a central position in determining everything that occurred in Java after 1830. It also gave them the opportunity to expand their colonial empire to other neglected islands.

The problems started when a long-standing conflict between the elites of the Yogyakarta sultanate of central Java became more heated as a transition of heir occurred during the British interregnum. The reappointed Sultan Hamengkubuwono II, after being forced to resign by the French-Dutch representative, enjoyed only one year of rule. The British then appointed a new sultan, Hamengkubuwono III, in 1812 and banished Hamengkubuwono II to the island of Penang, off the coast of the Malay Peninsula.

The British had earlier asked Diponegoro to accept the title of crown prince, but he declined. Hamengkubuwono III only reigned for two years before his untimely death. The British government then appointed Prince Jarot, or Raden Mas Sudama, the son of the official wife of Hamengkubuwono III, as Hamengkubuwono IV, sidestepping Diponegoro, who was the oldest son of Hamengkubuwono III from an unofficial wife. During this period, the sultan's mother, along with the chancellor (*patih*) Danureja IV, and a commander of the sultan's bodyguard, Wiranegara, formed a strong alliance within the palace. Diponegoro became the main critic of this clique.

The reign of Hamengkubuwono IV was also brief. The sultan died in December 1822, and Yogyakarta was handed back to Dutch control. In exchange, the Netherlands Indies government appointed Prince Menol, a three-year-old child, as Hamengkubuwono V. Diponegoro and three other distinguished personages were appointed members of the prince's guardianship. In reality, however, the tasks of the guardianship, with the exception of internal palace financial affairs, were taken over completely by Patih Danurejo. Danurejo worked closely with the colonial government and was hostile to Diponegoro. Diponegoro was left with a feeling of bitterness toward his many political opponents who had publicly humiliated him.

The situation became more complicated with the appearance of Dutch resident Smissaert, whose attitude offended the complicated Javanese rules of etiquette and customs. In routine meetings with the sultan inside the palace, for instance, Smissaert made it a habit to sit at the seat appointed specially for the sultan. The resident and his community and some sultanate elites also introduced Western ways into the palace, resulting in many changes in the daily lifestyle of the nobility. There were even reports of sex scandals between foreigners and the princesses inside the palace.

This situation was frowned upon by many *kraton* (palace) courtiers, who continued to uphold traditional Javanese values. Among them was Diponegoro, whose strict upbringing by his great grandmother, Kanjeng Ratu Ageng, had provided him with an image of how a good Javanese and good Muslim should behave.

The conflict among the elites resulted in political tensions that were difficult to control. Tension was heightened further as the Javanese people began to throw their support behind Diponegoro. The people's support of Diponegoro can be explained by analyzing several long-standing social and economic factors dating to the start of the nineteenth century. The leasing of appanage land owned by families of the sultan and the Javanese aristocracy to Europeans and Chinese started during the British period in 1814, and was continued by the Netherlands Indies government. The practice undermined the right of the Javanese community to work and live on the land. The opening of plantations on these leased lands caused the degradation of the people's status from farmers to laborers with meager incomes. In addition, many people were forced to move from their home villages.

At the same time, the introduction of a land-tax system by Stamford Raffles (1781–1826), along with the government's practice of administering tollgates by subcontracting through three to four Chinese tax-farmers, created more tension because the abuses of the traditional services system by local Javanese officials had

continued. People were further impoverished by various kinds of indirect taxes that were monopolized by Chinese *bandars*. Goldsmiths, coppersmiths, copper workers, and even the owners of Javanese musical orchestras, for example, had to pay an annual tax to the *bandar*, or they were sent to jail. Although the Netherlands Indies government denied that their tax system impoverished the Javanese populace—they even claimed to have eliminated twenty-four of the thirty-four types of tax once levied by the Javanese kingdom—the people still considered many of the taxes to be a burden.

The deepening social and economic grievances of the early 1820s became even worse when a cholera epidemic and harvest failure occurred in many parts of Java. During this period, Java's traditional belief system lent strong support to Diponegoro. People saw Diponegoro as the reincarnation of the mythical *ratu adil*, the "just king" in Javanese millenarian tradition. The *ratu adil* was expected to free people from their sufferings and bring back the glorious past. In the eyes of the Javanese people, Diponegoro not only brought hope to nativist Javanese, but he also represented the idea of *perang sabil*, or holy war within an Islamic frame.

Beginning in 1825, the policies of the colonial and sultanate elite did increasing damage to Diponegoro. For example, the government placed poles to designate the location of a planned new road that passed directly through Diponegoro's property without his permission. The event resulted in a spontaneous mobilization of people to defend Diponegoro's rights in mid-July 1825.

Diponegoro was further disappointed when, in early 1825, Patih Danurejo, acting as caretaker of the sultan, signed a thirty-year agreement with the colonial government to lease lands in the areas of Jabarangkah and Karangkobar without the consent of the guardianship board. After Diponegoro refused to meet with the representative of Resident Smissaert, the resident sent an order/invitation to meet with him on July 20, 1825. A day later, Smissaert sent an army of fifty men and two cannons to capture Diponegoro. Tegalrejo was destroyed, and Diponegoro retreated to the south, through Selarong, which then became the center of the struggle and the place where Diponegoro declared himself *erucakra*, another name for *ratu adil*, the just king.

Battles between the Dutch army, supported by local rulers, against the supporters of Diponegoro took place over a wide area that extended beyond the borders of Yogyakarta, especially in the areas around the Menoreh Mountains, Kedu, Bagelen, and Banyumas. The war also spread to the northern coastal areas of Java, such as Rembang, Lasem, Tuban, and Bojonegoro, and far to the east, crossing Surakarta as far as Madiun. Many areas in the Surakarta sultanate became battlegrounds for the war, as many local people and elites chose to support Diponegoro.

The widespread support of the Javanese people for Diponegoro cannot be underestimated. Although the Islamic groups became his main supporters, the largest war in Java's history also involved many other groups, from farmers to noblemen, from clergy to bandits. Furthermore, the soldiers called to the field of battles did not consist of men only; many of Diponegoro's troops were women, and it is known that at least one of his daughters became a commandant.

The war in Java prevented the Dutch from continuing their political and military expansion elsewhere in the archipelago, especially in islands outside Java. The Dutch tried various strategies, from battle to negotiation, but they failed to stop the struggle. A new approach known as the *Bentengstelsel* was then implemented to corner Diponegoro. Prior to that, however, the Dutch offered Diponegoro the status of prince, similar to the position of princely king *(pangeran adipati)* held by Mangkunegoro and Pakualam, if he would agree to stop the struggle.

By mid-1829, all of Diponegoro's most important supporters—Dullah Haji Abdulkadir, Pangeran Bei, Pangeran Joyokusumi, Pangeran Adikusumo, and Raden Basah Prawirodirjo—had either been killed or captured or had surrendered. Diponegoro decided to stop the war in February 1830, and he commenced with negotiation. Diponegoro was invited to the Dutch resident's house in Magelang on March 8, 1830. He was captured on March 28 during the negotiations, and was exiled to Manado, North Sulawesi. Diponegoro was later transferred to Makassar, South Sulawesi, where he remained until his death on January 8, 1855. During his years of exile, Diponegoro produced many works of literature on Java and Islam.

The Java War caused the deaths of more than 200,000 Javanese. The Dutch lost more than 8,000 European soldiers and 7,000 local soldiers, and not less than twenty million guilders were spent to finance the five-year war.

SEE ALSO *Java, Cultivation System.*

BIBLIOGRAPHY
Carey, Peter B. R. "Javanese Histories of Dipanegara: The Buku Kedhung Kebo, its Authorship and Historical Importance." *Bijdragen KITLV* 130 (1974): 259–288.

Carey, Peter B. R. "Pangeran Dipanegara and the Making Java War." Ph.D. diss., Oxford University, 1975.

Carey, Peter B. R. "The Origin of the Java War (1825–30)." *The English Historical Review* 91 (358) (1976): 52–78.

Carey, Peter B. R. "Waiting for the *Ratu Adil* (Just King): The Javanese Village Community on the Eve of the Java War

(1825–30)." Paper presented to the Second Anglo-Dutch Conference on Comparative Colonial History. Leiden, Netherlands, September 23–25, 1981.

Djamhari, Saleh As'ad. *Strategi Menjinakkan Diponegoro: Stelsel Benteng, 1827–1830.* Jakarta, Indonesia: Komunitas Bambu, 2003.

Greve, Ruud. *Pangeran Diponegoro: Beschrijving van leven en daden van broemde prins, 1785–1855.* Terschuur, Netherlands: Zevenster, 2004.

Kraus, Werner. "Raden Saleh's Interpretation of the Arrest of Diponegoro: An Example of Indoensian 'Proto Nationalist' Modernism." *Archipel* (69) (2005): 259–294.

Maryanto, Daniel Agus. *Pahlawan Diponegoro: Pahlawan dari Gua Selarong.* Jakarta, Indonesia: Grasindo, 2003.

Ricklefs, M. C. "Dipanegara Early Inspirational Experience." *Bijdragen KITLV* 130 (1974): 227–258.

Sagimun. *Pahlawan Diponegoro Berjuang: Bara Api Kemerdekaan Nan Tak Kunjung Padam.* Jakarta, Indonesia: Gunung Agung, 1986.

Soemoatmodjo, Soekesi. "Perang Diponegoro." In *Sejarah Perlawanan-perlawanan Terhadap Kolonialisme,* edited by A. Sartono Kartodirdjo, 123–162. Jakarta, Indonesia: Pusat Sejarah ABRI, 1973.

Yamin, Muhamad. *Sejarah Perang Diponegoro.* Jakarta, Indonesia: Balaipustaka, 1998.

Bambang Purwanto

JONSTON ISLAND

SEE *Pacific, American Presence in*

JORGE DA MINA

SEE *Colonial Port Cities and Towns, South and Southeast Asia*

JUSTIFICATION FOR EMPIRE, EUROPEAN CONCEPTS

The term *empire*, derived from the Latin word *imperium*, contains at least three overlapping senses: a limited and independent rule, a territory embracing more than one political community, and the absolute sovereignty of a single individual. All three of these components were in play when the European overseas expansion gathered speed in the late fifteenth century. And all three senses of the term would figure prominently in European justifications for empire.

Although it opened a Pandora's box of philosophical disputes, the original justification for Spanish colonialism was found in the bulls issued by Pope Alexander VI (1431–1503). These conceded to the Spanish monarchy the right to occupy the newly discovered Americas and to undertake the conversion of the indigenous population, thus making the Spanish monarchy the vicar of God in the New World. If the initial encounters with the inhabitants of the New World corroborated with the Christian hope of evangelizing to the entire world, it also lent new force to a more secular aspiration that focused on the increasing civilization of all humankind. Evangelization and this mission of civilization were the two complementary ideals that underpinned most justifications for European empire for nearly 500 years. This essay traces the many manifestations of these ideas and convictions in the imperial trajectories of the Western powers.

For conquest to serve as adequate proof of the righteousness of the Spanish cause, the conquest itself had to be justified. The wide-ranging debates that preoccupied generations of jurists who debated the legality of the conquest may be condensed into a single question: Had the wars with the indigenous population of the Americas resulting in European conquest, been just ones? In *On the American Indians*, Francisco de Vitoria (1486–1546) argued that war with native populations could not be justified on the basis of the jurisdiction given by a papal bull, or even a purported right to compel natives to obey natural law. Conflict could be justified in defending the innocent, however, especially in cases where cannibalism and human sacrifice were practiced.

War resulting in conquest also could be justified, according to Vitoria's logic, if indigenous rulers refused to allow missionaries to preach, or discouraged conversion by killing converts. The defense of the latter might instigate war in which the Spaniards could legally occupy the native territories and depose their governments. While critics of the Spanish wrangled over the legitimacy of the conquest of America and the dispossession of its inhabitants, other European powers were embarking on their empire-building missions and would devise different justifications to support their rule.

Like the Spanish, the English justified the conquest of Ireland by claiming that their aim was to convert its inhabitants to Christianity. They contended that this goal was impossible to realize so long as the Irish persisted in their barbarous ways. In the view of Sir Thomas Smith (1513–1577), the English were the new Romans who had come to civilize the Irish, just as the ancient Romans had once civilized the Britons. This historical vision bolstered the conviction that the Irish were culturally inferior to, and far behind, the English in

developmental terms. Through subjection, the English colonizers reasoned, the Irish could be made free. This was not regarded as a small task. In his book *Tragicall Tales* (1587), George Tuberville echoed England's dim view of Ireland, saying, "Wild Irish are as civil as the Russies in their kind;/ hard choice which is best of both, each bloody, rude, and blind" (Berry 1968, p. 28).

A similar rationale, the alleged responsibility to convert heathen Americans to Christian faith, extended to Britain's North American colonies. The true principal and main end of the colonial enterprise, according to one early seventeenth-century Virginian planter, Richard Hakluyt (1552–1616), was to preach and baptize into the Christian religion. Hakluyt exhorted Sir Walter Raleigh (1554–1618) in a similar vein, but added the civilizing mission that would become so important to imperialists in future centuries: "for to prosperity no greater glory can be handed down than to conquer the barbarian, to recall the savage and the pagan to civility, to draw the ignorant within the orbit of reason" (Pagden 1998, p. 35).

This is not to say that religious justification disappeared entirely and was superseded by a secular civilizing mission after the first age of European imperialism had drawn to a close. In late nineteenth-century Britain, many Christians viewed imperial expansion as being designed to support worldwide conversion. Some observers felt that the purported benefits of conversion justified the use of force. One missionary went as far as to remark in 1895 that the British army and navy were under God's Evangelical mission fused with, and complemented, other justifications for European expansion.

Unlike their Spanish counterparts, however, English and Dutch ideologues of empire rejected the notion that conquest itself justified rule. Hugo Grotius (1583–1645) distinguished the original acquisition of property through appropriation, which existed before the establishment of civil society and existed as a natural right, from the notion of ownership existing within civil society, and regulated by the laws made by the appropriate public authority. There were twofold implications of appropriation that served as the basis for a notion of divisible sovereignty: the public rights of sovereignty and the private rights of ownership.

Unlike the Spanish, but like Grotius, British theorists of empire were most concerned not with a king's jurisdiction over native populations, but with justifying the title to property they appropriated (or, more often, expropriated). In his *Two Treatises on Government* (1690), John Locke (1632–1704) asserted that ownership was acquired when a person had "mixed his labor with (it); and joined to something that is his own" (Pagden 1998, p. 45). This was part of a larger argument that drew on the Roman law of *res nullius*, which held that all empty things, including unoccupied land, remained the common property of all humankind until they were put to some use.

The arguments of Locke and Grotius formed the basis of most English attempts to legitimate their presence in America, both against the claims of the Iberian powers who appealed to the terms of the Treaty of Tordesillas (1494), which divided the New World among itself, and those complaints of the dispossessed native populations. Locke was most influential in the justification of the latter. America was in the same condition as that of the entire world before the founding of human societies when, he argued, "the inhabitants were too few for the country, and want of people and money gave men no temptation to enlarge their possessions of land, or contest for wider extent of ground" (Pagden 1998, p. 44). The major conclusion of Locke's meditations was that Europeans could disregard all aboriginal forms of government, and, consequently, deny their status as nations.

The English, by settling and cultivating the land, had acquired rights to possession that the native people had never enjoyed and certainly could not contest. In this way, Locke's version of the *res nullius* argument was the most frequent legitimation of British presence in America and would later be employed to justify colonization in Australia and Africa. It also would be used during the American Revolution (1776–1783) by those seeking to justify the continuation of British rule. "Because no nation ever planted colonies with so liberal or noble a hand as England has done," Scottish philosopher Adam Ferguson (1723–1816) argued in 1776, "(the Americans) should repay us for all the blood and treasure that we have extended in the common cause" (Paquette 2003, pp. 428–429). British statesman also appealed to *res nullius* in their disputes with Spain in the late eighteenth century, claiming that their occupation of the Mosquito Coast and Darien in Central America and the Nootka Sound in the Pacific Northwest was valid because Spain had neither cultivated nor populated those places.

The discourse of improvement then became a justification for the expansion of imperialistic governmental power in the nineteenth century. As historian Richard Drayton commented, "the rational use of Nature replaced piety as the foundation of imperial Providence, government became the Demiurge, and universal progress, measured by material abundance, its promised land" (Drayton 2000, p. 81).

Even where no formal empire existed, as in South America, British proponents of unhindered free trade with the newly independent states invoked the mission of improvement as a way to justify the incursion of their capital. In the 1820s and 1830s, a widespread conviction

A Bible Lesson in Colonial Massachusetts. *Christian hopes of evangelizing the entire world underpinned most justifications for European empire, and the alleged responsibility to convert heathens to the Christian faith extended to Britain's North American colonies. In this illustration, a European missionary preaches to Indians in the Massachusetts area.* © BETTMANN/ CORBIS. REPRODUCED BY PERMISSION.

arose that British industry and technological ingenuity could generate wealth from the fertile resources that Spain's primitive methods and indolence had squandered. Free trade would open markets that Britain could exploit with its superiority and excellence in machinery, skill of the artisan, and extent of capital it enjoyed. The rapid growth of British mining companies in Chile, for example, was premised on the conviction that the mines, if worked with moderate industry and knowledge of metallurgy, might yield considerably more than the quantity necessary for the supply of the whole world.

Such grandiose visions permeated parliamentary debates as well. In a speech urging diplomatic recognition of Spanish America as independent in 1824, Lord Ellenborough (1790–1871) remarked, "even the power of steam seemed to be discovered at the most favorable moment for giving faculties to the navigation of (South American) rivers and the working of precious mines"

(Paquette 2004, p. 87). The political language of improvement fused with the interests of British financiers to help bring about a series of free trade agreements that would stifle the development of independent Latin America's industry for much of the nineteenth century.

However much the mission of improvement and legal arguments were the predominant justifications of empire, the differences, real and imagined, between European and non-European cultures would emerge with increasing force and frequency to legitimize imperial rule. Long before Christopher Columbus (1451–1506) set sail, a vigorous, progressive Europe was juxtaposed with a more apathetic Asia and Africa. Although Pope Paul III's (1468–1549) early sixteenth-century bull (*Sublimis Deus*) left little doubt that "the [American] Indians are true men," assertions of their inferiority to Europeans remained pervasive and this theory was employed to justify the conquest, subjugation, and enslavement of indigenous populations.

Nonetheless, very few writers before the nineteenth century would justify empire on the basis of racial difference. They did not assume that those living east of the Ural Mountains or south of Crete implied subhuman status, if only because no reference existed in the Bible to separate acts of creation. In the absence of scriptural evidence, environmental explanations, the impact of terrain and climate specifically, gained in popularity. The most popular of these climatic theories was the one contained in Corneille de Pauw's (1739–1799) *Recherches philosophiques sur les Americains* (1768), who declared that the difference between Europe and America was best defined as the difference between strength and weakness, between civilization and savagery.

These explanations gradually led to the stage-based theory of history popularized by the leading figures of the Scottish Enlightenment. All societies, its proponents claimed, advanced through four stages evolving from a hunter-gathering society to a commercial society. An emphasis on cultural evolution linked physical environment and economic progress and could also be turned into a justification for empire. Although critical of Spanish conquest in the Americas, Scottish historian William Robertson (1721–1793) juxtaposed the science, courage, and discipline of the Spaniards to the ignorance, timidity, and disorder of the indigenous population to justify the vicious conduct of conquistadores in relation to the Aztec and Incan societies.

In the introduction to his *Historia del Nuevo Mundo* (1793), Juan Bautista Muñoz (1745–1799) argued that Spain had encountered in the New World "a field of glory worthy for its elevated thoughts"; and that, in spite of obstacles, "the genius along with the ardor of religious belief ensured the happy attainment of its most arduous enterprises" (Muñoz 1990, p. 25). Spain, in his view, far from destroying the New World's wealth, persevered heroically in the worst of conditions, until America's steadily increasing wealth sparked the emulation, competition, industry, commerce, and interest of all of Europe.

This notion of a hierarchy of civilization, the possibility of advancement toward the perfection achieved by Europe, and Europe's responsibility to accelerate the progress of the non-European world also inspired certain progressive, if paternalistic, late eighteenth-century political writers. Marquis de Condorcet (1743–1794) claimed in 1791 that the inhabitants of Africa, Asia, and America almost seemed to be waiting for Europe to civilize them.

In the early nineteenth century, racial attitudes emerged increasingly as part of the rhetoric that justified colonial rule. Catholics, half-castes, and Hindus were deemed irremediably degenerate, as their religions were thought to corrupt both their moral judgment and political institutions. Arguments of cultural superiority and civilizing mission were plentiful in nineteenth-century Britain. Empire came to express the protection and glorification of the British Crown, church, law, and trade. As Lord Palmerston (1784–1865) bluntly noted, Britain stood at the head of moral, social, and political civilization. "Our task," he said, "is to lead the way and direct the march of other nations."

Such national and cultural chauvinism increased and was given new impetus in the mid-nineteenth century with the emergence of social Darwinism. Coining the term "survival of the fittest" several years before Charles Darwin (1809–1882) set forth his theory, Herbert Spencer (1820–1903) developed an all-encompassing conception of human society and relations based on evolutionary principles. The centerpiece of Darwinism is the theory of natural selection, according to which only the fittest species in organic nature survive, whereas the unfit become extinct. Europeans employed this biologistic framework to justify their imperial rule over people whose races were considered inferior or less fit.

French political leader Jules Ferry (1832–1893) explicitly argued that "the superior races have rights over the inferior races." In his *Greater Britain* (1868), Charles Dilke (1789–1864) rejoiced over the "grandeur of our race, already girdling the earth." Josiah Strong (1847–1916), an American clergyman, wanted this Anglo-Saxon mantle shared with the United States and, in his *Our Country* (1885), praised the Anglo-Saxon instinct for colonizing, saying, "his unequalled energy, his indomitable perseverance, and his personal independence made him a pioneer" (Snyder 1962, p. 122).

Empire was justified because it served domestic goals as well. While an empire might have been built around notions of an exported social hierarchy, as historian David Cannadine has shown, it also served to reinforce the hierarchy at home. Possessing an empire bolstered the British perception that they still belonged—amid the upheaval wrought by mass democracy, industrialization, and urban growth to a traditional, agricultural, layered society.

If the legal and religious rationale for conquest, as well as the racial justifications for empire, have been discussed, other European concepts require further treatment. A pervasive justification for empire, existing from the Spanish Conquest until their dismantlement in the late twentieth century, involved the notion of empire as a trust. Finding indigenous societies to be lacking in human and political standards, Vitoria argued: "For their own benefit the king of Spain might take over the government of the country, nominating prefects and governors for their cities, and even giving them new rulers, if it were clearly necessary for their well-being." There was also a materialistic dimension to this trust in Vitoria's thought. The king, he argued, "is obliged to do for the pagans over whom he rules whatever he would be obliged to do for the good of his own people" (Hamilton 1963, pp. 133–134).

Such notions of trust persisted until the late eighteenth century. Speaking on the East India Bill in 1783, British statesman Edmund Burke (1729–1797) remarked that obligations stemmed from empire: "Such rights or privileges...are all in the strictest sense a trust; and it is the very essence of every trust to be rendered accountable; and even totally to cease when it substantially varies from the purpose for which alone it could have a lawful existence." This notion gathered force at the end of the eighteenth century. Imperialism's apologists pointed to their association with humanitarian policies, such as the abolition of slavery, in justifying the maintenance and expansion of territory. Writing of the acquisition of India in *The Expansion of England* (1883), J. R. Seeley (1834–1895) says, "aggrandisement might present itself in the light of a simple duty, when it seemed that by extending our empire the reign of robbery and murder might be brought to an end" (Snyder 1962, p. 120)—thus presaging Rudyard Kipling's (1865–1936) famous exhortation to Anglo-Saxons across the globe to "take up the white man's burden" (Snyder 1962, p. 87).

The question remained, however, about how this trusteeship could best be fulfilled. One of the main responses was that the expansion of commerce would benefit both the colonized and colonizer. Free trade was considered a vehicle for bettering the world, as well as a way to expand economic interests overseas. Capitalism was conceived as a moral force, helping to civilize the world through the spread of enterprise and a strong work ethic.

Palmerston believed commerce to be the best pioneer of civilization, saying that it improved humankind's sense of well-being. Others regarded this type of rhetoric with skepticism. Historian C. A. Bayly, for instance, said, "free trade was no more than a nostrum of a nation which had achieved superiority by the use of military force to break into other protected markets; the British could now afford to be free traders" (Bayly 1989, p. 237).

Free trade also would emerge as one of the main justifications for setting up the Belgian King Leopold II's (1835–1909) colony of the Congo in 1884. In exchange for recognizing the validity of his claims to sovereignty by other European powers, the King promised not to impose import duties on the goods of those nations in the newly established free state. Civilization, free trade, and fulfillment of European responsibility toward non-European people combined to justify such colonial ventures.

Different sentiments and justifications for imperialism as a trust also may be found in the history of Dutch imperialism. As a Christian nation, they believed that the Netherlands had a moral duty in Indonesia to uphold a policy that was manifested in the improvement of education, public health, agriculture, and the appointment of Indonesians to local administrative bodies. Similar notions would grow in strength after the Great War (1914–1918). Trusteeship dominated early twentieth-century debates, for example. It was the keystone of the mandate system proposed by the League of Nations in 1919, justifying the repartition of the collapsed German and Ottoman empires. Although the explicit purpose of making Britain and France trustees was to stifle slavery and forced labor, the demoralizing traffic in arms and spirits and other abuses were considered barbaric to European sensibilities. The mandatory power also was entrusted to promote the material, moral well-being, and social progress of the inhabitants.

The ethic of trusteeship served to justify empire at its most vulnerable point. In *The Dual Mandate in British Tropical Africa* (1922) F. D. Lugard (1858–1945) purveyed an alternate vision for the newly acquired tropical dependencies, thought to be unsuited for white settlement, based on his experiences as governor of Nigeria before the war. Lugard called for the development by the agency of natives through European guidance, a formula that demanded the government's intervention. It was a dual mandate because it called for the advancement of the inhabitants and the development of its material resources for the benefit of humankind. In this way, Lugard deflected criticism that tropical dependencies were maintained solely for British self-interest. He insisted that Africans, too, were benefiting from, as he put it, "the influx of manufactured goods and the substitution of law and order for the methods of barbarism"

(Lugard 1922, pp. 616–618), while a simultaneous reciprocal and mutual benefit accrued to Europe.

Arguments for trusteeship persisted until the bitter end of European empires. In Portuguese-controlled Angola, one apologist contended in the early 1950s that colonial rule had been characteristically paternal, slowly but surely improving the native's quality of living and bringing them toward the more refined European way of life. The rhetoric of trusteeship also permeated the creation of the colonial development schemes, the forerunners of contemporary development agencies. Britain's 1929 Colonial Development Act, though intended to help colonies to service borrowing for public works, was not altruistic in practice. It was primarily designed to give a boost to a decaying British heavy industry. Similarly, trade preference policies in the 1930s counteracted the slim benefits that development monies produced. In essence, they helped the dominions and harmed the colonial consumers who were likewise exploited by the 1939 policy of bulk-buying commodities, which led to the British economy being subsidized by colonial producers.

The Colonial Development Act had little practical effect. Between 1930 and 1939, only £18 million was spent on development, compared to the £145 million borrowed on the open market by the colonies. Furthermore, the government did nothing to remove the obstacles to investment in the colonies, nor did anything to make industrial production more profitable. In spite of the shortcomings in practice, the notion of empire as a trust was a common feature of the justifications for colonialism in all of the European empires at one time or another.

Some justifications for empire did not address the indigenous inhabitants who would be impacted and focused purely on the needs of European society and its economy. Proponents of such views often resorted to a political language that described colonization as a natural process arising from burgeoning wealth or population in a European country. Colonies were justified as a potential solution to the problems wrought by population expansion. Sir James Steuart (1713–1788), a Scottish political economist whose influence extended across Europe in the mid-eighteenth century, alleged that population must be reduced either by encouragements given to leaving the country, or by establishing colonies. To stay economically strong, he believed that the colony should check its population growth and facilitate the "preservation of wealth that they have already acquired."

Thomas Malthus's (1766–1834) early nineteenth-century demographic analysis, which stressed competition for increasingly scarce resources, justified the search for open territory where a surplus population could live. Observing the social unrest triggered by massive urbanization in the early nineteenth century, G. W. F. Hegel (1770–1831) also argued in the *Elements of the Philosophy of Right* (1821) that colonization could help to solve the problem generated by poverty by providing an outlet for the indigent population competing for scarce resources. European nations, he suggested, were driven to colonize by the pressures of burgeoning population, overproduction, and underconsumption. For Hegel, colonies represented an escape from the burdens and restrictions of European society and envisaged European peasants populating verdant and empty lands, making no mention of the people they might encounter there.

Demographic arguments persisted, especially among the nations without empires. One Italian politician in 1897 claimed that overpopulation forced large-scale immigration of Italians to rival European states and that the absence of space was a cause of poverty. Colonies would provide a much-desired outlet for this surplus population. Some believed that it was less safe and more expensive to bring under control 3 million hectares of land in Italy than to insure the prosperity of a large agricultural colony in Eritrea. Population, of course, was not the only surplus that flowed naturally to ultra-marine possessions. Capital, too, searched for new markets. In 1898 American financial analyst Charles Conant (1861–1915) spoke of the irresistible tendency of great states to expand and advocated new outlets for American capital. He argued, "The great industrial countries should turn to countries which have not yet felt the pulse of modern progress."

It must not be forgotten that one of the main justifications for imperialism was that of gaining advantage in the competition among the European powers. The European empires watched each other constantly. They measured their behavior against each other and borrowed from each other's practices. As Portugal's Marquês de Pombal (1699–1782) observed in the mid-1740s: "All European nations have augmented themselves and are augmenting even today through reciprocal imitation, each one carefully keeps watch over the actions taken by the others (and), through their ministers, they take advantage of the utility of foreign inventions" (Carvalho e Melo 1986, p. 158).

Under the mercantilist system, each state aimed to secure the advantages of colonial trade by depriving competitor nations of access. To achieve this goal, the creation of monopolies was necessary. The conquest and maintenance of colonies was justified not only by bringing commodities to the European colonizing power and opening new markets for domestic manufacturers, but also by depriving rival nations of the benefits of that territory. All of the European empires endeavored to create a closed, monopolistic trading system so that all benefits of colonization would accrue to itself alone, rendering the empire self-sufficient and economically independent of the rest of the world.

Seventeenth-century English commercial writer Charles Davenant (1656–1714) claimed that, in matters of empire, "whoever is the cause of another's advancement is the cause of his own diminuition" (Davenant 1704, pt. 1, p. 205). A nation could not remain, in his view, unarmed and inactive, while other nations enlarged their dominions. In the late eighteenth century, Scottish economist Adam Smith (1723–1790) would show that the mercantile system had rendered less secure the long-term prosperity of the colonial power because its commerce, instead of running in a great number of small channels, had been taught to run principally in one great channel. But even though mercantilist assumptions about the profitability of a colonial monopoly gradually dissipated in the early nineteenth century, the justification of empire based on international rivalry persisted.

Allusions and analogies to the natural processes reached their peak in the biologistic justifications for empire offered by adherents to social Darwinism. This set of ideas played a key role in both imperial rivalry among European states and in the justification of empire over non-European people. In the effort to be fittest among their peers, social Darwinists justified rising military expenditure and increased national efficiency. Walter Bagehot (1826–1877), harnessing biology to defend liberal democracy in the 1870s, emphasized cultural rather than individual selection. He sought to prove that the institutions and practice of liberal democracy were the guarantors of evolutionary progress. "In every particular state in the world," Bagehot wrote in *Physics and Politics* (1872), "those nations which are the strongest tend to prevail over the others; and in certain marked peculiarities the strongest tend to be the best."

In 1886 the Russian sociologist Jacques Novikov defined the foreign policy of a state as the art of pursuing the struggle for existence among social organisms. Competition with other European states urged the securing of colonies to guarantee the raw material, land, and potential markets against their rivals. Theodore Roosevelt's (1858–1919) *The Strenuous Life* (1900) warned against the possibility of elimination in an international struggle for existence. America, he said, could not shrink from hard contests for empire or else the bolder and stronger would pass them by and gain domination of the world. Successful imperial ventures thus were perceived to indicate the vitality, and hence fitness, of a nation.

Roosevelt's ideas echoed the sentiment of the so-called Doctrine of World Empires, which maintained that great nations possessed empires. Not possessing an empire, or losing an existing one, would be a sign of being a third-rate, or declining, power. In 1877 French publicist Pierre Raboisson declared, "The grandeur of empires always reaches its apogee when colonial expansion has reached its maximum, and their decadence always coincides with their loss of colonies" (Baumgart 1982, p. 70).

Similarly, Britain's Herbert Asquith (1852–1928) interpreted European expansion as normal, necessary, and a sign of vitality in a growing nation. As they had been for mercantile nations until the eighteenth century, possessing colonies was a sign of national strength and an asset in the constant state of conflict among European nations. Yet even within a biologistic framework, the growth and consolidation of empires did not always tend toward war, but also could be the harbinger of peace. In 1898, dividing the world between living and dying nations, Lord Salisbury (1830–1903) argued, "The living nations will eventually encroach on the territory of the dying, and the seeds and causes of conflict amongst civilized nations will speedily disappear" (Baumgart 1982, p. 72). In this way, biologistic conceptions of international relations made the acquisition of colonies imperative.

This essay has discussed European justifications for empire that persisted during its more than 500 years of world domination. The main justifications were evangelization, pursuit of the civilizing mission, racial superiority, trusteeship and development, and internal demographic and economic pressures. Yet while legions of the West's leading political thinkers collaborated in legitimizing empire, many others lent their intellectual prowess to debunking such justifications. Sometimes unfavorable attitudes toward empire arose from their lack of profitability rather than moral censure. The utility of colonies, or plantations, was among the most contentious and least resolved issues debated by seventeenth-century English economic writers.

Roger Coke derogated their value, asserting: "Ireland and our plantations rob us of all the growing youth and industry of the nation, whereby it becomes weak and feeble, and the strength as well as trade becomes decayed and diminished" (Paquette 2004, p. 77). William Petty (1623–1687) lamented on the treasury-draining impact of providing imperial defense for small, divided, and remote governments that are seldom able to defend themselves. He argued that defending these nations was too much of a financial burden and ultimately diminished national strength.

By the mid-eighteenth century, however, Denis Diderot (1713–1784), Immanuel Kant (1724–1804), and J. G. Herder (1744–1803) all opposed imperial rule over non-European people on ethical rather than economic grounds. The views of these Enlightenment, anti-imperialist thinkers on issues of human nature, cultural diversity, and cross-cultural moral judgments served to undermine justifications for European overseas expansion. They rejected imperialism outright as unworkable, dangerous, or even immoral.

Diderot and his collaborator Abbé Raynal (1713–1796), for example, rejected imperialism not only because of its unhappy consequences for subjugated non-Europeans, but for its adverse impact on Europeans as well, whose prospects for peace, economic stability, and freedom were diminished by the quest for, and maintenance of, empire. Furthermore, Herder, Kant, and Diderot, as scholar Sankar Muthu has recently shown, shared a commitment to human dignity, rooted in the humanity of each individual. These authors presaged the attacks on empire that intellectuals, most notably Marxists, pursued in the twentieth.

SEE ALSO *Christianity and Colonial Expansion in the Americas; Imperialism, Liberal Theories of; Imperialism, Marxist Theories of; Mission, Civilizing; Race and Colonialism in the Americas; Religion, Roman Catholic Church.*

BIBLIOGRAPHY

Andrews, C. M., and A. S. Kanya-Forstner. "Centre and Periphery in the Making of the Second French Colonial Empire, 1815–1920." *Journal of Imperial and Commonwealth History* 16 (3) (1988): 9–34.

Armitage, David. *The Ideological Origins of the British Empire.* Cambridge, MA, and New York: Cambridge University Press, 2000.

Baumgart, Winfried. *Imperialism: The Idea and Reality of British and French Colonial Expansion 1880–1914.* Translated by Ben V. Mast and Winfried Baumgart. New York: Oxford University Press, 1982.

Bayly, C. A. *Imperial Meridian: the British Empire and the World 1780–1830.* London and New York: Longman, 1989.

Berry, L. E. and R. O. Crummey, eds. *Rude and Barbarous Kingdom: Russia in the Accounts of 16th Century British Voyagers.* Madison and London: University of Wisconsin Press, 1968.

Brading, David A. *The First America: The Spanish Monarchy, Creole Patriots, and the Liberal State 1492–1867.* Cambridge, U.K.: Cambridge University Press, 1991.

Cannadine, David. *Ornamentalism: How the British Saw Their Empire.* Oxford, U.K., and New York: Allen Lane, 2001.

Canny, Nicholas P. "The Ideology of English Colonization: from Ireland to America." In *Theories of Empire 1450–1800*, edited by David Armitage. Aldershot, U.K.: Ashgate Variorum, 1998.

Carvalho e Melo, Sebastião de [later, Marques de Pombal]. *Escritos Económicos de Londres (1741–1742) (London Economic Writings).* Edited by José Bareto. Lisbon, Portugal: Biblioteca Nacional, 1986.

Davenant, Charles. *Essays Upon Peace at Home, and War Abroad.* 2 parts. London: 1704.

Drayton, Richard. *Nature's Government: Science, Imperial Britain, and the "Improvement" of the World.* New Haven, CT: Yale University Press, 2000.

Elliott, J. H. *The Old World and the New 1492–1650.* Cambridge, U.K.: Cambridge University Press, 1970.

Fieldhouse, D. K. *The West and the Third World: Trade, Colonialism, Dependence, and Development.* Oxford and Malden, MA: Blackwell, 1999.

Gallagher, John, and Ronald Robinson. "The Imperialism of Free Trade." *Economic History Review* 2nd Series 4 (1953): 1–15.

Hamilton, Bernice. *Political Thought in Sixteenth-Century Spain: A Study of the Political Ideas of Vitoria, De Soto, Suárez, and Molina.* Oxford, U.K.: Clarendon Press, 1963.

Hyam, Ronald. *Britain's Imperial Century 1815–1914: A Study of Empire and Expansion*, 3rd ed. Basingstoke, Houndmills, Hampshire, U.K., and New York: Palgrave/Macmillan, 2002.

Keene, Edward. *Beyond the Anarchical Society: Grotius, Colonialism, and Order in World Politics.* Cambridge, U.K., and New York: Cambridge University Press, 2002.

Lynn, Martin. "British Policy, Trade, and Informal Empire in the Mid-Nineteenth Century." In *The Oxford History of the British Empire*, Vol. 3: *The Nineteenth Century*, edited by Andrew Porter. Oxford, U.K., and New York: Oxford University Press, 1999.

Lugard, F. D. *The Dual Mandate in British Tropical Africa.* London and Edinbugh: Blackwood, 1922.

MacLachlan, Colin M. *Spain's Empire in the New World: The Role of Ideas in Institutional and Social Change.* Berkeley: University of California Press, 1988.

Marshall, P. J., and Glyndwr Williams. *The Great Map of Mankind: British Perceptions of the World in the Age of Enlightenment.* London: J. M. Dent & Sons Ltd., 1982.

Maxwell, Kenneth. "The Idea of Luso-Brazilian Empire." In *Naked Tropics: Essays on Empire and Other Rogues*, edited by Kenneth Maxwell. New York: Routledge, 2003.

Muñoz, Juan Bautista. *Historia del nuevo mundo.* New Edition. Valencia, Spain: University of Valencia, 1990.

Muthu, Sankar. *Enlightenment Against Empire.* Princeton, NJ: Princeton University Press, 2003.

Pagden, Anthony. *Lords of All the World: Ideologies of Empire in Spain, Britain, and France, c. 1500–c. 1800.* New Haven, CT: Yale University Press, 1995.

Pagden, Anthony. "The Struggle for Legitimacy and the Image of Empire in the Atlantic to c. 1700." In *The Oxford History of the British Empire; Vol. 1: The Origins of Empire*, edited by Nicholas Canny. New York and Oxford, U.K.: Oxford University Press, 1998.

Paquette, Gabriel. "Hegel's Analysis of Colonialism and its Roots in Scottish Political Economy." *Clio* 32 (4) (2003): 415–432.

Paquette, Gabriel B. "The Intellectual Context of British Diplomatic Recognition of the South American Republics, c. 1800–1830." *Journal of Transatlantic Studies* 2 (1) (2004): 75–95.

Platt, D. C. M. *Finance, Trade, and Politics in British Foreign Policy 1815–1914*. Oxford, U.K., and London: Clarendon Press, 1968.

Porter, Andrew. "Trusteeship, Anti-Slavery, and Humanitarianism." In *The Oxford History of the British Empire*, Vol. 3: *The Nineteenth Century*, edited by Andrew Porter. Oxford, U.K., and New York: Oxford University Press, 1999.

Robinson, Ronald. "The Moral Disarmament of the African Empire 1919–1947." In *The First British Commonwealth*, edited by Norman Hillmer and P. G. Wigley. London: Cass, 1980.

Scammell, G.V. *The First Imperial Age: European Overseas Expansion c. 1400–1715*. London and Boston: Unwin Hyman, 1989.

Semmel, Bernard. *Imperialism and Social Reform: English Social-Imperial Thought 1895–1914*. London: George Allen & Unwin, 1960.

Semmel, Bernard. *The Rise of Free Trade Imperialism: Classical Political Economy, the Empire of Free Trade, and Imperialism, 1750–1850*. Cambridge, U.K.: Cambridge University Press, 1970.

Snyder, Louis L., ed. *The Imperialism Reader; Documents and Readings on Modern Expansionism*. Princeton, NJ: Van Nostrand, 1962.

Stanley, Brian. *The Bible and the Flag: Protestant Missions and British Imperialism in the Nineteenth and Twentieth Century*. Leicester, U.K.: Apollos, 1990.

Stengers, Jean. "King Leopold's Imperialism." In *Studies in the Theory of Imperialism*, edited by R. Owens and B. Sutcliffe. London: Longman, 1972.

Stokes, Eric. *The English Utilitarians and India*. Oxford, U.K.: Clarendon Press, 1959.

Tully, James. *An Approach to Political Philosophy: Locke in Contexts*. Cambridge, U.K., and New York: Cambridge University Press, 1993.

Wesseling, H. L. "The Giant that was a Dwarf, or the Strange History of Dutch Imperialism." *Journal of Imperial and Commonwealth History* 16 (3) (1988): 58–70.

Gabriel Paquette

K

KANDY, COLONIAL POWERS' RELATIONS WITH THE KINGDOM OF

In the early sixteenth century, when the Portuguese arrived at the shores of Ceylon (Sri Lanka), the Sinhalese kingdom of Kandy was still under the domination of the neighboring Kotte kingdom—though the foundations for independence had already been laid. The kings of Kandy were attempting to establish themselves as autonomous rulers in the central mountains by wresting control of the region from the powerful Kotte rulers of the western lowlands. As the Kotte kingdom fell into a state of disarray, due mainly to the protracted succession crises of the early sixteenth century, Kandyan rulers began to establish their autonomy.

In 1521, with the support of the Kandyan king, the three sons of the Kotte king, Wijayabahu IV, engineered a coup, then executed their father and proceeded to divide up the Kotte kingdom. Mayadunne, the middle son, who established himself in Sitawaka, to the east of Kotte, enlarged his portion of the kingdom by annexing his younger brother's share, following the brother's death. Buvanekabahu, the eldest, who received the prime areas of the kingdom—including Kotte, the seat of the kingdom—sought the help of Kandyan kings in his struggle against Mayadunne, who was a potential threat for both, as Sitawaka was located adjoining to the Kandyan region. In 1582 Mayadunne's son Rajasinghe I defeated Karaliyedda, the Kandyan ruler, and annexed Kandy to Sitawaka.

It was following the fall of Sitawaka after the death of Rajasinghe in 1592 and the total subjugation of Kotte to the Portuguese in 1597 that Kandy emerged again as an important historical player. Konappu Bandara, son of a chief of Kandy, ascended to the throne of Kandy in 1592. He defeated the Portuguese plan to enthrone Karaliyedda's daughter, Kusumasana Devi (Dona Katerina), as the puppet queen of Kandy, and married her in order to secure a legitimate right to the Kandyan throne.

THE SOLE NATIVE KINGDOM

When the Portuguese annexed the Jaffna kingdom, which controlled the Jaffna Peninsula and parts of the northern tip of the island in 1621, Kandy emerged as the sole native kingdom that could claim to represent the continuance of precolonial traditions, including religious and social rituals. This enabled the Kandyan kings to occasionally call upon the support of natives in other regions outside of Kandy.

Portuguese attempts to occupy Kandy proved disastrous in the face of the guerrilla tactics of the Kandyans, who skillfully made use of the virtually inaccessible mountains that formed their kingdom's frontier. Kandyan kings even toyed with the idea of expanding their frontier at the expense of the Portuguese. In 1602 Wimaladharmasuriya I tried to obtain the support of the Dutch when he received General Spilbergen, the leader of a Dutch East India Company fleet, but met with no success. Rajasinghe II, however, managed to conclude the Westervolt treaty with the Dutch in 1638, as a result of which the Portuguese were expelled from the island in 1658.

The British Governor Interviews Kandyan Chiefs. *George Anderson, the newly appointed British governor of Ceylon (now Sri Lanka), and his assistants meet with native chiefs of Kandy on February 1, 1851, an event depicted in this nineteenth-century illustration.* © CORBIS. REPRODUCED BY PERMISSION.

KANDY AND THE DUTCH

Relations between Rajasinghe II and the Dutch were not cordial for long, however: things soured after the Dutch captured the fortified city of Galle on the southern coast of the island in 1640. In defiance of Rajasinghe's wishes, the Dutch were aiming to establish themselves as the successors to Portuguese possessions. The relationship turned into an open confrontation when Governor Van Goens captured Kalpitiya Harbor, which was Kandy's main access to the sea from the western coast. The Dutch then followed a policy of territorial expansion, although the Batavian administration of the Dutch East India Trading Company did not fully comply with this policy. From the point of view of Kandy, this was an open violation of the treaty of 1638, which precluded the Dutch from holding any territory against the wishes of the king. Dutch authorities, however, justified their claim on two grounds. First, they interpreted the treaty in a different manner by, apparently, deleting one important clause. Second, and mainly because the first claim was not convincing, they argued that they had the right to hold onto the territory they captured until the debt owed the Dutch for helping Kandy expel the Portuguese was fully paid. Estimated unilaterally by the Dutch, this debt was by no means affordable for Kandy. Thus, the Dutch were able to justify holding onto various territories for a long time.

Following the death of Rajasinghe II, Kandy's attitude toward the Dutch became more conciliatory. The Dutch also became less aggressive, as their economic interests demanded a peaceful atmosphere. Peaceful coexistence basically prevailed until the Kandy-Dutch war of 1761 to 1766. Dutch governors made a conscious effort to please the king. For example, they helped Kandy to bring Buddhist monks from Burma and Siam to perform higher ordination for Buddhist novices. They also accepted, at least nominally, the sovereign rights of the king even in Dutch territories. The Dutch, in turn, received permission to peel cinnamon free of any remuneration in Kandyan lands.

There were, however, occasions when this peaceful coexistence was tested. Repeated demands from Kandy to take part in the overseas trade and occasional unrest among the inhabitants of the Dutch territory caused problems. The Dutch stood firm against Kandy's wish to take part in trade. Nayakkars from South India, who constituted a significant group in the Kandyan court (because Kandyan kings frequently selected Nayakkar wives for the royal family), had a great interest in the trade between the two opposite coasts. Moreover, Kandyan chiefs either instigated or supported various rebellions in the Dutch territory, most significantly those involving cinnamon peelers. These issues lay the ground for the open confrontation that culminated in the war of 1761 to 1766.

When a Siamese prince was handed over to the Dutch to be deported following a conspiracy in the Kandyan court, a rumor spread that the Dutch were planning to enthrone the prince. Kandy then invaded the Dutch territory in 1761 under the pretext of responding to the grievances of inhabitants who had complained to the king.

War and the treaty that followed greatly weakened Kandy. Its access to the sea was completely denied after it lost the coastal portions of its territory. It also lost more territories in the interior, and was forced to recognize the sovereign rights of the Dutch over their possessions. The treaty in general was humiliating to Kandy, and as a result the kingdom did everything to baulk at its implementation.

KANDY'S SUBJUGATION TO THE ENGLISH

The English East India Company got hold of the Dutch possessions in Ceylon in 1796, benefiting from Napoleon's invasion of Holland. In place of the Dutch, the internally weakened Kandy now had to deal with agents of the ever more powerful British Empire. When the English occupied the Maritime regions, a bitter rivalry broke out among the court chiefs of Kandy, who divided themselves into two rival factions. A succession crisis after the death of King Rajadhi Rajasinghe, who left no son, added more fuel to this rivalry. While Nayakkars tried to enthrone the son of the brother of one of the queens, a move that was supported by a section of the court chiefs, Mahaadigar (prime minister) Pilimatalauve, the most powerful chief, planned successfully to enthrone an eighteen-year-old named Konnasami, the son of a sister of one of the queens-dowager.

The crisis in the court was extremely beneficial for the English, as each rival party tried to win their support. Pilimatalauve soon broke from the king and approached the English on his own. In 1803, hoping to exploit the situation, the British governor of Ceylon, Frederick North, mounted an expedition to occupy Kandy, which proved to be disastrous. The failure of the English adversely affected the career of Pilimatalauve. In 1810 he was executed following an aborted revolt, after which his nephew Ahelepola succeeded him. He too followed his uncle's path by revolting against the king. The execution of Ahelepola's family widened the gap between the two parties and gave the opportunity for the English to intervene. The intervention was masterminded by John D'Oyly, an expert on Kandyan affairs, who had built an efficient intelligence network and was in communication with the chiefs who had defected. The war against Kandy, proclaimed in January 1815, was strongly supported by Ahelepola. It was over in forty days, without any notable military engagements. The king was captured and the Kandyan Convention was signed, ceding the Kandyan kingdom to the British, but maintaining many of the rights of the chiefs.

However, the honeymoon between the British and the rebel Kandyan chiefs did not last long. Although the Convention has made provisions to safeguard the *ancien regime*, administrative measures that were taken to consolidate British rule greatly diminished the influence of the chiefs. While Britain planned to extend its rule from maritime areas to the Kandyan interior, the chiefs were unwilling to sacrifice their power and privileges. A rebellion in 1818 was the inevitable outcome of dissatisfaction among the chiefs and on the part of the principal Buddhist monks, who formed another significant element of the Kandyan polity.

Following their ruthless crushing of the rebellion, the British issued a proclamation in 1818 that effectively put an end to the erstwhile organization of the Kandyan kingdom. Unlike the Convention of 1815, this proclamation greatly curtailed the power and privileges of the Kandyan chiefs. It is fair to say, therefore, that the proclamation concluded the integration of the Kandyan kingdom into the British colonial sphere, by bringing an end to Kandy as a separate political formation.

SEE ALSO *Ceylon; Empire, British; Empire, Dutch; Empire, Portuguese.*

BIBLIOGRAPHY

Abeyasinghe, T. B. H. *Portuguese Rule in Ceylon, 1594–1612.* Colombo, Sri Lanka: Lake House, 1966.

De Silva, Chandra R. *The Portuguese in Ceylon, 1617–1638.* Colombo, Sri Lanka: H. W. Cave, 1972.

De Silva, Colvin R. *Ceylon under the British Occupation 1795–1833*, Vol. 1. New Delhi: Navrang, 1995. (First published in 1941.)

Dewaraja, L. S. *The Kandyan Kingdom of Ceylon, 1707–1760*. Colombo, Sri Lanka: Lake House, 1972.

University of Ceylon History of Ceylon, Vol. 3. Edited by K. M. de Silva. Colombo, Sri Lanka: University of Ceylon Press, 1973.

University of Peradeniya History of Sri Lanka, Vol. 2: *c1500–c1800*. Edited by K. M. de Silva. Peradeniya, Sri Lanka: University of Peradeniya, 1995.

Wickremesekera, Channa. *Kandy at War: Indigenous Military Resistance to European Expansion in Sri Lanka, 1594–1818*. Colombo, Sri Lanka: Vijitha Yapa, 2004.

Nirmal Ranjith Dewasiri

KARTINI, RADEN AJENG
1879–1904

Raden Ajeng Kartini has occupied a dominant space in the history of women emancipation in modern Indonesia. She was born April 21, 1879, in a small town on the northern coast of Central Java (part of present-day Indonesia). Kartini received a modern Dutch education provided to her by virtue of her aristocratic background and her family's acquaintance with reform-minded Dutch officials and women. Her education, along with her personal experiences, rendered her highly qualified to address issues facing contemporary Javanese women.

Kartini grew up in an aristocratic family of a regent *(bupati)* in Jepara in the northern part of Central Java. Her father, Sosroningrat, first married Kartini's future mother, an ordinary local girl, Ngasirah, a daughter of a coconut trader and religious scholar, in 1872 when he was a district officer in Mayong. In 1875, while Ngasirah was still alive, Sosroningrat also married Raden Ajeng Muryam, who eventually assumed the position of official wife *(garwa padmi)* because of her aristocratic background. This marriage helped pave the way for Kartini's father to succeed his father-in-law as regent of Jepara in 1881. Ngasirah never assumed the official wife position, one of rank and status, because of her non-aristocratic background. In a society where higher social status was socially and bureaucratically crucial, the status of wives became crucial in climbing the social ladder, including access to European education.

As the daughter of an aristocrat, Kartini received her early education directly from her mother, stepmother, and father, who taught her about religion, Javanese customs, and etiquette. At the age of six, Kartini was enrolled at a Dutch primary school located near her home in Jepara. Although the school served only Dutch and Eurasian children, Kartini was allowed to attend because her father was a regent. After school, Kartini received extra tutoring in embroidery, sewing, religion, and reading.

Unlike many other girls in the regency, Kartini was privileged to attend various functions and meet the Dutch and indigenous officials who visited her father. Most of these privileges came to an end by the time she completed her primary school education, because she was obliged to undergo an almost total seclusion inside the walls of her home, in accordance with aristocratic etiquette of the time.

Kartini's father allowed her an hour a day to receive sewing lessons from the wife of the Dutch assistant resident, Mrs. Marie Ovink-Soer, an energetic woman with feminist sympathies, which had an influence on the young Kartini. Kartini appealed unsuccessfully to her father to be allowed to join her elder brothers, who had been sent to Semarang for higher schooling. She and her two sisters were allowed in 1896 to attend an official ceremony near their home. Then, in 1898, they accepted an invitation to attend a celebration of Dutch Queen Wilhelmina's (1880–1962) coronation held by the governor general in Semarang.

In light of Kartini's early exposure to education and feminism, it is not surprising that she later protested against the custom of forced, early marriage, insisting that women be allowed "to be free... to study, not to be subject to any one, and, above all, never, never to be obliged to marry" (Symmers and Geertz 1964, p. 64)." Her conception of an ideal education focused on empowerment, enlightenment, and relevance, and she advocated open, nondiscriminative, government-sponsored schools. Her experiences and her understanding of the challenges of the changing times inspired her to emphasize the importance of education for all her compatriots, especially women. She was keenly aware of how poorly girls were represented in local schools; for many girls, their mothers would be their first teachers. Kartini also emphasized the importance of lifelong education.

Kartini's long seclusion and the gender-based unequal treatment she experience encouraged her to fight for women's emancipation in Java. More specifically, her access to such books as Goekoop de Jong's *Hilda van Suylenburg* (1898) and her extensive correspondence concerning feminism with Stella Zeehandelaar (b. 1874) and others helped her focus her ideas on women's emancipation and even independence in the larger context.

Kartini's great achievements resulted from her correspondence with various, mostly Dutch, officials and individuals. Although her direct encounters with visitors to her father and with other enlightened individuals had a strong impact on her search for emancipation, it is her correspondence in Dutch where Kartini's great vision is apparent. Along with Zeehandelaar, the individuals with whom Kartini maintained intensive, regular correspondence include Jacque H. Abendanon, the director of the Batavian Department of Education, Religion, and Industry; H. H. van Kol, a Dutch socialist parliamentarian; and Annie Glaser, an activist and educator; as well as G. K. Anton, P. F. Sijthoff, and Hilda de Booy-Boissevain.

Although Kartini advocated the prevention of marriage to a man with previous wives and children, in November 1903 she married the regent of Rembang, Joyoadiningrat, shortly after the death of his official wife. Joyoadiningrat had been close to Kartini's father, for they were about the same age. In July 1903 Kartini's father told her that Joyoadiningrat had made a proposal to marry her; she was given three days to reply. Kartini accepted the proposal on the condition that they have a simple wedding ceremony and that she be given the opportunity to pursue her ongoing project of providing tuition for girls in Rembang. She was, in fact, given full support and facilities to open classes for girls, including her stepdaughters, in her new home. In addition, her desire to open a vocational school was warmly received

Kartini's new life as an official wife of a regent seems, as she claimed in her letters, to have brought her strength and happiness. She was greatly impressed by the care and treatment her husband gave her. She shared with her husband the determination to improve the conditions of the Javanese people. She pursued her ideas with him in Dutch, and he encouraged her to write a book on the myths and legends of Java. Her health deteriorated after the delivery of her first child; Kartini died four days later on September 17, 1904.

Despite the limited impact of Kartini's ideas and actions on her compatriots, she was considered ahead of her time by contemporary social reformers and feminist sympathizers in the Indies. Kartini emerged at a time when the ideals of the Dutch colonial Ethical Policy had won the day in the colony. Indeed, Kartini was a product of the policy. Yet, she maintained a balance between indigenousness and modernity in envisioning the future of her society. More specifically, Kartini pioneered a movement to emancipate women from the patriarchal structure and enlighten the youth with modern education for all. Her insistence on freedom of choice and modern education for girls left a major impact on the future youth movement in the country. Because of her relentless efforts, women and girls were given an equal place as citizens. Future generations should be, she maintained, a melting pot of the best, both locally and universally.

Kartini was formally declared the major symbol of women's emancipation in Indonesia when her birthday, April 21, was declared women's national day. In addition, she was declared a national heroine in 1964. Kartini's ideas, more than her actions, have been a source of inspiration for the emancipation movement in Indonesia, because her life story and ideas closely resemble those of many other Indonesian women. Kartini's determination to "end darkness and open light" has become a slogan for freedom in Indonesia.

SEE ALSO *Daum, Paulus Adrianus; Ethical Policy, Netherlands Indies; Multatuli (Eduard Douwes Dekker).*

BIBLIOGRAPHY

Coté, Joost, ed. and trans. *Letters from Kartini: An Indonesian Feminist, 1900–1904.* Melbourne, Australia: Hyland House, 1992.

Geertz, H. and A.L. Symmers, ed. *Letters of a Javanese Princess* by Kartini. New York: Norton Library, 1964.

Soeroto, Sitisoemandari. *Kartini: Sebuah Biografi.* Jakarta, Indonesia: Gunung Agung, 1984.

Zainu'ddin, Ailsa Thomson, et al. *Kartini Centenary: Indonesian Women Then and Now.* Clayton, Victoria, Australia: Monash University, 1980.

Iik Arifin Mansurnoor

KENYATTA, JOMO
1891–1978

Jomo Kenyatta, the first president of the Republic of Kenya, was born Johnston Kamau in Kiambu, in the Central Province of Kenya. The history of his life traverses Kenya, Europe, and other parts of Africa that he visited as a nationalist leader and as the head of state. Kenyatta is best known for his part in the nationalist movement in Kenya in which he played various roles both within Kenya and abroad. He was the secretary general of the Kikuyu Central Association (KCA) from 1926 until 1940 when the organization was banned. In 1928, he served as the editor of one of the first African newspapers in Kenya, *Muiguithania* (The Reconciler). He represented the KCA in 1929 when he was sent to present to the Colonial office in Britain the KCA grievances on land, female circumcision, and the establishment of independent schools.

Between 1931 and 1946 Kenyatta was based in London, from where he toured many European countries including Russia, France, Italy, Denmark, Norway, and Sweden. He studied at Moscow University and at London School of Economics. He wrote articles in newspapers such as *The Manchester Guardian* and spoke at

Jomo Kenyatta (1889–1978). Prime Minister Kenyatta of Kenya waves to well-wishers in London as he leaves to attend the 1964 African Leader's Conference in Cairo. © HULTON-DEUTSCH COLLECTION/CORBIS. REPRODUCED BY PERMISSION.

his calls for *Harambee* ("to pull together") through which he urged Kenyans to redouble efforts in nation building. He urged Kenyans to "forget the past"—that is, the colonial encounter and its negative impact, and work together for national unity. Kenyatta, drawing from the nationalist movement, viewed poverty, ignorance, and disease as the major problems that Kenyans had to overcome in order to develop their nation and move forward.

His leadership was colorful, and Kenyatta always carried his flywhisk and wore the nationalist hat made of colorful beads, often accompanied with an entourage of singers at his public gatherings, which he addressed with great oratory skills. His leadership was, however, at times controversial. As the first president of Kenya, he ran the country as a de facto single-party state from 1966, becoming precursor to the later de jure one-party state from 1982 under the second president of Kenya, Daniel Arap Moi.

Kenyatta commenced political detention without trial in independent Kenya when he banned the opposition party Kenya Peoples Union (KPU) and detained all KPU members of parliament in1968. Under his regime, gender issues around women's leadership in Kenya were mainly silent, although he nominated at least two women to parliament among the twelve nominated members during his last two tenures as the president in 1968 and 1974. Despite the controversy associated with his leadership, Kenyatta is remembered as a great African statesman who remained in office during a time of prosperity for Kenya. He died on August 22, 1978, having led Kenya for fifteen years.

SEE ALSO *Nationalism, Africa; Nkrumah, Kwame.*

BIBLIOGRAPHY

Delf, George. *Jomo Kenyatta: Towards Truth About "the Light of Kenya."* Garden City, NY: Doubleday, 1961.

Slater, Montagu. *The Trial of Jomo Kenyatta*, 2nd ed. London: Secker and Warburg, 1962.

Wepman, Dennis. *Jomo Kenyatta: President of Kenya.* New York: Chelsea House, 1985.

Edith Miguda

public meetings where he addressed the plight of his people the Kikuyu, land hunger in Kenya, and the harsh colonial pass laws. He also represented the KCA demands that included direct representation of the African people in the legislative council. Kenyatta wrote anthropological works such as *Facing Mount Kenya.* He worked closely with George Padmore, the radical West Indian trade unionist in the 1930s, and was one of the founders of the Pan African Federation with Kwame Nkrumah.

Kenyatta returned to Kenya in 1947, joined the Kenya African Union (KAU), and was elected president of the organization in 1947. During his tenure, he attempted to dissociate KAU from Mau Mau but was arrested and detained between 1952 and 1962, accused of organizing the Mau Mau movement.

Kenyatta is remembered for his controversial trial at Kapenguria where the British colonial government detained him for seven years with hard labor. He denied being the leader of Mau Mau or adhering to any of the violent activities conducted by Mau Mau in Kenya.

At Independence, Kenyatta stood for and personified national unity and urged Kenyans to work hard through

KHOMEINI, AYATOLLAH RUHOLLAH
1902–1989

Ayatollah Ruhollah Khomeini, a Shi'i Muslim cleric and instructor, played a central role in the Iranian Revolution of 1978 to 1979 and orchestrated the establishment of

Ayatollah Khomeini (1900–1989). *Ayatollah Ruhollah Khomeini (center) waves to supporters on February 1, 1979, the day of his return to Iran from exile, after the abdication of the shah.* © BETTMANN/CORBIS. REPRODUCED BY PERMISSION.

Meanwhile, living conditions in Iran had worsened throughout the 1970s despite Iran's massive oil reserves. Iranians increasingly blamed the failures of the shah's economic policies, government corruption, and repression for the status quo, and looked to Khomeini, whose charisma and religious rhetoric proved to be effective unifying mechanisms. In Iran's diverse political spectrum, the only commonalities among the various groups were their resentment of the shah and their shared cultural background, of which Shi'i Islam is a major part.

In 1978, as Iranians were increasingly frustrated with the government and pushing for reform, a government-owned newspaper attacked Khomeini with dubious accusations. Students and merchants in Qom, the city where Khomeini had received his training, protested spontaneously and the army ended the demonstration with force, killing some seventy students. At the customary memorial gatherings held after forty days, more demonstrating mourners were killed; the initial incident led to a recurrence of demonstrations and deaths every forty days. Khomeini encouraged the demonstrations from France via his students' networks and cassette distributions. By January 1979, the shah's military backing was collapsing and he fled the country; Khomeini returned to Iran two weeks later.

From the time of Khomeini's return until 1982, circumstances in Iran were precarious and chaotic. During this period, religious and secular sectors struggled for control of Iran's future, and an Islamic theocracy was only one of several alternatives. Khomeini launched a number of measures to root out the opposition, including the Islamic Republic Party, the Revolutionary Guards, and tribunals. Khomeini also established the Council of Guardians, a body that has veto power over all legislation, and installed himself as supreme leader.

Although the Islamic regime under Khomeini sought a comprehensive, severe Islamization of society, it has been forced to reverse or soften many policies. For example, despite Khomeini's efforts to curtail women's rights in the early 1980s, women have successfully campaigned to overturn many of these rulings and have secured some legal advantages that they lacked under the shah.

SEE ALSO *Iran.*

BIBLIOGRAPHY

Abrahamian, Ervand. *Khomeinism: Essays on the Islamic Republic.* Berkeley: University of California Press, 1993.

Algar, Hamid, ed. and trans. *Islam and Revolution: Writings and Declarations of Imam Khomeini.* Berkeley, CA: Mizan Press, 1981.

Keddie, Nikki. *Modern Iran: Roots and Results of Revolution.* New Haven, CT: Yale University Press, 2003.

the Islamic Republic of Iran. Khomeini first became a well-known public figure when he spoke out during the 1960s against the failings and policies of Mohammad Reza Pahlavi (1919–1980), the shah of Iran, denouncing the government's corruption, repression, secularism, and alliance with the United States. Khomeini was further incensed when the government gave women suffrage and extended the legal privileges of Americans in Iran. Khomeini demanded the shah's resignation, after which the government soon deported Khomeini to Turkey.

The next year, Khomeini was expelled to Iraq, where he maintained contact with Iranians by smuggling into Iran cassettes of his sermons, through which he continued to condemn the shah's government. In 1978 Khomeini was deported to France, where it was easier to sustain these contacts. Throughout his years in exile, Khomeini increased his credibility and fame for his opposition to the shah due to both the wide circulation of his sermons and his network of former students who were rising in the religious ranks.

Martin, Vanessa. *Creating an Islamic State: Khomeini and the Making of a New Iran*. London and New York: Tauris, 2000.

Mottahedeh, Roy. *The Mantle of the Prophet: Religion and Politics in Iran*. New York: Simon and Schuster, 1985.

Elizabeth Brownson

KIAOCHOW

SEE *Shandong Province*

KINGMAN REEF

SEE *Pacific, American Presence in*

KNIL (KONINKLIJK NEDERLANDSCH-INDISCH LEGER)

SEE *Royal Dutch-Indisch Army*

KOREA, TO WORLD WAR II

The strategic location of the Korean Peninsula, situated at the far eastern edge of the Asian continent and a mere 210 kilometers (about 130 miles) from the Japanese archipelago, often compromised the state's ability to maintain its sovereignty. Nineteenth-century Russian expansion eastward only complicated Korea's already precarious position, particularly after Japan emerged as an imperial power and Korea's traditional ally, China, was weakened by domestic and foreign crises. The Korean Peninsula's division following the defeat of its colonial occupier, Japan, not only separated a people, but also Korea's agricultural south from its mineral-rich north.

Throughout most of its pre-1945 history, Korea participated in China's tributary system, whereby it recognized the Chinese emperor as the sole "Son of Heaven," followed the Chinese calendar based on his reign, and dutifully reported Korea's regal successions to the Chinese capital. Chinese imperial blessing in turn gained the Korean throne legitimacy, and selected Korean merchants were granted access to Chinese markets. Participation in this system also provided the Korean Peninsula with military protection, as long as the reigning dynasty in China was strong. Membership

had its drawbacks, as well, particularly during times of dynastic transition, as was the case in the mid-seventeenth century. At this time, Chinese political instability forced the Korean government to decide whether to remain loyal to the waning Ming dynasty, which had just helped drive the Japanese from the peninsula, or support the Manchu, who challenged, and eventually toppled, the Ming.

Korea's relations with Japan generally assumed an open, albeit cautious posture. The threat of "pirate" *(wako)* intrusions dominated the two states' diplomatic relations from the twelfth to seventeenth centuries. The late sixteenth-century invasions of the Japanese military leader Toyotomi Hideyoshi (1536–1598) still remain a bitter memory to Koreans. The two peoples resumed their trade relations from the early seventeenth century, after the new Japanese regime cooperated in returning kidnapped artisans and in assisting in Korea's battle against Manchu (now Qing) retaliation over Korea's remaining loyal to China's Ming dynasty. The twelve Korean missions to the Japanese capital over the Tokugawa period (1603–1868) were as much for trade as they were for reconnaissance. Additional Japanese-Korean trade took place through the Japanese island of Tsushima, which frequently sent missions to the southern city of Pusan.

Domestically, the Korean government depended heavily on the precepts of the ancient Chinese philosopher Confucius (ca. 551–479 BCE) to guide its legal, social, and political institutions. Korean elite wishing to secure a government position were required to pass a series of tests based on Confucian philosophy. The tenets of the ideology governed how social relations were maintained and administrative decisions made. An elite group, known as the *yangban*, comprised the kingdom's aristocracy, which surrounded and influenced decisions made by the king. Government positions were staffed from a pool of *yangban* who had successfully risen in the ranks by passing a series of civil service examinations that required the examinees to correctly interpret Confucian text passages.

In addition to the *yangban*, Korean society officially consisted of three commoner ranks: the farmers, artisans, and merchants. In practice, Korean society was much more complex, with the *yangban* divided into different ranks, and several groups, such as the slaves and the *paekchong* (a debased group discriminated against on account of their having participated in "unclean" occupations that involved animal butchering and leather works), holding ranks below the commoner.

The nineteenth and twentieth centuries were turbulent times for the Korean peninsula, in both its domestic and foreign affairs. Major domestic rebellions broke out in 1812, 1862, and 1894. The last uprising, led by the

Tonghaks (eastern learning), initiated a foreign crisis after the Korean government requested Chinese assistance to quell the rebellion. This move invited in Japanese troops, which led to the Sino-Japanese War (1894–1895). These challenges also demonstrated fundamental weaknesses in the central bureaucratic system, including, but not limited to, its ability to fairly tax its constituents. During the 1880s, reform-minded groups emerged that sought, among other things, more equitable participation in government and reforms in taxation and education. One of the more successful reform-minded groups was the Independence Club, which endeavored to strengthen Korean sovereignty: it convinced the king to declare his land an empire (i.e., a sovereign state); it printed a newspaper written in Korea's *han'gul* script; and it initiated other symbolic projects to emphasize this point. Their success threatened the established traditional system, and in 1898 the Korean emperor Kojong (1852–1919) ordered their two-year experiment to disband, thus rendering helpless the core of Korea's reform movement.

Japan's presence on the Korean Peninsula intensified toward the end of the nineteenth century. In 1875 it initiated a confrontation along Korea's west coast that drew the two governments into negotiations to modernize their traditional relations. Armed with demands similar to those brought by the American naval officer Matthew C. Perry (1794–1858), who demanded in 1853 that Japan "open" itself to the West, Japanese negotiators imposed upon the Koreans a similar "unequal" treaty that forced them to open ports to Japanese residence, to accept extraterritorial rights for Japanese residents, and to accept determined fixed import and export tariffs. Soon thereafter, the United States and several European states arranged similar treaties with the Korean government. Over the latter half of the nineteenth century, Japanese intellectuals influenced the core of the Korean reform movement and assisted them in failed coup attempts. The Japanese were also implicated in the 1895 murder of Korea's pro-Chinese Queen Min.

Following victories in war with the Chinese (1895) and the Russians (1905), the Japanese moved to first establish Korea as its protectorate (1905) and later to formally annex the peninsula into its growing empire. Thus began a thirty-six-year period of colonial occupation that ended with Japan's surrender to the Allied forces in 1945. Many Koreans battled the Japanese presence. Righteous armies fought Japanese colonizers up through annexation (1910).

A huge independence movement, formed in March 1919, kept Japanese police occupied throughout much of that year. A provisional government was formed in the spirit of this movement, but it soon split into militant and diplomatic factions, with the former migrating to China and Russia to join Communist activists, and the latter traveling globally to seek support for Korea's independence. Others, who believed that Korea's future could not be guaranteed unless the people were prepared, envisioned a less radical, and more gradual, path to liberation. Still others believed this vision to be a pipe dream: Korea's best hope for the future lay with it remaining in the Japanese empire.

The sudden and complete defeat of Japan left a political void on the Korean peninsula that was filled by occupation, with the United States occupying the south and the Soviet Union the north. The division, which was to have been temporary, remains in place to this day.

SEE ALSO *China, First Opium War to 1945; East Asia, European Presence in; Empire, Japanese; Occupations, East Asia.*

BIBLIOGRAPHY

Deuchler, Martina. *The Confucian Transformation of Korea: A Study of Society and Ideology.* Cambridge, MA: Council of East Asian Studies, Harvard University, 1992.

Duus, Peter. *The Abacus and the Sword: The Japanese Penetration of Korea, 1895–1910.* Berkeley: University of California Press, 1995.

Eckert, Carter J. *Offspring of Empire: The Koch'ang Kims and the Colonial Origins of Korean Capitalism, 1876–1945.* Seattle: University of Washington Press, 1991.

Kim, C. I. Eugene, and Han-kyo Kim. *Korea and the Politics of Imperialism, 1876–1910.* Berkeley: University of California Press, 1968.

Myers, Ramon H., and Mark R. Peattie, eds. *The Japanese Colonial Empire, 1895–1945.* Princeton, NJ: Princeton University Press, 1984.

Palais, James B. *Politics and Policy in Traditional Korea.* Cambridge, MA: Council of East Asian Studies, Harvard University, 1975.

Shin, Gi-Wook, and Michael Robinson, eds. *Colonial Modernity in Korea.* Cambridge, MA: Harvard University Asia Center, 1999.

Mark E. Caprio

KOREA, FROM WORLD WAR II

Japan's surrender to the Allied forces on August 15, 1945, left liberated Korea in an uncertain state. Though Koreans naturally anticipated full recovery of national independence, they were soon disillusioned. By September 1945 Korea was occupied once more, now by the armies of the United States and the Union of Soviet Socialist Republics (USSR), who soon agreed upon a joint trusteeship of Korea until the ushering in of self-rule. The line dividing

Kim Jong Il and Chung Dong-young. *Kim Jong Il (right), the leader of North Korea, shares a toast with Chung Dong-young, South Korea's unification minister, during a meeting in Pyongyang on June 17, 2005.* © UNIFICATION MINISTRY/HANDOUT/REUTERS/ CORBIS. REPRODUCED BY PERMISSION.

the northern (USSR) and southern (U.S.) zones of occupation was set at the 38th parallel, running north of Seoul and splitting the peninsula roughly in half.

Recent scholarship has argued that Korea was ripe for civil war in the wake of Japan's defeat, in response to centuries of economic and political inequities that had been reinforced and perpetuated under Japanese colonial rule. While the Soviet Union used emerging leftist political organizations and figures in the creation of a functioning administration in the north, American military authorities in the south opted to rely largely upon more conservative Korean elements, many of whom had in fact served the Japanese colonial regime.

In the course of preparing Korea for self-rule then, the politics of the Soviet-backed north and American-backed south grew increasingly polarized. These Soviet-American tensions played a part in polarizing postwar Korean society as well, with many leftists fleeing north and conservatives and large landowners fleeing south. The end result of this confused state of affairs was a

United Nations election in 1948—ostensibly to usher in a sovereign Korean state—that was boycotted in the north and by many in the south. From this election emerged the Republic of Korea (ROK) in the southern (American) zone. On August 15, 1948, American-backed Syngman Rhee (Yi Sung-man, 1875–1965) was inaugurated as the first president of the ROK. In response to this, in the north the Soviet-backed Democratic People's Republic of Korea (DPRK) was formed, with the Korean independence guerilla and Moscow-trained Kim Il Sung (Kim Il-sung, 1912–1994) at its head.

On June 15, 1950, the DPRK launched a massive attack across the 38th parallel in a bid at armed reunification. Though the origins of the resulting Korean War (1950–1953) are still hotly contested, scholarly consensus places the immediate cause of the conflict with Kim Il Sung. With United Nations and then Chinese Communist intervention on behalf of the ROK and DPRK respectively, the Korean War was fought to an armed truce in 1953, roughly along the same 38th parallel that had divided the ROK and DPRK prior to the war.

The Korean War had reverberations far afield, resulting in the strengthening of the North Atlantic Treaty Organization (NATO) alliance and a hardening of the Cold War. Set at ideological loggerheads and in a continuous state of armed tension, the postwar fortunes of North Korea and South Korea were tightly bound to the Soviet Union and United States respectively. Following the Korea War, and in view of Communist advances in Europe and China, the American strategic vision of Korea took a radical shift as the ROK became a major recipient of U.S. military and economic aid. The DPRK likewise became heavily dependent upon Soviet aid and expertise.

In the North, drawing upon Korea's shameful colonial past, Kim Il Sung increasingly emphasized national "self-reliance" *(juche)* in all spheres, while painting the ROK as an American puppet state, playing upon opposition frustrations in the ROK that under American occupation the south had never properly dealt with former Japanese collaborators. Kim also instituted a personality cult unrivaled even by the China of Mao Zedong (1893–1976) or the Soviet Union of Joseph Stalin (1879–1953).

In the wake of President Rhee's 1961 overthrow by a student movement violently opposed to his authoritarian politics, the ROK Army general Park Chung Hee (Pak Chong-hui, 1917–1979) seized power in South Korea. Park would go on to rule the ROK for eighteen years, his often repressive tenure overseeing the rapid industrialization of the ROK. Park also forged more intimate ties with Korea's former occupier, Japan, as well as with the United States, which Park saw as a vital source of the economic aid incumbent for development. In 1979 Park was assassinated by his intelligence chief in an ostensible bid to save South Korea from dictatorship. The result was a series of military leaders in the ROK before the ushering in of democracy there in the late 1980s.

Not all in South Korea were happy about the ROK–U.S. alliance. A rising and increasingly vocal populist movement in the 1980s perceived in the ROK's acquiescent stance toward the United States shadows of the traditional Chinese–Korean relationship, in which Korea was the tribute state. Such deference to the greater power is termed *sadae* (serving the great) in Korean, and this perceived Korean penchant for *sadae-ism* (toadyism) was seen as a historical source of Korea's weakness. Added to this was the frustration that under American tutelage Japanese collaborators had not only evaded prosecution but had been allowed to prosper. As a result, many leftists, and in particular the student activist movement, in South Korea revered North Korea's *juche*

ideology in view of Korea's experience of colonization and division at the hands of foreign powers.

Though less apparent than the ROK–U.S. alliance, the DPRK under Kim Il Sung remained highly dependent upon the Soviet Union. However, Soviet subsidies to the DPRK came to an abrupt halt with the collapse of the Soviet Union in 1991, and from that time North Korea, since 1994 led by Kim Il Sung's son Kim Jong Il (Kim Chong-il, b. 1941), has languished under a deepening economic crisis. The DPRK ultimately remains a highly authoritarian and secretive state whose society revolves around the personality cults of both Kim Il Sung and Kim Jong Il.

Since the 1990s, political dynamics on the Korean Peninsula continue to be volatile, if less predictable. Though the South Korean president Kim Dae Jung (Kim Tae-jung, b. 1925), who served from 1997 to 2002, initiated a "Sunshine Policy" regarding the DPRK that resulted in the first ever North-South summit in 2000, relations between the two Koreas continue to be characterized by tension and mistrust. The rise of the left-leaning opposition into national power in the ROK elections of 2002 has resulted in a resolve to finally deal with the issue of past Japanese collaboration, as well as more vocal debate regarding the costs and benefits of the ROK–U.S. alliance. However, though at times troubled, in the face of the continued perceived threat from North Korea, the ROK–U.S. alliance remains a mainstay of South Korean policy.

SEE ALSO *Occupations, East Asia.*

BIBLIOGRAPHY

Cumings, Bruce. *Korea's Place in the Sun: A Modern History.* New York: Norton, 1997.

Jager, Sheila Miyoshi. *Narratives of Nation Building in Korea: A Genealogy of Patriotism.* Armonk, NY: Sharpe, 2003.

Oberdorfer, Don. *The Two Koreas: A Contemporary History.* Reading, MA: Addison-Wesley, 1997; New ed., New York: Basic Books, 2001.

Stueck, William Whitney. *Rethinking the Korean War: A New Diplomatic and Strategic History.* Princeton, NJ: Princeton University Press, 2002.

Daniel C. Kane

KRUGER, PAUL
1825–1904

Known for his leadership of the Transvaal, significantly during the lead up to the South African War (1899–1902), Stephanus Johannes Paulus Kruger personified

Paul Kruger During the Boer War. *Paul Kruger (center, with pipe), president of the Transvaal from 1883 to 1900, visits Boer troops during the Second Anglo-Boer War.* © BETTMANN/ CORBIS. REPRODUCED BY PERMISSION.

the Afrikaner independent spirit. This father of Afrikaner nationalism, he was born in the eastern Cape Colony in 1825. In 1835 his family joined the Great Trek. Kruger developed his beliefs in the crucible of a developing Afrikaner nationalism. He fought Ndebele forces led by Mzilikazi (1795?–1868) at Vegkop in 1836, and went on to become a *veldkornet*, or district law enforcement officer, for the local government.

In 1883 Kruger became president of the Transvaal, following upon the state's victory over the British in the Anglo-Transvaal War (1880–1881). Combining his spiritual beliefs with a clear notion of Boer independence from British imperial encroachment, Kruger secured what he considered to be the republic's clear sovereignty from Britain in the Treaty of London in 1884. In 1886 gold was discovered at Witwatersrand, south of the capital at Pretoria. This, the largest gold deposit in the world, enabled the Transvaal to enjoy a new economic lease on life.

The Treaty of London did not halt Britain's imperial expansion. In 1890 diamond magnate Cecil Rhodes (1853–1902) established the colony of Rhodesia north of the Transvaal. Rhodes envisioned building a British "road to the north" from Cape Town to Cairo. He also argued for the destruction of the two Boer republics by suffocation, surrounding them with British territory. Rhodes's actions served to increase the tension between Kruger's government and Britain. This was played out in the winter of 1895 to 1896, when Rhodes sanctioned a raid into the Transvaal to overthrow the state government. Although the raid failed, it did succeed in driving Kruger to arm the republic (using capital from the gold mines), complete with the construction of forts around the Pretoria.

In 1899, following a summer of heated debate, the two republics declared war. Early and important victories went to the Boers, forcing Britain to send more troops while implementing a crash recruiting program at home. The tide began to turn in 1900, however, as new leadership in the British army helped secure the fall of the Orange Free State in March and the Transvaal Republic in June. With British troops spilling into his country, Kruger went on the run, finally leaving his beloved nation in October 1900. He went to the Netherlands seeking international assistance for his war with Britain. He received sympathy, but little else. Britain won the war in 1902, but gave the Boers substantial aid as part of the peace agreement. Paul Kruger died in exile in Switzerland in 1904, having never returned to the Transvaal.

A man of solid faith and solid nationalism, Kruger's folksy demeanor helped endear him to his fellow Afrikaners, many of whom he received on the front porch of his house near the capitol building in Pretoria. "Oom Paul" (Uncle Paul) remained a beloved figure in the Afrikaner national memory, helping to strengthen the growing mythology of apartheid.

SEE ALSO *Great Trek.*

BIBLIOGRAPHY

Fisher, John. *Paul Kruger: His Life and Times.* London: Secker and Warburg, 1974.

Kruger, Paul. *The Memoirs of Paul Kruger: Four Times President of the South African Republic, Told by Himself.* London: Unwin, 1902. Reprint, New York: Negro Universities Press, 1969.

Pakenham, Thomas. *The Boer War.* New York: Random House, 1979.

Shillington, Kevin. *A History of Southern Africa.* Harlow, U.K.: Longman, 1987.

Thompson, Leonard M. *A History of South Africa,* 3rd ed. New Haven, CT: Yale University Press, 2001.

Jeffrey Lee Meriwether

L

LANGUAGE, EUROPEAN

Language and empire were closely related, whether the quasireligious and legal language of papal donations concerning lands beyond Europe, or the speech and signs that Christopher Columbus (1451–1506) described in his writings about first encounters with natives in the New World. European gestures and classical and vernacular languages from that continent are a key part of the story and history of expansion, colonization, and empire. Words are the traces we have of the European empires that begin in earnest with the Portuguese expansion into Africa in the fifteenth century, and that ended formally with decolonization, a process that began with the American War of Independence in the 1770s, and finally ended with similar wars in the twentieth century, as well as peaceful independence in parts of Asia and Africa (often in the British Empire).

The Spanish humanist, Elio Antonio de Nebrija (1441–1522), author of the first grammar of the Castilian language (1492), reached the conclusion in his preface to that work that "language always accompanies empire." Nebrija's classical statement is a point of departure for how a few European languages became world languages owing to imperialism. European speech and writing also transmitted the Western languages of politics, radicalism, journalism, education, law, history, and more. Some postcolonial scholars have advanced arguments that what was actually transmitted was the language of "Orientalism" (a Western discourse of misunderstanding and undervaluing colonial "others"), as well as racism, sexism, fascism, capitalism, and globalism.

LANGUAGE PRACTICES AND REPRESENTATIONS

Portuguese practices at home later became usual in colonies overseas. Legal language was particularly important in this regard. On May 26, 1375, King Ferdinand I (1345–1383) of Portugal published a law by which all rural landowners were to cultivate their lands or rent them for cultivation (*Lei de Sesmaria*), a practice that Portuguese colonies in Africa and Brazil adopted. In Portugal, black slaves replaced in the fields men who were overseas.

Brazil was to be a key colony for the Portuguese, who claimed it during Easter week of 1500 as recorded by Pero Vaz de Caminha, one of the crew of Pedro Álvares Cabral (ca. 1467–1520). This same writer uses the power of language to represent themes that Columbus had expressed about the New World—the innocence that makes the natives ready to convert, the nakedness of the inhabitants, and the native signs that indicate gold and other riches, the will of God, and salvation. One curious passage in Caminha's account is that he has no doubt that if the *degradados* (banished Portuguese criminals) learned the natives' language then these new-found peoples would come into the Christian faith. Early on, sign language and the learning of native languages was an important part of converting local populations abroad. Later, however, the use of European languages became part of a practice of assimilation or domination (in the root sense of having lordship over the tributary or vassal population of natives).

Apparently, Cabral did not write about his voyage to Brazil and India. Various sources help to piece together the events of this journey. The key source is an anonymous text, written in Portuguese but translated into

Italian, that was included in one of the collections of voyages that were appearing in the first decade of the sixteenth century. In Lisbon in 1502 a volume was published that included descriptions of the voyages of Marco Polo (ca. 1254–1324), Nicolò de Conti (ca. 1395–1469), and Hieronimo di (Geronimo da) San Stefano (a Genoese who traveled to Pegu in Burma in 1495–96) and a volume titled *Paesi Nouamente retrouati et Nouo Mondo da Alberico Vesputio intitulato* (Newfound Lands …) was published in Vicenza, Italy, in 1507. This last source provided an example for the collections of Simon Grynaeus (1493–1541) and Giambattista Ramusio (1485–1557) and, more indirectly, of Richard Hakluyt the Younger (ca. 1552–1616) and Samuel Purchas (1577–1626), a compiler of travel books whose work included this 1507 narrative. Language was not simply about individual texts but about editing, translating, collecting, printing, and reading them. There is a collective as well as an individual context. Translation ensured that all European states gathered strength and that their knowledge and languages were enriched.

A few years earlier, Columbus, as described in the "Letter of Columbus," which Columbus probably wrote in 1494 to King Ferdinand and Queen Isabella of Spain about the "discovery," colonization and commerce of Hispaniola, remarked on how timid the natives were but then admitted that he took some of them by force and established a mutual understanding "by speech or signs." Before Walter Raleigh (ca. 1554–1618), Columbus used a language that identified the land in the New World as a woman and sometimes eroticized the female natives he encountered. The use of a language of signs, and the interpretation of those signs and of speech even before the Portuguese or Spanish learned the languages of the natives, represent the practice of traders but also may seem like overconfidence. From the beginning of the Iberian expansion, the language of gesture and of the spoken and written word became crucial in the enterprise. This passage from Columbus has implications that extend to this day.

The mediation of writing and reading seems to shape the images Columbus forms of the native after first contact. Perhaps it also has an effect on the transmission and editing of his account, as well as on the rhetorical relation between speaker or writer and audience, and between Columbus and the sovereigns (whom he has in mind and whom he addresses). This relation has a very material dimension, for Columbus proceeded to promise Queen Isabella (1451–1504) and King Ferdinand (1452–1516) of Spain vast riches and slaves in return for their "very slight assistance."

In this possible contract, in this quid pro quo, the natives are lost; they are transformed into slaves. These slaves, as many as sovereigns ordered to be shipped, would

La Malinche. *The Native American woman La Malinche worked as a translator and interpreter for Hernán Cortés. As such, she was a mediator, caught between languages.* **THE ART ARCHIVE/MIREILLE VAUTIER. REPRODUCED BY PERMISSION.**

be chosen from the idolaters, so that Columbus could have a clear conscience and could, with a highly imperfect knowledge of the language and culture of the natives, decide who among them practiced idolatry and who did not. Slavery was fine for those whom Columbus considered to worship idols instead of Christ. Columbus and other Europeans choose to interpret others in the framework of their church and legal dogma. Who was a pagan, idolater, heretic, or infidel was a decision based on an interpretative context that papal bulls helped to forge. It was also encoded in "encounter" narratives and the many other written documents that represented European expansion into lands "discovered" or "rediscovered."

The precariousness of the expansion of European languages and empires is a key part of the story. There was a certain defensiveness in the offensive stance of Europe. The Iberian powers (Spain and Portugal) had been largely under Muslim rule for hundreds of years before the Christian kingdoms started to push the Muslims back. It took until 1492 for Spain to reconquer its territory, and the year of Columbus's first voyage to America, the Spanish Crown ordered the expulsion of Moors (Muslims) and Jews. The spread of Castilians and

Portuguese involved the distinction between Portugal and Spain from each other, as well as the distinction between their languages.

DEFENDING THE NATIVES AND LEARNING AND PROTECTING THEIR LANGUAGE AND CULTURE

During the first three decades of the conquest (1492–1519), owing in part perhaps to the quick decimation of the natives, there was no Amerindian chronicler of the encounter. It was the Spanish Dominican missionary Bartolomé de Las Casas (1474–1566) who rose to write a defense of the native population. Las Casas also defended the natives of the New World against the arguments of Juan Ginés de Sepúlveda (1490–1573) at Valladolid, Spain, where in 1550 to 1551 King Charles I (1500–1558) convened theologians and philosophers. Stangely enough, Las Casas and Sepúlveda, who called on the Council for the Indies for the "debate" on colonization and the war against the American Indians, in the first instance, did not face each other, but read their arguments to a panel of theologians from the University of Salamanca. Las Casas insisted on a place for the Amerindians as members of a human civil society. The famous debate between Las Casas and Sepúlveda for the benefit of the Spanish king over Aristotle's (384–322 B.C.E.) concept of natural slavery and whether it applied to the aboriginal inhabitants of the New World demonstrates the dissention from within. A debate based on distinctions in language was to determine whether natives were considered barbarian or even human.

The question of the European representation of native peoples also relates to the Amerindian representation of the European arrival in, and colonization of, America. One of the difficulties presented by preconquest native documents, as in the case to the Nahuas of central Mexico, is that even the most informative among them were mostly redone under Spanish influence during the 1540s and after. The Europeans and their American settlers frequently wrote about the natives from the vantage of conquest and triumph. Europeans also had a myth that the Amerindians had no writing, and when the Europeans encountered evidence of writing, they tried to eradicate it because it posed a threat to the Bible.

The represented also represent. Examples are the annals of the Valley of Mexico (1516–1525), a Tupi taunt of French missionaries in Brazil (1612), and a seventeenth-century Algonquin account of Europeans entering North America. The representation of the natives and the Amerindian representation of the Europeans have left evidence only in the wake of Columbus's encounter with the world of the western Atlantic.

TRANSLATION, IDEOLOGICAL EDITING, AND THE BLACK LEGEND

Writers and translators in France and England made ambivalent and contradictory use of the example of Spain's colonization of the New World from Columbus's first voyage to the end of the War of the Spanish Succession (1701–1714). Translations of Spanish books about the New World, along with French and English texts on the same subject, suggest that historical changes occurred in the use of the example of Spain while, for the most part, ambivalence and contradiction remained. Legal and textual anxieties developed amongst the French and English over Columbus and Spain being the first Europeans to "discover" the "New World" and over the pope's division of that newfound land between Portugal and Spain. France and England tried to learn from Spain and to compete with it and circumvent its monopoly in the New World (1492–1547).

Texts in the period from the deaths of Henry VIII (1491–1547) of England and François I (1494–1547) of France to the year of the first narrative of the Spanish massacre of the French colonists in Florida (1548–1566) contain praise for Spain in England during the reign of Queen Mary I (1516–1558), as well as the first important French description of Spanish cruelty in the New World. In addition, the historian Richard Eden (ca. 1521–1576) used translation to advocate English colonization and then the imperial union of Spain and England.

Eyewitness accounts of the conflict between the French and Spanish in Florida—Thomas Hacket's (fl. 1560–1590) translation of Jean Ribault (ca. 1520–1565) (the original was lost) and Nicolas Le Challeux's narrative—also contributed to the debate on colonization. These are key texts with apparently different aims: Eden's work appears to be that of a champion of the potential alliance of England with Spain, whereas the Ribault and Le Challeux texts are French Protestant works that help to produce, in France and England, the Black Legend of Spain, an anti-Spanish attitude that blamed Spaniards for cruelty, greed, and fanaticism in their empire, especially in the Netherlands and the New World, in contrast with the White Legend (*leyenda rosa* or *blanca*), which idealized Spaniards. An analysis of these important texts suggests a shift in the representation of Spain in the 1560s, when the French and then the English, mainly because of the events in Florida and in the Netherlands, began to develop an intricate anti-Spanish rhetoric.

Having incorporated into the Spanish conquest of the New World the qualities of civility and *virtú*, Eden also followed Columbus in dividing the natives into good natives, or those who helped and acquiesced, and bad natives, or those who opposed the Europeans: the Spanish liberated the natives through religion and civility. Columbus represented the "bad natives" as cannibals and Amazons. The distinction between liberty and license, one that the English author John Milton (1608–1674) would later take up, is part of an imperial discourse in which the forces of empire liberate the indigenes from their primitiveness, barbarity, strife with treacherous neighbors, pagan beliefs, and laziness.

The imperial discourse of France and England would replicate this language of liberty for their own ends well into the twentieth century. Sometimes the French and English would cast the Spaniards as the treacherous party, as cannibals devouring the innocent natives. But the paternalism, Christian and secular, differed little from Eden's rendition on behalf of Spain. The narratives of the explorers included representations of the relations among the European imperial powers: Spain was still a powerful example that these practical French and English mariners contemplated. The captains and seamen wrote accounts of their experiences with the Spanish that were often framed in the language of romance and heroism but that frequently reflected what their own governments would tolerate or sanction unofficially.

Economic self-interest and the balancing of power in European politics affected these apparently straightforward narratives. Through their written accounts, explorers and pirates (depending on whether the reports were from the point of view of Spain or not), like John Hawkins (1532–1595) and Dominique de Gourges, justified their actions, the one for breaking Spanish laws and the other for wreaking revenge on Spain. English and French narratives were instrumental, their ends often being political and economic, even as they protested motives of religion and liberty.

From the mid-1550s, French and English translations were sending out mixed messages about the natives through Spanish eyes. In a history of discourse—and this applies in the historiography of expansion—translation is so central that there is sometimes a lag between event or original textual argument, representation, and its transmission into other languages. Latin was available to the elite, but most often the translation into Spanish and then into French and English or some variation on that process (Spanish to French, French to English) meant a greater and more popular dissemination than of the Latin original. Many Spanish authors decided to write in Spanish, and, for some, especially among the captains, adventurers, and settlers, the vernacular was the only option, or what might be called the confident option. Some of the texts on Spain were not French or English

translations but were histories and narratives of exploration, encounter, and settlement that involved imitation of, allusion to, and commentary on Spain.

The example of Spain was central in determining English attitudes toward the New World and its inhabitants. In addition to Hakluyt, who translated or commissioned translations from the Spanish, other principal translators were Richard Eden, John Frampton (fl. 1577–1596), and Thomas Nicholas (b. 1530s). Even though the English adapted Spanish writings that glorified the Spanish conquest for their own purposes—providing propaganda to encourage potential investors and settlers—they often adopted Spanish representations of the New World and its natives. The "Spanish" authors most translated into English, such as Peter Martyr (1499–1562), Gonzalo Fernandez de Oviedo (1478–1557), and Francisco López de Gómara (ca. 1511–1566), emphasized the glory of Spain in the face of Native American betrayal and barbarism, even if they sometimes advocated conversion and condemned Spaniards for mistreating the natives.

Even though Las Casas thought the work of his compatriots in the New World was important, he was not one to emphasize Spain's colonization of the New World and its treatment of the natives as full of glory. Those Spanish authors who glorified Spain were the most often translated into English. Only one edition of Las Casas's *Brevissima relación de la destruyción de las Indias* (Brief Account of the Destruction of the Indies, 1552) appeared in English (as *The Spanish Colonie,* 1583). This translation was filtered through the French translation from which the preface was taken. The preface encouraged support for the Dutch revolt against Spain.

Numerous translations of Spanish works concerning the New World also appeared in France. The French and English textual responses to the events in Brazil and Florida were staggered over the years, and this response complicated the way the Portuguese and Spanish texts moved into these languages (as well as into Dutch).

This historiography of expansion involved the production, dissemination, and reception of ideas about Spain. The earlier complaints against Spain were pale beside the propaganda that arose in the French and English languages from London through Amsterdam and Paris to Geneva. The anti-Spanish tracts of the 1560s and 1570s led up to the building of the Spanish Armada (1567–1588) and the intensification of rivalry with Spain as both France and England tried to expand and establish colonies. Columbus was to be a model and precedent, even in 1566 when the English navigator Humphrey Gilbert (ca. 1539–1583) planned to establish a colony in territory that Spain claimed.

In the wake of the Armada, works such as Richard Hakluyt's *Principal Navigations* (1589) and Marc

Bartolomé de Las Casas (1484–1566). *A famous debate took place in the mid-sixteenth century between Bartolomé de Las Casas, a Dominican missionary, and Juan Ginés de Sepúlveda on the concept of "natural slavery." This debate, based on distinctions in language, was to determine whether the natives of the New World were to be considered barbarian or even human.* **LIBRARY OF CONGRESS.**

Lescarbot's *L'Histoire de la Nouvelle France* (The History of New France, 1609) demonstrate that the ambivalent and contradictory representation of Spain in the New World was not simply a matter of religion. Once France and England established permanent colonies in the New World and Spain began to decline, the sustained intensity of anti-Spanish sentiment abated into periodic eruptions of the Black Legend of Spain. Language in the original and in translation could be a political weapon.

The language of key texts expressed religious, legal, and political ideas for and against the expansion into the New World that occurred in roughly the first six decades after Columbus's landfall in the western Atlantic. These ideas and practices intertwined in the texts and documents of the period. The textual evidence suggests that the English, while quick to "discover" the North American continent, soon lost momentum and, for the period in question and beyond, the French made this northern part of America a priority. Before and after Columbus, whether in Spain, France, England, or other western European countries, the merits and demerits of expansion played an important role in legal, religious, political, and economic debates.

One of the chief means of spreading anti-Spanish sentiment among other nations was the use, against

Spain, of the work of Las Casas, a critic of Spanish colonization but a supporter of the Spanish emperor and empire. Las Casas was a holy Spaniard who would never have approved of the use to which his work was put by these "heretics." The very ability the Spanish had in criticizing themselves became a weapon of intolerance and a tool to be used against an increasingly intolerant Spain. The French and English exploited Spain's self-criticism through vernacular translations, particularly of Las Casas. And Las Casas appeared in English-speaking countries as a weapon of propaganda late in the day. For instance, his account of the destruction of the Indies was printed four times in the period of the Spanish-American War of 1898. Language reproduces itself, persisting while changing shape.

LANGUAGE OF COLONIZATION, EMPIRE, LIBERTY, AND DECOLONIZATION

Las Casas had used language to defend the dignity and humanity of native peoples, although he was less concerned with the rights of African slaves. The spiritual dimension of the natives and their potential for conversion were mainstays of his argument. Contradictions, ambivalence, and opposition within the European states and their empires was expressed through language, so that Nebrija's yoking of language and empire is intricate.

In New England in the seventeenth century, John Eliot (1604–1690) acted as an apostle to the Indians and tried, by establishing communities of converts (fourteen towns, Natick being most notable among them), to allow them to pursue a Christian life. After King Philip's War (1675–76) between the English and the natives, the community was broken up and many of the Natick Indians deported to islands. Subscriptions from English parishes helped to enable that effort, as well as the establishment of the Harvard Indian College in 1655. Eliot also translated the Bible into the indigenous language (Algonquin in 1663). The natives themselves were torn between their own religion and language and the classical and vernacular European languages. This Eliot Bible was used as a means of converting the Indians, including by fellow educated natives, such as Harvard's first such graduate, Caleb Cheeshahteaumuck from the Wampanoag tribe (class of 1665). He lived with other students—English and native, in a dormitory called the "Indian College," founded under President Charles Chauncy and, as a result of neglect, torn down in 1698.

These residential schools continued well into the twentieth century, and there have been legal disputes over their negative effects in Canada. Mediators, such as La Malinche (Malintzin or Doña Marina, ca. 1505–ca.1529) a Native American woman, most likely Nahua, from the Mexican Gulf Coast, acted as go-betweens. La Malinche accompanied Hernán Cortés (ca. 1484–1547), played a key role as an interpreter in the Spanish conquest of Mexico, and was mistress to Cortés, whose son she bore. Another example of a mediator is Squanto (d. 1622), a Patuxet Indian who helped William Bradford (1590–1657) in Massachusetts. Translation also involved the transmission and transformation of native languages into European ones. One example of this is the codex in *Broken Spears,* a text often used in courses on colonization. The work is a collection of documents about the Spanish Conquest of Mexico by the Nahua (Mexicas or Aztecs) and translated into at least twelve languages. The debate here is whether the earliest of these documents were written in Nahuatl and how great the influence of the Spanish missionaries, their language and culture, were in this enterprise. Bernardino de Sahagún was a key figure in this translation and transculturation. Translation occurs between native and European cultures, but also between centuries.

Language is also about incommensurability and the abuse of power. The *Requiermento* (Requirement) was a document that the Spaniards read to natives, even though its language was incomprehensible to them, before massacring them. This warning was beyond understanding as an empty form that did not allow the natives to do as they should to protect themselves, and it served as a justification for what might be considered genocide today. The *Requiermento* might have been indebted to the *jihad* (holy war) that the Moors had used in the Iberian Peninsula; both were based on legal foundations.

Europeans tried to destroy or assimilate natives into their religion or language. Whether the last of the Mohicans or the last speaker of a dying language before the juggernaut of English, Portuguese, or Spanish, indigenous peoples since the expansion of European states have had to fight for their physical, cultural, and linguistic survival.

Conflicts between Europeans, and between natives and Europeans, are embodied and expressed through language. Recognition and misrecognition of empire, as well as the promotion of and opposition to empire, exist in language: empire and language are not simply linear or dual in their connection. For instance, Elio Antonio de Nebrija wanted Spain to teach Castilian Spanish and Christianity to the natives, but this view met with resistance. The mendicant friars and Jesuits preferred to write grammars of the indigenous American languages rather than teach the Indians Castilian.

It is ironic that, centuries later, Spanish became the language of nationalism in the construction of independent states in the former Spanish Empire in the Americas. In 1570 King Philip II (1527–1598) announced in a royal order that Nahuatl would be the official language of the natives in New Spain. *Coloquios y*

doctrina christiana (Colloquies and Christian Doctrine, 1524) shows this linguistic contestation. This work, a dialogue between Mexican elders and twelve Franciscan friars in 1524, was transcribed by Bernardino de Sahagún (1499–1590) in 1565 and involves mediation and transculturation. In this text, the Mexicas favor telling stories aloud, whereas the Spaniards prefer the letter and word as the foundation of understanding and knowledge.

The language of rights was as much a part of the quasilegal and legal framework as were the terms of papal donations and treaties. International law tried to set out a discourse of justice, liberty, and fairness, but also had to contend with conflict, slavery, and warfare. The Spanish legal scholar Francisco de Vitoria (ca. 1483–1546) helped to call into question the legitimacy of the Spanish conquest of the New World. The Dutch attempted to come to terms with the law as they tried to supplant the Portuguese and Spanish in the East and West Indies. *Mare Liberum* (Freedom of the Seas, 1609) by the Dutch scholar Hugo Grotius (1583–1645) considered the freedom of the oceans, which was key for trade and conquest. Slavery, as well as expansion, was closely related to liberty.

The tension between slavery and liberty is a main theme in the language of the European empires. Gomes Eannes de Azuzara (ca. 1410–1473), a chronicler attached to Prince Henry (1394–1460) of Portugal, described how in 1444 the Portuguese landed 235 African slaves near Lagos in south Portugal. The language of slavery would become a key element in European empires, and above all the topic of African slaves would be essential to the development of the New World and the consequent riches of Europe.

In the seventeenth century, the slave trade in the English, Dutch, and French colonies had ambivalent beginnings. People favored and opposed it. It created great profits and problems. Texts proliferated. The novel *Oroonoko, or, The Royal Slave* (1688) by the British author Aphra Behn (1640–1689) represented ambivalence to slavery, and during the eighteenth century, this attitude became more widespread. Montesquieu's *L'Esprit des lois* (The Spirit of the Laws, 1748) scorned the slave trade and disputed Aristotle's theory of natural slavery, which framed the language of many who had long justified slavery in the European empires. In 1758 Frei Manuel Ribeiro da Rocha, born in Portugal but resident in Brazil, produced a call for the abolition of slavery. The French writers Pierre Marivaux (1688–1763), Montesquieu (1689–1755), Voltaire (1694–1778), Denis Diderot (1713–1784), and Jean-Jacques Rousseau (1712–1778) all circulated ideas about the liberation of slaves and about freedom generally.

During the American Revolution (1775–1783), both the British and the Americans began to abolish slavery. In the *Declaration of Independence* (1776), Thomas Jefferson (1743–1826) may have omitted a condemnation of slavery because of the pressure of some representatives from southern colonies whose commerce depended heavily on slavery. Benjamin Franklin (1706–1790) had written a dialogue in 1760 that revealed the injustices of slavery in Europe and America. When Abigail Adams (1744–1818) wrote to her husband, future American president John Adams (1735–1826), in September 1774, she considered slavery in Massachusetts an iniquitous scheme and saw the irony of fighting for freedom while depriving others of it.

The American poet Phillis Wheatley (ca. 1753–1784), kidnapped from Senegal-Gambia, fashioned poetry in English about her condition. Her work was published in London with the support of her masters. Some readers were shocked that an African could write in English, but there was also interest in her work.

Women's writing about slaves and slavery in the dying years of the American Revolution and in its aftermath suggests some of the complex emotions of white Americans and the Africans they represent. Some of the letters and diaries tell tales of contesting and conflicting forces within and between these European Americans and in the minds, hearts, and communities of African Americans. *The Interesting Narrative of the Life of Olaudah Equiano, or Gustavus Vassa, the African* (1789) by the former slave Olaudah Equiano (ca. 1745–1797) was another text by an African-born writer in English, this time explicitly representing the abuses of the slave trade and slavery and advocating their abolition. In 1794, during the French Revolution (1789–1799), the convention of Paris declared the emancipation of slaves without abolishing the trade.

The language of slavery and freedom continued to be bound up with colonization and became part of the linguistic aspect of decolonization and independence. In 1820 the British philosopher Jeremy Bentham (1748–1832) advised the Spanish to rid themselves of Ultramaria, their overseas colonies, and to grant these possessions independence. In this way, they would do what the United States had done, but their act would be a lesson to the United States and Britain by moving Spain entirely beyond benefiting from slavery.

The British started to use the language of antislavery as its empire expanded, so that the contradictions in the language of empire persisted. British policy in China was not about reform, even if it did concern the trade in and the holding of slaves. Even between 1856 and 1858, while concerns over slavery were still pressing in the British government, a second Opium War in China was being fought. Some, like Richard Cobden (1804–1865), a free-trader and a member of parliament for Stockport (part of the greater Manchester area that was the center of the cotton mills), thought Britain was being hypocritical as there was a gap between its language and action. While the government and those against slavery appealed to morality, Britain was the greatest seller to Brazil of textiles that were made from cotton, which slaves produced. At the same time, Britain refused to receive sugar, another product based on slave labor. The language of the debates in the British House of Commons revealed how intense were the feelings aroused by slavery.

In the United States, the language of the debate over slavery also suggested contradictions and hypocrisy. Frederick Douglass's (ca. 1818–1895) speech before the American and Foreign Anti-Slavery Society in May 1854 underscored the ways African Americans were excluded from the rights and freedoms that the founders of the United States had set out. In his notes, Abraham Lincoln (1809–1865) thought that God might be punishing settlers of European backgrounds for enriching themselves through slavery. In a letter to James N. Brown in 1858, Lincoln said that he considered that the founders had included "the Negro" in the term "men" in their declaration of equality.

The language of slavery and freedom constituted a site of contestation in the rhetoric of the empire of liberty, as in Britain, and of the break with empire and decolonization in the United States. Abolitionists in the mother country and the former colony were still connected in their battle for the rights of slaves as part of a larger movement toward human rights, democracy, extended suffrage, and liberty.

The language of human rights in the debate over colonialism and decolonization continued into the twentieth century. The tensions between empires and colonies affected discourses and practices of freedom. If the Spaniards had made slaves of and decimated natives in the New World during the colonial era, the Nazis had enslaved and exterminated peoples in Europe during the twentieth century. In disbanding the substantial remains of the British Empire, Prime Minister Harold Macmillan (1894–1986) called for an end of abuses and advocated for a sense of equality and freedom for all. Mohandas Gandhi (1869–1948), Martin Luther King (1929–1968), and Nelson Mandela (b. 1918) all looked to the education they had in the European tradition and used it peacefully to oppose, curtail, and attempt to end the violence of racism. Civil disobedience, as Henry David Thoreau (1817–1862) had advocated in the nineteenth century, was part of the striving toward freedom.

Just before and after World War I (1914–1918), opposition to imperialism grew more intense.

Paradoxically, when these empires seemed most powerful, they declined. By 1941, Prime Minister Winston Churchill (1874–1965) and President Franklin D. Roosevelt (1882–1945) had established the Atlantic Charter, which set out the principles of self-government and liberty, opposition to the Nazis as forces of tyranny and slavery, and the right of self-determination for all peoples. The Soviet Union opposed what it saw as Anglo-American world domination or imperialism, whereas President Dwight Eisenhower (1890–1969) came to see the Cold War as a struggle of freedom against slavery. The Eastern European states might have considered the Soviets as a new version of Russian imperialism. Point of view in matters of language is always a key factor.

World War II (1939–1945), even more than the first, had shattered the western European empires. Nationalism, which had been so developed in Britain in the nineteenth and twentieth centuries, spread globally. The so-called white man's burden or the Social Darwinist imperialism of the late nineteenth and early twentieth centuries became diffuse and displaced. Language shifted to rights for all peoples in the United Nations Charter (1945) and the *Universal Declaration of Human Rights* (1948). Discourses of multiculturalism and postcolonialism developed from the 1960s. That did not mean that discourses of nationalism, racism, and intolerance disappeared, but they found new challenges, especially in the official government ideology of Western democracies, including those that had held vast overseas empires for many centuries.

An example of the legacy of colonization illustrates the persistence and the language of empire. In Australia, the High Court judgments in the Mabo case, published in June 1992, involved the complaint of Eddie Mabo (1936–1992), a native of Murray Island in the Torres Strait, that the state of Queensland's annexation of the Torres Strait in 1879 had not legally extinguished his customary ownership of a part of Murray Island that his family passed on to him. Concerning the Mabo case, two judges of the High Court of Australia, William Deane and Mary Gaudron, questioned the quality of the doctrine of *terra nullius*—a Latin phrase that came from Roman Law, meaning "empty land," a concept the Portuguese had used in claiming Africa. In the Australian legal system the doctrine of *terra nullius* was confirmed in 1979 and rejected in 1992. The colonial persisted in the postcolonial: perhaps the postcolonial reinterpreted the colonial.

In Australia, as in the Americas, the legacy of Portuguese and Spanish expansion, which was also to be found in empires like those of Britain, France, and the Netherlands, was being reinterpreted in the years leading up to the 500th anniversary of Columbus's landfall in the Americas. The relation of settler and aboriginal

cultures was being redefined in the courts. What constitutes *property* and what constitutes *appropriation* have become central questions in language, especially the language of rights and the law more generally.

Since about the mid-1980s, debates have intensified over whether we live in a neocolonial, rather than a postcolonial, age, and whether empires change their forms, as if the shape-shifting Greek god Proteus was one shape ahead of those that came after him. Ambivalence and contradiction remain in our use of language, as in the fifteenth century, when Europeans expanded and began their empires, however haltingly, in earnest.

SEE ALSO *Law, Colonial Systems of; Papal Donations and Colonization.*

BIBLIOGRAPHY

Bataillon, Marcel. *Études sur Bartolomé de las Casas.* Paris: Centre de recherches de l'Institut d'études hispaniques, 1965.

Breisach, Ernst. *Historiography: Ancient, Medieval, and Modern.* Chicago: University of Chicago Press, 1983.

Bueno, Salvador. "Al Lector." In *Viages en la Nueva España,* by Thomas Gage, 9–15. Havana, Cuba: Casa de las Américas, 1980.

Burke, Peter. "America and the Rewriting of World History." In *America in European Consciousness, 1493–1750,* edited by Karen Ordahl Kupperman, 33–51. Chapel Hill: University of North Carolina Press, 1995.

Canny, Nicholas P. *The Elizabethan Conquest of Ireland: A Pattern Established, 1565–76.* Hassocks, U.K.: Harvester, 1976.

Clendinnen, Inga. "'Fierce and Unnatural Cruelty': Cortés and the Conquest of Mexico." *Representations* 33 (1991): 65–100.

Davenport, Frances Gardiner. *European Treaties Bearing on the History of the United States and its Dependencies to 1648.* 4 vols. Washington, D.C.: Carnegie Institution of Washington, 1917–1937.

Duviols, Jean-Paul. *L'Amérique espagnole vue et rêvée: Les livres de voyage de Christophe Colomb à Bougainville.* Paris: Promodis, 1985.

Elliott, John. *The Old World and the New, 1492–1650.* Cambridge, U.K.: Cambridge University Press, 1970; reprint, 1992.

Elliott, John. "Final Reflections: 'The Old World and the New Revisited'." In *America in European Consciousness, 1493–1750,* edited by Karen Ordahl Kupperman, 391–408. Chapel Hill: University of North Carolina Press, 1995.

Gibson, Charles. "Introduction." In *The Black Legend: Anti-Spanish Attitudes in the Old World and the New,* edited by Charles Gibson, 3–27. New York: Knopf, 1971.

Greenlee, William Brooks, trans. *The Voyage of Pedro Álvares Cabral to Brazil and India: From Contemporary Documents and Narratives.* London: Hakluyt Society, 1938.

Hanke, Lewis. "A Modest Proposal for a Moratorium on Grand Generalizations: Some Thoughts on the Black Legend." *Hispanic American Historical Review* 51 (1971): 112–127.

Hart, Jonathan. "Strategies of Promotion: Some Prefatory Matter of Oviedo, Thevet, and Hakluyt." In *Imagining Culture: Essays in Early Modern History and Literature*, edited by Jonathan Hart, 73–94. New York: Garland, 1996.

Hart, Jonathan. *Representing the New World: The English and French Uses of the Example of Spain*. New York and London: Palgrave, 2001.

Hart, Jonathan. *Contesting Empires: Opposition, Promotion, and Slavery*. New York and London: Palgrave Macmillan, 2005.

Hume, Peter. *Colonial Encounters: Europe and the Native Caribbean, 1492–1797*. London and New York: Methuen, 1986; reprint, London: Routledge, 1992.

Ingalls, John J., ed. *America's War for Humanity Related in Story and Picture, Embracing a Complete History of Cuba's Struggle for Liberty, and the Glorious Heroism of America's Soldiers and Sailors*. New York: Thompson, 1898.

Juderías, Julián. *La Leyenda Negra y la verdad histórica* (The Black Legend and Historical Truth). Madrid, 1914.

Keen, Benjamin. "The Black Legend Revisited: Assumptions and Realities." *Hispanic American Historical Review* 49 (1969): 703–719.

Las Casas, Bartolomé de. *A Short Account of the Destruction of the Indies*. Translated by Nigel Griffin. Harmondsworth, U.K.: 1992.

Léry, Jean de. *History of a Voyage to the Land of Brazil, Otherwise Called America*. Translated by Janet Whatley. Berkeley: University of California Press, 1990.

López, Ignacio Escobar. *La Leyenda Blanca*. Madrid: Ediciones Cultura Hispánica, 1953.

Martínez, Miguel Molina. *La leyenda negra*. Madrid: NEREA, 1991.

McAlister, Lyle N. *Spain and Portugal in the New World, 1492–1700*. Minneapolis: University of Minnesota Press, 1984.

McCann, Franklin T. *English Discovery of America to 1585*. New York: King's Crown Press, 1951; reprint, New York: Octagon, 1969.

Morison, Samuel Eliot. *The European Discovery of America: The Northern Voyages, A.D. 500–1600*. New York: Oxford University Press, 1971.

Pagden, Anthony. *The Fall of Natural Man: The American Indian and the Origins of Comparative Ethnology*. Cambridge, U.K.: Cambridge University Press, 1982; corrected ed., 1986.

Pagden, Anthony. *Spanish Imperialism and the Political Imagination: Studies in European and Spanish-American Social and Political Theory, 1513–1830*. New Haven, CT: Yale University Press, 1990.

Pennington, Loren E. "The Amerindian in Promotional Literature, 1575–1625." In *The Westward Enterprise: English Activities in Ireland, the Atlantic, and America, 1480–1650*, edited by Kenneth R. Andrews, Nicholas P. Canny, and P. E. H. Hair, 175–94. Liverpool, U.K.: Liverpool University Press, 1978.

Pereira, Duarte Pacheco. *Esmeralso de Situ Orbis*. Translated and edited by George H. T. Kimble. London: Hakluyt Society, 1937.

Quinn, David B., and A. N. Ryan. *England's Sea Empire, 1550–1642*. London: Allen & Unwin, 1983.

Rego, António da Silva. *Portuguese Colonization in the Sixteenth Century: A Study of The Royal Ordinances (Regimentos)*. Johannesburg, South Africa: Witwatersrand University Press, 1965.

Rosenfeld, Jean E. *The Island Broken in Two Halves: Land and Renewal Movements Among the Maori of New Zealand*. University Park: Pennsylvania State University Press, 1999.

Rowse, Tim. *After Mabo: Interpreting Indigenous Traditions*. Melbourne, Australia: Melbourne University Press, 1993.

Sauer, Carl Ortwin. *Sixteenth Century North America: The Land and the People as Seen by the Europeans*. Berkeley: University of California Press, 1971.

Williams, John. *Politics of the New Zealand Maori: Protest and Cooperation, 1891–1909*. Auckland, New Zealand: Oxford University Press, 1969.

Jonathan Hart

LAW, COLONIAL SYSTEMS OF

Law has never been marginal to colonialism. When European powers began expanding their wealth through the acquisition and possession of territories in the New World, they necessarily did so with appeals to law. Whether they used military means of conquest, economic ties of ceded territory and fortified trading posts, or "peaceful" agricultural settlement, the processes by which expansion and colonization occurred and within which it was framed "the discourse of legalities" (Tomlins 2001, p. 38).

Initially, there were no internationally recognized rituals of claiming ownership by right of discovery. These had to be established through contest. The discussion over legality, "the quest for an apparently unassailable legitimation" (Pagden 1998, p. 52) for acquiring new lands and resorting to violence when expedient, extended over more than two centuries and had an enduring impact on subsequent conceptions of empire. In the sixteenth and seventeenth centuries, law was a technique of expansion as legal instruments recorded the facts of occupation and authorized colonizing ventures by private companies and groups.

The importance of law did not stop there. Colonies required administration; strategic decisions had to be made about how to introduce and extend legal control, and these gave rise to new forms of governance when law was imposed on newly acquired territories and subordinated peoples.

There was no single strategy employed. Possible strategies could and did include "aggressive attempts to impose legal systems intact" (Benton 2002, p. 2). But imposing top-down foreign law on other local legal systems was not the most obvious strategy followed. More commonly, in the interest of maintaining order, colonial administrators made conscious efforts to sustain indigenous legal forums and retain elements of existing legal institutions, thereby limiting the amount of legal change. European colonizers were in the process themselves of developing coherent systems of state law over alternative sources, such as customary and canon law, as they simultaneously expanded their borders. This fluid, complex, pluralistic model underscored the likelihood of multiple jurisdictions within colonial administrations.

Conquered and colonized groups, in turn, sought to respond to the imposition of law in ways that included accommodation, advocacy within the system, subtle delegitimation, and outright rebellion. These responses were compounded by factionalism and competition between colonial authorities. Thus, "multisided legal contests" were "central to the construction of colonial rule" (Benton 2002, pp. 2–3).

EARLY MODELS AND STRATEGIES: ROMAN AND CANON LAW

The impetus and basic model for colonization came from the Renaissance humanist fascination with Roman antiquity, which spread in the fifteenth century as Italian scholars became aware of the riches of classical antiquity. Although the English came later than other European powers to the project of empire building, they "were as much in thrall as the Spanish had been" to ancient models of Imperial grandeur (Pagden 1998, p. 35). Rome provided the model of imperial expansion through colonization. One of the first and most prominent theorists of colonization was Thomas Smith (1513–1577), professor of classics and law at Cambridge University, but he was one of many educated Europeans who were familiar with the idea that the Romans had advanced "their authority and civility throughout much of Europe" through colonization (Canny 1998, p. 7).

Ancient Rome also provided the European powers with the concepts and language of law. Although Islamic law must also have been influential on the development of ancient legal principles, by the Middle Ages Roman civil law...formed the basis for political and legal thought throughout Europe" (Stein 1999, pp. 66–67). In the thirteenth century, it combined with canon law and theology to become, for those who were in positions of authority, part of a common, shared learned culture. Roman law was then "readily exported...into areas that had never been part of the Roman Empire" (Stein 1999, p. 40). By the time Europeans were seeking expansion, the church was the main custodian of Roman legal tradition. The first step in developing an empire was to resort to the authority of the church.

Catholic powers, initially Spain, pursued their goals on the "highly questionable authority" of the pope, who

in the Bulls of Donation of 1493 conceded to the Spanish monarchs the right to occupy new regions, even those yet to be discovered. Pope Alexander VI (1431–1503) in fact divided the New World between the first discoverers, Spain and Portugal. For the Protestant powers, the Netherlands and England, papal authority was unavailable, although similar terms were used by the English monarchs to endow their adventurers and explorers with the rights of conquering new lands.

Roman law had "indelibly impressed its character" on the legal and political culture and thought of Europeans (Stein 1999, p. 2). It was a foundational concept of classical imperialism that any expansionist state had to legitimate its actions by appeal to either natural or divine law. "In the terms accepted by every legal system of classical or Christian origin, acts of appropriation necessarily involved the denial of those rights which all men held by virtue of their condition as men. Every such act therefore had to be explained so as to render those natural rights invalid" (Pagden 1998, p. 37). Imperial ambition, enslaving the indigenous peoples, or occupying their territories had to be argued for, defended, and identified in the language of legality, and tensions between secular and religious law in European tradition gave particular form to these defenses.

Theories of legitimation that we now call *colonialism* served as both justification for past actions of "discovery" and exploration, and as motivation for further conquest and colonization. They were mobilized when exploitation and spoliation had occurred sufficiently to attract attention within or between either the European powers or the colonists themselves. At first, the European powers who saw themselves as conquerors legitimated their actions with appeals to religious theology.

By the Middle Ages canon law had developed as an independent judicial system whose authority over religious belief and practice extended to include marriage and family, military service, slavery, and on occasion economic and commercial behavior. It made sharp distinctions between the legal status of Christians and non-Christians (heretics, apostates, Jews) in their relations with each other and their ability to participate in legal proceedings and exercise authority. It was this aspect of legality that was most referred to in discussions of expansion, over the rights of conquest, the rights of conquerors to take possession, and the rights of conquered peoples.

To the question "by what right or warrant we can enter into the land of these Savages, take away their rightful inheritance...and plant ourselves in their place...?" posed by Englishman Robert Gray (c. 1580– c. 1640) in the early seventeenth-century (Pagden 1998, p. 37), expansionists held up principles of Christian religious belief that overrode natural law. Imperial expansion and territorial acquisition were to be based on a Christian obligation to convert the heathen. There were those who believed that non-Christians could not bear rights in property or sovereignty: therefore their territories and the persons of the indigenous people of the New World were to be forfeited to the first "godly" (i.e., Christian) person they encountered.

The Americas were not the only places Europeans established communities. Merchants, such as those in the Dutch East India Company trading in calico and spices, and ship-owners trading in slaves and gold, were pursuing trade with Asian and African ports on an unprecedented scale, which led to the establishment of commercial and administrative outposts in these areas. They could often be fortified communities, although they were not colonies as such and traders did not need to legitimate their practices. The few settlements established on the African coast before the nineteenth century were often held by agreements about rent or tributes paid to local indigenous rulers, and Asian settlements in places of trade and commerce such as India were acquired and held by treaty. It was not until expansion could only occur with prolonged warfare that legitimation became a pressing moral and political concern.

Until the thirteenth century, canon law had little interest in defining the relation between Christians and infidels outside Europe. After that date, however, it began to develop principles that limited the church's jurisdiction over infidels and simultaneously established a special responsibility of the church to intervene to protect natural law. These principles would be tested with colonial expansion into the New World.

Spain and Portugal on the eve of expansion in the fifteenth century had complex legal systems where different religious groups—Christians, Jews, and Muslims—coexisted with separate legal authorities and followed the laws of their own communities. Compounding this complexity further was the tension between local customary law and the superior claims of royal legal authority. This "complex legal landscape" (Benton 2002, p. 45) was made even more complicated as these countries moved into new areas of control.

European expansion in the sixteenth century presented "unprecedented problems" to legal scholars whose existing notions of law (drawn from codified customs and Roman law) were intertwined with Christian theology. A concept of *ius gentium* (law of people), a law shared by all the peoples, had previously been confined to Christian European countries under the power of both emperor and pope. Expansion beyond these boundaries brought non-Christian people into the purview of European law. Were they to be included? Did Christian Europeans have the legal right to usurp or adjudicate the crimes of non-Christian peoples? The answers to these questions were found through reference to natural law.

However, at the points of contact, legal adjudication and the administration of justice were often limited to the European community, despite the difficulty of maintaining boundaries between those and the indigenous inhabitants. Portugal delegated its legal authority to private venturers or the ship's captain, and only sporadically attempted to assert royal supervision. Consequently, non-Christian indigenes were treated as either living outside the law or were subjected to "virtually unregulated disciplinary excesses" (Benton 2002, pp. 46–47).

One person who addressed this problem was a Spanish Dominican professor of theology, Franciscus Vitoria (ca. 1483–1546), who in 1532 laid down important principles for the natural rights of the heathen infidels living in territories conquered by Spain. Roman law provided the concept of justice developed by Christian philosopher Thomas Aquinas (ca. 1225–1274), and was at the heart of the argument proposed by Vitoria on the rights held by indigenous people. Vitoria argued that *ius gentium* was not based on a shared religion but rather was built on the nature of humankind: it was a set of rules to govern relations between one group of people and another, and was "what natural reason had laid down among all peoples" (Stein 1999, pp. 94–95). Similarly, under natural law indigenous people fully owned their lands and could not be deprived of them against their will. While Vitoria seemingly championed indigenous rights, recent scholars have pointed to the triumphant imperialism internal to Vitoria's logic. Vitoria's principles also contained the seeds of domination.

COMMERCIAL AND PROPERTY LAW

Over the course of the sixteenth century, as trade became increasingly important, rationales supporting commercial interests supplanted those advocating religious doctrine. As European nation-states grew, the interests of the Crown intertwined with those of merchants, and colonies became widely accepted as an essential means of providing economic well-being to the populace. Acquiring new lands and ensuring the conduct of trade and commerce required rules and regulations binding on the parties and protecting merchants from competition and encroachment from rival powers. Conflict and competition meant early theoretical arguments that legitimated European conquest and laid down principles by which colonization could proceed. These principles subsequently became the foundation of modern international law.

Colonization means appropriation, taking possession. Important in taking possession are the techniques of planning, explaining, and justifying the action of appropriation, whether it be territory, trade routes, or resources. Once a territory had been conquered either for Christian or commercial purposes, the key problem of how to develop it and keep it as a colony also became a matter of legality.

Religion and commerce were important as motivations for colonization, but when the theorists of expansion discussed the processes of acquisition, "the measures necessary for the realization of colonization's essential processes" (Tomlins 2001, p. 28), they turned to the techniques of geography and law. Geography's methods of mapping and surveying enabled colonists to take possession of the areas the maps represented and named. Law provided the documents that enabled the areas mapped and surveyed to be fenced, bought and sold, defended with arms, and "used, taxed and inherited" (Tomlins 2001, p. 30).

By the seventeenth century and continuing well into the eighteenth century, the most persuasive and frequently cited argument favoring appropriation of aboriginal lands in America was the theory of property, derived from the Roman law of *res nullius* (no thing) and perpetuated most effectually by the English philosopher John Locke (1632–1704). *Res nullius* held all things that were empty, including lands that were "unoccupied," remained common property until they were put to use, usually agriculturally. Though it was not uncontested, especially by colonists with other agendas, Locke's position powerfully legitimated colonists' acquisition of indigenous territory through the authority of natural law rather than legislative decree. To combat the claims of other European powers, it had also to be yoked to claims of prior discovery, which in law constituted the initial step toward legitimate occupation. Claims of possession could only be sustained, however, by prolonged occupation (i.e., by the establishment of colonies).

Colonialism is the term for political and economic relationships that are established with colonization, but constructed and legitimized through ideologies of progression and racism. Colonialism is intricately historical in its effects. While the process of "cultural distancing" (Benton 2002, p. 13) was uniformly set in motion by colonizing powers claiming legal jurisdiction over new lands and people, the process itself differed substantially in practice. The legal system and background of the colonizing power on one hand conditioned the meaning, as well as the means, by which law was extended to conquered peoples. On the other hand, subordinated colonized people could use legal strategies to exploit the tensions and complications aroused by the colonial setting of any dispute. One such instance where the ambiguities of jurisdiction were evident and powerfully felt

was the joint authority of Crown and church in the Spanish conquest of the Americas.

COLONIAL LAW AND CULTURE

In addition, "always, equally importantly and deeply," colonialism is a cultural process whose "discoveries and trespasses are imagined and energized through signs, metaphors and narratives" (Thomas 1994, p. 2). By the eighteenth century, colonialism was framed in terms of natural history, and by the nineteenth century in terms of an "overt, pervasive and extraordinarily confident racism, which was manifested in military operations . . . [And] in apartheid laws regulating marriage, residence and education" (Thomas 1994, p. 79). Not surprisingly the people who had been subjected to colonization "often perceived very clearly the close connections between jurisdictional claims and messages about cultural difference." Institutional frameworks that developed in colonial settings "link[ed] local cultural divisions to structures of governance" (Benton 2002, p. 15).

Law is implicated in colonialism as a technique of legitimation, authority, and dominance. It is also a sign system, language, and culture. Law could and did work both instrumentally in facilitating the colonial project and imaginatively as a resource of power and authority to be drawn on. It was in itself a language in which colonization could take place: "physical occupancy and legalized claim overlap[ped] as expressions of colonizing" (Tomlins 2001, p. 33). The charters given by the English monarch to establish colonies on the Chesapeake and in New England, for example, functioned to English audiences "as signs of colonization's legitimacy" and to the colonizers "as specifications of the process's limits and boundaries" (Tomlins 2001, p. 33).

Ensuring that the messages intended to be conveyed, through legal institutions and rituals, were indeed those actually received was always a problem for the colonizers. Within colonial encounters, cultural practices were often a result of interaction between colonizers and colonized, not necessarily of "domination" or "subordination," but rather the consequence of a complexity of cultural representation and interpretation and a sophistication in cultural adaptation. Colonialism also created new legal statuses as intermediaries acted to protect their interests against imposition by the colonial authorities, yet did so by acting within those very legal mechanisms, thereby simultaneously collaborating with the imposed legal order and yet resisting its effects.

Colonialism gave rise to particular state formations, such as, for example, *settler societies*, which are characterized by having nomadic or semi-nomadic indigenous populations displaced from the land and replaced with imposed formal centralized institutions of authority and government. Within these colonial states, conflicts often took the form of disputes about group rights and legal status, which in itself was a form of property. Where numbers mattered in the size and strength of the polity, indigenous subjects were held "inherently incapable of exercising the rights and responsibilities of citizenship" (Grimshaw 2001, p. 79).

The aim of the colonial project was to establish order, and colonial states were produced out of this "politics of legal ordering" (Benton 2002, p. 253), which could not be achieved without reference to previous local custom. Colonialism "required interaction" between the law that was being imposed and whatever indigenous law or custom already existed. The colonial state was an "arbiter over internal boundaries" in the face of "jockeying over alternative visions" of legal ordering (Benton 2002, p. 23).

Extending jurisdiction over new territories and new peoples created new relationships between the colonizers and the colonized, differences that were formalized in legal categories. Law also structured difference, "making rules about cultural interactions" (Benton 2002, p. 12). Jurisdiction marked new boundaries, made possible a shared identity of subjects before the law, and for colonizers and colonized to function within the law—as litigants, advocates, witnesses, and judges. Thus "the act of extending formal jurisdiction" (law) was frequently complex and difficult. "Colonizing groups in fact wished at times to restrict jurisdiction and thus to reinforce cultural divides" (Benton 2002, p. 12). In settler societies colonists expected political independence and democracy for themselves, often in advance of these developments occurring in their country of origin, yet they marginalized or excluded the indigenous people from those same "democratic" processes.

Nowhere was this more powerful than in the former English, Dutch, and German colonies in southern Africa, where formal union under a constitution into the Union of South Africa in 1910 brought in its wake the structuring of political rights on lines of racial difference. Through constitutional developments, court appointments, and racial legislation, the national government of this new country "showed, from the start, that it intended to govern in the interests of its white electorate" (Evans and Philips 2001, p. 91). New laws, passed almost immediately, reserved land for white ownership, entrenched an industrial color bar, removed existing political rights, and finally introduced full-fledged apartheid. Nonwhite voters were removed from electoral rolls, judicial and government institutions were "unscrupulously" manipulated, and all-white electorates elected all-white governments.

Such discriminations were resisted wherever they were set up. In some areas indigenous people struggled

for inclusion on equal terms, other groups fought to maintain the legitimacy of their own legal forums. (Benton 2002, p. 12). "Colonial rule magnified jurisdictional tensions," as the presence of cultural "others" challenged existing legal categories and exposed ambiguities in the law (Benton 2002, p. 253).

As settlement grew in the new areas following their colonization, settlers expected to be governed in the manner of metropolitan European governance (e.g., "claiming the rights of Englishmen" and developing categories of exclusion, hierarchies, and boundaries between populations). Law furnished the "means to design and implement those relationships" and "provided a potent medium for the imposition of meaning on the activities engendered" (Tomlins 2001, p. 29). Within colonial domains, law created the relationships and routines of social interaction, established authoritative identities, and constructed the culture within which human purpose, "habits of living," and "objects of industry" were constituted (Tomlins 2001, p. 30). Law had material importance.

Property and trade were central to colonial interests. At times "seemingly irrelevant cases of inheritance or marriage property could quickly become crucial to the production of labor, revenue collection, or the regulation of land markets" (Benton 2002, p. 22). Colonial states defined sites for setting rules about property and social identity and enforced definitions of property as it also acted to regulate exchanges. Simultaneously, laws of property, commerce, and civic duty in European countries developed concomitantly with the growth of those nation-states as imperial powers. Colonialism structured legal ordering within the metropolitan centers, as well as in the colonies where "local . . . elites often ran ahead of colonial administrators," for example, "in advocating a greater role for the colonial state in regulating property transactions of all kinds" (Benton 2002, p. 23). This in turn reflected back to the colonial power.

Nevertheless, colonial legal cultures exhibited localized variations conducive to an idea of colonialisms rather than a singular concept. While law could sometimes be used instrumentally, for most circumstances it is better understood as "an imaginative resource" that was "inherently ambivalent, contradictory" and not always in the control of colonial administrators (Tomlins 2001, p. 37). The act of colonizing required the movement of people, not just the process of legally claiming territory. It therefore also conveyed identifiable legal cultures distinguished by local variation, depending on where colonists came from and which stratum of society they belonged to. Law was something common people participated in; it was part of popular culture. Their usage of the law, and the meanings they attached to it, helped shape the diversity within law even within similar colonies.

Colonialism was not simply "a crushing progress" of triumph for the colonizers (Kirkby and Coleborne 2001, p. 3). There were also significant contradictions between policy, such as "rhetorical commitment[s] to equality among British subjects" formulated back in Europe or the British Colonial Office, and practice on the edges of empire where it "was often far less enthusiastically endorsed by settlers and administrators..." (Evans and Philips 2001, p. 94). Issues were perceived differently in different centers of power. A question such as that of extending the franchise (the right to vote) "held a more particular immediacy for Europeans in colonial communities...than it ever could for politicians and colonial officials in Britain" (Evans and Philips 2001, p. 94). It also represented different significance. In the colonies the franchise was "a potent indicator" of the colonists' anxiety "to maintain exclusive [white] minority rule" but a "measure of the Home Government's unwillingness to redress such discrimination in practice" (Evans and Philips 2001, p. 94).

COLONIAL ENCOUNTERS WITH INDIGENOUS AND LOCAL LAW

Encounters with local indigenous systems of law also prevented the imposition of a singular legal authority or a unitary colonialism. By 1820 a quarter of the world's population lived within Britain's empire. The continent of Africa was being carved up between the major imperial European powers of that time—France, Germany, and Britain. The nineteenth century was the great period of empire: the period when the largest proportion of the world's population lived under direct colonial rule. But this does not mean colonial power was unlimited. Introduced institutions were frequently appropriated to strategic effect by colonized peoples.

Colonial histories were shaped by indigenous responses of resistance and accommodation to colonization, as much as by the imposition of power from metropolitan authorities and local officials adhering to or departing from policy and previous practice. The colonizers, as well as the colonized, were exposed to new possibilities of action and departure from Old World corruptions. This was particularly the case within the English colonies of North America, where law became the medium of social transformation when colonists resisted the imposition of imperial constraints and asserted their legal independence through a newly acquired identity.

Similarly, in the common law jurisdiction in the Australian penal colony of New South Wales, colonists, whether convict or free, enjoyed access to the courts and economic freedoms denied to their counterparts in the imperial center. Married women, who in English law were denied economic rights and legal personhood under the common law doctrine of coverture, were in the colonies permitted to engage in economic activities, even to buy and sell land, as colonial societies developed congruently and in relationship with, yet independently of, the metropole.

The presence of indigenous populations and the political and symbolic importance of defining their legal status provided the biggest challenge to the colonial imposition of unitary legal authority and "stretched across the colonial world" (Benton 2002, p. 253). As Europeans encountered peoples who were non-Christians, legal boundaries closely following ethnic and cultural boundaries were "an important constraint and rhetorical resource used in shaping ethnic identities" (Benton 2002, p. 78). Thus, cultural difference—and relationships of power based on this difference that we call *colonialism*—became the heart of political difference in the development of the modern world.

Not least, European imperialism created new sites for struggle within and between indigenous and European women and men. Miscegenation complicated cultural categories, legal status, and property rights as it tied colonizers and colonized together in familial and kinship ties, as well as in economic and political obligation. It presented particular problems to the existing question for the colonizers of how and to whom to apply law.

To the usual problems of evidence and corroborating witnesses in cases of rape was added the problem of non-Christians taking oaths of truth-telling in courtrooms. Europeans did not expect to adhere to or be judged by tribal law, nor did they want to litigate in indigenous courts where such courts existed. At times, European colonizers sought to interfere with legal prohibitions where traditional practices were thought to be morally unacceptable. Colonial rule thus proceeded amidst "myriad conflicts over the definitions of difference, property, and moral authority" (Benton 2002, pp. 127–129). The outcome was inevitably unresolved and unresolvable.

Many of the legal issues of colonialism remain. In the twentieth century, law continued to shape colonized societies even after the colonial era was officially ended by the United Nations. Law was perceived as an instrument of development, capable of bringing about far-reaching social change through the constitution of modern nation-states and the facilitation of finance capital. Yet, in practice law could instead maintain structures and perpetuate conflicts that were instituted under colonialism. Here continuities with colonialism suggest that law, rather than being a legacy of the colonialist past, may more profitably be seen as "a living instrument for the reproduction of imperial international relations" (D'Souza 2001, p. 257). Contests over law are constitutive of larger international relationships. In the globalized world today, even "seemingly small struggles over cultural boundaries in the law" have the potential to profoundly affect power structures everywhere (Benton 2002, p. 265).

Indeed the legal politics that shaped the "global ordering" of the modern world continue in the contemporary postcolonial era as indigenous people of former colonies challenge the internal legal authority of the states in which they live with "competing legal pluralisms" (Benton 2002, p. 264). At the same time, the rise of transnational associations demands alternative jurisdictional boundaries. Colonialism is now implicated in the writing of the history of those nation-states that were once colonies, as scholars debate the legitimacy and accuracy of territorial acquisition by "peaceful" settlement, and legal authorities contest the very concept of "sovereignty"—whose "simple conjuring is held to change an ancient peoples' relationship with its land" (Borrows 2001, p. 190)—that has undermined indigenous ownership since the fifteenth century.

SEE ALSO *Divide and Rule: The Legacy of Roman Imperialism; Law, Colonial Systems of, British Empire; Law, Colonial Systems of, French Empire; Law, Colonial Systems of, Spanish Empire; Religion, Roman Catholic Church.*

BIBLIOGRAPHY

Benton, Lauren. *Law and Colonial Cultures: Legal Regimes in World History, 1400–1900.* Cambridge, UK: Cambridge University Press, 2002.

Borrows, John. "Because it does not make sense': Sovereignty's Power in the Case of *Delgamuukw v. The Queen* 1997, in *Law, History, Colonialism: The Reach of Empire*, edited by Diane Kirkby and Catharine Coleborne, 190–206. Manchester, UK: Manchester University Press, 2001.

Canny, Nicholas, ed. *The Oxford History of the British Empire*, Vol. 1: *The Origins of Empire: British Overseas Enterprise to the Close of the Seventeenth Century.* Oxford, UK: Oxford University Press, 1998.

D'Souza, Radha. "International Law—Recolonizing the Third World? Law and Conflicts Over Water in the Krishna River Basin," in *Law, History, Colonialism: The Reach of Empire*, edited by Diane Kirkby and Catharine Coleborne, 243–260. Manchester, UK: Manchester University Press, 2001.

Evans, Julie, and David Philips. '"When there's no safety in numbers': Fear and the Franchise in South Africa—the Case of Natal, in *Law, History, Colonialism: The Reach of Empire*, edited by Diane Kirkby and Catharine Coleborne, 91–105. Manchester, UK: Manchester University Press, 2001.

Fitzpatrick, Peter. "Terminal Legality: Imperialism and the [De]composition of Law," in *Law, History, Colonialism: The Reach of Empire,* edited by Diane Kirkby and Catharine Coleborne, 9–25. Manchester, UK: Manchester University Press, 2001.

Grimshaw, Patricia, Robert Reynolds, and Shurlee Swain. "The Paradox of Ultra-democratic Government: Indigenous Civil Rights in Nineteenth-century New Zealand, Canada and Australia," in *Law, History, Colonialism: The Reach of Empire,* edited by Diane Kirkby and Catharine Coleborne, 78–90. Manchester, UK: Manchester University Press, 2001.

Pagden, Anthony. "The Struggle for Legitimacy and the Image of Empire in the Atlantic to c.1700," in *The Oxford History of the British Empire,* Vol. 1: *The Origins of Empire: British Overseas Enterprise to the Close of the Seventeenth Century,* edited by Nicholas Canny, 34–54. Oxford, UK: Oxford University Press, 1998.

Seuffert, Nan, and Catharine Coleborne, eds. *Making Law Visible: Past and Present Histories and Postcolonial Theory.* Special issue, *Law Text Culture* 7 (2003).

Stein, Peter. *Roman Law in European History.* Cambridge, U.K.: Cambridge University Press, 1999.

Stoler, Ann Laura. "Rethinking Colonial Categories: European Communities and the Boundaries of Rule." In *Colonialism and Culture,* edited by Nicholas Dirks, 319–352. Ann Arbor: University of Michigan Press, 1992.

Thomas, Nicholas. *Colonialism's Culture: Anthropology, Travel, and Government.* Melbourne, Australia: Melbourne University Press, 1994.

Tomlins, Christopher, "Law's Empire: Chartering English Colonies on the American Mainland in the Seventeenth Century," in *Law, History, Colonialism: The Reach of Empire*, edited by Diane Kirkby and Catharine Coleborne, 26–45. Manchester, UK: Manchester University Press, 2001.

Young, Robert. *Postcolonialism: An Historical Introduction.* Oxford, UK: Blackwell, 2001.

Dr. Diane Erica Kirkby

LAW, COLONIAL SYSTEMS OF, BRITISH EMPIRE

British colonial expansion brought the administration of English common and statutory law to the newly acquired territories in America, Asia, Africa, and the Pacific. Common law had been developing in England since the twelfth century, and denominated a body of mostly unlegislated law founded on custom and precedent. Due to its centuries-long evolution, common law proved to be a stable and slow-to-change legal system. It formed the basis of jurisdiction in all three types of direct colonial holdings. Common law formed the basis of British jurisdiction in the trading posts along the Indian Ocean coast. British settlers brought it to the settlement colonies of North America, South Africa, and Australia. And it became the legal fundament of all British colonies of domination in Asia and in Africa.

Nevertheless, British administrators in all three types of colonies soon recognized the need to adapt their imported law according to local circumstances, and they amended English common and statutory law with colonial statutes in response to specific colonial situations.

Until the passing of the Colonial Laws Validity Act in 1865, such colonial laws were valid only if they were in no aspect "repugnant"—that is, contradictory—to the laws of the home country. Although often criticized for manifesting the principle of "nonrepugnancy," the Colonial Laws Validity Act recognized the validity of colonial legislation and declared "repugnant" laws invalid only to the extent of their conflict with British law (whereas such laws had been invalid in total before).

The Colonial Laws Validity Act and the nonrepugnancy principle governed colonial legislation in all British colonial holdings (regardless of colonial self-government) until the passing of the Statute of Westminster in 1931, which granted validity to any law passed in a dominion parliament. In British Crown colony holdings the Colonial Laws Validity Act remained valid until independence.

COLONIAL LAW IN TRADING POSTS AND FACTORIES

When European merchant companies started to establish trading stations and factories in territories under foreign authority, they took advantage of a practice relatively widespread in contemporary merchant societies—the practice of consular law. To further and protect their foreign trade, local sovereigns, particularly in Asia, recognized the right of foreign merchants (or other subjects) to live under their own legal system.

Thus, the British East India Company brought English law to its trading posts and factories in India. The company's founding charter of 1600 already made indirect reference to the principle of nonrepugnancy regarding the laws and punishments in future company territories. Company legal authority was vested in miniature governments and originally covered only British subjects. In 1661 legal authority over company servants and other Europeans was placed in the hands of Governor and Council. But with its power in the trading posts steadily growing, the company continuously extended its jurisdiction to legal cases involving European and indigenous subjects and finally assumed legal authority over the indigenous population as well. However, indigenous cases were generally handled by local judges according to local customary law—thus establishing a practice of legal pluralism.

COLONIAL LAW IN SETTLEMENT COLONIES

In colonial territories with a comparatively sparse indigenous population and continuous European immigration, English common and statutory law were claimed by the settlers as the one and only law of the new colonies. To live under English law was perceived as a privilege reserved for the white population, and the privilege was not readily shared with the indigenous inhabitants. The royally-appointed or (in case of chartered colonies) proprietarily-appointed Governor and Council constituted the highest legal authority in the colonies in civil as well as in criminal matters. Although theoretically bound by the principle of nonrepugnancy, slow communications and the practice of issuing "temporary" laws guaranteed considerable legislative freedom to Governor and Council.

English law was adapted to local colonial circumstances. In the North American colonies, the importation of African slaves required the implementation of European-designed laws regulating master-slave relations. In the Australian settlements, colonizers adopted the practice of *terra nullius* (nobody's land), thus not recognizing native claims to land and securing European land titles. Settlement colonies rarely produced legal pluralisms (and if so only in their weakest form), but they confirmed British law as the single legal system. It is important to note that self-government in settlement colonies did not override the principle of nonrepugnancy. Only with the Statute of Westminster did Britain's six dominions (Australia, Canada, the Irish Free State, New Zealand, Newfoundland, and South Africa) achieve full legal authority.

COLONIAL LAW IN INDIA AND OTHER COLONIES OF DOMINATION

With the acquisition of Bengal in 1757, the British East India Company (and with it the British government) was confronted with new challenges concerning the legal administration of its European and indigenous subjects in India. Legal pluralism as practiced in the factories and trading stations was advocated by the legal reforms of Warren Hastings (1732–1818), India's first governor-general, in 1772 (placing Muslims under Muslim civil law, Hindus under Hindu civil law, and all indigenous inhabitants under Muslim penal law) and the Regulating Act of 1773 (extending British jurisdiction over all British subjects, all company servants, and all other indigenous inhabitants who chose to submit to it).

Discovering the economic value of India beyond mere revenue collection, the British administrators began to interfere with the relatively untouched indigenous legal systems only in the second quarter of the nineteenth century. After the Indian Revolt of 1857, the British Crown took over the Indian holdings from the East India Company in 1858. A unified Indian Penal Code was introduced in 1860 and during the rest of the nineteenth century most fields of commercial, criminal, and procedural law had been fully codified—incorporating only little indigenous legal practice. Legal pluralism continued only in the fields of Hindu and Muslim personal laws. After Indian independence was achieved in 1947,

Warren Hastings. *Legal pluralism as practiced in Britain's colonial factories and trading stations was advocated by the legal reforms of Warren Hastings in 1772, placing Muslims under Muslim civil law, Hindus under Hindu civil law, and all indigenous inhabitants under Muslim penal law.* **LIBRARY OF CONGRESS.**

the legal system introduced by the British remained practically intact.

The legal practice that had evolved in colonial India became a role model for other British colonies of domination. Codification, the expansion of British law and the application of indigenous customary law in personal affairs, became the acknowledged practice. Labeled as *indirect rule*, the British made use of indigenous elites to administer law in their African colonies, thus keeping up a form of legal pluralism. However, local customary laws mostly survived only in altered forms as appendages to British state law.

PURPOSE AND SCOPE OF COLONIAL SYSTEMS OF LAW

The primary purpose of colonial law was the safeguarding of the colonizers' interests. The introduction of British laws regarding land and property secured British acquisition of and titles to land in settlement colonies and—later—secured investments in the plantation industry. British-designed slave laws regulated master-slave

relations in North America and provided a steady and reliable labor force. In trading stations, British law on a consular basis guaranteed personal security in an alien society and protected foreign trade.

Both in settler and nonsettler colonies, to fall under British jurisdiction had been viewed as a privilege not readily shared with the indigenous population. The resulting legal pluralism retained legal inequality in nonsettler colonies. The codification of colonial law—incorporating altered forms of local customary law—finally imposed a Europeanized legal system on many colonies of domination, much of which remained in place even in the postcolonial era.

SEE ALSO *Empire, British; Indian Revolt of 1857; Law, Colonial Systems of.*

BIBLIOGRAPHY

Anderson, David M., and David Killingray, eds. *Policing the Empire: Government, Authority, and Control, 1830–1940.* Manchester, U.K.: Manchester University Press, 1991.

Benton, Lauren. *Law and Colonial Cultures: Legal Regimes in World History, 1400–1900.* Cambridge, U.K.: Cambridge University Press, 2002.

Chanock, Martin. *Law, Custom, and Social Order: The Colonial Experience in Malawi and Zambia.* Cambridge, U.K.: Cambridge University Press, 1985.

Mamdani, Mahmood. *Citizen and Subject: Contemporary Africa and the Legacy of Late Colonialism.* Princeton, NJ: Princeton University Press, 1996.

Mann, Kristin, and Richard Roberts, eds. *Law in Colonial Africa.* Portsmouth, NH: Heinemann, 1991.

Mommsen, Wolfgang J., and J. A. de Moor, eds. *European Expansion and Law: The Encounter of European and Indigenous Law in 19th- and 20th-Century Africa and Asia.* Oxford: Berg, 1992.

Tomlins, Christopher L., and Bruce H. Mann, eds. *The Many Legalities of Early America.* Chapel Hill: University of North Carolina Press, 2001.

Washbrook, David A. "Law, State and Agrarian Society in Colonial India." *Modern Asian Studies* 15 (3) (1981): 649–721.

Roland J. Wenzlhuemer

LAW, COLONIAL SYSTEMS OF, DUTCH EMPIRE

Export of Dutch law to its various overseas possessions (Brazil, 1630–1654; New York, 1626–1664; and Dutch Guiana, 1627–1975) is best exemplified by experiences in the Netherlands Indies (present-day Indonesia) between 1602 and 1942. Although not the longest colonial undertaking of Dutch expansion overseas, it was the most important.

The law applying primarily to Dutch citizens in territories acquired by the Dutch East India Company (1602–1799) was basically the law of the fleet or "Ships Law." Subsequently supplemented by Dutch legal practice at Batavia (present-day Jakarta), it found expression in the *Statutes of Batavia* (1642), revised in 1766 as the *New Statutes of Batavia*. In the latter, attempts were made to incorporate Javanese law. These particularly concerned the special place of Islam with regard to marriage, divorce, and inheritance. On paper, local law remained valid. In practice, the increasing involvement of the Dutch East India Company administrative state in the island's political and economic life resulted in the demise of written courtly law with the resultant rise of the unknown and unknowable customary *(adat)* law.

The continuity of the Dutch colonial system of law was hampered by the political underdevelopment of the metropole. Until the early nineteenth century, the Dutch political entity consisted of seven heterogeneous provinces. Solely by virtue of their geographic position, they had been able to assert political independence from their liege lord, Philip II of Spain (1527–1598). A national Dutch state was created in 1816 as a result of international politics culminating in the Congress of Vienna. Even then, a legal basis for the kingdom was delayed by war with the southern Netherlands, which in due course would become Belgium. Only after a finished constitution was promulgated in 1838 could attention be turned to regulating law in the colony.

The Netherlands East Indies Constitution *(Regeringsreglemente)* of 1854 enshrined two basic principles. The first was the concordance principle, ensuring that Dutch persons residing in the Indies would be subject to the same laws and ordinances as those living in the metropole. The second was that of duality: Dutch laws applied to the Dutch and those considered as such; "native" law applied to the indigenous population. From the latter followed the doctrine of applicability, through which "natives" could legally become "Dutch," voluntarily or at the discretion of the government, temporarily or permanently. The assumption was that the natural superiority of Dutch law would attract enlightened "natives" *(inlander)*, which would ultimately result in legal unification. Ethnicity was a legal definition, albeit with far-reaching social effects. Criminal and commercial law were unabashedly European.

Traditional scholarship has empathized the importance of customary law *(adat recht)* as applying to the indigenous population. Based upon the work of Dutch legal scholar Cornelis van Vollenhoven (1874–1933) and his disciples at Leiden University, who were greatly influenced by the *Historische Rechtsschule* (Historical School of Law) of German jurist Friedrich Karl von Savigny (1779–1861), the Indonesian archipelago was divided into some seventeen so-called "law circles," each assumed to reflect the customary law of that region. Thus, to the two nonindigenous law systems—Dutch, plus after 1918 that of the Foreign Orientals (Sino-Indonesians)—came these mutually exclusive sets of oral laws. Under the circumstances, "forum shopping" and the "conflict of laws"—a determination of which set of laws were valid in cases between individuals from different ethnic or legal groups—almost overshadowed the law itself.

Recent scholarship tends to see the adoption of the *adat* either as an instrument of the nationalist project or as one providing the rationale for incorporating the bureaucratic nobility *(priyayi)* into the Dutch colonial system. The *priyayi* were declared to be the sole sources of *adat* canon. They constituted the "natural leaders" who were bound to the Dutch by "perks" in office.

The odd man out was religious law. Dutch penchant for seeing religion as the basis of indigenous law is attested to by the General Provisions on Legislation for the Netherlands Indies (1846–1848), which stated that for the natives, "their religious laws, institutions, and customs are to remain in force." Islamic features were recognized, but depended for their validity on being part of the customary law system rather than a system of *shari'a* (Islamic law) in its own right.

The combination of late state-building and early recognition of legal pluralism reduced Dutch imperialism to an extension of existing control rather than new projects. Particularly under Governor-General J. B. van Heutsz (1851–1924), the conqueror of Aceh, the borders of the Netherlands East Indies were pushed out over the greater part of the archipelago. With them came the complex system of legal plurality already established on Java. The fact that the Outer Islands' indigenous legal system was influenced at a far later date than that of Java led to a sharpening of the administrative contrast between the two with regard to both theoretical and practical results.

Although less elaborate, legal pluralism continued under the Republic of Indonesia. According to the constitution of 1945, "the regulations and state organs present at the moment of the birth of the Republic on 17 August 1945 remain in force," as long as they were not superseded by new laws and did not conflict with the contents of the constitution. The Indonesian Republic's founders were split between those extolling the virtues of the customary village ideal assumed to be ordered by the *adat* and those orientated to formal legality at the national level.

Certain paragraphs of the constitution conceived the state as a hierarchy of laws, others as a more *teori integralistik* (totalistic concept) in which the communal principles underlying *adat* came to the fore. Whatever the case, law under the "New Order" (1966–1998) was an opportunistic mixture of both, depending on the interests of the political and economic elite. Indonesia's self-proclaimed *rechtsstaat* (state bound by the rule of law) was belied by its proclaimed *Panca Sila* (the five principles mentioned in the constitution's preamble) basis stemming from its Indonesian historical and romantic ideas. Elements of the *adat* were specifically allowed. Yet they had to give way to the exigencies of the development state when they stood in the way of development, as in conflict with Western-style ownership rights and unlimited access to natural resources. The country's natural resources were placed under the disposal of the state apparatus without reference to indigenous ownership rules or access to society's commonly held goods. Access to the means of production was governed by the positive rules of the *rechtsstaat*.

SEE ALSO *Empire, Dutch; Law, Colonial Systems of.*

BIBLIOGRAPHY

Ball, John. *Indonesian Legal History, 1602–1848.* Sydney: Oughtershaw, 1982.

Benton, Lauren. *Law and Colonial Cultures: Legal Regimes in World History, 1400–1900.* Cambridge, U.K.: Cambridge University Press, 2002.

Burns, Peter. *The Leiden Legacy: Concepts of Law in Indonesia.* Jakarta, Indonesia: Pradnya Paramita, 1999; Leiden, Netherlands: KITLV, 2004.

Mommsen, Wolfgang J. *Theories of Imperialism.* Translated by P. S. Falla. Chicago: University of Chicago Press, 1980.

Mason C. Hoadley

LAW, COLONIAL SYSTEMS OF, FRENCH EMPIRE

The raison d'être of the French colonies was to benefit France. Royal ordinances of the eighteenth century defined the *système de l'Exclusif* whereby overseas territories were under the authority of metropolitan France. Any trade between France and its colonies was to be to the advantage of France. The principles of the French Revolution of 1789 and its legacy ran counter to these provisions of the Ancien Régime (France's prerevolutionary political and social system), especially after the consolidation of the French Republic in the 1880s. In theory, French law should have applied equally to all French territories, including those outside of metropolitan France, but this was not the case in practice. Deeply influenced by the Revolution, republican law was supposed to have been a means to emancipate colonized populations, but on the ground, the law was also used to coerce them.

A PATCHWORK OF RIGHTS AND LAWS

A combination of different legal regulations—formal laws, decrees voted on or issued from Paris, executive orders, and local customs—were maintained in French colonies to serve the interests of the colonizer. After the actual conquest of a territory, law was supposed to substitute the might of weapons. But in nearly every case, the rivalry between the French army and civil administration persisted. Algeria is a case in point. The military—the conquerors of 1830—were reluctant to obey the civil administration whose power was confirmed by law only in December 1896 and later in December 1900. In colonies like Algeria that were under direct French rule, the governor-general was omnipotent.

Colonies were ruled, on the one hand, through decrees issued by two different ministries (the Ministry of the Interior and the Colonial Office) in Paris and, on the other hand, by executive orders that made the representative of the French government the main source of the law. Most of the executive and judicial power in French territories resided with the governor-general, particularly in territories that were further away from France. While the French Empire was mainly under direct rule, protectorates were established. To maintain the appearance of autonomy, the French left indigenous sovereigns with symbolic legislative power and kept local legal institutions intact. After the conquest of Morocco in 1911, for instance, the sultan was retained as part of the state apparatus. He signed *dahirs* (decrees) drafted by his viziers—and approved by the French administration. But for all intents and purposes it was the French, through the resident general, who ruled the country.

As far as possible the French tried not to interfere in civil matters, as long as their authority was not challenged. They were particularly careful where religion was concerned. Courts were usually under the jurisdiction of indigenous judges but were invariably controlled by the French administration. All over the empire, when written law did not exist before their arrival, the French recorded traditional law, as was the case for the Berber and Kabyle populations in Algeria and Morocco.

THE LAW AS A MEANS TO EMANCIPATE

Since the Revolution of 1789, French law was conceived as a means to attain the republican ideal of equality among men, as stated in article VI of the Declaration of Human Rights of 1789. But by its very nature, colonization ran counter to this principle. Slavery still existed in many colonies. After a failed attempt to outlaw the practice under the first republic (the Convention of 1792 to 1795) in February 1794, the French abolitionist and statesman Victor Schoelcher (1804–1893) finally succeeded in banning it in 1848. The law was passed throughout the empire, but in colonies like Cambodia local rulers were reluctant to abandon such a lucrative institution. French officials formally denounced "inhuman" practices such as corporal mutilation and even cannibalism in Equatorial Africa or lethal punishment by strangulation in Indochina.

With the French Republic firmly entrenched at the end of the nineteenth century, true democrats supported the policy of assimilation, which was based on the principle that French law should apply in all French territories and that all the populations within the empire should be granted the same rights as any French citizen. In 1892 the standardization of customs duties was inspired by the same principle.

This trend prevailed from the 1870s to the mid-1890s. But after the creation of the Colonial Office in March 1894, opponents of assimilation gained ground on the pretext of respecting local traditions. Then the main obstacle to equality remained French citizenship, which was not often granted to individuals from the colonies. Despite the mobilization of almost one million colonial soldiers during World War I (1914–1918), timid legal reforms kept it difficult for them to obtain full citizenship. This fed a growing resentment among the indigenous elite, aware of their inferior status.

The Popular Front of Léon Blum (1872–1950), who led the first socialist government in France (1936–1937), focused its attention on domestic issues and devoted little energy to reforms in the colonies. Nevertheless, it imposed measures such as the prohibition of compulsory labor and the creation of a colonial inspector of work.

THE LAW AS A MEANS TO COERCE

Because the idea of the exploitation of the colonies for the profit of the colonizer never really disappeared, the "constraint" of French law was rarely applied on the ground. French settlers were needed to develop the new territories. But the French, historically strongly attached to their homeland, were rarely willing to venture overseas without the prospect of lucrative gain. Laws were put into place to minimize the risk for the new settlers.

After the "pacification" of Algeria in the late 1830s, for example, the administration provided each settler with a house on a plot of land, one third of which had already been cultivated. This was the first impetus to develop the

Mitidja, the most fertile land around the province of Algiers. To face the growing demand for land, local populations were confined to the smaller and less productive plots, which were divided among the tribes.

After the French defeat against Prussia and the loss of the provinces of Alsace and Lorraine under the Treaty of Frankfurt in May 1871, a law was passed in June 1871 allotting 100,000 hectares (about 247,100 acres) in Algeria to the natives of these provinces. The land had been confiscated from Moqrani, the chief of the Medjana area (d. 1871), who rebelled against the French during the Great Revolt of Kabylie from March 1871 to January 1872. This policy of confiscation reached its peak in July 1873 with the passing of a law that facilitated the dispossession of Algerians. In the same spirit, compulsory labor was imposed throughout the empire. In theory, locals could be made to perform public duties for anywhere from five days in Indochina to two weeks in Equatorial Africa.

French law was a means to justify colonization. The French, like Americans, were supposed to "civilize" indigenous populations but in reality merely exploited their colonies. Nevertheless, after independence, most of the colonies did benefit from French law, for instance with the adoption of the French Civil Code of 1804. Paradoxically, French influence was more significant after independence.

SEE ALSO *Empire, French.*

BIBLIOGRAPHY

Ageron, Charles-Robert, Catherine Coquery-Vidrovitch, Gilbert Meynier, and Jacques Thobie. *Histoire de la France Coloniale, 1914–1990.* Paris: Colin, 1990.

Benton, Laurent. *Law and Colonial Cultures: Legal Regimes in World History, 1400–1900.* Cambridge, U.K.: Cambridge University Press, 2002.

Frémeaux, Jacques. *Les Empires Coloniaux dans le Processus de Mondialisation.* Paris: Maisonneuve et Larose, 2002.

William Guéraiche

LAW, COLONIAL SYSTEMS OF, JAPANESE EMPIRE

Beginning in the mid-sixteenth century, European merchants and missionaries began visiting Japan. These Westerners, known to the Japanese as *Nanban* (literally, "southern barbarians"), earned tremendous profits, and their frequent visits opened a period of expanded commercial and cultural exchange between Japan and the West. Internally, Japan was divided by warring factions, which in 1600 were forcibly united under the Tokugawa shogunate, a type of military-civil administration. Its leaders grew suspicious of the foreigners' motives, and in the 1630s all Westerners were banned from Japan except a very restricted number of Dutch traders who were limited to port calls near Nagasaki.

For the next two hundred years, Japan's leaders quarantined the country from virtually all international contacts, cultivating instead a social system, culture, and politics centered on the divinity of the emperor and unquestioned obedience to imperial edicts. The legal system was relatively simple. Most disputes were resolved either by the intervention of *samurai*, the high-caste chieftains who supported the throne, or through customary practices of mediation, conciliation, and resolution. Renewed contact with expanding Western colonial powers in the mid-nineteenth century forced Japan to adopt a series of internal reforms, including legal modernization, which Tokyo then utilized in the construction of its own colonial empire in Asia.

THE MEIJI RESTORATION

In 1854 an American naval force coerced the ruling shogunate into signing a treaty that gave Western merchants open access to Japan, while obliging Japan to provide supplies for Western ships and suspending Japan's legal authority to control visiting foreigners. Recognizing Japan's vulnerability, and fearing invasion by one or more of the Western powers, the old Tokugawa leaders faced a crisis. Civil war erupted between conservative and reformist leaders in 1867 to 1868. The victorious reformers gained support from the young Emperor Mutsuhito (1852–1912), who took the throne in 1867.

Mutsuhito adopted the reign name Meiji ("enlightened rule"). With guidance from the reform clique, the Meiji emperor vowed to restore Japan's strength as a nation and to make it a peer of the Western powers. His first major reform, introduced in 1868, was the Five Charter Oath, which included a commitment to replace traditional methods of conflict resolution with a uniform system for administering justice. A rudimentary constitution was promulgated, placing Japan's sovereignty in the person of the emperor himself. Japan's brightest young scholars attended European and American universities, where their studies included administration and law. Upon their return, these students advised the Meiji government on how to rapidly transplant to Japan Western institutions that would build it into a political, commercial, and military rival of the great powers of the West.

Reform of Japan's traditional legal system was central to this plan. Continental European legal codes and procedures gained favor with Japan's reformers, in preference to Anglo-American jurisprudence, which relied upon a complex body of legal precedent and case law. The systematized procedures of continental law were practical, less complicated, and amenable to modifications that accommodated traditional Japanese social mores. For example, in 1875 a government decree provided a new criminal justice framework based in part on French law, but it also allowed for Tokugawa-era conciliation procedures as well.

Indeed, several features of French law were introduced in the early Meiji period, including the opening of courts to journalists, prohibition of torture in civil cases, restrictions on methods of torture in criminal cases, and the use of appeals procedures. Tokugawa-era orders, like the Code of a Hundred Articles of 1742, which instructed the governed on how they should act, were replaced by French-style laws that identified unacceptable behaviors and specified punishments for each offense. Japan's Penal Code and its Code of Criminal Instruction, both introduced in 1882, reflected French practices that emphasized aggressive investigations and inquisitorial procedures.

Over the next fifty years, German legal theories also gained ground in Japan. Early evidence of this came with the promulgation of Japan's first Code of Civil Procedure, adopted in 1890. Under this new system for civil actions, pretrial witness interviews were disallowed; interviews were reserved instead to the court itself during trial proceedings. Judges were assigned to lead trials, rather than act as referees between the parties, as they do in Anglo-American legal procedure. A German adviser to the Meiji court drafted Japan's first Commercial Code in 1893, which regulated sales, contracts, and bankruptcies. An updated Commercial Code adopted in 1899 remained in force until the 1930s. It legalized new commercial tools, including checks and promissory notes, and regulated freight and marine trade. Japan's judges and lawyers were selected according to the German practice of examinations, interviews, and apprenticeships overseen by officials from the Ministry of Justice. Finally, in 1922, the old French-style criminal procedures law was replaced by a German-influenced criminal code that remained in effect until Japan's occupation by the United States following its defeat in World War II (1939–1945).

LAW AND ORDER IN THE JAPANESE EMPIRE

With centralized legal systems borrowed from continental Europe and a uniform belief in the sovereignty and infallibility of the emperor, Japan embarked upon an ambitious foreign policy program designed to provide it with the resources and manpower necessary to rival the Western powers. Beginning in the 1880s, when elements of the Kuril and Ryukyu Islands were annexed, Japan's empire grew to include Taiwan (1895), Korea (1910), ports and privileges in mainland China, Germany's Pacific island possessions (following Germany's defeat in World War I), Manchuria in northeastern China, and, between 1940 and 1942, the mainland and maritime Southeast Asian colonies of the British, French, and Dutch.

From the beginning of its colonial expansion, Japan imposed legal distinctions on its nonmetropolitan territories. An 1899 government directive labeled such territories as *shokuminchi*, or colonies, where the executive orders of the imperial government would not generally be applicable or enforced. Instead, the colonies would be subject to special ordinances issued by local administrations. Important exceptions arose with the annexation of Taiwan and of Korea, which were designated as "sovereign colonies" to which selected elements of Japan's constitution and existing laws would apply. Voting rights were not included, but individuals in these colonies were regarded in law as Japanese nationals. In 1929, after acquiring some 1,400 Micronesian islands formerly owned by Germany, Japan saw that the complexity of colonial affairs demanded new solutions. It created a Ministry of Colonial Affairs to liaise between the imperial government at Tokyo and its far-flung colonial administrations.

Fundamental decisions were made to limit the legal protections afforded to conquered or annexed peoples. Most colonial subjects of Japan lived under martial law administered by military governors-general who exercised both civil and military authority. Civilian Japanese bureaucrats ran economic and public enterprises, while military garrisons of Japanese troops enforced Tokyo's policies. Military control was reinforced through strict enforcement of colonial ordinances by the *kempeitai*, or gendarmerie units, which spread throughout Japan's colonies. This police force, first developed to suppress anti-Japanese guerrillas in Taiwan in the 1890s, expanded its role from counterinsurgency to other important areas, including tax collection, curfew monitoring, and enforcement of racial segregation directives. Combining its extensive police powers with intimidation and retaliation, the *kempeitai* was widely feared. It often succeeded in securing local leaders' cooperation in maintaining internal security and the uninterrupted economic productivity of Japan's colonial territories.

Since Japan's colonial policies were not aimed at long-term goals such as political pacification or cultural assimilation, but rather at efficient economic exploitation, local institutions that did not cooperate were regularly destroyed or absorbed into Japan's governance scheme. When Korea's urban population proved difficult to control, for example, Japan reorganized the Korean army and police as units of its own military, and used the education system, the press, radio, and films to try to erase the distinctiveness of Korea's national identity and

replace it with obedience to Japan's emperor. Japan also imposed Meiji-style reform laws in Korea, such as changing traditional land-tenure practices and terminating the legal privileges of Korean social elites. These tactics reflected the breadth of Japan's political and social control of Korea as a colony, where the subjugated population had virtually no legal recourse against the occupying power.

The peoples added to the Japanese Empire were also stripped of any legal right to refuse service to Japan or to its colonial administrations. In 1918 Japan enacted a directive providing for its colonies a uniform legal system covering criminal, civil, and commercial matters, and also imposing military conscription duties. Colonial administrators publicly emphasized the obligations of Japan's subjects, rather than their rights. As the most heavily populated colonies, Taiwan and Korea bore the brunt of military service and labor levies.

In 1939, in preparation for expanding the empire in Southeast Asia, Japan adopted the Military Manpower Mobilization Law, which rendered all people in Japan's colonies susceptible to labor drafts and forced relocation for unlimited periods of time. Japan's subjects from Manchuria to Micronesia were registered, conscripted, and compelled to work on construction projects for both civilian and military installations. When more manpower was needed, Tokyo issued a directive forcing some 200,000 convicts out of Japan's prisons and into labor battalions that were dispatched to numerous Pacific islands to participate in airfield construction.

POSTWAR CHANGES AND INDIGENOUS PEOPLES

Following Japan's defeat in 1945, Allied forces occupied most of Japan's colonial territories. Japan itself was occupied principally by U.S. forces, which established a military-civilian government that ran Japan's affairs until 1952. During this period, Japan accepted a new constitution that conformed closely to the U.S. Constitution. It afforded personal rights to Japanese citizens and relegated the emperor to the role of a largely symbolic and powerless figurehead. Anglo-American jurisprudence was also introduced, including adversarial courtroom proceedings and separate police investigatory procedures. Japan joined the United Nations in 1956, subscribing both to the human rights clauses of the UN Charter and, later, to most major international legal rights and human rights conventions.

Indigenous ethnic minority populations in Japan's islands had long been neglected and legally disempowered by Tokyo. In the 1970s these minority peoples began to establish new legal and political identities, in part by launching claims to recognition under international human rights conventions. The Okinawan minority, who live in the Ryukyu island chain and number approximately 1.3 million people, and the Ainu *minzoku*, or folks, an aboriginal population that resides in northern Hokkaido and numbers approximately 50,000, have been among the most vocal minorities to demand recognition and rights from the Japanese government. While Tokyo has made some concessions to these minorities, and continues to assess the advisability of enacting special legislation to assist these groups, Japan's courts have begun to extend special legal recognition to them.

SEE ALSO *Empire, Japanese.*

BIBLIOGRAPHY

Anaya, S. James. *Indigenous Peoples in International Law,* 2nd ed. Oxford: Oxford University Press, 2004.

Beer, Lawrence Ward. *Freedom of Expression in Japan: A Study in Comparative Law, Politics, and Society.* Tokyo: Kodansha International, 1984.

Dudden, Alexis. *Japan's Colonization of Korea: Discourse and Power.* Honolulu: University of Hawaii Press, 2005.

Duus, Peter, Ramon H. Myers, and Mark R. Peattie, eds. *The Japanese Informal Empire in China, 1895–1937.* Princeton, NJ: Princeton University Press, 1989.

Duus, Peter, Ramon H. Myers, and Mark R. Peattie, eds. *The Japanese Wartime Empire, 1931–1945.* Princeton, NJ: Princeton University Press, 1996.

Henderson, Dan Fenno. *Conciliation and Japanese Law: Tokugawa and Modern.* 2 vols. Seattle: University of Washington Press, 1965.

Myers, Ramon H., and Mark R. Peattie, eds. *The Japanese Colonial Empire, 1895–1945.* Princeton, NJ: Princeton University Press, 1984.

Peattie, Mark R. *Nan'yō: The Rise and Fall of the Japanese in Micronesia, 1885–1945.* Honolulu: Center for Pacific Islands Studies, University of Hawaii Press, 1988.

von Mehren, Arthur Taylor. *Law in Japan: The Legal Order in a Changing Society.* Cambridge, MA: Harvard University Press, 1963.

Yamada, Y. "The New Japanese Constitution." *The International and Comparative Law Quarterly* 4 (2) (1955): 197–206.

Laura M. Calkins

LAW, COLONIAL SYSTEMS OF, OTTOMAN EMPIRE

The Ottomans were among the Turkish tribes that came to Anatolia (the Asiatic region in present-day Turkey) from Central Asia. They adopted Islam in the ninth and tenth centuries. From a modest nomadic state, they created a stable Middle Eastern empire lasting for more than six hundred years under one dynasty. The Ottoman Empire holds a special place in world history on account of the long duration of its existence and the extent of its realm, which comprised vast territories in the three continents of the ancient world—Europe, Asia, and Africa. The Ottoman Empire passed through several stages: the first Ottoman period (1281–1446), the classical age (1446–1566), destabilization (1566–1789), reform efforts (1789–1912), World War I (1912–1918), and collapse (1923).

By the fourteenth century, the Ottomans ruled the Balkans, and by the early seventeenth century, the empire had expanded as far as Vienna. It extended in Europe to embrace the Balkans, Greece, Albania, Serbia, and the greater part of Hungary and Austria. The Ottomans controlled the Black Sea, and in the north their empire included the Crimea. The Ottomans also controlled most of the Mediterranean, and in Africa the empire included Egypt, Libya, Tripoli, Tunisia, and Algeria. In Asia the Ottomans took in Asia Minor, Syria, Iraq, Palestine, the western shores of the Persian Gulf, and the west and south in Arabia. As early as 1399, the empire's eastern frontier had reached the Euphrates River.

In 1453 the last great Byzantine stronghold, Constantinople (now Istanbul, Turkey) fell to Sultan Mehmed II (ca. 1432–1481), the Conqueror. The Ottoman conquest of Egypt under Sultan Selim I (ca. 1470–1520) brought the caliphate to the Ottomans in 1517, the sultan becoming the supreme voice in all matters religious, not only for the Ottoman Empire but for most Muslims. Under Süleyman the Magnificent (ca. 1494–1566), the empire was the strongest power in Europe, stretching from the Atlantic shore of North Africa to the borders of Iran, Austria, Poland, and Russia. Buda, the capital of Hungary, was taken in 1541.

Geography and brilliant leadership were the two most important factors in the rise of the Ottoman Empire. The first ten sultans had remarkable personal abilities, functioning as kings in Europe and Turkish nomad lords in Anatolia. The empire was created through conquest, and in the early years the Ottomans were attracted to Europe by the booty to be gained there—the principal economic basis of life—and the interest of the Turkish Gazis (warriors of the faith) in expanding the rule of Islam. There was no one power in Europe to oppose this expansion.

Later, the Gazi state was transformed into a centralized bureaucratized empire led by all-powerful sultans. The importance of the nomad warriors decreased, and a new army was created by the regular, enforced recruitment of Christian boys *(devçirme)* for training and eventual employment in the military and civil service as slaves of the sultan. On arrival in Istanbul, the capital, they were converted to Islam.

The Ottoman Empire was based on expansion. The Ottomans neither colonized the territories they conquered nor carried Ottoman Islamic law to all the new settlements. They did, however, introduce an administrative system for collecting taxes to promote national economic growth. They also established fortresses and garrisons at strategic points and along the frontiers, but the armies returned home after conquests.

Islamic law applied to the Turks left behind in conquered territories and to the few converted natives. The rest of the population continued to live according to their existing laws in most respects. This was a multiethnic, culturally and legally pluralist, and decentralized empire. Cultural and religious differences functioned as structuring elements in the law. The different groups were identified by religion: Muslim, Orthodox, Christian, Armenian, and Jewish, though any Ottoman subject could become a Muslim. The system applied was the *millet* system, a term first used for Muslims and later for non-Muslim religious communities. Keeping *millets* as organized and legally recognized separate and distinct religious entries fostered religious separation.

Until the second half of the fifteenth century, the Ottoman Empire had a Christian majority under the rule of a Muslim minority. Eclecticism and pragmatism prevailed in the running of the empire. The principle of tolerance inherent in Muslim governmental tradition toward Christians and Jews was closely connected with a financial policy based on the payment of tribute by non-Muslims. However, tolerance of diversity meant that there was no one language and no single distinct culture within the empire.

Conversion to Islam was practiced only in those regions conquered by the Gazis in Eastern Thrace, and later in the furthest western frontiers in Albania and Bosnia. The vast territory between these two Gazi zones was allowed to remain Christian. Some non-Muslims, the *zimmis* (mostly Armenian, Greek, and Jewish communities and Christian groups given asylum), lived in and around Istanbul. In personal status and private law, their own religious laws and customs applied, their disputes being settled in their own community courts. Though *zimmis* had special legal status, they had a lower status than Muslims.

The second category of non-Muslims comprised the people of conquered lands in Europe whose own local indigenous laws applied in existing local courts. Non-Muslims could not become civil servants and paid special additional taxes *(cizye)* in these regions.

The third category of non-Muslims comprised foreigners, mostly residing in Istanbul and Izmir (Smyrna), who were concerned with trade. These foreigners had special status, including residence privileges and the right to have their disputes settled by consular courts. These privileges were first granted in 1537 to the French in conjunction with an offensive and a defensive alliance, and later to the Dutch and the English. Such foreigners were ruled by their own laws and paid no taxes to the empire.

The Ottoman legal system was pluralistic, the primary connecting factor in choice of law being religion. Public law and administrative structures were influenced by ancient Turkish political customs and by the organization of the Byzantine Empire and the Balkan states. In appearance, however, the Ottoman Empire was an Islamic state, and the fundamental Islamic distinction between master and slave, men and women, and believer and unbeliever was an essential aspect of Ottoman society.

The sultans settled Turks in sensitive regions for defense; elsewhere a program of conciliation and vassalage was adopted. Defeated kings kept their lands as tribute-paying vassals and contributed troops for Ottoman wars. When the vassals weakened and the Ottoman forces were firmly settled, direct control was instituted. The Crimea, for example, was a vassal state of the Ottoman Empire. Crimean Tatars accepted Ottoman sovereignty in 1475 and remained as vassals until 1774, defending the frontier against Russian encroachment.

The first Ottoman provinces were military governorships, with high officials *(bey)* ordered by the sultan to govern regions called *sancak*. In times of peace, the *bey* was the civil authority and oversaw the bureaucracy and taxation. In wartime, he was the general. In the Balkans, for example, many *sancaks* were created and a non-Turkish element came into the operation of the empire. To prevent the establishment of local interest groups and loyalties, the *beys* were subject to a rotation system.

Serbia (1459), Bosnia (1463), and Albania (1479) were under direct Ottoman rule for most of their time as Ottoman provinces. In Anatolia and the Balkans, the provinces were called *vilayet*. Hungary also became a regular province in 1541. Later the empire was divided into three *beylerbeyliks*: Rumelia, Anatolia, and Africa.

In the sixteenth century, throughout much of the Ottoman Empire, conquered lands—theoretically the property of the state—were converted to private ownership *(timar* lands) by the sultans. In *timar* lands, appointed landholders acted as imperial representatives for revenue collection. The *timar* system preserved much of the indigenous social order. Elsewhere, much of the land was *vakif* ("pious foundations") in the hands of the *ulema* (Islamic religious leaders), who could set aside income-producing properties for charitable purposes, paying no taxes.

Dubrovnik (in Croatia), Moldavia (a region in present-day Romania and Moldova), Walachia (in Romania), and the North African coastal regions were tributaries of the Ottoman Empire. Some of the tributary states later became *sancaks*. Turcoman principalities were governed as suzerainties. Over most of the Muslim world, direct rule applied.

The decline of the Ottoman Empire started in 1789. The most important factors in this decline were the growth of European imperialism and the resulting constant loss of land by the empire, and in the nineteenth century, growing nationalism among Christian ethnic groups in the empire. These factors fueled political separation in an empire made up of so many distinct ethnic and religious groups, and led to its dissolution. After World War I, the Ottoman Empire collapsed, to be replaced by the present Republic of Turkey in 1923.

SEE ALSO *Empire, Ottoman.*

BIBLIOGRAPHY

Benton, Lauren. *Law and Colonial Cultures: Legal Regimes in World History, 1400–1900.* Cambridge, U.K.: Cambridge University Press, 2002.

Gibb, Hamilton A. R., and Harold Bowen. *Islamic Society and the West: A Study of the Impact of Western Civilization on Moslem Culture in the Near East.* London and New York: Oxford University Press, 1950–1957.

İnalcık, Halil. *An Economic and Social History of the Ottoman Empire*, Vol. 1: *1300–1600.* Cambridge, U.K.: Cambridge University Press, 1997.

Lewis, Bernard. *The Emergence of Modern Turkey*, 3rd ed. London and New York: Oxford University Press, 2002.

McCarthy, Justin. *The Ottoman Turks: An Introductory History to 1923.* London and New York: Longman, 1997.

Örücü, Esin. "The Impact of European Law on the Ottoman Empire and Turkey." In *European Expansion and Law: The Encounter of European and Indigenous Law in 19th- and 20th-Century Africa and Asia*, edited by Wolfgang J. Mommsen and J. A. de Moor, 39–58. Oxford: Berg, 1992.

Wittek, Paul. *The Rise of the Ottoman Empire.* London: Royal Asiatic Society, 1938.

Esin Örücü

LAW, COLONIAL SYSTEMS OF, PORTUGUESE EMPIRE

Early modern Portuguese society was multicultural; it emerged from a period of reconquest against the Muslims and was home to communities of Jews. Through a slow process of conquest and political consolidation, from the twelfth to the fourteenth centuries, the Portuguese Crown claimed sovereignty over the territories that make up its modern borders. Conquest and political domination of the most western portion of the Iberian Peninsula was concomitant with the development of a legal system reflected in the Portuguese Law Code.

Up until the fourteenth century, several statutes had already been promulgated and in 1446 were codified in the so-called *Ordenações Afonsinas* during the reign of Afonso V (1432–1481). As new laws arose, it became necessary to amend old ones. In 1521 Dom Manuel I (1469–1521) promulgated the *Ordenações Manuelinas*, which became one of the crucial instruments in the governing of the overseas Portuguese colonies. There was rigid crown control of justice and of land ownership, solidified by the supremacy of royal agents over local authorities. The Casa da Suplicação and the Desembargo do Paço (both appeal courts located in Lisbon) constituted the highest level of the judiciary in the Portuguese Empire, and from their location in Lisbon they controlled the distant and often difficult colonial system. Various laws and institutions were created within this framework with the aim of controlling the problems posed by administering colonies.

Portuguese colonization followed two basic patterns. In Asia, the Portuguese would conquer cities and then monopolize trade, whereas in Africa and the Americas they occupied extensive territories in which European political organization was superimposed on existing indigenous societies. The development of commerce in East Asia naturally involved the need for specialized administrative entities and thus the Casa da India (House of India) was created in 1503 in Lisbon.

The creation of the Casa da India resulted in the centralization of overseas trade within Lisbon, which became the locus for all administration and trade with India. This included the export of goods to India, the import of Asian products and their distribution within Portugal and throughout Europe, and the collection of custom fees in the name of the king. Further, Lisbon became the administrative center for the naming of functionaries and the promulgation of crown directives. In the case of Africa, control of the slave trade was overseen by the Casa dos Escravos (House of the Slaves), created as a separate entity in 1486.

On the American continent, the colonial Portuguese administration produced a series of laws, provisions, and royal orders specific to that situation. The territory that was to become Brazil was an immense geographical expanse. Moreover, the indigenous peoples posed a new situation for the Portuguese legal codes. Coming under the banner of Christianization of the Indians, enslavement of Indians dates to the beginning of Portuguese colonization in the Americas in 1530. Though the enslavement of Indians was discouraged, it was only with the arrival of the Jesuits in 1549 that indigenous slavery was strenuously opposed.

The Jesuits established the *aldeamento* system, the practice of settling and Christianizing Indians in supervised villages. In the ensuing battle with secular Portuguese colonists over control of Indian populations, the Jesuits relied heavily on support from the crown. However, unlike the Spanish colonies in the Americas, the Indians never possessed their own colonial tribunal. Considered vassals of the Portuguese king, the Indians' complaints were made via petitions directly to the king, who ordered an investigation of the complaint. Officially, only Indians captured in "just" wars could be enslaved, although in reality indigenous slavery was practiced throughout colonial Portuguese America.

Thus, in the sixteenth century, after the promulgation of the *Ordenações Manuelinas* (codex, collection of laws written when D. Manuel I was the king), additional laws were created to regulate new colonial aspects not covered in the old legislation. This enormous quantity of laws led to the *Leis Extravagantes* (a complementary collection) compiled in 1569. Upon the unification of Iberia in 1580 under the Spanish Crown, Philip II of Spain (Philip I of Portugal, 1527–1599) carefully guarded his royal prerogatives and political authority over Portugal, though he showed good will toward the Portuguese by granting them a measure of autonomy in reforming their legal system.

After the unification, a commission completed the revision of the *Ordenações Manuelinas,* including the *Leis Extravagantes,* around 1595. It was not until 1603 that a new code—the *Ordenações Filipinas* (also a collection of laws written when Philip I was the king)—was issued. In the seventeenth century, the principal change for the colonies was the transformation of the old Conselho da India (1604) into the Conselho Ultramarino (Council for Oversea Affairs) in 1643. The expansion of this new administrative institution resulted from the increasing importance of Brazil over India; all matters and business pertaining to the colonies were now referred to the Conselho Ultramarino.

Consequently, the crown drew up a deliberate strategy of creating structures endowed with ill-defined jurisdictions intended to act as checks on one another. The repeated approvals and consultations required by the traditional administrative procedures hampered Portuguese rule on the periphery of its empire, especially in situations that required flexibility, as in the event of military threats.

Moreover, the temporary nature of administrative appointments throughout the empire gave the latter a makeshift quality that hindered the establishment of stable power structures and made it rely excessively on charismatic personalities. It seemed as if, instead of a strong empire relying on well-defined areas of responsibility, the crown preferred a precarious arrangement in which mutual vertical and horizontal surveillance among officials safeguarded the power of the supreme authority. A consistent royal policy of imposing overlapping jurisdictions and the accumulation of authority in chosen figures, paradoxically, led to a relatively weak but centralized empire in which the thicket of intermediate levels of authority became a structure capable of managing day-to-day matters, while the base structures required that a reasonable degree of decision making remained essential for the empire's survival.

In Brazil, the structure of Native American societies appeared politically disorganized to the Portuguese. This resulted in not only more direct political intervention, but also the barring of any form of self-government on the part of the Indians, thus making the importation of European political and administrative practice inevitable.

Soon after colonization began, the need for overseas appeals courts became apparent in order to process local cases, and additionally to alleviate the cumbersome and inefficient practice of appealing cases in the colonies all the way back to Lisbon. Thus the Tribunal da Relação (appeal court located in the colonies) was established in Goa (India) in 1544, in Bahia (Brazil) in 1609, and nearly a century and a half later in Rio de Janeiro (Brazil) in 1750. The judges were legal scholars who had studied at the University of Coimbra, Portugal's oldest and most prestigious university.

In Coimbra, legal studies were a process of socialization intended to engender loyalty to the crown. It is worthy of notice that during the modern period Coimbra possessed the only law school in the entire Portuguese Empire. All colonial judges, whether of metropolitan or colonial birth, attended this school. Legal training was not permitted for students whose parents plied manual trades or worked as retail merchants.

When, in 1640, Portugal once again became independent of Spain, control over the colonies intensified and *juizes de fora* (judges from outside) were appointed in the main towns for three-year terms. Whereas historians have traditionally regarded these judges as agents of the crown that impinged on municipal powers, more recently the *juizes de fora* have been considered homogenizers of the legal and administrative parameters imposed by the central authority. *Juizes de fora* were established in Goa in 1688, Bahia in 1696, Rio de Janeiro in 1703, and Luanda (Angola) in 1722. While their original duties were restricted to investigating losses to the Royal Treasury, they soon extended their purview to encompass all kinds of actions.

New analysis shows that the appeals courts lacked the power required to curb the excesses of unruly priests. The civil courts were indeed entitled to issue decrees to ecclesiastical courts, as well as intervene in them, but the courts exercised no decisive power over bishops. Appeals to Portugal were lengthy procedures, and pending final resolution, the bishop was free to do as he pleased. Lacking any institutionalized means of control, the civil court would resort to harassment or the withholding of priestly salaries. But the bishops possessed the far greater power to pronounce excommunication or interdict (a Roman Catholic form of censure), and did not hesitate to employ them in the pursuit of the church's goals.

There is no doubt that conflicts between the appeals courts and the other state organs hampered the courts' effectiveness in the conduct of their judicial business. Although personal clashes and spite contributed to this deplorable state of affairs, they do not suffice to explain it. Portuguese colonial administration was afflicted above all by an absence of well-defined spheres of authority, indeed often by contradictions between overlapping jurisdictions. The intentional powerlessness of local authorities made them dependent at all times upon edicts from a distant metropolis that they were forced to consult for every major decision. At times, the situation was aggravated by conflicting goals, as in the case of state-church disputes, but also, within the civil administration itself, by rivalry between the appeals courts and treasury officials.

SEE ALSO *Empire in the Americas, Portuguese; Empire, Portuguese.*

BIBLIOGRAPHY

Benton, Lauren. *Law and Colonial Cultures: Legal Regimes in the World History, 1400–1900.* Cambridge, U.K., and New York: Cambridge University Press, 2002.

Bethencourt, Francisco, and Kirti Chaudhuri, eds. *História da expansão Portuguesa.* 5 vols. Lisbon, Peru: Circulo de Leitura, 1998–2000.

Caetano, Marcelo. *O Conselho Ultramarino: Esboço da sua história.* Lisbon, Peru: Agência-Geral do Ultramar, 1967.

Mattoso, José, ed. *História de Portugal.* Lisbon, Peru: Editorial Estampa, 1993–1994.

Mommsen, Wolfgang J., and J. A. de Moor, eds. *European Expansion and Law: The Encounter of European and Indigenous Law in 19th and 20th Century Africa and Asia.* Oxford and New York: BERG, 1992.

Mommsen, Wolfgang J., and Jürgen Osterhammel. *Imperialism and After: Continuities and Discontinuites.* London and Boston: Allen & Unwin, 1986.

Schwartz, Stuart B. *Sovereignty and Society in Colonial Brazil: The High Court of Bahia and its Judges, 1609–1751.* Berkeley: University of California Press, 1973.

Carmen Alveal

LAW, COLONIAL SYSTEMS OF, SPANISH EMPIRE

Basing its legitimacy in Spanish America and Asia on the papal bulls of Alexander VI (1493) and Julius II (1508), the Spanish Crown asserted preeminent authority in these regions as the vicar of the Vicar of Christ (i.e., the pope). Accordingly, believing that *natural law* expressed divine will and that *positive law* (manmade law) must conform to natural law, the law system of the Spanish Empire was built on the twin pillars of church and state, on canon law and crown law. Acknowledging the inseparability of religious and secular power in the Spanish Empire, this entry will focus on secular law and authorities.

Although the institutional framework of the colonial legal system clearly originated in Iberia, the degree to which the formal and customary laws governing the colonies reflected Spanish political and legal hegemony is disputed by historians. Rather than being an absolutist system, throughout the Hapsburg and much of the Bourbon reigns, the legal system in Spain's colonies was a patchwork of laws and overlapping jurisdictions.

COUNCIL OF THE INDIES

At the apex of the institutional hierarchy was the Spanish Crown. Its policies were informed by reports from the Consejo Real y Supremo de las Indias (Supreme and Royal Council of the Indies), which was established in 1524, shortly after the conquest of the Aztec Empire. From its founding until the eighteenth century, the Council of the Indies possessed supreme legal, administrative, military, trade, finance, and, by way of royal patronage over the church in the colonies, religious authority. It was the primary executive and lawmaking body, as well as the final court of appeals. Immediately below the Council of the Indies, and located in the American and Asian kingdoms, were the archbishops, viceroys, and judges of the royal courts *(audiencias).*

THE VICEROY

Throughout the reign of the Hapsburgs, from 1521 to 1700, the colonies had two viceroyalties: New Spain and Peru. Between 1580 and 1640, when the Portuguese and Spanish crowns were united, the viceroyalty of Brazil was integrated into the imperial bureaucracy. Under the Bourbons, who ruled since 1713, two additional viceroyalties were created: New Granada (1717, 1739) and La Plata (1776).

As the alter ego of the crown, viceroys possessed broad executive and lawmaking powers, and they acted as the vice-patron of the church and the president of the viceregal *audiencia.* Predominately aristocrats without juridical training, viceroys could influence decisions and proceedings of the tribunal as its president, but could not decide the outcome of legal cases.

In addition, as the secular protectors of Indians, viceroys were ordered to designate at least one day each week to hear cases and to receive petitions brought by native subjects. Responding to the growing numbers of cases initiated by native subjects and the economic hardship of litigation, in 1585 the viceroy of New Spain, Don Luis de Velasco, the younger, Marqués de Salinas (1534–1617) established the General Court of the Indians (Juzgado General de Indios). As a specially designated court for the protection of native people, the Juzgado guaranteed that native people received abbreviated legal processes, summary judgments, and reduced or free legal services.

AUDIENCIA

Despite the legal protections proffered by the Juzgado, natives in New Spain recognized that having their case heard by judges or appealed to the *audiencia* could provide legal advantages, in certain cases. Similarly, native people in outlying provinces recognized the impracticality of bringing their cases before either the *audiencia* or the *Juzgado* in Mexico City, or the *audiencia* in Lima and relied on provincial *audiencia* judges to decide their cases. In the frontiers and outlying provinces, the provincial *audiencia* judges were generally the highest royal officials with whom the local population interacted. In addition to their judicial powers, *audiencia* judges generally possessed extensive executive and administrative authorities— being the first royal bureaucrats to arrive in newly conquered territories.

The earliest *audiencias*, or royal courts, were established in Santo Domingo (1511) and Mexico City (1527, 1530) to rein in the conquistadors. Thereafter, they were founded as need dictated to assert royal authority and to resolve disputes between crown subjects—Spaniards, Africans, and Indians alike—in outlying regions; in the viceroyalty of New Spain, including the Audiencia of Mexico and the lesser courts of Santo Domingo, Guatemala (1544), New Galicia or Guadalajara (1549), and Manila (1583); and in the viceroyalty of Peru, including the Audiencia of Lima (1542) and the lesser courts of Panama (1538, abolished in 1543, reinstated in 1567), Santa Fe de Bogotá (1549), La Plata or Charcas (1559), Quito (1563), and Chile (1565, disbanded in 1575, reinstated in Santiago in 1609). Under the Bourbons, the Audiencias of Buenos Aires (1661–1672, reinstated in 1783), Venezuela (1786), and Cuzco (1787) were also established.

JURISDICTIONAL CONFLICTS

Jurisdictional disputes were common among the secular and religious authorities of the sixteenth and seventeenth centuries because officials held overlapping authorities. Despite being structurally subordinate to the viceroy, for example, the *audiencia* judges who lived away from the viceregal capital were able to exercise their executive and administrative powers in relative autonomy, while those closer to Mexico City and Lima frequently challenged the executive and administrative authority of the viceroy.

Additionally, while archbishops were responsible for overseeing the evangelization of and upholding religious orthodoxy among the native population, and viceroys for the good governance and treatment of the native population, their respective interpretations of how to administer the native population brought them into frequent conflict with one another. On one hand, as colonial officials brought their disputes to the Council of the Indies, it allowed the council to assert royal authority in the colonies. On the other hand, recognizing the overlapping jurisdictions, native people learned to manipulate the tensions in the system, often to their advantage, as they appealed their cases from lower courts or challenged the legal interpretations and powers of parallel authorities.

LAWS

At the imperial level, laws derived from royal and viceregal provisions, mandates, and ordinances. In general, crown laws addressed specific concerns of particular petitioners and litigants and, therefore, generally were narrow in scope rather than universal. Moreover, generally responding to the initiative of petitioners and litigants, crown laws reflected the concerns and issues of Africans, Indians, and *castas* (mixed-raced people), as well as Spaniards.

As the imperial period progressed, the crown increasingly promulgated universal laws for common problems and aimed to standardize laws. The earliest bodies of laws issued were the Laws of Burgos (1512–1513) and the New Laws (1542), both of which aimed to establish standards for governance as well as conduct for Spanish colonists in their dealings with the native population. In addition, many jurists recognized the need to compile the laws and legal decisions that had been issued, and they attempted to collect the royal provisions, mandates, and ordinances into single texts, as reflected in *Recopilación* (compilation) of Juan Ovando; *Cedulario* (royal mandates collection) of Vasco de Puga (1563); *Compilación para las Indias de general* (general compilation of the indies) of Alonso de Zorita (1574); *Cedulario para las Indias en general, gobernación espiritual y temporal de las Indias* (general collection of royal mandates of the indies, the spiritual and temporal governance of the indies);

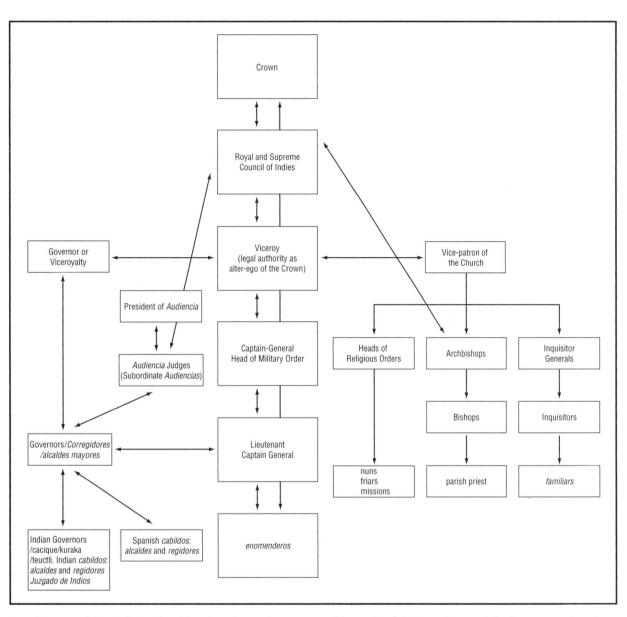

Legal System of Spanish Empire. *This chart depicts the institutional hierarchy of the Spanish empire's legal system in colonial territories.* **THE GALE GROUP.**

Recopilación para las Indias en general (general compilation of the indies) of Diego de Encinas (1596); *Autos, acuerdos, y decretos del gobierno real y supremo consejo de Indias* (decisions, agreements, and government decrees of the royal and supreme council of the indies) of León Pinelo (1658); and the *Recopilación de leyes de los reynos de las Indias* (1680) (compilation of the laws of the kingdoms of the Indies). Although most laws remained particular, as the legal system developed, royal officials increasingly aimed to universalize and standardize laws, and to have laws to mediate between the various communities under crown authority.

At the communal level, laws were based on the customary laws, traditions, and ordinances of the particular community. In issuing laws that addressed concerns or issues of a particular community, Castilian practice necessitated that royal law and legal decisions not ignore the rights, traditions, and practices of the community. Thus, each community had its own legal tradition, whether it was a locality, such as a village, town, or city; or a religious, political, or economic community, such as the body of friars, nobles, merchants, or military orders. Likewise, according to colonial legal practices with Castilian tradition, in 1530 the crown mandated that its officials protect native customs and traditions in their legal decisions—as long as the indigenous laws did not contradict Catholic doctrine or natural law.

LOCAL AUTHORITIES

In civil disputes involving persons from other communities or sojourners, Spanish officials—governors, *corregidores,* and *alcalde mayores*—adjudicated the cases. In the early sixteenth century, and later in frontier areas, when royal officials were not present, friars often adjudicated civil and criminal cases. Likewise, being charged with tutoring native people in Spanish political, legal, and religious norms, zealous friars, parish priests, and royal officials sometimes punished native people for practices that contradicted Catholic doctrine or natural law.

Nonetheless, according to law, within communities, local native authorities maintained their right of first instance and decided criminal and civil cases—using native customary law and practice. Ultimately, similar to the viceregal level, local authorities frequently disputed over jurisdictional authority, and asserted their autonomy from each other and those above them.

LAW AND NATIVE SOCIETIES

Despite royal protection of native custom, every aspect of native traditions and customary law was transformed during the imperial period. For example, although the authority and wealth of the native elite was explicitly protected, much of their political tradition was infused with practices, such as polygamy and belief in the elite's relationship to traditional deities, that contradicted Catholic doctrine. In prohibiting one aspect of native tradition, most elements of native tradition were impacted. Contributing further to the shifts, sometimes Spanish judges misunderstood native traditions and other times native people intentionally misrepresented their traditions (as part of a legal strategy). When decisions were rendered on these misunderstandings and misrepresentations, new legal and cultural practices emerged.

SEE ALSO *Empire in the Americas, Spanish; Native Americans and Europeans; New Spain, the Viceroyalty of.*

BIBLIOGRAPHY

Benton, Lauren. *Law and Colonial Cultures: Legal Regimes in World History, 1400–1900, Studies in Comparative World History.* New York: Cambridge University Press, 2002.

Borah, Woodrow. *Justice by Insurance: The General Indian Court of Colonial Mexico and the Legal Aides of the Half-Real.* Berkeley: University of California Press, 1983.

García Gallo, Alfonso. *Estudios de historia del derecho indiano.* Madrid: Instituto Nacional de Estudios Jurídicos, 1972.

Gomez, Thomas. *Droit de conquête et droits des indiens.* Paris: Masson & Armand Colins Éditeurs, 1996.

Kellogg, Susan. *Law and the Transformation of Aztec Culture, 1500–1700.* Norman: University of Oklahoma Press, 1995.

Margadant S., Guillermo F. *Introduction to the History of Mexican Law.* Dobbs Ferry, NY: Oceana; Mexico City: Libros Ocotepec, 1983.

Ots y Capdequí, José María. *El estado español en las Indias,* 3rd ed. Mexico City: Fondo de Cultura Económica, 1957.

Ots y Capdequí, José María. *Historia del derecho español en America y del derecho indiano.* Madrid: Aguilar, 1968.

Schäfer, Ernst. *El consejo real y supremo de las Indias: Historia y organization del consejo y de la casa de contratación de las Indias.* 2 vols. Vol. 1. Madrid: Marcial Pons Historia, 2003.

Solórzano Pereira, Juan de. *Política indiana* (1647). Madrid: Biblioteca Castro, 1996.

Tau Anzoátegui, Victor. *Nuevos horizontes en el estudio histórico del derecho indiano.* Buenos Aires, Argentina: Instituto de Investigaciones de Historia del Derecho, 1997.

Tau Anzoátegui, Victor. *El poder de la costumbre: Estudios sobre del derecho consuetudinario en América Hispana hasta la emancipación.* Buenos Aires, Argentina: Instituto de Investigaciones de Historia del Derecho, 2001.

Zavala, Silvio Arturo. *Las instituciones jurídicas en la conquista de América.* Madrid: Imprenta Heléncia, 1935.

R. Jovita Baber

LAW, CONCEPTS OF INTERNATIONAL

Colonialism has been a central preoccupation of international law since the very beginnings of the discipline. One of the first texts of modern international law, Francisco de Vitoria's work, *On the Indians Lately Discovered* (1532), addresses the complex legal problems that arose from Spanish claims to sovereignty over the Americas following Christopher Columbus's voyage. Drawing upon the naturalist and theological jurisprudence of the period, Vitoria argued that all peoples, including the Indians, were governed by a basic "natural law." The Indians, Vitoria argued, violated this law by, for instance, interfering with the Spanish right to trade in those areas, as a consequence of which it was legal to wage war against the Indians and dispossess them of their lands. This text establishes a clear pattern, for the conquest of non-European peoples and the exploitation of their resources were invariably justified by legal doctrines.

HISTORY

Contact between European and non-European peoples had taken place for thousands of years. As European presence into non-European areas intensified, beginning in the fifteenth and sixteenth centuries, legal doctrines were developed to manage more complex forms of inter-action between European and non-European states, and these extended, finally, to doctrines that could account for the acquisition of sovereignty over the non-European peoples. These doctrines, invariably, were created by Europeans, or adapted by Europeans, for their own purposes, although scholarship has shown that many principles relating to the law of treaties and the law of war, for example, were also developed and practiced by non-European states.

Imperial expansion intensified during the nineteenth century, and it was also during this period that positivism became established as the major jurisprudence of international law. Unlike naturalism, which argues that all states are subject to a higher universal law, positivism, in basic terms, asserts that the state is the creator of law, and cannot be bound by any law unless it has consented to it. There is no higher authority than sovereignty according to this system of jurisprudence.

Nominally, at least, under the system of naturalism, both European and non-European societies were bound by the universal natural law, which was the foundation of international law. Although non-European peoples had never been completely equal in this system of international law, positivist nineteenth-century jurists devised a series of formal doctrines that distinguished between "civilized states" that were full, sovereign members of international society, and "uncivilized states" that were not properly sovereign and were therefore deprived of international rights. In this way, racial and cultural criteria were used to exclude non-European societies from the realm of international law. Once non-European societies were so deprived of legal status, they lacked the personality to advance any legally cognizable objection to their conquest or dispossession, and were thus reduced to objects for conquest and exploitation.

During the latter part of the nineteenth century, when imperialism was at its height as European powers sought to expand and consolidate their empires, Western jurists developed and refined a variety of doctrines to justify imperialism. Under the doctrine of *terra nullius*, for instance, imperial powers claimed title to unoccupied lands by discovering them; often these lands were occupied by natives, but these peoples were deemed to be so inferior that they were considered less than human. As such, the lands could be simply possessed as belonging to nobody. War was a legitimate instrument of statehood during this period; as a consequence, Western states could acquire sovereignty over non-European peoples by military conquest. In other cases, imperial powers claimed that native chiefs had entered into treaties that gave those powers sovereignty over non-European territories and peoples. European states also used their superior military power to compel non-European states to provide them with extensive trading and other rights through unequal treaties. This practice was a source of enduring humiliation to the non-European states that were compelled to accept them.

Many of the legal doctrines used at this time dealt not so much with relations between European and non-European states (for the latter were regarded as simply lacking legal personality) but between European states who were intent on acquiring title over the non-European territories. These doctrines were developed in order to prevent conflict between European states over which states had proper title to a non-European state. Thus, at the Berlin Conference of 1884–85 the great European powers of the period met in Berlin to decide on the modalities by which Africa was to be occupied by European states. Within this scheme, certain non-European societies, such as China, were deemed to be "civilized" and yet possessing a sort of civilization of an entirely different character from that of the West. As a consequence, these societies too were excluded from the realm of international law, but deemed to possess certain rights under international law; they were quasi-sovereign.

Under the international law of the nineteenth century, non-European states could become incorporated into European international law only by being subjected to European sovereignty—by becoming colonies—or else, by changing their social, political, economic, and legal systems in such a manner as to ensure that they complied with European standards. This was the arduous task successfully undertaken by Japan, which was accepted into the "family of nations."

States such as Siam, which were never formally colonized, were nevertheless compelled to enter into unequal treaties, and to a system of capitulations, according to which foreigners were governed by their own law, rather than being subjected to the laws of the local sovereigns. By the end of the nineteenth century, European expansion had ensured that European international law had been established globally as the one system that applied to all societies.

The trauma of World War I (1914–1918) brought about many changes in international law and relations. The imperial character of the discipline was recognized and criticized by scholars and political leaders of the interwar period who denounced the international law of the nineteenth century that had legitimized colonial exploitation. The League of Nations attempted to formulate a new approach toward colonies that were now termed "backward territories." As a consequence, the territories of the defeated powers of the Ottoman Empire and Germany, rather than being acquired as colonies by the victorious powers, were placed under the authority of the Mandate System of the League of Nations. The purpose of this system was, through international supervision, to ensure "well-being and development" of the mandate territories; and it was even contemplated that some of these territories, such as Iraq, would become sovereign states.

Nationalist struggles in the third world had been profoundly affecting the international system, and by the time the United Nations had emerged, decolonization had become a central preoccupation of the international system. The United Nations responded by creating a number of institutional mechanisms for the furtherance of decolonization. The acquisition of independence by colonized states significantly changed the composition of the international community, as they became a majority in the United Nations system. These new states attempted to use their numbers in the General Assembly to establish a set of principles that would outlaw colonialism, and reverse its economic effects. The emerging law of international human rights provided one vehicle in which anticolonial initiatives could be furthered. Thus the right to self-determination was one of the principal human rights that the new states asserted and developed.

Further, the General Assembly passed a number of resolutions dealing with issues ranging from the outlawing of intervention, to the creation of a New International Economic Order.

The latter initiative was especially important, as the new states realized that political independence would be meaningless without corresponding economic independence. Thus the new states attempted to articulate a series of doctrines designed to enable them to regain control over their natural resources. Consequently, issues such as the terms on which a state could nationalize a foreign entity became particularly controversial. The arena of international economic law now became a central arena of struggle between the West and the new states, as the new states argued that this body of law had been created by the West to further its own interests. On the whole, the new states were unable to realize their ambitions to change international economic law, as General Assembly resolutions are not in themselves binding on states.

By the end of the 1980s, virtually all colonies had achieved independence. The end of formal colonialism, while extremely significant, did not, however, result in the end of colonial relations. Rather, in the view of third world leaders, colonialism was replaced by neocolonialism; third world states continued to play a subordinate role in the international system because they were economically dependent on the West and the rules of international economic law continued to ensure that this would be the case. U.S. and Soviet involvement in the affairs of third world states because of the ongoing cold war raised important issues as to the legal principles prohibiting intervention and the use of force.

The collapse of the Soviet Union and the intensification of globalization, together with civil wars in third world states—including the genocide in Rwanda—were prominent features of the 1990s, as was the view that democratic governance had become the international norm. The ascendancy of neoliberal economic policy and the creation of the World Trade Organization presented new challenges to third world states. International financial institutions such as the International Monetary Fund and the World Bank played an increasingly intrusive role in the economies of third world states, and indeed, attempted to use their considerable powers to reform the political and social structures of these states, this in the name of promoting good governance. In this way, these institutions attempted to use human rights law to further their particular policies. The demand made by the international financial institutions that these states reform their internal arrangements was compared by some scholars with the system of capitulations that had previously been used by European states to demand the reform of non-European states.

The twenty-first century war on terrorism suggests a new phase in the relations between the West (and the United States in particular) and the third world. Recourse by the Bush administration to the unilateral use of force, coupled with the intention to transform Middle Eastern states into democracies, raise new challenges to the law relating to the use of force, international humanitarian law, and human rights law, and it remains to be seen what impact the war on terrorism will have on international law.

THEORY

The conventional history of international law is based on the view that all the major doctrines and principles of international law originated in Europe, and were then gradually transferred to the non-European world as a consequence of European imperialism. Sovereignty is the foundation of international law, and the treaty of Westphalia of 1648 is traditionally viewed as articulating a version of sovereignty that has prevailed since then. The Westphalian model holds that all sovereigns are equal and, further, that intervention in the affairs of a sovereign state, most particularly in the exercise of its powers over its own territory, is prohibited. Colonization and decolonization, then, can be viewed as the processes by which Westphalian sovereignty was transferred to non-European states, which, upon acquiring independence, were viewed as formally equal with Western states.

More recent scholarship, however, has questioned some of these basic assumptions. Rather than viewing colonialism as peripheral to the discipline, this

The Palestinian Delegation in The Hague, February 23, 2004. *Delegates from Palestine attended a three-day hearing to discuss the legality of Israel's construction of a barrier wall in the occupied territories. The Israelis boycotted the hearing.*
MICHEL PORRO/GETTY IMAGES. REPRODUCED BY PERMISSION.

scholarship has argued that colonialism is central to the formation of international law. European international law could not have become universally applicable if not for colonialism. Colonialism justified itself as a civilizing mission. This project, then, was furthered through a structure of ideas by which European practices were asserted to be civilized and universal, and non-European societies were barbaric and particular.

International law participated in this mission by developing a set of doctrines by which distinctions could be made between the civilized and the uncivilized. This essential distinction having been made, the project then remained of civilizing the barbaric—and international law devised a set of doctrines, such as conquest or the protectorate regime—for the purposes of doing so. Further, scholars have argued that the very foundational doctrines, for example of sovereignty, were formulated in such a manner as to exclude the non-European world. This is most evident in the international law of the nineteenth century, when the question of who was sovereign was decided by using racial criteria. Sovereignty, then, might be viewed as containing within itself a series of mechanisms by which exclusion and discrimination can be

effected; and these mechanisms were developed for and animated by the purpose of disempowering the non-European world. Thus, while it is possible to view certain doctrines, such as conquest and the validity of unequal treaties, as being colonial because they were used for explicitly colonial purposes, this newer scholarship suggests that colonialism has shaped the very basic concepts of international law including those that appear to be neutral.

It is arguable that the standard of civilization that was such an important aspect of nineteenth-century law continues to shape international relations. Some scholars have called for the explicit reinstatement of the standard of civilization, civilization in this context being assessed by the extent to which a state complies with international human rights law. Others have argued that the civilizing mission continues today: the nineteenth-century division between the so-called civilized and uncivilized, excised from the vocabulary of international law on account of its racism, has now been reformulated in more acceptable ways in distinctions that play a profound role in contemporary international relations, between states that are developed and developing, liberal and nonliberal, postmodern and premodern.

Each of these distinctions refers to a particular set of concerns and areas of inquiry, and is supported by different doctrinal structures. In this way, even ostensibly neutral doctrines such as human rights, for instance, may be used for these purposes, to bring about transformations in the internal polities of a state. The ramifications of this scholarship are still being developed. Recent scholarship thus focused on questions of how colonial relations and structures of thought continue to operate in an ostensibly neutral setting. Further, jurists, principally from the non-European world, have continued their efforts to incorporate legal principles from very rich traditions of jurisprudence into the system of international law.

The war against terrorism launched by the United States, with its avowed attempt to transform the Middle East and its willingness to use preemptive force for the purposes of doing so, resemble in many ways a much earlier version of the civilizing mission. The question arises: How can international law respond to these challenges? The major issue remains whether international law has ever successfully rid itself of its imperial dimensions and whether or not it is possible to create a non-imperial international law.

SEE ALSO *Law, Colonial Systems of.*

BIBLIOGRAPHY

Alexandrowicz, Charles Henry. *An Introduction to the History of the Law of Nations in the East Indies.* Oxford: Clarendon Press, 1967.

Anand, R. P. *New States and International Law.* Delhi: Vikas Pub. House, 1972.

Anghie, Antony. *Imperialism, Sovereignty and the Making of International Law.* New York: Cambridge University Press, 2005.

Bedjaoui, Mohammed. *Towards a New International Economic Order.* New York: Holmes & Meier, 1979.

Gong, Gerrit W. *The Standard of "Civilization" in International Society.* Oxford: Clarendon Press, 1984.

Grovogui, Siba N'Zatioula. *Quasi-sovereigns and Africans: Race and Self-Determination in International Law.* Minneapolis: University of Minnesota Press, 1996.

Lindley, M. F. *The Acquisition and Government of Backward Territory in International Law: Being a Treatise on the Law and Practice of Colonial Expansion.* New York: Negroes University Press, 1969.

Onuma, Yasuaki, "When Was the Law of International Society Born? An Inquiry of the History of International Law from an Intercivilizational Perspective." *Journal of the History of International Law* 2 (2000): 1–68.

Vitoria, Francisco de. *Political Writings.* Edited by Anthony Pagden and Jeremy Lawrence. New York: Cambridge University Press, 1991.

Weeramantry, C. G. *Universalizing International Law.* Boston: M. Nijhoff Publishers, 2004.

Westlake, John. *Chapters on the Principles of International Law.* Cambridge, U.K.: The University Press, 1894.

Antony Anghie

LIBERIA

Liberia, a nation on the west coast of Africa, emerged out of America's antislavery and abolitionist campaign of the early nineteenth century. The abolitionist movement, which comprised blacks and white northern philanthropists and clergy, adopted a strategy of emancipation and colonization in its campaign. It focused not merely on abolishing slavery, but also on colonizing freed slaves in a territory of their own outside the United States, preferably in the continent of origin of their ancestors, Africa. Many elements within the abolitionist movement believed that colonization would provide ex-slaves the opportunity to live a decent and true life of freedom in a territory of their own. Yet, colonization was also intended to allay Southern fears of perceived threat that a large, free black population posed to white society. Colonization was thus a way of ridding America of unwanted black population.

EARLY U.S. INFLUENCE

The American Colonization Society (ACS), founded in December 1816, undertook the task of the colonization of free blacks in Liberia. The society raised money, and with additional financial backing from U.S. Congress, embarked on a project to plant a colony in West Africa where free blacks could be repatriated. In January 1822, the society established the first settlement on Cape Mesurado, which later became Monrovia. Although many American blacks opposed repatriation to Africa, emigrations to the region nevertheless continued, leading to establishment of other settlements. By 1850 about 5,000 settlers lived in various settlements, which had now become incorporated as the Commonwealth of Liberia with Monrovia as capital, named after James Monroe, the sitting president of the United States when the first settlement was established. As a result of the American antislavery naval patrol off the coast of West Africa, Liberia also became home to New World–bound slaves rescued aboard slave ships still illegally engaged in slave trafficking. By 1867 the U.S. Navy had resettled about 5,700 recaptives in Liberia.

Before 1848 the international status of Liberia was anomalous. It was neither a sovereign state nor a colony of the United States. A constitution of 1825 that gave administrative authority over the commonwealth to agents of the ACS made it a private colony. Liberia's status, however, changed on July 26, 1847, when it declared its independence under a constitution strikingly similar to that of the United States. Joseph Jenkins Roberts, who in 1842 had become the first black governor, was elected the first president of the sovereign state now called the Republic of Liberia. Before World War II (1939–1945), Liberia did not feature prominently in America's foreign and commercial relations. Even though Britain and other nations recognized Liberia's independence soon after it was declared, the United States did not do so until October 1862, a reflection of America's racial prejudice. Barring missionary and maritime activities in Liberia, the United States had no significant political and economic relations with the new African state. Despite historical ties, the United States lacked consistent interest in Liberia, and only responded sporadically to it, often during critical periods of challenge to its sovereignty.

Liberia did face such periods during its formative years. A number of times its sovereignty was threatened by European imperialism in Africa. Already active in the scramble for African territories in the nineteenth century, Britain and France desired to expand their conquests by annexing Liberia. Indeed, in 1883, Liberia lost a portion of its original territory in the area north of the Mano River to Sierra Leone, a British colony. Again, in 1895, the Liberian territory beyond Cape Palmas was annexed by the French colony of Ivory Coast. America's attitude to European colonial encroachment on Liberia was to oppose it and defend the nation's territorial integrity. On occasions, America's intervention in the incessant boundary disputes with the British and the French, whose colonial possessions literally encircled Liberia, did help to preserve its independence. For instance, in 1862, following an appeal from Monrovia, the United States sent a warship to West Africa to thwart possible British annexation of Liberia.

From the early years of the foundation of Liberia, the settlers faced constant uprising from the indigenous ethnic groups. The interior people were particularly fearful of the settlers' expansion and encroachment on their lands and the extension of government rule into their territories. In many instances, the United States provided Liberia with military assistance in putting down uprisings by indigenous groups such as the Kru and the Grebo.

U.S. INFLUENCE IN THE TWENTIETH CENTURY

Despite the United States' lack of consistent interest in Liberia, its sporadic support for the nation during critical times ensured that it exercised informal influence over the African nation. America's influence further increased when the Firestone Rubber Company established rubber plantations in the country in 1926. Liberia soon became an important source of rubber to the United States. Through its operations in the country, Firestone came to play a significant role in Liberia's political economy.

© MARYLAND CARTOGRAPHICS. REPRODUCED BY PERMISSION.

During World War II, Liberia assumed an unprecedented importance to the United States when it served America's economic and strategic needs. Liberian rubber and other products such as palm oil became of critical importance to the Allied powers after the Axis takeover of the traditional Far East market. Also, when the administration of President Franklin D. Roosevelt assumed the control of an air ferry operation across Africa through which American bombers and other military supplies reached the Allied forces in the Middle East, Liberian ports and airfields provided strategic points along the ferry route. Liberia's support for the American war effort was rewarded with American modernization projects in the country.

In the course of Liberian history, two distinct groups have constituted the society. First were the immigrant settlers called the Americo-Liberians, born and bred in the United States, and, therefore, Eurocentric in orientation and outlook. Second were the various indigenous ethnic groups original to the area. The Americo-Liberian minority group emerged as the dominant class with special privileges, to the detriment of the indigenous population, which it relegated to a subservient position. The Americo-Liberians developed commerce, education, and social services, and a political system tailored along American democracy. Many Americo-Liberians were successful farmers and wealthy merchants, controlling a booming trade along the coast. From independence in 1847, the Americo-Liberians exercised almost total economic and political dominance of Liberia. Their political party, the True Whig, held power until April 12, 1980, when a bloody coup d'état led by Master Sergeant Samuel Doe, an indigenous officer, terminated their unprecedented control of power.

SEE ALSO *Abolition of Colonial Slavery; African Slavery in the Americas; American Colonization Society.*

BIBLIOGRAPHY

Clegg, Claude Andrew. *The Price of Liberty: African Americans and the Making of Liberia.* Chapel Hill: University of North Carolina Press, 2004.

Gershoni, Yekutiel. *Black Colonialism: The Americo-Liberian Scramble for the Hinterland.* Boulder, CO: Westview Press, 1985.

Hyman, Lester S. *United States Policy Towards Liberia, 1822 to 2003: Unintended Consequences?* Cherry Hill, NJ: Africana Homestead Legacy Publishers, 2003.

Reef, Catherine. *This Our Dark Country: The American Settlers of Liberia.* New York: Clarion Books, 2002.

Saha, Santosh C. *Culture in Liberia: An Afrocentric View of the Cultural Interaction Between the Indigenous Liberians and the Americo-Liberians.* Lewiston, NY: E. Mellen Press, 1998.

Adebayo Oyebade

LI HONGZHANG
1823–1901

Li Hongzhang, a Chinese scholar-official, military leader, diplomat, and statesman, was born on February 15, 1823, in a village near Hefei Anhui Province. In 1844, he traveled to Beijing to study intensively under the direction of Zeng Guofan (1811–1872), his patron and mentor. Li became a *jinshi* (graduate of the highest order) in 1847, and he was admitted into the Hanlin Academy in 1849.

Li's rise began during the years of the Taiping Rebellion, when Qing government forces fought the forces of Hong Xiuquan (1812–1864), a self-proclaimed mystic and Christian convert who challenged Qing authorities. When the Taiping rebels reached the central provinces in 1853, Li returned to Anhui, where he raised a militia regiment, which was successful and attracted the attention of Zeng Guofan. Li was then appointed a circuit attendant *(daotai)* in Fujian Province, but in 1859 Zeng Guofan had him reassigned to the campaign against the Taiping. With the support of the "Ever Victorious Army"—a Chinese brigade, trained and commanded by foreigners, originally raised by Frederick Townsend Ward (d. 1862), later placed under the command of Charles George ("Chinese" Gordon, 1833–1885)—Li gained numerous victories, resulting in the surrender of Suzhou and the capture of Nanjing. Li was then appointed acting governor-general in Nanjing, where he established an arsenal.

In 1866 Li was ordered to suppress the Nian Rebellion (a remnant of the Taiping in Henan and Shandong) and finally succeeded. The next year, he was appointed governor-general of Huguang (the provinces of Hunan and Hubei) and held this post until 1870. After the Tianjin massacre (Catholic missionaries had been attacked by a group of anti-foreigners, who were disgusted by rumors of human sacrifice and the drinking of babies' blood), Li was appointed governor-general of the metropolitan province of Zhili, where he suppressed all antiforeign sentiments. To honor his services, Li was made imperial tutor and a member of the Grand Council. Most important, he was appointed superintendent of trade—and from that time until his death, he had a key role in Qing foreign politics: Li concluded several treaties and conventions (e.g., the Zhifu Convention of 1876 that ended the difficulties caused by the Margary affair, treaties with Peru and Japan, and the treaty with France to end the Sino-French War in 1886), and he directed Chinese policy in Korea. After the death of the Tongzhi emperor in 1875, Li played a major role in the coup d'état that put the Guangxu emperor on the throne.

Li was always aware of the necessity of strengthening the empire, modernizing transportation and industries, and reorganizing the armed forces. He raised a large armed force that was well drilled and well armed. Due to his prominent role in Qing policy toward Korea, Li was the leader of the Chinese forces in the Sino-Japanese War (1894–1895). China's defeat in this war undermined Li's position, and he was transferred to a nonpolitical post. In 1896 Li toured Europe and the United States.

Two years later, Li was appointed governor-general of Guangdong and Guangxi. In the aftermath of the antiforeigner Boxer Uprising (1900), he was urged to return to Beijing to negotiate a peace settlement with the allied powers, a multinational force that had suppressed the uprising. Li used all his power and ability to keep the indemnities as small as possible and to eliminate undue humiliations resulting from other conditions of the treaty. Li signed the treaty on September 7, 1901, and died in Beijing on November 7 of that year.

SEE ALSO *Qing Dynasty; Taiping Rebellion.*

BIBLIOGRAPHY

Chu, Samuel C., and Kwang-Ching Liu. *Li Hung-Chang and China's Early Modernization.* Armonk, NY: Sharpe, 1994.

Foster, John W., ed. *Memoirs of the Viceroy Li Hung Chang.* London: Constable, 1913.

Paine, S. C. M.. *The Sino-Japanese War of 1894–1895: Perceptions, Power, and Primacy.* Cambridge, U.K.: Cambridge University Press, 2003.

Monika Lehner

LIMA

On January 18, 1535, the Spanish conquistador Francisco Pizarro (ca. 1475–1541) founded La Ciudad de Los Reyes (The City of the Kings), or Lima, in the Rímac Valley, six miles inland from what would become the port of Callao. The valley had been part of Pachacamac, a precolonial Andean religious center. In contrast to Mexico, where the Spanish established and built their colonial capital upon the ruins of the imperial center of the Aztecs, Tenochtitlán, Lima was located far from the Andean Inca capital of Cuzco. Pizarro wanted a city and political center on the Pacific and conveniently connected to the sea routes to Panama, Cuba, and Spain.

In 1542 Lima was made the capital of the viceroyalty of Peru, in effect, the imperial political center of all of Spanish South America. From that year until the end of Spanish rule, forty-two viceroys resided in Lima in the Palace of the Viceroys, located on the north side of the Plaza de Armas. In the early twentieth century, this run-down colonial palace was reconstructed as the more stately, neocolonial Palacio de Gobierno, which became the residence of the president of the republic.

Pizarro set the first stone of Lima's cathedral on top of the Puma Inti Temple. "Pizarro ordered Juan Tello to distribute the plots in the order they were designed in the plan," wrote the Spanish soldier and historian Pedro de Cieza de León (ca. 1518–1560). "And they say that Juan Tello, who was knowledgeable in this, remarked that this land would be another Italy and in trade a second Venice because with such a quantity of gold and silver it was impossible for it to be otherwise" (1550/1998, p. 357). Lima, like all Spanish American cities, had been laid out according to a rational grid system inspired by Renaissance thinking on town planning. At the center of the city was a public square, the Plaza de Armas, with eight streets running outward from the corners of the square (and one additional street extending from the southern side of the plaza). Around the square were located the cathedral, the viceregal palace, and the houses of the municipal government. Proximity to the Plaza de Armas indicated the social prestige of the families who lived in fine houses of two stories. The orderliness of the city demonstrated the Spanish attempt to impose rational European structures upon a wild and natural America. In the early seventeenth century, Garcilaso de la Vega (1539–1616) commented, "The city was beautifully laid out, with a very large square, unless it be a fault that it is too big. The streets are broad and so straight that the country can be seen in four directions from any of the crossroads" (1617/1966, p. 776).

In 1593 Lima had a population of about 13,000 people. By 1614 the population had grown to over 25,000. Africans comprised the largest single group with 10,386, and with the addition of mulattos, the people the Spaniards called *negros* and *pardos*, exceeded 11,000. The next largest population group in the city was Spaniards, both American-born criollos and peninsular-born *chapetónes*, at 9,616. There were 1,978 native Andeans and only 192 mestizos (mixed Spanish-Indian offspring). The small number of mestizos suggests that many sons and daughters of mixed unions lived (and were therefore counted) as Indians or passed as Spaniards. At the beginning of the eighteenth century, there were more than 36,000 *limeños* (residents of Lima). By this time, Spaniards were in the majority with 56 percent of the population; Africans and mulattos made up 32 percent; and natives and mestizos constituted only 12 percent.

Compared to Mexico City, Lima was a small city but no less rich or monumental. In the mid-sixteenth century, the Spaniards had discovered the mountain of Potosí, the world's largest deposit of silver, which was controlled from Lima. Merchants, agriculturalists, and miners like Antonio López de Quiroga, acting as a business agent for others or on his own account, brought great sums of money to Lima. The Spanish historian Bernabé Cobo (1580–1657), in his mid-seventeenth-century *Historia de la fundación de Lima*, wrote of the "trade, splendour, and wealth" of the city. "The commerce and bustle which is always to be seen in this square is very great," wrote Cobo, referring to the Plaza de Armas. "The things to be found in this market are all that a well provisioned republic can desire for its sustenance and comfort" (quoted in Higgins 2005, p. 37).

There were in Lima in the seventeenth century fifteen or so *mayorazgos* (entailed estates) with incomes of 300,000 to 400,000 ducats yearly, but that was exceeded by the total income that flowed annually in salaries to ecclesiastics, royal officials, and military officers. The city's wealth was displayed in churches, houses, luxurious coaches, jewelry and gold and silver plate, tapestries, silks, brocades, fine linens, articles of worship, and African slaves.

The most impressive aspect of Lima in the seventeenth and eighteenth centuries was the size and splendor of its religious establishment. A contemporary report in 1613 stated that there were more than 400 secular priests, about 900 friars, and 1,366 nuns. They worked and lived in nineteen churches, monasteries, and nunneries. One in ten of Lima's inhabitants were clerics. Besides the cathedral and the palace of the archbishop, there were parish churches, monasteries, convents, the house and jail of the Inquisition, separate hospitals for Spaniards and Indians, a hospital for sailors, a house for orphans and another for abandoned women, a doctrinal school for Indians, and schools and colleges.

The church and monastery of San Francisco, with its beautiful twin towers, conventual buildings, and grounds, constituted a city within the city of Lima. It housed more than two hundred monks, with an additional large staff and numerous African slaves in its prime. The convent of the Nuns of the Incarnation housed more than four hundred religious women. "Many of the rich nobles' daughters came to learn good manners, and they leave to marry," wrote Pedro de León Portocarrero in the early seventeenth century. "In this convent there are splendid and intelligent women, endowed with a thousand graces, and all of them, both nuns and lay women, have Black women slaves to serve them" (quoted in Mills and Taylor 1998, p. 170).

Lima was also a city of manufactures and commerce. Artisans and merchants tended to concentrate on particular streets according to specialization. There was the street of the silversmiths, the hatters' ally, the street of the mantas (cloaks), and the main one, Merchants' Street, which had at least forty shops. Many observers described Lima as a city overflowing in wealth. "I am astonished at what they tell me about Castile," noted a resident of Lima in 1590, "that it is finished, and I believe it from what people say here. Here we go neither hungry nor thirsty, nor do we lack for clothing." Another Lima resident writing home to Spain was upset by the news of "the hardship that you suffer in Spain. Since we want for nothing over here, we can hardly believe it" (Kamen 2003, pp. 309–310).

Late colonial Lima was not the great city it had been during its seventeenth-century "silver age." Devastating earthquakes, particularly in 1655, 1687, and 1746, severely damaged the city. The quake of 1746 killed some 6,000 residents and brought down most of the important buildings in the city. After these earthquakes, and the great quake of 1940, few genuine "colonial" buildings remain in Lima.

In 1739 Spain established the new viceroyalty of New Granada (with the viceregal capital of Bogotá) and in 1776 the viceroyalty of La Plata (with the viceregal capital of Buenos Aires). This redesign of the political map of Spanish South America not only reduced the prestige and power of Lima but also broke its near commercial monopoly. Goods no longer had to be imported at Callao and Lima and transported by mule train up and down the Andes as far as the port city of Buenos Aires.

By 1812 the population of Lima was close to 64,000. About 18,000 were Spaniards. Spaniards were always a minority in their colonial capital. In this late colonial year, the large majority of *limeños* were African slaves and free blacks and mulattos—over 30,000 people. There were slightly more than 10,000 Indians living in the city and almost 5,000 mestizos.

During the wars of independence in the years leading up to 1821, Lima quartered the royalist army of some 70,000 men. Despite this occupation, Lima's Creoles demonstrated little interest in revolution and independence. Creole fear of African slaves, blacks and mulattos, and Indians and mestizos—the exploited and subordinated majority—produced a very cautious and conservative local elite. In 1821 when Lima, and Peru, was liberated from Spanish rule and the republic was established, it was the result of the invasion of Peru by a revolutionary general from Argentina, José de San Martín (1778–1850).

SEE ALSO *Inca Empire; Lima; Mining, the Americas; Pizarro, Francisco; Túpac Amaru, Rebellion of.*

BIBLIOGRAPHY

Cieza de León, Pedro de. *The Discovery and Conquest of Peru: Chronicles of the New World Encounter* (1550). Edited and translated by Alexandra Parma Cook and Noble David Cook. Durham, NC: Duke University Press, 1998.

de la Vega, Garcilaso. *Royal Commentaries of the Incas and General History of Peru* (1609/1617). Translated by Harold V. Livermore. Austin: University of Texas Press, 1966.

Doering, Juan Gunther, and Guillermo Lohmann Villena. *Lima.* Madrid: Editorial MAPFRE, 1992.

Higgins, James. *Lima: A Cultural History.* New York: Oxford University Press, 2005.

Kamen, Henry. *Empire: How Spain Became a World Power, 1492–1763.* New York: HarperCollins, 2003.

Mills, Kenneth, and William B. Taylor, eds. "Pedro de León Portocarrero's Description of Lima, Peru." In *Colonial Spanish America: A Documentary History,* 165–175. Wilmington, DE: SR Books, 1998.

Charles F. Walker
Thomas Benjamin

LINGGADJATI AGREEMENT

The Linggadjati Agreement was agreed upon by a Dutch delegation and representatives of the Republic of Indonesia on November 12, 1946, in the hill station Linggadjati (Linggarjati) near Ceribon on Java. The agreement was signed in Batavia (Jakarta) on March 25, 1947.

Dutch authorities returning to the Dutch East Indies after World War II (1939–1945) soon realized they were not in a position to restore Dutch authority on Java and Sumatra, which was controlled by the Republic of Indonesia. This Republic had proclaimed its independence on August 17, 1945. Lieutenant Governor-General H. J. van Mook (1894–1965), the highest-ranking Dutch administrator in the East, realized that negotiations with Sukarno (1901–1970), president of the Indonesian Republic, were inevitable. However, the Dutch government in the Netherlands, together with most Dutch political parties, was reluctant to talk to Sukarno, especially given his pro-Japanese stance during the war.

Under strong British pressure, the Dutch reluctantly started negotiations with the Republic of Indonesia. Van Mook studied events in French Indochina to find a solution for the Dutch problems in Indonesia. He wanted to recognize the Republic of Indonesia as having de facto authority over Java and Sumatra in exchange for the willingness from the Indonesian side to accept a federal Indonesian state that would be a partner with the Kingdom of the Netherlands. Within the federal Indonesian state the Dutch would at least control Borneo (Kalimantan) and the eastern part of the archipelago. The model for this proposal was the Fédération Indochinoise (Indochina Federation) and the Union Française (French Union), which were designed to maintain French control over Vietnam.

After the Dutch elections of May 1946, the newly formed Dutch coalition government decided to establish a "commission-general" in order to start negotiations with the Republic of Indonesia. The members of this commission-general were former prime minister Wim Schermerhorn (1894–1977), Max van Poll (1881–1948), and Feike de Boer (1892–1976). Their assignment was to adapt the constitutional arrangements for the Dutch East Indies to postwar realities without giving up the Dutch imperial mission.

The commission-general left for Indonesia in November 1946 and started negotiations with a delegation of the Republic of Indonesia, which included Sukarno and Sutan Sjahrir (1909–1966), in Linggadjati. Difficult and long negotiations followed on the future relationship between the Netherlands and Indonesia. In the end, van Mook laid down a compromise in which the "United States of Indonesia" would become a "sovereign and democratic state" within a Dutch-Indonesian Union, which would concentrate on economic and cultural cooperation. The United States of Indonesia would have three states: the Republic of Indonesia, East-Indonesia, and Borneo. The Dutch would recognize the Indonesian Republic as having all authority on Java and Sumatra.

Sukarno accepted this compromise in order to avoid a long and difficult armed struggle against the Netherlands and, with the knowledge of his Republic, would control the vast majority of the population of Indonesia and would therefore soon control the United States of Indonesia. The Dutch commission-general accepted the compromise because a possible war was avoided and a close future relationship between the Netherlands and Indonesia seemed to be assured.

In the Netherlands, conservative forces strongly opposed the Linggadjati Agreement. The commission-general seemed to have "given away" the Dutch East Indies to an irresponsible and unreliable group of Indonesian nationalists. The Dutch government decided to amend and to interpret the agreement in order to assure the Netherlands a reasonable future influence in Indonesia. The Dutch minister for overseas territories, J. A. Jonkman (1891–1976), issued a statement in parliament in which the Linggadjati Agreement was called merely a basis for further discussions and Dutch overseas ambitions were reasserted. The Social-Democratic Party and the Catholic Party proposed a motion that made clear that the future United States of Indonesia would be a part of a sovereign Dutch-Indonesian Union. Parliament passed this motion, by which the Netherlands definitely gave a new interpretation to the Linggadjati Agreement—without changing the precise words of the agreement itself.

Within the Republic of Indonesia, Sukarno faced his own problems in gaining support for the Linggadjati Agreement. Radical elements within Indonesia were supported by the leader of the army, General Sudirman (1915–1950), in opposing the agreement, which did not bring immediate and full independence to Indonesia. However, Sukarno succeeded in convincing the Indonesian Parliament that the Linggadjati Agreement was a stepping stone toward full independence. On March 5, 1947, the parliament accepted the agreement, but only with the explicit understanding that the Indonesian government should work toward the "liberation" of Borneo and East-Indonesia by making these areas a part of the Indonesian Republic "as soon as possible."

On March 25 the Linggadjati Agreement was finally signed by the Netherlands and Indonesia in the Rijswijk Palace in Jakarta. In reality, two different agreements were signed. The Dutch signed the agreement as interpreted by the Dutch government and the Dutch Parliament, which meant they agreed on forming a sovereign and powerful Dutch-Indonesian Union in which the United States of Indonesia and the Republic of Indonesia only played a minor role. The Indonesians signed the agreement in its more original form, accepting only a symbolic Dutch-Indonesian Union and wanting a fully sovereign United States of Indonesia in which the Republic of Indonesia would play a dominant role.

This fundamental difference of opinion on the future of Indonesia could not be bridged in the months following the signing of the Linggadjati Agreement. Finally, the Dutch government decided in June 1947 to fight a war against the Republic of Indonesia, hoping "moderate" Indonesians would grasp the opportunity to take over power in the Republic. The Dutch failed to understand that "moderate" Indonesians also desired full independence. In December 1948 a second war followed, after which international pressure, military failure, and the loss of political influence in Indonesia made the Dutch accept the independence of Indonesia along the lines of the original Linggadjati Agreement.

In December 1949 the United States of Indonesia was formed. The new country was linked with the Netherlands through a symbolic Dutch-Indonesian Union. This political construction only lasted for a few years: the United States of Indonesia was soon replaced by a unitary Republic of Indonesia. Indonesia left the Dutch-Indonesian Union in 1954.

SEE ALSO *Dutch-Indonesian Wars; Indonesian Independence, Struggle for.*

BIBLIOGRAPHY

Cheong, Yong Mun. *H. J. van Mook and Indonesian Independence: A Study of His Role in Dutch-Indonesian Relations, 1945–48.* The Hague: Nijhoff, 1982.

Doel, H. W. van den. *Afscheid van Indië: De val van het Nederlandse Imperium in Azië.* Amsterdam: Prometheus, 2001.

Lapian, A. B., and P. J. Drooglever, eds. *Menelusuri jalur Linggarjati: Diplomasi Dalam Perspektif Sejarah.* Jakarta, Indonesia, 1992.

Smit, C., ed. *Het Dagboek van Schermerhorn: Geheim verslag van Prof. Dr. Ir. W. Schermerhorn als voorzitter der Commissie-Generaal voor Nederlands-Indië, 20 September 1946–7 Oktober 1947.* Groningen, Netherlands, 1970.

Wal, S. L. van der, ed. *Officiële Bescheiden Betreffende de Nederlands-Indonesische Betrekkingen, 1945–1950.* 20 vols. Gravenhage, Netherlands: Nijhoff, 1971–1996.

Wim van den Doel

LITERATURE, MIDDLE EASTERN

Twenty-first-century Middle Eastern (primarily Arabic, Persian, and Turkish) literature encompasses a rich variety of genres, whose maturation has profited from internal and external influences upon this literature over the past fourteen centuries. Modern Arabic literature addresses the full range of human experience, often through a realist approach that employs the Arabic language in ways ranging from the most formal to the most colloquial. While Turkish and Persian literatures have both followed individual trajectories since the modern period, they too evince a similar range with respect to genre and employment of language.

Although today these three literatures appear as discrete entities, they share a long early religious, cultural, and political history. While pre-Islamic Persian and Turkish literatures would prove influential when taken up by writers in the first few centuries after Islam, pre-Islamic Arabic literature provided the first literary model. Pre-Islamic Arabic literature is characterized by the *mua'allaqat* (ca. mid 500s–early 600s CE), a collection of poems from the Arabian Peninsula renowned for their beauty. These poems are odes to the sorrows of lost love, using such tropes as abandoned campsites to evoke memories of a beloved. That of Imru al-Qays (c. mid-500s), perhaps the best known, begins: "Come, let us cry from the remembrance of a love and a home." Although poetic themes have changed over the centuries, the ode *(qasida)* has enjoyed continuing popularity through the twentieth century.

Poetry remained the dominant literary form during the "classical" period of the Abbasid (750–1258), with romantic praise of a beloved, whether male or female, the most common theme. A folk literature also emerged, involving heroic or adventure narratives; *A Thousand and One Nights* is the most renowned example. This collection of stories, of which "Ali Baba and the Forty Thieves" and "Aladdin" are perhaps the best known to Western readers, began to take shape around the year 1000. It drew together stories with roots in India, Persia, and the Arab world. Meanwhile, prose matured as a literary form, a development attributed to the Persian bureaucrats employed by the Abbasid court. Authors like Ibn Muqaffa (died ca. 760) and al-Jahiz (776–868/9) brought Persian narrative forms, stylistics, themes, and subject matter into the world of classical Arabic literature.

With the political fragmentation of the Muslim world in the 1200s, cultural contributions from Persia, India, western Asia, and North Africa intensified, entering the literature primarily through Sufi figures like the eminent Persian poet Hafiz (ca. 1352–1389). For the Levant and the Persian Gulf—the heart of the Arab world—the emerging Ottoman Empire provided the most significant influence. The Ottoman Empire aided the development of Arabic literature by, like the earlier Islamic empires, serving as a bridge joining peoples and cultures across its great geographic expanse.

Napoléon Bonaparte's (1769–1821) invasion of Egypt in 1798, often described as the beginning of the modern era, also marked the shift from domestic to external literary traditions as dominant influences on Middle Eastern literature. The introduction of European colonial regimes, coupled with the modernizing efforts of the Ottoman state, opened the region to European political, economic, and cultural influences on a much broader scale than in any previous historical moment. Whether in the form of European themes or genres, the incorporation of European words or the adoption of European languages wholesale, or literary responses to the new reality of colonial regimes, European influences on Middle Eastern literature began appearing toward the end of the century.

The most notable effect of European influence was the emergence of the novel as a primary literary genre of modern Arabic literature. Imported European novels first appeared in the mid-nineteenth century. By the late nineteenth century, the genre had attracted an upper- and upper-middle-class following. The reputed "first" Middle Eastern novel, Muhammad Hussein Heykal's (1890–1956) *Zaynab*, was published in 1913 and was followed by numerous novels published in Ottoman Turkish and Arabic.

The other characteristic genre of modern Arabic literature, the short story, also emerged in this period. Drawing upon the *hakawati* (story-telling) tradition found in folk literature, the modern short story has been employed to offer social and political commentary on the difficulties faced by ordinary citizens—particularly those in urban areas. Finally, the early and mid-twentieth century saw the blossoming of memoirs and autobiographic literature, which blended elements of the *tarjuma* (a type of formalized curriculum vitae often used to summarize the life achievements of eminent men), the literary inheritance of the *sira* (the narrative of the life of the Prophet Muhammad), and the more personal elements of naturalistic nineteenth-century poetry into autobiographic and memoir genre traditions.

Drama and poetry were also affected by nineteenth- and twentieth-century European literary movements.

Absurdist and existential dramatic styles have aided works whose political critiques needed to be safely cloaked in abstraction. On the other hand, an often gritty realism has enabled the production of a rich collection of novels and short stories, whose narratives are steeped in the daily lives of ordinary people. In poetry, the introduction of free verse style, breaking the tight conventions of the traditional forms, has spurred the emergence of new themes: the dramas of ordinary life, emotional responses to the loss of Palestine, and other topics grounded in the personal experience of the author rather than conventional rhetoric found in earlier eras.

A list of modern Middle Eastern literature must begin with the Egyptian author Naguib Mahfouz (Najib Mahfudh, b. 1911), who has exercised a peerless influence over twentieth-century Arabic literature. His best-known works include the Cairo trilogy (*Palace Walk, Palace of Desire, Sugar Street*), published from 1956 to 1957, and *Children of the Alley* (1959). A similarly eminent figure is Jordanian Abdelrahman (Abd al-Rahman) Munif (1933–2004), whose *Cities of Salt* (1984), an epic portrayal of the changes brought to a desert community by the advent of oil drilling there, was rewarded for its authenticity with bans in several countries.

The Palestinian short-story author Ghassan Kanafani (1936–1972) wrote a number of pieces that demonstrate the richness of the genre, of which "Men in the Sun" (1963) is the most widely known. Egyptian author Nawal el Saadawi (b. 1930) is best known in the United States for her activist writing on the oppression of women in the Arab world; within the region she is also known as a novelist, whose works, including *Woman at Point Zero* (1975), often treat similar themes. The books of Lebanese novelists Hanan al-Shaykh (b. 1945) and Ghada Samaan (b. 1942) are also often described as concerned with women's experiences, particularly during the Lebanese civil war: Samaan's *Beirut '75* (1974) can be found on university reading lists in Damascus, for example, while al-Shaykh's *Beirut Blues* (1995) uses the war to revisit themes of frustration and emptiness that she first addressed in *The Story of Zahra* (1986) and other works.

Some of the most well-known writers of contemporary Middle Eastern literature write in other languages: Palestinian novelist Anton Shammas (b. 1951) and emerging writer Sayed Kashua (Qashu', b. 1975) both write in Hebrew; Algerian author Assia Djebar (b. 1936) and Persian graphic writer Marjane Satrapi (b. 1969) write in French.

Poetry continues to play a significant role in modern Middle Eastern literature. The twentieth century was a time of great evolution in poetic styles, from the mysticism of the Lebanese-born writer Gibran Khalil Gibran

(1883–1931) to the gentle experiments with form and expression made by Egyptian author Ahmad Shawqi (1868–1932), the Palestinian poet Ibrahim Tuqan (1905-1941), and others in the interwar period. The best known figures of the later twentieth century have been those who have turned their mastery of language and rhythm to explore new poetic forms while expressing often sharply critical political and social commentary.

The Palestinian poet Mahmud Darwish (b. 1942) remains one of the most active voices in contemporary Arabic poetry; *Memory for Forgetfulness* (1982) is perhaps his most famous *diwan* (collection of poetry). The Syrian poet Nizar Qabbani (1923–1998), known for his often frosty relations with his own and other state governments, wrote political poetry in the guise of romance and quasi-erotic pieces. His works are often misrecognized as the latter in the West; translated collections of his poems often bear misleading references to love in their titles.

In addition to fiction, the genre of memoirs has proven particularly rich in the later twentieth and early twenty-first century. The best known and most frequently cited is eminent mid-century Egyptian author Taha Hussein's (1889–1973) autobiography, *The Days* (1929–1955), which follows the course of his life in three parts. Most other memoirs, however, focus on the author's childhood. In the late-twentieth century the genre began opening to women, following the publication of Moroccan writer Fatima Mernissi's (b. 1940) *Dreams of Trespass* (1994). (The childhood memoir of Turkish feminist and intellectual Halide Edib Adivar [1884–1964], *House with Wisteria*, was published in the mid-1900s.) Well-known Palestinian poet Fadwa Tuqan (1917–2003; *A Mountainous Journey*, 1985), Syrian author Siham Tergeman (*Daughter of Damascus*, 1994), and Moroccan short-story writer Leila Abouzeid (b. 1950; *Return to Childhood*, 1993) and others have published memoirs.

SEE ALSO *Clothing and Fashion, Middle East; Education, Middle East; Ideology, Political, Middle East.*

BIBLIOGRAPHY

Badawi, Muhammad. *A Short History of Modern Arabic Literature.* Oxford; Clarendon, 1993.

Cachia, Pierre. *An Overview of Modern Arabic Literature.* Edinburgh, U.K.: Edinburgh University Press, 1990.

Jayyusi, Salma, ed. *Modern Arabic Poetry: An Anthology.* New York: Columbia University Press, 1987.

Strauss, Johann. "Romanlar, ah! Romanlar! Les débuts de la lecture moderne dans l'Empire Ottoman." *Turcica* 26 (1994): 125–163.

Andrea L. Stanton

LONDON MISSIONARY SOCIETY

The London Missionary Society (LMS), established in 1795, was one of a number of voluntary foreign missionary societies formed throughout Western Europe at the end of the eighteenth century. The evangelical revivals that inspired lay humanitarian activity at home, coupled with an increased sense of Britain's moral responsibilities to populations in its growing empire, led to the wave of foreign missions that crested across the nineteenth century. The founders of the LMS had been preceded by the founders of the Baptist Missionary Society (1792), and were followed by evangelical colleagues who established organizations in Scotland and England—in Scotland, the Edinburgh and Glasgow Missionary Societies (both 1796), and in England, the Society for Missions to Africa and the East (1799), which from 1812 was known as the Church Missionary Society. The LMS joined with the Commonwealth Missionary Society to become the Congregational Council for World Mission in 1966, and that organization evolved into the Council for World Mission in 1977.

The nondenominational founding principles of the Missionary Society, as the LMS was known until it was renamed in 1818, were preserved throughout its institutional history despite the fact that the organization quite quickly became almost exclusively associated with the Congregational Churches in Britain. Membership of the society was based on annual subscription. Members met annually in May to deliberate, to vote on administrative decisions, to be introduced to and send off new missionaries and those on furlough, and to celebrate the life and work of the institution. The formal administrative work of the LMS was undertaken by a voluntary Board of Directors, administration was managed by a Home Secretary, and a Foreign Secretary exchanged personal and business correspondence with the missionaries employed by the society all over the world. In 1810 this core organizational structure was expanded to include a growing number of committees, some region-specific, which oversaw the increasingly complex work. These included an Examinations committee—the work of which was to screen and train mission candidates. In 1875 this group was joined by a Ladies' board, which functioned until 1891, when it was replaced by a ladies' examination committee after women were allowed to join the Board of Directors. These central committees were also supported by a network of voluntary local auxiliary groups, organized and supported mostly by women, that disseminated information about missions and raised the funds—in small increments—needed to support administrative and mission work. What seems clear is that women's decision-making power, both in Britain and in foreign work, lay in their ability to exercise

Robert Morrison (1782–1834). *The Scottish missionary Robert Morrison (right), the first Protestant missionary in China, is shown in the early 1800s with Chinese assistants as they prepare Morrison's translation of the Bible.* **HULTON ARCHIVE/GETTY IMAGES. REPRODUCED BY PERMISSION.**

skill in working within what was a male-dominated institutional organization. As such, women operated through familial and social networks, and when attempting to influence decision making were bound by the necessity of avoiding the sort of direct confrontations they were certain to lose.

The LMS sent its first missionaries abroad in 1796, to Tahiti, and by 1945 it had sent 1,800 men and women to engage in foreign mission work. LMS missions to the South Seas were marked by the establishment of small but vibrant Christian communities, like those that resulted in the self-governing church in Papua. They were also marked by dramatic events, such as the fate that befell John Williams, who joined the mission in 1817 and became one of the LMS's most famous martyrs. Williams's criticism of existing LMS practices, his broad travel and dynamic evangelism, and his violent death in Erromanga in 1839 made him an inspiration to future mission workers; the society subsequently named a series

of seven missionary boats after him, and wooden ship-shaped boxes labeled "the John Williams" were used by mission workers collecting the change that supported mission work. A mission venture was established in eastern Siberia in 1818 when two missionaries and their wives traveled to Irkutsk to evangelize the Buryat before moving on to work with Mongols in China. Other missions were established in Greece and Malta, in North America, and to the Jews in London during this era.

The main fields of LMS activity across the nineteenth century were India, China, Southeast Asia, the Pacific, Madagascar, Central and Southern Africa, Australia, and the Caribbean. The LMS hired a significant number of Scottish missionaries throughout its history. Because Scots tended to be better educated than their English colleagues, they made up the majority of the Society's medical missionaries and provided the hearts and hands for work in the east, where better-trained candidates were deemed necessary to counter the arguments of Hinduism and Islam. LMS work in India was first begun in 1798 outside of Calcutta; work was initiated after that in western India, and then in southern India, in 1805. LMS work in China was begun by Robert Morrison, who arrived in Canton (Guangzhou), the only port open to foreigners, in 1807; he and the colleagues who followed him focused on translation and publishing. However, the Qing Imperial government was successful in refusing Westerners entry to the rest of China until the mid-nineteenth century, and it was not until after 1843 that LMS workers began to slowly work their way into mainland China. LMS missionaries were present in the early days of the Sierra Leone settlement, but sustained LMS activity in Africa began in 1799 in Southern Africa, and spread north. A series of LMS missionaries in Southern Africa offered an important and sustained critique of settler actions, colonial activity, and imperial policy; David Livingstone, the society's most famous popular missionary, traveled north from there in his famous journeys as missionary and explorer. In each of the territories the LMS operated in, a combination of preaching, institution-building, and social outreach work was met by a variety of responses ranging from acceptance to adaptation, to outright rejection.

Both because of and in spite of the efforts of mission societies like the LMS, Christian churches were established throughout the world that exhibited beliefs and practices quite distinct from anything found in the West. Since their establishment, many of these churches have developed to a size and with a dynamism that has outstripped the Western church.

SEE ALSO *Missionaries, Christian, Africa; Missions, China; Missions, in the Pacific.*

BIBLIOGRAPHY

Over two thousand boxes of archival material generated by the LMS are deposited at the School of Oriental and African Studies at the University of London. For information about the collection, see *http://www.soas.ac.uk/library/index.cfm* and *http://www.mundus.ac.uk/sites/4.htm.*

Goodall, Norman. *A History of the London Missionary Society, 1895–1945.* London: Oxford University Press, 1954.

Lovett, Richard. *The History of the London Missionary Society, 1795–1895.* 2 vols. London: Oxford University Press, 1899.

Porter, Andrew. *Religion versus Empire? British Protestant Missionaries and Overseas Expansion, 1700–1914.* Manchester, U.K.: Manchester University Press, 2004.

Semple, Rhonda. *Missionary Women: Gender, Professionalism, and the Victorian Idea of Christian Mission.* Woodbridge, U.K.: Boydell and Brewer, 2003.

Thorne, Susan. *Congregational Missions and the Making of an Imperial Culture in Nineteenth Century-England.* Stanford, CA: Stanford University Press, 1999.

Thorogood, Bernard, ed. *Gales of Change: Responding to a Shifting Missionary Context: The Story of the London Missionary Society, 1945–1977.* Geneva: WCC Publications, 1994.

Rhonda A. Semple

LUANDA

SEE *Colonial Cities and Towns, Africa*

LUGARD, FREDERICK JOHN DEALTRY
1858–1945

Frederick Lugard was a British military and colonial administrator. Lugard had a successful military career: he joined the army in 1878 and in 1905 became a colonel (with the local rank of brigadier general). He served in the Afghan war (1879–1880), in the Sudan campaign against Mahdist forces (1884–1885), and in Burma (1886–1887). In 1888 he was wounded in combat during an expedition organized by white settlers against Arab slave traders in the region of Lake Nyasa. One year later he was recruited by the Imperial British East Africa Company (I.B.E.A.), which employed him in geographical explorations and in further initiatives to crush slavery and the slave trade in the mainland territory under the jurisdiction of Zanzibar.

Lugard's fate changed when the Company dispatched him into Buganda (1890) as its representative. Lugard succeeded in urging Kabaka Mwanga to accept the I.B.E.A.'s protection. Lugard's memorandums and his addresses to various bodies did much to prevent the evacuation of Uganda. In the dispute between Christian missions, that beside the denominational differences involved Anglo-French rivalry, Lugard supported and armed the Protestant party against the pro-French Catholics headed by Mwanga, but throughout the whole affair he was anxious to reach a friendly settlement.

In 1894, the young but already notorious captain was sent by the Royal Niger Company to the future Nigeria. Even more than Uganda, Nigeria, especially northern and western Nigeria, with its well-established political infrastructure, proved to be an excellent setting for implementing Lugard's colonial design, known as *indirect rule.* The core idea was to utilize tribal chiefs as part of the colonial administration, while preserving their cultural identity and social separation. Colonialism as a governmental structure was welcomed and supported by westernized African elites, the so-called "collaborators," who essentially endorsed the new system brought by

Lord Lugard at the London Zoo, June 1934. *Frederick John Dealtry Lugard (standing center), the British diplomat and colonial administrator of Africa, accompanies a delegation of West African chiefs on a visit to the London Zoo in 1934.* **HULTON ARCHIVE/ GETTY IMAGES. REPRODUCED BY PERMISSION.**

Europeans; for functions like justice, tax collection, and local public order the tribal chiefs were more suitable than anybody else because of their effective control of territory and inhabitants. Where necessary—for example in the Niger delta region, where stateless societies prevailed—the British administration did not hesitate to *invent* tribes, then create *warrant chiefs* in order to establish the model elaborated by Lugard—which in the meantime had become the dominant British approach in tropical Africa. Lugard combined administrative and military duties, overwhelming and subduing the African kingdoms and opposing rival European powers, mainly France and Germany. Between 1897 and 1899 he commanded the West African Frontier Force.

In 1900, when the Royal Niger Company's charter expired—thus concluding the private phase of colonialism—Lugard was appointed high commissioner of the Northern Territories of Nigeria. The expansion of British forces in the region was challenged by the powerful sultan of Sokoto and other Fula monarchs, who were galvanized by Islam. After Lugard mounted a campaign against them, however, both the emir of Kano and the sultan

of Sokoto were induced to accept British protectorate status. This eased the occupation of the entire region. At the end of Lugard's term in office, in 1906, the whole country was administered by the former rulers under the supervision of British residents.

After an interlude as governor of Hong Kong, in 1912 Lugard returned to Africa as governor of the Northern and Southern Provinces of Nigeria. There he achieved his greatest triumph as a colonial administrator, by unifying and amalgamating the two huge territories despite their profound differences. The operation was completed in a few years and on January 1, 1914, Lugard, by then Sir Frederick (and later Lord) Lugard, became governor-general of Nigeria, which he administered during World War I and up to 1919, when he retired.

In 1920 Lugard was named privy councilor. Between 1922 and 1936 he served as a member of the permanent mandates commission of the League of Nations, offering his great experience in colonial affairs to an international ambit. Lugard published a partly autobiographical book about the British colonial expansion (*The Rise of Our East*

African Empire, 1893), issued remarkable reports on Northern Nigeria, and expounded his ideas on colonial administration, which were perhaps influenced by George Goldie's enterprises and arguments, in *The Dual Mandate in Tropical Africa* (1922). The core of the doctrine he espoused in this seminal book is summarized by his assertion that "Europe is in Africa for the mutual benefit of her own industrial classes, and of the native races in their progress to a higher plane; that the benefit can be made reciprocal and that it is the aim of the civilized administration to fulfil this dual mandate." To some extent, however, indirect rule was the evidence that colonialism, despite its disruption of traditional statehood, was not omnipotent and needed to rely on the same personnel and institutions that had defended in vain their own power and the freedom of their polities.

SEE ALSO *Dual Mandate, Africa; Indirect Rule, Africa; Warrant Chiefs, Africa.*

BIBLIOGRAPHY

Perham, Margery. *Lugard: Master of Modern Africa.* Vol. 1: *The Years of Adventure, 1858–1898.* London: Collins, 1956.

Giampaolo Calchi-Novati

Patrice Lumumba (1925–1961). Patrice Lumumba, leader of the Congolese National Movement, addresses troops in Stanleyville, July 18, 1960. AP IMAGES. REPRODUCED BY PERMISSION.

LUMUMBA, PATRICE
1925–1961

Lumumba, the son of a poor peasant, was born in Onalua (near Katako-Kombe, in East Kasaï, Congo) on July 2, 1925, when Congo was under Belgian colonial rule. During his primary school years, Lumumba ran away or was expelled from several missionary institutions. But at the same time, he was ambitious and driven by real intellectual hunger. On arriving in Stanleyville (now Kisangani) in July 1944, he attended evening classes and became a voracious reader. He was employed in the postal service, but also had an active public life outside of work.

Lumumba became the founder and president of several Congolese cultural, social, and political organizations, including the local *Amicale Libérale.* In this capacity, he met the Belgian Minister of Colonies, Auguste Buisseret, when the latter was visiting Congo in 1954. Thanks to the minister's help, he participated in a delegation of Congolese visiting Belgium in 1956—a rare privilege for a black person at the time. Upon his return, Lumumba was arrested on the charge of theft while performing his duties as a postmaster. He was sent to jail and lost his job. However, these events did not break his spirit, nor impact his growing popularity among the Congolese.

After his release, in June 1957, he went to the capital, Léopoldville (Kinshasa), where he found a job as a salesman for a local brewery. More than ever before, Lumumba engaged in public and even outright political activities. In October 1958 he was co-founder and provisional president of the *Mouvement National Congolais* (MNC), which immediately became one of the most influential formations of nascent Congolese nationalism. In December 1958, he participated in the Pan-African Conference at Accra (Ghana's capital). In July 1959 internal disagreements led to the split-up of the MNC into two rival organizations, Lumumba's wing being more radical.

The so-called MNC-Lumumba was one of the few Congolese parties being organized on a non-ethnical basis; it stressed the necessity of Congolese unity, as opposed to confederalist or separatist tendencies. In a climate of growing hostility toward Belgian colonial rule, Lumumba was arrested once again after riots in Stanleyville in October 1959. On January 21, 1960, he was condemned to six months' imprisonment, but was released a few days later so he could attend the Round Table Conference, held in Brussels, where the Belgian government discussed the political future of the Congo with all Congolese parties. This conference decided to grant the country a quick and unconditional independence on June 30, 1960.

In the meantime, parliamentary elections were being held in May; they established MNC-Lumumba as the single most important party of Congo, but without gaining an absolute majority. Consequently, Lumumba became prime minister of the first Congolese government, while Joseph Kasavubu (1910–1969), the leader of another important party, the Abako, was designated as president. During the official ceremonies, held in Léopoldville on independence day in the presence of Belgian King Baudouin (1930–1993) and several prominent Belgian politicians, Lumumba caused serious turmoil by delivering an unannounced speech in which he stressed the many sufferings the Congolese had undergone during Belgian domination. This incident confirmed to the Belgian authorities and other Western powers, such as the United States, that Lumumba was a dangerous and extremist leader.

He was seen as a real threat to Western influence and as a promoter of communist rule throughout the entire African continent. Only five days after independence was declared, a rebellion in some units of the Congolese army led to unilateral Belgian military intervention and widespread chaos in the country. Moreover, the rich mining province of Katanga broke away from central authorities and declared its own independence. This secession was (in practice) supported by the Belgians. Lumumba's central government broke off diplomatic relations with Belgium and called for international help. This led to a United Nations (UN) intervention in Congo. By now the political and, in some circles even physical, elimination of the Congolese prime minister had become a priority for the Belgian and U.S. authorities.

Inspired by them, President Kasavubu dismissed the prime minister on September 5, 1960; Lumumba, in turn, immediately deposed the president. This political stalemate led Colonel Mobutu (1930–1997), then head of the Congolese National Army and protégé of Washington, DC, and Brussels, to take over power.

Lumumba, arrested and placed under home surveillance by Mobutu's troops (but protected by UN soldiers), made an unsuccessful attempt to escape to Stanleyville, where he could count on many followers. After his capture, Lumumba was finally handed over to his fiercest enemies, the secessionist authorities of Katanga. Only a few hours after his transfer to Katanga's capital, Elisabethville (now Lubumbashi), during which he was severely beaten and tortured, he was executed nearby on January 17, 1961.

The news of his death caused great indignation in many third world countries and in the Soviet bloc. The elimination of Congo's legal chief of government was seen as a plot of Western imperialist powers to curtail growing African and third world self-determination. Although the Belgian and U.S. authorities denied any participation in Lumumba's assassination, presented as an intra-Congolese affair, it is clear by now that both Western powers contributed to create the context leading to his elimination, without directly carrying it out. Immediately after his death, Lumumba became an icon of the third world's struggle against imperialism—even if he had been prime minister for only two months and not given much opportunity to exercise power.

SEE ALSO *Belgium's African Colonies; Decolonization, Sub-Saharan Africa; Nationalism, Africa.*

BIBLIOGRAPHY

De Vos, Luc, Phillipe Raxhon, Emmanuel Gerard, and Jules Gérard-Libois. *Les secrets de l'affaire Lumumba*. Brussels: Racine, 2004.

Omasombo, Jean, and Benoit Verhaegen. *Patrice Lumumba, jeunesse et apprentissage politique: 1925–1956*. Paris: Institut Africain-L'Harmattan, 1998.

Willame, Jean-Claude. *Patrice Lumumba. La crise congolaise revisitée*. Paris: Karthala, 1990.

Witte, Ludo de. *The Assassination of Lumumba*. London: Verso, 2001.

Guy Vanthemsche

M

MACAO

Macao (also Macau), a special administrative region of the People's Republic of China, occupies a small, hilly peninsula located on the west shore of the Pearl River (or Zhujiang River) on the southeast coast of China. Originally less than 15 square kilometers (5.8 square miles), the peninsula and the adjacent islands of Taipa and Colôane have expanded by land reclamation since the early twentieth century to 27 square kilometers (10.4 square miles). The population in 2004 was approximately 460,000, 95 percent comprising Chinese immigrants from the South China provinces, plus a small number of perhaps no more than 5,000 Macanese, the mixed-blood descendants of early Portuguese unions with Asian peoples.

Macao was founded in 1557 by Portuguese traders seeking a location for a permanent commercial settlement. Until the founding of Hong Kong nearly 300 years later, Macao was the only permanent European settlement in China. By 1600 Macao had become a thriving cosmopolitan city, its prosperity founded on the trade network from Goa in India, to Malacca on the Malay Peninsula, to Macao, and on to Nagasaki in southern Japan.

By the mid-seventeenth century the Portuguese seaborne empire declined precipitously under the assault of the Dutch, who took Malacca in 1641. In 1640 Japan expelled all foreigners and closed the country. Macao's prosperity collapsed, and the city survived as a center of local Southeast Asian trade. As the new colonial powers, led by Britain, arrived in pursuit of the China trade in the late eighteenth century, Macao's importance was revived as a temporary refuge for Europeans involved in the Canton (Guangzhou) trade. But when Hong Kong was founded by the British in 1842 in the wake of the first Opium War (1839–1842), Macao was relegated to a backwater, its inferior harbor increasingly unable to accommodate modern ships. By the early twentieth century Macao had acquired notoriety for gambling and various forms of vice. Its principal industries then included matches, fireworks, incense, furniture, and cheap toys. After World War II (1939–1945) Macao's economy remained stagnant, but the establishment of a gambling syndicate and the growth of tourism in the 1960s saw its slow revival.

China had never ceded sovereignty over the territory, and the Portuguese paid ground rent for the privilege of occupation. In the late nineteenth century Portugal attempted to claim formal sovereignty over Macao and a treaty in 1887 recognized Macao as a colony under perpetual Portuguese occupation. Its status remained ambiguous until the 1980s when Hong Kong's ultimate return to China in 1997 was settled with Britain. Negotiations between China and Portugal led to the return of Macao to Chinese control on December 20, 1999. The agreement preserved Macao's economy, society, culture, and quasi-autonomous government for at least fifty years.

From the 1980s Macao experienced rapid economic growth and expansion. Tourism and gambling grew vigorously with the construction of an airport, new hotels, and casinos. Fifty-five percent of municipal revenues derive from a tax on gambling. In 2002 the gambling monopoly was opened to bidding and new Las Vegas syndicates won places in Macao. Macao's robust economy has become an integral part of the Pearl River Delta economic region.

SEE ALSO *China, After 1945; China, First Opium War to 1945; China, to the First Opium War; Chinese*

Diaspora; Empire, Portuguese; Hong Kong, from World War II; Hong Kong, to World War II; Opium; Treaty Port System.

BIBLIOGRAPHY

Cheng, Christian Miu Bing. *Macau: A Cultural Janus.* Hong Kong: Hong Kong University Press, 1999.

Porter, Jonathan. *Macau: The Imaginary City, Culture, and Society, 1557 to the Present.* Boulder, CO: Westview Press, 2000.

Jonathan Porter

MACHEL, SAMORE
1933–1986

Born into a poor family in the Chilembene village of colonial Mozambique on September 29, 1933, Samore Moisés Machel worked hard to achieve eminence as a nationalist, statesman, and intellectual. Under his leadership as a freedom fighter, Machel helped dismantle the Portuguese's colonial clutch on his people of Mozambique. In his position as the first president of an independent Mozambique, Machel also is remembered for his unflinching opposition to white minority rules in neighboring South Africa, and Southern Rhodesia (later Zimbabwe).

In the 1940s Machel had his early education under the Catholic mission schools at his home province, then known as Adeia da Madragoa. With the Portuguese policy of assimilation, colonial education was under strict government control. Unlike some of his privileged comrades in the anti-colonial struggle, Machel was denied the privilege of a higher education because of his poor background. Nonetheless, he received good military training in several African and Western countries. The wider continental liberation struggles of the 1950s and 1960s, which corresponded with Machel's formative years, played a crucial role in his emergence as an African nationalist. Bitter from the exploitative Mozambican colonial experience, Machel, like the majority of African nationalists, equated Western capitalism with colonialism and oppression, whereas Soviet socialism stood for freedom and independence.

In 1962 Machel joined the left-wing Mozambican Liberation Front (FRELIMO), which had launched a guerrilla movement against Portuguese colonial rule in 1961 under the leadership of Eduardo Mondlane (1920–1969). Machel would eventually rise through the ranks and become the leader of the movement six months after Mondlane was assassinated in 1969. Under Machel, the FRELIMO intensified guerrilla attacks against white settlers in Mozambique, especially around the Cahora Bassa

Samore Machel. *The nationalist leader and president of Mozambique from 1975 to 1986, photographed with troops in Mozambique on June 25, 1980.* © BETTMANN/CORBIS. **REPRODUCED BY PERMISSION.**

and Vila Pery districts. As the popularity of FRELIMO increased among the Africans, the Portuguese national army started rethinking the repressive approach to the decolonization question in their African colonies, including Mozambique, Angola, Guinea-Bissau, and Cape Verde.

On April 25, 1974, the army overthrew the Caetano regime in Portugal and the incoming government of General Antonio de Spinola (1910–1996) immediately favored a ceasefire with FRELIMO. After about a year of negotiations, uneasy peace, and more bloodshed,

Mozambique gained its independence on June 25, 1975. Samore Machel was sworn in as president of the People's Republic of Mozambique on July 1, 1975.

In accordance with his ideological beliefs, Machel advocated for the formation of a new Mozambican society based on Marxism. He established a one-party state, declaring that his country would be a "revolutionary base against imperialism and colonialism in Africa." Machel provided the basis for the African Nationalist Congress (ANC), and the Zimbabwean liberation movements. Troubled by Machel's pro-Communist policies, several Western powers, including the United States, collaborated with the apartheid regimes in South Africa and Southern Rhodesia in funding an anti-Communist faction in Mozambique known as the Mozambique National Resistance (RENAMO). Mozambique had heavily depended on South Africa for its food and material needs. Therefore, the internationalized civil conflict amounted to a stranglehold that Machel needed to confront to keep his dreams alive. Heavy financial, material, and personnel contributions from the Soviet Union, Cuba, Tanzania, Zambia, and other African countries sustained the FRELIMO in the war, while Machel attempted to build a country tolerant to race and ethnic differences.

On October 19, 1986, Machel died in a suspicious plane mishap coming back from a meeting with President Kenneth Kaunda of Zambia (b. 1924). Joaquim Chissano (b. 1939), the current President of Mozambique, succeeded Machel as the new party leader. In 1994 he initiated the region's transition into multiparty politics.

SEE ALSO *Nationalism, Africa; Portugal's African Colonies.*

BIBLIOGRAPHY

Cabrita, Joao M. *Mozambique: The Tortuous Road to Democracy.* New York: St. Martin's Press, 2000.

Munslow, Barry, ed. *Samore Machel, an African Revolutionary: Selected Speeches and Writings.* Translated by Michael Wolfers. London: Zed Books; Totowa, NJ: Biblio Distribution Center, 1985.

Nelson, Harold D., ed. *Mozambique: A Country Study*, 3rd ed. Washington, DC: Foreign Area Studies, American University, 1985.

Newitt, Malyn. *A History of Mozambique.* Bloomington, IN: Indiana University Press, 1995.

Raphael Njoku

MADRAS

SEE *Colonial Port Cities and Towns, South and Southeast Asia*

MAGELLAN, FERDINAND
1480–1521

The Portuguese mariner Fernão de Magalhães, whom the world knows as Ferdinand Magellan, was given command of a Spanish fleet of five ships in 1518 to discover the Spice Islands for Spain. Magellan's five small ships, the Armada de Molucca, departed Seville in 1519 with about 260 crew members from "divers nations"—Greeks, Venetians, Genoese, Sicilians, French, Portuguese, Spaniards, and others—as the chronicler Antonio Pigafetta (d. ca. 1534) wrote. This three-year expedition was the most important European voyage of discovery after the voyages of Vasco da Gama (ca. 1469–1524) to India in 1497 to 1499 and Christopher Columbus (1451–1506) to America in 1492 to 1493.

Magellan's expedition was an expedition of many "firsts." It was the first voyage to pass from the Atlantic Ocean to the Pacific Ocean through what came to be known as the Strait of Magellan, the first European voyage to cross the Pacific Ocean, the first European "discovery" of the Philippines, and—most famously—the first circumnavigation of the globe. This 96,500-kilometer (about 60,000-mile) voyage opened the remaining crucial sea-lanes of the world to European ships, commerce, and colonial empires.

Ferdinand Magellan was born near Villa Real in Tras os Montes, Portugal, and educated in Lisbon at the royal courts first of King João II (1455–1495) and then of Manuel I (1469–1521). Beginning in 1505, Magellan began an eight-year career as a sailor and soldier in the Portuguese East Indies. In 1513 he joined the Portuguese invasion of Morocco. In India, Magellan lost his investment in trade. In Morocco, his horse was killed in battle. His requests to the king for compensation were refused. Charges of treason and corruption against Magellan for actions taken in Morocco were not reviewed by the king at Magellan's request but were later dismissed in North Africa. By 1517, when the king refused to increase Magellan's allowance or support a voyage to the Indies, the soldier-mariner was deeply distressed; his pride was wounded, his reputation insulted, and his ambition thwarted. When Magellan asked the king if he could offer his services to another kingdom, the answer was a surprising yes. A month later, Magellan arrived in Seville.

In Spain, the Portuguese mariner Fernão de Magalhães became known as Hernando de Magallanes. He offered the kingdom's powerful House of Trade extremely valuable knowledge. He claimed he had sailed on behalf of Portugal to the Spice Islands (the Moluccas), he knew where they where and how to find them, and he claimed that under the Spanish-Portuguese Treaty of Tordesillas (1494) these islands were located within the Spanish hemisphere.

In 1518 King Charles I (1500–1558; soon to be Charles V, the Holy Roman Emperor), gave Magellan a commission "to find in the domains that belong to us and are ours in the area in the Ocean Sea, within the limits of our demarcation, islands, mainlands, rich spices" (quoted in Thomas 2003, p. 496). The crown (and the banking House of Fugger) provided Magellan with the ships of the Armada de Molucca, salaries for the crew, trade goods, provisions, and more, all expenses coming to 8,751,125 *maravedís* (in current U.S. dollars, this expenditure would have a value of approximately one million dollars). The captain-general (Magellan) was paid 50,000 *maravedís* and an additional 8,000 each month.

Magellan left Spain in September 1519 with the *San Antonio*, the *Concepción*, the *Victoria*, the *Santiago*, and the captain-general's flagship, the caravel *Trinidad*. This small fleet immediately sailed to the Canary Islands to pick up more provisions. From this usual departure point for Spanish ships heading west, Magellan turned south and followed the coast of West Africa from Cape Verde to about Sierra Leone, and then let the south equatorial current take his ships across the Atlantic to the bulge of Brazil. From late November through December and January, the Armada de Molucca coasted southwest, reaching the bay at Rio de Janeiro and then the great estuary of the Río de la Plata. After determining that the River Plate was not the strait to the East Indies, Magellan continued sailing south and searching for a passage. Discontent among the crew, particularly the Spanish officers, led to a mutiny against the Portuguese captain-general that took control of three ships. The hesitation of the conspirators and the furious response of Magellan defeated the mutiny.

The search for the strait began in May 1520 and took months. During the search, the *Santiago* was shipwrecked in a storm in August. Magellan and his four remaining ships discovered the strait in October. Passage through the narrow, surging, and confusing network of fjords approximately 480 kilometers (about 300 miles) long was difficult and dangerous and took three of the ships thirty-eight days to accomplish. In midpassage, the *San Antonio* disappeared and returned to Spain.

Emerging from the strait into what was known as the Southern Sea, the smaller Armada de Molucca coasted northwest along the South American shore until reaching the site of the future Santiago de Chile and then turned due west. For ninety-eight days this small fleet sailed across more than 11,300 kilometers (about 7,000 miles) of relative calm. On this exceedingly long voyage, the crew ran out of food and water and ate rats, ox hides, and saw dust, and drank "yellow water." Scurvy, a malady caused by vitamin C deficiency, produced a swelling of the gums, as well as boils and lesions that seemed to make the skin fall off the bones. Pigafetta reported that twenty-nine crewmen died of scurvy, and nearly as many fell grievously ill. In March 1521 the crew heard the cry "Tierra!" (land). The fleet landed in the Marianas on the islands of Rota and Guam.

By April, Magellan and his steadily shrinking expedition arrived in what would later be named the Philippines. At Cebu Island, Magellan made a show of military force and forged an alliance with the local ruler Humabon. As the captain-general began to make himself lord of the natives, he became more and more insistent on encouraging his native allies to convert to Christianity and, where necessary, on requiring conversion by coercion and violence.

On the neighboring island of Mactan, Magellan found a chief, Lapu Lapu, who refused any cooperation with the Europeans. At the request of another native chief, Magellan brought sixty of his men, armed and armored, and attacked the village of Lapu Lapu. Although Magellan believed one European soldier could defeat a hundred native warriors, when the fight began the Europeans were outnumbered twenty-five to one, and the battle did not go as planned. Natives shot poisoned arrows at the unprotected legs of the European soldiers. The toxin disoriented and weakened the soldiers, which allowed natives to approach the wounded and do more damage. This is what happened to Magellan. Shot in the leg with a poisoned arrow, Magellan continued to fight for another hour or so, but eventually he lost his strength and was surrounded and attacked by several natives who hacked him to death. An additional eight European soldiers were killed in the battle before the surviving wounded and scared soldiers retreated to their ship. On April 27, 1521, European expansion met effective resistance. Facing Mactan Harbor today is a giant statue of Lapu Lapu. An obelisk nearby commemorates the battle: "Here on this spot the great chieftain Lapu Lapu repelled an attack by Ferdinand Magellan, killing him and sending his forces away" (Bergreen 2004, p. 287).

A few days after the battle, Magellan's ally Humabon hosted a feast that thirty Europeans attended, most of them officers, about one-quarter of the entire crew. Near the end of the banquet, the Europeans were attacked and most were killed. Learning of this tragedy, the remaining 115 crewmen in three small ships did not send a rescue party but, instead, set sail and left Cebu as quickly as possible. Once they were at sea, the crew of the *Concepción* concluded that their damaged and worm-eaten ship would not make the voyage. After its provisions, rigging, and other useful items were transferred to the other two ships, the *Concepción* was burned and scuttled. The *Trinidad* and the *Victoria* now proceeded to the Spice Islands as best they could.

From May to November 1521, the ever-smaller Armada de Molucca journeyed to Borneo, Palawan, Brunei, and Cimbonbon. As they traveled into the "East Indies," the crew entered more populated, commercial, and politically dangerous regions. They also found a guide to bring them to Ternate, Tidore, Motin, Makian, and Bacan, the primary islands of the Moluccas, the famed Spice Islands.

In November and December 1521 the crew traded what they had for 1,400 pounds of cloves, the most valuable spice on the European market. In late December the *Victoria*, under the command of the Basque sailor Juan Sebastián de Elcano (d. 1526), left for home with sixty crewmembers. The *Trinidad* attempted to sail back across the Pacific but foundered and turned around, then sailed to Portuguese Goa in India. The few surviving crew reached Lisbon and were immediately imprisoned. Only four sailors from this ship ever returned to Spain.

The *Victoria* passed Java and then sailed across the Indian Ocean to the Cape of Good Hope, then north to the Cape Verde Islands and finally Spain. Pigafetta noted that as the ship sailed north along the African coast, the crew had to throw the dead bodies of their mates into the ocean. When the *Victoria* reached Seville on September 8, 1522, there were eighteen survivors onboard. King Charles granted Captain Sebastián de Elcano a coat of arms that showed a globe, spices, Malay kings, and the legend *Primus me circumdedisti* (Thou first circled me).

After 1522, the great unknown was known. All the world's oceans were connected and they became highways for European ships, traders, missionaries, and colonists. This became clear in 1529 in Diego Ribero's world map, which accurately depicted the outlines of the continents of Africa, India, and America. This map also showed the route of the Magellan voyage. The most famous illustrations of the Magellan circumnavigation were the oval world maps made by Battista Agnese from 1543 to 1545. These gorgeous color manuscript maps on vellum showed the route of Magellan (in black ink) and the Spanish silver fleet (in gold). In 1543 Charles V ordered one of these maps to give to his son Philip. Paolo Forlani's engraved map of South America (ca. 1564–1572), although not the first to do so, clearly showed the strait connecting the Atlantic and the Pacific oceans and gave it the name Streto di Magaanes, the Strait of Magellan.

SEE ALSO *Cartography in the Colonial Americas; Columbus, Christopher; Empire, Spanish; European Explorations in South America; Gama, Vasco da.*

BIBLIOGRAPHY

Bergreen, Laurence. *Over the Edge of the World: Magellan's Terrifying Circumnavigation of the Globe.* New York: Perennial, 2004.

Perry, J. H. *The Discovery of the Sea.* New York: Dial Press, 1974.

Thomas, Hugh. *Rivers of Gold: The Rise of the Spanish Empire, from Columbus to Magellan.* New York: Random House, 2003.

Torodash, Martin. "Magellan Historiography." *Hispanic American Historical Review* 51 (2) (1971): 313–335.

Thomas Benjamin

MAJI MAJI REVOLT, AFRICA

The Maji Maji Revolt (1905–1907) was a pivotal event in the history of early colonial Tanzania. The revolt was the first manifestation of a united, interethnic opposition to colonial rule in Africa. Though the rebellion failed to oust the Germans from East Africa, it led the colonial administration to implement a series of reforms. The Maji Maji Revolt further engendered a protonationalist tradition that was tapped into in the 1950s during the country's modern nationalist period.

Following the Berlin Conference (1884–1885), Germany acquired several colonies in Africa, including the present-day countries of Tanzania, Rwanda, Burundi, and part of Mozambique. Like other colonial powers, Germany aimed to maximize the economic potential of its African colonies. In East Africa, the Germans exerted control through violent repressive tactics. They introduced a head tax in 1898 imposed on adult males to raise revenue for their administration. Like many other colonial powers, Germany relied on forced labor to build roads and other infrastructure. In 1902 the governor of German East Africa, Count Adolf von Götzen (1866–1910), ordered Tanzanian villagers to grow cotton as cash crop. Tanzanians resented so strongly this order because of the back-breaking work involved in cotton cultivation. These German policies were highly unpopular, and some villagers refused to work the land or pay the taxes. German policies also disrupted African social and economic relations as many men were forced away from their homes to work, and rural women were forced to assume new roles and contribute more to subsistence. The difficult conditions to which the natives were subjected were exacerbated by a drought that threatened the region in 1905. These circumstances, in combination with the effects of the government's agricultural, forest, and labor policies, led to open rebellion in July 1905.

The native Tanzanians turned to African spirituality and magic to drive the Germans out of Tanzania. The leader of the rebellion was a spirit medium named Kinjikitile Ngwale (d. 1905), who called himself Bokero and claimed to be possessed by a snake spirit called Hongo. Bokero began to spread the idea that the people had been called upon to eliminate the Germans. The revolt was named after a medicine called *maji* that purportedly gave African fighters immunity to German bullets. Although this "war medicine" was in fact nothing but water mixed with castor oil and millet, the dissemination of the *maji* ideology spread a message of common opposition and resistance to German colonial rule.

Believing themselves empowered with this medicine, Bokero's followers began the Maji Maji Revolt. Armed with cap guns, spears, and arrows, and wearing millet stalks around their heads, they set out from the Matumbi Hills in southern Tanzania and attacked German garrisons throughout the colony. Along with the Matumbi, the Mbunga, Kichi, Ngoni, Ngindo, and Pogoro joined the rebellion in German East Africa. Although fewer in number, German forces of European and native soldiers used superior firepower to their advantage, and several thousand Maji rebels were cut down by machine-gun fire. The magic water that they thought would protect them from the German guns failed. However, the fight in several areas was bitter.

When Kinjikitile Ngwale was executed by German troops on August 4, 1905, another spirit medium continued to lead the revolt. The rebellion continued when the Ngoni people joined in the revolt with a force of 5,000 but they were no match to German guns when they were attacked. The Germans destroyed villages, crops, and other food sources used by the rebels in a scorched-earth policy, leading to the deaths of an estimated 250,000 from famine. The defeat of the Ngoni marked the end of any serious resistance. By April 1906, the southwest of German East Africa was pacified, but it was not until August of 1907 that the rebellion was effectively stamped out.

The aftermath of Maji Maji Revolt had important implications for German rule until the end of World War I in 1918, when the area became British territory. The rebellion, which led to the death and displacement of hundreds of thousands of people, was a major challenge to German colonial rule in Africa. The colonial government instituted important administrative reforms in the wake of the rebellion. For the Africans in the region, the rebellion raised a nationalist consciousness that was called upon during the decolonization period.

SEE ALSO *Berlin Conference; Germany's African Colonies.*

BIBLIOGRAPHY

Iliffe, John. "The Organization of the Maji Maji Rebellion." *Journal of African History* 8 (1967): 495–512.

Iliffe, John, and G. C. K. Gwassa, eds. *Records of the Maji Maji Rising.* Dar es Salaam, Tanzania: East African Publishing House, 1967.

Sunseri, Thaddeus. "Reinterpreting a Colonial Rebellion: Forestry and Social Control in German East Africa, 1874–1915." *Environmental History* 8 (3) (2003): 430–451. Available from http://www.historycooperative.org/journals/eh/8.3/sunseri.html.

Chima J. Korieh

MALABAR, EUROPEANS AND THE MARITIME TRADE OF

In the sixteenth century, prior to the arrival of Europeans, the maritime region of Malabar on the southwest coast of India had the enviable reputation of being the most hospitable of trading havens in the Indian Ocean. Constituted by geography as a robust and self-contained coastal unit with access to a productive pepper-growing hinterland, the region was dotted with ports that carried on a thriving commerce in pepper and spices in the markets of the Indian Ocean. There was, in addition to the high-seas trade with West Asia, a substantial coastal trade that connected the Malabar ports with Kanara and Gujarat further north along the west coast of India and with the Coromandel in India's southeastern littoral. Malabar's exports consisted primarily of pepper and spices, while imports were rice and textiles from Gujarat and Bengal, as well as bullion and horses from West Asia.

Politically, the region was fragmented among a series of contenders and local suzerains, of whom the most influential was the *zamorin* of Calicut, followed by the rulers of Cannanore, Cochin, and Vynad. The actual business of commerce was, by and large, dominated by three merchant groups: (1) the *pardesis* or foreign merchants; (2) the Mapillas, the local Muslim merchant community; and (3) the Chetties, a Tamil merchant caste, who were prominent as money changers and coral merchants and transacted the trade with the Coromandel. The *pardesis* enjoyed a special status in most of the Malabar ports and especially in Calicut, where the *zamorin* scrupulously safeguarded their interests. It was not surprising, therefore, that this group played a major role in resisting the European offensive that came with the arrival of the Portuguese in 1499.

Shipping and seafaring in Malabar drew the appreciation of early European travelers and traders. The Mapillas were considered excellent sailors and ship owners, as well as courageous fighters. Coastal shipping was dominated by fast oar- and sail-powered *vallams* (a type of Indian boat). The fast-moving Malabar galleys, built in the shipyards of Cochin and Calicut, were also ubiquitous in the coastal circuit. Fleets of twenty to thirty Malabar galleys swarmed the Arabian Sea, pouncing on vulnerable ships.

East India Company Ships in Malabar. *Ships belonging to the British East India Company explore the coast of Malabar at Calicut in southwest India in this nineteenth-century illustration.* **HULTON ARCHIVE/GETTY IMAGES. REPRODUCED BY PERMISSION.**

Oceangoing vessels in Malabar seem to have been smaller, in terms of tonnage, than their counterparts in Gujarat.

The Portuguese discovery of the direct sea route to India, which they hoped to use to dominate the pepper traffic between India and Europe and to discover potential Christian allies, as part of their crusading zeal, was followed almost immediately by the articulation of superior claims to trade in the Indian Ocean and the establishment of a seaborne empire to enforce a monopoly on trade in pepper and spices. This took the form of constructing garrisons and fortified settlements in select Malabar ports, establishing pepper agreements with the rulers who were obliged to turn over a portion of their pepper production to the Portuguese at fixed prices, and imposing a policy of trading permits *(cartazes)* that local merchants were obliged to purchase, thereby confining them to designated routes and commodities. These measures specifically targeted *pardesi* merchants, who were forbidden from carrying pepper, thus turning over the traffic to Portuguese shipping.

Throughout the sixteenth and a considerable part of the seventeenth century, an overwhelming proportion of the pepper imported from Asia into Lisbon was procured from southwestern India. Against the total of approximately 17,300 quintals (1,907 short tons) of pepper imported into Lisbon in 1506, the average amount imported from Cochin alone in 1506 and 1507 was 13,214 quintals (1,457 short tons), while the total amount imported into Lisbon was 20,020 quintals (2,207 short tons) in 1513 and 20,415 quintals (2,250 short tons) in 1514. In the early part of the seventeenth century, this increased even further; between 1612 and 1634, pepper procured at Malacca (in present-day Malaysia) accounted for only 3.26 percent of the total amount shipped to Lisbon.

The arrival of the Portuguese completely altered the terms of trade in the Indian Ocean and introduced for the first time the idea of armed commerce. Malabar was probably the most traumatized region as a result of the European intrusion, and the consequence was a large-scale militarization of coastal society. The sixteenth century witnessed a state of endemic conflict, which threw into disarray existing patterns of trade and commercial activity on the Malabar coast. Local resistance to the

Portuguese took the form of occasional attacks on Portuguese ships and avoidance of the *cartaz*, thereby establishing a parallel network of ports. Two groups stand out in the annals of Malabar's resistance—the Mamales of Cannanore and the Kunajalis, the admirals of the *zamorin*. As coastal chieftains, who jealously defended their right to trade in the ocean, especially in the Maldives, they mounted an armed resistance that was sustained and successful. Endorsed by Malabar's rulers like the zamorin they were able to undermine the Portuguese monopoly.

The seventeenth century saw the entry of the Dutch and the English into the Indian Ocean and the waning of Portuguese influence in Malabar. By the beginning of the century, most of the commercial powers in the region had come to terms with the Portuguese. Calicut and Cannanore resumed their trade with the Red Sea. Coastal traffic with Gujarat and the Coromandel was renewed and the result was an overall expansion in the region's overseas trade.

Regular sailings of the Dutch into Malabar followed after their initial conquest of Kandy in Ceylon. In 1660 the Dutch took control of the fort of Coylan; in 1663 the capital fort of Cochin was occupied; and in 1664 the Dutch occupied Cannanore and Cranganore. At the same time, a treaty was entered into with the raja of Cochin. This agreement confirmed the raja's vassal status, and in theory ensured regular supplies of pepper at fixed prices. There was also a provision intended to exclude other competitors—Asian and European—from trade in those commodities.

All these arrangements did not immediately result in a substantial expansion of Dutch commerce, however. Dutch trade in Malabar never assumed the importance that it enjoyed in the contiguous region of the Coromandel. On the basis of available figures for Dutch exports of pepper from Malabar, it would appear that the Dutch shipped out of Malabar about 2,700 quintals in some years, to a high of 11,000 quintals in others. In most years, the exports were closer to 680 quintals. The English East India Company, on the other hand, began to step up its operations in Malabar from about the 1670s.

The total volume of European trade in Malabar in the seventeenth century appears to have been small. In all, the total European exports of pepper would have added up to more than 18,000 quintals (about 4 million pounds) in the last years of the seventeenth century. This constituted less than a quarter of the total pepper production, which continued to be absorbed into the trade of Asia. However, private European investment in the country trade of Asia became increasingly important in the last decades of the seventeenth century as the Dutch

joined Gujarati shipping in the Western Indian Ocean. In 1673 the Dutch made a profit of 177 percent on the sale of pepper in Bandar Abbas, and in 1701 the profit was 129 percent.

The Dutch also attempted to dominate the trade with the Coromandel by controlling the pepper supply in south Malabar and by restricting sailing through the Indo-Sri Lankan straits. This was found to be impossible because any restrictions on maritime sailing were subverted by the increasing transportations of pepper over land. The Bengal trade was a different story; the Dutch discouraged direct Malabar-initiated trade to Bengal, and Bengal merchants did not find it profitable to trade directly with Malabar.

European intrusion, first in the form of the Portuguese Estado and subsequently the Dutch and English East India companies, did not radically transform the trading structure of Malabar in terms of its orientation or its operational features. Admittedly, the consequences of periodic raiding, of the pass system (*cartazes*), which restricted trading and imposed conditions on free access to ports and the high seas, and of coercive mechanisms affecting price, supply, and distribution of pepper affected levels of trading activity from time to time, but on the whole these effects were temporary and only produced shifts in the relative status of ports.

In the eighteenth century, European trade in Malabar confronted a complex situation of competition and altercation with local rulers, especially the kingdom of Travancore, which by the middle of the century had successfully established a monopoly over Malabar's pepper trade. During the first half of the eighteenth century, the Dutch East India Company was forced to deal with increasing competition, initially from other Europeans and subsequently from the state of Travancore, which had begun to stake its claim to monopoly trade. The accession of Martanda Varma (1729–1758) to the kingdom of Travancore and his successive victories against the neighboring states and the Dutch East India Company in the Battle of Kolachel (1741) enabled him to take over the trade and production of pepper in Malabar and turn it over into a state monopoly.

The French settlement at Mahe (established in 1740) and the English settlement at Tellicherry became important centers of pepper trade. Activities at these settlements had the consequence of diverting pepper supplies and raising pepper prices. At the same time, there was on the part of Gujarati shipping a renewed interest in Malabar's trade, which gave a temporary but perceptible fillip to Calicut's fortunes. These developments, along with the expansion of the Travancore state and its policy of controlling the pepper trade, severely undermined the Dutch company's operations.

The decline of Travancore after the death of Martanda Varma was followed by a brief resurgence of British commercial expansion, which was deflected by the Mysorean invasions of Malabar in the 1780s. The region thereafter suffered long-term damage, which the expansion of English private interests and the growth of Bombay could not offset. For a brief period, the demands of the newly emerging colonial economy diverted Malabar's pepper production and trade to the markets of China and Europe, but even this by the first quarter of the nineteenth century was on the wane. The falling demand for pepper in the European markets and the growing interest in raw cotton as an export for China shifted the center of commercial gravity from Malabar to the ports of the north.

SEE ALSO *Colonial Port Cities and Towns, South and Southeast Asia; Coromandel, Europeans and Maritime Trade; Empire, British; Empire, Dutch; Empire, Portuguese; English East India Company (EIC); Indian Ocean Trade.*

BIBLIOGRAPHY

Arasaratnam, Sinnappah. *Maritime India in the Seventeenth Century.* Delhi and New York: Oxford University Press, 1994.

Bouchon, Geneviève. *"Regent of the Sea": Cannanore's Response to Portuguese Expansion, 1507–1528.* Translated by Louise Shackley. Delhi and New York: Oxford University Press, 1988.

Das Gupta, Ashin. *Malabar in Asian Trade, 1740–1800.* Cambridge, U.K.: Cambridge University Press, 1967.

Furber, Holden. *Rival Empires of Trade in the Orient, 1600–1800.* Minneapolis: University of Minnesota Press, 1976.

Nightingale, Pamela. *Trade and Empire in Western India, 1784–1806.* Cambridge, U.K.: Cambridge University Press, 1970.

Subrahmanyam, Sanjay. *The Political Economy of Commerce: Southern India, 1500–1650.* New York and Cambridge, U.K.: Cambridge University Press, 1990.

Lakshmi Subramanian

MALAYSIA, BRITISH, 1874–1957

Following the British founding of Singapore in 1819, Chinese and British economic involvement on the Malay Peninsula expanded because of the lure of profits from tin mines and plantation agriculture. In the west coast states, increased investment by merchants in the Straits Settlements (Singapore, Penang, and Melaka) coincided with ongoing succession disputes within several Malay ruling families. Contending Malay factions negotiated alliances with Chinese secret societies, which had mushroomed as thousands of men arrived from China in search of work. In addition, Straits Settlements investors backed different Malay contenders, hoping for commercial advantages. When the conflicts showed no signs of abating, they pressed for British intervention so that order would be restored and their capital would be safe. Their arguments were influential not only because industrializing Britain needed access to tin and forest products, but because London was concerned that some other European power would expand into the peninsula.

THE CREATION OF COLONIAL MALAYA

In 1873, when Sultan Abdullah of Perak asked for British help against his rivals, the Straits Settlements governor, Andrew Clarke (1824–1902), seized the chance to advance British interests. By the Pangkor Treaty of January 20, 1874, Abdullah gained British support in return for accepting a resident whose advice he was required to accept on all matters except religion and custom.

The Pangkor Treaty is significant not merely because it created new openings for economic expansion, but because it laid the groundwork for the extension of British rule across the entire peninsula. As a result of the murder of the first resident, most Perak chiefs were removed and a new Sultan installed, allowing the British to maintain the shell of the traditional Malay administrative structure while placing all effective power in colonial hands. This system of indirect control was extended to the other west coast states of Selangor, Negeri Sembilan, and eventually to Pahang. In 1896 they jointly became the Federated Malay States with the capital at Kuala Lumpur.

Britain's ambitions to acquire Siam's Malay vassals (Patani, Kedah, Perlis, Kelantan, and Terengganu) resulted in the Anglo-Siamese treaty of 1909, by which Bangkok relinquished authority over all the northern Malay states except Patani in return for diplomatic privileges. Johor remained independent until 1914, but its incorporation into British Malaya was simply a matter of time because its economy was so closely tied to financial interests in Singapore. In 1919, when Terengganu finally accepted a British adviser, the entire peninsula, consisting of the Straits Settlements, the Federated Malay States, and the Unfederated Malay States, came under colonial control.

COLONIALISM, ECONOMIC DEVELOPMENT, AND THE PLURALISTIC SOCIETY

The west coast of the Malay Peninsula experienced profound economic changes as a result of colonial expansion. Ports were developed, existing towns grew larger, roads were built to the mining centers and plantation areas, and by 1910 railways stretched from Johor to Penang. Malays

Federation of Malaya Constitutional Conference, London, 1956. *The Federation of Malaya gained complete independence from Britain in 1957 and later became part of the nation of Malaysia. Malayan delegates met with British officials in London in 1956 to discuss their country's future relationship with Britain.* © **HULTON-DEUTSCH COLLECTION/CORBIS. REPRODUCED BY PERMISSION.**

were outnumbered in many areas because so many Chinese and Indian laborers had arrived to work in the tin mines, rubber estates and other plantations, and to staff the civil service. These foreign Asians were concentrated in cities and on plantations. Economic development generally bypassed rural Malay communities.

The colonial presence was less evident along the east coast, which was never as important in colonial planning. It attracted fewer Chinese migrants and thus remained more "Malay" in character. Ironically, however, British expansion here met considerable resistance from Malay nobles and their peasant followers. In Pahang a major rebellion occurred in 1891, led by district chiefs alienated by a lessening of their former privileges. Local uprisings also occurred in Kelantan and Terengganu.

The extension of British control and expansion of a colonial economy was even slower in Borneo. In 1841 the Sultan of Brunei granted part of Sarawak to James Brooke (1803–1868), the first "white rajah," but both Brooke and his successor relied heavily on native chiefs. Development like that on the peninsula was not seen as

appropriate. Although a special place was given to the Ibans, ethnic divisions were less pronounced because many of the Chinese lived in rural areas. In Sabah the British North Borneo Company was anxious to operate profitably, but, apart from timber, most commercial ventures were unsuccessful. The administrations of both Sarawak and Sabah were theoretically autonomous, but the British government was always anxious to forestall the advance of some other European power and in 1888 Sabah, Sarawak, and Brunei all became British protectorates. Brunei accepted a resident in 1906.

Fundamental to the development of colonial government was the view that Malays were essentially farmers and fishermen, rather than laborers. The perception of the Chinese and Indians as being more economically astute locked Malays out of the colony's export sector. Occupational divisions were widened by religious differences because Malays were virtually all Muslim. The British also assumed that the Chinese and Indians were itinerants, and that there was no need to provide a common school system for all. A small number of upper-class Malays, Chinese, and

Indians did receive an English education because this was the path to advancement, but the majority acquired only basic schooling in the vernacular. Malaya thus became the classic example of a "plural society" where different ethnic groups met in the marketplace, but otherwise lived apart.

By the 1920s, however, a new generation of Malays was gaining access to educational training in teachers' colleges, and leaders of this group began to voice opposition to the economic dominance of the Chinese and Indians. Ethnic divisions were fueled by developments in China and India. Enthused by the revolutionary mood in their homeland, many Chinese joined either the Kuomintang or the Malayan Communist Party (MCP, formed in 1930). Indians took similar pride in the Indian independence movement, while Malays were caught up by the call for Islamic reform that urged Muslims to modernize education to compete with the West. Largely concerned with developing a unified economy and administration, the British gave little thought to the possibility of Malayan independence and how a new nation would deal with deepening ethnic distinctions. In the Borneo states education in any language proceeded much more slowly. Ethnic tensions were muted here because so many communities were only marginally affected by economic change.

WORLD WAR II AND INDEPENDENCE

Malaya's independence was precipitated by the outbreak of World War II (1939–1945). Japan attacked the peninsula in late 1941, and by February 1942 Malaya and Singapore were in Japanese hands. All British officials were imprisoned, and toward the end of the war there were hints that Japan might grant Malaya independence. Anxious to win local support, the Japanese generally treated Malays and Indians leniently, but the Chinese met systematic discrimination because of Japan's continuing military campaigns in China. It was, therefore, the Chinese groups, dominated by the MCP, which initiated wartime resistance against the Japanese. When the war ended, many British thought the Chinese should be rewarded with full citizenship, but it was difficult to eradicate suspicions resulting from years of separate ethnic and economic development. The British government's proposal for a "Malayan Union" that would make the Chinese and Indians citizens aroused unprecedented opposition among the Malays.

In 1946 a group of leading Malays formed the United Malays National Organization (UMNO). Basic to the UMNO's platform was retaining the status of Malay sultans and "special privileges" for Malays as the original occupants of the land. The Malayan Union was revoked in February 1948 and replaced by the Federation of Malaya, which united the peninsula under one government. Singapore was not included because the Chinese would then have outnumbered the Malays.

The Federation was seen as a victory for Malays, and many Chinese became sympathetic toward the MCP's aim of establishing a Malayan republic. The so-called Malayan emergency began in mid-1948 when the MCP embarked on a systematic campaign of violence against European interests. Since the communists were mainly Chinese, they received substantial help from rural Chinese settlements. From 1950 onward, the British forces began to resettle these communities into "new villages" and thus denied the MCP access to supplies. This strategy was successful, although the Emergency was not officially ended until 1960.

Two reasons for the ultimate failure of the communist insurrection were a new political alliance between Malay and Chinese leaders, and Britain's commitment to Malaya's independence. The formation of the Alliance, consisting of the UMNO, the Malayan Chinese Party (MCA), and later the Malayan Indian Congress (MIC) gave hope for multicultural politics. By 1955 the Alliance and its call for independence had overwhelming support. A constitution was developed for the new nation that created a federation of states with a strong central government, retaining certain privileges for Malays. On August 15, 1957, under its first Prime Minister Tuanku Abdul Rahman (1895–1960), Malaya was declared independent. However, the colonial division of Malayan society into three ethnic groups was complicated by the creation of Malaysia in 1963 and the incorporation of Sabah and Sarawak (and Singapore briefly, 1963–1965) because now non-Muslim and non-Malay groups in Borneo could also claim indigenous privileges.

SEE ALSO *Empire, British*.

BIBLIOGRAPHY

Andaya, Barbara Watson, and Leonard Y. *A History of Malaysia*, 2nd ed. Honolulu: University of Hawaii Press, 2001.

Butcher, John. *The British in Malaya, 1880–1941: The Social History of a European Community in Colonial Southeast Asia*. Kuala Lumpur and New York: Oxford University Press, 1979.

Chai Hon Chan. *The Development of British Malaya 1896–1909*. Kuala Lumpur and New York: Oxford University Press, 1964.

Harper, T. N. *The End of Empire and the Making of Malaya*. New York: Cambridge University Press, 1998.

Kaur, Amarjit. *Economic Change in East Malaysia: Sabah and Sarawak since 1850*. New York: St. Martin's Press, 1998.

Kratoska, Paul. *The Japanese Occupation of Malaya: A Social and Economic History*. Honolulu: University of Hawaii Press, 1997.

Loh, Philip Fook Seng. *Seeds of Separatism: Educational Policy in Malaya, 1874–1940*. Kuala Lumpur and New York: Oxford University Press, 1975.

Ramasamy, P. *Plantation Labour, Unions, Capital, and the State in Peninsula Malaysia*. Kuala Lumpur and New York: Oxford University Press, 1993.

Reece, Robert. *The Name of Brooke: the End of White Rajah Rule in Sarawak.* Kuala Lumpur and New York: Oxford University Press, 1982.

Roff, W.R. *The Origins of Malay Nationalism.* New Haven, CT: Yale University Press, 1967.

Sadka, Emily. *The Protected Malay States, 1874–1895.* Kuala Lumpur: University of Malaya Press, 1968.

Singh, D.S. Ranjit. *The Making of Sabah, 1865–1941: the Dynamics of Indigenous Society.* Kuala Lumpur: University of Malaya Press, 2000.

Tarling, Nicholas. *Britain, the Brookes, and Brunei.* Kuala Lumpur and New York: Oxford University Press, 1971.

Turnbull, C.M. *A History of Singapore 1819–1975.* Kuala Lumpur and New York: Oxford University Press, 1977.

Barbara Watson Andaya

MANCHU DYNASTY

SEE *Qing Dynasty*

MANDATE RULE

A *mandate*, defined in Article 22 of the Covenant of the League of Nations (1919), was a new form of political supervision created after World War I:

> To those colonies and territories which as a consequence of the late war have ceased to be under the sovereignty of the States which formerly governed them and which are inhabited by peoples not yet able to stand by themselves under the strenuous conditions of the modern world, there should be applied the principle that the well-being and development of such peoples form a sacred trust of civilization and that securities for the performance of this trust should be embodied in this Covenant. The best method of giving practical effect to this principle is that the tutelage of such peoples should be entrusted to advanced nations...[and] should be exercised by them as Mandatories on behalf of the League.

There were three types of mandates: A, B, and C. German colonies in Africa and the Pacific became B or C mandates under Britain, France, Belgium, South Africa, Australia, New Zealand, or Japan. The southern and largely Arabic-speaking provinces of the Ottoman Empire became A mandates, meaning their transition to self-determination would be faster and more assured than that of the B and C mandates. Britain received the mandates of Iraq and Palestine and Transjordan; France received the mandates of Syria and Lebanon.

SELFLESSNESS OR SELF INTEREST?

The texts of the mandates stated that "the Mandatory Power commands and governs only to educate." But Britain and France sought mandates according to their economic and strategic interests. France had concessions in Syria and Lebanon to build and maintain railroads, roads, port facilities, tramways, and public utilities and hoped to expand production of cotton and silk for its textile industry. A port or two in the eastern Mediterranean would also be welcome. Britain claimed Iraq, Palestine, and Transjordan for imperial communications needs and wished to control potential sources of oil in Iraq. Because the assignment of mandates indulged the self-interest of European powers, the mandates turned out to be "a cloak for a good measure of imperialism," as Elizabeth Monroe remarked in *Britain's Moment in the Middle East* (1963, p. 141).

France and Britain also claimed mandated territories on the basis of special relationships with minorities. France had ties to the Catholics of the Middle East, especially the Maronites in Lebanon. Britain had the 1917 Balfour Declaration that promised to facilitate the creation in Palestine of a national home for the Jewish people. Given that Jews were only about 10 percent of the population, this promise entailed colonization, which made Palestine unique among the mandated states. By patronizing religious minorities, both Britain and France sought to lay the basis for an especially strong and durable presence in the coastal areas; yet, by identifying with minority interests, Britain and France weakened their overall position in the region.

The newly created mandated states were inconvenient, inefficient, and irrational to most of their inhabitants. Trade barriers, separate administrative, legal, and security structures, and different currency zones, educational systems, and public works and transportation networks made the movement of goods, capital, and labor within the region more difficult than during the late Ottoman Empire. The imposition and replication of institutions, functions, and personnel in each new state was costly, not only in itself but in diminishing what might have been invested in the "well-being and development" of the peoples under mandate. Boundaries also created the basis for water diversion projects to benefit the users of one state at the expense of users in another. For example, the headwaters of the Quwayk River that fed Aleppo were across the border in Turkey, which in 1926 diverted much of the flow for its own use.

State boundaries were not the only divisions imposed by France and Britain. Within each new state, France and Britain mined veins of social diversity to strengthen their position overall. France divided Syria into a number of ministates on the basis, according to the French, of separatist feelings and different levels of

Removing the British Flag in Haifa, June 30, 1948. *After World War I, Great Britain was entrusted with the mandate of Palestine. Shortly after the state of Israel was proclaimed in May 1948, a British soldier hauls down the British flag in Haifa Harbor prior to the departure of the last British troops.* **AFP/GETTY IMAGES. REPRODUCED BY PERMISSION.**

development among various segments of the population: the State of the Alawis in the northwest, the State of Jebel Druz in the southeast, and direct French administration in the so-called Tribal Territory beyond the Euphrates. This multistate structure did not add up to an administration that met the needs or aspirations of the majority or allow for much local participation in governing. On similar grounds of ethnic separatism, France ceded the district (Sanjak) of Alexandretta to Turkey in 1939, contrary to its mandatory responsibility "that no part of the territory of Syria and the Lebanon [be] ceded or leased or in any way placed under the control of a foreign Power."

Britain divided Iraq and Transjordan into two jurisdictions each, one under so-called tribal administration and one under the central government. Cities and peasants within the orbit of cities were subject to one legal system; the transhumant countryside was subject to another. King Faisal (1885–1933) of Iraq complained that the small army

allowed him by Britain would be no match for any combination of tribal forces against him; thus he was reminded of his ultimate dependence on British protection. Designated tribal areas were subject to different voting laws, which worked against the election to parliament of nationalists who were generally from urban areas.

REBELLIONS AND THEIR IMPACT ON MANDATORY RULE

Mandatory rule was meant to accommodate the principle of self-determination, but it required force to be carried out. Major rebellions occurred in Iraq in 1920, in Syria from 1925 to 1927, and in Palestine from 1936 to 1939. These rebellions had a profound effect on the shape of mandatory rule.

The 1920 rebellion in Iraq caused Britain to adopt a model of indirect rule. Britain chose its wartime ally Faisal ibn Husayn to be king in 1921, deported his chief local rival for the throne, and conducted a referendum that legitimized his elevation by a suspiciously high 96 percent approval rating. On the Iraqi side, the rebellion brought together tribesmen and townsmen, Sunni and Shi'i, and provided the foundational myth for an Iraqi nationalism. King Faisal, poised uncomfortably between Britain and the population of Iraq, sought to gain as much freedom of action from Britain as was possible and to knit together the varied communities within the awkward British-drawn borders. Yet, he lamented in 1932 that "there is still . . . no Iraqi people but unimaginable masses of human beings, devoid of any patriotic idea . . . and ready to rise against any government whatever" (Batatu 1978, p. 25).

The 1925 to 1927 Syrian revolt began in Jebel Druz, crossed the borders of the ministates set up in Syria, and brought together townsmen and tribesmen, peasants and pastoralists, Muslim, Christian, and Druze, in Syria and parts of Lebanon. Like the Iraqi rebellion, it became a central event in a nationalist narrative. In its course, France bombarded Damascus and revealed for all to see, including the League of Nations, the hard edge of mandatory tutelage. Of course, the British had bombed Iraqi tribes during the rebellion in Iraq, but the bombing of a capital city familiar to Europeans through biblical references had a much more negative impact. The revolt caused both French and nationalists to moderate their positions. France saw the wisdom of indirect rule and of trying to co-opt nationalist leaders; the nationalist leaders saw that armed confrontation would not end the French mandate and began a strategy of "honorable cooperation."

Owing to the growth of a settler community in Palestine under British protection, there were more frequent and more obvious upheavals there than in the other mandated states. Important manifestations of strife between Jewish settlers and Arab inhabitants occurred in 1920, 1921, and 1929. From 1936 to 1939 there was a major Arab rebellion against British rule. As a result, Britain acknowledged in 1937 that "we cannot—in Palestine as it now is—both concede the Arab claim to self-government and secure the establishment of the Jewish National Home" (Palestine Royal Commission Report, 1937, reproduced in Smith 2004, p. 155). Another result was that Britain trained and armed Jewish auxiliaries while it disarmed the Arab community and killed or exiled its leadership.

THE END OF MANDATORY RULE

In 1932 Iraq was the first mandated state to gain formal independence. Britain maintained its interests by a treaty that allowed Britain to have military bases in Iraq, to be the sole supplier of arms and training to the Iraqi army, and to maintain its controlling interest in the Iraq Petroleum Company. Thus Iraq's independence caused

little immediate change in the politics of the country. Oil revenues paid in the form of rent started to accrue in significant amounts in 1932 and gave the state more resources to shore up support. In 1958 a revolution destroyed the monarchy and Britain's privileged position.

Syria, Lebanon, and Transjordan received independence after World War II. All the ministates that France had created in Syria were absorbed into the Syrian Republic. In Lebanon the 1943 National Pact cemented a system of power-sharing along sectarian lines, which gave Christians a slight edge. Owing to France's weak postwar status, it was unable to secure treaties with either Syria or Lebanon to guard its privileged position. A treaty maintained Britain's influence in Transjordan, renamed the Hashemite Kingdom of Jordan after the war. The British resident became the British ambassador to Jordan, but his influence and his duties changed little.

Palestine was a different story. Britain handed its mandate for Palestine to the United Nations in 1947, and the United Nations voted to partition Palestine into two states: one Jewish, the other Arab. Since the terms of the mandate had provided that a "Jewish agency shall be recognized as a public body for the purpose of advising and cooperating with the Administration of Palestine in such economic, social and other matters as may affect the establishment of the Jewish National Home," there was a governing structure ready to step in as a Jewish state. The Arab community in Palestine had no such structure. When Britain withdrew its forces from Palestine in May 1948, the leaders of the Jewish community in Palestine proclaimed the independent state of Israel, which was immediately recognized by the Soviet Union and the United States. The Arab state that was to be created in Palestine was neither supported nor enforced by the United Nations.

ASSESSMENT OF MANDATORY RULE

In a sense, mandatory rule achieved its goal everywhere but in Palestine. France and Britain created republics and constitutional monarchies respectively, which eventually gained independence. Syria, however, did not last long as a republic, nor did Iraq as a constitutional monarchy. And by tolerating election fraud and the opportunistic suspension of elections and parliamentary rule to get the sorts of administrations Britain and France could most easily work with, they set an example for the authoritarian governments that came after independence.

Jordan is still a constitutional monarchy, though for most of the period from 1957 to 1984, the king ruled without parliament and martial law was in force. Patterns of French patronage in Lebanon deepened sectarian divisions. Although the 1943 National Pact allowed sectarian leaders to work together for independence, by 1975 there was civil war in Lebanon fueled by sectarian identities. In

Palestine, Britain failed to create a governing structure that represented the interests of the whole population. Many regard the creation of a Jewish state, Israel, as a triumph; but Palestinians are still striving to have their losses recognized and to create a Palestinian state.

The economic and developmental impact of mandatory rule is debatable, but is largely seen as negative. The bulk of mandate budgets was spent on administration and security, leaving less for infrastructure, health, and education. After independence each former mandate acted to rectify such neglect. Iraq was most successful thanks to oil revenues beginning in 1934. In both Iraq and Syria, the mandate-period ruling elites were mainly large landowners. Thus land reform was not attempted until these elites, and the mandatory structures of government that supported them, were overthrown.

During the mandate period, public education was limited, especially in Lebanon and Palestine, where large private school or nonstate school sectors catered to special groups—Christians in Lebanon and Jews in Palestine—and taught in languages, French and Hebrew, that further estranged them from the regional majority. The generation educated in such schools under the mandate brought exclusivist outlooks to the independent states that came afterward. Finally, each mandate had its own army and security forces. In the postindependence period, armies have served as the central institution of state formation in all states except Lebanon, with deleterious effects on economic development and social support networks, on internal political processes, and on the conduct of regional affairs.

SEE ALSO *British Colonialism, Middle East; French Colonialism, Middle East; Iraq; Trusteeship.*

BIBLIOGRAPHY

Andrews, Christopher M., and A. S. Kanya-Forster. *The Climax of French Imperial Expansion, 1914–1924.* Stanford, CA: Stanford University Press, 1981.

Batatu, Hanna. *The Old Social Classes and the Revolutionary Movements of Iraq: A Study of Iraq's Old Landed and Commercial Classes and of its Communists, Ba'thists, and Free Officers.* Princeton, NJ: Princeton University Press, 1978.

Hourani, Albert. *Syria and Lebanon: A Political Essay.* London and New York: Oxford University Press, 1946.

Khoury, Philip S. *Syria and the French Mandate: The Politics of Arab Nationalism, 1920–1945.* Princeton, NJ: Princeton University Press, 1987.

Monroe, Elizabeth. *Britain's Moment in the Middle East, 1914–1956.* London: Chatto & Windus, 1963; 2nd ed., Baltimore, MD: Johns Hopkins University Press, 1981.

Owen, Roger, and Pamuk, Sevket. *A History of Middle East Economies in the Twentieth Century.* Cambridge, MA: Harvard University Press, 1999.

Smith, Charles D. *Palestine and the Arab Israeli Conflict,* 5th ed. Boston: Bedford/St. Martin's, 2004.

Thompson, Elizabeth. *Colonial Citizens: Republican Rights, Paternal Privilege, and Gender in French Syria and Lebanon.* New York: Columbia University Press, 2000.

Wakehurst, J. de V. Loder. *The Truth about Mesopotamia, Palestine, and Syria.* London: Allen & Unwin, 1923.

Wilson, Mary C. *King Abdullah, Britain, and the Making of Jordan.* Cambridge, U.K.: Cambridge University Press, 1987.

Mary Christina Wilson

MANDATE SYSTEM
SEE *Trusteeship*

MANDELA, NELSON
1918–

Born in Transkei, South Africa, on July 18, 1918, Nelson Rolihlahla Mandela is one of Africa's greatest nationalists, political activists, and statesmen. The son of Chief Gadla Henry Mphakanyiswa of the Thembu and his wife, Nosekeni Fanny of the amaMpemvu clan, Mandela's father named him Rolihlahla, which literally means "pulling the branch of a tree" or "troublemaker" in Xhosa. The English name "Nelson" was added later by a primary school teacher—an example of the imperial arrogance that characterized South Africa's colonial history.

Nelson Mandela's nature was deeply rooted in his chiefly upbringing in the royal house of the Thembu after the death of his father. Mandela's life, however, was defined by the struggle against racism, an inequality that defined white-black relations in South Africa until 1995, when the country became a democracy.

Mandela was educated at Healdtown, a Wesleyan secondary school, and the missionary University College of Fort Hare. His membership in the Student's Representative Council exposed him as a firebrand young radical and activist. He was suspended from college for joining in a protest boycott against the white racist policy of the institution. But it was only after he left Fort Hare and went to Johannesburg, where he completed his bachelor of arts degree by correspondence, took articles of clerkship, and commenced study for his law degree with the University of Witwatersrand, that he set out on the long task for national liberation.

Mandela was exposed daily to the inhumanities of apartheid, where being black reduced one to the status of a nonperson. Mandela joined a small but vocal group of African political activists with the aim of uprooting centuries of colonial rule that had concentrated all political

Nelson Mandela Leaves Prison. *Mandela, hand-in-hand with then-wife Winnie Mandela, parades past a jubilant crowd shortly after his release from prison on February 11, 1990.* © PATRICK DURAND/CORBIS SYGMA. REPRODUCED BY PERMISSION.

and economic power in the hands of the white minority. He joined the African National Congress (ANC), the premier black political organization, in 1942. Mandela and a small group of young African members of the African National Congress, including William Nkomo (1915–1972), Walter Sisulu (1912–2003), Oliver R. Tambo (1917–1993), and Ashby P. Mda, under the leadership of Anton Lembede (1913–1947), founded the African National Congress Youth League in September 1944. They argued that the political tactics of the old leadership of the ANC were proving inadequate.

Members of the ANC Youth League set themselves the task of transforming the ANC into a mass movement that would derive its strength and motivation from the working people in the towns and countryside, peasants, and professionals. Mandela's leadership impressed his peers, and he was elected the secretary of the Youth League in 1947. He became deeply involved in programs of passive resistance against the pass law, which made it compulsory for all black South Africans over the age of sixteen to carry, at all times, a pass book that stipulated where, when, and for how long a person could remain in a particular part of the country. He was also involved with other apartheid legislation that kept blacks in a position of permanent servility.

The victory of the National Party in the all-white elections of 1948 on the platform of apartheid spurred more radical action from black political leaders. At its 1949 annual conference, the ANC adopted the "Programme of Action." The Programme of Action, inspired by the Youth League, advocated boycotts, strikes, civil disobedience, and noncooperation, tactics that were accepted as official ANC policy. The Youth League called for full citizenship, direct parliamentary representation for all South Africans, the redistribution of the land, trade union rights, and free and compulsory education for all children, as well as mass education for adults.

In 1950 Mandela was elected into the National Executive Committee of the ANC. From this period, the ANC became more radical in its attempt to transform South African society. Mandela was elected national volunteer-in-chief when the ANC launched its Campaign for the Defiance of Unjust Laws in 1952. This initiative was conceived as a civil disobedience campaign that would ultimately culminate in mass defiance by ordinary people.

Mandela's role as volunteer-in-chief took him to many parts of the country to organize resistance to discriminatory legislation. Mandela played an important part in leading the resistance to the Western Areas removal scheme, which forced residents out of their homes in Sophiatown and relocated them to Meadowlands (now part of Soweto), and also to the introduction of the Bantu Education Act (1953), which enforced separation of races in all educational institutions including the curriculum. In recognition of his outstanding contribution during the Defiance Campaign, Mandela was elected to the presidency of both the Youth League and the ANC in Transvaal in 1952, and thus became a deputy president of the ANC.

Mandela was constantly under the radar of the white racist regime during the whole of the 1950s. He was brought to trial for his role in the Defiance Campaign and convicted of contravening the Suppression of Communism Act of 1950, for which he received a suspended prison sentence. Shortly after the campaign ended, he was also prohibited from attending gatherings and confined to Johannesburg for six months.

The Sharpeville Massacre on March 21, 1960, occurred when sixty-nine black South Africans, protesting against pass laws, were killed as the police opened fire on them. This marked a turning point in the struggle for liberation in South Africa. A state of emergency was declared at the beginning of April 1960, and several leading anti-apartheid politicians, black and white, were arrested. Following this, the ANC and the Pan Africanist Congress (PAC) were outlawed. The leadership of the ANC went underground. Mandela emerged at this time as the leading figure in this new phase of the struggle. It was during this time that he, together with other ANC leaders, formed a new section of the liberation movement known as Umkhonto we Sizwe (Spear of the Nation) as an armed wing of the ANC in 1961. Mandela was its commander-in-chief.

In 1962 Mandela left the country unlawfully and traveled abroad for several months. He was warmly received by senior political leaders in several countries including Algeria and Ethiopia. Anticipating an intensification of the armed struggle, Mandela began to arrange guerrilla training for members of Umkhonto we Sizwe. Not long after his return to South Africa in July 1962, he was arrested and charged with illegal exit from the country and incitement to strike. Mandela was convicted and sentenced to five years in prison.

Exasperated, the government mounted a massive treason trial against ANC leaders, Mandela among them. While serving his sentence, Mandela was charged with sabotage in the Rivonia Trial, which began on November 26, 1963. During the trial, he uttered these immortal words: "I have fought against white domination, and I have fought against black domination. I have cherished the ideal of a democratic and free society in which all persons live together in harmony and with equal opportunities. It is an ideal which I hope to live for and to achieve. But if needs be, it is an ideal for which I am prepared to die."

Mandela was sentenced to life imprisonment and started his prison years in the notorious Robben Island Prison, a maximum-security prison on a small island off the coast of Cape Town. Released on February 11, 1990, Mandela plunged wholeheartedly into his life's work, striving to attain the goals he and others had set out almost four decades earlier. In 1991, at the first national conference of the ANC held inside South Africa after being banned for decades, Nelson Mandela was elected president of the organization.

In 1993 Mandela was awarded the Nobel Peace Price, which he accepted on behalf of all people who have worked for peace and stood against racism. He became the first democratically elected president of South Africa in 1994 and served until June 1999.

After stepping down as president, Mandela continued to speak with the same moral force and devotion to democracy, equality, and commitment to conflict resolution, and he continued to work for the elimination of poverty, as well as the improvement of public health in Africa, especially with regard to HIV/AIDS. He remained an inspiration to fair-minded people all over the world.

SEE ALSO *African National Congress; Apartheid; Human Rights; Segregation, Racial, Africa.*

BIBLIOGRAPHY

Mandela, Nelson. *The Struggle Is My Life*, rev. ed. New York: Pathfinder, 1986.

Mandela, Nelson. *Nelson Mandela Speaks: Forging a Democratic, Nonracial South Africa.* New York: Pathfinder, 1993.

Mandela, Nelson. *Long Walk to Freedom: The Autobiography of Nelson Mandela.* Boston and New York: Little Brown, 1994.

Meredith, Martin. *Nelson Mandela: A Biography.* New York: Saint Martin's Press, 1998.

Chima J. Korieh

MANUMISSION

Slavery was not seriously questioned until the late eighteenth century. In fact, the exploitation of slave labor was crucial to the growth of most colonies. With the development of powerful antislavery movements, the problem presented itself in different forms. The most basic difference was between colonies in which Europeans and

Americans used slave labor and those in which the slave-owners were not European. Furthermore, within the first group we can distinguish between plantation colonies in which slavery was the base of the economy and those in which slaves were less numerous and slavery less important.

THE FIRST WAVE: SLAVE SOCIETIES

The first efforts at abolition took place in the northern United States, where slavery was not crucial to economic life. In 1780 a Pennsylvania act freed slave children born after that year on condition of service until age twenty-eight. This meant that anyone born to a slave mother after 1780 remained in servitude until age 28. This formula, known as a free womb act, became popular elsewhere. Connecticut and Rhode Island passed similar acts in 1784, New York in 1799, and New Jersey in 1804. As slavery became less important, private manumissions increased, as did pressure to be done with slavery. New York abolished slavery definitively in 1827, Pennsylvania only in 1847, and Connecticut in 1848. Only in Massachusetts and New Hampshire was manumission unconditional, and in both cases it occurred as a result of court interpretation of new state constitutions.

Many slaves were manumitted in exchange for military service. During the American Revolution (1775–1783), the British tried to undercut the colonists by freeing slaves. During the wars of independence in Spanish America, both sides freed slaves who enlisted. Real manumission for other slaves did not come until after independence. In Africa, slaves who served in colonial armies were often given freedom, though conditional on fulfilling an enlistment contract. Only in Haiti did a slave revolution win immediate and total manumission. Even there, new elites tried to sustain plantation production of sugar, but the former slaves refused plantation discipline and speedily became a free peasantry.

In 1833 Great Britain ended slavery in all of its colonies. Slavery did not exist in Britain itself. Compensation was provided for slave-owners, and a period of apprenticeship was set up to smooth the transition. Slave resistance to continued plantation labor forced a speedy end to apprenticeship in 1838. Where land was available, slaves withdrew to areas more suited to small-holder production than to plantations. On the island of Mauritius in the Indian Ocean, the slaves withdrew into highland areas not appropriate for sugar and within a decade, slave labor had been totally replaced by Indian indentured labor. Even where male former slaves continued to work for wages, freed women were withdrawn from the plantation and men were reluctant to work the long hours that marked slavery.

By Jacob Radcliff Mayor, and Richard Riker Recorder, of the City of New-York,

It is hereby Certified, That pursuant to the statute in such case made and provided, we have this day examined *one* certain *male* Negro Slave named *George* the property of *Iran D. Lacey* which slave *is* about to be manumitted, and *he* appearing to us to be under forty-five years of age, and of sufficient ability to provide *for himself* we have granted this Certificate, this *twenty-first* day of *April* in the year of our Lord, one thousand eight hundred and *seventeen*

New York City Manumission Certificate. This certificate of manumission, freeing a slave named George, was signed by New York mayor Jacob Radcliff and city recorder Richard Riker in 1817. © BETTMANN/CORBIS. REPRODUCED BY PERMISSION.

Other slave-owning societies followed. In 1848 France abolished slavery. Compensation was provided to former masters, but manumission took place within several months and was complete. Denmark ended slavery the same year, largely as a result of a slave revolt. The Dutch abolished slavery in their West Indian colonies in 1863, and Spain abolished it in Puerto Rico in 1873. In Cuba, many slaves were freed during the Ten Years' War (1868–1878). Spain abolished slavery in 1880, but conditional on a long period of apprenticeship. The slaves resisted apprenticeship, and in 1886 immediate and total manumission was granted.

Those emancipating slaves were generally more concerned to compensate masters for financial losses than slaves for unremunerated labor. Manumission often involved a period of struggle over the labor of former slaves. In many areas, slave labor was replaced by indentured labor, usually from India. When the planters on the Indian Ocean island of Réunion were denied the right to recruit labor in India, they imported African indentured labor and sought to keep the existing labor force in place with laws against vagabondage and begging. The Portuguese had a disguised slave trade on the cocoa plantations of São Tomé, an island off West Africa, until 1910. In many former slave colonies, master-and-servant laws were passed specifically to control former slaves.

They increased the control employers had over employees and made it difficult for former slaves to break contracts.

THE SECOND WAVE: NON-EUROPEAN MASTERS

Some colonies were primarily trading entrepôts. In these, slaves resident in areas under European administration were usually freed, but efforts were made to limit enforcement of these laws so as not to threaten the interests of their trading partners. As colonial rule was extended, the problem was that slave-owners were not European and were often important in the administration of the colony. Colonial governments thus were under pressure from humanitarian groups at home, but were reluctant to alienate local slave-owning elites.

The most important formula was worked out in India. The 1833 British Emancipation Act did not apply to India because India was ruled not by the British Crown but by a chartered company. Parliamentary pressure on the English East India Company, however, forced it to devise a formula that minimized change. The courts were no longer to recognize claims derived from slave status. No compensation was paid to slave-owners and no alternative employment was offered to the slaves. Slavery was fully abolished only in 1860, but Indian slave-owners were generally able to maintain their control over servile labor by developing other forms of bondage.

Colonial regimes faced the same dilemma elsewhere in Asia and Africa. In many cases, they turned to the Indian formula. On the Gold Coast, such a law, proclaimed in 1874, was poorly enforced. In French Africa, the regime prohibited all exchanges of persons and quietly asked administrators to stop recognizing slave status. They hoped that slaves would not notice, but in a six-year period an estimated one million slaves left their masters. In Northern Nigeria, the British freed only those who had been mistreated. Others were guaranteed the right to purchase their freedom.

The process was similarly slow in most Asian colonies. In Indonesia, the Dutch began to hesitantly extend antislavery laws to areas of indirect rule in 1874 and completed the task only decades later. The French abolished slavery in Cambodia in 1887. In Malaya and Burma, the British operated in a similar case-by-case manner. The process was completed only in 1915 in Malaya, and in 1926 in Burma. In Nigeria and the Sudan, slavery was only made illegal in 1936.

In most cases, no assistance was given to freed slaves, but former slaves everywhere asserted control over work and family. They usually rejected plantation discipline, preferring to become smallholders. Some former slaves accepted forms of continued dependency on rich patrons. Often, with little assistance, the success of former slaves depended on the options available to them. The most important was the availability of land or jobs.

SEE ALSO *Abolition of Colonial Slavery.*

BIBLIOGRAPHY

Cooper, Frederick. *From Slaves to Squatters: Plantation Labor and Agriculture in Zanzibar and Coastal Kenya, 1890–1925.* New Haven, CT: Yale University Press, 1980.

Foner, Eric. *Nothing But Freedom: Emancipation and its Legacy.* Baton Rouge: Louisiana State University Press, 1983.

Lovejoy, Paul, and Jan Hogendorn. *Slow Death for Slavery: The Course of Abolition in Northern Nigeria, 1897–1936.* New York and Cambridge, U.K.: Cambridge University Press, 1993.

Klein, Martin, ed. *Breaking the Chains: Slavery, Bondage, and Emancipation in Modern Africa and Asia.* Madison: University of Wisconsin Press, 1993.

Klein, Martin. *Slavery and Colonial Rule in French West Africa.* New York and Cambridge, U.K.: Cambridge University Press, 1998.

Miers, Suzanne, and Martin Klein, eds. *Slavery and Colonial Rule in Africa.* London: Frank Cass, 1999.

Miers, Suzanne, and Richard Roberts, eds. *The End of Slavery in Africa.* Madison: University of Wisconsin Press, 1988.

Reid, Anthony, ed. *Slavery, Bondage, and Dependency in Southeast Asia.* New York: St. Martin's Press, 1983.

Martin Klein

MAO ZEDONG
1893–1976

Mao Zedong was born on December 26, 1893, in Shaoshan, Hunan Province, China, and died on September 9, 1976. Mao was the most influential leader and theorist of the Chinese Communist Party (CCP) and of the People's Republic of China (PRC).

In the aftermath of the 1917 Russian Revolution, Mao, while staying in Beijing, started to study Russian Bolshevik theories and methods in a search for better ways to save a weak and divided China. The unsatisfactory settlement after World War I in the 1919 Treaty of Versailles concerning the transfer of German possessions in China to Japan triggered the anti-imperialist May Fourth Movement in China. This movement brought Mao closer to Marxism and Leninism.

Mao was one of the founders of the CCP, formed in July 1921. From 1924 to 1927, under the auspices of the United Front of the CCP and the Nationalist Party (Guomindang, GMD), Mao organized labor unions and peasant associations and participated in the Nationalist Revolution against warlords and foreign imperialists. Mao

Mao Zedong, November 12, 1944. *Mao Zedong (1893–1976), the future leader of Communist China, rallies a group of Chinese people to the Communist cause.* **HULTON ARCHIVE/GETTY IMAGES. REPRODUCED BY PERMISSION.**

stressed the central role of peasants in rural class struggles. It remained the core of his belief that the semicolonial status of China—foreign meddling and mauling inside China, the resulting lack of industrial development and a strong urban proletariat class, the warlord government—meant that the Chinese revolution would have to take the form of poor peasants versus rich landlords in rural areas.

From 1927, when a breach between the CCP and GMD occurred, to 1934, Mao established rural bases in Jiangxi and Fujian provinces in southeast China, and engaged in guerrilla warfare to resist the superior GMD forces. From 1934 to 1935, the CCP Red Army was driven out of its rural soviets (CCP's armed territories/ authorities in adoption of the name of the Soviet government) and forced to relocate to Yan'an, Shaanxi Province, in northwest China. The nearly 9,700-kilometer (6,000-mile) move became known as the "Long March."

In Yan'an, Mao consolidated his power and developed political, social, and economic models for the future China. After the eight-year war against Japan ended in 1945, civil war broke out between the CCP and the GMD, despite American attempts at mediation. The defeated GMD retreated to Taiwan, and the CCP's victory in the civil war led to the founding of the PRC in 1949, with Mao as its chairman.

In spite of constant friction in its relationship with the Soviet Union (USSR), which eventually resulted in an open split in the early 1960s, Mao chose to follow Russia's Stalinist system to implement socialism in the PRC—party supremacy in the government and the army, a state-planned economy with an emphasis on heavy industry, and agricultural collectivism. To achieve his goals, Mao initiated mass campaigns such as the Great Leap Forward (1958–1960, a disastrous social and economic movement that was intended to increase agricultural and industrial production through eradication of private land ownership, moral incentives, and mass labor) and the Cultural Revolution (1966–1976, a violent mass movement against the establishment, which brought about turmoil and enormous suffering to Chinese people).

Against the backdrop of the Cold War rivalry between the USSR and the United States, Mao's China, sympathetic to North Korea's pro-Moscow Pyongyang regime, went into the Korean War (1950–1953) in direct confrontation with the United States. In support of the GMD in Taiwan, the United States had adopted a non-recognition policy toward the PRC until the visit of American president Richard Nixon (1913–1994) to China in 1972 and the final normalization of Sino–American diplomatic relations in 1979.

From the early 1940s on, Mao's revolutionary ideology and methodology were labeled "Mao Zedong Thought." Central to Mao Zedong Thought is his application of Marxist and Leninist theories of world proletarian revolutions to the actual conditions of China. Mao's "Three Worlds" idea (1974) played an important role in forming alliances in world affairs among the third world countries of Africa, most of Asia, and Latin America.

As for Mao's legacy, some view him as an evil Chinese "Lord of Misrule," who was responsible for initiating tumultuous political, social, and economic changes that caused widespread suffering among millions of people. Some argue that Mao's contributions to the Chinese nation—the restoration of China's independence and sovereignty, the unification of China, and the construction of socialism—far exceed his errors. For ordinary Chinese, Mao remains an iconic figure, which attests that the Chinese have their own memories of their own past and their own leaders.

SEE ALSO *China, After 1945; Chinese Revolutions.*

BIBLIOGRAPHY

Cheek, Timothy. *Mao Zedong and China's Revolutions: A Brief History with Documents.* Boston: Bedford, 2002.

Jiang Xianzhi and Jin Chongji, eds. *Mao Zedong zhuan, 1949–1976.* 2 vols. Beijing: Zhongyang wenxian chubanshe, 2003.

Jin Chongji, ed. *Mao Zedong zhuan, 1893–1949.* 2 vols. Beijing: Zhongyang wenxian chubanshe, 1996.

Schram, Stuart. *Mao Tse-Tung.* New York: Simon and Schuster, 1966.

Snow, Edgar. *Red Star over China.* London: V. Gollancz, 1937.

Spence, Jonathan. *Mao Zedong.* New York: Viking, 1999.

Terrill, Ross. *Mao: A Biography.* New York: Harper, 1980.

Dong Wang

MARSHALL ISLANDS

The Marshall Islands are an archipelago of thirty-four low-lying atolls in the Western Pacific, lying in a double arc running north-south at latitude 5–14 North and longitude 162–173 East. In an area encompassing 800,000 square miles, the Marshalls has a total land area of only 70 square miles. The population of 50,000 (1999 census) is distributed throughout twenty-four inhabited atolls, but over two-thirds of Marshallese are crowded onto two atolls: Majuro, the capital, and Kwajalein, the site of a U.S. missile-testing base.

The Marshalls was first settled about 2,000 years ago, probably from central Melanesia. The Marshallese language, a member of the Micronesian language family, is closely related to the languages of its neighbors in the Carolines to the west. Although Marshallese share a common language and cultural tradition, minor differences distinguish the eastern chain (Ratak) from the western (Ralik). Marshallese have always been skilled navigators, employing celestial navigation systems similar to those used throughout Micronesia, as well as distinctive stick charts to map wave patterns. Paramount chiefs (*iroij*) once had absolute authority over their people and even today retain primary rights to the land.

The first recorded European visits to the Marshalls date back to the early sixteenth century. Two centuries later, the British sea captain John Marshall gave his name to the group. Otto von Kotzebue, a Russian naval commander, explored and mapped the archipelago on his visits there in 1817 and 1824. American Protestant missionaries began evangelizing the islands in 1857, just a few years before Adolph Capelle and Anton DeBrum arrived to establish the beginnings of the trade in dried coconut meat, or copra (the source of coconut oil).

To expand its copra trade interests in the area, Germany signed a treaty in 1878 with the most powerful chief in the Ralik group. The combined pressure of the German trade firms led to full German annexation of the Marshalls in October 1885. The Jaluit Company, formed by the merger of two large trading firms, was given full administrative authority over the Marshalls until 1906. Afterward, the German government directly administered the islands from its headquarters in Rabaul.

At the outbreak of World War I, Japan occupied all former German possessions north of the equator. After 1914, the Japanese Navy was responsible for the administration of the Marshalls, with its capital in Jaluit. In 1919 the Marshalls was officially entrusted to Japan as a League of Nations mandate, after which a government bureaucracy was set up to rule the islands. Japanese fortification of the islands began in 1940, and the military facilities were used in the Japanese invasion of Kiribati and Nauru.

In early 1944, U.S. forces captured Kwajalein and Enewetak, following which the U.S. Navy established a military administration over the other islands in the group. After the war, the Marshalls, together with the remainder of the former Japanese Mandate, were designated the Trust Territory of the Pacific Islands and placed by the United Nations under U.S. administrative authority. The capital was transferred from Jaluit to Majuro at that time. Between 1946 and 1958 the islands of Bikini and Enewetak were evacuated and used as sites for nuclear testing. From 1960 on, Kwajalein was developed into a defensive missile-testing site and supported a large American community.

In 1979, following ten years of negotiations with the United States over its political status, the Marshalls became self-governing under a parliamentary democracy, ending nearly a century of colonial rule. The constitution of the Republic of the Marshall Islands provides for an elected legislature as well as the Council of Iroij, with its twelve paramount chiefs as members. The independent status of the Marshall Islands was formalized in October 1986 when it signed the Compact of Free Association with the United States and was subsequently admitted as a member of the U.N.

SEE ALSO *Pacific, American Presence in; Pacific, European Presence in; Trusteeship.*

BIBLIOGRAPHY

Hezel, Francis X. *The First Taint of Civilization: A History of the Caroline and Marshall Islands in Pre-colonial Days, 1521–1885.* Pacific Islands Monograph Series, No. 1. Honolulu: University of Hawaii Press, 1983.

Hezel, Francis X. *Strangers in their Own Land: A Century of Colonial Rule in the Caroline and Marshall Islands.* Pacific Islands Monograph Series, No. 13. Honolulu: University of Hawaii Press, 1995.

Francis X. Hezel

MASSACHUSETTS BAY COMPANY

The Massachusetts Bay Company was formed in 1628 as a joint stock venture to trade in the fish and furs of New England. But from the beginning, a number of its leaders, notably John Winthrop (1588–1649), wanted to use it as a vehicle for promoting a Puritan religious commonwealth. The Puritans were dissatisfied with the progress of reform in the Church of England and were also alarmed at the outbreak of the Counter Reformation in Europe, to reestablish the supremacy of the Roman Catholic Church. Their last hope of reform was seemingly lost when King Charles I (1600–1649) dissolved Parliament and began a period of absolutist rule. Accordingly, Winthrop and his Puritan colleagues

bought out their more commercially minded colleagues in August 1629 and set sail for America in March 1630, taking the charter with them. But before leaving, the company held one last meeting at which Winthrop was elected governor with a council of eighteen like-minded assistants. The transformation of the company into a religious commonwealth was further strengthened on arrival in Massachusetts, where the General Court of the company, comprising the governor, council, and freemen, passed a resolution stating that thereafter only full church members could participate in the colony's affairs.

For the next eighteen months Winthrop and the assistants ran the colony almost as a theocracy. They made land grants to "the elect," as church members were known, allowing them to establish covenanted communities based on the congregational principle. They also issued laws and ordinances regarding everyday life, using the Bible as their guide. All of this contravened the charter, which stated that the laws of the company were to conform to those of England. The charter also stated that quarterly meetings of the General Court were to be held, and that the governor and council should be elected annually by the freemen of the company. Although the majority of the population wanted to live as good Puritans, they still cherished their rights as Englishmen. Hence it was not long before the authority of Winthrop and the council was challenged, first over the issue of taxation in 1632 and then over the general governance of the colony in 1634. Critical to the resolution of this controversy was the demand to see the charter, which Winthrop had in his safekeeping. Inspection of this confirmed that the General Court had the sole right to raise taxes, make laws, and hold elections. As a result, Winthrop lost his position as governor, though he retained his place on the council and duly returned during the Antinomian controversy in 1636 when Anne Hutchinson (1591–1643) challenged the qualifications required for membership of the elect. Nevertheless the principle of annual elections had been established, even if participation was still restricted to the elect. Since most church members now lived outside Boston, they opted to send representatives instead of attending the General Court in person. Another change was the decision of the representatives in 1644 to sit as a separate chamber, finally breaking the dominance of the governor and council. Massachusetts now had the makings of a constitution and a representative system of government, all based ironically on its royal charter as a joint stock company.

Meanwhile, the activities of the Massachusetts Bay Company had not gone unnoticed in England, where calls were made for an investigation into both its secular and spiritual activities. Several other parties had claims to the

John Winthrop Lands in Massachusetts. *John Winthrop (ca. 1588–1649), governor of the Massachusetts Bay Colony, lands in Salem in 1630 with other English migrants to Massachusetts in this nineteenth-century engraving.* © BETTMANN/CORBIS. REPRODUCED BY PERMISSION.

area, while the Anglican Church of Archbishop William Laud (1573–1645) was alarmed at the dissenting nature of the settlement. Proceedings were accordingly begun by King Charles I to annul the company's charter. Fortunately for the Puritans, the king soon found that he had other more pressing challenges at home and had to recall Parliament. The outbreak of the English Civil War in 1641 further shielded the Massachusetts Bay Company, especially when Oliver Cromwell (1599–1658) and the Puritan Independents emerged victorious. Massachusetts now had a friendly government in England that would protect its religious and civil polity. The 1650s proved a golden time for Massachusetts as an independent self-governing commonwealth.

The restoration of Charles II (1630–1685) to the throne in 1660, therefore, was a blow to the people of Massachusetts Bay. However, the second-generation Puritans followed their predecessors' example by attempting to keep the English authorities at bay. The colony accordingly declined the request of Charles II to appoint a governor. They also maintained the fiction that their charter only required nominal allegiance to the crown and that it gave the General Court a parallel authority to

that of Parliament. Hence, when the crown demanded compliance with the Navigation Act Laws of 1660, 1663, and 1673 to control colonial trade for the benefit of the mother country, Massachusetts simply passed a duplicate measure of its own. Clearly this situation could not continue, and in 1684 the crown began proceedings once more to annul the charter of the company. This was effected in 1685. In the future, Massachusetts was to be governed by a royal governor, Sir Edmund Andros (1637–1714), with an appointive council and no representative assembly. Equally distressing to the Puritans was the decision to subsume the colony into a new entity to be called the Dominion of New England. Fortunately for Massachusetts, King James II's (1633–1701) attempts to establish an absolute monarchy on both sides of the Atlantic were overturned by the events of the Glorious Revolution in 1689, which led to accession of William III and Queen Mary to the English throne. Nevertheless, there was to be no return to the old company charter of 1629. Under the new charter of 1691 the crown would appoint the governor. However, the skillful lobbying of Increase Mather (1639–1723), the province's most influential divine minister, ensured that Massachusetts regained much of what it had previously enjoyed. Not only would the freeholders elect an assembly, but their representatives in turn would nominate the governor's council, reflecting the old company charter whereby the freemen elected the council of assistants. It was this system of government that served the people of Massachusetts until the American Revolutionary War began in 1775.

SEE ALSO *Christianity and Colonial Expansion in the Americas; Empire in the Americas, British; Fur and Skin Trades in the Americas; Religion, Roman Catholic Church.*

BIBLIOGRAPHY

Labaree, Benjamin W. *Colonial Massachusetts: A History.* Millwood, NY: KTO, 1979.

Lovejoy, David S. *The Glorious Revolution in America.* New York: Harper, 1972.

Morgan, Edmund S. *The Puritan Dilemma: The Story of John Winthrop* (1958). 2nd edition. New York: Longman, 1998.

Morison, Samuel Eliot. *Builders of the Bay Colony* (1930). 2nd edition. Boston: Houghton Mifflin, 1962; reprinted 2004.

Richard Middleton

MAU MAU, AFRICA

Mau Mau is the term given to the insurgence that arose in Kenya as early as 1946 but was at its height between 1952 and 1956. The movement was rife in Nairobi, the Central Province, and in the settler provinces of the Rift Valley in Kenya. The effects of the movement were felt worldwide and impacted the postindependence politics in Kenya. At its height, the movement pitched the Kikuyu and the related Embu and Meru in guerrilla warfare against the British.

Mau Mau had economic and social origins arising from the urban squalor in Nairobi, whose population was growing at a very rapid rate without the necessary social services or infrastructure. This led to unsanitary conditions and low wages for the African workers. Another source of discontent lay in the loss of land that pushed many of the Kikuyu people into squatter farming in European farms where wages were extremely low and working conditions poor. Within the Kikuyu community, the rise of capitalism dispossessed the traditionally landless people, the *ahoi,* who were traditional tenants of those who had land. The *ahoi* were forced to seek wage labor in the urban centers and European farms, aggravating the sprawling, poor living conditions in these areas and heightening discontent with colonialism.

As discontent increased among Africans in general between 1944 and 1946, the Kikuyu transformed traditional Kikuyu oaths into a device for forging solidarity against Europeans. The period witnessed escalating violence that drew the attention of the colonial government to what administrative officials referred to as a "subversive organization, Mau Mau." Violence by the so-called Mau Mau reached alarming proportions by the first two months of 1952 during which cattle were maimed and mutilated in settler farms and crops were set on fire. Chiefs and their families and supporters, the African police, and Christians were attacked and killed as agents or as supporters of the colonial government.

On October 20, 1952, the colonial government declared a state of emergency following the assassination of a powerful Kikuyu chief by the Mau Mau. On the same date, African nationalist leaders including Jomo Kenyatta and AchiEng Oneko were arrested and detained. The declaration of the state of emergency forced Mau Mau leaders and Mau Mau adherents into the forests from which they waged guerrilla war against the British and the loyalists.

Both men and women entered the forests, revising some of the traditional gender relations as some women rose to hold positions as Mau Mau generals while men took up cooking responsibilities traditionally associated with women. By 1956, the British forces had stopped the military phase of the Mau Mau movement, especially when they rounded up, screened, arrested, and placed Kikuyu, Embu, and Meru in detention camps. The screenings and detention cut off the Mau Mau from their supply of food, clothing, hiding places, and ammunition. To circumvent arrest, some Kikuyu tried to emulate practices of other cultural groupings; for example, some removed their six lower teeth, a practice associated with the Luo people of Nyanza province, in the hope of passing as Luos. The Mau Mau movement is bound up with various facets of anticolonialism and tied to differently situated African peoples and communities in colonial Kenya. Many scholars and political leaders have interpreted Mau Mau as a nationalist liberation movement, and called Mau Mau freedom fighters. Others have termed it a peasant revolt against landlessness and Mau Mau as land struggle among the Kikuyu, a peasant war emerging out of the growing class struggles among the Kikuyu, or a religious and political movement. The movement, however, forced the British to rethink their policies in Kenya, especially regarding African representation in the governing of Kenya.

SEE ALSO *Anticolonialism; Britain's African Colonies.*

BIBLIOGRAPHY

Elkins, Caroline. *Imperial Reckoning: The Untold Story of Britain's Gulag in Kenya.* New York: Henry Holt, 2005.

Mau Mau Rebels Under Arrest, 1953. *Colonial police escort twenty-seven Mau Mau nationalists to court in Githunguri on April 14, 1953. The men were accused of setting fire to villages in the uplands district of the Kiambu near Nairobi, leading to the deaths of some 150 villagers.* © BETTMANN/CORBIS. REPRODUCED BY PERMISSION.

Odhiambo, Atieno, and Lonsdale John, eds. *Mau Mau and Nationhood: Arms, Authority and Narration.* Athens: Ohio University Press, 2003.

Throup, David. *Economic and Social Origins of Mau Mau, 1945–1953.* London: James Curry, 1987.

Edith Miguda

MEDICAL PRACTICES, MIDDLE EAST

The medical practices of the Middle East have a long history of interchange with the West. In the late medieval world a massive transfer of medical and scientific knowledge took place from the Arab-Islamic world to western Europe, while in the modern colonial period western European states *medicalized* many of the new states of the Middle East. Prior to the nineteenth century most of these places had not been constituted as countries, and much recent work in the history of medicine has concentrated on the imperial use of medicine as a form of repression and cultural subjugation in the creation of nation-states. Almost all of the Middle East—which is seen here as stretching from Morocco in North Africa to Iran—was occupied at some point in the nineteenth or twentieth centuries by imperial, primarily French and British, powers.

While the cultures of the Middle East evidently possessed distinct local medical practices, from the eighth century C.E. onward they all shared a medical culture that was based on three interlinking medical systems, whose composition varied from place to place and over time: Graeco-Arabic medicine, Qu'ranic medicine, and what Kathleen Malone O'Connor refers to as "vernacular medicine."

In the Medieval period Arabs and Persians were enthusiastic translators of Greek scientific knowledge. The term *Graeco-Arabic medicine* refers to the combination of Galenic and Hippocratic medical knowledge with indigenous Arabian medical beliefs, some of which were borrowed from Indian Ayurveda and other Eastern forms of medicine. Scientific learning was prized and promoted by the state in the Islamic world, which led classic Islamic physician-scholars, such as Ibn Rāzi, Ibn Sina, and Ibn Rushd, to refine and develop Greek medicine. Great emphasis was placed on diet, public health, and the connection between physical and spiritual well-being. This ethical approach to health fused with the growing field of Qu'ranic medicine, which advocated an approach to welfare that drew on the Qu'ran and the *hadith* (sayings) of Prophet Mohammed. In some cases this could involve the use of amulets inscribed with Qu'ranic verses, tinctures formulated from Qu'ranic ink, and prayer, but it also shared a belief in astrological medicine that was present in Graeco-Arabic healing. These treatments were supplemented by "vernacular medicine," which was primarily based upon pre-Islamic herbalism, and the science of pharmacology, which was very well developed in the medieval Arab-Islamic world.

Each of these forms of medicine shared an approach to health that stressed the importance of collective and individual efforts to prevent the spread of sickness, both through public health initiatives (such as hospitals) and the encouragement of righteous living. Arab-Islamic medicine was therefore profoundly holistic and it possessed a strong moral dimension, which is evinced in medieval literatures on medical ethics that discuss notions of justice, such as the question of whether it is acceptable for a doctor to charge for his services.

Many of the techniques and ideas of Arab-Islamic medicine were transferred to western Europe, often through Iberia, in an uncoordinated program of translation that transferred the knowledge generated by the "Golden Age" of Islamic science (1200 to 1600 C.E.). Texts such as Ibn Sina's *Canon of Medicine* became standard medical reference works across Europe, while the holistic ethos of Arab-Islamic medicine deeply influenced some European centers of medical learning, such as Montpellier. By the eighteenth century, however, western Europeans were confident that they had themselves developed a superior medical system. Known as *scientific medicine*, this was characterized by the emphasis on medicine's curative potential, often through surgical procedures, and was associated with Montpellier's great French rival, the Paris school of medicine.

Most Western colonists had little conception that the countries they occupied in the Middle East possessed complex medical cultures, let alone forms of medicine that had in fact played a formative role in the development of European scientific medicine. This European medicine was seen as a tool of progress that would reawaken the "primitive" cultures of the Middle East, and in most imperial ventures doctors played a large part in both establishing safe living conditions for the servants of the imperial state and in offering medical services that aimed to win over local populations. This process reached its apogee with the so-called *médecins aventuriers* in Morocco, who Maréchal Lyautey declared would "form the front-line of colonialism. In each settlement I will establish a native clinic.... Little by little, the gifts of civilisation will calm desires for independence" (Bidwell 1973, p. 16).

In neighboring Algeria, French doctors had played a large part in forging an Algerian state, often representing the only nonmilitary French authority with which Algerians came into contact. The French state promised Algerians a national health-service network that went beyond even the state's responsibility for medical provision in France, but budgetary constraints eventually led to Western medical knowledge being dispersed by competing groups of military, mission, and private doctors. The failure of this promise of universal healthcare, best seen in the tiny numbers of Algerians trained in medical professions, and the hostility of many Algerians toward drugs and vaccinations, which seemed to have little effect against the epidemics and plagues that ravaged the country, led to a disillusionment with Western medicine that was also apparent elsewhere in the Arab-Islamic world. A similarly nuanced approach to the reception of Western medical systems has been observed by Khaled Fahmy in his study of the development of a School of Midwifery in 1830s Cairo. Fahmy demonstrates how such training institutions represented both an extension of socioeconomic opportunity for Egyptian women and the means by which the modern state could gain greater oversight and control of its population. There were, however, states, such as Sudan, where Western medicine was seen in a more benign light, in part through the concerted efforts to recruit local doctors and to solve local problems.

Recent studies of eighteenth- and nineteenth-century Ottoman, Egyptian, and Persian medicine (see Murphey, Sonbol, Ebrahimnejad) have stressed the need to understand the medicalization of the Middle East as a complex process, in which both local and Western parties borrowed from each other, and where there were strong lines of continuity from traditional medical practices. This was especially evident in the case of medical education, where hospital-based training drew on the traditions of the *maristans* (traditional Middle Eastern hospitals) (Sonbol 1991, p. 6). Such education did, however, introduce novel notions of specialization, for whereas traditional Egyptian practitioners had often acted as doctors and herbalists, the Western system of distinctions between pharmacists, surgeons, and physicians became the regional norm (Sonbol 1991, pp. 44–45). With regard to Iran, Hormoz Ebrahimnejad goes so far as to assert that "the embryo of modernization in nineteenth-century Iran resided in the institutionalization of traditional medicine" (2004, p. 11).

Further illustration of this complex relationship comes in Daniel Panzac's work on the plague in this period. While plagues had been eradicated from western Europe by the eighteenth century, they continued to occur periodically throughout the Middle East. Panzac shows that the management of plagues in the Ottoman Empire was not only a central focus of the gradually more hierarchical exchange of medical knowledge between West and East, but also a major impetus for the establishment of international systems of disease management (in the form of quarantines and *cordons sanitaires*) that were forerunners of twentieth-century international health institutions.

On gaining independence all new states in the Middle East based their new, national medical systems on administrative models borrowed from the West. These systems were, however, much better resourced than had been the case in the colonial period, and in all of the Middle East there have been dramatic improvements in mortality rates and the near eradication of previously endemic diseases such as bilharzia and malaria. From 1950 to 1990, life expectancy rose from 41.8 years to 62.1 years in North Africa and from 45.2 to 66.3 years in West Asia, through a combination of improved nutrition, childhood immunization programs, improved water supplies, and increasing literacy (Barlow 1999, p. 3). As any visitor to a *souk* anywhere in the Middle East will see, Western, allopathic medicine exists alongside a continuing belief in traditional medical practices, such as herbalism, in a synthesis that precedes the contemporary West's interest in integrating scientific and complementary systems of medicine.

SEE ALSO *British Colonialism, Middle East; French Colonialism, Middle East; Literature, Middle Eastern; Western Thought, Middle East.*

BIBLIOGRAPHY

Barlow, Robin. "Health Trends in the Middle East, 1950–95." In *Studies in Middle Eastern Health*, edited by Joseph Winchester Brown and Robin Barlow. Ann Arbor: University of Michigan Press, 1999.

Bayouni, Ahmed. *The History of Sudan Health Services*. Nairobi: Kenya Literature Bureau, 1979.

Bidwell, Robin. *Morocco under Colonial Rule: French Administration of Tribal Areas, 1912–1956*. London: Cass, 1973.

Bürgel, J. Christoph. "Islam." In *Dictionary of Medical Ethics*, rev. ed., edited by A. S. Duncan, G. R. Dunstan, and R. B. Welbourn. London: Darton, Longman, and Todd, 1981.

Ebrahimnejad, Hormoz. *Medicine, Public Health, and the Qājār State: Patterns of Medical Modernization in Nineteenth-Century Iran*. Leiden, Netherlands: Brill, 2004.

Fahmy, Khaled. "Women, Medicine, and Power in Nineteenth-Century Egypt." In *Remaking Women: Feminism and Modernity in the Middle East*, edited by Lila Abu-Lughod. Princeton, NJ: Princeton University Press, 1998.

Gallagher, Nancy. *Medicine and Power in Tunisia, 1780–1900*. Cambridge, U.K.: Cambridge University Press, 1983.

Gutas, Dimitri. *Greek Thought, Arabic Culture: The Graeco-Arabic Translation Movement in Baghdad and Early Abbāsid Society*. London: Routledge, 1998.

Kamal, Hassan. *Encyclopedia of Islamic Medicine*. Cairo: General Egyptian Book Organisation, 1975.

MacLeod, Roy, and Milton Lewis, eds. *Disease, Medicine, and Empire: Perspectives on Western Medicine and the Experience of European Expansion*. London: Routledge, 1988.

Murphey, Rhoads. "Jewish Contributions to Ottoman Medicine, 1450–1800." In *Jews, Turks, Ottomans: A Shared History, Fifteenth through the Twentieth Century*, edited by Avigdor Levy. Syracuse, NY: Syracuse University Press, 2002.

O'Connor, Kathleen Malone. "Prophetic Medicine and Qu'ranic Healing: Religious Healing Systems in Islam." In *Studies in Middle Eastern Health*, edited by Joseph Winchester Brown and Robin Barlow. Ann Arbor: University of Michigan Press, 1999.

Panzac, Daniel. *La peste dans l'empire ottoman, 1700–1850*. Louvain, Belgium: Éditions Peeters, 1985.

Sonbol, Amira El Azhary. *The Creation of a Medical Profession in Egypt, 1800–1922*. Syracuse, NY: Syracuse University Press, 1991.

William Gallois

MEKONG RIVER, EXPLORATION OF THE

The mighty Mekong River flows for about 4,180 kilometers (2,600 miles) from its origins in the Tibetan highlands of western China to the South China Sea off the coast of southern Vietnam, passing through China, Burma (Myanmar), Laos, Thailand, and Cambodia. It was first mapped in the 1640s, in part by the Dutch merchant Gerrit van Wusthoff, who traveled upstream from a site near present-day Phnom Penh in Cambodia to Vientiane in what is now Laos. His report noted the severe navigational difficulties that he encountered, and for more than two hundred years, the full course of the river remained unmapped.

In the 1860s, however, soon after France had established its foothold in Indochina, French officials optimistically saw the Mekong as a gateway to the markets of central China. France established its protectorate over Cambodia in 1863, in part to gain access to this potential source of wealth. Preliminary explorations, echoing van Wusthoff, revealed that the river was not navigable between northern Cambodia and Laos because of daunting waterfalls and rapids. In Laos, moreover, the depth of the river varied sharply between the dry and rainy seasons, often rendering it impassable for shipping. These findings failed to dampen the fervor of the French, who were eager to map the river and to extend their influence into the unmapped and uncolonized parts of Asia.

In 1866 a forty-three-year-old French naval officer, Ernest Doudart de Lagree (1823–1868), who was posted to the Cambodian court, was placed in command of a twenty-two-man expedition. Second in command of the expedition was a fiery, ambitious, and talented naval officer, Francis Garnier (1839–1873), then only twenty-six. Garnier wrote a lively narrative of the expedition in 1869. Louis Delaporte (1842–1925), a talented French artist, also took part in the expedition and later produced an invaluable illustrated account.

The explorers set off confidently from Saigon (Ho Chi Minh City) in June 1866. Their stores included half a ton of rations, 700 liters (about 185 gallons) of wine, and 300 liters (about 79 gallons) of brandy, but no supply of sturdy boots.

After making a side excursion to the recently "discovered" Angkor ruins in northwestern Cambodia, the explorers proceeded north, where the rapids at Sambor in Cambodia and the Khone Falls in southern Laos impeded their progress. Returning to the river after marching around the falls, they proceeded upstream through several Lao-speaking principalities, reaching Luang Prabang—perhaps the first Europeans to do so—in April 1867. By then their supplies were running low, de Lagree was ill, and safe passage through northern Laos, Burma, and western China was by no means certain.

By October 1867, however, the explorers had reached western China. After traveling overland to Kunming, Garnier wanted to turn west to search for the sources of the Mekong, whereas de Lagree, who was seriously ill, argued that mapping the Red River, which flowed into northern Vietnam, would be more feasible and potentially more profitable for France. Leaving de Lagree to convalesce, Garnier attempted to reach the sources of the Mekong, but he was prevented from doing so by mistrustful local rulers. De Lagree died in March 1868, and the expedition came officially to an end. The surviving explorers, taking de Lagree's body with them, sailed down the Yangzi to Shanghai, reaching Saigon in July.

In a little more than two years, the expedition had mapped 6,700 kilometers (more than 4,160 miles) of Asian land and had reached parts of the world that had never been visited by Europeans. The expedition, however, brought no economic benefits to France, and it was poorly reported in Europe. Garnier, eager to salvage some glory for himself and for his country, lobbied for recognition when he returned to France, but only six hundred copies of his sumptuous two-volume account were ever published, while Delaporte limited his account to his travels in Cambodia. The posthumous account by a third explorer, Louis de Carné (1844–1871), was an amateurish production, filled with racialist remarks about the people of Cambodia, Laos, and China.

Francis Garnier became an imperial hero after he was killed in combat outside Hanoi in 1873. A second, condensed edition of his account, published in 1885, was a best seller in France.

SEE ALSO *French Indochina; Travelogues.*

BIBLIOGRAPHY

Osborne, Milton. *River Road to China,* 3rd ed. New York: Liveright, 1999.

Osborne, Milton. *The Mekong.* Sydney: Allen and Unwin, 2000.

David Chandler

MELANESIA

Melanesia is a region of the southwestern Pacific Ocean and forms, together with Micronesia and Polynesia, one of the three cultural areas of Oceania. Melanesia includes New Guinea, the Torres Strait Islands of northern Australia, the Solomon Islands, Vanuatu, New Caledonia, and the Fiji Islands. The name *Melanesia* derives from Greek words meaning *black islands* and refers to the dark complexions of the indigenous inhabitants.

Human beings have inhabited Melanesia for at least 40,000 years, and Melanesians were among the first peoples to develop agriculture, about 10,000 years ago. Scattered islands and rugged terrain led to the formation of small cultural groups, often isolated from each other, and over 1,000 indigenous languages are spoken in the region. Traditional Melanesian society was not based on a system of hereditary chiefs; instead, individuals became politically powerful through their own actions.

Although the coast of New Guinea was reached by the Portuguese possibly as early as 1512, most historians consider the Spanish expedition of Álvaro de Mendaña (1541–1595) as the first European contact. Mendaña reached what he called the Solomon Islands in 1568. Despite naming the islands after a legendary king of great wealth, the Spanish found no gold and consequently the islands held little interest for them. The Dutch arrived later and landed in Fiji and New Guinea in 1643. English explorers, including Captain James Cook (1728–1779), visited the New Guinea area in the 1770s at about the same time the French visited Vanuatu and the Solomon Islands.

Western colonization did not really begin until the nineteenth century, and even then was limited by the presence of tropical diseases and the resistance of the indigenous population. Missionaries started arriving around 1839, and by the 1850s the Dutch, British, French, and Germans began claiming parts of Melanesia. The Dutch claimed the western half of New Guinea, whereas the eastern half was divided between Germany and Britain. These countries also split the Solomon Islands, with the British taking Fiji as well. France claimed New Caledonia, Vanuatu, then the New Hebrides, which was jointly ruled by Britain and France. Britain later transferred its holdings in New Guinea to Australia, and after Germany's defeat in World War I (1914–1918), Australia acquired German New Guinea.

European colonialism united disparate ethnic groups under one administration, and imposed European languages, religion, economy, and political systems on top of the indigenous ones. Europeans introduced agricultural plantations using indigenous labor, and some Melanesians were brought to Australia in a form of slavery known as blackbirding. The British also brought laborers from India to Fiji.

Independence came late to Melanesia. Fiji became independent in 1974. The Australian territories in New Guinea became independent as Papua New Guinea in 1975, followed by the independence of the Solomon Islands in 1978 and Vanuatu in 1980. New Caledonia remains a French colony, and the western part of New Guinea is part of independent Indonesia, despite independence movements among the indigenous population. Postcolonial Melanesia has been troubled by ethnic conflicts, such as the recent coups in Fiji and secessionist movements in Papua New Guinea, Vanuatu, and the Solomon Islands.

SEE ALSO *Pacific, American Presence in; Pacific, European Presence in.*

BIBLIOGRAPHY

Lal, Brij V., and Kate Fortune, eds. *The Pacific Islands: An Encyclopedia.* Honolulu: University of Hawaii Press, 2000.

Oliver, Douglas L. *The Pacific Islands*, 3rd ed. Honolulu: University of Hawaii Press, 1989.

Scarr, Deryck. *A History of the Pacific Islands: Passages Through Tropical Time*, 2nd ed. London: Routledge/Curzon, 2001.

Michael Pretes

MERCANTILISM

Although the term *mercantilism* encompasses the diverse trade practices followed by European states from the sixteenth until the late eighteenth century, its core assumptions may be summarized: that wealth is an absolutely indispensable means to achieve geopolitical power; that such power is valuable as a means to acquire or retain wealth; that wealth and power constitute the dual ends of national policy; and that these two ends are compatible and, indeed, complementary. English commercial writer Charles Davenant claimed that, in "matters of empire, whoever is the cause of another's advancement is the cause of his own diminuition" (Davenant 1704, pt. 1, p. 205). A nation could not remain, in his view, "unarmed, sit still and suffer another country to enlarge its dominions" (Davenant 1704, pt. 1, p. 205). Mercantilism, then, refers to the collection of policies designed to keep the state prosperous through economic regulation.

EARLY TRADE POLICIES

The keystone of the mercantilist system was the complex network of regulations controlling the trade of colonies with each other and with the mother country, the chief object being to secure monopoly and prevent competitor nations from enjoying the produce of, and trading with, one nation's colonies. As another English seventeenth-century writer, Josiah Child, noted: "If [colonies] are not kept to the rules" then the "benefit of them would be wholly lost to the nation" (Child 1688, pp. 177–178). England's Navigation Act of 1651 set the pace and tone of interimperial trade relations. It represented a genuine departure from past policy. Designed originally to eliminate the Dutch as the principal shippers of English imports, the Navigation Act signaled a new attitude toward government regulation, and put the power of the state squarely behind national economic development. It forbade the importation of plantation commodities from Africa, America, or Asia, except on ships owned and operated by English subjects.

Under the terms of its 1696 amplification, foreign agents or states were forbidden from engaging in any facet of colonial trade, articles could not be shipped from the colonies to foreign nations, and colonial imports were limited to goods shipped from England, thus creating a monopoly. The term *monopoly* was applied to any trade where there was a legal or legally sanctioned restriction on entry. The goal was to free England from its reliance on foreign commodities and to give English manufactures a free hand in its dominions. Every other European empire endeavored to create a closed, monopolistic trading system in order that all benefits of colonization would accrue to itself alone, rendering the empire self-sufficient and economically independent of the rest of the world. If the attempt by every nation to create a monopoly by excluding the merchants of all other nations from its colonies was one pillar of the mercantile system, the attempt to exclude all merchants other than those of a single privileged company was the second.

After trade legislation, the privileged (sometimes referred to as monopoly or chartered) commercial company was the second mainspring of mercantilism in the seventeenth and eighteenth centuries. Companies were forged out of the cooperation of state power and market-oriented entrepreneurship. Their creation entailed the delegation of government authority and property rights to the company in an overseas dominion. In exchange for rights of sovereignty and exclusive economic access to a colonial territory, such companies were required to construct forts and garrisons to protect against the depredations of indigenous inhabitants, to provide naval power and protection from aggression by other European nations, and to conduct diplomatic relations with indigenous rulers. Louis XIV's reforming minister in the late seventeenth century, Jean Baptiste Colbert, had viewed companies as effective in colonial trade where the traffic was not well established and long sea voyages and financial risks were involved. Other nations followed suit and by the end of the seventeenth century the globe was divided into rival empires of trade.

CHANGING ATTITUDES

Just before the turn of the eighteenth century, attitudes toward the mercantilist trading system began to change. Whereas the mercantilists maintained that a nation could develop economically only by outstripping and impoverishing its neighbors in a zero-sum world, new political writers began to rethink trade, the sources of wealth, and the bases of geopolitical power. In France, a group of political economists called Physiocrats contended that all wealth derived from agriculture and argued for the virtues of laissez-faire, or free trade. Two leading Physiocrats, François Quesnay and Marquis de Mirabeau, in their widely circulated 1763 tract *Rural Philosophy*, asserted that nations that adopted agriculture "sooner or later came to enjoy the benefits of society, of union, of population, of good and equitable laws, and of the appropriate arts and skills" whereas the others had "grown old in a state of barbarism" (Meek 1973, p. 110).

Although many of the French economists were connected to the world of imperial administration, Baron Turgot urged Louis XVI to contemplate an unimperial future, calling for the West Indian sugar islands to become independent states, connected to France only by the bonds of identity of origin, language, and customs. More radically, Abbé Raynal urged European nations to relinquish colonial monopoly and to remove "every obstacle...that intercepts a direct communication" (Paquette 2004b, p. 206) between the Americas and all of Europe. Raynal contended that privileged companies never recovered the money and rights advanced to them through the duties they levied. For Raynal, the world historical purpose of commerce was to corrode relentlessly the fences of colonial fiefdoms until it produced a universal society without national boundaries. The trend away from privileged companies in France culminated in the 1769 suspension of the Compagnie des Indes.

It was the Scot Adam Smith who coined the terms *mercantile system*, which he used derisively. In *The Wealth of Nations* (1776), Smith contended that the fundamental error of the mercantilists was their confusion of wealth with money. Since they believed, mistakenly, that a favorable balance of trade was the primary means of acquiring wealth and money, they had been unable to conceive of the advantages to be derived from foreign trade. Similarly, he explained that the exclusion of foreign competition from the colonial trade might indeed have raised profits, but that this apparent advantage was offset by an accompanying rise in prices that subjected the nation to "an absolute and relative disadvantage in every branch of trade of which she has not the monopoly" (Smith 1976, vol. 2, p. 592). The mercantile system, then, "rendered less secure" the long-term prosperity of the colonial power because "her commerce, instead of running in a great number of small channels, has been taught to run principally in one great channel" (Smith 1976, vol. 2, p. 604).

Even before the appearance of Smith's treatise, the British Navigation Acts had been loosened somewhat by the creation of free ports in the British Caribbean in 1766. These were designed, primarily, to allow silver-laden vessels from Spanish ports to enter Britain, essentially making the de facto smuggling de jure. Such a reduction in restrictions was preceded by the Dutch free port at St. Eustatius (1737), the Danish example in St. Thomas and St. John (1763), French experiments in Martinique and Guadeloupe (1763–1765), and the Spanish Caribbean in 1765. The powers wielded by the British East India Company came under similar scrutiny, though the company was not dismantled. British statesman Edmund Burke observed with dismay that it did not seem to be only a company formed for the extension of British commerce, but in reality a delegation of Britain's sovereignty deployed to the East.

This late-eighteenth-century skepticism presaged further attacks on the various components of the mercantile system by the classical political economists of early-nineteenth-century Britain: David Ricardo condemned colonial trade restrictions on free trade grounds, arguing

ABBÉ RAYNAL

∎

Born in Saint-Geniez, France, on April 12, 1713, Guillaume-Thomas-François Raynal is noted for his influential writings on slavery in the New World. Educated by the Jesuits, Raynal initially joined the Roman Catholic order and worked at the Parisian parish of Saint-Sulpice. Abbé Raynal, as he is more commonly known, eventually left the Jesuits and started a writing career, beginning with a popular work on the history of the Netherlands and another on the history of the English Parliament.

In 1770 Raynal published the controversial six-volume *Philosophical and Political History of the Settlements and Trade of the Europeans in the East and West Indies*, which strongly condemned both the Roman Catholic Church and the French government. The fourth volume of the collection criticizes in detail the use and treatment of slaves in the North and South American colonies, and advocates the abolition of the slave trade. Raynal warned European leaders that if the slaves were not freed, bloody revolutions would soon commence, a prediction vindicated shortly thereafter by the Haitian slave rebellion of 1791.

Four years after its publication, the *Philosophical and Political History* was banned by the church, and in 1781 it was burned by the French public executioner, after which Raynal fled the country. Raynal was allowed to return in 1787, and two years later witnessed revolution in France, followed in 1794 by a formal decree eliminating slavery in the French colonies. Raynal died on March 6, 1796.

---

that the existence of such exclusive colonial markets neither affected profits nor were necessary for the employment of the mother country's surplus capital. James Mill opposed such colonial monopoly on utilitarian grounds, claming that the mother country was gaining at the expense of the colonies, thereby decreasing the sum of overall public welfare of the empire as a whole.

SHIFTS IN MERCANTILISM

Although the reservations voiced by the Physiocrats and Adam Smith were ascendant after 1760, some European powers clung to, and benefited from, the reinvigoration of the mercantile system. In Portugal, the powerful reforming prime minister, the Marques de Pombal, derided "all business which is done in foreign countries [as] insecure and very contingent" because the "ambition and greed inspired in other countries gives rise to frequent attempts to impede or usurp [that commerce]" (Carvalho e Melo 1986, p. 42). None of these dangers, Pombal reasoned, "threatens commerce which is conducted with colonies," potentially a "secure and perpetual" relation so long as the "exclusion of foreigners" and "care in watching over the colony's commerce and fertilizing it each day more in order to sprout new branches" (Carvalho e Melo 1986, p. 42) were maintained.

Trading companies became the basic building block in his grand design upon his rise to power in 1755 and were realized most fully in Brazil. In creating the companies of Grão Pará and Maranhão, Pombal sought to develop new export commodities (such as cotton and rice) and encourage the growth of colonial manufactures. These companies, which did not survive Pombal's political fall, were abolished in 1778 and 1779 and a freer trade between Portugal and northern Brazil was established. The companies had failed to achieve their economic objectives: Less than one-quarter of the shipments to the colonies were composed of national manufacturers while Portuguese textiles represented only 30 percent of total dispatched to the empire.

In the Spanish Empire, debates over colonial trade monopoly and privileged companies were particularly fierce. From the advent of its dominion in the New World, the Crown had zealously guarded its American dominions from foreign penetration. Until 1720 all ships had to pass through Seville, and between 1720 and 1765, through Cádiz. Foreign commercial ships were, in legislation at least, prohibited from entering Spanish American ports. Furthermore, in an attempt to guarantee markets for Spanish exports, the development of manufactures was strictly forbidden in the colonies. The early-eighteenth-century Spanish political economists, whose thought underpinned the changes that Spain imposed on the structure and functioning of its empire between 1759 and 1808, endorsed monopoly and trading companies: Geronimo Uztáriz attributed Spain's economic stagnation to the composition of its foreign and domestic trade and poor shipping facilities, both of which caused otherwise avoidable outflows of precious metals.

Spain had fallen behind its imperial rivals, but its plight was reversible. This realization unleashed the debate over the viability of Spain's mercantile system: On the one hand, Raynal's Spanish translator implored the reader to resist the French Abbé's siren call of liberty of commerce, warning that it often proved nothing but a chimera. On the other hand, in his 1794 preface to *Wealth of Nations,* Smith's translator mocked Britain for having granted trading companies sovereign power and the right to maintain garrisons and fortifications in overseas dominions. The so-called free trade decrees of 1765 and 1778 did away with some of the regulations constricting Spanish colonial commerce, represented the death knell of the Royal Havana Company, and seemed to prefigure a Smithian or physiocratic embrace of freer trade. Yet foreigners were still legally excluded from Spanish entrepôts and trading companies persisted: Less regulated trade did not prove to be the anticipated remedy for the deep-seated structural malaise brought on by belated industrialization and colonial undersupply. By the 1780s, such shortcomings of the new approach prompted the Crown to experiment with a combination of freer trade and regulated companies. A Philippines Company was empowered to conduct trade between Manila and the entire empire, as well as exclusive right to import slaves into Venezuela. In addition, widespread smuggling and Creole discontent conspired to render unworkable the mercantile system by the eve of Spanish American independence in 1808.

Although the trend was toward freer trade, it was hardly an inexorable and irreversible movement. Even in Britain, the old allegiance to the Navigation Acts, the bulwark of the mercantile system, persisted and even outpaced newfangled economic liberalism. One prominent writer accused Smith of not merely opposing monopoly, but favoring the "dismemberment of the empire" (Paquette 2004a, p. 200). Even when free trade was adopted in one area it sometimes proved to be a powerful inducement for protection in another, and the languages of these different systems mingled in the mouths of political writers and policymakers. Older views about the role of the state in international trade remained, as did the goals of economic self-sufficiency and the avoidance of reliance on foreign suppliers: In the aftermath of the American Revolution, English politician Lord John Sheffield famously remarked that "freedom of commerce is not a power granted to merchants to do what they please." Only after 1820 would liberal notions of wealth, trade, and empire fully take hold. When they finally did, they would underpin a new, nonmercantilist conception of colonialism: the imperialism of free trade.

SEE ALSO *Enlightenment Thought.*

BIBLIOGRAPHY

Anderson, Gary, and R. D. Tollison. "Apologiae for Chartered Monopolies in Foreign Trade, 1600–1800." *History of Political Economy* 15 (4) (1983): 549–566.

Blussé, Leonard, and Femme Gaastra, eds. *Companies and Trade: Essays on Overseas Trading Companies during the Ancien Régime.* Leiden, Netherlands: Leiden University Press, 1981.

Carvalho e Melo, Sebastião de [later, Marques de Pombal]. *Escritos Económicos de Londres (1741–1742)* (London Economic Writings). Edited by José Bareto. Lisbon, Portugal: Biblioteca Nacional, 1986.

Child, Josiah. *A Discourse About Trade.* London: 1668.

Crowley, John E. *The Privileges of Independence: Neomercantilism and the American Revolution.* Baltimore: Johns Hopkins University Press, 1993.

Davenant, Charles. *Essays Upon Peace at Home, and War Abroad.* 2 parts. London: 1704.

LaHaye, Laura. "Mercantilism." In *The Concise Encyclopedia of Economics.* The Library of Economics and Liberty. Available from http://www.econlib.org/library/enc/mercantilism.html.

Magnusson, Lars. *Mercantilism: The Shaping of an Economic Language.* London and New York: Routledge, 1994.

Maxwell, Kenneth. *Pombal: Paradox of the Enlightenment.* New York: Cambridge University Press, 1995.

Meek, Ronald L. *The Economics of Physiocracy: Essays and Translations.* Cambridge, MA: Harvard University Press, 1963.

Meek, Ronald L., ed. *Precursors of Adam Smith.* Totowa, NJ: Rowman and Littlefield, 1973.

Paquette, Gabriel B. "The Image of Imperial Spain in British Political Thought, 1750–1800." *Bulletin of Spanish Studies* 81 (2) (2004): 187–214.

Paquette, Gabriel B. "The Intellectual Context of British Diplomatic Recognition of the South American Republics, c. 1800–1830." *Journal of Transatlantic Studies* 2 (1) (2004): 75–95.

Rothschild, Emma. "Global Commerce and the Question of Sovereignty in the Eighteenth-Century Provinces." *Modern Intellectual History* 1 (1) (2004): 3–25.

Ruiperez, Mariano García. "El Pensamiento Economico Ilustrado y las Compañías de Comercio." *Revista de Historia Económica* 4 (3) (1986): 521–548.

Smith, Adam. *An Inquiry into the Nature and Causes of the Wealth of Nations.* 2 vols. Oxford, U.K.: Oxford University Press, 1976.

Smith, Robert Sidney. "*The Wealth of Nations* in Spain and Hispanic America, 1780–1830." *Journal of Political Economy* 65 (1) (1957): 104–125.

Stein, Stanley J., and Barbara H. Stein. *Apogee of Empire: Spain and New Spain in the Age of Charles III, 1759–1789.* Baltimore: Johns Hopkins University Press, 2003.

Viner, Jacob. "Power Versus Plenty as Objectives of Foreign Policy in the Seventeenth and Eighteenth Centuries." In *Revisions in Mercantilism,* edited by D. C. Coleman. London: Methuen, 1969.

Winch, Donald. *Classical Political Economy and Colonies.* Cambridge, MA: Harvard University Press, 1965.

G. B. Paquette

MERCENARIES, EAST ASIA AND THE PACIFIC

The most renowned mercenaries (soldiers hired into foreign service) in colonial Asia were those hired by both sides of the momentous military campaigns during China's Taiping Rebellion (1850–1864). As the most devastating civil war in human history, in which at least 25 million lives were lost, the Taiping Rebellion took place in the aftermaths of the Opium War, which ended with China's agreement to open its door to Westerners who subsequently flocked to China's coastal regions in search of adventure, profit, and Christian converts. Unsatisfied with their gains, the Western governments took advantage of the crisis faced by the ruling Qing dynasty and in the midst of the Taiping Rebellion dispatched a significant number of troops, military and naval, to force new, more conciliatory treaties upon the Qing court. Consequently, there was a large community of foreign nationals, both military and civilian, in China to be hired as mercenaries in the epic campaigns.

The Taiping rebels had 104 Western mercenaries in their service. The American J. I. Roberts for a while was the Taiping rebels' top adviser in charge of foreign affairs. On the Qing side, the desperate court in 1861 formed an Ever-Victorious Army, a bona fide mercenary military unit, to be recruited, trained, and led by an American adventurer from Salem, Massachusetts, Frederick T. Ward. Motivated primarily by lucrative financial reward, Ward vigorously worked to expand the Ever-Victorious Army, openly luring British and French expeditionary force soldiers to desert their units and join his mercenary army. Many answered his call, which displeased the British and French military officials.

Ward was killed in battle in 1862, at a time when his mercenary army had grown to 3,000 strong. The Qing court chose Henry Andrea Burgevine as Ward's successor. But the opportunistic Burgevine soon switched sides to the Taiping rebels for higher service fees. Eventually, a deeply religious Charles George Gordon, who came to China in 1860 to invade Beijing for more favorable treaties from the Chinese government, resigned his commission as an artillery major from the British Army and became the last commander of the Ever-Victorious Army until its successful ending in late May 1864. It was Gordon who made the mercenary unit a meaningful modern fighting force. Other well-known mercenaries during the late Qing period include the Frenchman Prosper Giquel, and two Brits, Sir Samuel Halliday McCartney and Horatio Nelson Lay.

The most legendary mercenary adventure in Asia in the twentieth century is the American Voluntary Group, popularly known as the Flying Tigers, that Claire Lee Chennault commanded for the Chinese cause against the Japanese aggression in the late 1930s and early 1940s.

SEE ALSO *Taiping Rebellion.*

BIBLIOGRAPHY

Hu, Guangbiao. *100 Foreigners Who Influenced China's Modernization* [yingxiang zhongguo xiandaihua de yibai yangke]. Taipei: Zhuanji Wenxue Press, 1984.

Spence, Jonathan. *To Change China: Western Advisers in China, 1620–1960.* New York: Little, Brown, 1969.

Maochun Yu

MEXICO

SEE *New Spain, the Viceroyalty of*

MEXICO CITY

Mexico City, once the dominant city in the Aztec Empire, became one of the most important cities in the Spanish Empire and, undoubtedly, in the history of global colonialism.

First founded as Tenochtitlán in 1325, the city fell in August 1521 to Spanish conquerors led by Hernán Cortés (ca. 1484–1547). Destroyed by the conquest, Tenochtitlán was not immediately selected as the site of the conquerors' new settlement; however, the strategic and symbolic advantages of the site outweighed its disadvantages, and within months the reconstruction and repopulation of the city were underway. The city was soon designated a center for imperial secular and clerical administration. In 1535 Tenochtitlán became the capital of New Spain, the first viceroyalty to be created in the Americas. In 1547 Mexico's bishopric was recreated as an archdiocese. In 1571 the city received a tribunal of the Holy Office (the holy office of the inquisition, charged with policing Catholic orthodoxy and, increasingly, the behavior of the faithful).

By the end of the sixteenth century, then, Mexico City exercised spiritual and temporal jurisdiction over a vast area comprising much of Central America, the Caribbean, and even the Philippines. The viceregal capital also acted as an important financial center and a conduit for the bullion that issued from the mines to the north of the city after the mid-1540s. A significant amount of this silver flowed through the city to the port of Veracruz and on to Spain. However, much also remained in the churches and merchant houses of New Spain's capital, fueling both local ostentation and, through lending activities, the continued economic growth of the region.

Throughout the colonial period, Mexico City would act as a centripetal force throughout the Spanish-speaking world, attracting both wealth and a disproportionate number of settlers. With an estimated population of 170,000 on the eve of Mexican independence in 1820, Mexico remained the largest city in Latin America and one of the colonial world's major centers throughout its colonial history.

SEE ALSO *Empire in the Americas, Spanish.*

BIBLIOGRAPHY

Bakewell, Peter. *A History of Latin America: Empires and Sequels, 1450–1930.* Oxford and Malden, MA: Blackwell, 1997.

Brading, D. A. *Miners and Merchants in Bourbon Mexico, 1763–1810.* Cambridge, U.K.: Cambridge University Press, 1971.

Marroquí, José María. *La ciudad de México,* 3 vols. México: Jesús Medina, 1969 [1900].

Morse, Richard. "The Urban Development of Colonial Spanish America." In *The Cambridge History of Latin America,* edited by Leslie Bethell, vol. 2, 67–104. Cambridge, U.K.: Cambridge University Press, 1987.

Jacqueline Holler

MICRONESIA

Micronesia is a region of the central Pacific Ocean. It forms, together with Melanesia and Polynesia, one of the three cultural areas of Oceania. Micronesia includes the islands of Guam and Nauru, and the Mariana, Caroline, Marshall, Gilbert, and Line islands. The name *Micronesia* derives from Greek words meaning "tiny islands." Most of these islands are atolls, or low coral islands fringing a partially enclosed lagoon.

Human beings have inhabited parts of Micronesia for at least five thousand years. Though Micronesia extends over a vast area, its people are excellent sailors and discovered and settled nearly every island in the region well before Europeans arrived. Traditional Micronesian society was based on a system of hereditary chiefs, with individuals divided into nobility and commoners.

The first European to visit Micronesia was the Portuguese Fernão de Magalhães (1480–1521), better known in English as Ferdinand Magellan. Employed by the king of Spain, Magellan entered the Pacific from the southern tip of South America and reached Guam in 1521.

Though Spain laid claim to Guam in 1565, it did not establish a settlement there until the mid-1600s. As

in other parts of Oceania, European colonialism really began in the nineteenth century. Though Spain was a weak colonial power at this time, it still controlled Guam, as well as the Mariana and Caroline Islands, though British and American traders and missionaries had become active on these islands. Britain claimed the Gilbert Islands and the nearby island of Banaba, while Germany claimed the Marshall Islands and Nauru.

After Spain's 1898 loss in the Spanish-American War, the United States acquired Guam and Spain and sold the Marianas and the Carolines to Germany. Germany lost all its colonies after its defeat in World War I, with the Marianas, Carolines, and Marshalls going to Japan, and Nauru being administered by Australia. Japan settled large numbers of its citizens in Micronesia, but lost these colonies after its own defeat in World War II; its Micronesian empire was transferred to the United States.

The small size and remote location of Micronesia's islands did not make it an especially attractive place for European colonialism. Export crops were largely limited to copra, a form of dried coconut used for its oil, and the islands of Nauru and Banaba were also important as sources of phosphate fertilizer. Micronesia was of strategic importance, given its location between the United States and Japan, the two naval powers of the Pacific, and both countries militarized islands under their control.

Today Micronesia is a mix of colonies, semicolonies, and independent states. The Gilbert Islands became independent in 1979 as the Republic of Kiribati, and Nauru is also an independent republic. Guam and the Northern Marianas are still colonies of the United States, while the Marshalls and Carolines are in "free association" with the United States, meaning that the United States maintains certain political rights in those places. The Caroline Islands were split into Palau and the Federated States of Micronesia, the latter consisting of the four states of Yap, Chuuk, Pohnpei, and Kosrae.

SEE ALSO *Federated States of Micronesia; Marshall Islands; Pacific, American Presence in; Pacific, European Presence in.*

BIBLIOGRAPHY

Lal, Brij V., and Kate Fortune, eds. *The Pacific Islands: An Encyclopedia.* Honolulu: University of Hawaii Press, 2000.

Oliver, Douglas L. *The Pacific Islands,* 3rd ed. Honolulu: University of Hawaii Press, 1989.

Scarr, Deryck. *A History of the Pacific Islands: Passages Through Tropical Time,* 2nd ed. London: Routledge/Curzon, 2001.

Michael Pretes

MINAS GERAIS, CONSPIRACY OF

This conspiracy, known in Brazilian history as the *Inconfidencia Mineira*, took place in Minas Gerais in 1788 to 1789, and involved members of the region's wealthy and cultured elites, most of them Brazilian-born. It occurred at a time of difficulties in the region's economy, connected to the decline of its previously opulent gold mining industry, and of resentment toward the Portuguese government for its oppressive system of taxation, especially the onerous tax on gold. However, while the conspiracy began as a protest against the policies of the metropolitan government, it became an anticolonial movement. Its intellectual authors, many of whom had studied at the Portuguese university of Coimbra or in France, were inspired by the American Revolution and dreamed of following its example by eliminating Portuguese rule, making Minas Gerais independent, and installing therein a republican form of government. Although it was thwarted before being put into operation, the conspiracy is generally considered the first attempt to overthrow the colonial order in Brazil.

The conspiracy failed when, at the start of 1789, Joaquim Silvério dos Reis went to the governor of Minas Gerais and reported to him a conspiracy against the colonial government. The governor, the viscount of Barbacena, and the viceroy of Brazil, Luis de Vasconcelos e Sousa, ordered an investigation, in which the leading suspects were duly imprisoned, tried, and found guilty. In April 1791 the new viceroy, the Count of Resende, presided over a trial at which eleven conspirators were sentenced to the gallows and seven others banished to Africa. The only one executed was Joaquim José de Silva Xavier, a junior army officer who had been very active in plotting rebellion, and who was known as "Tiradentes" (Toothpuller), a name that is sometimes given to the movement. He was hanged, beheaded, and quartered in Rio de Janeiro on April 21, 1792. The sentences of the others were commuted to banishment through a pardon granted in October 1791, which became public under the agreement of April 18, 1792.

The mainspring of the plot was the decline in gold mining in Minas Gerais in the second half of the eighteenth century, a decline that generated tensions of all kinds. It led among other things to a steady rise in the number of *quilombos* (settlements of runaway slaves) and of poor freedmen. This process was aggravated by the incessant growth of Minas Gerais's debt to the Royal Treasury and the imminent collection of the *derrama*— the tax assessed on the inhabitants' income, paid by the captaincy into the Royal Treasury. A new dimension to political protest came, however, from the successful overthrow of the colonial order in British North America in 1776 to 1783. The North American experience offered a new model to those who opposed Portuguese policies and sharpened perusal of Enlightenment writings like those of the *abbé* Raynal, the contemporary French critic of the European colonial system.

The conspirators' plans envisaged an end to control by the metropolis and an alternative form of government, either a republic or a constitutional monarchy; they also had schemes for improving economic life that included the removal of constraints on diamond mining, establishment of a mint and a gunpowder mill, and promotion of local initiative. On certain points there was disagreement, however. Some favored a general emancipation of the slaves, as they believed the new freedmen would be eager to defend the new regime; others feared the resultant loss of labor in the fields and mines. Yet others desired freedom only for slaves born in Brazil, not for the great majority who were born in Africa.

The principal actors in the conspiracy came from the upper echelons of regional society. According to the final report of the official investigation, the principal landowners, cattle breeders, mine owners, contractors, judges, and military officers of the region joined the movement, in addition to some of the prominent Brazilian intellectuals of the time. Among the conspirators were the poet Cláudio Manoel da Costa; Tomás Antonio Gonzaga, a poet and magistrate of Vila Rica; Inácio Alvarenga Peixoto, magistrate and landowner; the army officers Francisco de Paula Freire de Andrade, military commandant of the captaincy, and ensign Joaquim José de Silva Xavier; the clerics Luís Vieira da Silva, owner of one of the colony's best libraries, Carlos Correia de Toledo, and Oliveira Rolim; the young José Álvares Maciel, who had studied in Europe; and the contractors and merchants João Rodrigues de Macedo and Domingos de Abreu Vieira.

The Minas conspiracy was for many years ignored or mythologized, and historians have treated it in very different ways. The first mention of the episode occurs in the English writer Robert Southey's *History of Brazil*. Southey belittled the conspiracy, characterizing it as merely the first appearance of revolutionary ideas in Brazil and repudiating any similarity to the independence movement in the British colonies of North America. In the *História Geral do Brasil* (1854–1857), Francisco Adolfo de Varnhagem, the quasi-official historian of the empire during the reign of Pedro II, disparaged the plot. Concerned with stressing his era's continuity with the colonial period, he played down Brazil's conflicts with Portugal, especially in connection with the Bragança dynasty. At the beginning of the twentieth century, in a reaction against the acclaim showered on Tiradentes by the Republic (established 1889), Capistrano de Abreu attributed scant importance to the Minas Conspiracy in his chapters on colonial history, stressing its parallels to the Pernambuco uprisings of 1710 to 1711 or 1817. However, the discovery of new documents allowed Joaquim Norberto de Souza e Silva to offer a new interpretation of the movement in his *História da Conjuração Mineira* (1873), emphasizing Tiradentes's deeply mystical religious ardor. The Minas Gerais historian Francisco Iglesias later also upheld the importance of the movement, stressing that use of the term "conspiracy" was appropriate.

However, the most original contribution to the subject comes from Kenneth Maxwell. On the one hand, Maxwell paid great attention to the influence of European politics on the plot. On the other, he argued that the Minas Conspiracy was based more on economic than ideological issues and reconstructed the complex panorama in which the conspiracy arose, by analyzing internal divisions within the colonial administration, disputes between elites and administration, and the unique character of Tiradentes's career.

More recently, Laura de Mello e Souza has argued that the conspiracy was part of a tradition of protest in Minas Gerais that resurfaced throughout the nineteenth century. Examining common elements among the dissenting movements of the captaincy—the *Emboabas* war (1707–1709), the Pitangui (1717) and Vila Rica (1729) rebellions, the Curvelo "conspiracy" (1761)—she proposes a reconsideration of the Minas conspiracy as an intertwining of different protests against crown regulations, while downplaying its anticolonial character.

SEE ALSO *Brazilian Independence; Rio de Janeiro.*

BIBLIOGRAPHY

Maxwell, Kenneth. *Pombal, Paradox of the Enlightenment.* Cambridge, U.K., and New York: Cambridge University Press, 1995.

Maxwell, Kenneth. *Conflicts and Conspiracies: Brazil and Portugal, 1750–1808.* Rev. ed. New York: Routledge, 2004.

Silva, Joaquim Norberto de Souza e. *História da Conjuração Mineira.* Rio de Janeiro: Garnier, 1873.

Southey, Robert. *History of Brazil.* London: Longman, Hurst, Rees, Orme, and Brown, 1810–1819.

Souza, Laura de Mello e. *Norma e Conflito: Aspectos da história de Minas no século XVIII.* Belo Horizonte, São Paulo: Editora UFMG, 1999.

Varnhagem, Francisco Adolfo de. *História Geral do Brasil.* Belo Horizonte, São Paulo: Itatiaia/EDUSP, 1973. (Originally published in 1854–1857.)

Carmen Alveal

MINING, THE AMERICAS

Although a complex mosaic of factors underpinned Spanish imperialism in the Americas, there is abundant evidence that for the *conquistadors*—as for the monarchy that licensed their expeditions—the quest for gold was of fundamental importance. The tone was set at the outset, with Christopher Columbus's log entry for October 13, 1492, describing his first encounter with native Americans:

> I was attentive and sought to learn whether they had gold and I saw that some of them wore a small piece suspended from a hole they have in the nose. And I was able to understand by signs that, going to the south there was a King who had large vessels of gold and who had a great deal of it.

Cuba, located by taking this southward course, yielded little immediate treasure. Gold nose ornaments and bracelets were found in northern Hispaniola, however, as well as a river, promptly named "River of the Gold," "all full of gold, to such an extent that it was a marvel." For the next two decades, the economic life of Hispaniola was underpinned by gold. This was obtained not from mines but, first, from accumulated native treasure, and, as these stocks diminished, from placer deposits in riverbeds panned by native conscripts. The conquests of Panama and Costa Rica similarly provided access, by looting and barter, to the artifacts, and to a lesser extent the placer deposits, of more advanced native societies that for centuries had been accumulating gold objects produced by the sophisticated technique of lost-wax casting. Remittances of gold to Spain reached an early peak in 1511 to 1515, and, after a brief fall reflecting the rapid decline of the native labor force in the islands, boomed from the early 1520s as the conquest of Mexico yielded much treasure. In 1520, for example, Hernán Cortés sent objects worth 32,400 pesos to Charles I, which he described as "so marvelous that considering their worth and strangeness they are priceless." The unsentimental sovereign had them promptly melted down for their bullion value.

The subsequent conquest of Peru (1532–1533), where Francisco Pizarro found an enormous stock of decorative and even utilitarian gold and silver objects, produced even greater riches. Many of these treasures were not "Incan" in a strict sense, but the products of earlier cultures whose craftsmen had been masters of advanced hollow-case casting and soldering for at least 2,000 years. Pizarro melted down virtually everything he could get his hands on, producing at Cajamarca alone—in 1533, from Atahualpa's ransom—13,420 pounds of gold and 26,000 pounds of silver. The sack of Cuzco, in November 1533, revealed incredible treasures, including life-size animal and human gold figures, all destined for the melting pot. On every occasion that treasure was distributed, scrupulous care was taken to set aside the one fifth due to the crown. The first consignment of Peruvian booty—part of the Cajamarca yield—reached Seville in 1534 in the custody of Hernando Pizarro (Francisco's half-brother), who returned to his native Extremadura to recruit more men for the Peruvian adventure. As men flowed one way, the bullion that fired their imaginations continued to pour in, giving a significant boost to the volume and value of trade in each direction. One significant feature was that silver, which had represented less than 1 percent of the value of bullion reaching Spain in the 1520s, began to rival gold in the 1530s. Indeed, it exceeded gold by a ratio of 7 to 1 in terms of volume, although the greater value of gold (10 to 1 in this period) allowed the latter to retain its supremacy, at least in the short term.

By the late 1530s, despite the continuing subjugation of regions with large treasure stocks—for example, New Granada (modern Colombia)—the more far-sighted settlers realized that the bonanza of native gold was drawing to an end, and that in the future bullion would have to be secured by the development of mining. By the second half of the sixteenth century, New Granada was emerging as the major gold-producer in South America, particularly as miners invested in the purchase of black slaves to replace the diminishing native labor force in Cáceres and Zaragoza. This early boom fizzled out in the 1620s, but gold production increased in New Granada from the late seventeenth century, as new deposits were opened up. Calculating actual production is virtually impossible, but what is certain is that exports of gold to Spain reached an annual average of two million pesos by the late eighteenth century. Chile, Mexico, and Peru also emerged as significant producers of gold—responsible for about two million pesos a year between them—but were overshadowed from the 1690s by Brazil, where the discovery of gold in the rugged interior sparked off a gold rush in Minas Gerais, Goiás, and Matto Grosso. The boom lasted until the 1750s, drawing thousands of settlers from the coast, and estimated total production in the eighteenth century reached thirty million ounces (roughly the same as that yielded by the California gold rush of the nineteenth century). In Spanish America, by contrast, silver mining reigned supreme, following the beginning of the exploitation of fabulously rich deposits at Potosí in Upper Peru (modern-day Bolivia) in 1545 and Zacatecas (in Mexico) in 1548. All production figures are to some extent "guesstimates," but what is certain is that in the period 1500 to 1650, registered trade conveyed 181 tons of gold and 16,000 tons of silver from America to Spain. Small amounts of copper were also exported, and more was mined for local use, but

significant exploitation of this metal and of tin would not occur until the late nineteenth century.

CONSOLIDATION AND DEVELOPMENT OF SILVER MINING, 1550–1700

During the Habsburg period Spanish America's preeminent mining center was Potosí, standing at an altitude of over 4,000 meters (13,123 feet) in the mountains of Upper Peru. In 1550 to 1554 alone, it yielded no less than thirteen million pesos, outstripping neighboring Porco (where the Incas had mined silver), and other Andean centers including Castrovirreina, Oruro, and Cerro de Pasco (in production from 1555, 1606, and 1630, respectively). Its rich surface ores—in the first two decades some had a silver content as high as 50 percent—were smelted in ovens known as *guayras*, and by 1556 the crown was receiving over 450,000 pesos as its fifth. Revenue remained at this level until 1567, when a temporary recession was caused by the working-out of the rich surface ores—yields had fallen to 2 percent by 1570—making smelting uneconomical, particularly because of the high costs of obtaining fuel from distant forests. Registered output fell back sharply from ten million pesos in 1565–1569 to 6.4 million in 1570–1574 (a five-year period during which Zacatecas produced slightly more), reducing the profits of both the miners and the crown. However, the crisis was only temporary, for in 1571 the refining process that extracted silver from ore by amalgamation with mercury was successfully introduced at Potosí, permitting silver production to expand to forty-seven million pesos in the 1570s and sixty-four million in the 1580s. The royal fifth yielded more than a million pesos a year in the period 1579 to 1634, before the onset of a gradual, if uneven, decline in the second half of the century. In the period 1550 to 1629 registered production at Potosí totaled 371 million pesos, compared with 90 million at its nearest rival, Zacatecas.

Potosí's preeminence resulted from three factors. The first, and most obvious, was the abundance of ores yielding sufficient silver to make mining profitable, despite their falling value after the boom of the first two decades. Unlike the Mexican mining centers, Potosí also enjoyed a guaranteed supply of mercury from Huancavelica (in central Peru), where production of the precious liquid metal began in 1564. Getting the mercury to Potosí was not easy—it either had to be carried by mules and llamas along 1,200 kilometers (745.6 miles) of mountain tracks 5,000 meters (16,404 feet) high or shipped down the coast to Arica for an equally difficult overland journey—but the required annual supply of 5,000 *quintales* (hundredweight) was guaranteed. The miners of Mexico, by contrast, were almost entirely

How the Indians Mine Silver from the Rock. *This engraving, rendered circa 1600 by Theodor de Bry, was based on published accounts of New World mining activities by the sixteenth-century Spanish missionary José de Acosta.* © **STAPLETON COLLECTION/ CORBIS. REPRODUCED BY PERMISSION.**

dependent on shipments from Seville of mercury from the Spanish mine of Almadén (and occasional supplies from Huancavelica), the regularity of which was often affected by conflicts in the Atlantic between Spain and other maritime powers. Consequently, Mexican miners, and the merchants upon whom they relied for capital, were more reluctant than their Peruvian counterparts to invest in the extraction of ores in times of uncertainty, because only those of high grade were worth processing by smelting when mercury was unavailable. Potosí's third, and most decisive, advantage was the system of draft Indian labor, the *mita*, implemented in 1573 by viceroy Francisco de Toledo, which provided for the delivery of thousands of natives to work in its mines and refining plants. By 1578 the annual draft had been fixed at over 14,000, one-seventh of the adult male population of a series of provinces selected by Toledo. Despite subsequent revisions downward to 4,000 a century later, as disease and migration took their toll on the dwindling native population of the contributing provinces, the system gave the Potosí miners a guaranteed supply of fixed-price labor. Some of the Europeans allotted quotas of Indians were actually able to receive substantial incomes without mining or refining any silver, by agreeing with native community leaders that cash compensation might be sent to them instead of laborers. The *mita* system, which also supplied a smaller number of conscripts to the Huancavelica mercury mine, theoretically reconciled the notional "freedom" of the native population with the crown's desire to provide the mining industry with a subsidized labor force. In reality it resulted in widespread and systematic abuse of the conscripts, many of whom either died from overwork or mercury poisoning or were prevented from returning to their communities at the end of their year of service at Potosí.

The rapid increase in Potosí's output in the last quarter of the sixteenth century resulted in a parallel growth in bullion remittances from Peru to Spain, from nearly five million pesos in 1571–1575 to a peak of twenty-four million in 1591–1595. In the latter period a further ten million arrived from Mexico. Enormous though they were, these remissions did not represent total production, for some silver remained in America to finance local trade or for manufacture into jewelry, some was diverted to Asia in return for Chinese silks shipped through Manila to Acapulco, and an incalculable amount lubricated contraband trade. The first two decades of the seventeenth century witnessed the onset of what would become by mid-century a sustained fall in silver remissions to Spain, reflecting to some degree gradual falls in production at Potosí and Zacatecas. At Potosí, for example, the fifth yielded one million pesos for the last time in 1649, falling to 800,000 in 1659, 624,000 in 1669, and 622,000 in 1679. By 1700 it brought in 434,000, and it continued to slide until 1736 when, in an attempt to revive the industry, the crown halved the tax to a tenth. This measure promptly reduced the revenue to a mere 183,000 pesos, but thereafter tighter fiscal controls coupled with an increase in silver output gradually raised the yield to 400,000 by 1780. Production difficulties in both Mexico and Peru, reflecting increasing problems in maintaining adequate supplies of labor (because of native depopulation) and mercury (because of frequent international conflicts), were partly responsible for the decline in the volume and value of transatlantic trade in the late Habsburg period. However, the fundamental cause was not economic decline in America. Rather, as France, England, and the Dutch Republic seized Caribbean islands and engaged in contraband and direct attacks on Spanish shipping both in the Caribbean and in the Pacific, a growing amount of private silver was retained in America to finance regional and contraband trade. At the same time, the bulk of the crown's diminishing taxation revenue was diverted into expenditure on defense. In Peru, for example, total crown revenue in 1653 was 3.7 million pesos, of which 490,000 was spent on defense costs and 1.7 million was remitted to Spain. In 1686 to 1690, by contrast, average annual revenue had fallen to 3.1 million pesos, but defense costs had multiplied threefold, to 1.3 million pesos a year, and thus remittances to Spain averaged a mere 150,000. A similar trend can be seen in Mexico, which by 1700 was providing 3.9 million of Spanish America's total bullion production of 8.3 million pesos. Although output at Zacatecas, which accounted for 40 percent of total

Mexican production in the seventeenth century, fell by half in the second quarter of the century, and the industry as a whole was depressed in 1635 to 1690 (mainly because of a shortage of mercury), the fall in output was much less severe than the downward curve in official transatlantic trade. There, too, a greater proportion of silver was being retained to pay for a more sophisticated defensive-administrative apparatus, and to finance the creation of an economic infrastructure that was becoming more developed than that of Spain itself.

MINING IN THE BOURBON ERA (1700–1810)

Registered bullion output increased fourfold in Spanish America in the eighteenth century, with Mexico recording an increase of 600 percent and Peru (including Upper Peru, which was transferred to the new viceroyalty of the Río de la Plata in 1776) an increase of 250 percent. In Mexico the first surge forward occurred in the first three decades, with output rising from 3.9 million pesos in 1700 to an average of 10.2 million in the 1720s. It grew more modestly to an average of thirteen million in the 1750s, and then declined (to an average of 11.9 million in the 1760s) before recovering to 17.2 million in the 1770s. Thereafter, the spectacular growth continued, with production averaging 19.4 million in the 1780s and 23.1 million in the 1790s, a level maintained in the first decade of the nineteenth century (22.7 million a year), before the onset of insurgency in 1810 reduced output in 1810–1814 to a mere 9.4 million a year. The record year was 1804, when Mexico registered 27 million pesos (two-thirds of all American production) and the single mining center of Guanajuato produced as much silver as Peru and Upper Peru combined.

In South America total output declined in the first quarter of the eighteenth century (from 6.4 to 3.5 million pesos a year), before the onset of a steady increase to a high point of 10 million pesos a year by century's end. By then Potosí was producing about 3 million pesos a year (as it had in the 1650s). Potosí's primacy was under threat, however, from the central Peruvian center of Cerro de Pasco, where output grew rapidly in the last quarter of the century—partly because merchant capitalists based in Lima invested there rather than at Potosí, following the separation of the latter from the viceroyalty of Peru. In Mexico, too, long-term investment by prominent merchant families was far more important in promoting growth than the attempts made by the crown in the 1780s to promote technical innovation and acquaint miners with new processing and engineering techniques. The Spanish mining specialist Fausto de Elhuyar succeeded in establishing a School of Mines in Mexico in 1792, while his brother Juan José had some success in introducing new technology in the Mariquita silver district before his death in 1796. However, the expedition to Peru and Upper Peru led by the Swedish scientist Thaddeus von Nordenflicht in 1788–1810 achieved little, partly because the conservative mining community reacted with hostility to his attempts to persuade them to adopt expensive new machinery for the amalgamation of their ores.

The bulk of Spanish America's mining production during the boom period of the late eighteenth century—over 20 million pesos a year, representing 62 percent of registered output—continued to be remitted to Spain, with the balance being consumed within the American economic system. According to some estimates, about half as much again of official production escaped registration and taxation, disappearing into the increasingly complex channels of contraband trade established primarily in the Caribbean and the Río de la Plata by traders from England and British America. Whether by these informal routes or by reexport from Spain to pay for the manufactured goods required in America that peninsular industry was unable to provide, most American bullion ended up in the countinghouses of Britain, Holland, and other European countries, feeding the increasing international demand for the silver required for trade with Asia. In relative terms, the importance of treasure imports into Spain diminished in the last quarter of the eighteenth century, from an average of 76 percent of the total value of goods arriving from America to an average of 56 percent. This shift was due to the gradual liberalization of trade during the reign of Charles III, which promoted the production and export of agricultural goods—mainly sugar, hides, cotton, coffee, and indigo—in parts of Spanish America hitherto regarded by the crown as of secondary importance, precisely because of their inability to provide significant quantities of precious metals. Nevertheless, the boom in American silver production meant that the volume of bullion reaching Spain continued to grow. Trade in all commodities came to an abrupt standstill in 1796, with the outbreak of what turned out to be prolonged hostilities between Spain and Britain, which in the commercial sphere led Charles IV to grant permission in 1797 for Spanish American ports to trade with neutral ships. When the crown withdrew that permission in 1799, the emerging agricultural regions, notably Venezuela and the Río de la Plata, began to demand genuine free trade in order to preserve their newfound prosperity, gradually realizing that they would first have to win their political independence in order to secure commercial freedom. The majority of the inhabitants of silver-producing Mexico and Peru, by contrast, remained loyal to the royalist cause in 1810.

SEE ALSO *Potosí.*

BIBLIOGRAPHY

Andrien, Kenneth J. *Crisis and Decline: The Viceroyalty of Peru in the Seventeenth Century.* Albuquerque: University of New Mexico Press, 1985.

Bakewell, Peter J. *Silver Mining and Society in Colonial Mexico: Zacatecas, 1546–1700.* Cambridge, U.K.: Cambridge University Press, 1971.

Bakewell, Peter J. *Miners of the Red Mountain: Indian Labor in Potosí, 1545–1650.* Albuquerque: University of New Mexico Press, 1984.

Barrett, Elinore M. *The Mexican Colonial Copper Industry.* Albuquerque: University of New Mexico Press, 1987.

Boxer, Charles R. *The Golden Age of Brazil, 1695–1750: Growing Pains of a Colonial Society.* Berkeley and Los Angeles: University of California Press, 1962; reprint, 1969.

Brading, David A. *Miners and Merchants in Bourbon Mexico, 1763–1810.* Cambridge, U.K.: Cambridge University Press, 1971.

Brading, David A., and Harry E. Cross. "Colonial Silver Mining: Mexico and Peru." *Hispanic American Historical Review* 52 (1972): 545–579.

Cole, Jeffrey A. *The Potosí Mita, 1573–1700: Compulsory Indian Labor in the Andes.* Stanford, CA: Stanford University Press, 1985.

Fisher, John R. *Silver Mines and Silver Miners in Colonial Peru, 1776–1824.* Liverpool: Centre for Latin American Studies, University of Liverpool, 1977.

Garner, Richard L. "Long-Term Silver Mining Trends in Spanish America: A Comparative Analysis of Mexico and Peru." *American Historical Review* 93, no. 4 (1988): 898–935.

Klein, Herbert S. *The American Finances of the Spanish Empire: Royal Income and Expenditures in Colonial Mexico, Peru, and Bolivia, 1680–1809.* Albuquerque: University of New Mexico Press, 1998.

McFarlane, Anthony. *Colombia before Independence: Economy, Society, and Politics under Bourbon Rule.* Cambridge, U.K.: Cambridge University Press, 1993.

Sharp, William F. *Slavery on the Spanish Frontier: The Colombian Chocó, 1680–1810.* Norman: University of Oklahoma Press, 1976.

Tandeter, Enrique. *Coercion & Market: Silver Mining in Colonial Potosí, 1692–1826.* Albuquerque: University of New Mexico Press, 1992.

John Fisher

MISSIONARIES, CHRISTIAN, AFRICA

When the Jesus movement moved from Palestine to the Greco-Roman world Africa became one of the major centers of Christianity, before the Islamic incursion in the seventh century, which disrupted the growth of African Christianity.

EARLY CONTACT WITH AFRICA

When the Portuguese first made contact with Africa in the fifteenth century, they were in search of four things. Number one, they were in search of a sea route to the spice trade in the Far East because Muslims controlled the land route through the Levant and the breadbasket in the Maghrib. Second, the Portuguese wanted to participate in the lucrative Trans-Saharan gold trade. Third, they initiated the "Reconquista" project to recover Iberian lands from the Muslims. Finally, they sought to reconnect with the mythical Christian empire of Prester John for the conversion of the heathens. The Portuguese monarch secured papal bulls, granting him powers to appoint clerical orders in the shoe-string empire discovered between 1460 and 1520, stretching from Cape Blanco to Java. But Portugal was a small country and lacked the manpower to control and evangelize large territories. They occupied the islands and coastal regions of Africa, and traded from their *feitoras* (trading posts). Cape Verde Islands became the center of missionary enterprise and a refueling depot. Iberian Catholicism was a religion of ceremonies and outward show, formal adherence supplanted strong spiritual commitment. Court alliances used religion as an instrument of diplomatic and commercial relationship.

A missionary impact that insisted upon the transplantation of European models remained fleeting, superficial, and ill-conceived. Evangelization succeeded among the *mestizo*, mixed-race, children of the traders. Incursions into the kingdoms of Benin and Warri (part of present-day Nigeria) soon failed as the Portuguese found pepper from India more profitable to trade in. The only enduring presence of Christianity was in the Kongo-Soyo kingdoms (in present-day Angola), lasting until the eighteenth century.

In this region, some of the indigenous population was ordained to the priesthood, especially the children of Portuguese traders and some of the servants of white priests; however, the force of the ministry weakened with the changing pattern of trade, internal politics, and the disbanding of the Jesuits. A charismatic indigenous response to Iberian Christianity was manifested in the popularity of Vita Kimpa, a girl who claimed possession by St. Anthony and was martyred. Celebrated cases such as the conversion of the Monomotapa, the chief of Mashonaland in present-day Zimbabwe, were soon overshadowed by the counter-insurgence of the votaries of the traditional cults.

Iberian presence on the East African coast was dogged with competition from Indians and Arabs. The thirteen ethnic groups of Madagascar warred relentlessly against the Portuguese, while the Arabs of Oman recaptured the northern sector. Finally, other European countries challenged Portugal for a share of the lucrative trade that had turned primarily into slave trading. Memories of Iberian missionary exploits of yesteryear are broken statues and a syncretistic religion, *Nana Antoni*, in Cape Coast.

MISSIONARIES IN THE EIGHTEENTH AND NINETEENTH CENTURIES

In the eighteenth century, twenty-one forts dotted the coast of West Africa because of intense rivalry; some had chaplains, many did not. These were poorly paid with shoddy trade goods. The Dutch and Danish experiments that employed indigenous chaplains (Quaque, Amo, Protten, Capitein) equally failed. The gospel bearers enslaved prospective converts. In the next century, abolitionism and evangelical revival catalyzed the revamping of old missionary structures and the rise of a new voluntarist movement. Spiritual awakenings emphasized the Bible, the event of the cross, conversion experience, and a proactive expression of faith. Evangelicals mobilized philanthropists, churches, and politicians against the slave trade, to be replaced by treaties with the chiefs, legitimate trade, a new administrative structure, and Christianity as a civilizing agent.

Various groups of black people campaigned for abolition: in America, liberated slaves became concerned about the welfare of the race and drew up plans for equipping the young with education and skills for survival; Africans living abroad, like Ottabah Cuguano and Olaudah Equiano, wrote vividly about their experiences; and entrepreneurs like Paul Cuffee (1759–1817), a black ship owner and businessperson, created a commercial enterprise between Africa, Britain, and America.

Motives for abolition varied: religion, politics, commerce, rational humanism, and local needs each played a role. In England, the Committee of the Black Poor complained about the increasing social and financial problems caused by the number of poor liberated slaves. In America, those who fought on behalf of the British forces in the American Revolution (1775–1781) were relocated in Nova Scotia. They complained about their excruciating conditions. They had absorbed the liberal constitutional ideals of individual enterprise, personal responsibility, equality before the law, and freedom to practice one's religion as the Republicans against whom they had fought. In the West Indies, "Maroons" had successfully rebelled against their slave owners and established communities of free people.

In 1787 the British government founded Sierra Leone as a haven for liberated slaves, but the colony nearly foundered because of inhospitable climate, poor soil, and attacks from local chiefs. In 1792, the Nova Scotians were dispatched to Sierra Leone, followed by the

Reading Lesson in the Congo. *A class of boys learns to read the local language in 1930 at the Jesuit school of Kwango in the Belgian Congo.* **ROGER VIOLLET/GETTY IMAGES. REPRODUCED BY PERMISSION.**

Maroons in 1800. They arrived with their own Baptist and Methodist spiritualities before any British missionary society was founded, and with a clear vision to build a new society under the mandate of the gospel that avoided the indigenous chiefs, who had been compromised through the slave trade. They set the cultural tone of industry and caused a mass evangelization of thousands of freed slaves in Sierra Leone between 1807 and 1864.

These freed slaves became agents of missionary enterprise throughout the west coast, serving variously as educators, interpreters, counselors to indigenous communities, negotiators with the colonial agents, preachers, traders, and leaders of public opinion in many West African communities. Others served in the Niger Mission. Samuel Adjai Crowther, made a bishop in 1864, signified their achievement. Furthermore, the American Colonization Society recruited enough African Americans to found Liberia in 1822, and from this period until the 1920s African Americans were a significant factor in the missionary enterprise to Africa.

African Christianity exploded because of an increase in the number of missionary bodies, men and women voluntarily sustained by all classes of society in various countries. The appeal of the gospel increased with education, translation of the scriptures into indigenous languages, and charitable institutions such as medical care and artisan workshops. These forces domesticated the message and equally changed the character of Christian presence.

As America warmed to foreign missions in the 1850s, it brought enormous energy, optimism and vigor, and human resources. The reasons included availability of technological power, civil and religious liberty at home, and other racial theories such as chosenness, covenant, burden, responsibility, civilization, manifest destiny—ideas that linked missions to the imperial ideology. The Roman Catholics revamped their organization and fund-raising strategies for missions in such a way that the rivalry with Protestants influenced the pace and direction of the spread of the gospel.

However, these changes coincided with new geopolitical factors: competing forms of European nationalism had changed the character of the contact with Africa from informal commercial relations into formal colonial hegemony. The Berlin Conference of 1884–1885 partitioned Africa and insisted on formal occupation. It introduced a new spirit that overawed indigenous institutions and sought to transplant European institutions and cultures. Collusion with the civilization project diminished the spiritual vigor of the missionary presence and turned it into cultural and power encounters. This explains the predominant strategy of the missionary movements in southern Africa of forming enclaves and tight control of ministry that spurned the cultural genius of the people. The Catholic missionary presence in the Congo colluded with the brutality of King Leopold until an international outcry in 1908 forced him to sell the colony to Belgium. The abusive Portuguese presence in Angola, Mozambique, Guinea Bissau, and Cape Verde Islands would later provoke an anti-clerical and Marxist response after the forced decolonization.

Indeed, the dominant aspect of the story became forms of African Christian initiatives, hidden scripts, and resistance to the system of control. First, malaria-bearing mosquitoes killed many white missionaries, compelling the recruitment of West Indian blacks for missions. Second, as missionaries sowed the seed of the gospel, Africans appropriated and read the translated scriptures from an indigenous, charismatic worldview. Native agency became the instrument of growth, giving voice to the indigenous feeling against Western cultural iconoclasm and the control of decision making in the colonial churches. Using the promise in Psalm 68:31 that Ethiopia shall raise its hands to God, Ethiopianism became a movement of cultural and religious protest. It preached emancipation and the hope that Africans would bear the burden of evangelization and build an autonomous church devoid of denominations and free of European control.

REVIVAL IN THE TWENTIETH CENTURY

In the twentieth century, a network of educated Africans was woven across West Africa to evangelize and inculturate an African Christianity. Typical of their ideology was *Ethiopia Unbound* by the Gold Coast lawyer Casely Hayford and *The Return of the Exiles* by Wilmot Blyden of Liberia. David Vincent rejected his English name, reclaimed the Yoruba name Mojola Agbebi, wore only African clothes, and left the white religious establishment by founding the Native Baptist Church without foreign aid. Products of missionary enclaves in Southern and Central Africa did the same; some were attracted to the black ideology and charismatic spirituality of the American African Methodist Episcopal Church. Racial tension thickened as World War I (1914–1918) approached. Both World War I and World War II (1939–1945) intensified African confidence, quest for education, and charismatic responses to the gospel. Four types of spiritual movements were prominent in the postwar eras, with Pentecostalism gaining prominence in the mid- to late twentieth century.

Christianity Adapted to the Local Culture. Often a diviner from the traditional religion appropriated some aspects of Christian symbols and the Christian message to create a new synthesis that was able to respond to the needs of the community. In seventeenth-century Kongo, Kimpa Vita started as an *nganga*, traditional diviner, a member of the *Marinda* secret cult, to claim possession by a Christian patron saint, St. Anthony. People perceived her as an *ngunza* or Christian prophetess; but the authorities executed her as a witch. Nxele and Ntsikana achieved an identical status among the Xhosa in the nineteenth century in spite of their differences. Nxele preached about one God for the whites and another for the blacks, and explained the massive European migration into the southern hemisphere as a punishment for killing their God's son, a potential danger for the Xhosa. He turned his half-digested Christianity into a resistant religion. Ntsikana advised his people to ignore Nxele's militant notions but apply the gospel to cure the moral challenges in the primal religion, and build an organized, united community so as to preserve the race in the face of the incursions of land-grabbing Europeans. Ntsikana's spirituality could be detected in the rich language of his hymns retained in Methodist hymn books. Religious revivalism contested the political threat by the religion of invading white immigrants.

Prophet-Driven Christianity. A prophet emerged from the ranks of the Christian tradition emphasizing the ethical and pneumatic components of the canon to intensify the evangelization of the community or contiguous communities. Sometimes, the tendency was to pose like an Old Testament prophet sporting a luxurious beard, staff, flowing gown, and the cross. Some would-be prophets inculturated aspects of traditional religious symbols or ingredients of the culture, and supplanted the indigenous worldview with the Christian. The examples include Wade Harris, whose ministry started in 1910; Garrick Braide, who operated between 1914 and 1918; Joseph Babalola, who left his job as a driver in 1928 in West Africa; and Simon Kimbangu, whose ministry lasted through one year, 1921, in the Congo. Each was arrested by the colonial government and jailed: Harris remained under house arrest until death; Braide died in prison in 1918; Kimbangu's death sentence was commuted to life imprisonment and exile at the intervention of two Baptist missionaries. He died at Elizabethville in 1951. Babalola was released through the plea of some Welsh Apostolic agents.

The Indigenous Church. A wave of African indigenous churches arose all over Africa at different times before World War I and especially during the influenza epidemic of 1918. Dubbed as *Aladura* in West Africa, *Zionists* in Southern Africa, and *Abaroho* in Eastern Africa, some caused revivals, others did not; but they tended to emerge from mainline churches by recovering the pneumatic resources of the translated Bible. They deployed traditional Christian religious symbols. Soon differences appeared based on the dosage of traditional religion in the mix: the nativistic forms were neopagan; the vitalistic used occult in the quest for power; the revivalists clothed primal religion in Christian garb; the messianic leader presumed to be one or the other of the Trinity. Sunday and Sabbath worshippers emerged among them. Scholars note their creativity and enduring contributions to African Christianity. They served as political safe havens for the brutalized Africans.

Charismatic Movements. Sometimes charismatic movements arose within churches challenging doctrine, polity, liturgy, and ethics, and those churches seeking to enlarge the role of the Holy Spirit within their faith and practices. Hostile church leaders often excluded the attackers who wanted to form new churches or ministries, while charismatic movements remained within the churches. Some were short-lived revival movements; others became permanent. Examples include the Ibibio Revival that occurred within the Qua Iboe Church in eastern Nigeria in 1927; the Kaimosi revival that occurred within the Friends Africa Mission/Quakers in western Kenya in 1927; the Balokole revival that swept through the Anglican church in eastern Africa from 1930; and the Ngouedi revival that occurred among the Swedish Orebro Mission in 1947 and resulted in the Evangelical Church of Congo (EEC).

The Pentecostal Movement. Excluded members of charismatic movements birthed contemporary Pentecostalism in Africa. The young people, nicknamed as *aliki* in Malawi, began to conduct large revival meetings in the 1960s but especially from the 1970s in many African countries. They traveled from one place to another, denouncing with fire and brimstone sermons the sinfulness and evils of everyday urban life. The phenomenon became even more pronounced in the 1980s. They challenged the predominance of either voodoo or Islam or Roman Catholicism. Later, the movements in various countries linked through the activities of the students'

organization, FOCUS (Fellowship of Christian University Students), and the migrations of students within the foreign-language educational programs.

Most revivals occurred during the period between 1914 and 1950 when missionary control reigned supreme, colonial power and white settlers colluded, and labor problems and racial exploitation predominated. Charismatic religiosity provided a survival technique for Africans in the midst of the disquiet of those years and stamped African Christianity with an identity that contested missionary control and its monopoly of Christian expression.

CHANGES IN THE MID- TO LATE TWENTIETH CENTURY

In the same period of the early to mid-twentieth century, many religious forms flourished. The mainline denominations engaged in strong institutional development with schools, hospitals, and other charitable institutions; evangelized the hinterland areas; essayed to domesticate Christian values by confronting traditional cultures; and, in the Kikuyu case, triggered a rebellion that had enormous consequences. Education enabled many people to access newspapers and magazines and remain connected with Asia and Europe. A number of cultic and esoteric religious organizations advertised their wares in magazines and newspapers. It became the pastime of the literate few to scour newspapers and magazines for advertisements and mail orders for amulets, charms, rings, and other cultic paraphernalia from Asia to ensure success in examinations, gain promotion, and ensure security in the competitive and enlarged horizon of urbanity. Freemason and Rosicrucian lodges dotted the urban capitals of various countries.

Islam expanded more in the wake of improved transportation and commercial opportunities created by colonialism than many jihads would have accomplished. Since most of the African population still lived in the rural areas, traditional religion predominated many countries. Certain forces challenged missionary Christianity in Africa: the two world wars weakened missionary resources and encouraged black nationalism. The decolonization process that followed ineluctably produced new state ideologies that challenged the missionary heritage; religious nationalism compelled the mission churches to indigenize their structures and message. Missionary response to nationalism was informed by individual predilections, the negative racial image of Africans, and some liberal support. Regional variations abound as those in the settler communities responded with fright and the bulwark of apartheid laws.

The wind of change exposed the weak roots of the missionary infrastructure: few indigenous clergy, a dependency ideology, undeveloped theology, poor infrastructure, and above all little confidence in indigenous leaders. From the 1950s, some hurried to train indigenous priests and to ally with nationalists, because the educated elites were products of various missions and their control of power could aid their denominations in the virulent rivalry for territory. This strategy entangled Christianity in the politics of independence.

Matters went awry when the elites grabbed the politics of modernization, mobilized the states into dictatorial one-party structures, castigated missionaries for under-developing Africa, promoted neo-Marxist rejection of the dependency syndrome, and seized the instruments of missionary propaganda such as schools, hospitals, and social welfare agencies. The implosion of the state challenged the churches, but the failure of the states produced a rash of military coups and regimes, abuse of human rights, and economic collapse. Poverty ravaged many African countries. The militarization of societies intensified interethnic conflicts and civil wars. Refugee camps filled to the brim. Natural disasters such as drought in the Horn of Africa worsened matters. Part of the problem could be traced to weak leadership, and part to external forces that used the continent as fodder in the cold war, patronized dictators, exploited the mineral resources, and manipulated huge debts that have burdened and crippled many nations permanently.

African Christianity grew rapidly against the backdrop of poverty and the legitimacy crisis. As civil society was decimated, Christianity remained the survivor. Christian leaders were chosen in one country after another to serve as the presidents of consultative assemblies that sought to renew hope and banish the pessimism that imaged African problems as incurable. Other developments include: (1) African Christian theologies from the mid-1970s enabled a critique of inherited theologies; this sustained a black revolution against apartheid in South Africa, Namibia, and Zimbabwe; and (2) the charismatic movements that exploded in the 1970s, and have continued to change shape in every decade, absorbing American prosperity preaching in the 1980s, and reverting to traditions of holiness and intercessory prayer in the 1990s. This form has a "fit" that answers to questions raised within the primal worldviews; it provides mechanisms for coping with economic collapse; it revitalizes and sets missionary message to work with inexplicable power of the Holy Spirit.

The missionary movement has charismatized the mainline churches, flowed from urban centers into rural Africa, engaged the public space, and experimented with new forms of ministerial formation. A third development is the rise of Christian feminist theology, challenging the churches to become less patriarchal. Through many publications and programs, churches are being compelled to ordain women and increase their participation in decision-making processes. Contemporary Africa resembles the early Christianity in the Maghrib.

SEE ALSO *Berlin Conference; Religion, Western Perceptions of Traditional Religions; Religion, Western Presence in Africa.*

BIBLIOGRAPHY
Hastings, Adrian. *The Church in Africa, 1450–1950.* Oxford: Clarendon Press, 1994.
Kalu, Ogbu U., ed. *African Christianity: An African Story.* Pretoria: University of Pretoria, 2005.
Sundkler, Bengt, and Christopher Steed, eds. *A History of the Church in Africa.* New York: Cambridge University Press, 2000.

Ogbu Kalu

MISSION, CIVILIZING

Studies of Western colonial history focus on the consequences of Europe's expansion into Africa and the Americas. Atlantic historians examine the impact of transporting domesticable livestock to the Americas, the forcible spread of Christianity to Indians, the impact of European diseases on Amerindians, the ceremonies that Europeans employed to indicate that newly discovered lands belonged to their kingdoms, and the contributions of Africans transported to the New World. African historians focus on the Berlin Conference (1884–1885) and investigate European encroachments into African territories. Europe's colonization of America occurred without as much pretense and formality as its carving of Africa.

The Spanish exploration of America started with the expedition in 1492 of Christopher Columbus (1451–1506). Amidst the chaos that Columbus's voyage brought, one result was certain; when the Spaniards arrived in America, they ran roughshod over numerically superior Amerindian armies and changed their lives forever. One explanation for this lopsided victory is the Indians' lack of literary development and therefore inability to understand global methods of warfare, surprise attacks, or diplomatic deception. Without technological achievements, the European conquerors enjoyed a distinct advantage over the virtually defenseless locals. Basically, the Europeans understood how to manipulate inexperienced and nonworldly peoples. Francisco Pizarro (ca. 1475–1541) brought a European army of 168 men to attack an Incan army consisting of eighty thousand soldiers. Pizarro's superior experience in warfare and deception allowed the miniscule army of terrified Europeans to capture Atahualpa (ca. 1502–1533), leader of the Incas, and therefore scatter and dismay the enemy's battalions.

Equally important to explaining the Europeans' success is that when Columbus, Pizarro, and Hernando Cortés (ca. 1484–1547) arrived, they inadvertently transmitted devastating diseases to the Amerindian populations. The prior isolation of the Amerindians contributed to their susceptibility to contracting the lethal smallpox virus. Consequent of the sudden impact of disease, many native populations became divided and faced civil war. Epidemics caused massive depopulations of people who could have been soldiers able to ward off the European intrusions. The status of the native medical professions had been relatively ineffectual, and doctors stumbled over finding remedies for what remains today a deadly virus. In a sense, Amerindians simply lacked the technologies that would have helped them fight back.

After the United States removed the British from North America, European powers started searching for fresh lands and subjects to impose on culturally and to exploit economically. Precipitated by the discovery of new African lands in the 1880s, European interest in Africa increased radically. Between 1874 and 1877, the Welsh-born journalist and explorer Henry Morton Stanley (1841–1904) uncovered the terrain of the last remaining uncharted river basin in Africa, within the Congo region.

King Leopold II (1835–1909) of Belgium founded the International African Society in 1876, after which he invited Stanley to assist in researching, acquiring, and uplifting the archaic African territories. Portugal, France, England, and Belgium simultaneously scrambled to formulate a distinct Congo state under their direction. The European powers wheeled and dealt the Congo region callously. Portugal signed an agreement with Great Britain on February 26, 1884, intended to strangle the Congo's access to the Atlantic Ocean. This pattern of dominating and shifting foreign territories eventually led to each major world power possessing a portion of African land.

In November 1884 German chancellor Otto von Bismarck (1815–1898) called together fourteen Western nations, including Russia and the United States, to discuss the future of Africa and to divide and conquer the continent at a peace table. The Berlin Conference officially shifted the European focus from the Americas to Africa. Bismarck's avowed motive for holding the Berlin Conference—scientific exploration—differed drastically from what occurred once negotiations broke down and centered on carving spheres of influence in Africa. Bismarck sought to oversee Germany's expansion and

to demonstrate Germany's ever-growing authority to negotiate the outcome of world affairs. Unfortunately, for indigenous populations numbering over one thousand, each Western power demanded a slice or a chunk of African territory without regard to the impact of artificially dividing territories on a generic map.

The series of conferences, often termed the "Congo Conferences," concluded on February 26, 1885. The result of the conferences was the signing of the Berlin Act. One major problem with the Western powers signing the act had been their division of African territory despite the ambassadors' lack of knowledge about the linguistic and tribal boundaries of indigenous populations. This separation threatened to arouse hatred and to cause warfare among distinct populaces. Ironically, although the Europeans referred to the creation of African spheres of influence in the Berlin Act, the slave trade became internationally prohibited. At the conference, France and Belgium ultimately received control of the Congo region to establish "democratic" Congolese states. France embarked on a program of massive African colonization after the signing of the Berlin Act. Additionally, every nation consented that in order to receive recognition as possessor of an African territory, a Western power would have to demonstrate tangible control over the terrain and population.

By 1895, French government officials had recognized their possession of African territories as an opportunity for rejuvenating the empire. France's unstable Third Republic (1870–1940) promulgated the ethnocentric idea that the French were the most civilized and enlightened people in the entire world. The British also issued ethnocentric declarations asserting their superiority based on pseudo-scientific phrenological experiments. From a political perspective, the Third Republic's noble ideals became a pretext for spreading French business and culture into the African interior. Improvements in European science and technologies allowed French policies to take hold.

French penetration into Africa became enabled by the steam engine that powered freighters, and by the construction of railways in Africa's interior. The Berlin Act stipulated the opening of the Congo and Niger rivers to all nationals. Technological innovation transformed the Congo, Niger, Senegal, and Gambia rivers into navigable and easily passable waterways. These advancements allowed trade ships to maneuver freely inside of Africa's interior regions. Medical advancements provided cures for many of the perilous diseases afflicting French workers in Africa. With the advent of vaccinations, the discoveries of Louis Pasteur (1822–1895) and Robert Koch (1843–1910), and the knowledge that mosquitoes spread yellow fever and malaria, suddenly carving spheres of influence in Africa seemed attainable and highly lucrative.

In order for the French people to accept their nation as a colonial power, racial doctrines were disseminated throughout the country. The French had learned the consequences of colonial rebellion from the bloody Haitian independence movement, and the British had learned the serious consequences of tyrannical governance from the American colonies. Despite these lessons, French explorers still viewed Africans as dark savages mired in barbarism and anarchy, and as incapable of leaving their ancient customs behind.

Because of the growing demand for raw materials, for manpower, and for economic expansion, between 1895 and 1935 French colonial administrations entrenched themselves in several African nations. These territories included: Mauritania, Senegal, Guinea, Côte d'Ivoire (Ivory Coast), Niger, Upper Volta (now Burkina Faso), French Sudan (now Mali), Tunisia, Morocco, and Dahomey (now Benin). One major consequence of French colonial administrative policies was the rebellions that developed as backlashes against imperial rule in Africa and the Americas. Racist policies of assimilation caused significant bloodshed on both sides and symbolized the exploitive nature of European-African colonialism.

SEE ALSO *Berlin Conference; Scramble for Africa.*

BIBLIOGRAPHY

Boahen, A. Adu, ed. *Africa Under Colonial Domination, 1880–1935.* Berkeley: University of California Press, 1985.

Conklin, Alice. *A Mission to Civilize: The Republican Idea of Empire in France and West Africa, 1895–1930.* Stanford, CA: Stanford University Press, 1997.

Diamond, Jared. *Guns, Germs, and Steel: The Fates of Human Societies.* New York: Norton, 1997.

Harris, Joseph. *Africans and Their History: Past and Present,* 2nd rev. ed. New York: Meridian, 1998.

Mintz, Sidney W. *Sweetness and Power: The Place of Sugar in Modern History.* New York: Viking, 1985.

Thornton, John. *Africa and Africans in the Making of the Atlantic World, 1400–1800,* 2nd ed. Cambridge, U.K.: Cambridge University Press, 1998.

Jonathan Jacobs

MISSIONS, CHINA

Though earlier missionizing in China had met with little success, during the sixteenth century Catholic missionaries succeeded in establishing Christianity as a permanent minority religion. From the beginning there was a link between colonialism and Christian missions in China, as power and profit mingled with spirituality and proselytizing. In 1517 the first Portuguese ships arrived in search of trade, casting anchor at the riverfront of Canton. They proceeded to terrify the Chinese populace by firing their cannons in salute and were then driven a hundred miles to the south, where they established the colony of Macao sometime around 1557. This colony became the base of early missionary operations in China.

Infused with the spirit of the Counter Reformation, Portuguese merchants frequently made room on their ships for Catholic missionaries, many of whom were members of the newly formed Society of Jesus. These Jesuits, as Society members are called, became the leading Catholic missionary force: 920 members of this remarkable group served as missionaries in China between 1552 and 1800. By almost any standard, China in the sixteenth and seventeenth centuries was the greatest country in the world, so the Jesuits soon realized that missionizing in China, unlike in Latin America or South India, required accommodation rather than forced conversion. This led the highly educated Jesuits, many of whom came from eminent European families, to cultivate their closest counterparts in China. These were the Confucian literati or scholar-officials. In appealing to this group, they attempted to forge a Confucian–Christian synthesis. Other missionary orders, most notably Franciscans, toiled in the provinces among the common people.

As leaders in the exploratory voyages of the early sixteenth century, Portugal dominated the eastward route to China. This Portuguese monopoly (*padroado*) is reflected in the fact that more than one-third of the 314 Jesuits in China during the premodern period of the mission were Portuguese. The Italian city-states provided 99 Jesuits, including the most famous China missionary of all, Matteo Ricci (1552–1610), whose respect for Chinese culture endeared him to the Chinese. The second-largest contingent of Jesuits (130) sent to pre-1800 China was provided by the French, who refused to submit to the Portuguese monopoly. The Sacred Congregation for the Propagation of the Faith (or the Propaganda) was established by Pope Gregory XV in 1622 in order to reduce these troublesome nationalistic and interorder religious rivalries.

Initially the Chinese showed some degree of receptivity toward the missionaries, and this led to the baptism of approximately 300,000 Christians out of a population of 150 million during the early seventeenth century. With the fall of the native Ming dynasty and the conquest of China by the Manchus in 1644, however, the cultural atmosphere became more conservative and it is believed that in the eighteenth century the number of Christians in China declined by one-third. With a decline in the conversions of eminent literati, the Jesuits began focusing on the Manchu court in an attempt to convert the emperor and powerful officials. This effort, however, met with only limited success. Additional damage to the mission in China was caused by Rome's dissolution of the Society of Jesus in 1773 (it was not reestablished until 1814).

As the Catholic mission flagged, Protestants entered the field on the ships of the emerging Protestant colonialist powers. The movement was led by Anglo-Saxon Evangelicals from Great Britain and the United States who sponsored missionary societies, notably, the London Missionary Society (LMS; founded in 1795), the Church Missionary Society (founded in 1799), and the American Board of Commissioners for Foreign Missions (founded in 1810).

The first Protestant missionary to serve in China was Robert Morrison of the LMS, who worked in Macao and Canton from 1807 to 1834. Unlike the Catholics, the Protestants emphasized the translation of the Bible into Chinese. By 1839 European colonialist nations like Great Britain had grown powerful enough to inflict humiliating defeats on a stagnating China. The Chinese were forced to open treaty ports to both colonialist traders and Christian missionaries.

The most famous Protestant missionary in China was the Englishman James Hudson Taylor, who arrived in 1854 and led the movement to penetrate the Chinese mainland. Taylor forged the creation of the China Inland Mission (CIM), which became the largest sponsor of Protestant missionaries in China. After World War I, the United States replaced Great Britain as the primary sponsor of Protestant missionaries in China.

Around 1900 the CIM's emphasis on evangelism began to be challenged by the Social Gospel movement led by the Young Men's Christian Association. This was a movement fueled by faith in modern science, with an emphasis on education, medicine, famine relief, and public health. The period 1900 to 1914 saw rapid growth in Protestant missionizing, with the number of Protestant missionaries peaking in the 1920s at 8,000, serving a total population of almost 500 million. However, the great age of missions in China was ending, and in the 1920s two indigenous movements began to challenge the missions in a way that foreshadowed the missions' end. One was Chinese nationalism, which found expression in the Christian Three-Self movement (the three "selfs" being self-government, self-support, and self-propagation). Combining love of country with love of church, this was a reaction against the belief of Western missionaries that Chinese culture was irreconcilable with Christianity, and against their refusal to treat Chinese Christians as equals. The other was the emergence of indigenous evangelical groups, such as the Little Flock, led by Watchman Nee (Ni Duosheng), and the

Matteo Ricci and Convert. *The Catholic presence in China was established in the late sixteenth century primarily through the work of the Italian Jesuit Matteo Ricci. Ricci (left) is shown with a convert and colleague in this mid-seventeenth-century illustration from a Chinese manuscript.* **HULTON ARCHIVE/ GETTY IMAGES. REPRODUCED BY PERMISSION.**

True Jesus Church, founded by Barnabas Tung in 1909 or 1910.

The missionaries' penetration into China provoked a powerful resentment that exploded in the xenophobic Boxer Rebellion of 1900, during which hundreds of missionaries and Chinese Christians were killed. In 1950 the new Communist government of mainland China expelled most foreign missionaries, though the link between foreign missionaries and colonialism was exploited for propagandistic purposes as late as the Cultural Revolution of 1966–1976. Because foreign mission boards and missionaries had always been reluctant to relinquish control of the Chinese churches to Chinese Christians, the missionaries' expulsion by the Communists turned out to be a blessing in disguise for the development of an indigenous Christianity in China. Although many scholars believed that Christianity in China had been eradicated by the Communists, the churches simply went underground and in fact continued to flourish.

SEE ALSO *Boxer Uprising; Catholic Church in Iberian America; Religion, Western Perceptions of Traditional Religions; Religion, Western Perceptions of World Religions; Religion, Western Presence in the Pacific.*

BIBLIOGRAPHY

Bays, Daniel H., ed. *Christianity in China: From the Eighteenth Century to the Present.* Stanford, CA: Stanford University Press, 1996.

Latourette, Kenneth Scott. *A History of Christian Missions in China.* New York: Macmillan, 1929.

Mungello, D. E. *The Spirit and the Flesh in Shandong, 1650– 1785.* Lanham, MD: Rowman and Littlefield, 2001.

Standaert, Nicolas, ed. *Handbook of Christianity in China, Vol. 1: 635–1800.* Boston: Brill, 2001.

Whyte, Bob. *Unfinished Encounter: China and Christianity.* London: Collins/Fount, 1988.

Zetzsche, Jost Oliver. *The Bible in China: The History of the Union Version, or, The Culmination of Protestant Missionary Bible Translation in China.* Sankt Augustin, Germany: Monumenta Serica Institute, 1999.

D. E. Mungello

MISSIONS, IN THE PACIFIC

The relationship of Christianity and colonialism in the Pacific Islands has varied. At different times and in different places Christian missionaries have been defenders of the independence of indigenous governments, supporters and opponents of imperial expansion, willing partners and critics of colonial administrations, and backers of nationalist and independence movements.

Christianity was brought to the Pacific Islands by missionaries from Western Europe. From the 1660s Spanish Roman Catholic priests, from their base in the Philippines, began missionary work in several island groups of the North Pacific. In the South Pacific, missionary activity was dominated by evangelical Protestantism. The first permanent mission was commenced by British missionaries of the London Missionary Society (LMS), which sent its first agents to eastern Polynesia in 1797. During the nineteenth century, many other branches of Western Christianity established missions in the Pacific Islands. These included Anglicans, Methodists, Roman Catholics, Presbyterians, French Reformed, Lutherans, and Seventh-day Adventists.

The great majority of Protestant missionaries of this period were British and American; Roman Catholics were mainly French. Having already been exposed to

Missionary and Converts in Tahiti, Circa 1845. *The London Missionary Society sent its first agents to eastern Polynesia in 1797, and during the 1800s many other branches of Western Christianity established missions in the Pacific Islands. This missionary posed for a photograph with two Tahitian converts in French Polynesia around 1845.* HENRY GUTTMANN/HULTON ARCHIVE/GETTY IMAGES. REPRODUCED BY PERMISSION.

Western trading contact, the islanders embraced Christianity, largely by choice and for reasons that seemed valid to them at the time. Through the agency of Pacific Island teachers, Christianity spread rapidly in the eastern and central Pacific (Polynesia and Micronesia). In each island group, the first mission to introduce Christianity usually received the support of the majority of the population. The evangelization of the more populous and fragmented societies of the southwest Pacific (Melanesia) was a much slower process and, in the island of New Guinea, is incomplete at the beginning of the twenty-first century.

With the exception of Australia, Christianity was planted in the region before the extension of European colonial rule. In Australia, the founding of the first convict colony in 1788 was accompanied by the introduction of British Christianity and the beginnings of missionary work, on a small scale and initially with little success, among the Aboriginal people.

In the Pacific Islands, the early Protestant missionaries supported independent indigenous governments. Seeking to create Christian societies, they encouraged converted island chiefs to promulgate codes of law that combined indigenous custom with the ideals of evangelical Christianity. In some island groups, such as Tonga and Hawaii, missionaries assisted in the creation of monarchies with a Western-style constitution and machinery of government. When indigenous governments proved unable to deal with aggressive Western powers or to provide political stability, missionaries began to favor annexation by their respective countries. Because of this they were widely seen as trailblazers of empire. In New Zealand, for example, Protestant missionaries played an important role in gaining acceptance of the Treaty of Waitangi (1840), through which the Maori tribes accepted British sovereignty and New Zealand became a white settler colony.

Between the 1840s and the 1890s almost every island group in the Pacific was brought within one of the Western colonial empires: Britain, France, Germany, and the United States. Missionaries did not oppose imperial expansion in principle. Despite tensions, they usually cooperated with colonial governments, especially those of their own nation, and colonial administrators often encouraged their subject peoples to accept Christianity. Missions were almost entirely responsible for the provision of primary education and medical services in island villages. Missionary paternalism fitted well with the authoritarian rule and limited expectations of colonial governments, but sometimes missionaries were critical of government policies that they regarded as unjust or harmful to the islanders.

After the end of World War II in 1945, the Protestant and Anglican missions moved slowly toward their goal of creating self-sustaining island churches with an indigenous ministry. This process paralleled moves by Western colonial powers in the postwar years toward decolonization. In every island group, these missions had evolved into self-governing churches before the achievement of political independence in the 1960s and 1970s. The Roman Catholic missions, committed to a celibate and Latin-educated priesthood, moved more slowly toward the indigenization of their leadership.

In each island group, the churches often helped to create a sense of national identity. Their schools and theological colleges produced many of the first generation of political leaders. In the Anglo-French condominium of the New Hebrides (since 1980 the independent state of Vanuatu) and the French overseas territories of French Polynesia and New Caledonia, the Protestant churches were deeply involved in independence movements.

As newly independent Pacific Island states assumed responsibility for village education and health services, the older churches began withdrawing from these areas,

which in turn reduced their need to rely on overseas funding. They turned their attention toward rural development, social services, and the creation of a theology that was based upon indigenous religious concepts and ways of thought. For the first time, they were also seriously challenged by such bodies as the Mormons, Baha'is, and Pentecostals.

Almost all Pacific Island political leaders claim a Christian affiliation, as have the leaders of the armed coups that brought down several postindependence governments. In many island groups, large sections of the dominant churches have formed a comfortable relationship with ruling elites, but within the churches there are also radical voices that challenge the status quo and campaign on such issues as political corruption, social justice, and the protection of the natural environment.

SEE ALSO *Religion, Roman Catholic Church; Religion, Western Perceptions of Traditional Religions; Religion, Western Perceptions of World Religions; Religion, Western Presence in the Pacific.*

BIBLIOGRAPHY

Garrett, John. *To Live Among the Stars: Christian Origins in Oceania.* Geneva: World Council of Churches; Suva, Fiji: Institute of Pacific Studies, University of the South Pacific, 1982.

Garrett, John. *Footsteps in the Sea: Christianity in Oceania to World War II.* Suva, Fiji: Institute of Pacific Studies, University of the South Pacific; Geneva: World Council of Churches, 1992.

Garrett, John. *Where Nets were Cast: Christianity in Oceania since World War II.* Suva, Fiji: Institute of Pacific Studies, University of the South Pacific; Geneva: World Council of Churches, 1997.

Gunson, W. N. "Missionary Interest in British Expansion in the South Pacific in the Nineteenth Century." *Journal of Religious History* 3 (4) (1965): 296–313.

Harris, John W. *One Blood: 200 Years of Aboriginal Encounter with Christianity: A Story of Hope,* 2nd ed. Sydney: Albatross, 1994.

David Hilliard

MITA

Meaning "turn" in Quechua, the word *mita* designated, in the Inca Empire, a system of temporary labor imposed upon the indigenous communities. It applied to rotating or intermittent work performed for the public interest, such as the construction of ways and fortresses, the harvest of Inca lands, the tending of the pasture of the llamas and vicuñas (an animal similar to the llama, but with wool that is of higher value than that of the llama), and the exploitation of gold and silver mines.

In contrast to taxes the Inca were required to pay in exchange for their residence, the mita entailed long-distance displacements of newly conquered populations. These men and women were moved to other regions, where they were forced to work. They were called *mitimaes* or *mitayos*, which means "foreigners." While the majority performed hard labor, some worked as craftsmen and defenders of the frontiers.

The duration of the services and the age of the workers were strictly regimented by the *ayllus* (the basic social entity of the Inca Empire, the "familiar clan"). The ayllus and the fruits of the mita or products derived from mita labor were distributed among the poorest people and regions to compensate everyone's needs and balance their economic situation with that of the richest regions of the empire.

From 1552 onward, the Recopilación laws justified the mita as a compulsory work service that would benefit the Spanish colonists, who had experienced a decline in workers in the mining industry. Supported by the Spanish king, the mita entailed a predetermined minimum salary, which was applied to all men over twenty years of age and below fifty.

The Spanish would then adopt the mita and implant it for the exploitation of gold, mercury, and silver, and for the development and cultivation of tambos, postal services, land, textile factories, public works, and domestic service.

When the viceroy Francisco de Toledo visited the mines of Potosí in 1573, the mining entrepreneurs, claiming a decrease in silver production, convinced the viceroy that mining productivity levels would only reach previous levels if forced labor could be provided. Gold and silver mining produced precious metals, essential to mercantilism and the world economic circuit.

Toledo decided to establish the mita, compelling the surrounding regions to provide Potosí with yearly rotating drafts of forced Indian labor at low wages. The viceroy intended the mita as temporary provision until the Indians voluntarily returned to the mines. According to the system, each displaced Indian would work for one week, followed by two weeks of rest, during the course of a year.

The mita was controversial since its introduction, and especially as wages became increasingly lower and the working conditions deteriorated. Specifically, the toxicity of the cinnabar dust and extreme working conditions in the Huancavélica mine contributed to an increased mortality rate.

Thousands of Indians escaped from their lands because the obligation to serve was based on territorial circumscriptions and not on personal status. Because the abandonment of the mines could lead to economic collapse, Spain was reluctant to abolish the mita. Finally, in 1812, Las Cortes de Cádiz abolished the system.

SEE ALSO *Inca Empire; Mercantilism; Mining, the Americas.*

BIBLIOGRAPHY

Bakewell, Peter. *Miners of the Red Mountain: Indian Labor at Potosí, 1545–1650.* Albuquerque: University of New Mexico Press, 1984.

Cole, Jeffrey A. *The Potosí Mita, 1573–1700: Compulsory Indian Labor in the Andes.* Stanford, CA: Stanford University Press, 1985.

Tandeter, Enrique. *Trabajo Forzado y Trabajo Libre en el Potosí Colonial Tardío.* Buenos Aires: CEDES, 1980.

Cristina Blanco Sío-López

MODERN WORLD-SYSTEM ANALYSIS

On the surface, world-system analysis, as eloquently formulated by the American sociologist Immanuel Wallerstein (b. 1930) in the 1970s, appears deceptively simple. Wallerstein's world-system analysis is a grand narrative of world historical development from the sixteenth century to the present, with boundaries, structures, member groups, rules of legitimation, and coherence. The world-system is dynamic and constantly evolving, with "conflicting forces which hold it together by tension, and tear it apart as each group seeks externally to remold it to its advantage" (Wallerstein 1974, p. 347).

Wallerstein's modern world-system is specifically a capitalist world economy with *capitalism* defined as "the *endless* accumulation of capital" (Wallerstein 2004, p. 24). Using a metaphor that recalls the theories of Scottish economist Adam Smith (1723–1790), Wallerstein defines the *world-system* as a geographical division of labor. While the basic linkage is economic, the system is reinforced by political and cultural factors.

THE TRIPARTITE WORLD-SYSTEM

Wallerstein's world-system divides the nations and areas of the world into three units, designated *core, peripheral,* and *semiperipheral* (in the past some areas remained external to the system). These normative units are systemic and relational within the capitalist world economy. All parts of the system are dependent upon and interact with each other; any change in the system will impact upon the system as a whole.

Core nations dominate the economic structure of their historical time and strive to maintain or expand this authority. One fundamental element of a core nation is the ability to produce and distribute products. Another characteristic is a strong state machinery linked to a unified national culture. The state supports economic influence wielded by private businesspeople, merchants, and financial institutions, which play a vital role in core nations. Culture often serves as an ideological justification for dominance. The state also provides military force to protect and expand economic interests. Contemporary core nations dominate high technology, financial institutions, and high-profit industries. Within the context of the world-system, core nations compete among themselves for economic advantage.

Peripheral areas or nations (often colonies from the sixteenth to the twentieth centuries and defined as underdeveloped or semideveloped for a brief time in the twentieth century) serve the interests of the core nations. Peripheral areas provide agricultural products, luxury goods, raw materials, and cheap sources of labor. At times peripheral areas gained prominence, serving as key geographically located posts to protect trade routes between the core and the periphery. Peripheral areas are dependent upon core nations and have often been a source of conflict between core nations. Core methods of domination range from various forms of colonialism to anticolonial imperialism and economic dependency.

Last in the tripartite world-system are semiperipheral nations and areas. These serve as intermediate trading areas between the core nations and the peripheral areas. They also have small manufacturing sectors, geared to either local or international trade, and some capital accumulation.

Historically, some areas remained external to the world-system either by choice or neglect. By the twentieth century virtually every region on the globe had been consolidated into the modern capitalist world-system.

A closer examination of the three components of the world-system reveals the complexity of this analytical framework. Core, periphery, and semiperiphery are, in Wallerstein's apt phrase, "a relational concept." What binds these three units into a system is interaction that generates an ever-changing systemic dynamic. While there is an economic hierarchy of core, periphery, and semiperiphery, the actions of one have an impact upon the others. Moreover, while the defining structural process remains constant, the individual parts of the system change over time.

One reason is the changing nature of the products of significance in the world economy. An example is the indigo industry, which was, for a brief period, an important product in the eighteenth- and nineteenth-century world economy. More broadly, in the sixteenth and seventeenth centuries, agricultural production dominated the economic world-system. By the late eighteenth century manufactured goods were the product of choice, and since the last decades of the twentieth century high technology production characterizes the core nations.

Within this paradigm, world-system analysis stresses dynamic interaction and change. Core nations can become semiperipheral or even peripheral nations. One classic example is Spain, which devolved from a core nation in the sixteenth century to a semiperipheral nation in the eighteenth century.

Conversely, a semiperipheral area can rise, over time, to core status. In the case of Atlantic North America, the colonies developed from external (the pre-Columbian period) to peripheral (the fifteenth to seventeenth centuries). After independence the United States evolved from a semiperipheral nation (the eighteenth to mid-nineteenth centuries) to a core nation (the mid-nineteenth to mid-twentieth centuries) and recently to hegemonic power (the late twentieth century).

One historical dynamic is the competition of core nations for advantage in the world-system economically, politically, culturally, and often militarily. Wallerstein identifies several struggles between core nations that result in warfare reverberating around the globe. Importantly, peripheral areas and semiperipheral areas are not passive participants in the system. In many cases they strive to rise in status and often rebel, at times successfully, against the power and control of the core nations and the hegemon. This creates policy disputes over strategy and tactics within the core nations. In the late eighteenth century, for example, Spanish diplomacy toward the rebelling British colonies was caught between the desire to weaken the power of England and the fear that the colonial rebellion would set a precedent for Spain's own colonies.

HEGEMONY

One other important concept plays a crucial role in the world-system: *hegemony*. During various historical times, one core nation accumulated sufficient power to dominate the other core nations. According to Wallerstein, *hegemony* "refers to those situations in which one static combines economic, political, and financial superiority over other strong states, and therefore has both military and cultural as well as economic and political power" (Wallerstein 2004, p. 94). Because of its superior means of production and distribution, strong financial institutions that lend credit to both domestic industry and externally to peripheral and semiperipheral areas, and the financial prowess to support military action, the hegemon dominates the world-system.

Wallerstein identifies three periods of hegemonic domination in the modern world: the United Provinces (Netherlands) in the mid-seventeenth century, Great Britain in the mid-nineteenth century, and the United States in the mid-twentieth century. In each of these cases, the hegemon, from a position of dominant economic power, advocated freer trade. The economic, military, and, at times, ideological burdens of maintaining a position of superiority, however, threaten the hegemonic power, which must pour resources into retaining its dominant position in the world-system.

Wallerstein's argument that the Dutch were the first hegemonic power, due to their application of science to agricultural production and their dominance over sea distribution, has generated lively scholarly debate. The idea of hegemony, moreover, has influenced the study of twentieth-century U.S. diplomatic historiography, particularly in interpreting the relationship between the United States and Latin America. Historians Thomas J. McCormick and Thomas Schoonover, for example, have applied world-system theory to examining the means of U.S. hegemonic control and the rivalry between the United States and other core powers.

INTELLECTUAL ANTECEDENTS

World-system analysis arose during the 1970s, primarily through the writings of Immanuel Wallerstein. Wallerstein identifies four intellectual antecedents that emerged between 1945 and 1970 as promulgating the emergence of world-system theory: (1) the study of Latin American history, contemporary politics, and foreign relations, from which arose the conceptualizations of core/periphery and *dependency theory;* (2) the Marxian idea of an "Asiatic mode of production"; (3) the historical debate about the transition from feudalism to capitalism; and (4) the scholarship of Fernand Braudel and the Annales school of historiography.

Latin American scholars strove to understand the economic and social structures of their region and its relationship to the United States. As succinctly stated by the nineteenth-century Mexican statesman Porfirio Díaz (1830–1915): "Poor Mexico. So far from God and so close to the United States." Emphasizing informal imperialism, *dependency theory* focuses on the subjugation by core nations of peripheral and semiperipheral economies through new forms of domination, such as financial coercion (dollar diplomacy) and, at times, military action. Since the 1940s international organizations, such as the International Monetary Fund, have been created by core powers to continue this dependency. Any

economic development was primarily in the service of the core nations.

Second, the "Asiatic mode of production" stresses the role of large, bureaucratic, and autocratic empires in the world-system. For example, during the Cold War, China regulated its economy to combat the capitalist world-system.

A third contribution to world-system theory was the debate on the timing and nature of the transition from feudalism to capitalism. Did internal factors within individual nations, such as consolidation of political power under a strong central government, or external factors, such as the expansion of trade, take precedence in the emergence of capitalism?

Finally, Wallerstein pointed to the scholarship of French historian Fernand Braudel (1902–1985) and the Annales school of scholars that he inspired. The Annales school emphasized *total history.* Rejecting disciplinary constraints, total history sought to capture the spirit of particular historical ages. This approach provided, according to Wallerstein, a theoretical framework for shaping world-system analysis. Braudel's work introduced two ideas that influenced Wallerstein's theory. First, Braudel's multidisciplinary approach to the interaction of nations provided a method for understanding history. Second, Wallerstein's theory was influenced by the Annales school's notion of *longue durée* (the long duration), which maintained that historical trends must be studied over long periods of time.

From economics, Wallerstein appropriated the theory of the Kondratieff Wave to explain economic fluctuations within the world-system. Nikolai Kondratieff (1892–1938), a Russian economist, postulated that cycles of upward and downward swings, approximately fifty years each, fluctuate in the world economy between expansion and contraction. Wallerstein takes careful note of the complexity of this theory (i.e., some elements of the economy prosper during periods of retraction and others suffer during expansion cycles). Wallerstein's reliance on the Kondratieff paradigm has generated criticism from scholars who question the validity of the Kondratieff Wave theory.

COLONIALISM IN THE WORLD-SYSTEM

Wallerstein dates the origins of the world economy to the late fifteenth and early sixteenth centuries. Determining the date of any historical movement is always an intellectual arena for dispute, and, as noted above, Wallerstein's timeline for the decline of feudalism and the rise of capitalism has become part of a longstanding historiographical debate. During this transition, technological and political changes allowed for the expansion of capitalism. Areas such as the Americas, which were external to the European economic sphere, became accessible and, over time, were consolidated into the world-system. Stronger state governments, advances in sailing techniques in the "era of exploration," and the maturation of economic institutions all combined to incorporate the entire globe.

The subtitle of Wallerstein's first volume on the development of the modern world-system is significant: *Capitalist Agriculture and the Origins of the European World-Economy in the Sixteenth Century* (1974). Not only does he date the advent of the modern world-system in the sixteenth century, but he emphasizes the idea that capitalism can be applied to agricultural economies. During this time, mercantilism, that is, the economic nationalism revolving around trade, became the preferred European state policy.

Colonialism is one form of interstate relationship within the capitalist world-system. Colonialism emerged as a political method of incorporation of external areas. Wallerstein argues that "incorporation into the capitalist world-economy was never at the initiation of those being incorporated. The process derived rather from the need of the world-economy to expand its boundaries" (Wallerstein 1989, p. 129). A colony serves the economic interests of a core nation. It can be a source of needed raw materials for the core, such as the production of indigo in the North American colonies or silver in Spain's Latin American colonies; a source of luxury goods; a market for goods manufactured in the metropole; or any combination of the three.

Colonies also served as way stations for commerce on the trade routes that linked the world-system and as bases to protect the trade routes or disrupt the commerce of rival core powers. At times, a colony can also be one part of a broader trade system, such as the various seventeenth- and eighteenth-century triangular trade routes. One example is the India-China-Britain triangular trade of the eighteenth century. Britain purchased tea from China, which was paid for with Indian raw cotton, and later with opium imported into China. In turn, Britain curtailed Indian domestic production of finished cotton goods and encouraged the Indian merchants to import British cotton manufactures.

Incorporation into the world-system induced changes in the economic, and even cultural, patterns of the peripheral and colonial areas. The nineteenth century saw the famous competition of European core powers for colonies in Africa and the Middle East.

Colonialism took several forms between the sixteenth and the twentieth centuries, ranging from settler colonies to political control by a small group of core citizens over a large native population. While economic factors were central, the creation of colonies was buttressed and sanctified by the religious and ideological worldview of the core nations. This worldview included racism, which justified dominance and often made peripheral populations feel culturally inferior. Both Catholic and Protestant colonizers sought to expand their religious spheres of domination.

Competition between core powers to consolidate areas external to the world-system was the catalyst to colonialism. At first, European powers competed for control of precious raw materials (i.e., the fabled gold and silver of the Americas and the fisheries and pelts on and off the coast of North America). Soon agricultural goods, such as sugar from the Caribbean and tobacco, indigo, and, later, cotton from North America, became valued imports to the core powers.

As labor-intensive agricultural products became more important, the transport and trade of a labor force became an increasingly vital factor in the world-system and a source of rivalry between core powers. The west coast of Africa was incorporated into the world-system as a source of slaves, making the slave trade a central component in the sixteenth- and seventeenth-century world economy and an integral part of the famous Atlantic triangular trade network between Africa, the Americas, and Europe.

Struggles between core powers, and their attempts to maintain a balance of power without any one power achieving hegemony, resulted in wars on the European continent. These wars expanded into the colonies. Treaties terminating such conflicts reflected the significance of the world-system. The Treaty of Utrecht of 1713, for example, which ended the War of the Spanish Succession (1701–1714), gave England access to the slave trade dominated by the Spanish.

By the middle of the eighteenth century, policymakers in the major European core nations—England, France, Spain, and the Netherlands—realized that conflicts in the peripheral colonial areas were as important toward maintaining the balance of power within the world-system as wars on the continent. In the late 1750s, for example, the Duc de Choiseul (1719–1785), French minister of foreign affairs, wrote to Charles III, king of Spain (1759–1788) and of Naples and Sicily (1735–1759): "The King [of France] believes that it is possessions in America that will in the future form the balance of power in Europe, and that, if the English invade that part of the world, as it appears they have the intention of doing, it will result therefrom that England will usurp the commerce of the nations, and that she alone will remain rich in Europe." Until the early nineteenth century, France and Spain fought to deny England hegemony.

IMMANUEL MAURICE WALLERSTEIN

Born in 1930, American sociologist Immanuel Maurice Wallerstein is best known for the development of *world-systems theory*—a comprehensive theoretical framework and methodology for the study of social change in the context of the global system of nations. World-systems theory has reshaped the sociology of development and has made Wallerstein one of the discipline's single most influential scholars.

Wallerstein's career began at Columbia University, where he served as an instructor (1958–1959), assistant professor (1959–1963), and associate professor of sociology (1963–1971). He then moved to McGill University in Montreal, serving as professor of sociology from 1971 to 1976. Wallerstein joined the State University of New York at Binghamton in 1976, where he was a distinguished professor of sociology until 1999, at which time he was named professor emeritus. In 2000 Yale University appointed Wallerstein as a senior research scholar. In addition, he has served as director of the Fernand Braudel Center for the Study of Economies, Historical Systems, and Civilizations since 1976, and has written and edited many books.

Wallerstein maintains that a new form of Western colonialism, neocolonialism, pursued mostly by the United States and various multinational corporations, has replaced old forms of colonial domination with indirect domination achieved through economic and political means. Examples of methods used to obtain indirect domination include the provision of economic aid, as well as monetary and trade policies.

In a slightly adapted version of the introductory essay to *The Essential Wallerstein* (New Press, 2000), posted on Yale University's Web site in 2006, Wallerstein explains: "World-systems analysis allowed me to range widely in terms of concrete issues, but always in such a way that the pieces might be fit together at the end of the exercise. It is not that world-systems analysis enabled me to 'discover the truth.' It is rather that it enabled me to make what I considered to be plausible interpretations of social reality in ways that I believe are more useful for all of us in making political and moral decisions. It is also that it enabled me to distinguish between what are long-lasting structures and those momentary expressions of reality that we so regularly reify into fashionable theories about what is novel, as for example, the enormous recent production concerning so-called 'globalization.' "

In a careful study of India, Wallerstein traces the colonization of the Mughal Empire, which ruled much of the Indian Subcontinent during the sixteenth and seventeenth centuries. The decision to incorporate India as part of the British Empire illustrates the dynamics of the globalization of the world-system and the conflicts between the core powers. Contributing to Britain's decision to colonize was competition with France, which also sought Indian riches.

Demonstrating the linkage between private business and government in the world-system, three actors participated in the colonization of India: the British East India Company, the British government, and individual traders. In the mid-eighteenth century, a debate arose in England over the economic costs of colonialism (i.e., whether the costs of colonial rule outweighed the trade advantages). This debate, in one form or another, occurred in all core colonial powers until the demise of formal colonialism.

Within world-system analysis, colonies are not passive participants. In virtually every colony, antisystemic forces disputed colonial status. Responses ranged from petition to revolution and warfare. Beginning with the British North American colonies and the Spanish and French colonial empires in the late eighteenth and early nineteenth centuries, anticolonialism gained momentum. The successful anticolonial rebellion against the French in Haiti in 1804, moreover, reinforced a racial fear of slave rebellions into the consciousness of European powers and the United States.

By the late nineteenth century, anticolonial rebellions were occurring worldwide, and in the twentieth century, core nations realized that the costs of colonialism outweighed the advantages. By the twenty-first century, formal colonialism was essentially a relic of the past. While many colonies rebelled against colonial status, most did not reject the basic structure of the capitalist world-system. Ultimately, core nations found new methods of controlling the economies of the newly independent nations in the periphery and semiperiphery. These methods included economic coercion and military intervention.

GLOBALIZATION

In the 1990s the idea of *globalization* entered into public discourse. World-system and globalization theory stress a global economic interaction, but *globalism* and *globalization* are not synonymous terms. Globalization is one form of core domination in the world-system. Both globalism and globalization emphasize a global perspective in understanding the world economy and take into account private business as an important element in the dynamics of the global economy. However, Wallerstein asserts that in globalization theory, "the pressures on all governments to open their frontiers to the free movement of goods and capital is unusually strong" (Wallerstein 2004, p. 93).

At the dawn of the twenty-first century, Wallerstein observes that the modern world-system is in crisis, which he defines as difficulties that cannot be resolved. Several factors contribute to this crisis. First, the revolutions of 1968, demonstrations by students throughout the Western world who organized to condemn both United States hegemony and the collusion of the Soviet Union, challenged the fairness of the world-system, and these challenges have continued in antiglobalization activism.

Second, less and less of the earth's population live in rural areas, which were, for centuries, a prime source of cheap industrial labor; hence, the costs of production have risen. Even the current trend of "runaway factories" (corporations moving their production facilities to peripheral areas with cheap labor) is not secure, because corporations and governments must pay the high costs of moving and often the expense of maintaining political stability in these areas. Wallerstein suggests that a choice exists between constructing a new world-system based on the same hierarchical privileges of the old system, or constructing a new more democratic and equalitarian system.

SEE ALSO *Anti-Americanism; Hegemon and Hegemony.*

BIBLIOGRAPHY

McCormick, Thomas J. "World Systems." In *Explaining the History of American Foreign Relations*, 2nd ed., edited by Michael J. Hogan and Thomas G. Paterson, 149–161. New York: Cambridge University Press, 2004.

Wallerstein, Immanuel. *The Modern World-System*, Vol. 1: *Capitalist Agriculture and the Origins of the European World-Economy in the Sixteenth Century.* New York: Academic Press, 1974.

Wallerstein, Immanuel. *The Modern World-System*, Vol. 2: *Mercantilism and the Consolidation of the European World-Economy, 1600–1750.* New York: Academic Press, 1980.

Wallerstein, Immanuel. *The Modern World-System*, Vol. 3: *The Second Era of Great Expansion of the Capitalist World Economy, 1730–1840s.* San Diego, CA: Academic Press, 1989.

Wallerstein, Immanuel. *World-Systems Analysis: An Introduction.* Durham, NC: Duke University Press, 2004.

Martin Haas

MOLUCCAS

In the history of the Moluccas (a group of islands in present-day Indonesia), three regions are to be distinguished: the North Moluccas, with its sociopolitical center in the small islands of Ternate and Tidore off the west coast of Halmahera; the South Moluccas, with its center in the Banda Islands; and the Central Moluccas, with its center in the island of Ambon and three adjacent small islands off the southwest coast of Seram.

Ternate and the adjoining islands were the natural habitat of the clove tree, while the Banda Islands were the natural habitat of the nutmeg tree, producing nutmeg and mace. Until the sixteenth century the production of cloves, nutmeg, and mace remained restricted to these islands. From ancient times, cloves, nutmeg, and mace had been much sought-after spices for which extremely high prices were paid in the markets of Asia, the Middle East, and Europe. In the course of time, foreign traders found their way to the Moluccas, also called the Spice Islands. Javanese merchants were almost certainly the first to do so, followed by traders from South Asia and the Middle East and, finally, in 1512, by the Portuguese.

By the end of the fifteenth and into the early part of the sixteenth century in Ternate-Tidore and in the Banda Islands, trade contacts with the distant outside world went hand in hand with the introduction of Islam. Furthermore, state formation occurred in the North Moluccas, resulting in the beginning of the sixteenth century in four principalities: Ternate, Tidore, Jailolo, and Bacan. Of these, Ternate and Tidore were the most important. Ternate and Tidore were well-matched rivals, and continuously opposed each other; Ternate usually had the backing of Bacan, whereas Jailolo sided with Tidore.

No state formation occurred in Banda. In the sixteenth century, Bandanese society comprised more than twenty villages without a central authority. Bandanese village chiefs, usually known as *orang kaya* (literally, "rich men"), every now and then waged war on one another, but conferred with each other when common interests vis-à-vis foreigners came into play. Banda did exhibit a kind of supravillage order. The villages were organized into two mutually opposed groupings: the Uli Lima, or League of Five, and the Uli Siwa, or League of Nine. Each village belonged to either the League of Five or the League of Nine, and the villages were distributed in such a way as to make for a dual territorial division. The two leagues regarded each other as opponents.

The same clear-cut order of villages existed in the Central Moluccas. Before the sixteenth century, the Central Moluccan islands, with a relatively uncivilized population, were unimportant. However, because Ambon was an intermediate station in the sailing route between Banda and Ternate-Tidore, the Ambonese came in contact with foreigners. As a result, early in the sixteenth century the villages of Hitu, the northern peninsula of the island of Ambon, began to cultivate cloves. At about the same time, Islam found acceptance in Hitu.

Such was the situation in the Moluccas when the Portuguese arrived in the early 1500s, the first Europeans to reach the region.

THE PORTUGUESE

After Afonso de Albuquerque (ca. 1460–1515), the governor of Portuguese India, conquered Malacca (Melaka) in 1511, he immediately sent three ships to the Moluccas. Consequently, the inhabitants of Banda, Ambon, and Ternate had become acquainted with the Portuguese by 1512. The crew of one of the Portuguese ships did not return to Malacca, but at the invitation of the ruler of Ternate settled on that island. The Ternatans were impressed by the knowledge, skills, and arms of the Portuguese and invited them to establish a permanent trading station in Ternate.

Meanwhile, the Spaniards also showed interest in the Moluccas. In 1521 two Spanish ships managed to reach Tidore via the Pacific. The Tidorese, being afraid that the Ternatans in cooperation with the Portuguese would dominate the clove trade, welcomed the Spaniards. Although the Spanish ships stayed in Tidore only for a short time, the Ternatans and Portuguese felt threatened by a potential alliance between the Tidorese and the Spaniards.

Amongst other concerns, the possibility of Spanish–Tidorese cooperation induced the Portuguese in 1522 to construct a fortress in Ternate. Eventually the Portuguese also established trading stations and forts elsewhere in the Moluccas, but until 1575 these were subordinate to the fortress in Ternate.

Portuguese authorities pursued a dual purpose in the Moluccas: (1) purchasing large quantities of cloves, nutmeg, and mace for the benefit of the Portuguese Crown, while pushing as many competitors as possible out of the market; and (2) aiding the Catholic Church in its missionary activities, in particular in areas where the progress of Islam could be checked. The building of forts served this dual purpose. Trade was conducted from the forts, which at the same time served as military bases that could provide protection to those amongst the native population who had chosen to embrace Christianity.

The policies pursued by Lisbon in the Moluccas were hampered by deficient political, administrative, and military organization, by lack of dedicated servants of the crown, by lack of manpower and other resources, and by long lines of communication. Portuguese authorities in Goa (on the west coast of India), the Portuguese headquarters in Asia, sent a series of commanders to the Moluccas for terms of three years. The commander had to recruit his own subordinates to sail with him to Ternate. A large number of those who enlisted for service in the faraway Moluccas were regarded as the dregs of Portuguese society in Asia. Once in the Moluccas, most of the Portuguese tried to become as rich as possible by private trade, to the detriment of the crown that they were supposed to serve. Control from distant Goa was highly ineffective.

Some of the Portuguese serving in the Moluccas never returned to Goa. Instead, they started families in the Moluccas with local Moluccan women or with imported slave women. They supported themselves, in part, through private trade, buying spices from the local population and selling them to the agents of the Portuguese Crown or to Asian traders if they offered to pay more. Slaves belonging to these Portuguese households tended gardens and did some fishing, thus supplying the day-to-day livelihood of the household. Slaves also grew spices for their masters. The resident married men, called *casados,* became the backbone of the Portuguese presence in the Moluccas. Some *casados* also became advisors to Moluccan rulers.

The Portuguese were unable to realize their agenda in the Moluccas by exercise of power alone, but they could take advantage of rivalries and chasms in Moluccan society. Thus, in Ternate, when Ternatan and Portuguese interests conflicted, there were always ambitious Ternatans who were willing to enhance their position in Ternatan society by means of Portuguese assistance. Moreover, the alliance with the Portuguese provided the principality as a whole with opportunities for political and military ascendancy within Moluccan society.

Tidore and Jailolo tried to counter the effects of the Portuguese presence in the area by entering into an alliance with the Spanish, who, from 1527 to 1534 and 1544 to 1545 were once again upon the Moluccan stage. This tactic had little effect, however, because the Spanish at that time were unable to maintain their position in the region. The Ternatan-Portuguese ascendancy was used to bring the kingdom of Jailolo to its knees, and in 1551 Jailolo was finally overwhelmed by combined Ternatan and Portuguese forces.

In Ambon, the Portuguese capitalized on the tension between the League of Five and League of Nine. Initially, the Portuguese were on friendly terms with the Muslim villages of the League of Five in Hitu. But in the 1530s the Portuguese angered the Hituese, who sought support from Muslims in Java and Ternate. The Portuguese in their turn made allies of the pagan villages of the League of Nine, which due to the efforts of Jesuit missionaries had gradually converted to Christianity. Thus, the long-standing antagonism between the League of Five and the League of Nine turned into a conflict of Muslims versus Christians. Facing a surging tide of Muslim Hituese, in 1575 the Portuguese started construction on a fort in Leitimor, the southern peninsula of the island of Ambon. This fort eventually became the nucleus of the city of Ambon, the present capital of the Moluccas.

The Portuguese never built a trading station or fort in Banda. But regularly, usually once a year, a Portuguese ship would visit Banda to purchase nutmeg and mace in competition with other traders.

Conflicting interests and Portuguese contempt for Islam prevented the formation of long-lasting and close cooperation between the Portuguese and their most valuable ally, Hairun, the sultan of Ternate (1535–1570). In 1570 Hairun was stabbed to death by order of the Portuguese commander Diogo Lopes de Mesquita, who considered Hairun an obstacle to the Portuguese expansion in the Moluccas. The murder of Hairun by the Portuguese led to a permanent rupture. The Ternatans thereafter seized every opportunity to attack the Portuguese, who were finally forced to surrender their fortress in Ternate in December 1575. They withdrew to Ambon, where they had shortly before begun construction on the fort in Leitimor. After 1575 the fort in Ambon served as the European base of power in the Moluccas.

After the Portuguese had been chased off Ternate, the sultan of Tidore, Gapi Baguna (at least 1571–1599), fearful of political and military domination by the Ternatans, invited the Portuguese to establish a military post in Tidore. This way he hoped to divert the clove trade from Ternate to his own island. In 1578 the Portuguese built a fort in Tidore, thereby reestablishing themselves in the North Moluccas. But they were never to regain their former position of power there.

THE DUTCH UNITED EAST INDIA COMPANY (VOC)

In 1599 Dutch ships appeared in the Moluccas. The Dutch presented themselves as opponents of the Portuguese, and Portugal's Moluccan enemies, all Muslims, gave the Dutch a warm welcome. The Bandanese, Hituese, and Ternatans signed contracts agreeing to supply their spices at good prices to the Dutch, while the Dutch promised to support the Moluccans against their Portuguese enemies. But only after the Verenigde Oost-Indische Compagnie (VOC, or United East India Company) was founded in 1602 in the Netherlands did the Dutch obtain a firm footing in the Moluccas. In 1605 they succeeded in capturing the Portuguese forts in Ambon and Tidore, thereby bringing the role of the Portuguese in the Moluccas to an end.

The VOC was both a commercial company and a military power. In Asia, the company could enter into contracts, erect fortifications, and administer subject territories on behalf of the Dutch Republic.

Soon the VOC recognized the unparalleled opportunities the Moluccas offered: the Moluccan Islands were the sole producers of precious cloves, nutmeg, and mace; and they comprised a limited territory with a small population (in the relevant spice-producing regions no more than about 100,000 people in total), making the Moluccas easy to control. Here was a chance to force the population to produce spices in a limited territory exclusively for the VOC. The VOC would thus have a monopoly of the sale of these spices in the Asian and European markets.

With such a monopoly the profits would be driven up because the VOC as the sole buyer of the spices could maintain low costs, while as the sole supplier the VOC could enforce high prices in the world market. However, the prevention of smuggling was crucial for the maintenance of this monopoly. The monopoly required that the Moluccas be closed to all free trade, and the VOC took care that its employees did not engage in spice trading. Within fifty years this program was realized.

At first, the Spaniards tried to thwart the Dutch by conquering from Manila in 1605, with the help of Tidore, the former Portuguese fortress on the west coast of Ternate and by erecting a garrison in a fort in Tidore. To protect themselves and their Ternatan allies, the Dutch constructed a fortress in 1607 on the east coast of Ternate. The Dutch and the Ternatans were unable to drive the Spaniards from Tidore or from the western and southern half of Ternate, but they succeeded in bringing about conditions under which the costs of the Spanish strongholds in the Moluccas exceeded the benefits, with the result that Spain voluntarily withdrew from the Moluccas in 1663.

The English also caused problems for the Dutch. English ships began appearing in the Moluccas in 1604, but in 1623 the VOC, using all the forces at its disposal, pushed the English altogether out of the region.

The greatest resistance that the VOC encountered in enforcing its monopoly came from the Moluccans themselves. To achieve its goals the VOC behaved unscrupulously in the Banda Islands. Because the Bandanese continued to sell their nutmeg and mace to anyone who offered higher prices, the VOC conducted a military campaign against the Bandanese in 1621 and broke all resistance. Survivors were shipped into slavery to Batavia, and only a small number of Bandanese escaped the Dutch by taking refuge on faraway islands. The VOC divided the conquered land into parcels that were given in hereditary tenure to Dutchmen, who exploited the land with slave labor. Until the nineteenth century the tenants were obliged to deliver their nutmeg and mace at prices fixed by the VOC.

The Dutch action in the Banda Islands caused shockwaves elsewhere in the Moluccas. In Banda, the VOC had shown that it was capable of doing anything to safeguard its interests.

Subsequently, the Dutch, not without difficulty, had everything their own way in Ternate and Ambon. Having broken all overt and covert resistance, and having managed to keep away all Asian traders from the Moluccas, the Dutch signed contracts from 1652 to 1657 with the rulers of the North Moluccas in which the Moluccans conceded that they were subordinate to the VOC. The North Moluccan rulers also promised to entertain no relations with other nations or rulers; to keep out all foreigners; to offer no asylum to enemies of the VOC; to neither carry on trade in or cultivate spices; to assist with the tracking down of spice trees; to supply goods and render services to the VOC as its subjects; and to recognize the VOC's right to construct fortifications where it deemed necessary.

At the same time, the population of Ambon and three adjacent small islands was obliged to grow a quantity of cloves as stipulated by the VOC and to supply this to the company at a fixed price. Hence, on these four islands a cultivation system was introduced under the strict supervision of the VOC, which was to supply the entire world market with cloves. The village chiefs were instrumental in the implementation of this system. The company assured itself of their cooperation by paying them 10 percent of the price paid to the producers coming under their authority. The village chiefs were also expected to ensure that villagers rendered services due to the VOC. These services imposed a heavy burden on the villagers.

In taking over the Portuguese authority in Ambon in 1605 the VOC inherited a number of native Christians. They had been allies of the Portuguese, but for the Dutch they were subordinates who were obliged to grow cloves and perform *corvée* services just like Muslims. The Christian villagers were granted minimal education and pastoral care.

In the North Moluccas, the main objective of the VOC after 1657 was to isolate the principalities of Ternate, Tidore, and Bacan as much as possible from the outside world. The character of the European settlements in the area developed from that of trading posts to that of guard posts for the prevention of the growing and smuggling of cloves. Within this system of indirect rule, however, the Dutch failed to exercise effective control over Tidore because they neglected to establish a garrison there. Tidore and its dependencies were nominally under Dutch authority, but in reality this principality mostly managed to escape Dutch oversight.

Toward the end of the eighteenth century, the VOC's power was definitely waning, and the company was increasingly confronted with such problems as piracy and the rise to power of Nuku, a prince of Tidore who in 1779 had been passed over for succession. Prince Nuku subsequently decamped to the areas east of Halmahera, where he rallied many supporters to his cause. Together with British private traders operating from India, he became involved in spice smuggling. Eventually, in 1797, he succeeded in conquering Tidore with his fleet and with the assistance of two English ships.

BRITISH INTERREGNUM

Soon after the French Revolution broke out in 1789, Britain and France went to war with each other (the Napoleonic Wars, 1793–1802, 1803–1814). The Netherlands became a satellite state of France and had to pay a price in Asia. In 1796 Ambon and Banda passed into British hands, and in 1801, with the support of Nuku of Tidore, the British took control of Ternate.

The British maintained a system of compulsory cultivation and delivery of spices, but at the same time young clove and nutmeg trees were transplanted to other British colonies. In the long run, therefore, the Moluccas would no longer be the sole producer of cloves, nutmeg, and mace.

In 1803 the Moluccas again fell into Dutch hands. Extremely bad times followed for the Moluccas as the islands were put in a state of defense against the British. In various ways, the population was more heavily burdened than ever before.

In 1810 Ambon, Banda, and Ternate fell again in British hands. After the hardships of the foregoing years, the second British interregnum (1810–1817) was a relief for the Moluccas. The British resident, William Byam Martin (1811–1817), demonstrated a sincere interest in the well-being of the population and displayed an aversion to the use of force. The spice monopoly was maintained, but without its excrescences. For the Moluccans, the British administration in every respect compared favorably with the Dutch administration.

After the Napoleonic Wars in Europe, the Moluccas were handed over once again to the Dutch in 1817. Disappointed with the return of the Dutch, rebellion broke out in the Ambon Islands, and it took the Dutch six months to quell the uprising.

DUTCH COLONIAL GOVERNMENT

The return of Dutch rule did not imply a simple reversion to the former situation of the VOC period. The

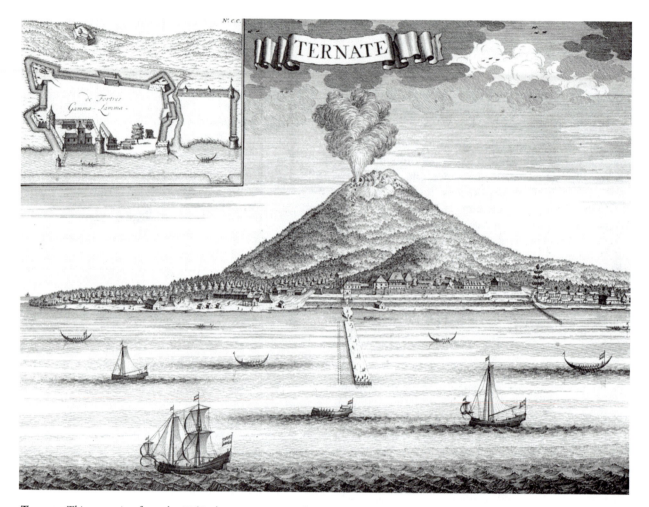

Ternate. *This engraving from the 1740s shows an eruption of Mount Gamalama on the island of Ternate in the North Moluccas in Indonesia. A nearby Dutch fort appears in the inset on the upper left.* © CORBIS. REPRODUCED BY PERMISSION.

Dutch monopoly on the world supply of cloves, nutmeg, and mace had completely broken down. This development had important consequences for the Moluccas. Although the system of compulsory cultivation of spices continued for the time being, there was in effect no longer any policing of the prohibition on the cultivation of cloves beyond Ambon. As the production of cloves, nutmeg, and mace beyond the Moluccas rose, the prices for these products on the world market fell, with the result that the Dutch government began to take losses on the spices it was obliged to purchase in Ambon and in Banda, and the monopoly on clove and nutmeg production was officially lifted on January 1, 1864. In the nineteenth century, after the Moluccan spices lost their former high value on the world market, the Moluccas became an economically undesirable area.

With the new colonial government, direct involvement in production and trade was no longer the first matter of importance. As the nineteenth century progressed, the emphasis became more on good government in support of the advancement of private trade and commerce. With the expansion of the colonial state, administration became more and more an end in itself. The result for the Moluccas was that an interest was now also taken in parts of the larger islands of Halmahera, Seram, and Buru and in the southern islands, which had never had any economic value to the Dutch. Efforts were made to place those islands wholly under Dutch authority and under regular colonial rule. This aim was realized in the twentieth century.

Early in the nineteenth century, there was also a clear break with the previous VOC period in the areas of church, mission, and education. The VOC had never shown any interest in missionary activities, but from 1814 onward, missionaries, first under the protection of the British and then under the protection of the Dutch, made their appearance again in the Moluccas, for the first time since the Portuguese left in 1605.

Another important development was that in the second half of the nineteenth and the first half of the twentieth centuries the educational system was gradually extended in the Central Moluccas. Although the separation between schools and churches made it possible for Muslims to take advantage of the educational facilities, it was almost exclusively the Ambonese Christians who benefited from them. Thus the extension of education increased the social distance between Christian and Muslim Ambonese.

As the colonial state's need for Indonesian officials increased and the educational system in Ambon came to offer more and more training facilities, the number of Ambonese taking up positions as officials in the colonial government grew. Other Ambonese found employment with the church, with the missions, in the educational system, in health care, and with private companies. Men with only an elementary-school education could enlist in the colonial army, which especially after 1875 made systematic attempts to recruit Ambonese soldiers. This eagerness of Christian Ambonese to serve in the colonial apparatus or in the Dutch private sector, within and outside the Moluccas, remained strong until the end of the colonial period. The Moluccas, and in particular Ambon, was transformed from a supplier of spices to a supplier of personnel for the Dutch.

The prewar nationalist movement advocating Indonesian independence did not pass by Ambonese society. From the early 1920s onward this movement drew supporters from among better-educated Ambonese emigrants. The majority of them, however, still expected a perpetuation of the colonial system and desired little more than an improvement in social opportunities for Ambonese within this system. On the Ambonese islands themselves, the chiefs of both Christian and Muslim villages were conservative and on their guard against anything likely to undermine their authority. Hence, they tried as much as possible to counter all forms of political activity in their villages in cooperation with the Dutch administrative apparatus.

At the end of the nineteenth and the beginning of the twentieth centuries, missionaries operating in Halmahera were assiduous in pointing out the detrimental effects of Ternatan and Tidorese rule on the local population in the North Moluccas. They became advocates for the suppression of the influence of autonomous principalities and for improvement in the administrative control of the colonial government. At the beginning of the twentieth century, there was an acceleration in the dismantling of authority exercised by the autonomous governments. From 1907 to 1910 the principalities of Ternate, Tidore, and Bacan were forced to sign away their formal independence, and the self-governing territories were thereby incorporated more closely into the colonial state. This was a formal ratification of a process that had begun earlier and paved the way for the subsequent remodeling of the formal autonomy of Ternate, Tidore, and Bacan according to the norms of the colonial state.

Although part of the pagan population of Halmahera embraced Christianity, in the North Moluccas the level of education did not surpass elementary school. Thus the development of the North Moluccas lagged far behind that of the Central Moluccas, and the nationalist movement gained no foothold there.

The South Moluccas, with the exception of the Banda Islands, had always been of marginal significance, and remained so in the nineteenth and twentieth centuries.

WORLD WAR II AND DECOLONIZATION

The defeat of the Dutch by Japan in 1942 dealt Dutch prestige a serious blow. When the Dutch returned to the region in 1945, it looked as though the old regime would be reestablished. Large numbers of Christian Ambonese again entered the service of the Dutch colonial apparatus as officials and soldiers.

The end of colonial rule in 1949 caused few problems in the North and South Moluccas. The Central Moluccans reacted differently. In Ambon, the transfer of power led to the proclamation of an independent Moluccan Republic in April 1950. But the uprising got no support outside the Central Moluccas, and the Moluccan Republic, dominated by Ambonese Christians, was short-lived. From 1950 to 1951 the Indonesian army crushed the rebellion, although hard-core rebels continued fighting a guerilla war in Seram until 1965.

SEE ALSO *Dutch United East India Company; Empire, Dutch; Empire, Portuguese; Pacific, European Presence in.*

BIBLIOGRAPHY

Andaya, Leonard Y. *The World of Maluku: Eastern Indonesia in the Early Modern Period.* Honolulu: University of Hawaii Press, 1993.

Chauvel, Richard. *Nationalists, Soldiers, and Separatists: The Ambonese Islands from Colonialism to Revolt, 1880–1950.* Leiden, Netherlands: KITLV Press, 1990.

Cribb, Robert B. *Historical Atlas of Indonesia.* Honolulu: University of Hawaii Press, 2000.

Ellen, Roy. *On the Edge of the Banda Zone: Past and Present in the Social Organization of a Moluccan Trading Network.* Honolulu: University of Hawaii Press, 2003.

Meilink-Roelofsz, M. A. P. *Asian Trade and European Influence in the Indonesian Archipelago Between 1500 and about 1630.* The Hague, Netherlands: Nijhoff, 1962.

Wright, H. R. C. "The Moluccan Spice Monopoly, 1770–1824." *Journal of the Malaysian Branch of the Royal Asiatic Society* 31 (4) (1958): 1–127.

Chris F. van Fraassen

MOMBASSA

SEE *Colonial Cities and Towns, Africa*

MONEY IN THE COLONIAL AMERICAS

Money, as it is understood today, originated three thousand years ago in China, where coins known as *cash* were introduced to represent the tools and lengths of cloth previously used for exchange. The practice spread in the ancient world as a number of Greek states adopted coinage, and in 285 B.C.E. the Romans began to produce their famous *denarius.*

As the power of Rome spread, its coins replaced primitive tribal "tool" currencies—in Britain, for example, iron bars—establishing a tradition that resulted in all of Europe having adopted a monetary regime based upon silver coins by the Middle Ages. In Spain the regular minting of gold coins, too, began in the fourteenth century, and the Lisbon mint began to produce the gold *cruzado* in 1457 from gold obtained by barter in West Africa.

Christopher Columbus (1451–1506) carried this monetary tradition with him to the New World in 1492. During the first three decades of Spanish exploration and settlement a variety of Old World coins circulated in the Caribbean. The most important were the *maravedí* (the smallest unit of Spanish account currency) and the *real* (a unit worth thirty-four *maravedís*), particularly after 1497, when Queen Isabella I (1451–1504) approved currency regulations making the standard unit of account the *peso de oro* worth 375 *maravedís*. Her regulations also specified the bimetallic relationship between gold and silver as 1:10, although this ratio was frequently adjusted and by the eighteenth century became 1:16.

Gold, derived from both treasure and alluvial deposits, was much more abundant than silver in the Caribbean and Central America. However, the conquest of Mexico and Peru not only increased the volume of gold bullion in circulation, but also made available vast quantities of silver, first as booty and by midcentury from mining. At Cajamarca, for example, the ransom given to Francisco Pizarro (ca. 1475–1541) by the Inca ruler Atahualpa in 1533 yielded 6,087 kilograms (13,420

pounds) of gold and 11,793 kilograms (26,000 pounds) of silver (one fifth of which—the *quint*—was sent to Spain for the king).

As the magnitude and wealth of the mainland territories became clear, King Charles I (1500–1558) of Spain ordered in 1535 the creation of the first American mint in Mexico, beginning the production of America's first silver coin, the peso of eight *reales*, known to posterity as the *piece of eight*. Santo Domingo was granted a mint in 1542, and others opened shortly thereafter in Lima (1565), La Plata (1573), Potosí (1574), and Panama (1580), followed in the seventeenth century by Santa Fe de Bogotá (1620) and Cuzco (1697). The expansion of the frontiers of empire in the eighteenth century, coupled with a dramatic increase in silver production, led to further mints opening in Popayán (1729), Guatemala (1731), and Santiago (1743). Later still, in the first two decades of the nineteenth century, several more mints were established in Mexico, Venezuela, and New Granada, partly in response to the movements of armed forces during the independence period.

During the almost three centuries that coins were minted in Spanish America, there were several significant attempts to standardize coinage and its production. From 1729 all mints were under direct crown control. More significantly, during the reign of Charles III (1716–1788), a sustained campaign was mounted to call in old coins, many of which were clipped and defaced, for replacement by the ubiquitous peso.

A number of mints, notably those in Peru and New Granada, produced gold as well as silver coins, as did mints in Brazil, where major gold finds from the late seventeenth century inaugurated the "golden age" (1690–1750) and the establishment of mints in Salvador, Rio de Janeiro, and Minas Gerais (literally, "General Mines"). By the mid-eighteenth century peak, they were processing over 3,000 kilograms (6,614 pounds) of gold a year, as gold replaced sugar as Brazil's principal export to Portugal (and indirectly to Britain) before production began to fall.

In Spanish America, by contrast, the late colonial period saw Mexico and Peru exporting record quantities of silver—up to thirty million pesos a year—to Spain. Although no longer as important as in the 1580 to 1630 period, when bullion accounted for 80 percent of the value of exports to Spain, it continued to dominate transatlantic trade (56 percent of its value), as well as lubricating complex networks of regional trade in the Americas and beyond. Chinese silks and porcelain, for example, entered Mexico and Peru, via Manila, in large quantities in exchange for silver.

In addition to registered trade, from which the crowns of Spain and Portugal derived customs dues as well as the *quint* (lowered to a tenth in Spanish America in 1736 to stimulate mining output), vast but unquantifiable quantities of unregistered gold and silver entered the channels of contraband trade, particularly in the Caribbean, where Jamaica (British from 1656) traded extensively with the Spanish islands and the northern coast of South America. Given Spain's perennial inability to supply either slaves or manufactured goods in the quantities and at the prices required by increasingly sophisticated Spanish-American consumers, ships from British America also began to penetrate this market in the seventeenth century.

British America, like Brazil, had been largely ignored by Spain because of the failure to find there either easily assimilated natives or precious metals. The early British settlers in Virginia, too, were disappointed that gold did not materialize, despite assiduous prospecting. Economic salvation came, of course, in a different guise, with the introduction in 1614 of tobacco from Trinidad; by 1620, 22,680 kilograms (50,000 pounds) of tobacco had been shipped to England for sale at high prices.

Given the scarcity of currency, and the fact that the few silver coins that trickled in from Spanish America were too valuable for small purchases, the early colonists adopted tobacco as the first legal currency in 1619. A century later "tobacco notes" became legal tender in Virginia, and "rice notes" were introduced in South Carolina. The first mint was established in Boston in 1652, producing mainly small silver coins (shillings, sixpences, and threepenny pieces), and other states soon followed this example.

After independence, Vermont and Connecticut began to issue copper cents, thus beginning the dollar system (the word *dollar* is derived from the German *thaler*, which the Massachusetts authorities had recognized in 1642 as worth five shillings, like the Spanish peso). And so began the monetary empire of the United States.

SEE ALSO *Mercantilism; Mining, the Americas.*

BIBLIOGRAPHY

Davies, Glyn. *A History of Money: From Ancient Times to the Present Day,* 3rd ed. Cardiff, U.K.: University of Wales Press, 2002.

Jones, J. P. *The Money Story.* Newton Abbot, U.K.: David & Charles, 1972.

Moreyra Paz Soldán, Manuel. *La moneda colonial en el Perú: Capítulos de su historia.* Lima, Peru: Banco Central de la Reserva del Perú, 1980.

Vilar, Pierre. *A History of Gold and Money, 1450–1920.* Translated by Judith White. London: NLB, 1976.

Wiseley, William. *A Tool of Power: The Political History of Money.* New York: Wiley, 1977.

John Fisher

MONGOLIA

In 2005 Mongolia was home to 2.5 million people on a 1.5-million-square-kilometer (972,445-square-mile) landlocked high plateau, averaging 1,580 meters (almost 1 mile) above sea level. The country has thick forests and mountains in the north, but 90 percent of the land is arid steppes and deserts, unsuitable for farming. It traditionally has been occupied by migrating herders of sheep, goats, cows, horses, and camels, living in a harsh, dry climate. The country's population is quite homogeneous. Nearly 90 percent are of Khalkha Mongol, with the largest minority being Kazakh Turks in the west. Not included in this modern definition of Mongolia are large populations of Mongols in China (Inner Mongolia) and Russia (Buryatia and Kalmykia), who number another 6 million.

Mongolia traces its origins to the election of a young warrior named Temujin, who in 1206 was elected in a *kuriltai* (council) as Khan. Temujin chose the mystic name of Chinggis (Genghis) Khan, which perhaps means "universal or great khan." This great military leader established the Mongolian Empire of the thirteenth and fourteenth centuries, the largest empire in world history. It stretched from Siberia, Korea, and China to Afghanistan and North India through Tibet, Central Asia including the Silk Road cities, Russia, Turkey, and Iraq to the borders of Egypt and Germany. The Mongols promoted trade, art, and cultural exchange throughout the empire, which is why historians call this period of history Pax Mongolica.

Chinggis reorganized his nomadic warriors to establish a political-military system totally loyal to him. Then he turned against the Jin Empire in North China, where his army developed siege techniques to attack fortified cities. Chinggis devastated the Jin capital (modern Beijing), but the subjugation of China was completed only by his grandson, Kubilai, who in 1279 became the emperor of a new Mongol dynasty called Yuan. Chinggis himself spent much time fighting the Qara Khitai (Western Liao or Tangut) state over the next twenty years.

The murder of Mongol envoys in 1218 in the Muslim Central Asian state of Khawarism was the defining reason that the Mongolian Empire expanded westward from East Asia into the Middle East and Europe. Chinggis, with a nomadic army of 200,000, wiped out the country. He sent small detachments of Mongol cavalry west to defeat the Georgians. These crossed into Russia, through the Crimea and Ukraine. The Khan also made a political-religious alliance with Tibetan Buddhists, which initiated more than 700 years of cultural and religious connections between the two peoples.

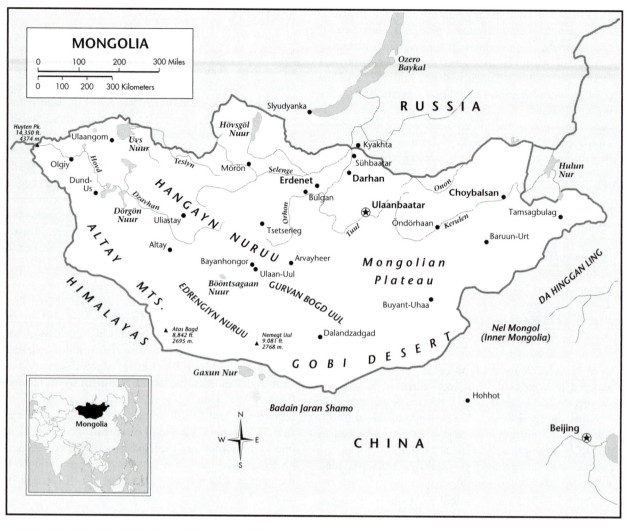

© MARYLAND CARTOGRAPHICS. REPRODUCED BY PERMISSION.

Chinggis died in 1227, dividing up his empire between his four sons.

His son Ogedei was elected Great Khan. He expanded the empire further into Russia, Korea, China, Iran, and Syria. He built the empire its first sedentary capital called Karakorum in the heart of the Mongol homeland steppe. This capital was visited by Western writers such as John of Plano Carpini, William of Rubruk, and Marco Polo. During the imperial period the Mongol rulers in the four major parts of the empire usually came to promote the religion and arts of the peoples they ruled. This was particularly true in Islamic and Buddhist countries.

In West Asia the Mongol Ilkhans remained in power only until 1335. However, Mongol rule—"the Golden Horde"—persisted in Russia until 1502 when it was destroyed by the Muscovite state, but did not embrace Russian Orthodoxy. The Mongols' administrative

practices greatly influenced Russia, and often this heritage, also known as Tatar, is credited with explaining Russia's distinctive culture from that of other European nations.

When the Mongols were deposed in China in 1368 by the Ming dynasty, they returned to the Mongol steppe in disunity. In the late 1500s they became Tibetan Buddhists, which impacted greatly on Mongol culture. In the seventeenth century the Manchu people made an alliance with the Mongol nobles to conquer China and establish the Qing dynasty. Over three centuries the alliance disintegrated into full political and economic domination. With the fall of Manchu rule in China in 1911, Mongolia was able to establish a weak autonomous government under a Buddhist religious leader with strong ties to Republican China.

In 1921 Mongolia underwent a communist revolution with the aid of Siberian Bolshevik forces, and became a loyal Soviet satellite from 1924 to 1990. In 1990 the country experienced a peaceful democratic revolution, and in the twenty-first century seeks to develop its rich mineral and animal resources through free market and democratic institutions.

SEE ALSO *China, After 1945; China, First Opium War to 1945.*

BIBLIOGRAPHY

Baabar, B. *History of Mongolia*. London: White Horse Press, 1999.

Gerhard, Peter. *Pirates of the Pacific, 1575–1742*. Lincoln: University of Nebraska Press, 1990.

Khan, Paul. *The Secret History of the Mongols: The Origins of Chingis Khan*. Boston: Cheng and Tsui, 1998.

Man, John. *Genghis Khan, Life, Death, and Resurrection*. New York: St. Martin's Press, 2005.

Morgan, David. *The Mongols*. Cambridge, MA: Blackwell, 1986.

Rossabi, Morris. *Khubilai Khan: His Life and Times*. Berkeley: University of California Press, 1988.

Spuler, Bertold. *The Mongols in History*. Translated by Geoffrey Wheeler. New York: Praeger, 1971.

Weatherford, Jack. *Genghis Khan and the Making of the Modern World*. New York: Crown Publishers, 2004.

Alicia J. Campi

MONROE DOCTRINE

The Monroe Doctrine was enunciated by President James Monroe (1758–1831) in an annual message to the U.S. Congress in 1823. The main concern of Monroe and his secretary of state, John Quincy Adams (1767–1848), was the future of Hispanic America. Hispanic America had struggled for independence from Spain, and new republics sprang up from Mexico to Chile, influenced in part by the examples of French and U.S. republicanism. The United States welcomed the emergence of the new republics in most respects; but the absolute monarchies in Europe, notably Russia and the briefly resurgent monarchical regime in France, looked askance at the creation of the new states and sought to isolate them diplomatically.

While the United States began the process of recognizing the Spanish American republics in 1822, France in 1823 urged Spain to reimpose the power of the House of Bourbon in Spanish America. A program of reconquest backed by the Holy Alliance (Russia, Prussia, and Austria) and endorsed by the Vatican was a matter of deep anxiety in Spanish America, the United States, and Britain, which was aiming to establish strong commercial ties with the fledgling republics. Indeed, the British

foreign secretary, George Canning (1770–1827), even proposed that Britain and the United States should together warn Spain and France against intervention. Adams, meanwhile, had a secondary anxiety: the drive of Russia to extend its influence along the Pacific coast of North America from Alaska to California, then still part of Mexico.

The Monroe Doctrine amounted to a statement that the United States would treat any attempt to extend European influence in the "New World" as a threat to its security. This was, in effect, an assertion that the Western Hemisphere was closed to European colonization, whether by powers like Russia with new expansionist aspirations or by old colonial powers like Spain, which aimed to recuperate colonies lost in the wars of independence. The immediate impact of the Monroe Doctrine was limited, both because the powers of mainland Europe were too preoccupied with events closer to home to put up a united front in the Americas, and because Spain was too debilitated by the effects of warfare at home and in the former colonial empire to launch a project of reconquest.

Enjoying some support from the British, the most formidable naval power of the century, the Monroe Doctrine remained in place. It was insufficient, however, to prevent brief interventions in the 1860s by Spain in Santo Domingo and France in Mexico. There were two reasons for this: the weakness of the U.S. Navy, which was smaller than the Chilean navy; and deep divisions in the United States, which culminated in the American Civil War (1861–1865). Only after the consolidation of the frontier in the West and the assertion of the United States as a major naval power in both the Atlantic and Pacific oceans could the Monroe Doctrine be applied without British support.

The final defeat of Spain in the Caribbean and the Pacific during the War of 1898 meant that the United States could now assert an ascendancy in northern Latin America and the Caribbean and consolidate U.S. influence in southern South America. Complemented by the Roosevelt Corollary, enunciated by President Theodore Roosevelt (1858–1919) in 1904, the Monroe Doctrine was used by successive U.S. administrations to justify interventions ostensibly designed to preempt European, especially German, invasions of small nations, usually to collect outstanding debts. Thus the Monroe Doctrine provided the main rationale for a sequence of interventions in Cuba, the Dominican Republic, Haiti, Nicaragua, and the port of Veracruz (Mexico) during the next three decades. These interventions achieved the goal of forestalling European involvement at the expense of awakening widespread and, in some countries, sustained nationalist movements.

European Potentates Observe Naval Might. *This cartoon, in which figures representing the countries of Europe observe the naval power of the United States, appeared in the* New York Herald. © **BETTMANN/CORBIS. REPRODUCED BY PERMISSION.**

SEE ALSO *United States Interventions in Postindependence Latin America.*

BIBLIOGRAPHY

Collin, Richard H. *Theodore Roosevelt's Caribbean: The Panama Canal, the Monroe Doctrine, and the Latin American Context.* Baton Rouge: Louisiana State University Press, 1991.

Niess, Frank. *A Hemisphere to Itself: A History of US–Latin American Relations.* Translated by Harry Drost. London: Zed, 1990.

Perkins, Dexter. *A History of the Monroe Doctrine,* rev. ed. Boston: Little, Brown, 1955.

Christopher Abel

MUHAMMAD 'ALI
1769–1849

Muhammad 'Ali was an energetic and ambitious Ottoman governor of Egypt from 1805 to 1848. During his long career he managed to augment Egypt's wealth, introduce long-lasting changes to its society, and embark on an expansionist policy that gravely threatened the Ottoman Empire. Due to European opposition, however, the mini-empire he had founded had to be dismantled; in exchange, the Ottoman sultan granted him hereditary rule of Egypt and the Sudan.

Said to be of Albanian origins, Muhammad 'Ali had been a tobacco merchant when in 1801 he joined an irregular military force dispatched to Egypt by the Ottomans to evict the French army, which had occupied the country three years earlier. Following the French evacuation, Muhammad 'Ali seized effective control of Cairo and forced the sultan in Istanbul to appoint him officially as governor of Egypt with the title of Pasha (1805).

Muhammad 'Ali moved fast to centralize control by inviting many friends and relatives to settle in Egypt and by appointing them in key positions within the provinces. He then initiated a radical overhaul of the agricultural sector. Aware of Ottoman attempts to dislodge him from Egypt, he attempted to raise troops from the Sudan in 1818. When these attempts proved unsuccessful, he started conscripting peasants from the Egyptian countryside (1820–1821) and soon appointed European

Muhammad ʿAli. *Considered the founder of modern Egypt, Muhammad ʿAli is often depicted as a strong man who stood up against Western imperialism.* © BETTMANN/CORBIS. REPRODUCED BY PERMISSION.

officers to train them. He also founded many schools, factories, and hospitals to serve this army. Using these well-trained troops he grudgingly lent a helping hand to the sultan in his fight against the rebellious Greek insurgents. After initial successes, a combined British, French, and Russian navy sank the entire Egyptian and Ottoman fleet in October 1827.

Following the Greek debacle, the Pasha resolved not to get embroiled in the sultan's struggles. In 1831 he even invaded Syria to establish a buffer area between his power base in Egypt and the sultan's in Anatolia. His troops faced ineffective resistance and soon crossed into Anatolia and gravely threatened Istanbul. Alarmed at his vassal's surprise advance, the Ottoman sultan sought help from Britain, and when this did not materialize he turned to the Russians who were only too eager to interfere in Ottoman affairs. In time, the British saw the Pasha's bid for independence and expansionist policies as undermining the peace in Europe and seriously threatening their interests in Asia. In 1840 they convened a European conference in London that forced the Pasha to withdraw from Syria, southern Anatolia, Crete, and Arabia. Finally, in 1841 the Ottoman sultan issued a rescript ordering

him to reduce the size of his army, but also bestowed on him the hereditary rule of Egypt and the Sudan.

For the remaining years of his reign Muhammad Ali devoted all his energy to domestic policy. After his death in 1849 the governorship of Egypt was passed on according to the 1841 rescript to the oldest male member of Muhammad ʿAli's family, but in 1867 Ismail, his grandson and third successor, managed to change the conditions of hereditary rule to maintain the governorship in his own line. When the British occupied Egypt in 1882 they kept members of Muhammad ʿAli's family as titular governors of Egypt under the titles first of khedive (1882–1914), then sultan (1914–1923), then king (1923–1952). In 1952 a military coup lead by Gamal Abd al-Nasir forced King Farouk, the last of Muhammad ʿAli's descendants, to abdicate the throne, and in 1953 the monarchy was abolished and Egypt was declared a republic.

Dubbed as the "Founder of Modern Egypt," Muhammad ʿAli is often depicted as a strong man who stood up against Western imperialism. Having imperial designs himself, however, it is probably more correct to see his legacy as changing Egypt's relationship with the Ottoman Empire, instituting long-lasting socioeconomic changes in Egypt, and establishing a dynasty that ruled over Egypt and the Sudan for 100 years.

SEE ALSO *Egypt; Empire, Ottoman; Empire, Russian and the Middle East.*

BIBLIOGRAPHY

Dodwell, Henry. *The Founder of Modern Egypt: A Study of Muhammad Ali.* Cambridge, UK: Cambridge University Press, 1931.

Fahmy, Khaled. *All the Pasha's Men: Mehmed Ali, His Army and the Making of Modern Egypt.* Cambridge, UK: Cambridge University Press, 1997.

Lufti al-Sayyid Marsot, Afaf. *Egypt in the Reign of Muhammad Ali.* Cambridge, UK: Cambridge University Press, 1984.

Rivlin, Helen. *The Agricultural Policy of Muhammad Ali in Egypt.* Cambridge, MA: Harvard University Press, 1961.

Tucker, Judith. *Women in Nineteenth-Century Egypt.* Cambridge, UK: Cambridge University Press, 1985.

Khaled Fahmy

MULTATULI (EDUARD DOUWES DEKKER)
1820–1887

In his novel *Max Havelaar of de koffieveilingen der Nederlandsche Handel-Maatschappij* (Max Havelaar or the Coffee Auctions of the Dutch Trading Company; 1860) the Dutch writer Multatuli offered a critical description of the colony of the Netherlands Indies (present-day Indonesia). This novel hails as the most important work of Dutch literature, and Multatuli as the most important Dutch author.

Multatuli (literally, "I have sustained a lot") is the pseudonym of the eccentric Eduard Douwes Dekker, who was born in Amsterdam in 1820 and died in Nieder-Ingelheim, Germany, in 1887. Dekker entered the service of the Dutch colonial government in 1839 in Batavia (present-day Jakarta), worked in faraway parts of the archipelago, and rose to a high administrative post.

In 1856, shortly after his appointment as assistant resident of Lebak in west Java, Dekker became involved in an official conflict. The controversy related to the exploitation of the native population, which was being ill-treated by its own leaders, and the manner in which Dutch authorities attempted to deal with this problem. Dekker advocated immediate radical action. His superiors, however, were convinced of the importance of the role of traditional leaders as representatives of Dutch authority toward the native population, and they held dear to their circumspection and tact. They refused to arrest chiefs before inquiries were made or to criticize them openly. To Dekker their attitude exemplified weakness and ignorance. Dekker resigned his post after the highest Dutch authority in the region, the governor-general, ruled against him.

Back in Europe, Dekker, using the name Multatuli, wrote an idealized autobiography in *Max Havelaar*, drafting what became a self-portrait. With this work, Multatuli revealed himself to be a phenomenal stylist and a writer with strong powers of persuasion. In opposition to Havelaar—presented as the ideal administrator who is available to the population day and night and who allows himself to be led by his conscience—Multatuli places the fictitious figure of Batavus Droogstoppel. Droogstoppel, a comical character, is a coffee broker who has become rich because of the colonial system; a hypocritical smooth talker who is only interested in his own benefit, Droogstoppel is a personification of the worst aspects of Dutch colonialism.

In a peroration, Multatuli dedicates the book to King Willem III (1817–1890). The message of the book is twofold: (1) the population of the Dutch East Indies deserve better treatment, and (2) Max Havelaar (in actual fact, Dekker) must be rehabilitated. If the Dutch government would not buy into Multatuli's program, it would face a moral defeat, rendering the Netherlands nothing more than "a pirate state on the sea, between Eastern Friesland and the river Schelde" (Multaluti 1982, p. 319).

Apart from his trouble in Lebak, Multatuli also describes Havelaar's (and Dekker's) earlier career. At the age of twenty-two, he was assigned to an independent administrative position in Natal (Sumatra), but he was not successful. Dekker was suspended from this post in 1844 on suspicion of fraud; eventually Dekker's bookkeeping was proved to be poor, but no evidence of fraudulent intent was found. Nonetheless, Dekker had to live down the bad reputation incurred in Natal, and he served in lowly jobs for years. He would only work at a higher level again in 1848 to 1851, when he served successfully in Menado (Sulawesi) as the first secretary under a progressive resident. Dekker was promoted to assistant-resident of Ambon, but after a few months he contracted an obscure disease, and had to return for a time to the Netherlands, where he remained from 1852 to 1855.

Although Multatuli tells the story of Havelaar, rather than Dekker, in *Max Havelaar*, broadly speaking Multatuli's narrative is historical. The author does, however, see things from his own perspective. Thus, Multatuli represents the Natal incident as the revenge of a superior toward whom Havelaar had not shown adequate meekness. His direct superior in the Lebak affair is represented as a ridiculous figure, and the governor-general—from that time on Multatuli's greatest enemy—is depicted as incompetent and lazy.

As an author, Multatuli's power was foremost in the field of literature—in his style, his imagination, and his lively sense of humor. His writing raised a number of social issues, and he pleaded for innovation in many areas. He insisted, for example, on equality and challenged—albeit with a paternalistic attitude—discrimination against Jews, Eurasians, and women. Multatuli is considered the Netherlands' first feminist writer. He also took up the cudgel for the Dutch worker, whom he referred to as *"de witte slaaf"* ("the white slave"; *Volledige werken* 3, p. 119).

Multatuli also questioned traditional relationships of authority, and the validity of values that had been passed down from earlier generations. Although Multatuli was not the first atheist in the Netherlands, he did eventually become the most discussed. His alter ego, Dekker, a trendsetter until the end, was the first Dutchman to opt for cremation.

Multatuli's political ideas were less modern. He wanted to abolish the Netherlands' recently introduced parliamentary democracy and return to absolute monarchy, with the king as an enlightened despot. For the Dutch East Indies, Multatuli advocated enhanced enforcement of the colonial laws, which he believed would radically improve the lives of the native population. Only later did he suggest a revolution, although not a revolution that would bring Indonesians to power in Indonesia. He imagined an independent empire called Insulinde, where the government would stay in European hands—for example, those of Eduard Douwes Dekker.

Multatuli's books earned much admiration, not only from lovers of literature, but also from freethinkers, socialists, and anarchists. Others, however, sharply denounced his work and personal character. It has been reported that in later years new colonial administrators traveled to the East Indies with copies of *Max Havelaar* in their suitcases. The more ethical policies that governed Dutch colonial politics at the beginning of the twentieth century, with the goal of making the interests of the population of the Dutch East Indies prevail over those of the Netherlands, were influenced by Multatuli. To this day, Max Havelaar is an icon for humanity, ethics, conscientious actions, and self-sacrifice, particularly in the relations between developed and developing countries.

SEE ALSO *Anticolonialism, East Asia and the Pacific; Empire, Dutch.*

BIBLIOGRAPHY

Beekman, E. M. "Dekker/Multatuli (1820–1887): The Dialogic Truth from the Tropics." In *Troubled Pleasures: Dutch Colonial Literature from the East Indies, 1600–1950,* 202–252. Oxford: Clarendon Press, 1996.

Francken, Eep. "Multatuli, Kolonialist Zonder Moederland." In *Antipode. Jaarboek vir Nederlandse studies,* Stellenbosch, South-Africa: Suider-Afrikaanse Vereniging vir Neerlandistiek, 1993.

Francken, Eep. "Beekman over Multatuli." *Over Multatuli* 40 (1998): 73–77. Amsterdam: Lubberhuizen.

King, Peter. *Multatuli.* New York: Twayne, 1972.

Multatuli. *Max Havelaar, or the Coffee Auctions of the Dutch Trading Company* (1860). Introduced by D. H. Lawrence; translated by Roy Edwards; edited by E. M. Beekman. Amherst, MA: University of Massachusetts Press, 1982.

Multatuli. *Max Havelaar of de koffiveilingen der Nederlandsche Handelmaatschappy* (1860). 2 vols. Edited by A. Kets-Vree. Assen-Maastricht, Netherlands: van Gorcum, 1992.

Multatuli. *Volledige werken.* 25 vols. Edited by G. Stuiveling, with the assistance of Hans van den Bergh, B.P.M. Dongelmans, and Dik van der Meulen. Amsterdam: van Oorschot, 1950–1995.

Eep Francken

MUSLIM BROTHERHOOD

The Society of the Muslim Brotherhood is an international Islamic political and social welfare organization that was founded by Hasan al-Banna' (1906–1949) in

Hassan al-Banna'. *The Egyptian social and political activist and founder of the Muslim Brotherhood.* **AFP/GETTY IMAGES. REPRODUCED BY PERMISSION.**

1928 as a means of resisting British imperial influence in Egypt. Al-Banna' was a schoolteacher in Ismailia, where there was a large British presence due to the city's location on the strategically important Suez Canal.

Al-Banna' became convinced that the way to throw off imperial rule was through renewed adherence to Islamic principles expressed in the Sharia, the Islamic legal tradition. The Brotherhood thus helped Muslims establish social welfare programs for the poor, the creation of medical clinics, food distribution centers, and primary schools. In addition, it encouraged land redistribution, unemployment payments, unionization, and the replacement of foreign investment with local. They promoted Islam as an alternative to Western materialism, claiming that it offered spiritual comfort and social justice.

In the 1930s the group branched out into Syria and, in 1939, became a recognized political party in Egypt. In the 1940s, as economic conditions worsened and the masses became increasingly alienated from Egypt's rulers, the Brotherhood's membership swelled to 500,000. The Brotherhood's activities came to include violence against foreigners, their businesses, and their supporters. The government responded by suppressing them.

In 1948 members of the Brotherhood were implicated in the assassination of Prime Minister Mahmud

Fahmi al-Nuqrashi (1888–1948). In 1949 the Brotherhood issued pamphlets that called for "Muslim rule"; shortly after they were distributed, an unidentified man shot al-Banna'. Many Egyptians believe that the government workers who took al-Banna' to the hospital were instructed not to treat him; they consider his murder to be politically motivated. In 1952 members of the Brotherhood helped to overthrow the pro-British monarchy and establish a republic.

Collusion with the new government ended with an attempted assassination of President Gamal Abdel Nasser (1918–1970) in 1954. Thousands in the Brotherhood were imprisoned as a result, including the editor of the Brotherhood's journal—*Sayyid Qutb* (1906–1966). Qutb's ideas had a profound influence on the Brotherhood's ideology and attitude toward the West. The West's adoption of the secularist separation of church and state, he argued, had caused "spiritual schizophrenia." Westerners segregated spirituality from their daily lives and, in his view, alienated themselves from life's real meaning. Most troubling to him, however, was the West's attempt to impose their beliefs on Muslims through imperialism.

Qutb wanted to bring spirituality back into daily life by creating a government and social structure based on Sharia. He believed that Muslims were obligated to fight those who prevented the establishment of this government, that their mission was religiously legitimate as jihad, and that those who died in this fight were not truly dead, for their influence lived on.

In the 1970s and 1980s, the Brotherhood produced several splinter groups that embraced Qutb's radical call for action. One of these assassinated President Anwar al-Sadat (1918–1981) in 1981; another became the Palestinian group known as Hamas in 1988. The mainstream Brotherhood has become more moderate since the 1990s; members seek to influence government policy through democratic processes. In Egypt, several members have held office as independents, while the Brotherhood now functions as an opposition party in Jordan.

SEE ALSO *Egypt; Islamic Modernism.*

BIBLIOGRAPHY

Berman, Paul. "The Philosopher of Islamic Terror." *The New York Times Magazine* 23 (March 2003).

Cleveland, William L. *A History of the Modern Middle East*, 2nd ed. Boulder, CO: Westview Press, 2000.

Mitchell, Richard P. *The Society of the Muslim Brothers*. New York and Oxford: Oxford University Press, 1993.

Indira Falk Gesink

N

NAGASAKI

The history of Nagasaki, Japan, has been inexorably tied—both positively and negatively—to European expansion and Western colonialism. The founding of the port of Nagasaki was directly related to the initial wave of European expansion into Asia. Portuguese explorers rounded the tip of Africa and sailed into Asia just after the turn of the sixteenth century in search of trade goods and opportunities to proselytize. By 1511 they had established fortified stations at Mozambique, India, and Malacca (in present-day Malaysia), and in 1555 they finally built a base at Macao in southeastern China.

By this time, Portuguese traders had already reached Japan. In 1543 Portuguese sailors had drifted ashore at a small island south of Kyushu. Six years later, Jesuit missionaries went to Japan in an effort to convert as many Japanese as possible to Catholicism. The Jesuits exhibited early proselytizing successes in Japan. Part of this success was attributable to the promise of the annual Portuguese China Ship coming from Macao to ports in Japan, where the local daimyo supported Christianity. At the time, the Ming government of China had banned foreign trade, thus allowing the Portuguese an opportunity to control the silk-for-silver trade between China and Japan as third-party intermediaries.

In 1571 a permanent home for the Portuguese China Ship was established at Nagasaki, a heretofore small fishing village with a shallow harbor that had recently been dredged by the Jesuits. A port town was constructed at Nagasaki to handle the needs of foreign trade and to serve as a haven for harassed Christians in Japan.

Christian churches were built on the former sites of Buddhist temples and by the end of the first decade, the local Christian daimyo, unable to protect Nagasaki against attacks by non-Christian daimyo and desirous of the benefits of Western trade, agreed to donate the port town to the Jesuits. The Jesuits administered the town until 1587, when Toyotomi Hideyoshi (1536–1598), the military ruler of Japan, issued an edict calling for the expulsion of Christian missionaries and the destruction of all Christian churches in Nagasaki. Some churches were torn down, but the expulsion order was not enforced. After bribing the necessary officials, the missionaries were able to continue their work, albeit with more discretion. Hideyoshi, while condemning the missionaries, appreciated their role as interpreters and intermediaries in Western trade, and did not want to jeopardize this profitable venture.

Nagasaki was made a public territory, with Japanese officials coming to the town from time to time, but, in actuality, foreign missionaries and local Christian merchants continued to handle day-to-day administrative concerns and foreign trade. Spanish Franciscan, Dominican, and Augustinian missionaries from Manila soon joined the Jesuits in Nagasaki and proselytizing efforts expanded. They were followed in 1609 and 1613 by Dutch and English traders, who established themselves on the island of Hirado, just north of Nagasaki.

For a short time, the Portuguese, Spanish, Dutch, and British traded side by side, but Japanese government crackdowns on Christianity and poor business decisions by the English resulted in the departure of all but the Dutch from Japan by 1639. In 1641 the Dutch were forced by Japanese officials to move from Hirado to the manmade island of Dejima in Nagasaki Harbor. At the same time, Japanese leaders imposed a maritime prohibition policy *(sakoku)* on its own people, prohibiting them from leaving the country and restricting foreign trade to a few designated merchants.

Later in the seventeenth century, both the Portuguese and English tried to reestablish trade relations with Japan but to no avail. The policy remained in effect and all foreigners who strayed into Japanese waters were taken to Nagasaki, where they were imprisoned until they could be deported. Christianity was strictly prohibited upon punishment of death; therefore, all remaining Japanese Christians went underground with their beliefs.

By the early nineteenth century, the Russians, English, and Americans were all knocking on Japan's door, but Japanese officials refused to alter the country's maritime trade policy until forced to do so by Commodore Matthew Perry (1794–1858) and his armed American fleet in 1853 and 1854. Perry's forced opening of Japan, along with the British defeat of China in the Opium War a decade earlier, represented the beginning of the second phase of Western imperialism in Asia.

A commercial treaty followed in 1858, which opened three Japanese ports, including Nagasaki, to foreign trade and residence in July 1859. Landfill was brought in from neighboring islands to fill in the eastern side of the harbor, and a foreign settlement was constructed. The Russians, who later used Nagasaki as a winter port for its Asiatic Fleet, lived in a separate area across the harbor. Soon the settlements were filed with missionaries, sailors, merchants, and government officials. The latter were needed because extraterritoriality—the right to try westerners according to Western law—was a provision of the new treaties. Also included in the treaties were a "most-favored nation" clause and the right of Western nations to determine tariff duties on most Japanese goods. Nagasaki remained a designated treaty port until the so-called Unequal Treaties were revised in 1899.

Even though Nagasaki became a free port in 1899, the number of westerners in the city continued to grow until the Russo-Japanese War (1904–1905). It was also at this time that Nagasaki became renowned as the setting of Giacomo Puccini's (1858–1924) famous opera *Madama Butterfly* (1904), which came to represent to some the West's colonial attitude toward East Asia.

From 1905, however, Nagasaki's fortunes began to decline, and by the end of World War I most European and American merchants had left and fewer warships called at the port. This left only a limited number of missionaries and government officials to cope with the rising influence of militarism, as Japan itself became an ever-stronger imperial force in the struggle for East Asia and the Pacific.

Nagasaki was spared from much of the conventional bombing that most Japanese cities suffered during World War II, but on August 9, 1945, a 10,000-pound (4,536-kilogram) plutonium bomb was detonated over the city, killing more than seventy thousand people. A week later, the war was over, and by September American occupation officials had arrived to take control of Nagasaki. American officials stayed until 1952, when Japan regained its independence. Since this time, Nagasaki has depended on Mitsubishi Shipyards and historical tourism to support its economy.

SEE ALSO *Empire, Japanese; Japan, Colonized.*

BIBLIOGRAPHY

Boxer, Charles. *The Christian Century in Japan, 1549–1650.* Berkeley: University of California Press, 1951.

Burke-Gaffney, Brian. *Starcrossed: A Biography of Madame Butterfly.* Norwalk, CT: EastBridge, 2004.

Doeff, Hendrik. *Recollections of Japan.* Translated and annotated by Annick M. Doeff. Victoria, British Colombia: Trafford, 2003.

Hoare, James E. *Japan's Treaty Ports and Foreign Settlements: The Uninvited Guests, 1858–1899.* Folkerstone, U.K.: Japan Library, 1994.

Marx, Joseph. *Nagasaki: The Necessary Bomb?* Toronto, Ontario: Macmillan, 1971.

Paske-Smith, M. *Western Barbarians in Japan and Formosa in Tokugawa Days, 1603–1868.* Kobe, Japan: J. L. Thompson, 1927.

Lane R. Earns

NASIR, GAMAL ABD AL
1918–1970

Of an Upper Egyptian family and the son of a postal clerk, Abd al Nasir was educated in Cairo and graduated as an officer from the military academy in 1938. He served in Sudan and later with distinction in the Palestine War in 1948–1949. In late 1949 Nasir formed a group calling itself the Free Officers who seized power in the early hours of July 23, 1952. Composed of young officers with a broad nationalist program, the new regime, although fronted by General Muhammad Naguib (1901–1984), was effectively led by Colonel Nasir. A contest with Naguib for power in March 1954 saw Nasir consolidate his position, serving as prime minister from 1954–1956 and president from 1956, a position he effectively held until his death.

Gamal Abd al Nasir. *The Egyptian president (center) was greeted by cheering crowds when he returned to Cairo from Alexandria in 1956 after his announcement that he had nationalized the Suez Canal Company.* **HULTON ARCHIVE/GETTY IMAGES. REPRODUCED BY PERMISSION.**

Under Nasir's leadership the revolution sought to transform Egyptian society. In 1953 political parties were dissolved and a republic established. Thereafter, political life was restricted to a series of government parties, the most important being the Arab Socialist Union set up in 1962. Nasir tolerated little political opposition and particularly repressed Communists and Muslim Brothers, many of whom served long terms in prison. Committed early to land reform, the regime went on to embrace an economic program of state-sponsored industrialization, nationalization, and public employment. Initially successful, these policies produced substantial inefficiencies by the late 1960s.

On the international stage, Nasir played a leading role in the non-aligned movement formed at the Bandung Conference in April 1955. His decision to nationalize the Suez Canal on July 26, 1956 led to the Suez crisis and war with Britain, France, and Israel. A Czech arms deal in 1955 had already signaled Nasir's move away from the West, and the Soviet decision to finance the dam reinforced this trend. After the diplomatic triumph of Suez, Nasir adopted a strong Arab nationalist and pro-African foreign policy.

In 1958 Egypt and Syria merged to form the United Arab Republic, although the union lasted only three years. Nasir's revolutionary call to the Arab world led him into conflict with both conservative Arab monarchies and progressive republics, but he continued to be an inspiring figure to the Arab masses during the 1960s. Following a game of diplomatic brinkmanship in June 1967, Israel launched a surprise attack and inflicted a stunning defeat on Egypt. Nasir immediately offered his resignation but, after massive public demonstrations, resumed office and pursued less radical policies. He died suddenly on September 28, 1970.

A charismatic, inspiring third world leader, personally charming if somewhat reserved, Nasir spoke in the language of the people and was passionately committed to the welfare of ordinary Egyptians and the cause of Arab unity on his terms. Many of his policies were repudiated by his successor, Anwar Sadat (1918–1981), but Nasir's memory remains revered by many in the Arab world. His legacy has been kept alive by journalist and personal confidant Mohamed Hassanein Heikal (b. 1923) and a Nasserist Party operates in Egypt based on his political ideals. Nasir's *Philosophy of the Revolution* provides an important statement of his early political thought.

SEE ALSO *Egypt.*

BIBLIOGRAPHY

Heikal, Mohamed Hassanein. *The Cairo Documents; the Inside Story of Nasser and His Relationships with World Leaders, Rebels, and Statesmen.* Garden City, NY: Doubleday, 1973.

Lacouture, Jean. *Nasser: A Biography.* Translated by Daniel Hofstadter. New York: Knopf, 1973.

Nasser, Gamal Abdel (or Nasir, Gamal Abd al). *Philosophy of the Revolution.* Buffalo, NY: Smith, Keynes and Marshall, 1959.

Anthony Gorman

NATIONALISM, AFRICA

Nationalism, a universal human construct, has been studied extensively because of its resiliency as a major societal force. The literature on nationalism is complex, conflicting, inchoate, contradictory, and at times paradoxical, sentimental, and perplexing. It is not surprising that because of its multifaceted nature and manifestations, nationalism has become notorious for its indefinability. Although nationalism has universal properties, it also exhibits unique characteristics that are determined by historical forces—political, sociocultural, and economic.

Nationalism is such a powerful force in human affairs that even those who regard it as an unmitigated disaster created by human genius have themselves sometimes resorted to nationalistic sentiments, perhaps in moments of frustration and weakness, to make their points. The truth is, like it or not, nationalism will never fade away. The fad of internationalism, regarded by some as a more progressive and rewarding movement, is increasingly becoming a forlorn hope.

This entry is a modest effort to present the meaning and dimensions of nationalism in modern Africa. This restriction in no way supports the views of those who argue that modern African nationalism is a phenomenon that started after 1935 and that Africans learned it from the colonizers. The antecedents of the movement are as old as African history itself. However, its modern manifestations, no doubt complicated by the impact of Europe, are more relevant to contemporary Africa.

MEANING

Generally, European colonial administrators and early Western scholars did not fully understand, and could not appreciate the existence of, African nationalism as a major political and socioeconomic force. Thus, Lord Milverton's (Arthur Frederick Richards, 1885–1978) view, expressed in 1956, that African nationalism was "just the craving for power by a small group of individuals," reflected a general European sentiment on the subject (Kohn 1965 [A], p. 9).

When by the 1960s the regaining of African independence had become a fait accompli, two British imperial historians, John Gallagher and Ronald Robinson, embellished the same sentiment rather flamboyantly but equally incorrectly. For them, the majority of Africans who were "peace loving" and "good natured" saw colonialism as a good thing and generally welcomed it. The few who resisted it were atavistic and backward-looking individuals who were engaged merely in "romantic, reactionary struggles against the facts, the passionate protest of societies which were shocked by a new age of change and would not be comforted" (Robinson and Gallagher 1962, p. 640). The authors were, however, perceptive enough to recognize that these earlier movements differed from the later and "defter nationalisms" that "planned to reform their personalities and regain their powers by operating in the idiom of the westernizers" (Robinson and Gallagher 1962, p. 640).

Several later Western scholars continued to argue that African nationalistic resistance was directed against the cruel forms and seamier aspects of the European presence and not against colonialism as such, and that individuals and groups resisted colonialism for selfish motives and not because of any nationalistic impulses. Recent historiography, however, shows that African resistance movements were a natural reaction against the imposition of alien rule; that they were propelled by a desire to protect African sovereignties; and that when they failed to do so, the advocates of resistance resolved to regain their independence by conciliation, force, or both.

Modern African nationalism, then, began as an attempt by African nationalities to not submit to European rule during the scramble for Africa. When that failed, the nationalities, now grouped under new multination states created by colonialism, reorganized under the leadership of the new, more radical Western-educated elite (the nationalists) to terminate colonial rule. And when that succeeded, the nationalists began to wrestle with the difficulties of solidifying the multi-nation states that they inherited.

In the final analysis, modern African nationalism was initially a response to European political, socioeconomic, and biological imperialism. It was, in the words of K. A. Busia, "a demand for racial equality" that "is its most conspicuous attribute" (Kohn 1965 [A], p. 13) or in those of Ndabanigi Sithole, "a struggle against white supremacy" (Kohn 1965 [A], p. 13). Even so, what is most fascinating is the movement's later hardheaded pragmatism, which, having grudgingly accommodated the European presence, moderated its anticolonial pos-ture and used the framework provided by the colonizers to attempt to construct a developmental synthesis. It is hoped that this synthesis will make Africa more relevant in a competitive and even callous modern world.

Indeed, as Godfrey Uzoigwe wrote: "The genius of African nationalism ... is its superb pragmatism which enabled it to beat Europeans at their own game and allowed them to depart with honor. African nationalism triumphed over colonialism because it won the game of collaboration" (Uzoigwe 1975, p. 383). In other words, African nationalists won the support of grassroots people and that of other elitist and resisting groups who, hitherto, had been passive toward colonialism. Once that happened, European colonizers had no group with whom to do business except African nationalists, whom, gener-ally, they resented. Even in those parts of Africa where the colonizers had depended on the support of prefabri-cated European collaborating groups—Algeria, Kenya, Angola, Mozambique, Southern Africa—it was becoming clear by the 1960s that the game was up and that it was time to create an exit strategy. It was to the credit of Africa's victorious nationalists that there was no attempt to humiliate the westernizers.

DIMENSIONS

Modern African nationalism may be profitably studied under three broad categories that, paradoxically, conflict with one another: *micronationalism*, *mezzonationalism*, and *meganationalism*.

Micronationalism. This is the nationalism of Africa's original, pre-twentieth-century nationalities, however, they may have evolved by the time of the European scramble, partition, and conquest of Africa at the close of the nineteenth century. These nationalities, which earlier scholarship erroneously called *tribes* but which recent scholarship describe as *ethnic groups*, are estimated

to number about three thousand. They ranged from the ancient empires, kingdoms, and societies of the Nile Valley and the Horn of Africa, which have been in existence for thousands of years, to those of Africa south of the Sahara, which trace their origins back hundreds of years.

Micronationalism demanded the complete loyalty and devotion of all citizens—not always successfully due to the existence of contentious issues that influenced the nature of their relationships—because of supposed com-mon origins expressed in consanguinity, culture, lan-guage, religion, history, historic charters, geographical contiguity, or a combination of all or some of the above. Once consolidated, a nationality, usually made up of independent communities, became apprehensive and sus-picious of stranger elements. This attitude accounted, perhaps, for the absence of the notion of naturalized citizenship in Africa.

Some scholars regard the later multination states created by colonialism as the best paradigm for studying modern Africa, since the so-called original nationalities as presently constituted are fictitious. They are regarded as fictitious because, being creations of European colonial-ism, they do not deserve to be regarded as original African nations. Admittedly, in several areas European boundary-making, during and after the partition, did tinker with the territorial integrity of Africa's original nationalities, but it did not completely erase their essences. After all, these nationalities were in existence long before the coming of Europe, and were functioning on the bases of historic charters, social structures, politi-cal cultures, and pan-associations that bound them together. These nationalities were thus distinguished from their neighbors, and cannot be said to be fictitious colonial creations. It is important to note that African countries today are faced with the problem of national-ities of varying intensity, some of maximum severity (as in Nigeria), some of medium severity (as in Uganda), and some benign (as in Ghana).

It was these original nationalities that challenged the European conquest during the phase of primary resis-tance, the aim being the prevention of colonization. This first stage of European confrontation with the African nationalities and communities was largely complete by the first decade of the twentieth century. The confronta-tions, lost by the African nationalities, have been well studied. Being attempts by resisters to protect their lands and sovereignties, it is incorrect not to regard them as expressions of nationalism. The resistances took various forms and were not always physical. There were, for example, groups like the Baganda in present-day Uganda who used cooperation with the invaders to cut deals for themselves in the colonial dispensation. There were also those like the Banyoro, also in Uganda, with whom no deals were possible. However, both cooperators and resisters were incorporated by the colonizers into larger territorial states, often with new names invented to encompass the new aggregations that became the current multination states.

The failure of the primary resistance movements, far from signaling acceptance of foreign domination, was followed in many of the new states by secondary resistance movements. These movements used guerrilla-style hit-and-run tactics, or, as in the case of the Banyoro, passive resistance to continue to oppose foreign domination. By the 1920s these revolts were also mostly over. Colonialism had become a fait accompli.

However, between the 1920s and the regaining of independence, Africa's defeated nationalities regrouped in the urban areas of the new nations to form voluntary ethnic organizations. These organizations enabled individuals to adjust to changes brought about by colonialism and, more importantly, to create a niche for themselves in the sociocultural, political, and economic arithmetic of their new countries. To be sure, they were not yet in the business of seeking the overthrow of colonialism, especially before the 1950s. There were, indeed, groups like the Hausa-Fulani of northern Nigeria that for a period in the 1950s opposed the regaining of independence by Nigeria because of fear of southern Nigerian domination after independence.

And even after independence was regained, the resiliency of Africa's original nationalities was apparent. The result, in part, is the chaos that Africa is experiencing today. The 1963 charter of the Organization of African Unity (OAU), now called the African Union (AU), included clauses affirming the inviolability of the colonial boundaries and requiring that member states not interfere in the internal affairs of other states. These clauses were an admission that the new nations had not yet solidified and that the forces of micronationalism were strong and needed to be curbed. Africa's postcolonial history shows that the forces of micronationalism, far from being curbed, are more resilient than ever. The effort to dismiss them as "tribalism" has so far failed to gain serious traction. All over Africa, devotees of the original nationalities are bent on receiving what they perceive to be their fair share of the "national cake." That is why ideology tends to count less than ethnicity in the final analysis, and why it matters from what group the president of an African country comes.

Mezzonationalism. This is the nationalism of the new multination states that were created by colonialism. Mezzonationalism challenged colonialism at three levels: political, economic, and sociocultural.

Politically, mezzonationalism may be seen as a subtler continuation of the earlier secondary resistance movements that failed to stop the consolidation of colonial rule. Initially, adherents of this form of nationalism used constitutional means to challenge the absolutism, the flaunted omniscience, the vaunted omnipotence, the arrogant arbitrariness, and what mezzonationalists regarded as the vengeful character of the colonial state. They were encouraged by the aftermath of several crucial developments that occurred during the climax of colonialism (1914–1945). These included World War I, the rise of Soviet Communism, Italian Fascism, German Nazism, the Great Depression, and World War II. The goal of mezzonationalism was to regain not the independence enjoyed by Africa's pre-European nationalities but an independence that eventually would be based on the continent's new multination states.

Before 1945, there was no concerted effort to overthrow colonialism. Indeed, as C. R. L. James (1901–1989) indicated, such a thought was not contemplated by himself, George Padmore (1903–1959), or Jomo Kenyatta (ca. 1899–1978) as they met in London in the 1930s to ponder the fate of Africa. In short, they did not believe that by the 1960s most African states would have become independent. Colonial protests, therefore, before 1945 sought greater participation in colonial governance and the general amelioration of the colonial state.

In the interwar years (1918–1939), African nationalists were emboldened by clauses in the Treaty of Versailles that expressed the new notion of colonies as a "Sacred Trust." They were also encouraged by President Woodrow Wilson's (1856–1924) fourteen points, which eloquently endorsed the right of small nations to self-determination. The interwar period further witnessed the resurgence of Afrikaner nationalism in South Africa and the rise of settler nationalism in various parts of Africa. These European collaborators with colonialism demanded and got generous concessions from their respective governments, concessions that further ignited African nationalist protests.

Another major impetus in the development of African nationalism during this period was Italy's unprovoked invasion and occupation of Ethiopia in 1935, an aggression that united Africa and its diaspora more than any other event. The complacent attitude of the European countries and the League of Nations toward this invasion gave Africans food for thought.

The Atlantic Charter of 1941, between the United States and the United Kingdom, also encouraged this new form of nationalism in Africa. By this charter British prime minister Winston Churchill (1874–1965) and U.S. president Franklin Delano Roosevelt

(1882–1945) declared on behalf of their countries to "respect," after their victory in World War II, "the right of all peoples to choose the form of government under which they will live." And yet in November 1942 Churchill declared that he was not prepared to preside over the liquidation of the British Empire. African nationalists retorted that if it was wrong for Germans to control and govern the French, it should also be wrong for Europeans to control and govern Africans, but this view made no impression on the Allied powers. This hypocrisy helped to demonstrate to African nationalists that Europeans had no intention of leaving Africa soon.

The aftermath of the war, especially the creation of the United Nations (UN), changed that perception. The charter of the UN, which replaced the discredited League of Nations, was anticolonial; it replaced the "mandated territories" of the League of Nations with "trusteeship territories." Further, each colonial power was required, despite stiff opposition, to make annual reports on each of their colonies to the UN. In addition, colonial peoples could send delegations to the UN to air their grievances. A major aspect of the aftermath of World War II was, indeed, the weakening of colonialism and the colonial system. This was the reverse of what happened after World War I. While the colonial powers and colonialism emerged stronger after World War I, they emerged very much weakened after World War II. In fact, colonialism was in decline globally. African nationalists, aware of these developments, worked diligently after 1945 to build greater political consciousness among the African masses. Once they were able to do so, it became clear that the days of colonialism were numbered.

Economically, the role of nationalists in Africa was limited. They were, however, able to use the economic difficulties that Africans faced during this period to try to win the masses to their side. The post–World War I economic boom was short-lived. The years 1921 and 1922 witnessed an acute economic crisis, followed by an unprecedented economic boom from which the African colonies also benefited. The ten years of boom, burst, and boom (1919–1929) were followed by the Great Depression (1929–1933), which affected the colonies most adversely.

Africa's nationalists capitalized on this adversity. Their diatribes resonated well with the masses because it had become clear that the economic policies of the colonizing nations were not geared toward African economic development. The colonizers' policies: (1) discouraged industrialization and the acquisition of Western managerial skills; (2) maintained low capital investment in the continent, with the exception of South Africa; (3) encouraged the export of African raw materials at prices determined by the colonizers, and the importation

of European manufactured goods at prices also arbitrarily determined by the colonizers; (4) made use of forced labor, often undisguised, to ensure that Africans participated in the colonial economy on terms favorable to the colonizers; and (5) encouraged land alienation, the plantation economy system, low-wage labor, unfair taxation, and blatant exploitation by the European commercial companies. The reality was that the colonial economy, as an extension of the economy of the respective colonial powers, had either destroyed African economies or transformed and subordinated them. This led to African unrest expressed through strikes and boycotts of foreign stores. Of course, the African nationalists carefully ignored the beneficial aspects of this economy because they were in the business of convincing and galvanizing Africans to change from passivism to activism in their fight to undermine colonialism.

Socioculturally, mezzonationalists realized, unlike the colonizers, that African colonial society was not a blank slate upon which Europeans wrote whatever they pleased. Mezzonationalists refused to accept the notion that the relationship between Africans and their colonizers amounted to the relationship between the exiled nobleman Prospero and his brutish servant Caliban in Shakespeare's *The Tempest* (ca. 1611), a relationship between gods and lesser mortals. It is true that the colonial period witnessed what may be described as the triumph of Albinism, that is, white supremacy, a euphemism for racialism, which was engaged in the "noble" goal of the "civilizing mission." The clear implication, of course, was that what was African was inferior and uncivilized and what was European was superior and civilized. The great mission, therefore, of the colonial enterprise at the sociocultural level was to rid Africans of the seamier side of their cultures, which the westernizers believed had degraded them, and to gradually regenerate the Africans through the process of westernization.

African nationalists saw clearly the dichotomy between theory and practice, and they denounced the underlying philosophy behind the colonizers' mission. In short, that philosophy was regarded by them as unadulterated racism. That was why Busia and Sithole described racism and white supremacy as the major forces that characterized African nationalism. That was why mezzonationalism opposed racial segregation, whether of the Afrikaner apartheid variety or of the other varieties, however nuanced they might have been. That was why African nationalists preached the ideal of Negritude, the beauty of being black, and mocked the "been tos"— those who after a fleeting acquaintance with European culture in an European country returned to their own countries and began to dress, talk, and carry themselves in a comical effort to out-Europe the Europeans. Some African nationalists stressed cultural purity, but where that was not possible, they stressed the boycott, or as Nigerian activist Mazi Mbonu Ojike (1914–1956) put it rather felicitously, to "boycott the boycottables." And some, who may be described as cultural maximizers, hoped for a cultural synthesis of the best of the old (African) and the new (European).

Throughout the colonial period, these views notwithstanding, there was a continuity of African institutions—which some nationalists exploited as a counterweight to colonial culture. The colonial society, then, was characterized by three cultures—(1) Western, which acted as the superstructure; (2) African, which acted as the substructure; and (3) mixed, that is, culture practiced by those who were no longer at ease because, having been unable to fully assimilate European culture or fully abandon African culture, had found themselves in a morass of cultural and intellectual confusion. In fairness to mezzonationalism, it generally acknowledged the beneficial aspects of Western education, Western Christianity, Arab Islam, and particularly the role that Christianity played, unwittingly, in the development of nationalism. But it also noted the complications that these forces had brought with them, their hypocrisy, and their tendencies toward a suffocating, totalitarian holism that blinded them to some of the noble and beneficial aspects of African cultures.

African mezzonationalism used a variety of media to articulate grievances. These included newspapers and periodicals, literary output in the African languages, student unions, ethnic unions, youth leagues and youth movements, trade and labor unions, and political party organizations. Notable among these media was the National Congress of British West Africa (NCBWA), formed in 1920 by Casey-Hayford (Gold Coast) and Dr. Akinwade Savage (Nigeria). Members of the NCBWA were gentlemen and constitutionalists, and their movement flourished between the 1920s and 1930s before it was overtaken by events. Since the NCBWA was elitist and purely urban, its impact was limited because of lack of popular appeal. Generally, the pace of African anticolonial movements accelerated after 1945.

Mezzonationalism faced three major obstacles. The first was the colonizers' counterpoise intended to undermine it. When it became clear that the momentum generated by Africa's nationalist movement had become irreversible, European colonial governments began to create what they described as a "responsible middle class" to whom political power would be "safely" transferred—that is, those whom they trusted to protect their interests after independence. They also decided to slow down the process of decolonization by giving way in small steps. And most importantly, they adopted the usual and effective tactic of divide and rule.

The divide-and-rule tactic became very purposive when the colonizers discovered that the ethnic unions and trade unions, which had merged to form political parties, had also developed conflicting agendas. The trade unions, for example, supported the faction that was in alliance with conservative trade unions in the colonial countries against those who were allies of radical unions funded by socialist countries. The trade unions also succeeded for a while in using traditional rulership and indirect rule to curb the aspirations of the Western educated elite; when that tactic collapsed by the 1930s, they turned to ethnicity and settler nationalism to achieve the same goal.

Mezzonationalism's second obstacle was created by micronationalism. This was a major concern, but as the anticolonial movement gained strength after 1945, the ending of colonialism seemed to take precedence over all else. The admonition of Ghanaian statesman Kwame Nkrumah (1909–1972), "Seek ye first the political kingdom," seemed to have had a particularly strong appeal. Even so, in negotiations leading to the transfer of power, efforts were made to protect not only minority interests but also those of the micronationalities. There was, at least, a temporary unity that obscured real problems that were soon to arise in the postcolonial state. The great achievement of micronationalists, mezzonationalists, and the colonizers was their ability to construct an acceptable modus vivendi before colonial rule was officially terminated.

The third obstacle to mezzonationalism was that posed by white settlers. Nationalistic settlers demanded independence from their respective metropolitan governments in the fashion of South Africa in 1910, promising to look after the interests of the majority of nonwhite Africans, just as white South Africans had promised but conspicuously failed to deliver. African nationalists were aware that the successive South African governments, far from being sanctioned for their deliberate failure, were supported by European and American governments for a variety of essentially selfish and, sometimes, racist motives. It is in this context that the nationalist armed struggles that characterized the 1960s and early 1970s should be understood.

The arrogant and generally racist settlers were apparently unaware of, or unconcerned about, the absurdity of their position. They believed that while it was right for them to govern themselves in Africa as a minority group and wrong to be governed from Europe, it was right and proper for them to govern the African majority. Indeed, Rhodesian prime minister Ian Smith (b. 1919) and his Rhodesian Front had the confidence to declare the independence of white Rhodesians unilaterally in 1965 and were shocked when their action was universally

Kwame Nkrumah, 1957. *The Ghanaian nationalist Kwame Nkrumah was carried on the shoulders of triumphant Ghanaian officials after he became the first leader of independent Ghana in 1957.* © BETTMANN/CORBIS. REPRODUCED BY PERMISSION.

condemned. When they were forced to face reality by a combination of nationalist armed struggle and international pressure, Smith saw it as a betrayal; his memoirs, interestingly, are titled *The Great Betrayal* (1997).

In Kenya, although the Mau Mau Revolt of the 1950s was a military failure, it was the catalyst that made possible the independence of Kenya in 1963. In North Africa, the brutal ebullition of the French-Algerian *colons* (settlers) was suppressed by a combination of the armed struggle of Algerian nationalists and the government of French president Charles de Gaulle (1890–1970). In Angola, Mozambique, and Guinea-Bissau, independence had also to come through armed struggle and international pressure. This was the case in Namibia and South Africa as well.

Mezzonationalism took longer in these countries than in the others to regain independence—and had to resort to long-drawn armed struggle to do so—because the settlers, although a minority, were nevertheless strong enough militarily and numerically to deal effectively with

African nationalist armed resistance. But even so, not even the strongest and most numerous of the settlers— in South Africa—were strong enough to halt and reverse the awesome march of African nationalism.

Meganationalism. The interests of this type of nationalism are regional, continental, and biological. Inevitably, these interests conflict with one another, as well as with those of micro- and mezzonationalism. The issue of whether meganationalism can be legitimately regarded as *nationalism* may be a nice point, but since this form of nationalism was and still is a powerful expression of anticolonialism, protection of geopolitical and economic interests, and racial solidarity, its credentials as a nationalistic movement are as good as any other.

Regional nationalism in Africa manifested itself in the creation of such regional geopolitical blocs as the Brazzaville Group (moderate and pro-French), the Monrovia Group (moderate and largely English-speaking), and the Casablanca Group (radical and

Nnamdi Azikiwe. *Nigerian statesman and nationalist leader Nnamdi Azikiwe answers questions at a news conference in London in August 1968. Azikiwe served as president of Nigeria from 1963 to 1966.* AP/WIDE WORLD PHOTOS. REPRODUCED BY PERMISSION.

opposed to the moderates). These groups, however, had one thing in common: the unity of African states as a powerful force against neocolonialism and as a positive organization for African political, economic, and sociocultural development. They differed on how this goal could be best achieved. Unfortunately, this division sometimes degenerated into incivility and name-calling. Self-designated moderates castigated self-designated progressives and radicals as "socialists," "communists," "militants," and "dictators;" and the so-called radicals dismissed the so-called moderates as "sluggards," "traditionalists," "feudalists," "stooges," and "agents of imperialism." Western ideological and intellectual divisions thus became major factors in the development of meganationalism.

Continental nationalism, epitomized by the OAU, was not isolated from these divisions. It is to the credit of meganationalism that the OAU was formed at all. The most important exponents of continental unity included Nigerian president Nnamdi Azikiwe (1904–1996, popularly called "Zik of Africa") and Kwame Nkrumah. The OAU charter, modeled on that of the UN charter, continues to guide the relationships between African states and between Africa and the rest of the world. It is a document remarkable for its tameness. It had to be so because it had to take into account the interests of mezzonationalism and the continent's international geopolitical imperatives.

The OAU suffered from other difficulties. It was handicapped by the economic and military relationships of some of its members with the former colonial rulers. In addition, the organization was torn by ideological differences within its ranks. And, in spite of the declaration of nonalignment and positive neutrality, by nonaligned nations meeting in Bandung, Indonesia, in 1955 in an effort to stay out of the Cold War, there was a perplexing but, perhaps, understandable inconsistency in the postcolonial foreign policies of African states, especially during the Cold War, with moderates generally supporting the former colonial rulers and radicals generally supporting the socialist countries of Europe, Asia, and Latin America.

Biological nationalism is a form of nationalism that exhorts people, in the famous appeal of Prussian statesman Otto von Bismarck (1815–1898) to the German people, to "think with your blood." The assumption is that consanguinal (blood) relationships, based on some vague common ancestry, should take precedence over other interests. So long as people have been imbued with that state of mind, it did not much matter how pure or watered down the blood is. Thus, proponents of settler nationalism, Pan-Africanism, and the Arab League—all expressions of biological nationalism—were appealing to their supporters to think with their "bloods."

The nationalism of Pan-Africanism and the Arab League (an organization of Middle Eastern Arabs and North African nations founded in March 1945) are discussed here in biological terms because of their emphasis on racial solidarity—Pan-Africanism perhaps more so than the Arab League. It is true that the formation of the OAU de-essentialized the racial factor, which has been its cornerstone, by limiting membership to independent African states. The result was the inevitable sidelining of black Africans in the diaspora, who founded and led the Pan-Africanist movement until the 1950s, and the inclusion of North Africans, who emphasize their cultural and consanguinal relationships with Arabia.

It was not surprising that the sixth Pan-African Congress, which met in Dar es Salaam, Tanzania, in 1974, did not fare well. Since then, efforts to revive the movement have been unsuccessful. The new Pan-African movement, which aims to bring race back to the forefront and has produced what it calls its "Black Agenda," has largely been ignored. What is clear is that Pan-Africanism, whether of the old or new variety, faces a serious dilemma because of its inherent contradictions. First, it has failed to reconcile the tensions between the continental unity ideal and the demands and realities of national independence. Second, it has been unable to articulate how a movement in a continent comprising six different racial groups could be taken seriously if it is concerned with the interests of one race, which it purports to stand for the whole. Third, it has been unable to find a proper role for Africans in the diaspora all over the world, to whom the Pan-African movement genuinely wishes to appeal.

The Arab League, too, faces contradictions. First, it is estimated that about 70 percent of so-called Arabs inhabit the African continent and yet the focus of the Arab League is not Africa but the Middle East. Second, North Africa faces a major crisis of identity created largely by European colonialism. The Arab League's biological nationalism is, in part, a response to the European impact. But this crisis has become exacerbated as Arabism, Pan-Africanism, and Westernism compete for the allegiance of North Africans.

The third contradiction within the Arab League is the paradox represented by the Egyptian political leader Gamel Abdel Nasser (1918–1970). On the one hand, he contributed much toward the struggle for the independence of Africa; on the other hand, more than anyone before him, he emphasized the Arabness of Egyptians and of North Africans. Before Nasser, "Egyptians," writes Peter Mansfield, "did not regard Egypt as an Arab state at all" but as "primarily" and "African" state whose "interests ... were localized in the northeast of the continent" (Mansfield, 1969 pp. 114-115). For Nasser's successors in Egypt, and for other North African leaders with the notable exception of Libya's Mu'ammar Gadhafi (b. 1942), Africa seems to be a gigantic footnote to their interests in the Middle East, their formal participation in African organizations as African states notwithstanding.

SUMMARY

To summarize, meganationalism, in all its manifestations, is basically a reaction against European domination and racism. With the regaining of independence, its anti-imperialistic rhetoric has become considerably moderated. The emphasis now is on the reinvention of Africa in such a way that it will achieve the ultimate goal of economic and political unity. Such unity will enable the continent to attain a level of economic growth, military strength, and intellectual achievement so that it can become a force for good in world affairs.

Mezzonationalism, too, has moderated its anti-imperialistic tone. But, having replaced the colonizers in government, the African leadership has become much burdened by its inheritance. Africa's leadership inadequacies, coupled with the mess left by the colonizers, has led African governments to pursue policies that have galvanized the forces of micronationalism, which are now threatening the corporate existence of many African countries. The conclusion, then, is that it is important to revisit the crucial role of micronationalism in the future political, economic, and sociocultural development of African countries. The new approach will no longer be premised on ethnicity as an unfortunate, backward-looking, and divisive force, but rather on its positive attributes, because diversity in unity is preferable to a nebulous and chaotic unity.

SEE ALSO *Anti-colonial Movements, Africa; Assimilation, Africa; Decolonization, Sub-Saharan Africa; Organization of African Unity (OAU); Pan-Africanism.*

BIBLIOGRAPHY

Berman, Bruce T. "Ethnicity, Patronage, and the African State: The Politics of Uncivil Nationalism." *African Affairs* 97 (1998): 305–341.

Campbell, Horace. *Pan-Africanism: The Struggle Against Imperialism and Neo-Colonialism, Documents of the Sixty Pan-African Congress.* Toronto, Ontario: Afro-Cairo, 1975.

Coleman, James S. *Nigeria: Background to Nationalism.* Berkeley: University of California Press, 1958.

Davidson, Basil. *The Black Man's Burden: Africa and the Curse of the Nation-State.* New York: Three Rivers, 1992.

Eley, Geoff, and Ronald G. Suny. *Becoming National: A Reader.* New York: Oxford University Press, 1996.

Esedebe, P. O. "Origins and Meanings of Pan-Africanism." *Présence Africaine* 73 (1970).

Falola, Toyin, ed. *The Dark Webs: Perspectives on Colonialism in Africa.* Durham, NC: Carolina Academic, 2005.

Geiss, Emmanuel. *The Pan-African Movement: A History of Pan-Africanism in America, Europe, and Africa.* London: Methuen, 1974.

Hodgkin, Thomas L. *Nationalism in Colonial Africa.* London: Muller, 1956.

Hutchinson, John, and Anthony D. Smith, eds. *Nationalism.* New York: Oxford University Press, 1994.

Kohn, Hans. *Nationalism: Its Meaning and History.* Rev. ed. Princeton, NJ: Van Nostrand, 1965 (B).

Kohn, Hans, and Wallace Sokolsky. *African Nationalism in the Twentieth Century.* Princeton, NJ: Van Nostrad, 1965.

Langley, J. Ayodele. *Pan-Africanism and Nationalism in West Africa, 1900–1945: A Study in Ideology and Social Classes.* London: Oxford University Press, 1973.

Legum, Colin. *Pan-Africanism: A Short Political Guide.* New York: Praeger, 1962.

Mansfield, Peter. *Nasser's Egypt.* Baltimore, MD.: Penguin, 1965.

Mazrui, Ali A. "Africa Between Nationalism and Nationhood: A Political Survey." *Journal of Black Studies* 13, no. 1 (1982): 23–44.

Nnoli, Okwudiba. *Ethnic Politics in Nigeria.* Enugu, Nigeria: Fourth Dimension, 1978.

Osahon, Naiwo. *God Is Black.* Lagos, Nigeria: Heritage, 1993.

Padmore, George. *Pan-Africanism or Communism? The Coming Struggle for Africa.* New York: Roy, 1956.

Robinson, Ronald E., and John Gallagher. "The Partition of Africa." In *The New Cambridge Modern History; Vol. 11: Material Progress and World-Wide Problems, 1870–1898,* edited by F. H. Hinsley. Cambridge, U.K.: Cambridge University Press, 1962.

Robinson, Ronald E. "Non-European Foundations of European Imperialism: Sketch for a Theory of Collaboration." In *Studies in the Theory of Imperialism,* edited by Roger Owen and Bob Sutcliffe, 117–141. London: Longman, 1972.

Sithole, Ndabaningi. *African Nationalism.* New York and Cape Town, South Africa: Oxford University Press, 1959; 2nd ed., 1968.

Smith, Ian Douglas. *The Great Betrayal: The Memoirs of Ian Douglas Smith.* London: Blake, 1997.

Snyder, Louis L. *Encyclopedia of Nationalism.* Chicago and London: St. James Press, 1990.

Suzman, Mark. *Ethnic Nationalism and State Power: The Rise of Irish Nationalism, Afrikaner Nationalism, and Zionism.* New York: St. Martin's Press, 1999.

Uzoigwe, Godfrey N. "From the Gold Coast to Ghana: The Politics of Decolonization." In *Transformation of a Continent: Europe in the Twentieth Century,* edited by Gerhard L. Weinberg, 377–459. Minneapolis, MN: Burgess, 1975.

G. N. Uzoigwe

NATIVE AMERICANS AND EUROPEANS

In 1492 Christopher Columbus (1451–1506) set sail to find a western overseas passage to Asia and to carry the cause of Christendom to its far shores. When his ships reached what he thought was Asia he named the people he met *Indios* and reported that they were suitable to be commanded to work, plant, and support Spanish colonies. The people that Columbus brought into being, the Indians, however, did not really exist, for the people had their own ideas about whose land it was and what kind of people they were. In many ways the story of contact between Native Americans and Europeans involves the latter's attempts to subject the native people to their rule, whereas the former sought to maintain their own independence and integrity in the face of the invasion of the Americas.

Just two years after Columbus's landfall, the Treaty of Tordesillas (1494) granted Portugal much of present-day Brazil and assigned Spain the remainder of the Americas. In the late 1490s and early 1500s adventurers, petty nobles, and plain folk left Spain to find their fortunes in the Caribbean. The islands of Cuba, Jamaica, and Hispaniola proved most attractive where local Arawaks and Tainos helped adapt the newcomers to their surroundings. But the Spaniards wanted gold and silver, not maize and cassava, so they forced the native people to dig for treasure they hoped would make them rich. Precious metals proved hard to find, however, and the native people suffered terribly.

Contact with the Arawaks and other nations prompted a wide-ranging debate in the Vatican and in the courts and universities of Spain. To questions about whether or not the so-called Indians were men or beasts,

The Indians Pour Molten Gold into the Mouths of the Christians. *This engraving, rendered in the 1590s by Theodor de Bry, was included in de Bry's edition of* La historia del mondo nuovo (The History of the New World) *by Girolamo Benzoni, originally published in 1565.* © **STAPLETON COLLECTION/CORBIS. REPRODUCED BY PERMISSION.**

Pope Alexander VI (1431–1503) decreed in 1493 that they were capable of conversion to Christianity, and in 1537 the papal bull, *Sublimis deus*, asserted that they were rational people fully capable of understanding the Christian faith. Against popes and royal officials, however, any number of conquerors and landowners argued that native people were little better than animals suited only for hard labor on plantations and in mines.

Word of fabulous wealth to the west of Cuba spread. In 1519 Hernan Cortés (1484–1547) followed the rumors to the coast of present-day Mexico. He and his 400 soldiers marched inland and became embroiled in the politics of the city-state of Tenochtítlan, which, with the support of neighboring cities Texcoco and Tlacopan, governed much of modern Mexico through networks of trade and tribute. The arrival of Cortés, however, offered an opportunity to those leaders who chafed under Tenochtítlan's rule. Cortés exploited their intrigues ably and built for himself a powerful network of allies as he marched inland to challenge Tenochtítlan's ruler Moctezuma II (1466–1520).

On his arrival in Tenochtítlan Cortes seized Moctezuma and attempted to govern through him. To the crowds who feared that the gods had abandoned their great city, Moctezuma counseled patience. Cortés's efforts to smash local temples and to erect crosses to Jesus and the Virgin Mary, however, exacerbated tensions, and, after the Spaniards massacred a number of people at a holy celebration, the Mexicans attacked. Cortés sent Moctezuma out to calm the people but a stone hurled from the crowd struck and killed him, leaving the Spaniards with neither their hostage nor any leverage. Cortés led his men through a harrowing retreat out of the city and into the arms of his allies in Tlaxcalan, and by the middle of 1521 Cortés was ready to return with Tlaxcalan's support. Meanwhile a smallpox epidemic had swept through Tenochtítlan and decimated the people. By August Cortés was in possession of the city and the vast networks of tribute and alliance that it commanded, and he doled out towns and territories to the soldiers who had served in his command and to his allies to maintain their support.

Taking his cues from Cortés, in 1532 Francisco Pizarro (1475–1541) took a small party of horsemen and foot soldiers from his base in Panama to invade the Incas, whose territory stretched 3,000 miles down South America's western edge. When the invaders arrived, the empire was in the throes of civil war because two men, Huascar (d. 1532) and Atahualpa (1502–1533), were battling to succeed Huayana Capac (d. 1535) as emperor, who stepped down in 1525. As they marched toward the Andes, Pizarro's troop received an invitation to meet with Atahualpa, who thought they might be useful in his struggle with Huascar. The meeting was tense. Some 40,000 Inca warriors surrounded the group of Spaniards. Sizing up the situation, Pizarro seized Atahaulpa in a bloody affray. For eight months Pizarro ruled the empire through Atahaulpa but ordered the emperor killed when word of a plot to overthrow the Spaniards reached his ears. Each side in the civil war sought to enlist Pizarro, and as the various ethnic groups that had been gathered under the empire sensed their opportunity to throw off the Inca yoke, they, too, turned to the Spanish for assistance. Like Cortés, Pizarro relied on the fractured and hierarchical political system of the people he faced to facilitate his conquest.

Just as Cortés inspired the conquest of Peru, so did his example drive the conquest of the Mayas. In 1527 one of Cortés's captains, Francisco de Montejo (1479–1553), landed on the Yucatan peninsula where Montejo ordered the ships destroyed to ensure the men's devotion to the conquest he was planning. Owing to the independence of the various Maya cities, there was no one leader for Montejo to capture or kill. Instead, it took years for the Spanish to prevail. Disease, famine, and drought, however, worked where warhorses and arquebuses did not, and in 1542 Maya resistance began to yield to the Spanish invasion.

Other conquistadores moved into what is today the southern United States. Francisco Vazquez de Coronado (1510–1554) set out in 1540 with several hundred men to find the golden cities of Cíbola, but instead he found fields of maize and people who were happy to send him

on his way with indications that Cíbola was just a little farther east. Coronado reached the grassy prairies of present-day Kansas before he realized there was no Cíbola and returned to Mexico in 1542. Hernando de Soto (1500–1542) had a similar experience in the American south when he landed in Florida in 1539 and spent the next few years searching in vain for precious metals and great cities like had been found in Mexico and Peru, only he died in 1542 as it dawned on him that his quest had been in vain.

The Spanish aspired to govern the peoples they conquered in ways that resembled the feudal order of Europe. The Crown organized settlers in what was called the republic of Spaniards, who enjoyed various rights of citizenship, property, and life, whereas beneath them lived and toiled the republic of Indians, who served as a kind of New World peasantry. Both Cortés and Pizarro relied on an institution known as the *encomienda* that enabled Spaniards to own a village's or several villages' labor and to command various levels of tribute in maize, cacao, cotton, or cattle and horses. The coercive and feudal aspects of the *encomienda*, however, had close analogues in the societies they had conquered. From the Incas to the people Coronado and Soto met, leaders appropriated tribute, typically either foodstuffs or more specialized prestige items, from the people they governed. Village leaders would then hand over a portion of their tribute to regional leaders who would then pass goods on to the highest leaders in the land. But if the notions of hierarchy and tribute that made Spanish and aboriginal notions of social organization and government remarkably similar, the coercive power of the Spanish was of an altogether different order.

While the Spanish created a hybrid feudal and aboriginal network of chiefly power and payment of tribute to rule their colonial societies, the Portuguese battered the aboriginal populations of Brazil into submission in order to enslave them. The process began in 1532 when the Portuguese established a permanent settlement called São Vicente. So long as the trade in tropical wood remained the primary meeting point between the invaders and the native people, relations were relatively cordial. But the Crown required that the colony pay its own way, so when the small fort was built so, too, was a sugar mill, and sugar cane brought from the Madeiras Islands was planted shortly thereafter.

From São Vicente a number of other settlements spread and by the mid-sixteenth century sugar plantations were Brazil's mainstay. In the absence of settlers willing to do the work and with African labor costing more than planters were willing to spend, landowners took on the Crown and the Vatican to argue for the right to enslave the native people. Under pressure to make a

Wars between Native Americans and Europeans in North America

War	Date
First Powhatan War	1609–1611
Second Powhatan War	1622
Pequot War	1636
Third Powhatan War	1644–1646
Apalachee 'Revolt'	1647
King Philip's War	1675
Bacon's Rebellion	1676
Pueblo 'Revolt'	1680
Franco-Iroquoian War	1690s
King Williamm's War	1689–1697
Queen Anne's War	1702–1713
Yamasee	1715
King George's War	1743–1748
French and Indian War	1754–1763
Pontiac's 'Rebellion'	1763

These wars, rebellions, and revolts constitute many of the important and well-known Euro-Indian conflicts. Euro-Amerindian conflict from the fifteenth to the eighteenth century was almost endemic. There were thousands of attacks, raids, rebellions, and wars during these centuries.

THE GALE GROUP.

profit, the Crown relented and thousands of people found themselves forced to toil in the sugar fields under pain of death. There was no accommodation of aboriginal governance and no respect for the nations' autonomy—only hard labor for the profit of the empire.

Fisherman's tales and the ongoing search for the passage to Asia led the French into the present-day St. Lawrence River in 1534. Instead of China Jacques Cartier (1491–1557) found a bustling trading fair at Tadoussac and important allies at a town called Stadacona. On a second voyage the following year he pushed further up the river to a series of dangerous rapids just past the town of Hochelaga, the site of present-day Montréal. He and his men wintered at Stadacona before returning to France to raise interest in founding a colony. The settlement Cartier founded near Stadacona in 1541 collapsed, however, because of cold and famine, and it would be a long time before the French braved the shores of the St. Lawrence.

When they did return some seventy years later, diseases had decimated the land. The aboriginal population was neither large enough nor concentrated enough to allow for a Spanish-style conquest. Instead, the French had to use trade with far-flung populations to build relationships and alliances. In 1603 various Algonquian-speaking peoples and their Huron trading partners agreed to make a place for Samuel de Champlain (1567–1635)

and the French, and they connected the French to a vast trade network that reached from the Atlantic to the Great Lakes to the Hudson Bay. In 1608 Champlain founded Québec where Stadacona had once stood to give the French a permanent foothold in the trade, and while the town succeeded as a trading post, it was less attractive as a destination for settlers.

The men who conducted the fur trade on behalf of France, the *coureurs de bois*, as well as the voyageurs, who transported the furs and other goods by canoe, extended the empire's reach up the network of lakes and rivers of the mid-continent. The good relations they cultivated with people enabled France to deploy small garrisons and settlements, such as outposts like Detroit and Michilimackinac on the Great Lakes and Cahokia and Kaskaskia on the Mississippi River, to secure their claims to the empire. At the same time Jesuit and Recollet missionaries followed the traders into the country to convert France's important trading partners to Catholicism. Indeed it was the fur trader Louis Jolliet (1645–1700) and the priest Jacques Marquette (1637–1675) who opened the Mississippi River to France in 1673 that made possible the settlement of Louisiana in 1699.

As in Canada, so in Louisiana, too, did French leaders adopt a policy of alliance with the native people. Pierre Le Moyne (1661–1706), *sieur d'Iberville*, founded Biloxi in 1699, and the friendships he crafted through exchange of gifts and ritual smoking of tobacco enabled the French to build outposts at Mobile, and, in 1718, New Orleans. The local people, too, saw advantages in their relationship with Iberville. English slave raiders who worked among the Chickasaws to the north had preyed on the Choctaws for years. When Iberville came and offered guns and ammunition, the Choctaws became fast friends of the French.

So long as the French settlements were confined to the coast and to New Orleans, the trade relationship effectively maintained a large system of alliances until the 1720s when the French sought to duplicate the tobacco plantation economy that was generating such profits in the English colonies. As settlers encroached upon land that belonged to the Natchez, the Natchez plotted to drive them back. The fatal blow came on November, 28 1729, when most of the area's settlers were killed. Some months later a small French force from New Orleans backed by a large party of Choctaw warriors arrived to find the Natchez huddled inside of two forts with a number of women and slaves that they had captured. Choctaws brokered a solution by convincing the Natchez to hand over the captives and allowing the Natchez to escape across the Mississippi River. Although the brief war spelled the end of the Natchez nation, French expansion in Louisiana also stalled.

While Champlain was founding Québec, the English were building a permanent colony in Virginia. The Powhatan nation saw in English cloth, tools, and guns a source of great power and sought to use gifts of food to enlist the English as allies. The Virginians, led by John Smith (1580–1631), in some ways accepted their new role and Smith became recognized as a Powhatan leader. The English, however, did not want to be partners; they wanted to be conquerors, and so what good relations had been built unraveled as settlers encroached on Powhatan land and abused the people.

The Powhatans struck back in the hopes of teaching the unruly settlers a lesson, and from 1610 to 1613 small raids and ambushes brought terror to the countryside. Things changed when the tobacco economy took off. The settlers began to seize land in earnest and to threaten Powhatan survival. In response a war leader named Opecancanough (1554–1644) organized an uprising that aimed to drive the English back into the sea. On March 22, 1622, his warriors killed nearly 500 settlers, one quarter of the settler population, and over the following year took another 500 lives. The English responded by using trade to forge alliances with nearby nations and by burning Powhatan towns and fields, ambushing the people, and cutting off all contact. For ten years the hostilities simmered and ended only with Opecancanough's recognition of English power.

Lessons learned in Jamestown made English colonization different from both the hierarchical policies of the Spanish and the strategy of trade and alliance-building developed by the French. Instead, the English, while always maintaining trading relationships, preferred to prevent any kind of social connection. Where both the Spanish and the French recognized native people as members of their colonial societies, to the English such people were always undesirable outsiders, and it was the English who developed what we know today as the reservation where they isolated native people from the flow of colonial life.

The English experience in New England offers the clearest example of their exclusionary policies. A local Wampanoag leader named Massasoit (d. 1661) enlisted the newcomers on his side against his native rivals, and he provided them with maize and other food to get them through the first winters. In spite of the Puritan governors' official policies of drawing stark boundaries between settlers and native people, trade ties laced across the countryside to tie all kinds of people together in relationships, some of which, particularly in the 1630s and 1640s when immigrants from England flooded the countryside, ended in violence.

The Pequots were the first to feel the crushing tide of settlers and the colony's leaders were anxious to make war on a people they saw as in league with the devil.

The Town of Secota. *This engraving of Secota, Powhatan town in present-day Virginia, was rendered by Theodor de Bry and published in 1590. The image is based on a watercolor by John White, an early European settler in Virginia.* © ARCHIVO ICONOGRAFICO, S.A./CORBIS. REPRODUCED BY PERMISSION.

When a trader turned up dead, the governor accused the Pequots of the murder and dispatched a small force to kill every male Pequot they could find. After the force returned to Boston, the Pequots struck back and killed nine settlers. Narragansetts and Mohegans, who thought they could improve their standing in the Puritans' eyes by fighting on their side, helped the colonials surround the main Pequot town in May 1637. While the warriors launched fire arrows into the roofs of the homes, the settlers shot down all who fled the flames. At the end of the day nearly 1,000 Pequots lay dead. The New Englanders rounded up what few survivors they could find and sold them into slavery in the West Indies.

Expansion continued apace and threatened the land of those who had formerly fought for the Puritans. Metacom (1639–1676), whose father Massasoit had originally helped the settlers get on their feet, regretted the loss of land and the abuse that he saw happening to the Wampanoags and Narragansetts. After three Wampanoags were hanged on charges of murder in 1675, Metacom, or King Philip as he was known to the colonists, ordered a series of retaliatory raids. Farms burned and families perished before militias from Massachusetts, Connecticut, and Rhode Island surrounded Metacom's town. Other defeats followed, Metacom was killed and dismembered, and the survivors were again sold into slavery.

The wars of conquest that characterized the sixteenth and seventeenth centuries, of course, did not mean that all first nations came under European control right away. Indeed, the different patterns of colonization followed by the Spanish, the French, and the English, and the different patterns of resistance offered by native people across the Americas meant that free native communities experienced quite different histories depending on where they were located. In Mexico, for example, the Yaquis, who lived near the Zacatecas silver mines of northern Mexico, struggled to balance their place in the republic of Indians with their own desire for autonomy and independence. In the aftermath of a devastating smallpox epidemic, they asked Jesuits to settle among them in the 1620s. The priests reorganized the Yaquis and concentrated what had been eighty scattered settlements into eight principal villages. But Jesuit control of surplus agricultural produce spurred many Yaquis to migrate abroad in search of work in the mines or on ranches. In 1740 a rebellion against the Jesuits and those Yaquis who worked closely with the Spanish was crushed, but the continuing exodus of Yaquis from the villages caused the Crown to expel the Jesuits in 1767 and restore to the Yaquis a measure of self-government and independence.

French losses in European wars meant that the English often confronted native people who were unaccustomed to the harsher nature of English colonization. After the Treaty of Utrecht ended the War of Spanish Succession in 1713, England obtained from France what is today Nova Scotia. A subsequent treaty granted the Mi'kmaq people rights to use the land while at the same time making them subjects of the Crown. The presence of the French in Canada, however, enabled the Mi'kmaq to have access to firearms and supplies, and so rather than conquer them as they had done to native people elsewhere on the continent, the English sought trade ties with the native people that were orderly and mutually beneficial. The more tolerant approach taken by the English in this case reflected both the power of the Mi'kmaq as well as the perpetuation of a French-style model of contact and coexistence.

In the present-day United States, the English pattern of exclusion and isolation continues unabated. Whereas some nations took up arms to fight the United States, particularly under the leadership of the Shawnee war leader Tecumseh (1768–1813) in the early nineteenth century, the Cherokees sought to accommodate the demands of Euroamerican culture in order to make a safe place for themselves. After becoming dependent on the deerskin trade and losing land to settlers, the Cherokees invited missionaries to build schools so that their children could learn to read and write to better defend the nation's interests. Leaders also reformed the nation's laws to bring them into conformity with Anglo-American norms, and in 1827 a Cherokee constitution modeled in part on the federal constitution created an elected assembly, a supreme court, and an elected executive officer. Such changes enhanced the Cherokee's ability to resist their expulsion from their homeland in northern Georgia and eastern Tennessee, and their victory in a U.S. Supreme Court case in 1832 offered hope that they would retain a measure of their sovereignty. The federal government, however, pursued its plans to remove the Cherokees to Oklahoma, which it accomplished in 1839.

In some ways what happened to the Cherokees in 1839 was analogous to what happened to the Incas in 1532. Contact and colonization were ongoing processes that, while varying from time to time and from place to place, often ended in similar ways. But it is important to recognize the differences, for just as there were no real Indios to greet Columbus, it is also difficult to generalize about the very complicated history of contact between native people and Europeans in the Americas.

SEE ALSO *Encomienda.*

BIBLIOGRAPHY

Clendinnen, Inga. *Ambivalent Conquests: Maya and Spaniard in Yucatan, 1517–1570.* Cambridge, U.K., and New York: Cambridge University Press, 1987.

Cortes, Hernan. *Letters from Mexico.* Edited and Translated by Anthony Pagden. New Haven, CT: Yale University Press, 1986.

Dickason, Olive. *The Myth of the Savage and the Beginnings of French Colonialism in the Americas.* Edmonton: University of Alberta Press, 1984.

Jennings, Francis. *The Invasion of America: Indians, Colonialism, and the Cant of Conquest.* New York: Norton, 1975.

Meinig, D.W. *The Shaping of America: A Geographical Perspective on 500 Years of History.* New Haven, CT: Yale University Press, 1986.

Stern, Steve J. *Peru's Indian Peoples and the Challenge of Spanish Conquest: Huamanga to 1640.* Madison: University of Wisconsin Press, 1982.

Todorov, Tzvetan. *The Conquest of America.* New York: Harper and Row, 1984.

Wood, Peter, Gregory A. Waselkov, and M. Thomas Hatley, eds. *Powhatan's Mantle: Indians in the Colonial Southeast.* Lincoln: University of Nebraska Press, 1989.

James Taylor Carson

NEGRITUDE

Negritude is an African diasporic, self-affirming idea that evolved into an artistic and cultural movement and later became a lightening rod for controversy and ideological disputes. The (re)valorization of the black world, the affirmation of the humanity of black people, and the glorification of the richness of black culture had antecedents in the works of earlier thinkers and scholars such as Edward Wilmot Blyden (1832–1912), Martin Delany (1812–1885), and W. E. B. Du Bois (1868–1963), and writers of the Harlem Renaissance such as Claude McKay (1890–1948) and Langston Hughes (1902–1967), who reclaimed "blackness" with pride, reinvested it with positive meanings, and rejected the negativity heaped on it by racism, slavery, colonialism, and imperialism.

The strong argument for a rethinking and revaluing of black identity and culture grew in the nineteenth century among black intellectuals and precursors of black nationalism and Pan-Africanism, such as Blyden, who were responding to the biological racism of European writers and philosophers, such as G. W. F. Hegel (1770–1831) from Germany, that placed blacks outside of historical progress and development.

The redefinition of black identity and the celebration of black heritage picked up steam early in the last century and jelled into a cultural movement of the 1920s, the Harlem Renaissance, which grew in New York City but had a profound impact beyond the United States, particularly in the Caribbean and Europe, where it fueled the activities of a group of young black students from the colonies. A member of the group, Aimé Césaire (b. 1913) of Martinique, wrote a dissertation on the Harlem Renaissance.

Post–World War I (1914–1918) Europe witnessed a gathering of blacks from the French Caribbean and West Africa who fought alongside French and African-American soldiers in World War II (1939–1945). In the early 1930s, they founded journals and other publications as outlets for their political, cultural, and artistic works—the moderate, proassimilationist *Revue du monde noir* (Review of the Black World, 1931) was followed three years later by the radical, antiassimilationist, and proliberation review, *L'Etudiant noir* (The Black Student), founded by Césaire, Léopold Sédar Senghor (1906–2001) of Senegal, and others.

These activities morphed into a cultural and artistic movement of reaffirmation of black identity and heritage that took its name, *negritude*, from Césaire's 1939 poem "Cahier d'un retour au pays natal" (Notebook of a Return to My Native Land). Césaire's conceptualization of the term *negritude* was imbued with the historical context of a black world whose unity is "measured by the compass of suffering." But as the movement evolved,

Aimé Césaire. *The Martinican writer and politician attends a rehearsal of his 1966 play* Une saison au Congo (A Season in the Congo) *in Paris in October 1967.* **ROGER VIOLLET/GETTY IMAGES. REPRODUCED BY PERMISSION.**

some of its proponents invested the concept with new meanings. Senghor for one gave the concept an ontological base that is anchored in black essences. The biologism that was injected into the concept caught on with French intellectuals and artists who championed African art and culture, in particular Jean-Paul Sartre (1905–1980), whose preface to Senghor's 1948 poetry collection presented negritude thinking as the black man's descent into self in search of essences.

Senghor's ontological positioning of the idea of negritude became even more controversial when he went further to engage in a comparative analysis that assigned emotion to the black man and reason to Europe. This racialized dichotomy earned Senghor some criticism from black Francophone intellectuals and writers (e.g., Stanislas Adotevi) that became even more acerbic in the writings of intellectuals from Anglophone Africa, including Nigerian author Wole Soyinka (b. 1934), South African author Ezekiel Mphahlele (b. 1919), and others.

SEE ALSO *Assimilation; Decolonization, Sub-Saharan Africa; Nationalism, Africa; Pan-Africanism.*

BIBLIOGRAPHY

Adotevi, Stanislas Spero. *Négritude st Négrologues* (new edition). Paris: Le Castor Astral, 1998.

Kesteloot, Lilyan. *Black Writers in French: A Literary History of Negritude.* Translated by Ellen Conroy Kennedy. Washington, DC: Howard University Press, 1991.

Senghor, Léopold Sédar. The *Foundations of "Africanité or "Négritude" and "Arabité."* Translated by Mercer Cook. Paris: Présence Africaine, 1971.

Obioma Nnaemeka

NEOCOLONIALISM

Neocolonialism is what the Marxist theorist and economist Harry Magdoff called quite simply "imperialism without colonies" (1972, p. 144). It has also been referred to as "informal imperialism," "the imperialism of free trade," and particularly in the context of Latin American history, "dependency." Neocolonialism can generally be defined as the ability of a powerful state to secure economic, strategic, and other benefits from a weaker state without possessing or directly governing it in any formal, legal, or institutional form as a colony.

The concept of neocolonialism has been widely employed since the 1970s in historiography to describe and explain the policies and behavior, primarily, of Great Britain and the United States in specific parts of the world during the nineteenth and twentieth centuries. From the time of its invention in the 1950s, however, this historical concept has been and remains controversial among scholars of imperialism and colonialism. Those who adopt the concept of neocolonialism believe it is useful in explaining an apparent anomalous historical development: that the essential characteristics of imperialism can exist without possession and control of a territorial empire. Critics of the concept, on the other hand, argue that there is an important difference between territorial colonialism and the political and economic influence or even dominance of a strong state over a weaker one. "Informal imperialism" creates more problems than it solves," writes Winfred Baumgart. "If subjected to logic it creates no clear border line. It is synonymous with any form of dependence and it is therefore unacceptably vague" (1982, p. 6).

Reference to any asymmetrical relationship between a strong and a weak state using the terminology of imperialism since the mid-twentieth century has more polemical than descriptive power. For some time now, Western colonialism has been widely assumed to be, and depicted as, morally wrong and evil in academic and popular literature, as well as in documentaries for television and in feature films. Those scholars, political activists, and statesmen who have employed the term *neocolonialism* during the past several decades have been,

for the most part, ideological radicals influenced by the strong theoretical currents of Marxism, structuralism, dependency, and postcolonialism more than their critics who have followed a more empirical approach.

There was scattered criticism of British and American "exploitation" and "bullying" in securing trade agreements, taking over important sectors of the national economy, and cozying up with or strong-arming local elites and their governments in the last decades of the nineteenth century and the early twentieth century. The related ideas of neocolonialism, informal empire, and dependency emerged in academic and political discourse in the era of decolonization after World War II (1939–1945). It is interesting to note that while these ideas and concepts appeared almost simultaneously during the postwar era of decolonization, they actually developed in isolation of one another, from different historiographical and theoretical traditions.

INFORMAL IMPERIALISM

Let us begin with the British and the concept of *informal imperialism.* By the early-to-mid nineteenth century, the British state possessed the military power and financial resources to seize, conquer, or annex more territories and peoples and expand its already worldwide colonial empire. In a number of different cases, however, British statesmen opposed the assumption of new colonial annexations. John Gallagher and Ronald Robinson in their seminal article "The Imperialism of Free Trade," published in 1953, challenged the mid-Victorian view that the new policy that favored trade over rule was anti-imperialist. Gallagher and Robinson argued that although the means may have changed, the ends were the same. For the British state and merchants, the rule was: "Trade with informal control if possible; trade with rule when necessary" (Gallagher and Robinson 1953, p. 13).

H. S. Ferns (1953) and later Peter Winn (1976) adopted this model to demonstrate Britain's "informal empire in Argentina and Uruguay. The Gallagher and Robinson model stimulated considerable interest and research regarding British influence in many parts of the world. With respect to China, D. K. Fieldhouse noted that the two Opium Wars of the nineteenth century were excellent examples of the imperialism of free trade. These wars demonstrated that "where economic considerations were allowed to predominate and where an indigenous political structure could provide the essential framework of order, economic forces did not necessarily lead to formal empire" (1973, pp. 476–477). Robinson and Gallagher (1961/1981) directed their research to Africa and the Victorians and explained, this time, how the British imposed formal rule on territories that previously had been under informal control. Their argument, in this case, was strategic rather than economic. The British Crown sought to protect the routes to India round the Cape and through the Suez Canal.

In the nineteenth century, Great Britain was the "superpower" of the age. In 1815 the British state had concluded a "hundred years' war" with France over the balance of power in Europe, control of North America, maritime supremacy in the Atlantic, and more. By mid-century, the British Empire had some 40,000 British troops stationed in India and a force of 200,000 Indians in arms. The British Indian army was deployed not only in India and Afghanistan, but also in garrisons from the Red Sea to China. The total strength of the British army in 1848 was only 130,000 men. This meant that in most colonies, local settlers and natives were recruited into military service to man the posts in Quebec, New Zealand, Cape Town, Jamaica, and Peshawar on the Northwest Frontier.

Also by midcentury, the British Royal Navy had 129 warships serving exclusively its foreign stations and guarding the world's main shipping routes. This overseas navy was divided into seven squadrons for the key regions necessary to dominate the high seas: North America, South America, the West Indies, the East Indies, Gibraltar, Cape Colony, and West Africa. By the nineteenth century the Royal Navy had expanded its responsibilities to not only protect British merchant shipping but the merchant marine of all peaceful countries. British warships escorted unarmed trading ships through wartorn regions and during the 1860s cleared out the pirates in the China Sea. In 1851 the Royal Navy had bases at Gibraltar, Malta, Aden, Bombay, Trincomalee, Seychelles, Mauritius, Calcutta, Singapore, Hong Kong, Sidney, the Sandwich Islands, Valparaiso (Chile), the Falkland Islands, Cape Town, Buenos Aires, Rio de Janeiro, Ascension, Trinidad, Jamaica, Antigua, Bermuda, Halifax, and Newfoundland.

The first steam-powered battleship ever built was a Royal Navy ship put into service in 1844. In the second half of the nineteenth century, the Royal Navy created ironclad steam-powered battleships with enormous guns and self-propelled torpedoes, true behemoths— *Warrior* (1860), *Devastation* (1871), *Inflexible* (1875), *Dreadnought* (1879), and dozens more with names like *Invincible, Indomitable,* and *Indefatigable.* The designer of the *Inflexible* wrote: "Imagine a floating castle which the progress of invention in artillery has finally driven us to resort to" (quoted in Herman 2004, p. 459). This navy did indeed rule the waves and police that era's new world order.

During the first half of the nineteenth century, the British superpower, particularly in the first decades following the defeat of France, used its military and commercial power and influence for a number of purposes. One of these was to bring an end to the Atlantic slave trade. Britain abolished its own trade in slaves in 1807, and after the defeat of Napoléon Bonaparte (1769–1821) at Waterloo, Belgium, in 1815, Britain exercised its considerable influence in trade treaties with Portugal, Spain, France, the Netherlands, and other countries to reduce or end their slave trades. These treaties generally gave the British Royal Navy the right to enforce the terms of the treaties. As a result, warships were maintained on the African coast and in the West Indies to inspect cargo ships suspected of carrying slaves. In the 1830s Britain abolished slavery in its American plantations and liberated more than 600,000 Africans and New World blacks. The British abolition influenced the French, who freed the slaves in their Caribbean colonies, Martinique and Guadeloupe, in 1848.

Lord Palmerston (Henry John Temple, 1784–1865), as foreign secretary in the 1830s and 1840s and prime minister of Britain from 1855 to 1865, endeavored to shut down the Atlantic slave trade, bring an end to human slavery, and open the world's markets to free trade for the benefit of both Great Britain and, he believed, the less fortunate peoples of the world. Palmerston, and "Palmerstonianism," accepted the idea that commerce was more important, and more moral, than colonialism. When he rejected the annexation of Abyssinia (Ethiopia) in the 1840s, Palmerston declared: "all we want is trade and land is not necessary for trade; we can carry on commerce very well on ground belonging to other people" (quoted in Lynn 1999, p. 108).

Palmerston, however, was not opposed to the annexation of new colonies when they were deemed necessary. The Palmerstonian approach is clearly what historians have in mind when they refer to the "imperialism of free trade." Under Palmerston, British consuls, goods, investments, merchant colonies, fashions, and even sports became influential in Latin America, the Ottoman Empire, West Africa, Persia, and China. British cultural influence expanded significantly when more than twenty-two million English, Welsh, Irish, and Scottish men and women left home between 1815 and 1914 and sailed for the Americas, Australia, New Zealand, India, South Africa, Egypt, and who knows where.

The British state and statesmen took actions in the hope of economic gain, strategic advantage, and moral progress without knowing the long-term outcome of their endeavors. The nineteenth-century British superpower sought economic penetration and political influence not only in the new nation-states of Latin America but in the crumbling empires of the Ottomans and the Chinese, and the generally weak and divided coastal states of tropical Africa. The British exercised more power in these regions, particularly in Egypt, which became a protectorate due to the strategic significance of the Suez Canal.

Britain, the first power to do so, followed by France, Germany, Russia, Japan, the United States, and Italy, established a system of international treaties, which the Chinese called *capitulations*, that opened specific Chinese ports to foreign trade, imposed a free-trade regime at these ports, and gave foreigners legal privileges and immunities in these ports. By 1878 there were six so-called treaty ports in China. The treaty port system did not fully open the interior of China to foreign trade, and thus the promise of an unquenchable market was never realized. The system did encourage China to promote industrialization in the 1890s, and it fueled the fire of the Boxer Rebellion in 1900. Humiliation at the hands of foreigners promoted nationalism and revolution and finally led to the abrogation of the treaties in 1943. Compared to Latin America, British trade with China by the late nineteenth century, and with the Ottoman Empire and tropical Africa, was a pittance.

This first age of commercial and financial globalization was made possible, to a considerable extent, because of the Pax Britannica, a long peace supervised by a great power willing to sustain a stable and open international order using its military and financial resources. As a result, during the first half of the nineteenth century, the volume of world trade more than doubled. During the second half, the volume of world trade increased by a factor of ten times. In 1827 Britain exported £50 million (British pounds) in goods, most of which went to the United States and western Europe. Four decades later the value of British exports had reached £180 million (with about £50 million going to the "captive markets" of the British Empire—India, Australia, Canada, Hong Kong, Singapore, and New Zealand). In the new age of globalization, Britain sold more of its cottons, woolens, and steam engines to the "free markets" of the United States, Europe, and Latin America. Britain's largest customer was still the United States at £22 million. Latin America purchased £12 million worth of goods, while tropical Africa imported less than £9 million.

By 1890 Great Britain had more registered shipping tonnage than the rest of the world combined. By 1913 the total value of British commerce was £1,294 million, with £525 million in exports and £769 in imports. On the eve of World War I (1914–1918), Great Britain had a nominal trade imbalance quite contrary to the economic nostrums of the day, which demanded that industrial nations export their surplus manufactures and maintain a trade surplus in order to avoid the perils of overproduction, declining profits and wages, labor

unrest, and worse. One is reminded of the persistent trade imbalances of the present-day superpower, the United States, and the heretical idea that free trade regimes may over time be more likely to promote world development (however unevenly) at the expense of tax-payers, workers, and consumers at home.

Latin America offers an excellent testing ground for the arguments for and against "informal imperialism." After Gallagher and Robinson's groundbreaking article in 1953, a number of scholars focused on making the case of Britain's informal empire in Latin America and in specific countries of Latin America. In the nineteenth century, British consuls, merchants, financiers, and others invaded the ports and backlands of Latin America. A flood of cheap British textiles in the 1820s, it is claimed, destroyed the infant industrialization of the region. British exports to Latin America increased from £5 million in the 1840s to £55 million by 1913. (British imports from Latin America, primarily basic foodstuffs, fibers, and minerals, were valued at £76 million in 1913, or nearly 140 percent the value of Britain's exports.) British investment in Latin America increased from £30 million in 1826 to over £80 million by 1865 and £1,180 in 1913. These monies built railroads, docks and ware-houses, processing plants, public utilities, and refurbished mines.

Gallagher and Robinson and the "informal imperialism" thesis pursued by other historians was quickly subsumed in a scholarly dispute that has continued to this day under different terms and concepts. H. S. Ferns (1960), a Canadian historian who at first embraced "informal imperialism" as a model for Latin America, turned around a few years later in a research monograph to argue that Great Britain did not have the power to force Argentina to pay a debt, or a dividend, or to export or import any particular commodity. The commercial relationship between Argentina and Great Britain, Ferns concluded, resembled one of mutual advantage more than informal imperialism.

Ferns and other historians of Argentina demonstrated that that country had the most diversified exports and sustained a high level of export expansion, which translated into national economic growth for several decades. By 1913 Argentina was the wealthiest country in Latin America (as measured by per capita gross national income) and one of the wealthiest countries in the world with a real income higher than Austria-Hungry, Finland, Portugal, and Italy. The countries of Latin America that participated most intensely in the international economy—Argentina, Uruguay, Cuba, and Chile—also had the highest national incomes.

Thirteen other Latin American countries also adopted similar export-led growth models, but these economies produced modest, and in a number of cases quite poor, results in terms of growth and development. The problem is often attributed to the failure of the model, which in turn is portrayed as the critical element of Latin America's era of neocolonialism. It is difficult to escape from the conclusion, writes economic historian Victor Bulmer-Thomas, "that any model adopted by the thirteen countries ... would have shown a poor rate of return. Political instability, administrative incompetence, poor transport systems, lack of capital, shortages of labor, and the small sizes of internal markets would have overwhelmed any conceivable alternative to export-led growth in the nineteenth century" (Bulmer-Thomas 1994, p. 153).

MARXIST THEORIES OF NEOCOLONIALISM

Also beginning in the 1950s, another approach to neocolonialism appeared, this time in the literature of the scholarly and activist left. The Marxist economist Paul Baran (1957) argued for the first time in Marxist literature that the capitalism of the advanced industrial countries was responsible for the impoverishment of the third world. Contrary to the analysis of Karl Marx (1818–1883) and Friedrich Engels (1820–1895), as well as that of V. I. Lenin (1870–1924), Baran proposed that poverty was not the inevitable condition of human beings, but had been introduced into the third world by capitalism via colonialism and neocolonialism.

As Harry Magdoff (1972) would note later, a common feature of all Marxist approaches is the understanding that imperialism survived decolonization intact. Unlike the "informal imperialism" thesis, which focused on the power of the imperial state to control or favorably influence trade, the Marxist theory of neocolonialism assumes that imperial control continues through foreign (capitalist) investment. Thus when we look at mid-to-late nineteenth-century Latin America, British and then U.S. investment in railroads facilitated the production and exchange of primary products—unprocessed raw materials and foodstuffs—transported to port cities, and not the creation of an integrated national market. The "insidious" aspect of foreign investment, from the Marxist point of view, is its seductive appeal to local elites to remake their values to conform to those of the capitalist investors, entrepreneurs, and merchants from Britain and the United States.

The prominent African anticolonialist leader, Marxist theorist, and first president of independent Ghana, Kwame Nkrumah (1909–1972), applied the concept of neocolonialism to independent Africa in his book of the same name in 1965. "The result of neocolonialism is that foreign capital is used for the exploitation rather than the development of the less developed parts of the world," wrote Nkrumah. "Investment under neocolonialism increases rather than decreases the gap between the rich and the poor countries of the world" (1965, p. x).

DEPENDENCY THEORY

By the 1960s and 1970s, a third model of neocolonialism had appeared in the scholarly literature. This model came to be called *dependency theory,* a sweeping historical and analytical explanation of economic development and underdevelopment that derived from the structuralist theories elaborated by Raúl Prebisch (1901–1986), who headed the United Nations Economic Commission for Latin America in the 1940s and 1950s. In contrast to the idea of informal imperialism (which charged that control of trade was more important than control of territory) and contrary to the Marxist notion of "imperialism without colonies" (which held that capitalist investment was the instrument for enriching the industrial countries and impoverishing all of the rest), dependency theory claimed a radical inheritance from Marxism but focused the neocolonial connection on patterns of unequal trade.

The Spanish and the Portuguese in their colonial empires in the Americas first set the pattern of unequal trade through mercantilist decrees and monopoly trading systems that required their American colonies to produce and export primary products, luxury foodstuffs, and minerals in exchange for more valuable manufactured goods from Europe. In the nineteenth and twentieth centuries, Great Britain, and increasingly the United States, replaced the old colonial powers and dominated Latin American markets. Although the commercial relationship was less than grand in the first half of the nineteenth century, business picked up during the last several decades of the century. Latin American countries, as a result of the rise of stable governments and collaborating elites, the growth of foreign demand, increased foreign investment, and the ability of Latin American producers to increase production of coffee, sugar, wool, cotton, nitrates, copper, and more, became part of the new globalized world order of the late nineteenth century. Latin America's role was to produce primary commodities for the factories and consumers of the industrialized countries of western Europe and the United States and, in turn, to purchase the manufactured goods of these nations and indefinitely put off their own industrialization.

It is difficult to find a textbook on Latin American history today without the obligatory chapter or section on "neocolonialism." Benjamin Keen's perennial *A History of Latin America* (5th ed., 1996) has long had a chapter entitled "The Triumph of Neocolonialism," which refers to the era 1870 to 1914. John Charles

Chasteen, in his concise history of Latin America, *Born in Blood and Fire* (2nd ed., 2006), calls his chapter on the period 1870 to 1930 simply "Neocolonialism." These textbook authors, and many others, employ dependency analysis, Marxist theory, and informal imperialism explanations in their narratives regarding how "despite many transformations, neither Latin America's subordinate relationship to European countries nor its basic social hierarchy—created by colonialism—had changed" (Chasteen 2001, p. 180).

Neocolonialism, the unhealthy alliance between foreign governments, financiers, merchants, and entrepreneurs, on the one hand, and collaborating Latin American governing officials, bureaucrats, landowners, and military officers (the so-called comprador elites) on the other, is given as the explanation for all the ills of late nineteenth-century Latin American societies: that is, authoritarian dictatorships or presidencies; small, powerful oligarchies; latifundia and the decline of peasant landholding; the rise of debt servitude and the decay of the standard of living for most rural families; and national economies tied to one or two commodity exports that were vulnerable to fluctuations, and therefore the cycles of boom and bust that most national economies suffered during the age of the "neocolonial order."

Dependency theory was popular and influential in academia and in progressive activist circles in the 1970s and 1980s. During this same period, critics of the approach went to the archives and tested the theory. Over time, in books and articles, the key components of dependency theory were undermined and discredited. "Once the disjuncture between radical theories and archival realities became evident," writes Rory Miller, "historians found themselves in a cul-de-sac" (1999, p. 446). An almost discouraged Florencia E. Mallon asked: "What is a progressive scholar to do? If we continue to commit to emancipatory, bottom-up analysis and yet can no longer simply ride one of our various Marxist or Marxian horses into the sunset, what are the alternatives?" (1994, p. 1491). The alternative she suggested, and one that many have taken up in Latin American studies, is *postcolonialism* and a turn from the political and economic to all things cultural. Thus, in a recent collection of essays, Gilbert M. Joseph notes that "today, with theories of imperialism and dependency under attack and the once-discredited diffusionist model recycled (yet again) in 'neoliberal' form by the managers of the 'New World Order,' Latin Americanists across a variety of disciplines and a new generation of historians of U.S. foreign relations (once known as 'diplomatic historians') are challenged to study the region's engagement with the United States in innovative ways" (Joseph et al. 1998, p. 4).

AMERICAN IMPERIALISM

Scholars and political activists have viewed and studied Great Britain and the United States quite differently through the prism of neocolonialism. The most striking difference between the two powerful modern nation-states and their histories is that Great Britain in the nineteenth and twentieth centuries had a vast colonial empire and exercised what some scholars and anticolonial leaders believed was and is "informal imperialism" through unequal treaties, investments, powerful consuls, the threat and occasional use of gunboats, and so on. The United States, on the other hand, despite picking up a few scattered islands at the end of the nineteenth century, never followed the western European model in creating a serious and substantial overseas colonial empire. The question for scholars, progressives, and radical activists, then, was not about "informal imperialism" (a concept invented specifically for Britain to contrast "informal colonies" from formal colonies). Since the United States did not have a real colonial empire, the question was more fundamental regarding the nature of the United States. Was the United States an empire or not?

The United States was created in an anticolonialist revolution in 1776 against the British Empire, and American statesmen and public opinion have long expressed anticolonial sentiments. In *The Federalist*, Alexander Hamilton (1755/57–1804) noted that:

> The world may politically, as well as geographically, be divided into four parts, each having a distinct set of interests. Unhappily for the other three, Europe, by her arms and by her negotiations, by force and by fraud, has, in different degrees, extended her dominions over them all. Africa, Asia, and America, have successively felt her domination. The superiority she has long maintained has tempted her to plume herself as the Mistress of the World, and to consider the rest of mankind as created for her benefit. (Hamilton 1787)

But no longer, proclaimed Hamilton, would this stand. "Let Americans disdain to be the instruments of European greatness!"

During the nineteenth century, the United States was an expansionist, and at times aggressive, state that acquired contiguous territory within the continental boundaries of North America. American constitutional law provided for the full and equal incorporation of new territorial acquisitions, thus continental expansion did not create western colonies but, in time, new self-governing states with representation in Congress and full citizenship for their settler population. This continental expansion was imperial if not colonial. The American state used military force, bribes, and other means to defeat and remove the indigenous peoples from their lands and reset-tle them on much smaller and poorer "reservations." From 1835 to 1836, American settlers to the Mexican province of Tejas (in fact, Coahuila y Tejas) rebelled, defeated the Mexican Army, and established the break-away Lone Star Republic. Ten years later, an American president annexed Texas and used a border incident to invade and defeat Mexico and annex nearly one-half of its national territory, the most important being the fertile valleys, gold fields, and seaports of California.

When presented with opportunities for overseas annexations, the United States generally turned away, with the early exception of Alaska, which was considered a "folly" at the time. During the last decades of the nineteenth century, as the United States began to grow into an economic powerhouse, American capital invest-ment began to increase in Mexico, Cuba and other Caribbean countries, Central America, and Colombia. American-financed railroads reaching into Mexico brought American merchants, manufactures, planters, settlers, and missionaries to Mexico, and, in turn, they carried Mexican cattle, copper, cotton, silver, coffee, rubber, and much more to the United States. By 1910 Americans owned 130 million acres in Mexico, or 27 percent of the land.

The Mexican petroleum industry was dominated by two foreign interests, the California oilman Edward Doheny (1856–1935), who brought in Texas oilmen and Standard Oil, and the British oil magnate Weetman Pearson (1856–1927). Mexico's primary export industry, mining, by the early twentieth century was in the hands of American and British investors. Americans held over 80 percent of the capital in the mining industry and owned outright seventeen of the thirty-one largest mining enterprises in the country. British investors held nearly 15 percent of the total capital and operated ten of the largest mines. "By 1910 more than 40,000 Americans resided in Mexico" (Hart 2002, p. 272). By 1913 total U.S. investment in Latin America had reached $1.6 billion, which was still far below total British investment in the region at $5 billion.

In 1898—America's "imperial moment"—the administration of President William McKinley (1843–1901) responded to a bloody crisis in Cuba, went to war with Spain, and seized Cuba, Puerto Rico, and the Spanish Philippines. A great debate immediately ensued between "imperialists" and "anti-imperialists" in Congress, the press, and across the United States regard-ing what course the country should take. The imperialists argued that history had determined that all great nations were imperial states and needed colonies like Cuba for resources, markets, the outward thrust of power, and so

on. The anti-imperialists claimed that overseas coloniza-tion was anti-American, and on the key issue, Cuba, they won. The U.S. Congress voted to give the Cuban people their independence after a short military occupation. Congress in 1898 also annexed the Hawaiian Islands, and President McKinley determined that the Philippine people were not ready for self-government. In 1903 the United States obtained the rights to build and defend a canal across the new nation-state of Panama, which became the most important strategic point in the defense of the United States.

Over the next thirty years the United States inter-vened repeatedly in the internal affairs of Caribbean and Central American nations in an attempt to maintain peace and order, collect international debts, prevent European intervention, protect American business inter-ests, promote democracy and good government, and—incidentally—improve public health and sanitation. Several countries, such as Cuba, Panama, Nicaragua, Haiti, and the Dominican Republic, became protecto-rates, were occupied by the U.S. Marines for years at a time, and had their armies and national guards trained and created by the United States from which, in some cases, presidents and dictators often arose.

These "Yanqui [Yankee] Years" (1898–1933) have often been pointed to as America's "imperial detour." By the 1920s, with Latin American governments increas-ingly critical and angry, and the Republican governments of the decade coming to realize that military interven-tions were expensive but did not really create any kind of long term stability, the U.S. State Department issued the Clark Memorandum in 1930. This statement, prepared by Undersecretary of State Joshua Reuben Clark Jr. (1871–1961), repudiated the Roosevelt Corollary to the Monroe Doctrine of 1905, which declared that only the United States could enforce the collection of debts owed to foreigners in the Western Hemisphere. At the same time, the Herbert Hoover (1874–1964) administration began to withdraw troops from Nicaragua and Haiti. When Franklin D. Roosevelt (1882–1945) was inaugu-rated president in 1933, he called for a "good neighbor policy," which, at the next Pan-American Conference, meant that the United States supported the noninterven-tion resolution of the Latin American members.

For a considerable number of historians, theorists, and political activists, the Yanqui Years have no signifi-cance. For most progressives and radicals, whether they are Marxists, dependency theorists, postcolonialists, Indian rights activists, antiglobalization activists, or inter-national Zapatistas, the United States has been an empire from its very founding. As Gilbert Joseph points out, to argue that the United States briefly had an empire "is to perpetuate false notions of 'American exceptionalism' and to engage psychologically in denial and projection. Such arguments also ignore structures, practices, and discourses of domination and possession that run throughout U.S. history" (Joseph et al. 1998, pp. 5–6). The United States was born, the historian Howard Zinn (2003) reminds us, of an invasion of America, massacres of Indians, and a powerful drive born in civilizations based on private property. This empire, from Jamestown to Baghdad, has no justification and no good deeds on its record.

The idea of an American imperium became an increasingly important subject of serious debate and writing in the decades following World War II and again in the decades following the end of the Cold War. In both eras, the idea of an American empire was fueled by unparalleled military and economic strength, seemingly unbounded cultural influence, and the more than occasional American covert and overt interventions overseas to remake the world in the image of itself. In both eras, domestic and international discussion of an American empire focused on the good it did (using its power to maintain a liberal global order) and the bad (supporting unpopular dictatorships, undermining populist regimes, and fighting the wrong wars in Vietnam and Iraq). The contributors to these debates extended beyond the radical left to include establishment liberal politicians, conservative and neoconservative intellectuals, foreign policy experts, diplomatic historians, and government officials.

By the end of the 1960s, Americans, and much of the rest of the world, had had enough of American imperium. The Richard Nixon (1913–1994) administration began withdrawing U.S. combat forces from South Vietnam, negotiated an "honorable peace" with the North in 1973, and removed all American forces from the county that same year. Two years later, Phnom Penh, the capital of Cambodia, fell to the Khmer Rouge, a repressive Communist organization, and Saigon (now Ho Chi Minh City) fell to the North Vietnamese army. During the 1970s, the Organization of Petroleum Exporting Countries (OPEC) raised the price of petroleum while Americans waited in line to fill up their gas tanks, North Korea captured an American spy ship, the United States returned the Panama Canal to Panama, the Soviet Union invaded Afghanistan, and radical students in Iran took American embassy officials hostage. By 1980 Americans, at any rate, did not see themselves in any imperial manner.

At the end of the Cold War, however, the age of the unipolar hyperpower was at hand. Although the United States cut its defense expenditures during the 1990s, its military budget was still greater than all of the military budgets of the next fifteen most powerful states combined. By 2000 the U.S. military budget reached nearly

$300 billion, a figure that paid for ten active army divisions, three active marine divisions, nine thousand M1 Abrams tanks, thirty active and reserve air wings, eleven aircraft carriers deployed in nine carrier battle groups, a garrison of some 100,000 troops in Europe, and about the same number of troops in South Korea and Japan. To begin to put some of these numbers in comparison, the U.S. Marine Corps had more troops and combat power than the entire army of Great Britain, France, or Italy.

The end of the Cold War nuclear standoff favored democratization and economic liberalization, but it also brought unscrupulous nationalism, ethnic cleansing, related wars, and a new wave of terrorism. In an increasingly disorderly world, some historians, public intellectuals and even government officials offer the suggestion that the United States, following the example of Great Britain in the nineteenth century, needs to accept its place in history, assume its imperial burden, and "export its capital, its people and its culture to those backward regions which need them most urgently and which, if they are neglected, will breed the greatest threats to its security" (Niall Ferguson, quoted in Urquhart 2003, pp. 8–9).

Radicals and neoconservatives who deplore or welcome the idea of an American empire mistake "the politics of primacy for those of empire," according to Joseph S. Nye Jr. (2003, p. 70). In the run-up to the Iraq war in 2002 and 2003, the United States could not obtain the votes of Mexico and Chile for a second Security Council resolution at the United Nations. When the time came for the invasion of Iraq, the parliament of Turkey refused to allow its territory to be used as a second front for the Fourth Infantry Division of the U.S Army, severely disrupting the Pentagon's battle plan.

The United States has been largely unsuccessful in sharing the postwar burden of funding reconstruction and bringing in European or other allies to assist in training Iraqi troops and police. When these limits to Washington's power are highlighted, the debate often returns to definitions. In this day and age, "empire," we are reminded, is a metaphor. All empires, historian Anthony Pagden argues, involve the exercise of imperium or sovereign authority, usually acquired by force. Had there been an American imperium, the parliamentarians of Turkey would not have had any choice but to agree to the request of the Pentagon. Pagden also notes that in order to survive for very long, all empires have to win over their conquered populations. "An Empire," he writes, quoting the Roman historian Livy (ca. 59 B.C.E.– 17 C.E.), "remains powerful so long as its subjects rejoice in it" (Pagden 2005, p. 48). The parliamentarians of Turkey not only refused the Pentagon's request because they could, they did so because they considered American policy in the second Gulf War illegitimate.

In the postcolonial and post–Cold War era, American army and marine divisions, air wings, and carrier battle groups can deliver unbelievable lethal force. American loans, trade concessions, and military assistance can be very tempting. In the final analysis, however, Washington, D.C., is not Rome or London. When a powerful state called upon a weaker allied state to provide a favor, the concept of neocolonialism (or the metaphor of "empire") would predict that Chile would vote with the United States in the United Nations and that Turkey would allow the Fourth Infantry Division to enter Iraq from the north. These predictions would have been wrong.

SEE ALSO *Boxer Uprising; Capitulations, Middle East; China, Foreign Trade; Chinese, Imperial Maritime Customs; Egypt; Empire, British; Empire, United States; Extraterritoriality; Hegemon and Hegemony; Imperialism, Cultural; Imperialism, Free Trade; Imperialism, Liberal Theories of; Imperialism, Marxist Theories of; Modern World-System Analysis; Nkrumah, Kwame; Open-Door Policy; Postcolonialism; Treaty Port System.*

BIBLIOGRAPHY

Abernethy, David B. *The Dynamics of Global Dominance: European Overseas Empires, 1415–1980.* New Haven, CT: Yale University Press, 2000.

Bacevich, Andrew J. *American Empire: The Realities and Consequences of U.S. Diplomacy.* Cambridge, MA: Harvard University Press, 2002.

Baran, Paul. *The Political Economy of Growth.* New York: Monthly Review Press, 1957.

Baumgart, Winfred. *Imperialism: The Idea and Reality of British and French Colonial Expansion, 1880–1914,* rev. ed. Oxford: Oxford University Press, 1982.

Brown, Judith M., and Wm. Roger Louis, eds. *The Oxford History of the British Empire; Vol. 4: The Twentieth Century.* Oxford: Oxford University Press, 1999.

Bulmer-Thomas, Victor. *The Economic History of Latin America Since Independence.* Cambridge, U.K.: Cambridge University Press, 1994; 2nd ed., 2003.

Chasteen, John Charles. *Born in Blood and Fire: A Concise History of Latin America.* New York: Norton, 2001; 2nd ed., 2006.

Ferns, H. S. "Britain's Informal Empire in Argentina, 1806–1914." *Past and Present* 4 (1953): 60–75.

Ferns, H. S. *Britain and Argentina in the Nineteenth Century.* Oxford: Oxford University Press, 1960.

Fieldhouse, D. K. *Economics and Empire, 1830–1914.* London: Weidenfeld and Nicolson, 1973.

Fieldhouse, D. K. *The Colonial Empires: A Comparative Survey from the Eighteenth Century.* New York: Delacorte, 1966; 2nd ed., London: Macmillan, 1982.

Ferguson, Niall. *Empire: The Rise and Demise of the British World Order and the Lessons for Global Power.* New York: Basic Books, 2003.

Ferguson, Niall. "Hegemony or Empire?" *Foreign Affairs* 82 (5) (2003): 154–161.

Ferguson, Niall. *Colossus: The Price of America's Empire.* New York: Penguin, 2004.

Ferguson, Niall. "The Unconscious Colossus: Limits of (and Alternatives to) American Empire." *Dædlus* 134 (2) (2005): 18–33.

Gallagher, John, and Ronald Robinson. "The Imperialism of Free Trade." *Economic History Review,* 2nd series, 6 (1953): 1–15.

Haber, Steven H., ed. *How Latin America Fell Behind: Essays on the Economic Histories of Brazil and Mexico,* 1800–1914. Stanford, CA: Stanford University Press, 1997.

Hamilton, Alexander. *The Federalist* No. 11: "The Utility of the Union in Respect to Commercial Relations and a Navy." 1787. Available from the Library of Congress at http://thomas.loc.gov/home/histdox/fed_11.html.

Harris, Lee. "The Intellectual Origins of America Bashing." *Policy Review* 116 (2002). Available from www.policyreview.org/dec02/harris.html.

Hart, John Mason. *Empire and Revolution: The Americans in Mexico since the Civil War.* Berkeley: University of California Press, 2002.

Herman, Arthur. *To Rule the Waves: How the British Navy Shaped the Modern World.* New York: HarperCollins, 2004.

Joseph, Gilbert M., Catherine C. LeGrand, and Ricardo D. Salvatore, eds. *Close Encounters of Empire: Writing the Cultural History of U.S.–Latin American Relations.* Durham, NC: Duke University Press, 1998.

Keen, Benjamin. *A History of Latin America,* 5th ed. Boston: Houghton Mifflin, 1996.

Knight, Alan. "Britain and Latin America." In *The Nineteenth Century; Vol. 3: The Oxford History of the British Empire,* edited by Andrew Porter, 122–145. Oxford: Oxford University Press, 1999.

Loomba, Ania. *Colonialism/Postcolonialism,* 2nd ed. London: Routledge, 2005.

Louis, Wm. Roger, ed. *Imperialism: The Robinson and Gallagher Controversy.* New York: New Viewpoints, 1976

Lynn, Martin. "British Policy, Trade, and Informal Empire in the Mid-Nineteenth Century." In *The Nineteenth Century; Vol. 3: The Oxford History of the British Empire,* edited by Andrew Porter, 101–121. Oxford: Oxford University Press, 1999.

Magdoff, Harry. "Imperialism Without Colonies." In *Studies in the Theory of Imperialism,* edited by Roger Owen and Bob Sutcliffe, 144–170. London: Longman, 1972.

Mallon, Florencia E. "The Promise and Dilemma of Subaltern Studies: Perspectives from Latin American History." *American Historical Review* 99 (5) (1994): 1491–1515.

Miller, Rory. "Informal Empire in Latin America." In *Historiography; Vol. 5: The Oxford History of the British Empire,* edited by Robin W. Winks, 437–449. Oxford: Oxford University Press, 1999.

Nkrumah, Kwame. *Neo-Colonialism: The Last Stage of Imperialism.* London: Heinemann, 1965.

Nye, Joseph S., Jr. "U.S. Power and Strategy After Iraq." *Foreign Policy* 82 (4) (2003): 60–73.

Osterhammel, Jürgen. "Britain and China, 1842–1914." In *The Nineteenth Century;* Vol. 3: *The Oxford History of the British Empire,* edited by Andrew Porter, 146–169. Oxford: Oxford University Press, 1999.

Pagden, Anthony. "Imperialism, Liberalism, and the Quest for Perpetual Peace." *Dædalus* 134 (2) (2005): 46–57.

Platt, D. C. M. "The Imperialism of Free Trade: Some Reservations." *Economic History Review* 2nd series 21 (1968): 296–306

Platt, D. C. M. "Economic Imperialism and the Businessman: Britain and Latin America Before 1914." In *Studies in the Theory of Imperialism,* edited by Roger Owen and Bob Sutcliffe, 295–311. London: Longman, 1972.

Platt, D. C. M. "Dependency in Nineteenth-Century Latin America: An Historian Objects." *Latin American Research Review* 15 (1) (1980): 113–130.

Porter, Andrew, ed. *The Nineteenth Century;* Vol. 3: *The Oxford History of the British Empire.* Oxford: Oxford University Press, 1999.

Robinson, Ronald, and John Gallagher, with Alice Denny. *Africa and the Victorians: The Official Mind of Imperialism.* London: Macmillan, 1961; 2nd ed., 1981.

Simes, Dimitri K. "America's Imperial Dilemma." *Foreign Affairs* 82 (6) (2003): 91–102.

Stern, Steven J. "Feudalism, Capitalism, and the World-System in the Perspective of Latin America and the Caribbean." *American Historical Review* 93 (1988): 829–872.

Urquhart, Brian. "World Order & Mr. Bush." *The New York Review of Books* 50 (15) (2003): 8–12.

Winn, Peter. "Britain's Informal Empire in Uruguay during the Nineteenth Century." *Past and Present* 73 (1976): 100–126.

Woddis, Jack. *An Introduction to Neo-Colonialism.* London: Lawrence and Wishart, 1967.

Young, Robert J. C. *Postcolonialism: An Historical Introduction.* Oxford: Blackwell, 2001.

Zinn, Howard. *A People's History of the United States: 1492–Present,* new ed. New York: HarperCollins, 2003.

Thomas Benjamin

NEOCOLONIALISM IN LATIN AMERICA

The term *neocolonialism* is used by some authors to describe the relationship of nominally independent countries in Latin America with *metropolitan* or *developed* countries from independence in the 1820s to the present. These authors, often referred to as the *dependency analysts*, stress a continuum whereby Latin America was kept in a condition of economic and, often, political subordination, and its resources were—or so it is claimed—organized in such a way as to promote the interests of developed countries rather than to assure the development of poor ones.

In the half-century after independence, the dominant international power, the United Kingdom, played a controversial role in the continent. The dependency analysts stress, with varying degrees of subtlety and insistence, that British "informal imperialism" replaced Iberian formal empire. They argue further that Latin American governments opened up markets to an influx of British manufactured imports, which served only to sabotage nascent cottage and artisan industries that could otherwise have served as stimuli to a transition to factory industrialization. In other words, Latin American elites, who embraced fashionable ideas of free trade that were rooted in prevailing assumptions that both partners in an international trading relationship benefited equally, were deceived. There was, in practice, no such equality, because Britain enjoyed the advantages of greater experience in international business, control of shipping lines, and a flourishing shipbuilding industry, and could threaten to use the Royal Navy when challenged. A system of international trade, reinforced by commercial treaties that were a precondition of diplomatic recognition of independent nations, was geared to British needs.

This argument is rejected by liberal authors. Some argue that Latin America enjoyed no opportunities for industrialization and development in this period. The region was a marginal component in the international economy of little sustained interest to the British. Indeed, factory industrialization was barely an option for Latin America, owing to shallow markets, an absence of cheap, accessible coal deposits, and costly internal communications. Latin American authors, in particular, contend that deep-seated rigidities, notably the interaction of *latifundios* (vast landed estates) geared more to prestige than to profit, and *minifundios* (small, nonviable plots), aborted possibilities of significant growth in agriculture, and precluded the emergence of both a surplus for reinvestment in factory manufacturing and significant rural markets for industrial products.

The consolidation of the world economy between circa 1870 and the global depression (1929–1933) brought considerable growth to Latin America, associated with the export of foodstuffs, minerals, and later oil. The continent was the recipient of a substantial injection of foreign capital and new technology, as well as a considerable influx of European immigrants. According to dependency analysts, this was a period in which international economic relationships were revised in such ways as to guarantee continued subordination of Latin America to the major industrialized countries, which came to include the United States, and, less important

Venezuelan President Hugo Chavez. *President Chavez delivers an address in Guayaquil, Ecuador, on July 26, 2002. Chavez is a vocal opponent of neocolonialism: he often refers to U.S. foreign policy in Latin America as "North American Imperialism."* © REUTERS/CORBIS. REPRODUCED BY PERMISSION.

to Latin America, Germany and France. For the first time, Latin America was exposed to new capitalist practices, especially the consolidation of U.S. corporate business in agriculture, mining, oil, and banking. While not uniform in their diagnoses, dependency analysts placed a heavy stress upon the sharpening of social and economic inequalities during these decades.

Foreign capital, technology, and skilled management were concentrated in the external sector, and domestic capital was lured by it, frequently leaving the sector producing food staples for domestic consumption—cereals, beans, poultry, vegetables—starved of capital, credit, and technology. Latin American allies of foreign firms in both the state and domestic business cooperated in practices that perpetuated low incomes and little welfare for majorities of the population, while an excessive proportion of profits in powerful foreign-owned businesses was repatriated to the developed countries. Small countries, especially in the Caribbean and Central America, where monocrop export production operated

by U.S.-based enterprises was dominant, were vulnerable to unpredictable shifts in the price and demand for their export commodities, which played a part in fostering political instability. This, in turn, provided the United States with pretexts for naval interventions.

The progressive erosion of economic independence and the emergence of distorted, lopsided economies where balanced growth was impossible condemned Latin America to the "deepening" of underdevelopment, so that its economies served European and U.S. needs, rather than those of most of its own citizens. What dynamic diversification was bought about by external linkages, through, for example, greater access to borrowing from Wall Street in the 1920s, tended to benefit domestic minorities and foreign business at the expense of the regions and sectors where capitalism lacked dynamism.

Liberal authors held a radically different view. They claimed that Latin America enjoyed considerable benefits from the normal forces of the market and of competition, and, that, far from being exploitative, foreign connections brought new, tantalizing opportunities for Latin American entrepreneurs and taxable wealth that consolidated and modernized Latin American states. The incipient transnational firms engaged in communications, sugarcane milling, and meatpacking supplied an invaluable example to Latin American businessmen of how business could be organized so as to lower the costs of production and explore economies of scale. Thus Latin America was the fortunate beneficiary of a long period of "export-led growth" and of the cumulative effects of small technical changes that promoted output and productivity. Latin American nations did not achieve a transition to "developed" status, because the opportunities for one did not exist.

The 1930s and early 1940s were decades of considerable flux, in which Latin American statesmen and businessmen were compelled to reappraise their priorities. Historians debate how far international capitalism withdrew from Latin America during these years, and how far they represented a mere hiatus in its advance. Some dependency analysts argued that the combined crises of the depression and World War II (1939–1945) provided the leaders of the continent with new opportunities to reorient its economies along inward-looking lines.

Some of this writing flies in the face of the empirical evidence. Ad hoc manufacturing growth and extemporized responses to acute problems of unemployment and incomes during the depression crisis are over-easily confused with coherent and consistent strategies of industrialization and development from within, which were impossible in countries where economic instability went hand in hand with a high turnover of incumbents in political office. Yet dependency analysts and their critics

Hyundai Plant in Mexico. *This Hyundai factory in Tijuana, Mexico, is a maquiladora,* a special manufacturing facility established by the Mexican government for trade with the United States and other countries. *Maquiladoras* are usually located just a few miles past the U.S.-Mexico border. © **STEVE STARR/CORBIS. REPRODUCED BY PERMISSION.**

converge in seeing this period as critical to the understanding of contemporary Latin America. Most agree that a paucity of investigation at national, sectoral, regional, and workplace levels precludes more than a shallow interpretation of these decades. What was manifest, however, was that sustained crisis in Europe meant that the external ascendancy, economic and political, of the United States across the continent was undisputed.

SEE ALSO *Neocolonialism.*

BIBLIOGRAPHY

Abel, Christopher, and Colin M Lewis, eds. *Latin America, Economic Imperialism, and the State.* Atlantic Highlands, NJ: Athlone, 1991.

Albert, Bill. *South America and the World Economy from Independence to 1930.* London: Macmillan, 1983.

Bulmer-Thomas, Victor. *The Economic History of Latin America since Independence,* 2nd ed. Cambridge, U.K.: Cambridge University Press, 2003.

Cardenas, Enrique, José Antonio Ocampo, and Rosemary Thorp, eds. *An Economic History of Twentieth-Century Latin America;*
Vol. 1: *The Export Age: The Latin American Economies in the Late Nineteenth and Early Twentieth Centuries.* Basingstoke, U.K.: Palgrave, 2000.

Cardoso, Fernando Henrique, and Enzo Faletto. *Dependency and Development in Latin America.* Translated by Marjory Mattingly Urquidi. Berkeley: University of California Press, 1979.

Haber, Stephen, ed. *Political Institutions and Economic Growth in Latin America: Essays in Policy, History, and Political Economy.* Stanford, CA: Hoover Institution Press, 2000.

Thorp, Rosemary. *Progress, Poverty, and Exclusion: An Economic History of Latin America Since Independence.* Washington, DC: Inter-American Development Bank, 1998.

Christopher Abel

NETHERLANDS MISSIONARY SOCIETY

In the seventeenth century the Dutch, under the colors of their East India Company (VOC, 1602) and West India

Company (WIC, 1625), gained a foothold in Southeast Asia, Africa, and America. Everywhere they brought the Reformed Church with them. For two centuries the two companies paid all expenses of church life in their dominions, but the close ties between church and state also prevented the Christian faith from expanding beyond the boundaries of the Dutch possessions. In Southeast Asia during these centuries Protestantism was adopted by indigenous populations only in Ceylon and in eastern Indonesia, where the island of Ambon was the main center. The large congregation of Batavia (present-day Jakarta) consisted mainly of Europeans and Eurasians. The military power of the VOC was occasionally used to protect Christian populations from their enemies, mostly Muslims, but not for spreading Christianity.

This situation was changed by political, cultural, and religious developments in Europe toward the end of the eighteenth century. The WIC and VOC were liquidated and their overseas possessions were taken over by the Dutch state (1791, 1799). At the same time, in the Netherlands as elsewhere in Europe, the separation of church and state was effectuated (1796). The Netherlands Reformed Church (NRC) could have taken advantage of this turn of events by starting missions in its own right, unhampered by a state pursuing its own interests. But it was weakened by the separation, and by a reorganization (1816) that encroached upon its reformed character and brought about a century of confessional strife. Consequently in the Netherlands, as in other European countries (Great Britain, Germany, and France), this task was taken up by missionary societies. Inspired by activities of the Moravian Brothers and following the lead of the London Missionary Society, in 1797 a number of Dutch pastors and laypeople founded the Nederlands Zendeling Genootschap (NZG, Netherlands Missionary Society).

The Netherlands Missionary Society was of an ecumenical nature, but throughout its history members and leadership were mainly Dutch Reformed. During the first half of the nineteenth century it was the only missionary society in the Netherlands, but between 1847 and 1859 the strengthening of confessionalism led to the foundation of a number of sister organizations. At home, these events were accompanied by passionate polemics, but in the mission field the various societies respected each other. After 1900, Society director Dr. J. W. Gunning (1862–1923) made overtures to the other societies that had their roots in the NRC. This led to increasingly close cooperation and ultimately to the merging of these societies into the Mission Board of the NRC (1951).

MISSIONARY WORK OVERSEAS

The beginnings of work overseas were slow. Between 1795 and 1815 the Netherlands, being in the sphere of influence of revolutionary and Napoleonic France, was almost continuously at war with England and consequently cut off from its overseas possessions. When peace came it left Holland with only the Indonesian Archipelago, the territory of modern Indonesia. After a short spell of activities in former Dutch possessions like Ceylon and South Africa, Dutch missionary work concentrated upon this area. But because the mission was not broadly based in Dutch society, the Netherlands Missionary Society and its Dutch sister societies were not able even to adequately serve the Netherlands Indies. The German Rhenish Mission Society (RMG) and (at a later stage) the American Christian and Missionary Alliance had to lend support, occupying a number of areas left vacant by the Dutch missionaries.

Society missionaries arrived in the Indies from 1814 onwards. During the first decades they were employed by the government to minister to the existing Protestant communities, who at that time numbered 40,000. Gradually the government organized these communities into the Protestant Church of the Netherlands Indies. This left the missionaries free to work among non-Christians. For the first time in Dutch mission history, systematic mission work was started among Muslims (East Java, 1848). In addition, the Society started work in North Celebes (Minahasa, 1831), East Sumatra (1890), and Central Celebes (Poso, 1892). At the time, the last mentioned region did not yet belong to the Dutch sphere of influence. The same was the case with a number of mission fields served by other societies, like Batakland (North Sumatra, 1857) and New Guinea (1855). These statistics point to another difference between the nineteenth-century Dutch missions and the Reformed Church in the preceding centuries: the Netherlands Missionary Society and other societies did not hesitate to establish mission posts in territories not (yet) administrated by the colonial government. In the case of Batakland, this did not prevent the RMG mission from prospering, whereas in New Guinea, Central Celebes, and other regions conversions were extremely few until colonial law and order was established.

MISSIONARY THEORY AND PRACTICE

Throughout the nineteenth century the missionaries' attitude toward non-Christian religions and non-Western culture was rather negative. Islam was viewed as the greatest enemy of the Christian faith; tribal religions were considered to be the result of a degeneration process. In this paradigm, "dark(ness)," "blind(ness)," and "sunk low" were the words most frequently used in describing the religious and moral state of the people evangelized. Consequently no elements from indigenous religion or culture were incorporated into church worship; newly converted were told to keep away from traditional feasts as well as from cultural expressions like music and dance; in haircut and dress they were urged to follow Western customs as much as the tropical climate could permit.

The emphasis on personal conversion denied the collectivistic nature of traditional society. However, the missionaries' view on religion as a matter of the heart caused them to use the local language, at least when working among language communities of a sufficient size. This policy contrasted with that pursued by the Reformed Church during the preceding centuries and by the established Protestant Church, which almost exclusively used Malay, as well as with that of present-day Indonesian churches, which increasingly adopt the national language, Indonesian, in worship and church organization. The missionaries not only preached the Gospel in the vernacular, but in many cases they also were the first to reduce it to writing and publish grammars and dictionaries, all in preparation of the Bible translations, which were to be the crown of their linguistic studies.

Toward the turn of the century missionary theory, and increasingly missionary practice, began paying more respect to indigenous culture. In the face of the refusal of the indigenous population to convert on the terms set by the mission, A. C. Kruyt (1892–1932 in Central Celebes) and other missionaries embarked on a new course. During the first decades of the twentieth century, Dutch and German missions no longer ignored or suppressed indigenous culture, but endeavored to study it and to conserve it in a purified form, that is, after having eliminated the elements that were considered pagan. In this way a (rather artificial) Christian culture was created. Language was viewed as a core element of this culture, and linguistic studies were intensified. Because the motives for using the vernacular were not only religious, but also ideological, not only Islam-tinged Malay but also Christian Dutch was discouraged. In this way the missionaries cut their flock off from developments in the outside world: from Indonesian nationalism, of which Malay was an important vehicle, and from higher education, which during the colonial era was only taught in the Dutch language. The negative effects in the field of politics and economics were felt after Indonesia became an independent state.

The relationship between the Netherlands Missionary Society (indeed the Dutch mission in general) and the colonial state and ideology was rather ambivalent. The missionaries often denounced injustices done to the population among whom they lived and whose language they spoke. On the other hand, the missionary societies depended on the colonial state for permission to work in a given region; in most fields mission work bore fruit only after pacification; in Muslim regions it would have been simply impossible without government

protection (which was often only grudgingly given). From 1900 onward mission activities in the fields of education and medical care were generously subsidized. Despite their harsh criticism of colonial policy, the missionaries shared the conviction of the superiority of Western civilization, which served as a justification for the colonization of non-Western peoples.

Because the colonial government hardly created structures that could become the nucleus of an independent Indonesian state, the mission only reluctantly set up church structures that would enable Christian communities to function independently. In both cases the reason given was that Indonesians were not yet mature enough to staff such structures. In this respect a new course was set by Hendrik Kraemer (1888–1965). He persuaded the missionaries to grant autonomy to local and regional churches. In this way a number of churches in West and Central Indonesia became independent before an independent Indonesian state came into being. In most of East Indonesia, however, when World War II came and the Dutch missionaries were interned, there were not even Indonesian ministers authorized to administer the sacraments, nor was there a church organization. Here the churches became independent after the state.

CONCLUSIONS

When the Netherlands Missionary Society first entered the territory of present-day Indonesia, in 1814, there were approximately 40,000 Protestant Christians in that region, less than 1 percent of the total population. In 1942 this number had grown to 1.8 million Christians, or 2.5 percent, of whom only 100,000 belonged to the churches that had come into being on the four mission fields served by the Netherlands Missionary Society. (In 2000 these numbers were approximately 16 million and 600,000, besides approximately 5 million Catholics.) Among these, one-half (33,000) of those converted to Christianity from Islam. Moreover, in the 1870s the Society had surrendered its most promising mission field, the Minahasa, to the Protestant Church. The NZG was important not on account of its size, but because during the 150 years it was in the vanguard of Dutch missions as regards to the quality of the education of its missionaries and the theoretical reflection on missionary practice.

SEE ALSO *Dutch United East India Company; Dutch West India Company; Religion, Western Presence in East Asia; Religion, Western Presence in Southeast Asia.*

BIBLIOGRAPHY
Akkeren, Philip van. *Sri and Christ: A Study of the indigenous Church in East Java.* Translated by Annebeth Mackie. London: Lutterworth, 1969.

Kraemer, Hendrik. *From Missionfield to Independent Church*. The Hague: Boekencentrum, 1958.

Rauws, Joh, and H. Kraemer et al., eds. *The Netherlands Indies*. New York: World Dominion Press, 1935.

Th. van den End

NEW CALEDONIA

New Caledonia (Nouvelle Calédonie) is a French overseas territory in the Southwest Pacific located between Australia and Fiji. It is 18,575 square kilometers (7,172 square miles) in size; the area comprises a main island (Grande Terre), the Loyalty Islands (Iles Loyaute), and several sparsely populated atolls with a total population of 213,769 (42% native origin [Kanak]; 37% European origin [Caldoche]). Natural resources include nickel (providing about 25% of the world's supply) and large-scale export crops such as coffee.

Captain James Cook sighted Grande Terre and dubbed it New Caledonia in 1774. British whalers and sandalwood traders soon followed, bringing diseases such as smallpox, dysentery, and leprosy that devastated the local population. As trade expanded in the region so did the number of missions, further eradicating local practices and traditions. French Marist missionaries arrived in 1843, and under the pretext of protecting the native peoples—when in reality it was to counteract British influence in the region—Napoleon III annexed New Caledonia in 1853.

Desperate to replace their failed penal colony of Guiana, the French began deporting convicts to New Caledonia in May 1864 and political exiles associated with the Paris Commune in 1871. By the time deportation was halted in 1897—in an effort to hasten free colonization—nearly 21,000 convicts had been exiled. As increasing numbers of free settlers arrived, native villages were displaced to make way for cattle grazing, which led to numerous revolts against French rule, all of which were violently repressed.

In 1956 New Caledonia's status changed from a colony to an overseas territory and Kanaks were given the right to vote the following year. This did not forestall political radicalization, however, and increasing demands for land reform and independence sparked a wave of violence between Kanaks and Caldoches in the mid-1980s. This unrest prompted France to grant New Caledonia a unique status somewhere between an independent country and overseas department. Thus, a fifty-four-member territorial congress elected by popular vote is responsible for taxation, labor law, and health, while the French Republic retains authority over foreign affairs, justice, and the treasury. Vote on a referendum for independence will occur in 2014.

SEE ALSO *Empire, French.*

BIBLIOGRAPHY

Foucrier, Annick, ed. *The French and the Pacific World, 17th–19th Centuries*. Burlington, VT: Ashgate, 2005.

Lyons, Martyn. *The Totem and the Tricolour: A Short History of New Caledonia since 1774*. Sydney: New South Wales University Press, 1986.

Stephen A. Toth

NEW FRANCE

The name *New France* was first applied to the northeastern portion of North America in a map prepared by the explorer Giovanni da Verrazano (1485–1530). It reflected the overseas ambitions of Verrazano's master, King François I (1494–1547), as well as the presence of Breton and Norman fishermen in the coastal waters of the region. The French navigator Jacques Cartier (1491–1557) staked a claim to the Saint Lawrence River in 1534, and later in the sixteenth century French and Basque fur traders established regular relations with the native peoples of the region. Only at the time of Samuel de Champlain (ca. 1570–1635), however, were year-round French settlements established, first in Acadia (present-day Nova Scotia) in 1604 and then in "Canada" (now Quebec) in 1608.

Through the first half of the seventeenth century, New France consisted of a few small posts owned by the Company of New France and allied to indigenous nations from whom the settlers purchased beaver and other furs. In 1663 King Louis XIV (1638–1715) dissolved the company and took over direct rule of New France, reorganizing colonial administration along the lines of a French province. France then provided Canada with a substantial injection of soldiers, settlers, and capital, with the result that the colony soon developed a European aspect, with the towns of Quebec and Montreal bracketing agricultural settlements along the banks of the Saint Lawrence.

The flow of immigration was numerically modest and almost exclusively French and Catholic; immigrants, drawn from across the western half of France, were mostly poor, predominantly male, and disproportionately urban in origin. A census in 1681 numbered the French-Canadian population at 9,742; by the end of French rule in 1760, it had risen to approximately 76,000.

Through the seventeenth century the French fully occupied only a small territory along the Saint Lawrence and around Port Royal in Acadia, but French influence extended over a vast and growing portion of the continent.

QUEBEC, *The Capital of* NEW-FRANCE, *a Bifhoprick, and Seat of the Soverain* COURT.

1. *The* Citadel. 2. *the* Castle. 3. *Magazine.* 4. *y* Recolets. 5. *Urfulines.* 6. *Jefuits.* 7. 7. Cathedral *of* Our Lady. 8. *The* Palace 9. *y* Seminary. 10. *The* Hôtel Dieu. 11. *S.* Charles River. 12. *The* Common Hospital. 13. *The Hermitage of the* Recolets. 14. *The* Bishop's House. 15. *The* Parish Church *of the* Lower Town. 16. *The* Upper Town 17. *y* Lower Town. 18. *The* Platform & Battery *of* Cannon 19. *The* Isle *of* Orleans. 20. Point Lievi.

Quebec, the Capital of New-France. *This view of Quebec, rendered by the American engraver Thomas Johnston in 1759, was probably based on a map published in 1718.* © BETTMANN/CORBIS. REPRODUCED BY PERMISSION.

Fur traders and missionaries traveled inland along canoe routes that led through the Great Lakes and into the Mississippi watershed. Cavalier de la Salle (1643–1687) reached the Gulf of Mexico from Canada in 1683, establishing a French claim that would later be followed up with the founding of Louisiana on the Gulf of Mexico in 1699.

New France's inland empire, enveloping the British colonies by the early eighteenth century, was French only in a very special and limited sense, for this was really Indian territory, largely beyond the control of French sovereignty, law, and culture. A few hundred French maintained a degree of influence thanks, in part, to their commercial role making European goods available to avid native customers. Equally important—and inseparable from the economic connection—was the central role they played in the alliance system that emerged in the interior as tribes sought to maintain a common front, first against the Iroquois and later against the British.

By the early eighteenth century, it was becoming evident that, on purely mercantilist principles, the North American colonies were far less valuable to France than its booming sugar plantation possessions in the West Indies. After a disastrous attempt to finance colonial development through private investment, Louisiana became synonymous with speculation and waste. Canada, where settlers were free of direct taxation, generally cost the crown more than it produced by way of revenue from the fur trade. And Acadia, on the exposed Atlantic shore, proved impossible to defend in the long run.

The imperial logic shaping policy toward New France was of a different order in the eighteenth century—strategic rather than economic—and it had everything to do with the growing Anglo–French rivalry. The great arc of French territorial claims, from the Gulf of Saint Lawrence, through the Great Lakes and the Mississippi River to the Gulf of Mexico, was designed at least in part to keep the much more populous and economically viable British colonies hemmed in along the seaboard. Taking the form of a great alliance system connecting hundreds of native nations to the French crown, this larger New France represented a valuable military resource in times of war.

Throughout its history, New France was intermittently at war, first with the Iroquois League between 1609 and 1701. In later struggles, against the Fox of the Great Lakes and the Natchez and Chickasaws of Louisiana, the French seemed determined to exterminate entire enemy nations, effectively giving the lie to any notion that France's approach to empire was entirely benign.

After 1689, the intensifying rivalry between Britain and France embroiled the North American colonies increasingly in Europe's dynastic struggles. Though the Anglo-American side enjoyed an immense superiority in numbers and economic power, the French-Canadians were more thoroughly militarized and, in the case of the fur-trade veterans, skilled in wilderness travel; furthermore, they could usually count on support from their network of native alliances. Accordingly, New France specialized in the techniques of "*la petite guerre*" (small guerrilla war) with parties of Indians and Canadian militia raiding vulnerable outposts on the frontiers of New England, New York, and Pennsylvania. Ruthlessly targeting civilian settlers, this strategy succeeded for a time in keeping the enemy off-balance, but it contributed to a growing determination on the part of the British to defeat and utterly destroy New France.

After a series of French victories early in the Seven Years' War (1754–1763 in America, where it was known as the French and Indian War), Britain was persuaded by her American colonies to mount a major assault aimed at conquering Canada. With the Europeanizing of the struggle, Canada's native alliances and frontier raiding traditions became a marginal factor. While the navy sealed off approaches to the Saint Lawrence, a huge (by colonial standards) British and American army launched a three-pronged attack. While one force headed west to capture inland posts before doubling back toward Montreal, a second army made its way straight north along the heavily fortified Lake Champlain corridor. Meanwhile, a third, amphibious, army sailed in from the east to lay siege to Quebec in 1759. The famous battle on the Plains of Abraham brought a dramatic conclusion to the eastern campaign, but New France's fate was sealed, not so much by a single clash of arms, but by the relentless and convergent advance of three overwhelming forces. The British attackers met at Montreal, and there the governor of New France surrendered on September 8, 1760.

With the end of New France confirmed by the peace settlement at Paris in 1763, the French Canadians found themselves uneasy subjects of a Protestant monarch. The transition was more difficult for the native nations of the western interior, who lost much of the leverage they had maintained in a context of contending empires; without the support of the French alliance, they had reason to dread the onslaught of British settlers.

SEE ALSO *Company of New France; Empire in the Americas, French; Quebec City.*

BIBLIOGRAPHY

Eccles, W.J. *The French in North America, 1500–1783.* Markham, Ontario: Fitzhenry and Whiteside, 1998.

Greer, Allan. *The People of New France.* Toronto: University of Toronto Press, 1997.

Harris, R.C. *Historical Atlas of Canada*, 3 vols. Vol. 1, *From the Beginning to 1800.* Toronto: University of Toronto Press, 1986.

Havard, Gilles, and Vidal, Cécile. *Histoire de l'Amérique française.* Paris, Flammarion 2003.

White, Richard. *The Middle Ground: Indians, Empires and Republics in the Great Lakes Region, 1650–1815.* New York: Cambridge University Press, 1991.

Allan Greer

NEW SPAIN, THE VICEROYALTY OF

After a decade of conquest, exploration, and administrative turmoil, Spain created the viceroyalty of New Spain in 1530 in order to centralize its control over the territories of the Aztecs, Mayas, and other indigenous groups of Mesoamerica, while curbing the evolution of powerful local fiefdoms among the conquistador class. This move coincided with efforts by the nascent Spanish monarchy to unite the Iberian kingdoms and counter the power of the nobility and municipal government in the metropolis. Bureaucratic control from Spain evolved in fits and starts throughout the Habsburg period (until 1700) as the viceroyalty expanded to include all of today's Mexico, the Caribbean, most of Central America, the Philippines, and the western, southwestern, and southeastern United States.

In theory, the elaborate bureaucratic hierarchy radiated power downward from the king to the Council of the Indies, the viceroy, the *audiencias* (judicial and administrative tribunals), provincial administrators called governors, *corregidores* or *alcaldes mayors,* and municipal councils. In practice, however, this chain was often broken or circumvented under the Habsburgs, the ruling dynasty in Spain that began with Charles V in 1518 and continued through 1701. The Harsburgs' continental entanglements, distant from America in an era of slow sailing ships, and lack of capital and coercive power forced them to impart a good deal of latitude to colonial officials and elites who were in turn expected to maintain social control and remit a modicum of revenue to the crown.

In essence, a weak colonial state governed informally through mechanisms that rewarded New Spain's elites by allowing them to exploit indigenous peoples and maximize profit. Tribute, paid by Indians in commodities and labor through the institution of *encomienda*, became partly monetized in silver coinage and eventually passed from the control of conquistadors to the crown through middle-level officials called *corregidores* who took a share of the tribute they collected and extracted other resources from native communities.

Officially, however, the viceroy and other colonial officials were charged with ensuring fairness to the natives; in many cases, they executed this responsibility through an evolving body of protective legislation for these "wards" of the state. Laws were more easily disregarded by lower officials whose livelihood depended upon extracting resources from the natives, particularly in areas distant from the seat of government in Mexico City. For example, Spain never exercised much control in the northern regions of the viceroyalty; even the establishment in 1776 of a special administrative jurisdiction, the Provincias Internas, did little to bring the area under effective domination.

The civil bureaucracy had a counterpart in the Catholic Church, where spiritual conquest by Franciscans, Dominicans, Augustinians, and Jesuits played a key role in justifying conquest and incorporating Indians into the Spanish orbit. The only Spaniards theoretically permitted to live in native communities, these missionaries performed the work of conversion while they imposed Spanish practices in economic activities and daily routines. This major acculturation effort was carried out in villages, either in Mesoamerican communities that predated the conquest or in pueblos created by relocating more dispersed or demographically low populations.

The humanistic efforts of the early church to provide education and social services gradually gave way to less zealous, more avaricious priests who, along with *corregidores*, conspired to extract resources from the natives. Some clerics played a broker role, defending their flocks either out of common interests or altruism. Scholars debate the nature and extent of conversion, as well as the degree of blending of religious traditions, but by the end of the colonial period, native practices and beliefs were greatly transformed by Catholicism.

Even the most benevolent activities of the clergy could do nothing to stem the steep population decline of the Indians that resulted from epidemic diseases brought by the invaders. The rates of demographic decline varied somewhat by region and ecology, but they ranged as high as 90 percent over the first hundred years of Spanish rule. This demographic fact coincided with imperial humanitarian efforts to check extreme exploitation of Indians. In addition to outlawing Indian slavery, the crown legislated an end to the *encomienda* by the mid-sixteenth century.

Facing new extractive pressures, Indian villages used or modified Spanish institutions—*cofradías* (confraternities) and *cabildos* (town councils)—to keep resources in their communities. And through these institutions, preconquest indigenous nobility (in the cases of the Nahuas in central Mexico, Mixtecs and other groups in Oaxaca, and Mayas in southern Mexico) continued to exercise power in the Indian sphere, at least for a while. Indigenous leaders or *caciques* served as another broker between their communities and Spaniards, walking a fine line between satisfying Spanish demands and mitigating abuses to their people. Although New Spain experienced no large-scale indigenous rebellions against colonial rule, opposition played out on multiple levels throughout three centuries of Spanish rule, as illustrated by occasional uprisings in peripheral areas populated by semisedentary groups, village riots against abusive officials, and everyday forms of resistance, such as pilfering and work slowdowns.

No longer able to squeeze labor and tribute from *encomienda*, Spaniards turned first to agriculture and from the 1540s to silver mining in Zacatecas and other areas north of Mexico City. Agriculture remained the chief economic activity throughout the colonial period, although silver dominated exports. Agricultural estates (haciendas) came to dominate the production of wheat, cattle, sheep, and sugar, while Indian villages produced corn for the market, along with other mainly subsistence crops. The Spanish landlord class devised new means of acquiring labor, coerced and free, from Indians, and they imported African slaves. Haciendas and villages (albeit with considerable regional differences) coexisted in a kind synergy that allowed Spaniards to profit modestly in a chronically weak domestic market and Indian villages to preserve some autonomy and land.

Strict mercantilist policies governed silver mining and transatlantic trade; although Spain never achieved monopoly control, New Spain's silver was the motor that sustained the Habsburgs' ill-fated imperial ventures. In the seventeenth century, however, silver exports from New Spain declined. Scholars still debate the nature of this seventeenth-century "depression," but most agree that

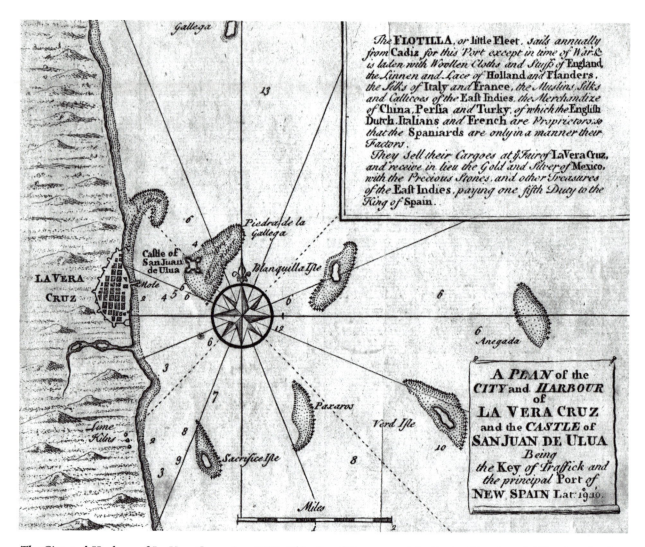

The City and Harbour of La Vera Cruz, circa 1750. This plan of Veracruz and the Castle of San Juan de Ulua describes the city as "being the key of traffick and the principal port of New Spain." Founded by the Spanish in the sixteenth century, Veracruz remains one of Mexico's most important ports. **HULTON ARCHIVE/GETTY IMAGES. REPRODUCED BY PERMISSION.**

silver production did not decline significantly, leaving open the question of what happened to the retained bullion. Did it fuel domestic, intercolonial, or Pacific trade, or did it go into conspicuous consumption? Regardless, it did not promote any profound transformation in New Spain's agrarian-based economy, and the triad of *hacendados* (proprietors of haciendas), miners, and merchants continued to monopolize wealth and power in the colony.

Over time, the Spanish, Indian, and African worlds commingled to produce biological and cultural *mestizaje*. This mixing, however, took place within an increasingly stratified patriarchal society based on race, class, and gender divisions, in which Spaniards born on the Iberian Peninsula *(peninsulares)* or in New Spain *(criollos)* lived in urban (thus civilized) spaces, and dominated politics, economic activity, and society. At the same time,

a rich baroque culture developed, blending artistic and musical traditions of the various ethnic groups.

Habsburg rule in seventeenth-century New Spain was characterized by (1) local oligarchic control of limited markets in an agrarian economy that functioned largely in the tributary mode described by Eric Wolf (1959); (2) declining silver remittances to the metropolis; and (3) forms of social control flexible enough to keep Indians, mixed groups, and blacks in their place without excessive force.

The Bourbons, a French royal family who claimed the Spanish crown in the eighteenth century, focused their sights on a more lucrative prize. They became determined to extract more wealth from New Spain by stimulating mining production, creating a more efficient bureaucracy to collect taxes, and appropriating a share of the Catholic Church's immense assets in money and rural and urban properties. These measures resulted in some success in channeling capital to the metropolis, but they were limited by persistent mercantilist structures in trade and manufacturing. In fact, metropolitan Spain never moved beyond its primarily agrarian economy and narrow tax base.

Nor did a profound capitalist transformation unfold in New Spain's agrarian economy, where domestic relations of production did not change. Market demand grew along with demographic recuperation as the Indian population doubled in the eighteenth century while non-Indian numbers tripled. Rising land values and a fall in real wages accompanied these processes. Landowners in the most dynamic regions moved aggressively to appropriate village lands, provoking protests, lawsuits, and even peasant riots. Social tensions escalated throughout the colony, exacerbated by epidemics and subsistence crises, as the Bourbons sought to limit Creole political participation, local autonomy, and popular forms of cultural and religious expression.

The crown responded with militarization and more repressive responses to opposition, upsetting the balance or "moral economy" often achieved in the give-and-take of Habsburg rule. Even elites became alienated by progressive royal usurpation of assets they had controlled, and by the imposition of peninsular bureaucrats to replace Creoles. Spain's increasing involvement and expenditures in European warfare at the end of the eighteenth century further strained Bourbon legitimacy in the eyes of the colony. Creole patriots celebrated their distinctive natural history and mixed heritage in writings that extolled the Aztec past and the Virgin of Guadalupe, Mexico's own saint.

Napoléon Bonaparte's (1769–1821) temporary removal of the Bourbon king in 1808 provoked a complex chain of events in New Spain. A popular uprising that began in 1810, directed against *peninsulares* and advocating the abolition of tribute, attracted thousands of lower-class peasants and workers. The uprising was put down by elites—not only *peninsulares* but also Creoles shocked by the prospect of a genuine social revolution. Only when Creoles decided that they could retain their power and property without provoking social upheaval did they opt for an independent Mexico in 1821. Their dominance, however, did not end the cultural resistance of rural ethnic and peasant communities to the state at the local level.

Spain had the great fortune to be one of the pioneering European empires, but its misfortune was that it acquired this empire before the emergence of the modern centralized state. Slow and difficult communication, lack of central military and bureaucratic control, and no modern coercive or persuasive means of establishing legitimacy and nationalistic beliefs hampered imperial rule. The Habsburg government had to adapt to these circumstances and, often reluctantly, did so. The crown issued voluminous laws, but these were more like exhortations, expressing what the crown would ideally want, than prescriptions. The two Habsburg centuries saw the durability of a shifting unwritten contract between the crown and colonial elites in which the latter had the tacit freedom to extract as much as they could, while honoring the legitimacy of church and state, and acknowledging that both deserved a share of the surplus produced.

The Bourbons, great error was a premature desire to create a modern, central, and dominant nation-state based on closer ties between peninsular Spain and its American colonies. They meddled constantly in previous understandings and introduced technological improvements, but never had the courage or the means to change basic social relations or modes of production. This paradox alienated sectors of the elite, and the Bourbons gradually sowed the seeds of a loss of legitimacy and the movements for independence.

SEE ALSO *Empire in the Americas, Spanish; Encomienda; Government, Colonial, in Spanish America; Haciendas in Spanish America.*

BIBLIOGRAPHY

Archer, Christon. *The Birth of Modern Mexico, 1780–1824.* Wilmington, DE: Scholarly Resources, 2003.

Brading, D. A. *The Origins of Mexican Nationalism.* Cambridge, U.K.: Cambridge University Press, 1985.

Cope, R. Douglas. *The Limits of Racial Domination: Plebeian Society in Colonial Mexico City, 1660–1720.* Madison: University of Wisconsin Press, 1994.

Farriss, Nancy. *Maya Society Under Colonial Rule: The Collective Enterprise of Survival.* Princeton, NJ: Princeton University Press, 1984.

Gibson, Charles. *The Aztecs Under Spanish Rule: A History of the Indians of the Valley of Mexico, 1519–1810.* Stanford, CA: Stanford University Press, 1964.

Hoberman, Louisa Schell. *Mexico's Merchant Elite, 1590–1660: Silver, State, and Society.* Durham, NC: Duke University Press, 1991.

Lockhart, James. *The Nahuas After the Conquest: A Social and Cultural History of the Indians of Central Mexico, Sixteenth through Eighteenth Centuries.* Stanford, CA: Stanford University Press, 1992.

MacLeod, Murdo J. "The Primitive Nation State, Delegations of Functions, and Results: Some Examples from Early Colonial Central America." In *Essays in the Political, Economic, and Social History of Colonial Latin America,* edited by Karen Spalding. Newark: University of Delaware, 1982, 53–68.

Meyer, Michael C., William L. Sherman, and Susan M. Deeds. *The Course of Mexican History,* 7th ed. New York: Oxford University Press, 2003.

Stein, Stanley J., and Barbara H. Stein. *Silver, Trade, and War: Spain and America in the Making of Early Modern Europe.* Baltimore: Johns Hopkins University Press, 2000.

Van Young, Eric. *The Other Rebellion: Popular Violence, Ideology, and the Mexican Struggle for Independence, 1810–1821.* Stanford, CA: Stanford University Press, 2001.

Weber, David J. *The Spanish Frontier in North America.* New Haven, CT: Yale University Press, 1992.

Wolf, Eric. *Sons of the Shaking Earth.* Chicago: Chicago University Press, 1959.

Susan M. Deeds

NEW YORK

New York, or New Amsterdam as it was called for the first forty years, was founded by the Dutch West India Company in 1625 as the political and commercial center for its colony of New Netherland. The settlement, however, lacked any obviously profitable enterprise except the export of furs, and growth was slow. By 1630 there were still only three hundred inhabitants in the entire colony.

Development was also restricted by the company's monopoly over the economy and political life. New Amsterdam was governed by an unelected mayor chosen by the senior company official, the Director General. Some liberalization occurred in the economic sphere after 1639, which encouraged a trickle of immigrants to the town, though most were not of Dutch descent, being Scottish, Flemish, Walloon (from southern Belgium and adjacent parts of France), and in a few cases Jews. Some Africans also arrived, mostly as slaves, so that New Amsterdam from its earliest days was a multicultural society. By 1660 the city had a population of thirteen hundred.

The conquest of New Amsterdam by the English in 1664 resulted in few immediate changes. Affairs remained in the hands of a small elite who controlled not only the commerce of the town but most of the land outside. The city could not in any case flourish while its hinterland remained open to attack from the French and from Indians, and its divisions and weakness were cruelly exposed during the Glorious Revolution of 1689, when the city and province were split by factional disputes during the governorship of Jacob Leisler (1649–1691).

As a result, emigration to the area remained modest. Nevertheless, a healthy trade in flour and wheat developed, so that after 1700 New York's merchants were able to challenge the hegemony of Boston for the North American coastal and Caribbean trades. Commerce also stimulated other activities, and by the middle of the eighteenth century the city had twelve thousand inhabitants. However, New York's greatest period of expansion began with the conquest of Canada in 1760, which finally removed the threat of invasion. With its fine harbor and access to the interior, the city rapidly caught up with Philadelphia as the most important center for finance, commerce, and immigration in English-speaking North America.

SEE ALSO *Dutch West India Company; Empire in the Americas, Dutch; Thirteen Colonies, British North America.*

BIBLIOGRAPHY

Archdeacon, Thomas, J. *New York City, 1664–1710: Conquest and Change.* Ithaca, NY: Cornell University Press, 1976.

Barreveld, Dirk. *From New Amsterdam to New York: The Founding of New York by the Dutch in July 1625.* San Jose, CA: Writers Club Press, 2001.

Goodfriend, Joyce D. *Before the Melting Pot: Society and Culture in Colonial New York City, 1664–1730.* Princeton, NJ: Princeton University Press, 1991.

Harris, Leslie M. *In the Shadow of Slavery: African Americans in New York City, 1626–1863.* Chicago: University of Chicago Press, 2004.

Richard Middleton

NEW ZEALAND

New Zealand is an island country in the South Pacific, within the Polynesian cultural region. New Zealand is about two-thirds the size of California. The country consists of two main islands of varied topography, with high mountain ranges, volcanoes, and agriculturally productive plains. The capital is Wellington, and Auckland is the largest city.

The indigenous Polynesian inhabitants, the Māori, arrived in New Zealand about one thousand years ago, probably from the Tahiti area. They brought a typical Polynesian culture, as well as many important food plants. Within a few hundred years they were well established on the warmer North Island, with many villages and forts. The colder South Island received only limited settlement.

The first European to sight New Zealand was probably the Dutch explorer Abel Janszoon Tasman (ca. 1603–1659) in 1642, but finding the Māori hostile he did not land. It was not until 1769 that the British captain James Cook (1728–1779) explored the islands, landed, and met the Māori. Within the next seventy years both the British and French established small settlements and traded with the Māori; missionaries also arrived and had complex effects on the indigenous population.

The British government, prompted by unregulated settlement and French and American interest in the region, formally concluded a treaty with the Māori to annex New Zealand and join it to the New South Wales colony in Australia. The Treaty of Waitangi, signed by Māori leaders in 1840, granted the British sovereignty but guaranteed Māori land rights. In practice, however, the treaty favored the settlers, and the Māori gradually lost control of most of their territories.

British settlement continued apace during the nineteenth century, and settlers came to outnumber the Māori. Māori resistance to the loss of their lands culminated in a series of wars between the Māori and settlers in the 1860s. Disagreements among the Māori resulted in the British gaining the upper hand, and peace was fully restored in 1881. By then the country was already self-governing.

British society in New Zealand came to resemble that of the mother country, with a pastoral, wool-based economy and British political institutions replacing indigenous ones. New Zealand sent troops to support the British in World War I (1914–18), giving the country a sense of its own distinctiveness. After World War II (1939–45), New Zealand became a colonial power in its own right with the acquisition of the former German colony of Samoa, as well as other Polynesian territories. Immigration to New Zealand from other parts of Polynesia and from Asia also began to change the cultural makeup of the society.

Since the late 1960s, there has been a resurgence of Māori cultural pride and a revival of the Māori language. The Māori name for New Zealand, Aotearoa, meaning "the land of the long cloud" (but technically referring only to the North Island), is now frequently used. Māori have also pressed for restoration of lands illegally seized during the colonial era and for financial compensation. The New Zealand government is now negotiating a series of settlements with Māori groups. Some of these claims, such as that of the Ngāi Tahu on the South Island, have already been settled, and claimants have received land and resource rights and financial compensation.

SEE ALSO *Black bird Labor Trade; Empire, British, in Asia and Pacific; Exploration, the Pacific.*

BIBLIOGRAPHY

Denoon, Donald, Philippa Mein-Smith, and Marivic Wyndham. *A History of Australia, New Zealand, and the Pacific.* Oxford: Blackwell, 2000.

Durie, Mason. *Te Mana, Te Kawanatanga: The Politics of Maori Self-Determination.* New York and Auckland, New Zealand: Oxford University Press, 1998.

King, Michael. *The Penguin History of New Zealand.* Auckland, New Zealand: Penguin, 2003.

Ward, Alan. *An Unsettled History: Treaty Claims in New Zealand Today.* Wellington, New Zealand: Bridget Williams, 1999.

Michael Pretes

NKRUMAH, KWAME
1909–1972

Kwame Nkrumah, the first head of state of independent Ghana, was born on September 21, 1909, in Nkroful in what was then the Western Province of the Gold Coast, later to become Ghana. He was a Pan-Africanist, a nationalist, and a crusader for decolonization whose political ideologies and cultural canons not only empowered Ghanaians, but also molded the antiracist and anticolonial ideas of other Africans, including those in the diaspora.

Nkrumah was the prime minister of Ghana from 1957 to 1960 and the president from 1960 to 1966. No matter how he is assessed, there can be no doubt that he was a visionary whose ideas and achievements were far ahead of his time. Indeed, so long as there is a history of African nationalism and decolonization to be told, Nkrumah would forever remain the great frontispiece that unfolds that epic.

Nkrumah was self-disciplined and lived an ascetic life. His father was a goldsmith and his mother was a trader. He attended the local Catholic primary school in Half Assini, his father's community, then qualified in 1926 to attend the Prince of Wales College at Achimota, near the colonial capital of Accra. Having being trained as a teacher at Achimota, he taught at a Catholic primary school and later became the headmaster of a school in Axim, near his place of birth. Nkrumah inspired his students by forming literary clubs and academic societies for them.

In 1935 he traveled to the United States to study. He earned a bachelor of science degree from Lincoln University in 1939 and a bachelor of theology from Lincoln Theological Seminary in 1942. In 1945 he obtained master of science degrees in education and philosophy from the University of Pennsylvania. He also took courses at the University of Pennsylvania toward a doctoral degree in philosophy, but moved to London in 1945 to study law. Overall, Nkrumah was a dedicated intellectual devoted to the cause of African liberation. A voracious reader of socialist and Marxist literature, Nkrumah wrote some fifteen books that diagnosed the African condition with timeless prescriptions.

Nkrumah's sojourn overseas is crucial to understanding his maturation as a Pan-Africanist and a vigorous anticolonialist. While in the United States, he experienced firsthand a systemic racism that shaped his views about white domination. He experienced acute poverty, and did several menial jobs to survive. He also acquired organizational abilities when he joined the African Students Association, which sought to empower black students.

Nkrumah sharpened his oratorical skills by preaching in African-American churches and speaking at gatherings. Involved in the West African National Secretariat in London, he became acquainted with the larger quest among Africans for decolonization. He also joined the socialist and Marxist clubs and attended lectures on political ideologies, especially socialism, at the London School of Economics and Political Science.

Nkrumah became involved in the Pan-Africanist movement under the authoritative leadership of W. E. B. Du Bois (1868–1963). Nkrumah served as a co-secretary of the last major Pan-African meeting, held in Manchester, England, in 1945, and, with the West Indian socialist and anticolonialist George Padmore (1903–1959), Nkrumah drafted the declaration of decolonization that was issued by the conference. He also interacted with future African leaders, including Dr. Hastings Kamuzu Banda (1898–1997), Kenneth Kaunda (b. 1924), Jomo Kenyatta (1891–1978), Joshua Nkomo (1917–1999), Juluis Nyerere (1922–1999), and countless others. These undertakings and peer associations convinced Nkrumah about the need for African liberation. By 1947 he had helped produce a number of Pan-Africanist publications, including the *African Interpreter*, *New African*, and *Pan African*, using them to agitate for African liberation.

During the post–World War II period, revolutionary nationalism gripped Africans as much as it had shaped the consciousness of peoples under European imperialism. In the Gold Coast, nationalism crystallized into the formation of a political party known as the United Gold Coast Convention (UGCC), led by Dr. J. B. Danquah (1895–1965). The leadership of the UGCC invited Nkrumah to become the general secretary of the party. As a result, Nkrumah returned to the Gold Coast on December 10, 1947, establishing a turning point in African nationalism and liberation. On January 20, 1948, Nkrumah was appointed the general secretary of the UGCC.

In 1948 several ex-servicemen, protesting for end-of-service benefits, were shot and killed, leading to several days of anticolonial protests throughout the Gold Coast. Panic-stricken, the British colonial government passed the Riot Act on March 1, 1948, with Governor Gerald Creasy declaring a state of emergency. Eleven days later, Nkrumah and other leaders of the UGCC were arrested

and sent to the faraway Northern Territories, where they were detained until April 12, when Creasy bowed to popular demands and released them.

Within a year, ideological problems arose between Nkrumah and the UGCC. Nkrumah wanted to shift the reformist and elitist bent of the UGCC toward a path of revolutionary politics that would involve and empower the masses to seek the complete overthrow of colonial rule. Nkrumah also wanted immediate self-government, unlike the UGCC, which favored a gradual pace toward independence. Consequently, on June 12, 1949, Nkrumah broke away and formed the Convention People's Party (CPP).

The CPP used a series of strategic nonviolent actions, including strikes, boycotts, and protests, which Nkrumah referred to as "Positive Action." He also established the *Evening News,* a newspaper that became the voice of the party, enabling the CPP to engage in populist politics. The CPP was a broad-based party: it successfully recruited women, rural dwellers, and the youth, groups that had been marginalized by the elitist posturing of the UGCC. Nkrumah's formation of the Committee of Youth Organization (CYO) on February 26, 1949, energized young people throughout the country who embraced his populist ideas.

Meanwhile, the outcome of the 1948 revolution forced the British government to rethink the political future of the Gold Coast. It appointed A. K. Watson to investigate the revolution and make recommendations. After a thorough investigation, the Watson Commission recommended that a constitution be drafted as a prelude to independence. The drafting of the constitution was chaired by Justice Henley Coussey, a highly respected jurist of the Gold Coast High Court.

On November 7, 1949, the Coussey Committee released its constitutional report. Nkrumah found the committee's work to be woefully inadequate because its prescription for self-government was limited. Disappointed, Nkrumah organized a nation-wide strike, scheduled for January 1, 1950. Fearing the whirlwind of populist action being unleashed by Nkrumah, the colonial government arrested about two hundred CPP and CYO leaders.

Even though Nkrumah was in prison, the CPP won a landslide victory in municipal council elections held in 1950 in the principalities of Accra, Cape Coast, and Kumasi. Consequently, Governor Noble Arden-Clarke freed Nkrumah and others, and Nkrumah became the leader of government business in a government dominated by Africans. Nkrumah became the prime minister in 1952. He led the Gold Coast to independence in 1957, attaining a republican status in 1960.

Apart from his role as the agent of Gold Coast independence, Nkrumah championed the liberation of the continent by organizing a series of Pan-African meetings in Accra. These were attended by future African leaders, including Robert Mugabe (b. 1924) of Zimbabwe. Nkrumah wanted to unify the continent into a sovereign state. But the emergent neocolonialism and exclusivist nationalism of some African leaders derailed his ideal of a united Africa. All the same, he was able to forge organic political unity with Guinea in 1959 and Mali in 1960; he was also instrumental in the formation of the Organization of African Unity in 1963.

Clad in kente cloth and a *batakari* smock, powerful symbols of Ghanaian culture, Nkrumah's ideas of cultural renaissance incubated the popular ideologies of "African personality," "Black is Beautiful," and "I am Black and Proud"; indeed, he inspired the empowerment and re-conscientization of blacks all over the globe. Apart from his autobiography, Nkrumah wrote a number of books that deal with the postcolonial political economy of Ghana and Africa as a whole and offer a cultural prognosis of the African condition in the context of neocolonialism. That Nkrumah's Ghana became a site of political pilgrimage in the 1960s is not in dispute. Overnight, his political magnetism attracted stalwart pilgrims, including W. E. B. Du Bois, Malcolm X (1925–1965), and Martin Luther King (1929–1968), to Ghana.

Nkrumah is also the "father" of Ghana in the sense that he provided Ghana with infrastructure that no Ghanaian leader has been able to match. Without Nkrumah's foresight, Ghana would be a provincial backwater today. Nkrumah built several industries based on the country's natural resources. To harness the rapid industrialization of a newly independent Ghana, he built the industrial township of Tema and the dam at Akosombo to supply power and water. Numerous roads were constructed to link different parts of the country, and the country's colonial-era railway system was improved to facilitate the transportation of produce, especially cocoa, from the interior to the coastal ports.

Nkrumah also built hundreds of educational institutions, including elementary schools, secondary or high schools, teacher training colleges, technical schools, and research institutes for the sciences and humanities. He established two new universities—the Kwame Nkrumah University of Science and Technology and the University of Cape Coast—and expanded the University of Ghana. In order to make education universal in Ghana, Nkrumah provided free education for the inhabitants of the Northern Region, an area that had suffered from underdevelopment during the colonial period. Nkrumah also established scholarships for overseas higher education to train personnel to assist in the country's educational

endeavors. In addition, adult and civic education were introduced nationwide to complement literacy and the civic duties of the citizenry. Mobile vans fitted with public-address systems also disseminated information on public health, etiquette, and social mores.

Historians disagree on the events that led to Nkrumah's overthrow. Certainly, his political demise was due in part to his authoritarian tendencies, including his declaration of a one-party state and the imprisonment of his political opponents. This tendency is best exemplified by Nkrumah's response to his opponents efforts immediately after independence in 1957 to either kill him or remove him from power. Nkrumah used state instruments to marginalize them, an action that troubled a section of the Ghanaian population. In addition, his internationalization of Pan-Africanism, his outspoken championing of socialism, and his political flirtations with the Soviet Union at the peak of the Cold War helped bring about his political downfall.

On February 24, 1966, a group of elite officers of the Ghanaian armed forces and police—sponsored by the American Central Intelligence Agency (CIA)—staged a coup while Nkrumah was in Vietnam attempting to broker peace between warring Vietnamese factions. After the coup, Nkrumah lived in exile in neighboring Guinea, where he spent his time writing about anti-colonialism and neocolonialism. Afflicted with cancer, he sought medical help in Romania, where he died in 1972.

SEE ALSO *Pan-African Congress; Pan-Africanism.*

BIBLIOGRAPHY

Arhin, Kwame. *The Life and Work of Kwame Nkrumah.* Trenton, NJ: Africa World Press, 1993.

Birmingham, David. *Kwame Nkrumah: Father of African Nationalism.* Athens: Ohio University Press, 1998.

Davidson, Basil. *Black star: A view of the Life and Times of Kwame Nkrumah.* Boulder: Westview Press, 1989.

Nkrumah, Kwame. *Ghana: Autobiography of Kwame Nkrumah.* London: Panaf, 1973.

Nkrumah, Kwame. *Consciencism: Philosophy and Ideology for Decolonization.* New York: Monthly Review Press, 1970.

Rathbone, Richard. *Nkrumah and the Chiefs: The Politics of Chieftaincy in Ghana, 1951–60.* Athens, OH: Ohio University Press, 2000.

Kwabena Akurang-Parry

NORTH AFRICA

The modern historiography of North Africa is dominated by controversy over European colonization in the nineteenth and twentieth centuries, which has colored the view of the past 3,000 years. Beginning with the French capture of Algiers in 1830, this colonization was the second such wave in modern times. The first began with the capture of Ceuta by the Portuguese in 1415; it followed on from the Reconquista, the annexation of Muslim Spain by the Christian kingdoms of Portugal, Castile, and Aragon that was completed in 1492 with the fall of Granada to the newly united kingdom of Spain.

By 1492 the Portuguese were in possession of Ceuta and Tangier, together with Arzila and Larache on the Atlantic coast of northern Morocco. By 1515 they had occupied Agadir, Agouz, Safi, Mazagan, and Azemmour on the coast of southern Morocco, whereas the Spaniards had taken Melila, Mers el-Kébir, Oran, Bijaya, and Tripoli along the Mediterranean coast, and garrisoned the port of Algiers; Tunis was captured in 1535. By 1575, however, only Mazagan remained to the Portuguese in southern Morocco, whereas Spain had lost everything east of Oran. By 1700 Tangier, Arzila, and Larache had been evacuated; Mazagan, Mers el-Kébir, and Oran would be evacuated as well by 1800. By 1830 only Ceuta and Melila were left to Spain.

The motives of Portugal and Spain were various. In the case of Portugal, crusading zeal served the purpose of trade, as the Moroccan ports became links in the chain that led to sub-Saharan Africa and the Indies. In the case of Spain, such zeal served the purpose of defense against the counter-crusade of Muslim pirates operating out of North Africa. Both the Iberian conquests and the piracy were symptomatic of the weakness of central government by the Wattasids, Ziyanids, and Hafsids, the dynasties ruling Morocco from Fez, western Algeria from Tlemcen, and eastern Algeria, Tunisia, and Tripolitania from Tunis. Lack of control of their largely tribal territories exposed the coast to invasion while leaving resistance to the people. It was through such resistance that the political vacuum was eventually filled, in Morocco by a Mahdist movement that reunited the country under the Saadian dynasty. Along the Mediterranean coast, the feat was performed by pirates from the Ottoman Aegean. 'Aruj (d. 1518), his brother Barbarossa (d. 1546), and their successors not only drove the Spaniards from Algiers, Bijaya, Tunis, and Tripoli, but as admirals of the Ottoman fleet, conquered the region for the Ottoman Empire. By the end of the sixteenth century the modern political divisions of North Africa had been established with the formation to the east of Morocco of three Ottoman provinces ruled from Algiers, Tunis, and Tripoli. By the beginning of the nineteenth century, all three were effectively independent under rulers of Turkish origin.

This enduring political achievement, that stemmed from the conflict with Spain and Portugal and provided the framework for the subsequent colonization of North Africa by France, Italy, and Spain, meanwhile, introduced 200 years of dependence upon Europe, both as an enemy and as a trading partner. As an enemy, Christian Europe provided rich pickings for state-sponsored piracy in the Mediterranean, where the so-called Barbary corsairs ran a profitable business in raids upon European shipping and European coasts for captives held to ransom and goods that were frequently sold back to European merchants. In Morocco, the expulsion from Spain in 1610 of the Moriscos, Muslims whose forcible conversion to Christianity had never been accepted as genuine, led to the creation of a pirate base at Salé, from which the so-called Sallee rovers operated in the Atlantic as far as the British Isles and Iceland. By the eighteenth century, however, such piracy was increasingly regulated by diplomacy, whereby various flags were exempted from attack in return for tribute. Growing numbers of European merchants were represented by consuls, whereas North African Jews with European connections acted as agents for the sultans, deys, beys, and pashas—the rulers of these so-called Barbary states. Morocco's capitals were inland and, for many years under the 'Alawite dynasty that succeeded the Saadian in the middle of the seventeenth century, trade with the infidel was restricted. But in 1760 the port of Mogador (now known as Essaouira) was created for the export of grain to provide the sultan with much-needed revenue.

North Africa thus lay on a frontier between two civilizations. In the eyes of Thomas Shaw (1694–1751), chaplain to the English consulate at Algiers in the 1720s, the Ottoman provinces were quite well governed, but socially and economically reminiscent of the primitive world of the Bible. Scientifically they had fallen far below the standards of mediaeval Islam, whereas Roman civilization was a thing of the past. William Lempriere (d. 1834), traveling from Gibraltar to Marrakesh in the 1780s, saw mainly desolation and despotism. These themes acquired a fresh significance in the nineteenth century, when the sense of European superiority was translated into conquest and colonization. The bombardment of Algiers by the British fleet in 1816 was a statement that piracy could no longer be tolerated, and that the North African states were no longer free to act in defiance of Europe. In relation to Europe, however, their rights were at a discount. When the dey of Algiers sued the French government for payment of debts outstanding from the supply of grain to France in the 1790s, the case gave rise to a diplomatic incident. In 1827 the flicking of the French consul with the flywhisk of an angry dey became the justification for the French capture of Algiers in 1830. As an expedient to keep the government of Charles X (1757–1836; King of France 1824–1830) in power it failed; but as a triumph of civilization over barbarism it became the justification for the conquest and colonization of the dey's dominions under the new name of Algeria.

Whatever it meant in practice, this notion of a civilizing mission sustained the French Empire in North Africa almost to the end. It depended upon a definition of the barbarism it was designed to overcome, a mental exercise that began in 1830 and continued down to 1950. Blame for the perceived backwardness of the region was variously apportioned between the Turks and Oriental despotism in general, Arab nomads who had ruined the agriculture of Roman Africa, and Islam—a religion that had stupefied the population. The thesis found its final expression after World War II (1939–1945), when the formation of the French Union generated a series of publications to which Eugène Guernier (b. 1882), editor of *L'Encyclopédie Coloniale et Maritime*, contributed *La Berbérie, l'Islam et la France*. This was a history of North Africa in which the native inhabitants, the Berbers, of the same race and customs as the Spaniards, and thus completely different from the Arabs, had profited from Roman civilization and Christianity, but succumbed to poverty and superstition under Islam; the task of France had been to return the land and people to the European fold.

Guernier's version of North African history is a colonial myth. The state of affairs in 1830, however, remains contentious: a comparatively prosperous economy and society going its own way in its own time; a backward economy and society structurally unable to progress; or one whose natural development had been inhibited by a long history of confrontation with external enemies. What is important is not the weakness of the states created in the sixteenth century, but their durability. Over the centuries their governments had taken increasing control of their territories and inhabitants while becoming ever more firmly identified with their societies. It was this structure that the French took over and adapted.

They did not do so without destruction. Like the Portuguese and the Spaniards before them, the French in Algeria encountered the opposition of tribal peoples left without central government by the removal of the Turkish elite. Within ten years, confrontation had escalated into war for the interior of the country with the Mahdist leader Abdelkader (1808–1883), whose defeat and final surrender in 1847 was only accomplished by a huge army and the ruthless devastation of the countryside. Invasion of the mountains of Great Kabylia completed the conquest in 1857, but major revolts down to 1871 entailed further loss of life and livelihood. In 1848

Alexis deTocqueville (1805–1859) declared that the country had been depopulated and its civilization ruined.

However true, his statement was an attack on the policies of the monarchy of Louis Philippe (1773–1850, King of France 1830–1848) by a partisan of the Second Republic, symptomatic of a conflict over Algeria that continued under the Second Empire and the Third Republic. In that conflict, the ideal of liberty, equality, and fraternity mingled with the concept of a colony of settlement by immigrants from the mother country and the alternative vision of a colony of exploitation by capital investment and technical assistance. The battle over these principles was waged between Paris, the army, and the settlers within the framework of the Constitution of 1848, which declared Algeria to be an integral part of France and subject to its laws. Within that framework, the slogans of assimilation and association acquired different meanings. In principle, the assimilation of the country into the departmental and communal structure of government in France required the integration of the conquered population into the French nation; but for the settlers it applied only to themselves as citizens distinct from native subjects. To the Saint-Simonians in the army under the Second Empire, believing in progress through technology, association meant partnership with the native population; but to the settlers it meant apartheid.

The outcome was a series of compromises that favored the settlers after the establishment of the Third Republic in 1870. The native population was given the vote in local elections on a limited franchise with minority representation; most, however, were placed in so-called mixed communes under administrators rather than mayors. As Muslims they were declared to be subjects and not citizens unless they agreed to live entirely under French as distinct from Islamic family law, while as subjects they were penalized by a special criminal code. A further anomaly was the continued separation of Algeria from France under a governor-general, reinforced by the creation of a representative assembly of the settlers in 1903. As full citizens, this pursued their civilizing mission at the expense of the indigenous majority, acquiring land for the production of wine and grain and raising taxes for their own benefit. The Muslim population was increasingly impoverished. Attempts by Paris to rectify a system so out of line with metropolitan France came to nothing.

Saint-Simonianism may have failed in Algeria, but the ideal of association lived on in a second generation of imperialists who believed in the creation of a French empire to compensate for defeat in the Franco-Prussian War of 1870–1971. In a climate of international rivalry, they acquired Tunisia in 1881 and Morocco in 1912, but on terms very different from Algeria. So, too, was the political philosophy. The occupation of Tunisia, ostensibly to regulate the country's debts and prevent tribal incursions into Algeria, was followed in 1883 by the establishment of a protectorate over a theoretically sovereign state in which a French resident-general directed the government on behalf of the bey. In Morocco, the French gained control of the finances of the country by the Act of Algeciras (1906) before establishing a French and Spanish protectorate by the Treaty of Fez in 1912. A French resident-general was installed together with a Spanish commissioner for a Spanish zone along the Mediterranean coast, and a Committee of Control for Tangier. In Tunisia the first resident, Paul Cambon (1843–1924), set out to complete the reform of government begun by the beys and their ministers over the past fifty years, by inviting the Tunisians to participate in the modernization of their country. In Morocco the struggle of the sultans, defeated by France at the Battle of Isly in 1845 and by Spain at Tetouan in 1860, to bring the tribal people of the mountains and the desert under their administration, while losing control of foreign trade to European merchants and consuls, was taken over by the new French resident, Marshal Louis-Herbert-Gonzalve Lyautey (1854–1934). Although, as in Algeria, this meant a campaign of conquest that culminated in a major war in the Spanish zone in 1926, Lyautey aimed to win the support of the Moroccans by promotion of the sultan as the embodiment of state and society. In both Tunisia and Morocco, this combination of separate statehood with paternalism was a victory for association over assimilation.

The partition of Morocco between France and Spain extended into the Sahara, where Spain was allocated the tiny enclave of Ifni and a narrow strip to the north of a line that fixed the Moroccan frontier at 28° N. To the south along the coast was the Spanish Sahara, while to the east was an immense extension of Algeria that began with the occupation of the oasis of Touat in 1900 and ended with that of Tindouf in 1934. Morocco was thus excluded from the Sahara, although its southeastern frontier with Algeria remained undefined. Meanwhile the Italians invaded Libya in 1911. Resistance in what had been an Ottoman province since 1835 was nevertheless so fierce that by 1921 the Italians had conceded autonomy to the Sanusiyya order in Cyrenaica, and constitutional representation in Tripolitania. Such liberalism was terminated in 1922 by the Fascists, who for the next ten years fought the Sanusiyya in Cyrenaica before undertaking a program of settlement by land distribution on the French model.

Ironically, by the 1930s the French had abandoned such a program not only in Algeria, but in Tunisia and Morocco, where it had been introduced in the 1900s and 1920s. The economy of the three countries now depended upon the export of wine, grain, and olive oil, together with phosphates and iron ore. But the economies of scale required by the overseas market had put an end to the original vision of a countryside densely populated by European farmers. The settler population of Algeria, now native to the country, had moved into the cities, leaving their original smallholdings to be amalgamated into large estates. The result, said Jacques Berque (1910–1995), was a land without people, and in the case of the Muslim population, a people without land. Across North Africa that population was outgrowing its means of subsistence, leaving the countryside for work in France, and like the settlers, crowding into the cities. This transformation of society was the background to the advance of North Africa to independence.

Agitation started in Algeria and Tunisia before World War II in Morocco during the 1930s. It began as an extension of the French debate over assimilation and association, but ended with a demand for independence. In Tunisia and Morocco it called on the protectorate to prepare the nation for eventual independence in the spirit of association; in Algeria it called for citizenship in the spirit of assimilation. But in 1934 the Destour or Party of the Constitution founded by the Young Tunisians in 1920 was eclipsed by the Neo-Destour, a mass party aiming at immediate independence. In 1943 the Moroccans followed suit with the Istiqlal or Independence Party. In pursuit of assimilation, the Young Algerians concentrated on the question of citizenship, against the demand by Islamic scholars in the 1930s for the association of the Muslim population with the French on equal terms. But both demands were overtaken by the formation in 1936 of the Algerian People's Party, which, like the Neo-Destour, called for independence.

The French treated this agitation as the work of an unrepresentative minority of basically loyal subjects. But the transformation of traditional society accomplished by colonization gave the new nationalists new supporters, and their movements continued to grow. In Algeria assimilation was gradually implemented with an extension of the franchise leading up to the concession of citizenship in 1947 and its final introduction in 1959. Reprisals for the killing of Europeans at Setif in 1945, however, escalated into war after the outbreak of rebellion in 1954. The impatience of extremists and the military reaction to their terrorism cut short the slow but steady progress toward a peaceful compromise. It precipitated the end of French Algeria in 1962, when the Europeans refused counter-assimilation into an independent Algerian nation, and left *en bloc*. The war likewise cut short French resistance to the independence of Tunisia and Morocco, which became sovereign in 1956.

At independence, the French version of North African history gave way to a nationalist account of liberation from oppression, rapidly clouded by the disappointment of conflicting hopes for democracy, socialism, and Islam under the rule of autocratic kings and presidents. In Algeria dissatisfaction with the performance of the one-party state culminated in Islamist terrorism during the 1990s, but in slow progress toward plural democracy in the only country to have had some experience of representative government throughout the colonial period. Stability has nevertheless been maintained by regimes working through parliamentary institutions to complete the modernization of government in the colonial period, and provide a secure framework for national politics. In Libya, where Britain took over from Italy after World War II, the monarchy set up by the United Nations in 1950 relied on British and American assistance until 1969, the military coup of the anti-Western Colonel Muammar Gaddafi (b. 1942) and a more lasting constitutional experiment in nation-building.

Even in the case of Libya, however, the ties with Europe have been unbreakable. Not only has Europe remained North Africa's main trading partner, taking oil and gas from Algeria and Libya and sending tourists to Morocco and Tunisia, but since independence the flow of immigrants from Europe into North Africa has been reversed by the emigration of North Africans to Europe to escape the poverty of a rapidly growing population. The problem of assimilation has thus been exported to metropolitan France and its neighbors, whereas North Africa has benefited in receiving remittances from these émigrés, from technical assistance and trade agreements. Economic growth, however, has yet to outstrip the rise in population, which poses a problem for Europe as well as North Africa. But while North Africa might welcome association with the European Union, the sense of a cultural barrier remains, and Europe has yet to agree on a constructive approach to removing it.

SEE ALSO *Missionaries, Christian, Africa; Nationalism, Africa; North Africa, European Presence in; Scramble for Africa.*

BIBLIOGRAPHY

Abun-Nasr, J.M. *A History of the Maghrib in the Islamic Period.* Cambridge, MA, and New York: Cambridge University Press, 1987.

Ageron, Charles Robert. *Modern Algeria: A History from 1830 to the Present.* Translated by Michael Brett. London: Hurst & Co., 1991.

Brett, M., and E. Fentress. *The Berbers.* Oxford: Blackwell, 1996.

Guernier, E. La *Berbérie, l'Islam et la France.* Editions de l'Union Française, Paris, 1950.

Hermassi, E. *Leadership and National Development in North Africa: A Comparative Study.* Berkeley: University of California Press, 1972.

Hess, A.C. *The Forgotten Frontier: A History of the Sixteenth-Century Ibero-African Frontier.* Chicago: University of Chicago Press, 1978.

Laroui, Abdallah. *The History of the Maghrib.* Princeton, NJ: Princeton University Press, 1977.

Le Gall, M., and K. Perkins, eds. *The Maghrib in Question.* Austin: University of Texas Press, 1997.

Morocco: From Empire to Independence. Oxford: Oneworld, 2003.

Pennell, C.R. *Morocco since 1830: A History.* New York: New York University Press, 2000.

Perkins, J. *A History of Modern Tunisia.* New York: Cambridge University Press, 2004.

Ruedy, J. *Modern Algeria. The Origins and Development of a Nation.* Bloomington: Indiana University Press, 1992.

Segrè, C. G., *Fourth Shore: The Italian Colonization of Libya.* Chicago: University of Chicago Press, 1974.

Thomson, A. *Barbary and Enlightenment. European Attitudes towards the Maghreb in the Eighteenth Century.* Leiden, Netherlands; New York: Brill, 1987.

Michael Brett

NORTH AFRICA, EUROPEAN PRESENCE IN

Africa, located between Europe and Asia, has been of strategic importance to world powers throughout history. Additionally, the Red Sea was an important artery of commerce and a highway for the spread of ideas. European presence in North Africa dates back to the invasions of Alexander, Caesar, and Ptolemy during Greco-Roman times. Closer to our time, European presence in North Africa dates to the fifteenth century, when Spain established a hold on the North African coast and occupied Mellila (1494) and Ceuta (1580). Spain again invaded Morocco in 1859–1860. European presence in the nineteenth century altered the status quo and history of North Africa.

European presence in North Africa impinged on the practice of Islam, African tradition, and various forms of social practice. It resulted in conflict between local peoples and colonial administrations. Resistance to colonial domination exacerbated racism and discrimination against Muslims. Not surprisingly, a disparate group of North Africans (both religious and secular), led by an educated elite, revolted against the European presence. Resistance was sustained and fierce, especially in reaction to the exploitation of labor and resources, racism, and control over North African economies.

EUROPEAN POLICIES

Europeans controlled the most fertile land in North Africa. In Algeria, for example, 26,153 European families owned 2,345,666 hectares (5,796,375 acres) of land, while 630,732 Muslim families farmed 7,349,100 hectares (18,160,361 acres). Despite revolts in Kabylia (1871) and other areas (1880s), French colonists increasingly displaced Algerians from the coastal plains and valleys to the Algerian highlands and steppes. The French also imposed a 3 percent direct tax on Algerians, who did not benefit from tax revenue despite harsh punishments for late payments. In addition, North Africans were subject to the *indigenat* laws, which required Muslims to carry passes.

Nationalist agitation began before the onset of decolonization, but accelerated after World War II. The various European powers recruited over 160,000 North and West Africans to fight in the war. France's defeat in 1940 and the Allied invasion of North Africa in 1942 weakened the aura of French invincibility and emboldened nationalists. In the Maghreb—Algeria, Morocco, and Tunisia—agitation for independence intensified after 1942. The nationalist struggle was long, violent, and bloody, as the substantial, often violently racist European populations were determined to stay in power at any cost.

ALGERIA

France invaded Algeria in the time of Charles X (1830) and that invasion culminated in a long, brutal war that Frantz Fanon chronicles in his classic *Wretched of the Earth* (1961). The European population in North Africa helped supply France's wartime needs during World War I and maintained its political control after World War II. By 1940, Europeans owned 2.7 million hectares (5.94 million acres) of land as compared to the 1.6 million hectares (3.5 million acres) they had owned in 1890. European immigrants, who made up 2 percent of the population, controlled one-third of all profitable agricultural land. Generally, both settlers and metropole largely ignored Algerian demands for equal rights, and whatever limited land reforms the French government initiated were blocked by the powerful Algerian settler population.

Different Algerian leaders advocated different approaches to decolonization. Ferhat Abbas (who from 1922 to 1926 published articles denouncing colonialism) favored federation with France. However, when Sheikh Ahmed Ibn Badis (founder of a nationalist reformist religious movement in 1928) died in 1940 and Massali al-Hajj (leader of the Parti du Peuple Algérien) was imprisoned, Abbas became more militant.

Ferhat Abbas sent appeals (such as the *Manifesto of the Algerian People*) to Marshal Pétain (governor-general of Algeria, 1941) and the American envoy, Richard Murphy, demanding agrarian reform, education, participation in government, and independence. France's Fourth Republic initiated some limited reform but the French administration in Algeria thwarted all efforts.

Charles de Gaulle's initiatives of March 1944, which aimed to give equal rights to Algerians, curtail discriminatory legislation, and open up civilian and military careers to all, were resisted by the French settlers. Frustration led Algerians to form new organizations, such as the Friends of the Declaration of Independence (Amis du Manifeste de la Liberté or AML, founded in Sétif in 1944), to carry on the nationalist struggle. In 1945 the Algerian Peoples' Party (Parti du Peuple Algérien or PPA) rejected federation with France and from May 1, 1945, anti-French demonstrations occurred in Sétif, leading to serious clashes on May 8, 1945. The brutal tactics police used to suppress the demonstrations incensed the crowds, which attacked Setif's armed garrison. Disturbances spread to Annaba, Gulma, and parts of Oran, and in reprisal the French bombed villages by air and sea. Abbas and other leaders were blamed for the disturbances and arrested and Sétif became the symbol of the Algerian nationalist struggle.

In 1945 Algerians secured the right to elect thirteen representatives to the French Constituent Assembly. The following year, Abbas, freed from jail, organized the Democratic Union for the Independence of Algeria (Union Démocratique du Manifeste Algérien or UDMA), which sought to make Algeria a republic federated with France. The UDMA won eleven out of thirteen seats in France's Constituent Assembly. Also in 1946, Massali al-Hajj launched another party, the Mouvement pour le Triomphe des Libertés Démocratiques (Movement for the Triumph of Democratic Liberties or MTLD), to agitate for an Algerian national assembly and French withdrawal from Algeria. The Fourth French Republic responded to nationalist demands by passing the Algerian Statute (1947), which gave fiscal but not political autonomy to Algeria.

Mohamed Belouizdad, Ahmed Ben Bella, and others formed the Organisation Secrète (Secret Organization or OS) in 1948, to protest electoral fraud in the Algerian assembly elections and the repression of Algerian leaders. The OS advocated militant action against colonial rule. Ben Bella and other OS leaders were arrested after an attack on the Oran post office, but Ben Bella escaped and fled to Cairo. In 1954 the revolutionaries formed the Comité Révolutionnaire d'Unité et d'Action (the Revolutionary Committee of Unity and Action or CRUA), to work toward Algerian independence. On

October 10, 1954, CRUA was renamed the National Liberation Front (Front de la Libération Nationale or FLN); under that name, it became the most potent force for Algerian freedom.

The FLN attacked targets in Algeria, destroyed infrastructure (police stations and barracks), and detonated bombs in Algiers. The French government arrested MTLD and FLN leaders and launched punitive raids against the "rebels."

In 1956 a group of liberal Europeans and FLN representatives met to declare a truce and to pledge to protect civilians. In July of that year, the FLN absorbed the Algerian Communist Party and made Casbah an important military base. In both Algeria and Cairo, the FLN intensified its independence struggle, tying down the huge French army in Algeria. After six more years of conflict, the Evian Agreements of May 1962 ended the Algerian war for independence.

TUNISIA

Following the 1930 Eucharistic Congress at Carthage (organized by Carthage's archbishop, Monsignor Lemaître, to celebrate a century of French/Catholic activity in Algeria), nationalist stirrings in Tunisia began to intensify. Habib Bourguiba, Mahmud Matiri, and other leaders of the Destour (Liberal Constitutional Party) launched the newspaper *L'Action Tunisienne* to spread their nationalist message. After *L'Action* was banned on April 27, 1933, Bourguiba and other leaders formed the Neo-Destour party in 1934. This was suppressed by the French colonial administration and Bourguiba was imprisoned for his role in disturbances at Bordj Le Boeuf.

In January 1938, the Neo-Destour and the General Confederation of Tunisian Workers (Confédération Générale des Travailleurs Tunisiens or CGTT) organized riots in Bizerte. Police killed 112 and wounded 62 and arrested Bourguiba and other leaders, thus stifling nationalist activity.

In 1942 the new Tunisian ruler, Munsif Bey, rekindled nationalist hopes when he received nationalist leaders in his palace and demanded the establishment of a consultative assembly with a Tunisian majority. After German troops arrived in Tunisia later that year, Munsif Bey formed a new government with Neo-Destour sympathizers (chief among them Muhammad Shanniq). However, Free French authorities deposed the bey as an Axis supporter after the Allies retook Tunis in 1943.

After Bourguiba was released by the Germans in 1943, he returned to Tunisia and issued a proclamation denouncing Italian fascism. In March 1945, Bourguiba secretly left Tunisia for a North African and North American tour to seek support for the nationalists. A year later, police broke up the Congress of August 23, 1946,

organized by Destour, Neo-Destour, and the Union Générale Tunisienne du Travail (UGTT) to coordinate nationalist activities. When demonstrations, strikes, and violence continued, the French in July 1947 asked Mustafa Ka'ak to form a new Tunisian government (with himself as prime minister), in which French and Tunisian ministers would share power. But co-sovereignty became problematic soon after its implementation because the French insisted on holding on to de facto control. Prime Minister Shanniq and other Tunisian ministers went to Paris in October 1951 to demand Tunisian independence; when the French resident-general, Hautecloque, demanded the Shanniq government's dismissal, riots broke out in Tunisia on January 15, 1952. Bourguiba was arrested on January 18, 1952, and in March, Shanniq and other Tunisian ministers were also arrested. The frightened bey appointed two successive prime ministers (in March 1952 and March 1954) who were amenable to French demands, but this was unacceptable to the nationalists, who dismissed any form of compromise after January 1952. The Neo-Destour party formed a united front with the UGTT to fight police actions, but most Neo-Destour leaders were arrested.

Tunisian guerrillas attacked settlers, and in turn the Red Hand, a settler terrorist organization, attacked Tunisian political leaders. When the Red Hand assassinated Farhat Hashdad on December 5, 1952, the violence that ensued eventually forced the French government to begin the process of granting autonomy to Tunisia. The French concluded an agreement with Bourguiba on April 22, 1955, but several Tunisian leaders denounced it because it ensured French control over Tunisia's foreign affairs, army, police, and senior administrative posts, as well as sectors of the economy. In June 1955, Bourguiba returned from France to Tunisia and on March 20, 1956, the French agreed to grant Tunisia independence. The Neo-Destour Party won eighty-eight of ninety-eight assembly seats in the March 25, 1956, election and on July 25, 1957, the assembly abolished the monarchy and declared a republic with Bourguiba as head of state.

MOROCCO

In Morocco, economic depression increased support for anticolonial and nationalist demands, especially after 1934. The Great Depression and the attendant hunger and unemployment hit Moroccans hard. Even affluent merchants and professionals found themselves marginalized by French settlers and businesses. From its creation, Allal al-Fasi's Committee for Action (formed January 1937 to champion Moroccan independence) was constantly harassed by the government. Appropriation of Moroccan lands and French plans to divert the Sebu River's waters

ALGERIAN WAR OF INDEPENDENCE

In 1830, during the reign of Charles X, the French invaded Algeria, beginning a more than 130-year-long occupation of the North African country. French settlers moved to the country and began farming much of the available arable land, displacing native Algerians in the process. A highly profitable colony, Algeria was largely controlled by the French colonialists, known as *colons,* both economically and politically. Though limited actions were taken in the first half of the twentieth century to include more Algerians in the administration of the country, these efforts were largely seen as ineffectual.

Lacking a meaningful voice in their own country, many Algerians looked to overthrow the French-supported government; eventually, various opposition leaders joined forces to create the Front de Libération Nationale. In late 1954 Algerian rebels began to attack French installations, but their efforts were soon redirected toward attacking French civilians, in hopes of gaining more attention, beginning with the Philippeville massacres in which 123 people were killed. French forces in turn killed over 1,000 Algerians, setting off a spiral of new violence throughout the country. France quickly responded by sending in nearly 500,000 troops, who by early 1958 were generally in control of the country. But world opinion soon began to side with the oppressed Algerian population and many in France became tired of

the military operation and the loss of so many young soldiers. As the Fourth French Republic vacillated, at times negotiating with the rebels and at other times conducting serious campaigns against them, French colonists and the military, both determined in their opposition to Algerian independence, threatened to attack the French mainland. These threats, while they were not carried out, contributed to the collapse of the Fourth Republic.

With little hope for diplomatic or military resolution, in 1960 De Gaulle proposed a referendum in France to allow the citizens of Algeria the opportunity to vote on independence, which passed the next year with three-quarters approving the measure. Feeling betrayed, the French colonists and the military again sought to overthrow the government, but this time were stymied. On July 1, 1962, Algerians voted for independence, which was granted two days later by Charles De Gaulle. According to the Evian Accords, which formally settled the war, French colonists were given the option of receiving Algerian citizenship or returning to France; thousands decided to return to the mainland. In return for promising to aid the Algerian government financially, France won access to oil fields in the Sahara, an arrangement that kept French influence in Algeria alive long after the country's independence.

---

angered nationalists, who staged violent demonstrations. The French occupied the *medina* (the Muslim quarter) of Fez, surrounded Qaraouiyine University, and forced nationalist leaders like Allal al-Fassi and al-Wazzani into exile.

Even with the arrest and exile of its leaders, nationalist opposition continued. A new nationalist movement developed, composed of Abderssalem Bennouna and Abdel Khaled Torres's National Reform Party and the Maghreb Unity Party (based in the French zone) of Mekki Nacri. Nationalists in northern and southern Morocco began to work together after the beginning of World War II. France's defeat in 1940, the landing of British and American troops in 1942, and the destruction of the pro-Vichy (pro-Nazi) French administration in Morocco all strengthened the nationalist cause. At the same time, a restrictive war economy caused untold hardships.

Nationalist agitation in Morocco only increased under the inflexible administration of the Gaullist French resident-general, General Puaux. By December 1943, a coalition of merchants and professionals had founded the Istiqlal (Independence) party. Istiqlal collected signatures for an independence manifesto that it submitted to the French, American, British, and Soviet governments on January 11, 1944. The nationalists, referring to the Atlantic Charter and Moroccan support against the Vichy regime, demanded Moroccan autonomy under Sultan Mohammed Ibn Youssef.

The sultan secured General Puaux's retirement and the eventual return from exile of nationalist leaders like Allal al-Fasi and al-Wazzani. In exchange for his signature on several French reform decrees that he (and Istiqlal) had opposed, Ibn Youssef won French, and later British, consent for a trip through the Spanish zone to visit Tangier. This visit, the first by a Moroccan sovereign since 1899, was met with popular acclaim in the French zone. In a speech to Moroccan notables, French and Spanish officials, and the diplomatic community (on April 10, 1947), the Sultan emphasized the need for reform in Morocco rather than delivering the expected platitudes concerning French rule.

By 1951 a National Front had unified rival parties and gained support from the Arab League, Egypt, and the United Nations. In large towns workers resorted to strikes and violence, while in the countryside, peasants supported demands for reform. Trade union activity began in earnest in Casablanca, though unions were prohibited. Abderrahim Bouabid and Tayyib Bouazza started to organize a national trade union movement in 1949, but news of the murder of Ferhat Hashdad (a Tunisian trade union leader) led to riots instead in Casablanca. On December 8, 1952, the local French administration deposed Sultan Ibn Youssef and replaced him with Ben Arafa. Nationalists interpreted the French action as an assault on Islam and violence broke out in Casablanca and other cites such as Fez, Port Lyautey, and Marrakesh. Mass protests occurred in many Moroccan towns and many activists died in clashes with French troops. Then, in 1955, a guerrilla war began.

Faced with these disturbances and unable to count on Sultan Ben Arafa or the antinationalist support of several Berber chiefs (such as al-Glaoui of Marrakesh), the Fauré government in France arranged the Aix-les-Baines Conference, which brought together Morocco's representatives. Conference participants agreed on Ben Arafa's departure (without abdication), the formation of a throne council, and a national union to negotiate with France. Following this, the French started negotiations with Sultan Mohammed Ibn Youssef and restored him to his throne as Mohammed V, king of independent Morocco. After negotiations with Istiqlal, Morocco became independent on March 2, 1956.

LIBYA

Libya came under European control much later than the other Middle Eastern countries, and only briefly. From the mid-nineteenth century, Libya was under Turkish suzerainty. By the 1880s it was divided into the province of Tripoli (Tripolitania and Fezzan) and Benghazi (with Cyrenaica) and ruled by local governors under Ottoman control and supported by an 8,000-man garrison. Turkish officials, assisted by the Sanusiyya brotherhood (founded in the 1830s), worked with local chiefs to collect taxes. The Sanusiyya and its *zawiya* (lodges) maintained peace and settled disputes between the Turkish authorities and the people.

Even after World War II, Libya had many characteristics that made its political situation unique. Without a ready constituency of disaffected people, nationalist movements in Libya had to work with the colonial administration. However, the tide changed after fascist Italy invaded Libya and colonized the country. Public lands owned by the Turkish administration were seized by the Italian colonizers. Land seizures accelerated after General de Bono (the Italian governor of Tripolitania) started a program of demographic colonization that provided land to carefully selected Italian peasants. The Tajura plains, the Khums hills, the Tarhuna mountains, and the central Jaffara plains were all seized and large tracts of Libyan land were given to Italians (and other Europeans) for agricultural purposes. In 1938 some 20,000 Italians settled in Libya, and in 1939 another 12,000 did. Thus, by 1939 about 120,000 Italians lived in Libya, making up around 12 percent of the population.

Furthermore, after the Italian conquest many Bedouins were kept in conditions akin to concentration camps. Umar al-Mukhtar, leader of the Cyrenaican resistance, was captured and hanged in 1930. Italian rule of Libya lasted until early in 1943, when British forces gained control of both Tripolitania and Cyrenaica.

Following World War II, British military administrators governed Tripolitania and Cyrenaica, while the French controlled the Fezzan. In November 1949, the U.N. General Assembly resolved that Libya would become independent in two years. With U.N. help, Sayyid Muhammad Idris, the Sanusi leader, was accepted by the Tripolitanians and, later, by Cyrenaicans, as their leader. In December 1951, Libya became the first North African colony to achieve independence.

EGYPT

In Egypt, the interwar years witnessed increased anti-colonial militancy and effective political organization for independence. Economic deprivation led to strikes and demonstrations, which were exacerbated by the arrest of Sa'ad Zaghlul and two colleagues on March 8, 1919. Students from Al-Azhar University, supported by transport workers, judges, and lawyers, staged a revolt in 1919. This resulted in Britain abolishing its protectorate and recognizing Egypt's independence on February 28, 1922, on four conditions: namely, British control of imperial lines of communication through Egypt and between the Mediterranean and Red Sea, responsibility for defending Egypt against external attack, British protection of foreign interests in Egypt, and control of the "Anglo-Egyptian condominium" of the Sudan.

Egyptian nationalists accepted this partial independence because the Wafd Party (formed in 1918 by Zaghlul Pasha) was weak. The Great Depression

Indian Troops in Egypt. *British officers lead a line of Indian soldiers from their camp in Egypt in March 1940. These troops were the first from the British Empire to take up occupation in North Africa.* © HULTON-DEUTSCH COLLECTION/CORBIS. REPRODUCED BY PERMISSION.

increased popular discontent and civil strife, and in 1936 an Anglo-Egyptian treaty (with Zaghlul's successor, Nahas Pasha) made concessions to Egyptian nationalists.

Britain used Egypt as a military base during World War II and drove Germany out of North Africa by 1943. Nationalism intensified in Egypt after the war. The creation and expansion of the state of Israel strained Anglo–Egyptian relations, as Arabs held Britain responsible for giving Arab Palestine to Israel. Furthermore, Britain's continued occupation of the Suez Canal Zone (resumed in 1952) energized the Muslim Brotherhood (founded in 1922), which became a force in Egyptian politics during the late 1940s and 1950s.

The Israeli defeat of Egypt in 1948–1949 discredited the Egyptian monarch and Nahas Pasha. In 1952 a group of young military officers opposed to the monarchy and British control of the Suez Canal Zone seized power in a bloodless coup d'état and formed a new government under General Muhamed Naguib. Egypt was declared a republic on February 10, 1953; in 1954 General Naguib, who many nationalists considered too conservative, was replaced

by Lt. Col. Gamal Abdel Nasser (1918–1970) following a palace coup. Gamal Abdel Nasser then became president. Britain agreed in July 1954 to evacuate its troops within twenty months. They kept this agreement, but the United States and various Western European powers grew increasingly hostile to Nasser's anti-Western rhetoric and policies. After the United States and Britain retracted offers to provide financial aid for the construction of the Aswan Dam, Nasser turned to the Soviets for aid and nationalized the Suez Canal.

Nasser's actions galvanized Britain's determination to get rid of him by any means possible. His radical nationalism was viewed as a type of communism, and thus a threat to Western supremacy. At the same time, the Israeli leadership regarded Egypt as a threat to Israeli security.

In November 1956 Israeli troops invaded the Canal Zone under a secret agreement with Britain and France. The invasion was condemned worldwide, and when the United States opposed it, Israel and its British and French allies quickly withdrew. Egypt then emerged as a truly independent state for the first time in modern history.

862

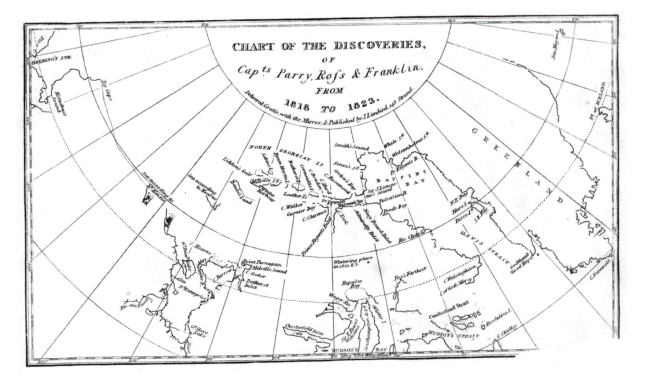

Chart of the Discoveries of Captains Perry, Ross, and Franklin. *This map, drawn circa 1845, charts the discoveries in the Artic of the British explorers William Parry, John Ross, and John Franklin. An expedition led by Franklin in search of the Northwest Passage disappeared near King William Island around 1848.* **HULTON ARCHIVE/GETTY IMAGES. REPRODUCED BY PERMISSION.**

SEE ALSO *Independence and Decolonization, Middle East; Secular Nationalisms, Middle East.*

BIBLIOGRAPHY

Bernard, Stéphane. *The Franco-Moroccan Conflict, 1943–1956.* New Haven, CT: Yale University Press, 1968.

Hoisington, William A. *The Casablanca Connection: French Colonial Policy, 1936–1943.* Chapel Hill: University of North Carolina Press, 1984.

Lucas, Scott, ed. *Britain and Suez: The Lion's Last Roar.* Manchester, U.K.: Manchester University Press, 1996.

Salem, Norma. *Habib Bourguiba, Islam and the Creation of Tunisia.* London: Croom Helm, 1984.

Smith, Tony. *The French Stake in Algeria, 1945–1962.* Ithaca, NY: Cornell University Press, 1978.

Edmund Abaka

NORTHWEST PASSAGE TO ASIA

The Northwest Passage was long sought by European explorers to shorten the distance and time that merchant ships needed to travel from Europe to Asia. Most explorers attempted to locate a sea channel in the Arctic waters to the north of Canada. The route that was eventually discovered runs from the Atlantic Ocean below Iceland and Greenland, through the Arctic archipelago in northern Canada, and along the northern coast of Alaska into the Pacific Ocean.

Spanish explorers were the first to try to locate this mythical passage from the Pacific side beginning in 1539, but the British soon surpassed them in the sheer number of exploration parties coming from the Atlantic. Martin Frobisher (ca. 1535–1594) discovered Frobisher Bay (1576–1578), John Davis (1543–1605) found Cumberland Sound (1585), and Henry Hudson (1565–1611) explored both the Hudson River and later the Hudson Bay (1609). All of these efforts failed, however, to find a passageway. It is often forgotten that Captain James Cook's (1728–1779) famous expedition of 1776 to 1779, which ended with his death in the Hawaiian Islands, began as a search for a Pacific route to the Northwest Passage.

Disasters were common. In 1845 Sir John Franklin (1786–1847) led a large expedition that completely disappeared. Later explorers determined that Franklin's ships became icelocked near King William Island. After abandoning their ships and making their way back by land, the entire 129-man party died by 1848. One reason for the total loss may be that they had been provisioned with eight thousand tins of food sealed with lead. After 138 years, laboratory tests on three bodies from this ill-fated expedition discovered lethal levels of lead poisoning.

Finally, after more than three hundred years of failure, an exploring party led by Robert McClure (1807–1873) completed the Northwest Passage by a combination of sea and land routes from 1850 to 1854. In 1906 the Norwegian explorer Roald Amundsen (1872–1928) spent a total of three years completing the voyage by sea. The first single-season passage was not accomplished until 1944, however, by Canadian Henry Larsen (1899–1964).

On July 1, 1957, the U. S. Coast Guard cutters *Storis*, *Bramble*, and *Spar* began to search for a deeper channel through the Arctic Ocean. Their success was a historic end to the more than 400-year challenge to find a deepwater route that would let large ships make the Northwest Passage. Upon its return to Greenland, *Spar* also became the first U.S.-registered vessel to circumnavigate the North American continent, beating *Storis* home by several weeks.

For all of the negatives that global warming may entail, it may also open the Northwest Passage for increasingly long periods of time. It has been hypothesized that by 2015 an ice-free commercial route will appear in the Arctic during the summer months. If true, this passage will allow ships traveling between Europe and Asia to shave more than four thousand miles off the normal route through Panama. In addition to avoiding delays and canal fees, many large container and tanker ships cannot fit in the almost century-old Panama Canal, forcing them to take the longer and more treacherous route around South America's Cape Horn.

SEE ALSO *European Explorations in North America; Exploration, The Pacific.*

BIBLIOGRAPHY

Cookman, Scott. *Ice Blink: The Mysterious Fate of Sir John Franklin's Lost Polar Expedition.* New York: Wiley, 2000.

Day, Alan Edwin. *Search for the Northwest Passage: An Annotated Bibliography.* New York: Garland, 1986.

Bruce Elleman

NYERERE, JULIUS
1922–1999

Julius Nyerere was the first prime minister of Tanganyika when the country attained self-government in 1961 and the first president of the United Republic of Tanzania (1964–1985), the name of the country following the union between Tanganyika and Zanzibar in 1964. He

Julius Kambarage Nyerere, July 11, 1966. President Nyerere of Tanzania holds the Freedom Torch, presented to him by Tanzanian youths who carried the torch from Nyerere's birthplace to Dar es Salaam. HULTON ARCHIVE/GETTY IMAGES. REPRODUCED BY PERMISSION.

was born in a chiefly family among the Zanaki people of North Western Tanganyika. He studied at Makerere University in Uganda where he trained as a teacher. He later studied history and economics for his master's degree at the University of Edinburgh.

Nyerere was a nationalist figure during the colonial times who brought together a number of different nationalist factions into one political organization termed the Tanganyika African National Union (TANU). Nyerere became a well-respected leader among his fellow Tanzanians, as well as across Africa and internationally. He played the role of a unifying leader to the diverse population of Tanganyika and later Tanzania, both as a nationalist leader and in his roles of president. He earned the title *mwalimu* (teacher) in Tanzania, a title with which he came to be referred internationally.

Nyerere is remembered for specific virtues and principles that he upheld and practiced as a leader. He was a great orator. He was often described as a humble leader, which earned him great respect worldwide. Nyerere had great concern for egalitarianism and was passionately committed to equality as the basis of African socialism. As a result, he rejected any assertion of privilege to the educated few and the elites.

In 1967 he released the Arusha Declaration, in which he defined African socialism and discouraged the emergence of an African capitalist class, while emphasizing localization through state and cooperative ownership. He established collective communities, *Ujamaa*, (villagization) as the backbone of the practice of African socialism, which was people centered with a collective effort toward development. As cooperative villages, peasants in the Ujamma villages were expected to live together, work collectively in the agricultural farms, and market their produce collectively with the aim of benefiting all members.

Nyerere often spoke of *uhuru na kazi*, meaning freedom and hard work as defining characteristics of independence and development. He gave meaning to his policy for the development of Tanzania through many speeches, which he delivered within Tanzania, across Africa, and at international forums. Nyerere's speeches touched on issues of development, democracy, freedom, education, and peace.

His speeches are indicative of his belief in the mutual reinforcement of freedom and development; he argued that freedom depends on development and development on freedom. He advocated for people-centered development, often reiterating that "development means the development of people." On education, Nyerere advocated education as a lifelong pursuit that leads to self-reliance and liberation. He supported the liberation struggles of other African countries and provided domicile in Tanzania for a number of African liberation movements, including the African National Congress (ANC), and Mozambique's *Frente de Libertação de Moçambique* (FRELIMO) or Mozambique Liberation Front.

Nyerere retired from the presidency in 1985 and from active politics in the early 1990s. He devoted the rest of his life to the pursuit of peaceful resolution to conflicts in Africa, serving as the chief mediator in the Burundi conflict in 1996. He died of leukemia on October 14, 1999, in London. Nyerere's life, teachings, and career remain an inspiration in the search for freedom and justice in Africa.

SEE ALSO *African National Congress; Nationalism, Africa.*

BIBLIOGRAPHY

Legum, Colin, and Geoffrey Mmari, eds. *Mwalimu: The Influence of Nyerere.* Trenton, NJ: Africa World Press, 1995.

Nyerere, Julius. *Freedom and Development: A Selection of Writings and Speeches, 1968–1973.* New York: Oxford University Press, 1973.

Edith Miguda

NZG (NEDERLANDSCH ZENDELING GENOOTSCHAP)

SEE *Netherlands Missionary Society*

O

OCCUPATIONS, EAST ASIA

The term *occupation* generally refers to the temporary stationing of troops by a victorious military force in the territory and possessions of a defeated state. The purpose is to pressure the occupied state into meeting the occupier's postwar demands. Once the stated goals are met the occupying military will repatriate (return to its country of origin) and the occupied territory will regain its sovereignty. In this sense, occupation resembles *trusteeship*, a post–World War I strategy that temporarily entrusted the territory of the defeated Axis powers to the victorious Allies, with the goal of nurturing the people to sovereignty. Occupation differs from *colonization*, which does not set specific goals and thus is not governed by temporal restraints.

The history of the U.S. presence in the Philippine Islands demonstrates the thin line distinguishing occupation from colonization. The first encounter with these islands by U.S. forces was as a battleground during the Spanish-American War (1898). After the United States took control of the islands from Spain, it engaged in battle with local independence-minded Filipinos. The debate in the United States at this time centered on the extent to which the United States would develop its presence on the islands. America's decision to establish a government to administer the islands determined the status of the United States as an indefinite colonizer rather than a short-term occupier.

American colonial activity in the Philippines coincided with similar imperial activities throughout East Asia by the United States and other world powers. Although these powers colonized certain territories outright, they also established occupations in others. This is particularly apparent in China. Over the latter part of the nineteenth century, no country was strong enough to colonize China outright. Consequently, the world's colonial powers signed agreements with China's weak government that permitted their occupation of designated territories. For example, the protocol signed between the Chinese and Great Britain, France, Germany, the United States, Russia, and Japan following the antiforeigner Boxer uprising (1898–1901) permitted the occupying countries to station twenty thousand troops in Beijing. The troops were meant to protect the occupiers' people and interests, and to pressure the weak Chinese government to carry out other conditions in the agreement. The Chinese government also signed agreements with the occupying powers that granted them lease rights in parts of the Shandong Peninsula and Lüshun (Port Arthur) for set periods of time (usually ninety-nine years).

The introduction of the trusteeship as a form of occupation, popularized after World War I as an answer to anti-imperialist sentiment, gained for the Japanese the former German territories in the South Pacific and on mainland China. These postwar Japanese occupations were intended to last just long enough for Japan to guide the people living in the trusteeship territories to sovereignty. On the basis of this premise (and the open-door policy) the world powers forced Japan at the Washington Conference (1920–1921) to relinquish its possession of China's Shandong Peninsula, which it had acquired from the Germans. Japan controlled its South Pacific acquisitions until the last year of War World II, when it was forced to relinquish most of these islands to the United States.

Japanese Soldiers at the Great Wall of China, 1933. Beginning in the 1930s, Japan began to occupy territories on the Asian continent, first Manchuria and then other parts of China. In this photograph, Japanese soldiers plant the flag of Japan on the first gate of the Great Wall in Shanhaiguan near Qinhuangdao in eastern China. © BETTMANN/CORBIS. REPRODUCED BY PERMISSION.

Beginning in the 1930s, Japan began to occupy territories on the Asian continent, first Manchuria in northeastern China and then other parts of China. In the early 1940s the Japanese took control of Malaya (Mayasia), the Dutch East Indies (Indonesia), Singapore, and the Philippines, all of which were former Western colonies in Southeast Asia. These expansion efforts closely resembled occupations, for Japan's stated plan was to liberate these territories from their Western colonial rulers and prepare them for their eventual independence once a government friendly to Japan had been established. Japan's defeat in World War II left nationalists in these territories in a precarious situation: Japan's overthrow of previous colonial administrations provided indigenous nationalist movements with room to expand, but Japan's continued presence prevented nationalist leaders from developing the people's national identity and allegiance.

The term *occupation* is most often associated with the postwar imposition of Allied troops in Axis territories

and their former colonies. The Allied powers originally envisioned a joint-trusteeship, with the various Allied countries cooperating in the occupation of a single region. This configuration worked better in Europe, where the Allies divided such cities as Berlin and Vienna into occupying zones. Joint-trusteeship worked less well in Asia, where the Korean Peninsula was partitioned by the United States and Soviet Union, resulting in the formation of two very different halves of the same peninsula.

East Asia experienced two forms of postwar occupation that differed in length and purpose. One type of occupation saw the Allied powers attempting to reestablish control over their former colonial possessions. The United States returned to the Philippines even before Japan's surrender and granted the islands their independence in 1946, after a year of occupation. The Dutch and British eventually failed in their attempts to regain their colonial possessions, bringing independence to former British and Dutch possessions. French attempts to retain control of Vietnam forced it to retreat to the south and establish an indigenous government backed by French, and later United States, occupations.

The United States and the Soviet Union established occupation administrations in northeast Asia to demilitarize the Japanese. The two occupiers also hoped to spread their respective political ideologies. The Americans took over Japan, including the island of Okinawa, and southern Korea beginning 1945; the Soviets occupied northern Korea and several northern islands that Japan had gained through treaty with Russia in the late eighteenth century. Japan and northern Korea were administered indirectly—that is, by issuing directives through indigenous governments. This approach differed from the one used in southern Korea and Okinawa, where the occupying powers installed military governments to administer the territories directly.

The formal postwar occupation of Okinawa ended by 1972, when the United States returned the island to Japan. The occupations of southern and northern Korea both ended in 1948, and the occupation of Japan ended in 1952. However, the continued presence of U.S. troops in America's former occupied territories, as well as the continued possession by Russia of four of the Kuril Islands claimed by Japan, as well as the continued division of the Korean peninsula into north and south, represents critical legacies of these occupations.

SEE ALSO *Boxer Uprising; East Asia, American Presence in; East Asia, European Presence in; Empire, Japanese; Japan, Colonized; Pacific, American Presence in; Pacific, European Presence in; United States Colonial Rule in the Philippines.*

BIBLIOGRAPHY

Armstrong, Charles. *The North Korean Revolution, 1945–1950.* Ithaca, NY: Cornell University Press, 2003.

Iriye, Akira. *Across the Pacific: An Inner History of American-East Asian Relations.* Chicago: Imprint Publications, 1992.

Oh, Bonnie B.C., ed. *Korea Under The American Military Government, 1945–1948.* Westport, CT: Praeger, 2002.

Takuma Eiji. *Inside Ghq: The Allied Occupation of Japan and Its Legacy.* Translated by Robert Ricketts and Sebastian Swann. New York: Continuum, 2002.

Mark E. Caprio

OCCUPATIONS, THE PACIFIC

Pacific oral history and archaeology suggest that territorial occupations occurred often in the Pacific. In historic times, for example, New Zealand Maori forces occupied the Chatham Islands and eliminated the indigenous Moriori population. In the late nineteenth century, Tongan warrior chief Ma'afu occupied eastern Fiji and Kamehameha of Hawaii conquered most of that archipelago. As a political concept, however, occupation is tied to a notion of the territorial state; this type of occupation only emerged after European powers and the United States had agreed upon a final division of the Pacific islands. This division largely followed the end of the Spanish-American War in 1898. Although, preceding this, German traders had already moved into the Marshall Islands and the new German state had declared this archipelago a protectorate in 1885 despite Spanish claims.

Occupation principally occurs as a reflex of war, and at the outbreak of World War I in 1914 both Australia and New Zealand sent squadrons north to occupy German's Southwest Pacific colonies, aiming particularly to seize cable and wireless communication centers. The Australians occupied German New Guinea and Nauru while New Zealand forces took Western Samoa. In the North Pacific, Japan moved quickly into the Marshall Islands and also the Marianas and Carolines—the other Micronesian archipelagoes that Germany had acquired from Spain in 1898. German forces, realizing the difficulty of defending these distant colonies, quickly withdrew. Australian, New Zealand, and Japanese militaries occupied these territories until their seizure was regularized as League of Nations C-class mandates.

World War II (1939–1945) occasioned even greater occupation of colonial territories. In late 1941 and early 1942, the Japanese moved swiftly to occupy American-controlled Guam and Wake, Dutch New Guinea, Australia's Territory of New Guinea, parts of Papua and Nauru, and British-held Solomon Islands and Gilbert Islands. In response, the Allies (mainly U.S. forces assisted by Australia and New Zealand) rushed troops into the rest of the Pacific including Samoa, Fiji, Tahiti, New Caledonia, and Ellice and Cook Islands in order to protect lines of communication between Australasia and North America. The largest number of U.S. forces occupied the New Hebrides (then a joint British and French Condominium colony), carving out two large advance bases that supported the subsequent invasion of Japanese-occupied Guadalcanal.

These Allied occupations were friendly insofar as military forces consulted, at least officially, with existing colonial administrations. In the New Hebrides (Vanuatu), however, U.S. military commanders, frustrated with colonial incompetence, assumed much of the day-to-day administration of the archipelago.

Bypassed behind the frontline, the Japanese occupied a number of islands (including much of New Guinea) until the end of the war in 1945. Distracted by battle, neither Japanese nor Allied forces concerned themselves much with Pacific Island populations apart from recruiting native labor corps. The huge U.S. presence in the New Hebrides and the Solomon Islands, however, helped spark several postwar social movements, including the Maasina Rule on Malaita and the John Frum movement on Tanna.

The United States assumed control of Micronesia as a strategic trust territory under the aegis of the new United Nations. This U.S. Navy administered these islands until 1951 when authority passed to the U.S. Department of the Interior. The Trust Territory eventually dissolved as the Northern Marianas became a U.S. Commonwealth (1975) while the remaining districts gained separate nationhoods—the Federated States of Micronesia and the Marshall Islands in 1986, and Palau (Belau) in 1994—although these have signed "compacts of free association" that give the U.S. oversight of their foreign affairs.

Since World War II, Pacific occupations have been less frequent. In 1963 Indonesia occupied Western New Guinea—the last remnant of the Dutch East Indies colony—and, in the 1990s, Australian and other forces occupied Bougainville Island (part of Papua New Guinea) and Guadalcanal (Solomon Islands), to help settle a secessionist war and civil unrest.

SEE ALSO *Empire, Japanese; Pacific, American Presence in; Pacific, European Presence in.*

BIBLIOGRAPHY

Grattan, C. Hartley. *The Southwest Pacific since 1900.* Ann Arbor: University of Michigan Press, 1963.

Lindstrom, Lamont. *The American Occupation of the New Hebrides (Vanuatu).* Macmillan Brown Centre for Pacific Studies Working Paper 4. Christchurch, New Zealand: Macmillan Brown Centre, 1996.

Lindstrom, Lamont, and Geoffrey M. White. *Island Encounters: Black and White Memories of the Pacific War.* Washington, DC: Smithsonian Institution Press, 1990.

Poyer, Lin, Suzanne Falgout, and Laurence M. Carucci. *The Typhoon of War: Micronesian Experiences of the Pacific War.* Honolulu: University of Hawaii Press, 2001.

Lamont Lindstrom

OCEANIA

Oceania is usually considered to include the central and southern Pacific, but excludes the North Pacific and Australia. It consists of three principal areas: Polynesia, Micronesia, and Melanesia. It is significant that whereas the names *Polynesia* and *Micronesia* have geographical origins ("many islands" and "small islands," respectively), the name *Melanesia* refers to the skin color of its inhabitants ("black islands"). This usage reflects eighteenth- and nineteenth-century classifications, which regarded Polynesians and Melanesians as Asiatic, or even Semitic, while defining Melanesians as similar to Africans.

These traditional distinctions are problematic. Linguistic research, for example, has revealed extensive Polynesian influence in parts of the western Pacific, and has divided Melanesians into Austronesian and non-Austronesian language speakers. Formal colonial rule in the Pacific, however, tended to follow island group boundaries rather than geographical categories.

Few islands featured desirable resources, such as precious minerals or coal; thus, most attracted only limited European settlement and developed plantation economies in combination with nonrenewable resources, such as sandalwood. The British colony of New Zealand developed the most extensive European settlement. In most other cases, colonial rule in this region had more to do with international rivalry and the nineteenth-century "scramble" for empire than with an interest in Oceanic resources.

Most Oceanian colonies were politically independent by the 1970s, but the United States, France, and Britain continue to rule several "territories," which have various degrees of self-determination. In other areas, Australia or New Zealand is the governing power. So familiar to westerners through tourist images of pristine beaches and attractive islanders, Oceania also experienced medically and environmentally devastating nuclear testing by France and the United States from the 1940s to the 1990s.

At the beginning of the twenty-first century, Oceania faces the challenges of poverty, resource depletion, environmental degradation, and political instability. Several of the regions' countries could disappear entirely under the rising sea levels prompted by global warming. Unsustainable tourist development is also taking its toll. Oceania remains both desirable and vulnerable to Western power.

SEE ALSO *Pacific, American Presence in; Pacific, European Presence in.*

BIBLIOGRAPHY

Campbell, I. C. *Worlds Apart: A History of the Pacific Islands.* Christchurch, New Zealand: Canterbury University Press, 2003.

Fischer, Steven R. *A History of the Pacific Islands.* New York: Palgrave, 2002.

CALOUSTE GULBENKIAN

Calouste Sarkis Gulbenkian, a significant figure in the early years of the oil industry, was born to a prominent Armenian family in Istanbul, Turkey, on March 23, 1869. Receiving his early education in Istanbul before studying in Europe, he eventually earned an engineering degree from King's College, London, in 1887. While traveling in Baku, Azerbaijan, the twenty-two-year-old Gulbenkian took an interest in the region's oil fields, which led to the publication of his book *La Transcaucasie et la peninsule d'Apcheron: Souvenirs de voyage*, an examination of Baku's oil industry. Officials from the Ottoman Empire took notice of Gulbenkian's work and hired him to make a detailed report on the empire's potential oil resources.

As European nations began to make the transition from coal-burning machines to oil-burning ones, many countries looked to gain a foothold in the Middle East. Sensing the importance of oil reserves, Gulbenkian began a career in the burgeoning oil industry, helping foreign countries acquire oil rights and invest capital in the Middle East region. The Armenian brokered deals with major European oil companies, including Royal Dutch Shell and the Anglo-Persian Oil Company (later to become British

Petroleum), often keeping a five-percent stake, which earned him the nickname "Mr. Five Percent."

In addition to pursuing his business interests, Gulbenkian also offered economic advice to Ottoman embassies in Paris and London. He advised other countries in the Middle East as well—for example, he served as Iran's representative in France. Gulbenkian negotiated the 1928 Red Line Agreement, a division of the oil rights in the former Ottoman Empire between British, American, Dutch, and French companies, and helped American oil companies acquire rights to the oil fields discovered in Saudi Arabia.

Gulbenkian's interests were not confined to the oil industry, however. He was renowned for his fine arts collection as well as for his numerous donations to charitable causes and his support of the Armenian community worldwide. In his final years, Gulbenkian lived in Portugal, where he died on July 20, 1955. His will contained provisions for the construction in Lisbon of the Calouste Gulbenkian Museum and for the establishment of the Calouste Gulbenkian Foundation, dedicated to supporting the arts, education, and the sciences.

Howe, K. R. *Where the Waves Fall: A New South Sea Islands History from First Settlement to Colonial Rule.* Honolulu: University of Hawaii Press, 1984.

Howe, K. R., Robert C. Kiste, and Brij V. Lal, eds. *Tides of History: The Pacific Islands in the Twentieth Century.* Honolulu: University of Hawaii Press, 1994.

Jane Samson

OIL

As long ago as 5,500 years ago, despite its economic insignificance, oil was a valued commodity. Vents where natural gas burned and oil seeped even served as places of worship in ancient times.

In about 1272 Marco Polo (1254–1324), while traveling through Baku, observed oil seeps being worked in hand-dug wells. In 1888, Calouste Sarkis Gulbenkian (1869–1955), engineering graduate of King's College in London and son of an Armenian kerosene merchant,

journeyed to Baku. There he saw that oil was being drilled, but also subjected to enormous waste. He also found that Robert Nobel (1829–1890) of the Swedish Nobel family had organized the best production and transportation system for getting Baku's oil to market. In 1891 he published *La transcaucasie et la peninsule d'apcheron: souvenirs de voyage* in which he presented details of the oil industry of Baku. The book quickly brought an invitation from finance ministers of the Turkish sultan to make a report on oil prospects in Mesopotamia.

In late 1900 William Knox D'Arcy (1849–1917), a financier made wealthy by Australian gold mining interests, was asked to fund oil exploration in Persia. Although D'Arcy never visited Persia, through his agent he did obtain a concession to search for oil there. The concession was granted by the Qajar dynasty, valid for sixty years and covering all of Persia except for the five provinces on the northern border with Russia.

Drilling began in 1902 in Chiah Surkh on the border with Iraq. By 1904 dry holes were draining away D'Arcy's fortune. In 1905 with the support of the first sea lord, Admiral John Fisher (1841–1920), the Scottish

An OPEC Meeting in Caracas. *Ministers from member nations of the Organization of Petroleum Exporting Countries gathered in Venezuela for a summit on September 26, 2000.* © REUTERS/CORBIS. REPRODUCED BY PERMISSION.

oil firm, Burmah Oil Company, eventually traded D'Arcy his concession in exchange for his wildcatting outlays and 170,000 shares of Burmah Oil.

On May 26, 1908, drilling at a new site in southwestern Persia, oil was struck just as Burmah Oil and D'Arcy were considering abandoning the concession. The new well at Masjid-I-Suleiman marks the beginning of the oil industry in the Gulf region—it was to also create a new strategic importance for the Middle East.

On April 14, 1909, a new company, Anglo-Persian Oil Company (APOC) was organized to develop the oil. The search for oil in Persia was spurred on by the British Admiralty's decision, just prior to World War I (1914–1918), to stop fueling the navy with coal and to switch to oil. In 1914 the Admiralty, led by Winston Churchill (1874–1965), signed an agreement with APOC to supply it with fuel oil. In addition the British government bought a controlling interest in the company.

In 1921 the Qajar dynasty was overthrown in a coup led by Raza Kahn (1878–1944), an officer in the Cossack Brigade. He soon became Reza Shah Pahlavi and initiated a program of modernization. He changed the name of the country in 1925 to Iran. APOC then changed its name to the Anglo-Iranian Oil Company (AIOC).

During the 1920s Gulbenkian was active in numerous deals developing oil in the Middle East. These included the 1920s Red Line Agreement that bound the partners in the oil business to collaborate in developing an oil business within the bounds of the former territories of the Ottoman Empire. He also was instrumental in the formation of the Iraq Petroleum Company to developed oil in Iraq first discovered near Kirkuk, in 1927.

During the 1920s French, Dutch, and American companies joined the search for oil in the Middle East. Oil was found in Bahrain in 1932, in Saudi Arabia in 1935, and in Kuwait in 1938.

During World War II (1939–1945) Reza Shah was forced to abdicate in favor of his son Muhammad Reza (1919–1980) when Iran was occupied by the British and used as a conduit for supplying the Soviets. After the war, the British withdrew; however, Iranian nationalists, many secular and many religious, used both the occupation and the business of AIOC to fuel nationalist hatred. One point at issue was that, by 1950, AIOC's oil revenues had increased tenfold, but the income to Iran had increased only fourfold.

Muhammad Mossadegh (1880–1967) emerged as the leader of Iranian nationalism. Muhammad Reza Shah was forced by political pressures to appoint Mossadegh as prime minister. In 1951 Gulbenkian, having been a representative of the Iranian government and its oil interests for decades, advised Iran not to nationalize the Anglo-Persian Oil Company. But, Mossadegh attempted to nationalize foreign oil interests in Iran. In response AIOC withdrew from Iran and organized a boycott of Iranian oil. The shah attempted to replace Mossadegh, but was unable and forced to flee the country. However, he was brought back in 1953 after a coup against Mossadegh engineered by the Central Intelligence Agency (CIA) was successful.

After World War II Gulbenkian helped to create the Stroke 54 Documents, which absolved American companies from the Red Line restrictions. This allowed them to get the Saudi Arabian concession. The concessions to explore for oil in Saudi Arabia, Kuwait, and Qatar were granted in the 1930s; however, these fields were not developed until after World War II.

In 1948 Americans found enormous fields in Saudi Arabia. Thereafter oil flowed in increasing amounts out of Middle Eastern fields. The seven major oil companies (the Seven Sisters) in the Middle East were: Exxon, British Petroleum, Standard Oil of California, Dutch Royal Shell, Texaco, Gulf, and Mobile. In the 1950s nationalism demands moved the oil royalties to a fifty-fifty split. Thereafter oil properties were nationalized and new deals made with oil companies. In 1973, following another of the Arab-Israeli wars, the Arab states engaged in petroleum politics. Using crude oil to punish the West for its support of Israel, an oil crisis was created. The resulting Arab oil embargo caused enormous transfers of wealth and enough oil market turbulence that a number of Western leaders experienced election defeats.

Oil revenues since 1945 have grown, but have floated up and down in price with global supplies or demand. Much of the oil revenue of the Middle East has been spent on armaments destroyed in wars with little going to a mushrooming population. This has contributed to political instability across the region.

By 2005 it was estimated that two-thirds of the world's oil reserves were located in the Middle East and North Africa, the Arabic-Islamic extension of the Middle East. Demand for oil was growing globally in both the West and in China necessitating policies of oil security and price stability. These policies have been seen as anti-Muslim and invasive by Islamic radicals and are believed by some to have contributed to increased Islamic terrorism.

SEE ALSO *Arabia, Western Economic Expansion in; Iran; Iraq; United States Policy Towards the Middle East.*

Oil Wells in Flames in Kuwait. *In early 1991, as the first Gulf War drew to a close, retreating Iraqi forces destroyed Kuwaiti oil wells by setting them on fire.* © PETER TURNLEY/ CORBIS. REPRODUCED BY PERMISSION.

BIBLIOGRAPHY

Bamberg, James. *The History of the British Petroleum Company; the Anglo-Iranian Years, 1928–1954*, Vol. 2. Cambridge, U.K., and New York: Cambridge University Press, 1994.

Bamberg, James. *British Petroleum and Global Oil, 1950–1975: The Challenge of Nationalism.* Cambridge, U.K., and New York: Cambridge University Press, 2000.

Cordesman, Anthony H. *Energy Developments in the Middle East.* Westport, CT: Praeger, 2004.

Ferrier, R. W. *The History of the British Petroleum Company; the Developing Years, 1901–1932*, Vol. 1. Cambridge, U.K., and New York: Cambridge University Press, 1982.

Hewins, Ralph. *Mr. Five Per Cent: the Biography of Calouste Gulbenkian.* London: Hutchinson, 1957.

Noreng, Oystein. *Crude Power: Politics and the Oil Markets.* London and New York: I. B. Tauris, 2002.

Roberts, Gwilym, and David Fowler. *Built by Oil.* Reading, U.K.: Ithaca Press; Concord, MA: Paul & Co., 1995.

Yergin, Daniel. *The Prize: The Epic Quest for Oil, Money, and Power.* New York: Simon and Schuster, 1993.

Andrew J. Waskey

OPEN DOOR POLICY

The Open Door policy was an effort by the U.S. government to preserve China's territorial and administrative integrity at a time when it seemed the major imperial powers intended to carve China into a series of concessions, perhaps presaging the end of a unified China.

In the aftermath of the Spanish-American War (1898), America looked more eagerly at the elusive China market. America had gained Wake, Guam, and the Philippines and, earlier, Midway, Samoa, and the Hawaiian Islands—all stepping stones on the way to China. And China seemed the answer to prevent a recurrence of the economic depression that had just ended.

In September 1899 U.S. secretary of state John Hay proposed an "Open Door" policy in China in which all nations would have equal trading and development rights throughout all of China. He sent notes to the British, German, and Russian governments and in November to the French, Italian, and Japanese governments. Acting in the spirit of the most-favored-nation concept, which America had secured nearly six decades earlier, Hay wrote carefully, seeking not to criticize the increasing spread of spheres of influence. He sought to retain equal opportunity for trade and industry, especially for such latecomers as the United States.

The notes in 1899 did not result in much. No government would commit itself before others did, and Russia and Japan explicitly rejected America's suggested policy. Interestingly, Hay announced in March 1900 that every government had accepted the policy, although Japan did challenge Hay's statement. And, after the Boxer Rebellion of 1900, Hay sent a second note that sought to preserve China.

But America's Open Door policy could not halt the rising tide of imperialism. Japan ignored the policy in expanding its control in Manchuria after the Russo-Japanese War, again with the infamous 21 Demands in January 1915, and with the secret treaties Japan negotiated with Britain and France during World War I (1914–1918) giving it the German concession in China. Indeed, the Washington Naval Conference (officially termed the Conference on Limitation of Armaments) had as a goal guaranteeing China's territorial and administrative integrity—the purpose of the Open Door policy—but the resulting Nine Power Treaty was long on phrases and short on action.

During World War II (1941–1945), when the Western Allies renounced their "unequal treaty" rights and China regained its territorial integrity, the Open Door policy became a dead issue.

SEE ALSO *China, First Opium War to 1945; Qing Dynasty; Scramble for Concessions.*

BIBLIOGRAPHY
Campbell, C. S. *Special Business Interests and the Open Door Policy.* Hamden, CT: Archon Books, 1968.

Hunt, Michael H. *Frontier Defense and the Open Door: Manchuria in Chinese–American Relations, 1895–1911.* New Haven, CT: Yale University Press, 1973.

McCormick, Thomas J. *China Market; America's Quest for Informal Empire, 1893–1901.* Chicago: Quadrangle Books, 1967.

Tomimas, Shutaro. *The Open Door Policy and the Territorial Integrity of China.* Arlington, VA: University Publications of America, 1976.

Charles M. Dobbs

OPIUM

Opium, or *Papaver somniferum,* has been cultivated and consumed by human beings since at least the third millennium B.C.E., when inhabitants of Mesopotamia began growing and ingesting it. From its likely origins in ancient Mesopotamia, opium use spread westward to Egypt and other parts of the eastern Mediterranean by the first millennium B.C.E., and eastward into Persia, India, and China by the first millennium C.E.

The European explorations of the fifteenth and sixteenth centuries encountered a preexisting opium trade in Mughal India, centered principally in areas surrounding Calcutta and Bombay (Mumbai). The Portuguese gradually entered the trade, progressively displacing Indians and Arabs from the increasingly lucrative China market. By the seventeenth and eighteenth centuries, the Dutch, English, and French had joined the opium commerce, which came to involve all of Asia and parts of Europe and its colonies around the globe as the nineteenth century unfolded.

At that point, opium had become a crucial commodity that had a major impact on the economic, social, and political circumstances in India, China, and Great Britain. The twentieth century witnessed the spread of opium cultivation to the Golden Triangle (Burma [Myanmar], Thailand, and Laos), to the Golden Crescent (Iran, Afghanistan, and Pakistan), and even to Columbia. At the same time, consumption of opium and its most popular derivatives, morphine and heroin, extended to every corner of the globe.

Medically, opium serves as an analgesic, relieving pain, especially for those who did not or do not have access to modern therapeutic procedures. People with respiratory disorders, particularly tuberculosis, self-medicated with opiates to control coughing. Opium produces constipation and was thus taken to treat diarrhea and dysentery, common symptoms of numerous maladies that were otherwise untreatable in premodern times. In addition, people believed that opium helped to mitigate the symptoms of malaria and to energize exhausted laborers.

In addition to medical usage, people consumed opiates to demonstrate social status. When the price of opium soared, only the well-to-do could afford such a luxury. In the nineteenth century particularly and later as well, many intellectuals, from China to England, viewed opium as an agent of enlightenment that could expand the powers of the mind and bring tranquility to the soul. As English author Thomas de Quincey (1785–1859) put it, "Whereas wine disorders the mental faculties, opium introduced amongst them the most exquisite order, legislation and harmony." French writer Jean Cocteau (1889–1963) claimed that opium smoking generated "the ultimate siesta." The drug also served as a sort of social lubricant, bringing together friends and neighbors at community opium establishments or "dens," much as people in the early twenty-first century meet at coffee houses, tea houses, or local taverns.

Most recreational users claim that opium alters one's mood, produces a feeling of euphoria, reduces the stress of everyday life, and acts as an aphrodisiac (though some consumers admit to reduced sexual performance). For both medical and recreational users, the perceptions of opium's powers may well outstrip the actual performance of the drug or even produce a result opposite to the one desired.

GLOBAL OPIUM PATTERNS, 1800–1950

The vast majority of opium production and consumption during the nineteenth and the first half of the twentieth century occurred in Asia. Britain, India, and China accounted for most drug activity there. National governments, local drug lords and officials, opium growers and merchants, colonial opium monopolies, and drug prohibitionists clashed over the suitable role opium should play on a continent whose inhabitants had increasingly become attracted to the drug.

By early twentieth century, pharmaceutical companies in the Europe, North America, and Japan began producing morphine and the precursor chemicals needed for the manufacture of opium derivatives for sale in the nonindustrial world, chiefly in China. Decades of global

prohibitionist activism, World War II (1939–1945), postwar decolonization, and the 1949 Communist revolution in China destroyed traditional opium trafficking and consumption patterns. These circumstances, plus an emerging tolerance for drug use in most of the industrial world by the 1960s, set the stage for new centers of opium production and consumption.

Nineteenth-century opium trafficking was chiefly an Asian phenomenon. Nearly all opium growing was done in Turkey, Persia, India, and China, while most consumption took place in China, though people in other parts of Asia, Europe, and North America also became regular opiate users. Opium probably had the largest impact on China, where the Qing/Manchu government (1644–1911) had historically prohibited the drug, a ban that brought China into conflict with Britain, which supplied more than 90 percent of the foreign-produced drug.

Chinese demand for opium resulted in an outflow of silver to pay for it. That in turn increased the price of silver, which peasants had to purchase with copper in order to pay their taxes. Just as important, the Chinese tribute system of international relations, which regulated foreign access to China, began to break down. The British East India Company—the only British organization permitted by the Chinese to conduct trade in their country, and then only in Canton (Guangzhou)—lost its London monopoly on the China trade in 1834, thus permitting (under British law) any British company to enter the China market. But even as mercantilism gave way to free trade in Britain, China continued to insist on conducting foreign trade through the tribute system. These points of disagreement—the impact of drugs and the system of international relations—produced the First Opium or Anglo-Chinese War (1839–1842).

China's defeat and the ensuing Treaty of Nanking (Nanjing, 1842), which made no reference to the opium trade, opened China to the outside world and the European system of international relations. China resisted opening its doors while the drug trade continued, generating the Second Opium War (1856–1860), another defeat for China, and yet another set of treaties, one of which—the Treaty of Tientsin (Tianjin, 1858)—allowed the import of opium upon the paying of a tariff. By this time, China was well on the way to becoming the world's largest opium producer. By the end of the century, probably more than ten million Chinese were addicted to the drug and millions more were periodic users. Millions of farmers had become producers of the drug, and tens of thousands of transporters and retailers emerged to get the product to users, while government officials at all levels reaped the taxation (some legal, some illegal) rewards.

Chinese Opium Den, circa 1900. *Men smoke opium through pipes as they read and relax in an opium den in China. During the nineteenth century the effects of opium smoking on Chinese society were devastating, leading to government prohibitions on its use and importation.* © HULTON-DEUTSCH COLLECTION/CORBIS. REPRODUCED BY PERMISSION.

Beyond China, the British government used opium profits to cover the expenses of governing India, while millions of Indian farmers produced opium for the burgeoning global market, which included all the colonies in Southeast Asia, particularly those locations where large concentrations of ethnic Chinese lived. But the drug had also caught on in England and the United States, where Americans became enthusiastic consumers of patent medicines, most of which contained some form of opium. In addition, colonial regimes in Southeast Asia came to depend on opium taxation to finance their administrative costs.

But even while global opium production and consumption soared, an international opium prohibition movement emerged to check nonmedical use of opiates and other drugs. In 1905 the British government informed China that it would consider ending its exports of opium to China if Beijing would undertake a serious anti-opium campaign. This offer by London represented

the culmination of a decades-long prohibitionist crusade in England and America, led by missionaries and assorted other reformers, much in the spirit of the progressive movement then in full swing in the United States. Should Britain be convinced of a serious Chinese effort, then London would end its export of opium to China by 1917.

Although Beijing launched an anti-opium movement in 1906 that initially succeeded beyond almost everyone's expectations, and though the British promised and did in fact bring an end to opium exports as prearranged, Chinese politics ultimately doomed the effort. First, the Manchu Qing government feared mobilizing the common people in the antidrug campaign for fear it could easily become a nationalist anti-Manchu movement. Next, the Empress Dowager Cixi (1835–1908), the nation's principal leader, died in 1908, and three years later China's dynastic government collapsed forever. Successor regimes had little interest in the campaign, and by 1916 the country had fallen into the hands of warlords, almost all of whom used opium to finance their organizational operations. Moreover, those political movements dedicated to crushing warlordism, ending foreign privileges in China, and modernizing the country—the Nationalists *(Guomindang)* and the Communists—both relied on opium revenue to some extent from the 1920s to the 1940s, even as they attacked the practice officially.

Meanwhile, several international anti-opium conferences held before and after World War I (1914–1918) to bring about an end to illicit drug trafficking began alerting the wider world to the perils of drug use. In the United States, the Harrison Act of 1914 began a prohibitionist drug campaign in a country that had liberally and legally consumed opiates. Great Britain agreed to end its export of opium to colonies in Southeast Asia by 1936, a pledge it honored. The League of Nations, created in 1919 by the Treaty of Versailles to deal with thorny international issues, sponsored numerous anti-opium conferences, which generated anti-opium treaties.

Between the world wars, heroin was quickly replacing opium as the drug of choice in much of China, and although all the industrial nations provided the necessary chemicals to produce heroin in China, by the mid-1930s Japan came to dominate the traffic in heroin and its precursor drugs there. A growing split surfaced between Tokyo on the one side and London, Washington, D.C., and Nanjing (China's capital from 1928 to 1949) on the other, which resulted in Japanese trafficking becoming a prominent rationale with which to brand Japan an outlaw nation. World War II and various independence movements destroyed traditional drug marketing patterns in Asia, and the Chinese Communist victory in 1949 and its subsequent genuine antidrug campaign obliterated nearly overnight the largest consumer market for opium (at least until the 1980s). By the mid-twentieth century, the vast majority of the world's opium was used to produce legitimate medicines.

OPIUM ACTIVITIES SINCE 1950

Nonetheless, there remained a demand for opiates, particularly in the industrial world. With India and China no longer producing the drug, other centers of cultivation and new patterns of trafficking emerged to fill the vacuum. Drug users proliferated in the 1960s as countercultural movements across the globe extolled the benefits of getting high, often with opiates. Two principal production sites surfaced to meet the growing demand for opium, the Golden Triangle and the Golden Crescent. The countries of these regions were relatively poor, possessed vast remote and mountainous regions difficult for a government to access or control, and had all

experienced considerable political instability. By the 1990s, Columbia entered the opium growing business.

After World War II, the United Nations and member governments supported drug prohibition movements, at least verbally. Like the League of Nations, the United Nations sponsored antidrug conferences, promoted antidrug treaties, and disseminated antidrug measures. In practice, however, the United Nations merely served as a launching platform for its members' antidrug public relations campaigns.

By the 1970s, the United States had commenced its "war on drugs," a reaction to the growing popular notion that drug use had somehow become an acceptable part of one's lifestyle. Popular culture began addressing drug issues, one example being the motion picture *The French Connection* (dir. William Friedkin, 1971), which chronicled the movement of illicit heroin from Marseilles, France, to the New York consumer market and the marginally successful police effort to thwart such trafficking. "Just Say No" campaigns in the United States and elsewhere aimed to reduce drug use, and did realize some success in the 1980s and 1990s. By the late twentieth century, though opiates still attracted addicts and recreational users, other illicit hard drugs, such as cocaine and methamphetamines, began to capture a larger share of the illegal drug market.

International affairs have continued to have an impact on the drug trade. The Cold War (1945–1991) between the United States and the Soviet Union tended to undermine global antidrug operations because Washington often found itself allied with drug traffickers. Thus the U.S. government turned a blind eye to the drug activities of Chinese nationalist remnants in Burma, where they plied their trade into the 1970s, and worked closely with the Hmong of Laos (also in the opium business) during the Vietnam War (1957–1975). In addition, the United States supported the mujahideen (Islamic guerilla fighters) in Afghanistan, who cultivated and marketed opium to help finance their war against the Soviet Union, which had invaded and occupied their country in the late 1970s and 1980s. After the Soviet withdrawal from Afghanistan in the 1980s and the American defeat of the militant Islamic Taliban government in 2001, opium cultivation once again became a significant source of income for Afghan tribes. This policy of overlooking the drug-related activities of America's conditional allies extended to Latin America, where Washington was predisposed to support governments that opposed Soviet or Cuban activities in the region.

These political marriages of convenience date back to World War II, when the United States worked with drug traffickers in Burma in an effort to defeat the

Japanese, and extend into the early twenty-first century, when the U.S. government worked with drug traffickers in Afghanistan to remove the Taliban and capture the Saudi-born terrorist Osama bin Laden (b. 1957). As long as consumers demand illegal opiates for recreational purposes, poverty will drive producers to meet those demands. And as long as governments advance agendas deemed more critical than illicit drug eradication, and prohibitionists continue to dominate drug policy in governments around the world, producers and consumers of opium will continue to achieve their agendas.

SEE ALSO *China, First Opium War to 1945; China, to the First Opium War; Opium Wars.*

BIBLIOGRAPHY

Bello, David Anthony. *Opium and the Limits of Empire: Drug Prohibition in the Chinese Interior, 1729–1850.* Cambridge, MA: Harvard University Press, 2005.

Booth, Martin. *Opium: A History.* London: Simon and Schuster, 1996.

Brook, Timothy, and Bob Takashi Wakabayashi, eds. *Opium Regimes: China, Britain, and Japan, 1839–1952.* Berkeley: University of California Press, 2000.

Courtwright, David. *Forces of Habit: Drugs and the Making of the Modern World.* Cambridge, MA: Harvard University Press, 2001.

Madancy, Joyce A. *The Troublesome Legacy of Commissioner Lin: The Opium Trade and Opium Suppression in Fujian Province, 1820s to 1920s.* Cambridge, MA: Harvard University Press, 2003.

Reins, Thomas D. "Reform, Nationalism, and Internationalism: The Opium Reform Movement in China and the Anglo-American Influence, 1900–1908." *Modern Asian Studies* 25 (1) (1991): 101–142.

Trocki, Carl A. *Opium, Empire, and the Global Political Economy: A Study of the Asian Opium Trade, 1750–1950.* New York: Routledge, 1999.

Walker, William O. *Opium and Foreign Policy: The Anglo-American Search for Order in Asia, 1912–1954.* Chapel Hill: University of North Carolina Press, 1991.

Walker, William O., ed. *Drugs in the Western Hemisphere: An Odyssey of Cultures in Conflict.* Wilmington, DE: Scholarly Resources, 1996.

Thomas D. Reins

OPIUM WARS

In the early nineteenth century, British merchants began to smuggle opium from India into China in order to balance their purchase of Chinese tea, porcelain, silk, and other goods for export to Britain. The British resorted to opium smuggling because Britain had no more silver for the China trade, and China, a country with a self-sufficient economy, was not interested in any Western product but silver.

The effects of opium smoking on Chinese society were devastating, and the drain of silver, which was spent on purchasing opium, greatly decreased the Chinese government's revenues. In an effort to stem the tragedy, the imperial government made opium illegal in 1836, and the traffic in opium thus became a criminal activity. However, British traders still smuggled massive amounts of opium into Guangzhou (Canton) by bribing local Cantonese officials.

In order to enforce the imperial government's prohibitions on the importation of opium, the imperial commissioner, Lin Zexu (ca. 1785–1850), was sent to Guangzhou by the Chinese emperor. Lin Zexu clamped down on all traffic in opium and destroyed all the existing stores of opium confiscated from British merchants at Guangzhou in March 1839. Great Britain, which had been looking for a means to end China's restrictions on foreign trade since the middle of the eighteenth century, responded by sending warships in June 1840 to attack Guangzhou and Xiamen, but the British effort was not successful.

From January 1841 to July 1842, however, British troops captured, in succession, Guangzhou, Xiamen, Dinghai, Zhenjiang, Ningbo, and Wusongkou. The British also captured the Chinese fleet anchored off Nanjing. British forces encountered fierce resistance from the Chinese, but China had only old and outdated weapons and artillery at their disposal. Finally, on August 29, 1842, the Chinese were forced to sign the "unequal" Treaty of Nanjing.

The Treaty of Nanjing opened five ports—Guangzhou, Fuzhou, Xiamen, Lingbo, and Shanghai—to conduct foreign trade as "treaty ports." In addition, a war indemnity of 21 million *taels* (1 Custom *tael* = 0.0378 kilograms = 0.10127 avoirdupois *pounds*) of silver was to be paid to Britain, and Hong Kong was surrendered to the British. The treaty further stipulated that all customs duties must be negotiated with other countries, and import duties were lowered from 65 percent to 5 percent. The treaty abolished the decree designating Guangzhou as the sole port for foreign trade and allowed British merchants to engage in free trade in China. Finally, the treaty allowed British merchants to bring their families to live in the treaty ports, and the Chinese local authorities had to provide housing or other establishments, which British merchants could rent.

To supplement the Treaty of Nanjing, the British forced the Chinese to sign the Treaty of the Bogue in 1843. According to this supplemental treaty, all British citizens would be subject to British, not Chinese, law if they should commit any crime on Chinese soil.

Chinese Militia, 1860. *Chinese militia armed with clubs and shields stand ready for battle during the Second Opium War.*
HULTON ARCHIVE/GETTY IMAGES. REPRODUCED BY PERMISSION.

Furthermore, any Chinese person who either dealt with the British, or lived with them, or was employed by them did not come under Chinese jurisdiction either.

In addition, the so-called most-favored-nation clause was included. This gave the British the same privileges extorted from China by any other country. Within a few years, several other Western powers signed treaties with China and received similar commercial and residential privileges. The treaties opened the Chinese markets and resources to Western capitalism, caused the inflow of cheap Western industrial products, and toppled China's self-sufficient economy. However, the terms of the treaties also speeded up the development of capitalism in China. At the same time, the treaties opened China to the outside world against the will of the Chinese people, turning China into a semifeudal, semicolonial state, with Western domination of China's treaty ports after the war.

The second Opium War (1856–1860) is also called the Arrow War. On October 8, 1856, Chinese officials boarded the *Arrow*, a Chinese-owned but British-registered ship, in Guangzhou. The British quickly responded to the "Arrow Incident" and attacked Guangzhou. France soon joined British action under

the pretext of seeking revenge for the execution of a French missionary, Father August Chapdelaine (1814–1856), by local Chinese authorities in Guangxi Province. The United States and Russia also sent envoys to Hong Kong to help the British–French alliance.

The joint English-French troops attacked again and occupied Guangzhou in late 1857. They maintained their colonial rule in the city for nearly four years. The coalition then cruised north to briefly capture the Dagu forts near Tianjin in May 1858. From there, they threatened to invade Beijing.

On June 23, 1858, the Chinese were forced to sign the Treaty of Tianjin, to which Britain, France, Russia, and the United States were party. The major points of the treaties were: Britain, France, Russia, and the United States would have the right to station legations in Beijing, and ten more ports would be opened for foreign trade, including Niuzhuang, Dengzhou, Tainan, Danshui, Chaozhou, Qiongzhou, Hankou, Jiujiang, Nanjing, and Zhenjing. Foreign vessels, including warships, would have the right to navigate freely on the Yangzi River. In addition, foreigners would have the right to travel within China's interior for the purpose of travel, trade, or missionary activities. China was also to pay an indemnity to Britain and France of two million *taels* of silver each, and compensation to British merchants of two million *taels* of silver.

China subsequently attempted to block the entry of diplomats into Beijing. In order to force China to comply with the terms of the new treaty, British and French allied forces landed at Beitang on August 1, 1860, and successfully attacked the Dagu forts on August 21. On October 6, the coalition occupied Beijing and burned the city's Summer Palace (Yihe Yuan) and the Old Summer Palace (Yuanming Yuan), completely destroying the Old Summer Palace. The Chinese emperor finally ratified the Treaty of Tianjin in the Convention of Beijing on October 18, 1860.

The opium trade was thereafter legalized. In addition, Christians were granted full civil rights that were previously denied to them on the grounds of religious belief, including the right to own property. They were also allowed to proselytize and spread their faith unhindered. The contents of the Convention of Beijing stated that: China should recognize the validity of the Treaty of Tianjin; China would open Tianjin as a trade port; the district of Jiulong Si was ceded to Britain; Chinese laborers were permitted to emigrate to work overseas; and the indemnity to Britain and France would increase to eight million *taels* of silver each.

SEE ALSO *China, First Opium War to 1945; Opium.*

BIBLIOGRAPHY

Chesneaux, Jean, Marianne Bastid, and Marie-Claire Bergère. *China from the Opium Wars to the 1911 Revolution.* Translated by Ann Destenay. New York: Pantheon, 1976.

Holt, Edgar. *The Opium Wars in China.* London: Putnam, 1964.

Gentzler, J. Mason, ed. *Changing China: Readings in the History of China from the Opium War to the Present.* New York: Praeger, 1977.

Gibson, Michael. *China: Opium Wars to Revolution.* London: Wayland, 1975.

Inglis, Brian. *The Opium War.* London: Hodder, 1976.

Melancon, Glenn. *Britain's China Policy and the Opium Crisis: Balancing Drugs, Violence, and National Honour, 1833–1840.* Burlington, VT: Ashgate, 2003.

Polachek, James M. *The Inner Opium War.* Cambridge, MA: Harvard University Press, 1992.

Waley, Arthur. *The Opium War Through Chinese Eyes.* Stanford, CA: Stanford University Press, 1958.

Wong, J. Y. *Deadly Dreams: Opium, Imperialism, and the Arrow War (1856–1860) in China.* Cambridge, U.K.: Cambridge University Press, 1998.

Yong Liu

ORGANIZATION OF AFRICAN UNITY (OAU)

In 1963 the leaders of thirty-two newly independent African states gathered in Addis Ababa, Ethiopia, to establish the Organization of African Unity (OAU), primarily intended to promote unity and cooperation among African states, uphold self-government and respect for territorial boundaries, and eradicate all forms of colonialism from Africa. From thirty-two member states in 1963, the membership of the organization increased to fifty-three in 1994. With this growing membership also came more achievements, problems, and challenges.

BACKGROUND OF THE OAU

The consciousness and movement for African unity is traceable to the ideas of Pan-Africanism, which originated among African descent in the Diaspora—in the United States, the Caribbean, and Europe. Pan-Africanists, both at the 1945 Manchester Conference in London and the 1958 All Africa People's Conference in Accra, unanimously spoke against the prevailing racism and colonialism. They called on Africans to unite in their fight for liberation. In 1957 Ghana became the first country in sub-Saharan Africa to gain independence. In his independence speech, President Kwame Nkrumah (1909–1972) declared that the independence of Ghana was meaningless unless it leads to the total liberation of the African continent. From 1957 to 1963, Africa's unrelenting struggle for freedom resulted in the liberation of thirty-two African states. However, the continent, as Haile Selassie (1892–1975), then emperor of Ethiopia acknowledged, lacked the mechanism that would enable it to speak with one voice. So, formation of an African organization became a necessity.

Undoubtedly, African leaders agreed to the need for African unity, but were divided on the choice of a unanimous strategy. According to April Gordon and Donald Gordon, the disagreement centered on whether full continental political unity should be established immediately at the founding of the OAU, or whether it should be accomplished progressively through a minimalist or building block approach. These two approaches to African integration were hotly and passionately debated and considered throughout Africa. Two groups emerged. The first group, led by Nkrumah, was known as the Casablanca Group (named after the Moroccan city). Otherwise called the radicals, the Casablanca Group called for a political union of African countries, patterned after the federal model of the United States. Again, it suggested that African development be based on socialist planning. The second group, Monrovia Group (named after the capital of

OAU Charter Conference, May 1963. *Delegates from independent African nations met in 1963 in Addis Ababa, Ethiopia, to discuss efforts to oppose colonialism and promote independence and unity among African peoples. The meeting concluded with the signing of a charter forming the Organization of African Unity.* © BETTMANN/CORBIS. REPRODUCED BY PERMISSION.

Liberia), was led by Abubakar Tafawa Balewa (1912–1966), prime minister of Nigeria. The group, otherwise known as the conservatives, in contrast, called for the creation of a looser organization and market-driven development. This division threatened to derail the course of continental integration. Nevertheless, the 1963 meeting united the opposing groups.

On May 25, 1963, Nkrumah of Ghana, Emperor Haile Selassie of Ethiopia, and Gamal Abdel Nasser (or Gamal Abd al-Nasir) of Egypt (1918–1970), convened a meeting of thirty-two newly independent African countries in Addis Ababa, Ethiopia, to deliberate on the desired African union. Delegates at the meeting understood that to wipe out all forms of colonialism from Africa, unity was crucial. Thus, the charter establishing OAU was signed on May 25, 1963, with the objectives of eradicating all forms of colonialism from Africa; promote unity and solidarity; coordinate and intensify cooperation and efforts to achieve a better life for the people of Africa; promote international cooperation and undertake collective and joint provision of resources and man power,

which would enable Africa to achieve rapid development. The most important objectives that drove the OAU from its inception in 1963 to the economic predicament of the 1980s was the need to protect the fragile sovereignty recently achieved by African states, and to help those still under colonial or racist rule to achieve sovereign independence. In these respects, OAU recorded commendable breakthroughs. From 1963 to 1994, the Coordinating Committee for the Liberation of Africa provided financial and military support to independence movements in Angola, Algeria, Namibia, Zimbabwe, Mozambique, Guinea-Bissau, Príncipe, São Tomé, and white minority-ruled South Africa. A total of twenty-one countries were ultimately liberated, with South Africa becoming the fifty-third member on May 23, 1994. Nevertheless, OAU failed to pay equal attention to the issue of economic development.

SHORTCOMINGS OF THE OAU

Even though the OAU effectively pursued the goal of African liberation, it failed to confront the postcolonial challenges of endemic poverty, war, genocides, human rights and environmental disasters, or political instability and failures. The organization provided inadequate answers to these problems, and, as the Tanzanian President, Julius Nyerere (1922–1999) noted, the OAU was basically a talking club of African leaders with no power to back up its resolutions. Under the ruthless dictatorship of Hastings Banda (1898–1997) of Malawi, Emperor Bokassa I (1921–1996) of Central African Republic, Idi Amin (1924–2003) of Uganda, Mobutu Sese Seko (1930–1997) of Zaire, and Sani Abacha (1943–1998) of Nigeria, the OAU was helpless. Except for the courageous step taken by Nyerere to unseat Idi Amin in 1979, the OAU's principle of state sovereignty and nonintervention simply meant that the organization looked the other way while ruthless dictators abused the people and enriched themselves. Civil wars in the Democratic Republic of Congo, Nigeria, Liberia, and Sierra Leone, among others, resulted from a struggle for power and allocation of resources. The ensuing division, instability, and uncertainty arrested sustainable development in Africa. Under this circumstance, as author S.K.B Asante noted, African states were not taken seriously by the international community as an important and effective partner in the global economy, and were increasingly swept aside by the intensification of economic globalization.

METAMORPHOSES OF THE OAU

Mindful of the harsh prospect of marginalization, and the ineffectiveness of the OAU in providing the way forward, African leaders, in 1999, convened for an extraordinary session of the OAU in Sirte, Libya. The session discussed ways of repositioning the OAU not only to align with the emerging global, political, and economic developments, but articulate the preparation necessary to promote Africa's social, economic, and political potentials within the context of globalization. With the theme of strengthening OAU capacity to enable it to meet the challenges of the new millennium, the Sirte summit demanded, among other things, for the speedy establishment of all the institutions provided by the treaty establishing the African Economic Community (AEC) in Abuja on June 3, 1991 (called the Abuja Treaty) namely, African Central Bank, the African Monetary Union, the African Court of Justice, and the Pan-African Parliament.

Based on the Sirte Declaration, the Constitutive Act of African Union was adopted by the Assembly of Heads of States and Government of OAU at its thirty-sixth ordinary session in Lome, Togo, on July 11, 2000. Two-thirds of the member states ratified it. Meanwhile, the OAU remained operational for a transitional period of one year following a decision adopted in Lusaka,

Zambia, on July 10, 2001. The next year, in Durban, South Africa, the OAU was replaced with the African Union (AU). The inaugural session of the new organization took place immediately at the same venue on July 9 and 10, 2002.

The AU was formed not only to accomplish greater unity and solidarity among African countries, but to ensure the acceleration of the political and socioeconomic integration of the continent. Of course, in the context of globalization, particularly since the 1990s, stronger integration in Africa became a precondition to improve its overall political and economic integration of Africa in the unavoidable world economy. As authors Jeffrey Herbst and Greg Mills rightly stated, AU might be seen as a mere baptismal name, or even a departure from the past disappointments of OAU. It might also be described as an old lady with a new dress, as Theodore T. Hodge noted. But what is remarkable, at any rate, is that AU opens a new chapter in African history when the paradigm of sustainable development is eventually identified and placed at the center of the continent's developmental concerns.

On the whole, efforts at African integration, symbolized in OAU, achieved the mission of ridding the continent of colonialism, but failed to achieve similar results in the social and economic spheres. Since the 1980s as a consequence, the postcolonial economy of Africa remained fragile. Frustrated with the apparent failure to address persistent socioeconomic problems in Africa, the OAU metamorphosed into AU, determined to take advantage of developmental opportunities implicit in the contemporary globalized economy.

SEE ALSO *Nkrumah, Kwame; Nyerere, Julius; Pan-Africanism.*

BIBLIOGRAPHY

Asante, S.K.B. *Regionalism and Africa's Development: Expectations, Reality, and Challenges.* New York: St. Martin's Press, 1997.

Gordon, April A. and Gordon Donald L. ed. *Understanding Contemporary Africa,* 3rd ed. Boulder, CO: Lynne Rienner, 2001.

Herbst, Jeffrey, and Greg Mills. *The Future of Africa: A New Order in Sight?* Oxford; New York: Oxford University Press for the International Institute for Strategic Studies, 2003.

Maluwa, Tiyanjana. "The Constitutive Act of the African Union and Institution Building in Postcolonial Africa." *Leiden Journal of International Law,* 16 (2003).

Wolfers, M. *Politics in the Organization of African Unity.* London: Methuen, 1976.

Ogechi Emmanuel Anyanwu

OTTOMAN EMPIRE: FRANCE AND AUSTRIA-HUNGARY

The Ottoman Empire was the preeminent Muslim state of the early-modern and modern periods. Arising in Anatolia in the thirteenth century, the Ottomans came to dominate the Middle East, North Africa, and Southeastern Europe. Although often perceived as a Middle Eastern power only, the Ottomans were an integral part of Europe.

The Ottoman Empire's relations with France and Austria (later Austria-Hungary) were often linked. For most of its history, the Ottoman state had good relations with France and fought with Austria. There were a number of factors that drove this dynamic. Most importantly, the Ottoman presence in the Balkans was a direct threat to the security of the Austrian Habsburg Empire. France too was often in conflict with the Habsburgs, and this brought the Ottomans and French together diplomatically and, sometimes, militarily. France also became deeply involved in the Ottoman territories, first through trade, then through investment. Only in the twentieth century did conditions change such that the Ottoman Empire allied with Austria-Hungary against France.

THE FIFTEENTH CENTURY

The Ottoman conquest of Constantinople in 1453 established the Ottomans as a world empire. The victorious Sultan Mehmed II, "the Conqueror," fully understood the significance of capturing the Byzantine capital. Wanting to preserve the city's role as a center for world trade, Mehmed sent his personal troops into the city to protect the Byzantine palace and major marketplaces from looting. Mehmed's campaigns into the Balkans began to concern the Austrian Habsburgs, but initially there was little direct contact. As for relations with France, French merchants began to increase their trade in the eastern Mediterranean in this period.

Mehmed's death in 1481 led to a succession struggle between his sons Bayezid and Cem. The civil war that followed Mehmed's death pitted Bayezid, who was supported by the janissary slave soldiers, against his brother Cem, who garnered the support of the traditional Turkish aristocracy. Bayezid emerged victorious, and Cem fled. After seeking refuge in Cairo and among the Knights of Saint John on Rhodes, Cem was sent to France, where he was kept as a "guest" at Bayezid's request. This included an annual remittance from the Sublime Porte, the Ottoman seat of government, to Paris to cover Cem's expenses. Cem spent the rest of his life as a pawn in international diplomacy, as the Christian powers used his claim to the Ottoman throne as a potential threat against Bayezid.

THE SIXTEENTH CENTURY

The sixteenth century opened with a period of Ottoman expansion that greatly affected the Porte's relationships with France and Austria. The questions surrounding Ottoman expansion—How far would they go? When would they advance? Could they be stopped?—became vital to the states of Europe. Sultan Selim "the Grim" (1512–1520) defeated Shah Ismail Safavi at Chaldiran (1514), ending the threat of Persian expansion into Anatolia, and conquered the Mamluks in Cairo, which brought the central Islamic lands under Ottoman rule (1517). The conquest of the Levant was the fulfillment of Ottoman plans to secure control of east–west trade. The Ottomans now held all the major entrepôts for silk and spices in the eastern Mediterranean, and their navy dominated the sea.

Under Selim's son, Süleyman "the Magnificent" (1520–1566), the Ottoman Empire became a major participant in the diplomacy of Europe. Süleyman was deeply interested in events and developments in Europe, and quickly moved to expand the empire to the west, especially into Hungary. This brought the Ottomans into direct conflict with the Habsburgs in Austria. At the same time, Süleyman developed closer economic and diplomatic ties with France. Relations with both states were complicated by the advent of the Protestant Reformation.

This period was one of competition for supremacy between three strong rulers: Süleyman, Francis I of France (1494–1547), and Charles V (1500–1558), the Habsburg heir in Spain elected Holy Roman Emperor in 1519. Francis and Charles battled for control of northern Italy and supremacy in western Europe. Charles's focus on the west led him to put his brother, Archduke Ferdinand (1503–1564), in charge of the eastern portions of the empire. The Ottoman–Habsburg rivalry took place in two areas: in the western Mediterranean against Charles and in Hungary against Ferdinand.

Süleyman's advances into Hungary were a direct threat to the Habsburgs in Austria. Süleyman first attacked Hungary in 1526. On August 28, 1526, a hastily mustered Hungarian force led by the young King Louis II met the larger and better-armed Ottoman army at Mohács, a plain on the Danube south of the Hungarian capital at Buda. The Hungarians were no match for the Ottomans, whose artillery was particularly devastating. Over 10,000 Hungarian foot soldiers were killed, along with most of the nobility and bishops. King Louis fell from his horse while fleeing the battle and drowned. Within days, Ottoman forces occupied Buda and Pest. Süleyman, however, quickly withdrew, holding only the eastern third of Hungary.

Louis's death led to a succession struggle in Hungary. The majority of the nobles elected John Zapolyai as king, and he quickly acknowledged Ottoman suzerainty. However, Ferdinand of Austria, Louis's brother-in-law, also claimed the Hungarian throne and occupied Buda in 1528. Securing control of Hungary became vital to Habsburg defense planning. Süleyman marched into Hungary to support Zapolyai in 1529, retaking Buda, and continued westward to besiege Vienna that fall. The siege began too late in the season and Süleyman was forced to raise the siege and march home. Hungary was divided into three parts: Ottoman, Habsburg, and royal Hungary under Zapolyai. In 1553 a treaty recognized both Zapolyai and Ferdinand as rulers over their respective territories in Hungary in exchange for annual tribute to the Porte.

Full Ottoman annexation of royal Hungary came in 1541, prompted by Habsburg military action. In 1538 Zapolyai and Ferdinand concluded the Treaty of Varád by which Ferdinand would inherit Zapolyai's lands in exchange for aid against Ottoman attacks. The agreement became problematic when Zapolyai had a son shortly before his death in 1540. The Porte recognized the child as king, obviating Ferdinand's claims. Habsburg armies again tried to take Buda, and in August 1541 Süleyman marched to relieve the city. This time, however, he installed an Ottoman governor and provincial administration for Hungary. Ferdinand took full control of the western third of Hungary, already under Habsburg rule.

In the western Mediterranean, conflicts with their mutual Habsburg enemies led Süleyman and Francis I to ally. France already had an amicable relationship with the Porte, having been granted its first capitulation, or trade agreement, in 1535. This agreement allowed French merchants to conduct business in the Ottoman realms and granted them extraterritoriality. In the same year, Charles V captured Tunis, prompting Süleyman to accept Francis's offer of an alliance. Joint French-Ottoman naval operations against Charles commenced, and plans were made, but never carried out, for a joint attack on Habsburg territories in Italy. Poor relations with Charles ensured that Francis would remain on good terms with the Ottomans through the 1540s. Naval operations continued and the Ottoman fleet wintered in Toulon in 1543.

Conflict with Charles also led Süleyman to support the Protestant Reformation. Charles was the leading Catholic king, and tried to suppress the spread of the Reform movement and bring the rebellious northern German princes back to the Roman church. Süleyman saw support for the Protestant princes as a way to strike at Charles and weaken the Habsburgs. The Protestants took advantage of Ottoman support and the growing Ottoman threat in the East to come to an agreement with Ferdinand. In exchange for help defending his lands they received religious tolerance for their churches.

Charles V abdicated the throne in 1556 and divided his empire between his son, Philip II, who inherited Spain, the Netherlands, and Spanish holdings in the New World, and Ferdinand, who became Holy Roman Emperor. Philip II signed the Peace of Cateau-Cambresis with Henry II of France in 1559, thus ending the Habsburg–French rivalry. This, combined with domestic difficulties, led Süleyman in 1562 to make peace with Ferdinand, who agreed to pay annual tribute to the Ottomans.

Ottoman–French trade relations were advanced with a new capitulation agreement in 1569. This agreement opened all Ottoman ports to French merchants and required all other western merchant vessels to sail under the French flag. French merchants took quick advantage of the new situation, and came to dominate Levantine trade.

THE SEVENTEENTH CENTURY

The seventeenth century opened and closed with major Ottoman wars with Austria. Border raiding by both empires' garrisons escalated into a full-scale imperial war in 1592. This war, usually called the Long War, lasted until 1606. The Habsburgs took a number of Ottoman fortresses and won several major victories in the early years of the war, and anti-Ottoman rebellions broke out in Transylvania and Wallachia. The tide shifted after the Ottoman victory at Mezo Keresztes in 1596, yet the Ottomans were unable to press their advantage and the war devolved into a stalemate. By 1605 Habsburg anti-Protestant policies had alienated much of the population in Hungary and Transylvania, and those regions rebelled against Vienna. The war ended with the treaty of Sitva Torok in 1606.

France remained a major trading partner with the Ottomans in the seventeenth century, but began to face serious competition from the rising trade powers of England and the Netherlands. French merchants had relied on the Venetian model of establishing close relationships with officials at the Porte to ensure trade access in the empire. As power in the Ottoman state became more decentralized, however, local officials and notables acted more independently. French merchants could no longer count on pressure from the central government to solve difficulties they were having in the provinces. English merchants were particularly successful in establishing themselves at the local level, and England's share of Ottoman trade increased.

Despite the growing competition from England, French merchants remained a vital part of the Ottoman

The Second Siege of Vienna. *Merzifonlu Kara Mustafa Paça besieged Vienna in 1683, but after several years the siege proved disastrous for the Ottomans. The European coalition finally defeated the Ottoman army, and the Treaty of Karlowitz was signed in 1699, marking the beginning of the permanent Ottoman withdrawal from Europe.* © BETTMANN/CORBIS. REPRODUCED BY PERMISSION.

economy. The relationship between France and the Porte remained cordial, especially as France came to replace Venice as the dominant western power in Levantine trade. French ships were even used to transport Ottoman officials. In the eighteenth century France came to dominate coastal shipping in the empire. France also continued to encourage the Ottomans to harass the Habsburgs in Austria, as French–Habsburg rivalry continued in the west.

Ottoman decentralization was halted in mid-century by the Köprülü family of viziers who reasserted the power of the central government. Part of their program was to revitalize the military, and this resulted in two major campaigns against Austria. The first began in 1663 under the personal leadership of Grand Vizier Fazil Ahmed Köprülü. Although the Habsburgs won the only major battle of the war, at Saint Gotthardt on August 1, 1664, the Ottomans came out ahead in the Treaty of Vasvar, which ended the war a few days later. The Habsburgs withdrew from the territories they had captured, and again agreed to pay annual tribute to Istanbul.

The most important Ottoman western campaign of the seventeenth century was the siege of Vienna in 1683. Grand Vizier Kara Mustafa Pasha set out with a huge army to try to take the city that even Süleyman had not been able to capture. Delayed by sieges of smaller forts along the way, the Ottoman forces arrived at Vienna too late in the campaign season and with too little artillery to be successful. The siege was raised by an army led by Jan Sobieski, the king of Poland.

The Habsburgs and their allies capitalized on the victory at Vienna by forming a Holy League to force the Ottomans out of Europe. Austrian forces took Pest in 1685 and Buda in 1686. By 1688 the Hungarian nobles had elected the Habsburg emperor king of Hungary, and Austrian forces had captured Belgrade. The Habsburg advance was halted by a new war with France and this allowed the Ottomans to regroup and counterattack. The Ottoman counteroffensive ended at the Battle of Slankamen (August 20, 1691) and the battle lines held along the Danube until 1699, when the Treaty of Karlowitz was negotiated. The Habsburgs gained Hungary and Transylvania as well as the right to look after the conditions of Catholic subjects of the Ottomans. Karlowitz was the beginning of the end of Ottoman rule in the Balkans. Austria was now the dominant power in southeastern Europe.

THE EIGHTEENTH CENTURY

The Ottoman Empire and France maintained their close relations throughout most of the eighteenth century. Because of their own conflicts with Austria, the French often encouraged the Ottomans to fight the Austrians. Austria for its part was not averse to trying to take territory in the Balkans, but was usually unable to successfully fight the Ottomans on its own. Most often Austria allied with Russia, which emerged in this century as the major threat to the Ottoman Empire.

The Ottomans first faced an Austrian-Venetian alliance in the war of 1716 to 1718. The Ottoman army made a very poor showing, and the war ended with the Ottomans ceding territory in the Treaty of Passarowitz (1718). The problems with their army set the Ottomans on a path of attempted military reforms, which led to a better force in the next contest with Austria and their ally Russia, in 1736 to 1739. The treaty that ended this conflict returned most of the territory the Ottomans lost at Passarowitz. Austria again joined Russia in attacking the Ottomans in 1788, but this war too ended with a negotiated peace at Sistova based on *status quo ante bellum* in 1791.

Because of good relations with France, the Porte often looked for French aid in its attempts at military reform. The Ottomans brought in a number of French military advisors, especially for help with new military technologies. Claude-Alexandre, Comte de Bonneval (1675–1747) and Baron Francois de Tott (1730–1793) both introduced modern artillery and military engineering as advisors to the Ottoman army.

The French Revolution and the rise of Napoleon affected the Ottoman Empire as it did the rest of Europe. Austrian and Russian involvement in the wars against France gave the Porte some space to continue its reform efforts. The Ottomans finally clashed with France in 1798, when Napoleon invaded Egypt. The Egyptian campaign was designed to strike against France's main enemy, Britain, but also led to the severing of amicable ties with the Ottomans. French troops handily defeated the Ottoman Mamluk forces in Egypt, and the French occupied the country for three years. The Ottomans then found themselves allied with Britain and Russia against their long-time friend, France. A joint Ottoman-British force recaptured Egypt, and with the French evacuation of the country relations were normalized with the Peace of Amiens, 1802.

THE NINETEENTH CENTURY

The dominant issue of Ottoman relations with France, Austria, and the other European powers in the nineteenth century was the "Eastern Question." In the sixteenth and seventeenth centuries the European states worried about Ottoman expansion. Now the concern was what would happen if the Ottomans withdrew from the Balkans or if the empire completely broke apart. As the nineteenth century progressed nationalist movements in the Balkans worked to secure their independence from the Ottomans.

The European Powers each had different views about what should happen to the Ottoman Empire. Russia wanted to dismember it and annex Slavic areas in the Balkans. Britain and France usually worked to shore up the Porte in the face of Russian aggression. For France, the need to counter Russian interests and preserve their economic investments in the Ottoman Empire offset their support for Balkan nationalist movements. The fate of the Ottoman Empire became a major issue in the balance of power that the European states tried to maintain.

Austria also had conflicting interests with regard to the Eastern Question. The Habsburgs did take some land from the Ottomans, gaining control over Bosnia-Herzegovina in 1879. Despite this, Austria was less inclined to break the Ottoman state apart than other European powers. Although they had been the traditional enemy of the Ottomans, the multiethnic nature of the Habsburg state made any new national states in the Balkans a threat to the cohesiveness of their own empire. The creation of the dual monarchy of Austria-Hungary in 1867 did not change this attitude, especially among the Hungarians who did not want to be outnumbered by Slavs and Romanians in the new state.

Great Power diplomacy affected internal developments in the Ottoman Empire. Muhammad Ali, the modernizing governor of Egypt, used French support in his bid for greater independence from the Porte. France also supported the establishment of Maronite power in Lebanon in the 1840s and again in the 1860s. France took territory directly from the Ottomans as well, occupying Algeria in 1830, and Tunisia in 1881.

The balance of power broke down in 1853 with the Crimean War. The proximate cause of the war was a dispute over who would have preeminence at the Church of the Holy Sepulcher in Jerusalem. This dispute pitted Catholic France and Austria against Orthodox Russia. Both sides made demands of and threatened the Ottoman sultan. In 1853 Russia invaded the Ottoman Danubian provinces, and France and Britain sent troops to assist the Porte. When Austria entered the war Russia backed down. War fever was running high, however, and the British and French still had troops on the move. They decided to attack Russia in the Crimea, nominally in support of the Ottomans. The war was incredibly bloody, and dragged on for three years, ending in the Treaty of Paris (1856).

Adding to their diplomatic interest in maintaining the balance of power, the European states were heavily invested financially in the Ottoman Empire. The Ottomans were already involved in the world capitalist system through trade, but industrial development in the nineteenth century deepened that integration. Modernization programs in industry and infrastructure were financed by foreign capital, mostly from France, Britain, and Germany. The great military expenditures of the Crimean War also necessitated large foreign loans. By the 1870s the Porte could not pay its loans, and in 1881 the European powers established the Ottoman Public Debt Administration, which came to oversee state finances and ensure repayment to European debtors.

THE TWENTIETH CENTURY

The Ottoman Empire did not survive long into the twentieth century, nor did its long-time opponent, Austria-Hungary. Both multiethnic empires were broken apart in the aftermath of World War I. France would emerge from the war a victor, and, together with Britain, would oversee the dismantling of both empires.

In 1912 the new national states in the Balkans—Greece, Serbia, Montenegro, and Bulgaria—joined together to force the Ottomans out of Europe once and for all. Success against the Ottomans led the allies to fight against each other as well. A negotiated settlement was reached in 1913.

The rise of Serbia posed a problem for Austria-Hungary, which ruled a large irredentist Serb minority. Common opposition to Russia brought the Ottomans, Habsburgs, and Germany together. The alliance with Germany led long-time Ottoman ally, France, to oppose the Ottomans.

France and Britain finally "answered" the Eastern Question after World War I, when they imposed the Treaty of Sevres on the defeated Ottomans in 1920. The remaining portion of the empire was broken up, with the Arab provinces under the control of Britain and France through League of Nations mandates. Anatolia was divided into European spheres of influence. In the same way, the victors broke apart Austria-Hungary, giving some territory to existing Balkan national states, and creating new states in Austria, Hungary, Czechoslovakia, and Yugoslavia.

SEE ALSO *Empire, Ottoman.*

BIBLIOGRAPHY

Brummett, Palmira. *Ottoman Seapower and Levantine Diplomacy in the Age of Discovery.* Albany: State University of New York Press, 1994.

Goffman, Daniel. *The Ottoman Empire and Early Modern Europe.* Cambridge, U.K.: Cambridge University Press, 2002.

Hurewitz, J. C. *Diplomacy in the Near and Middle East: A Documentary Record, 1535–1914.* Princeton, NJ: Van Nostrand, 1956.

Imber, Colin. *The Ottoman Empire, 1300–1650.* New York: Palgrave Macmillan, 2002.

Ingrao, Charles W. *The Habsburg Monarchy, 1618–1815,* 2nd ed. Cambridge, U.K.: Cambridge University Press, 2000.

Kortepeter, C. Max. *Ottoman Imperialism during the Reformation: Europe and the Caucasus.* New York: New York University Press, 1972.

Quataert, Donald. *The Ottoman Empire, 1700–1922.* Cambridge, U.K.: Cambridge University Press, 2000.

Sugar, Peter F., ed. *A History of Hungary.* Bloomington: Indiana University Press, 1994.

Zürcher, Erik J. *Turkey: A Modern History.* Rev. ed. London: Tauris, 2004.

Mark L. Stein

UNIVERSITY OF RHODE ISLAND

3 1222 00886 2081

The Natio

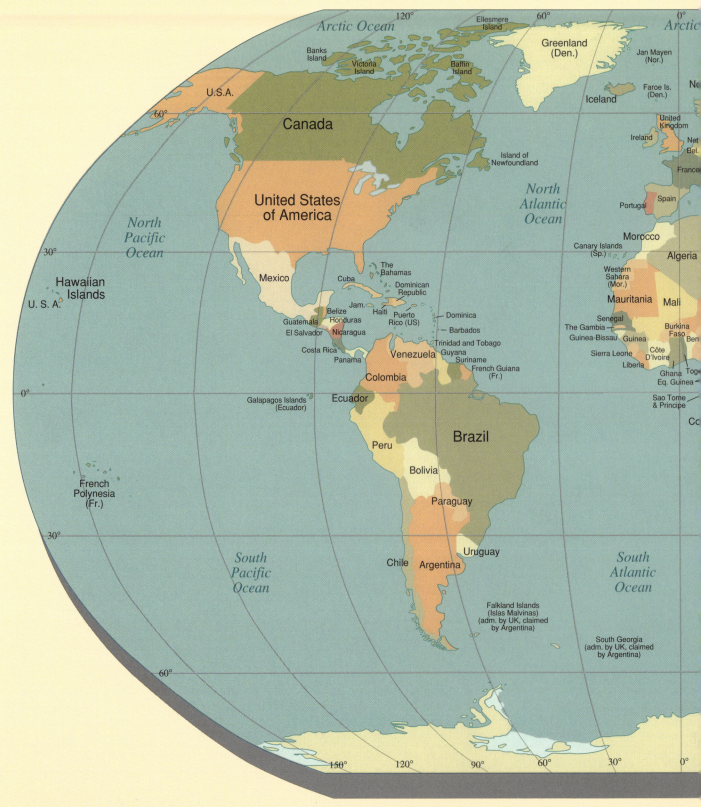

© MAGELLAN Geographix℠Santa Barbara, CA (800) 929-4MAP